Selected Awards and Honors

Chosen as a "Perfect Thing" by the editors of *Outside*
Official selection of the American Alpine Club Book Club
Winner of the National Outdoor Book Award
Winner of the Banff Mountain Book Award
Winner of the NCTE George Orwell Award
Winner of the American Society of Journalists and Authors
Outstanding Book Award

More praise for

Buried in the Sky

"Will surely stand as one of the most distinguished works within [the] genre.... This is reportage of the highest quality."   —Jim Perrin, citation for winning the Banff Mountain Festival Book Award in Mountaineering History

"A significant departure for mountaineer literature. . . . Impeccably researched ... finally humanizes the unsung heroes of the mountaineering world and their hopes and dreams for a better life."
                    —citation for winning the National Outdoor Book Award

"It's a testament to the thrills in this book that I scoured the notes, eager to learn how the authors wrote their account. . . . The authors' commendable documentary about the people who carry the gear is overtaken by the chilling adventure story of one terrible day on the mountain."   —*Smithsonian*

D0017359

"Exhaustive reporting and elegant delivery [give] the book its rich texture."   —Grayson Schaffer, *Outside*

"A work of obsessive reporting. [Zuckerman and Padoan] weave a narrative that is hair-raising and moving, but also precise."
—Matthew Power, *Men's Journal*

"Zuckerman and Padoan distinguish themselves by the depth of their research, especially into the lives and culture of the Nepali and Pakistani climbers and high-altitude workers."   —Kate Tuttle, *Boston Globe*

"Zuckerman and Padoan offer glimpses into the climbing culture that are as rare as the thin air the climbers breathe. . . . A provocative perspective on one of the world's most expensive and deadly athletic adventures."   —*Kirkus Reviews*

"A judiciously crafted chronicle of the devastating series of incidents that left 11 dead, this narrative is well organized and chilling."
—Ingrid Levin, *Library Journal*

"*Buried in the Sky* is by turns enlightening, fascinating, gripping, and heartbreaking, well-written in the best tradition of mountaineering narratives."   —Laura Hadley, *Daily Herald*

"An absorbing book that goes beyond the typical mountaineering tale. . . . This book is mesmerizing."   —Sharon Haddock, *Deseret News*

"The Sherpas climb off the page and carry a narrative that is as fast and as gripping as their superhuman ascents." —Michael Kodas, author of
High Crimes: The Fate of Everest in an Age of Greed

"Fast-paced and well-researched . . . a must-read for anyone fascinated by the people and politics of high-altitude mountaineering."

—Catherine Hollis, *Bookpage*

"This compelling story brought back from K2's slopes is a worthy tale about a little-known aspect of these high-stakes climbs."

—Colleen Kelly, *Minneapolis Star Tribune*

"A revelatory look at Sherpa history and culture . . . highly recommended."

—David Pitt, *Booklist*

"Unraveling the story through interviews in multiple languages across several countries has given the writers the depth and compassion to write a truly gripping account." —Milbry C. Polk, *Explorer's Journal*

"*Buried in the Sky*'s biggest surprise and ultimate triumph: By the end, the reader cares more about the inner life of Chhiring Sherpa than his adventures on top of one of the world's most dangerous mountains."

—Alex Tomchak Scott, *Williamette Week*

"A harrowing tale of adventure and survival." —Jeffrey St. Clair, *Counterpunch*

"I admired *Buried in the Sky* and enjoyed it, too. Because the authors did their homework and wrote their story well, and most of all, because credit is given at long last to those who deserve it most."

—Peter Matthiessen, author of *The Snow Leopard*

"*Buried in the Sky* reveals the heroic deeds of the Sherpa. . . . [It] brings to light how immensely strong, loyal, and talented the Sherpa climbers are. Finally credit is given, where credit is due." —Ed Viesturs, best-selling author of *No Shortcuts to the Top* and *K2: Life and Death on the World's Most Dangerous Mountain*

"An informative and inspirational book. . . . I couldn't put it down." —Jamling Tenzing Norgay, son of Tenzing Norgay and author of *Touching My Father's Soul*

"A compelling account of the men who have literally shouldered the rest of the world's mountaineers up K2." —Norman Ollestad, author of *Crazy for the Storm*

"Through phenomenal research, Zuckerman and Padoan have dug deeper than anyone else into one of the most mysterious tragedies in mountaineering history. Thanks to their efforts, the heroism and humanity of the Sherpa climbers who saved lives shine through the chaos and grief of that awful day on K2." —David Roberts, coauthor of *K2: Life and Death on the World's Most Dangerous Mountain*

BURIED in the SKY

▲▲▲

The Extraordinary Story of the
Sherpa Climbers on K2's Deadliest Day

PETER ZUCKERMAN

and

AMANDA PADOAN

W. W. NORTON & COMPANY

NEW YORK · LONDON

For Abrar, Almas, Asam, Dawa, Jen Jen,

Nima, Rahmin, Umbreen, and Zehan

Copyright © 2012 by Peter Zuckerman and Amanda Padoan

First published as a Norton paperback 2013

For information about permission to reproduce selections from this
book, write to Permissions, W. W. Norton & Company, Inc.,
500 Fifth Avenue, New York, NY 10110

For information about special discounts for bulk purchases, please
contact W. W. Norton Special Sales at specialsales@wwnorton.com or
800-233-4830

Manufacturing by RR Donnelley, Harrisonburg
Book design by Ellen Cipriano
Maps by Adrian Kitzinger
Production manager: Anna Oler

Library of Congress Cataloging-in-Publication Data
Zuckerman, Peter.
Buried in the sky : the extraordinary story of the Sherpa climbers on
K2's deadliest day / Peter Zuckerman and Amanda Padoan. — 1st ed.
p. cm.
Includes bibliographical references and index.
ISBN 978-0-393-07988-3 (hardcover)
1. Mountaineering—Pakistan—K2 (Mountain)
2. Mountaineers—Pakistan—K2 (Mountain)
3. Mountaineering accidents—Pakistan—K2 (Mountain)
4. Sherpa (Nepalese people)
5. Sherpa (Nepalese people)—Social life and customs.
I. Padoan, Amanda. II. Title.
GV199.44.P182Z84 2012
796.522095491—dc23
2012008490

ISBN 978-0-393-34541-4 pbk.

W. W. Norton & Company, Inc.
500 Fifth Avenue, New York, N.Y. 10110
www.wwnorton.com

W. W. Norton & Company Ltd.
Castle House, 75/76 Wells Street, London W1T 3QT

Contents

PART I: AMBITION

PART II: CONQUEST

PART III: DESCENT

List of Maps

List of Characters

More than seventy people endeavored to climb K2 in 2008. What follows is a list of the climbers, expedition coordinators, rescuers, staff, and weather consultants who played a significant role during the disaster as described in this book.

NAME	AFFILIATION
AAMIR MASOOD	Pakistani Fearless Five pilot
ALBERTO ZERAIN	Basque independent climber
"BIG" PASANG BHOTE★	South Korean K2 Abruzzi Spur Flying Jump
CAS VAN DE GEVEL	Dutch Norit K2 Expedition
CECILIE SKOG	Norwegian K2 Expedition
CHHIRING DORJE SHERPA	American K2 International Expedition
CHRIS KLINKE	American K2 International Expedition
COURT HAEGENS	Dutch Norit K2 Expedition
DREN MANDIĆ★	Serbian K2 Vojvodina Expedition
ERIC MEYER	American K2 International Expedition
FREDRIK STRÄNG	American K2 International Expedition
GERARD (GER) McDONNELL★	Dutch Norit K2 Expedition

Go Mi-sun (Ms. Go)	South Korean K2 Abruzzi Spur Flying Jump
Hoselito Bite	Serbian independent climber
Hugues d'Aubarède*	French-led Independent Expedition
Hwang Dong-jin*	South Korean K2 Abruzzi Spur Flying Jump
Iso Planić	Serbian K2 Vojvodina Expedition
Jelle Staleman	Dutch Norit K2 Expedition
Jehan Baig*	French-led Independent Expedition
Jumik Bhote*	South Korean K2 Abruzzi Spur Flying Jump
Karim Meherban*	French-led Independent Expedition
Kim Jae-soo (Mr. Kim)	South Korean K2 Abruzzi Spur Flying Jump
Kim Hyo-gyeong*	South Korean K2 Abruzzi Spur Flying Jump
Lars Flato Nessa	Norwegian K2 Expedition
Marco Confortola	Italian K2 Expedition
Maarten van Eck	Dutch Norit K2 Expedition
Muhammad Hussein	Serbian K2 Vojvodina Expedition
Nadir Ali Shah	Serbian K2 Vojvodina Expedition
Nick Rice	French-led Independent Expedition
Park Kyeong-hyo*	South Korean K2 Abruzzi Spur Flying Jump
Pasang Lama	South Korean K2 Abruzzi Spur Flying Jump
Pemba Gyalje Sherpa	Dutch Norit K2 Expedition
Predrag (Pedja) Zagorac	Serbian K2 Vojvodina Expedition
Roeland van Oss	Dutch Norit K2 Expedition
Rolf Bae*	Norwegian K2 Expedition
Shaheen Baig	Serbian K2 Vojvodina Expedition

SULEMAN AL FAISAL	Pakistani Fearless Five pilot
TSERING LAMA (CHHIRING BHOTE)	South Korean K2 Abruzzi Spur Flying Jump
WILCO VAN ROOIJEN	Dutch Norit K2 Expedition
YAN GIEZENDANNER	French-led Independent Expedition

★ = Climbers who died on K2 in August 2008

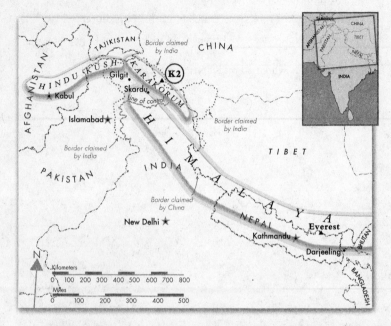

Karakorum, Himalaya, and Hindu Kush: K2 and the surrounding peaks rose from the sea as the Indian continental plate plowed under Eurasia. Still growing, the Karakorum is earth's youngest mountain range. The weather is much harsher than in the Himalaya.

Author's Note

by Peter Zuckerman

Many climbing accounts describe a death-defying struggle up fixed lines. But how did those ropes get there? Who performed the rescues? When your life hangs from a knot, it helps to know who tied it.

But some stories get buried. Western journalists seldom speak Ajak Bhote, Balti, Burushaski, Shar-Khumbu tamgney, Rolwaling Sherpi tamgney, or Wakhi. Reporters can't usually track down indigenous climbers by dialing telephone numbers or sending e-mails, and writers on a deadline rarely have time to trek to remote villages. As a result, testimony from high-altitude workers isn't broadcast far. Survivors of the Death Zone have imperfect recall, and the media maelstrom makes recovery—and accuracy—elusive as families, fans, friends, and publicists all assert claims on a story. Trauma and oxygen deprivation compound the confusion. As in war, eyewitnesses who were standing next to each other sometimes report different versions of the events.

Nonetheless, Amanda and I have tried to get at the truth and to be straightforward about our reporting. We researched for two years. We took seven trips to Nepal, trekking to regions rarely visited by Westerners and off-limits to journalists. We took three trips to Pakistan and obtained unprecedented access to military and government officials, thanks largely to Nazir Sabir, president of the Alpine Club of Pakistan. In total, we interviewed more than two hundred people and spent countless hours at kitchen tables in France, Holland, Ireland, Italy, Norway, Serbia, Spain, Switzerland, and the United States. We relied on more than a thousand photographs and videos. This book re-creates a true story. Please see the background notes for further information on methods and sources.

The death of Amanda's friend Karim Meherban was a catalyst for this book. Nursing a newborn, Amanda couldn't do all the research herself, so I was brought in as coauthor. Amanda and I are cousins, and we've been writing together since I was twelve. Before *Buried in the Sky*, I had a comfortable job as a daily newspaper reporter. I had never strapped on crampons. But when I learned about this story, I had no choice but to quit my job, grab a notebook, and head to the Himalaya. The characters were too inspiring, the goal too important, and the journey too compelling to resist.

Portland, Oregon
November 2011

BURIED
IN THE SKY

▲▲▲

Prologue

The Death Zone

The Bottleneck of K2, Pakistan
The Death Zone: about 27,000 feet above sea level

Hanging off the face of a cliff, an ice axe the only thing between him and death, a Sherpa climber named Chhiring Dorje swung to the left. A massive ice boulder ripped off above, hurtling toward him.

It was the size of a refrigerator.

The underbelly caught, and the mass flipped, cartwheeling down. It tore past, skimming Chhiring's shoulder, then vanished.

Brooof. It slammed into something below, shattering.

The mountain shook with the impact. Powder shot up in a column.

It was about midnight on August 1, 2008, and Chhiring had only a hazy idea of where he was: on or near the Bottleneck of K2, the deadliest stretch of the most dangerous mountain. At roughly the cruising altitude of a Boeing 737, the Bottleneck stretched away from him into the darkness below. In the starlight, the channel seemed bottomless as wisps of fog slithered into the abyss. Above, a lip of ice curled like the barrel of a crashing wave.

Oxygen depletion had turned Chhiring's mind to mush. Hunger

and exhaustion had broken his body. When he opened his mouth, his tongue froze; when he gasped for breath, the moistureless air scoured his throat and lashed his eyes.

Chhiring felt robotic, cold, too tired to think of what he'd sacrificed to get to K2. The Sherpa mountaineer, who had summited Everest ten times, had been consumed by the mountain for decades. A far more difficult peak than Everest, K2's summit is one of the most prestigious prizes in high-altitude mountaineering. Chhiring had gone despite his wife's tears. Despite the climb costing more money than his father had made in forty years. Despite his Buddhist *lama* warning him that K2's goddess would never tolerate the climb.

Chhiring had made it to the summit of K2 that evening without using bottled oxygen, vaulting him into an elite group of the most successful mountaineers, but the descent wasn't turning out as planned. He had dreamed of the achievement, a heroic reception, even fame. None of that mattered now. Chhiring had a wife, two daughters, a thriving business, and a dozen relatives who depended on him. All he wanted was to get home. Alive.

Normally, descent would be safer. Climbers usually go down during the early afternoon when it's warmer and daylight shows the way. They rappel, leapfrogging off the ice while attached to a fixed line to control their speed. In avalanche-prone areas around the Bottleneck, climbers descend as quickly as possible. This cuts exposure time, minimizing the chance of getting buried. Getting down fast was what Chhiring had planned on, depended on.

Now it was black and moonless. The fixed lines had vanished, severed by falling ice. Turning back wasn't an option. Without rope to catch him, Chhiring had only his axe to arrest a fall. And more than one life was in play: another climber was hanging from his harness.

The man suspended below him was Pasang Lama. Three hours earlier, Pasang had given up his ice axe to help more vulnerable climbers.

He had thought he could survive without it. Like Chhiring, Pasang had planned to rappel down the mountain using the fixed lines.

When the ropes through the Bottleneck disappeared, Pasang had figured it was his time to die. Stranded, he was unable to climb up or down without help. Why would anyone try to save him? A climber who attached himself to Pasang would surely fall, too. Using an ice axe to check the weight of one mountaineer skidding down the Bottleneck is nearly impossible. Stopping two bodies presents twice the difficulty, twice the risk. A rescue would be suicidal, Pasang thought. Mountaineers are supposed to be self-sufficient. Any pragmatic person would leave him to die.

As expected, one Sherpa already had. Pasang assumed Chhiring would do the same. Chhiring and Pasang were on separate teams. Chhiring had no obligation to help. But now Pasang hung three yards below him, attached to Chhiring's harness by a tether.

After dodging the block of ice, the two men bowed their heads and silently negotiated with the mountain goddess. She responded a few seconds later. The sound was electronic, the amplified pluck of a rubber band run through distortion pedals. *Zoing.* It continued, echoing louder, longer, faster, lower-pitched, from the left, from the right. The climbers knew what it meant. The ice around them was calving. With each *zoing*, fractures zigzagged across the glacier, ready to drop cinder blocks of ice.

If the men sensed one coming, they could shuffle to the side and contort themselves away. Failing that, they could sustain a hit. But eventually a mass the size of a bus would break off. Not much to do when that happens, except pray. Chhiring and Pasang had to get down before the falling ice crushed them.

Chuck. Chhiring hacked his axe into the ice. *Shink.* He kicked, stabbing the ice with his crampons. He descended like this for a few feet—*chuck, shink, shink, chuck, shink, shink*—and jammed himself against the slope so that the man attached to him could move to the same rhythm.

Pasang punched the hard ice with his fist, trying to compact it into a dent he could grip. Shallow and slick, the hold couldn't bear his weight. As Pasang extended his leg downward, he leaned on the safety tether that tied him to Chhiring. *Shink.* Pasang kicked in his crampons, relieving the pressure on the tether.

The weight on the rope threatened to pry Chhiring off the mountain's face, but he managed to cling on as they maneuvered around the bulges, cracks, dips, and lumps. Sometimes he and Pasang went side by side, holding hands, coordinating their movements. At other times Pasang went first, while Chhiring braced in a holding position with the axe and controlled the safety tether between them.

Rocks and chunks of ice spun at them, dinging their helmets, but they were halfway down and thought they'd survive. The night was windless—minus four degrees Fahrenheit—almost warm for K2. The lights of high camp were smoldering below. Chhiring and Pasang didn't expect it to happen.

A chunk of ice or rock knocked Pasang on the head. Batted off the ice, he swung like a piñata.

The force of Pasang's body on the rope peeled Chhiring from the slope.

The men tore downward.

Chhiring gripped his axe with both hands and slammed it into the mountain. The blade wouldn't catch. It cut surgically through the snow.

Sliding faster, Chhiring heaved his chest against the adze of his axe, digging into the slope. No good. Chhiring fell faster, another seven yards, another ten.

Pasang punched the slope with his fists and tried to grip, but his fingers skated along the ice.

The men dropped farther into the darkness.

Their shrieks, muffled by snow, must have funneled up the Bottleneck to the southeast face, but the survivors there heard nothing. They were deaf to the thud of falling bodies. All of them were lost. Dazed and hallucinating, some wandered off-route. Others calmed themselves enough to make a measured decision between two grim options: free-climb down the Bottleneck in the darkness or bivouac in the Death Zone.

Gerard McDonnell, who hours before had become the first Irishman to summit K2, cut a shallow ledge to sit on and another to brace his feet. Patience wouldn't stop an avalanche, but at least he had a perch to wait out the night.

Another climber, an Italian named Marco Confortola, squished in beside him. To stay awake, they forced themselves to sing. With hoarse voices, the men crooned the songs they could remember, anything to avoid dying in their sleep.

Earlier, a French summiter had made a promise to his girlfriend. "I'll never leave you again," Hugues d'Aubarède had told her via satellite phone. "I'm finished now. This time next year, we'll all be at the beach." That night, he slid down the Bottleneck to his death. His Pakistani high-altitude porter, Karim Meherban, strayed off-route, reaching the crown of the glacier that hulks over the Bottleneck. He slumped down and waited to freeze.

Farther down, a Norwegian newlywed had just lost her husband to several tons of ice. This climb had been their honeymoon. Now she was clawing down the mountain without him.

Many of the alpinists considered themselves to be among the best in the world. They hailed from France, Holland, Italy, Ireland, Nepal, Norway, Pakistan, Serbia, South Korea, Spain, Sweden, and the United States. Some had risked everything to scale K2. Their climb had devolved into a catastrophe. The final toll was bleak: within twenty-seven hours, eleven climbers had died in the deadliest single disaster in K2's history.

What had gone wrong? Why had the climbers continued up when they knew they'd never make it down before nightfall? How had they made so many simple mistakes, such as failing to bring enough rope?

The story became an international media sensation, landing on the covers of the *New York Times*, *National Geographic Adventure*, *Outside*, and in more than a thousand other publications. It ricocheted around the blogosphere and inspired speculation, documentaries, a stage-play revival, memoirs, and talk shows.

Some considered the climb an example of hubris, a waste of life fueled by machismo or madness: thrill-seekers trying too hard to get noticed by corporate sponsorship; lunatics climbing in a final act of escape; oblivious Westerners exploiting the lives of impoverished Nepalis and Pakistanis in a bid for glory; the media feeding off deaths to sell papers and products; gawkers observing the spectacle for entertainment.

"You want to risk your life?" a response to one of the *New York Times* stories said. "Then do it in service of your country, or family, or neighborhood. Climbing K2 or Everest is a selfish stunt that benefits nothing."

"Heroes my ass," sniffed another; ". . . these egomaniacs should stay off mountains."

Other people saw courage: explorers pitted against the adversity of nature; lost souls embracing risk to find meaning in an empty world.

"Climbing can expand the view of human potential for all of us," read a letter to the media from Phil Powers, executive director of the American Alpine Club.

Paraphrasing Teddy Roosevelt, another letter read, "Far better to dare mighty things, to win glorious triumphs, even though checkered by failure, than to rank with those poor spirits who neither enjoy nor suffer because they live in a gray twilight that knows not victory nor defeat."

Others raised basic questions: What do men and women do when they are on top of a mountain, dying? And why are some people driven to take such risks?

Before they were trapped on the mountaintop; before the deaths and funerals; before the rescues and reunions; before the fistfights and friendships; before the recriminations and reconciliations—everything had seemed perfect. The equipment was checked and rechecked; the routes, established; the weather, cooperative; the teams, intact. The moment they had spent so much time and training and money to reach—summit day—had finally come. They were going to conquer K2, stand on top of the most vicious mountain on earth, howl in triumph, unfurl their flags, and call their sweethearts.

Chhiring and Pasang, as they fell into the blackness, must have wondered: How did this happen?

PART I

AMBITION

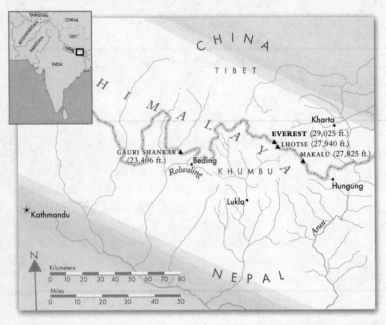

Rolwaling, Khumbu, and Arun regions of Nepal: The Sherpas in Chhiring's village of Beding (center) believe they are protected by a goddess who inhabits the mountain of Gauri Sankar. Pasang grew up in Hungung (far right), which became a war zone as the Maoists wrested control from Nepal's monarchy.

1

Summit Fever

Rolwaling Valley, Nepal
12,000 feet above sea level

His walk was more of a jog. He didn't drive a car; he rocketed through traffic on a black Honda Hero motorcycle. In the seven languages he spoke conversationally, Chhiring Dorje Sherpa talked so quickly it seemed as though each sentence were one long word punctuated by exclamation points. Everything about him was accelerated: his eating, his thinking, his climbing, his praying. He couldn't control the pace. Speed was hardwired into his DNA.

His first name meant "long life," but its pronunciation to English speakers—CHEER-ing—personified him. Cheerful determination radiated from Chhiring. It got him noticed. Clients praised his you-can-do-it, let's-rock-'n'-roll, give-me-your-pack attitude. It was contagious. How could you sit still in camp when every few minutes he would lurch up, stride forward, chop his arms through the air, make a pronouncement, plop down, and spring up again? There was a reason this thirty-four-year-old dynamo rarely drank coffee. He was caffeinated enough.

"Chhiring was always crazy," said his father, Ngawang Thundu

Sherpa. "He was a naughty child, and I knew he'd be a naughty adult."

"We have relied on his climbing for income," explained Chhiring's younger brother, also named Ngawang Sherpa. "Without his money, we wouldn't be where we are. But Chhiring became too ambitious. I was always telling him: 'Slow down.'" The family complained that Chhiring's line of work offended the gods and disrupted village life. His relatives wouldn't state the obvious: Chhiring's job could get him killed.

The summit of K2 was a long way from where Chhiring started. Before he climbed mountains, Chhiring lived in Beding, a remote village in Nepal. Wedged between India and Tibet, "like a yam between two boulders," Nepal is on the collision zone between two continental plates. This region of Southeast Asia used to be flat, submerged beneath the Tethys Sea, but for sixty-five million years, the Indian plate, moving north at twice the speed of a growing fingernail, has been jacking up the Tibetan crust, lifting the ancient seabed. It's now earth's highest mountain range. Nepal hosts a third of the Himalaya, including the south side of Everest.

Chhiring describes his birthplace as "mostly rock and ice." About 12,100 feet above sea level, the village of Beding seldom appears on maps, and when it does, it is plotted at different locations and, like many remote villages, goes by different names. Beding is about thirty miles west of Everest in a valley known as Rolwaling. Getting there takes a trek. First, travelers must jostle over a jeep track that ends near a cliff. Afterward, they zigzag up switchbacks, ford rivers, and wobble over chain-link bridges. After six days of lugging their own food and shelter, travelers see the village *chorten*, a shrine painted with unblinking blue eyes, rimmed in red. Symbolizing Buddha's gaze, the eyes stare down on Beding, inspiring the devout and spooking evil spirits.

Glaciated peaks surround the village, which is constructed of rocks, wood, mud, and dung mortar. A film of gray dust off the moraine coats the children. The air smells of threshed grass, blue smoke billows from fire pits, and the clouds seem so close you could jump up and punch them. Goats, sheep, cows, and yak-hybrids called *dzos* graze on steep terraces that resemble giant staircases. Below, the Rolwaling River shoots iridescent spray into the air.

Sherpas inhabit Beding and the other villages of the Rolwaling Valley. Although *sherpa*, with a lowercase *S*, is used colloquially as a job description, *Sherpa* is also an ethnicity, just as Greek, Hawaiian, and Basque are. And the Sherpas are a tiny ethnicity at that: The 150,000 Sherpas in Nepal make up less than one percent of the country's population.

Chhiring's village is often described by a list of what's missing: antibiotics, electricity, machinery, public sanitation, roads, running water, telephones. Residents lack formal education. Some don't know how to spell their names or read a clock, and many are told when they were born not by day but by season. A calendar's main function is to track dates commemorating the life of Buddha.

The Sherpas of Rolwaling seldom characterize themselves this way. They prefer to recognize what they have: faith and a self-reliant community. The gods are near, and neighbors are family. In Beding, locals take time to chat, drink tea, and play *Carrom*, a hybrid of billiards and shuffleboard in which players flick pucks at targets. They have a sophisticated knowledge of folklore, farming, and the region's topography, and they speak an unwritten language that combines eastern and central dialects of Tibetan, reflecting their long journey into Nepal. Rolwaling Sherpi tamgney is spoken nowhere else.

As with many Sherpa communities, the residents of Rolwaling rotate among three villages according to the season. The winter village heats up too much in the summer, the summer village cools down too much in the winter, and the central village, Beding, is more hospitable for crops and livestock in the fall. Residents live off the land, growing and eating astonishing amounts of potatoes. As Buddhists, they follow a tradition variously described as Tantrayana, Vajrayana, Nyingma, or, by detractors, Lamaism.

Written history on Rolwaling is hard to come by, and the legends vary, depending on the imagination of the storyteller. Anthropologist Janice Sacherer has studied the Sherpas of Rolwaling since the 1970s. "Piety they have," she said while discussing the challenges of studying their folklore. "Consistency they do not."

According to Tibetan scripture, Rolwaling is a *beyul*, a sacred valley formed as a refuge for Buddhists during times of turmoil and hidden until divinely revealed. Guru Rinpoche, who converted Tibetans to Buddhism in the seventh century, is credited with finding the *beyul* of Rolwaling, or even creating it with a giant horse and plow. Five centuries later, when Mongols were invading Tibet, the ancestors of the Sherpas moved to Nepal, and Buddhist visionaries told followers about the *beyuls* on the southern flanks of the Himalaya. Full of caves and rock monuments with spiritual properties, the *beyuls* are tributes to Guru Rinpoche and his consort, Yeshi Tsogyel, who aimed to peacefully enlighten all sentient beings.

At the hands of Chhiring's father and his elderly friends, however, these legends take on a less Buddhist tone. According to them, the Rolwaling Valley is the center of the universe and the cradle of life. The world began eight hundred years ago, before time was linear. Guru Rinpoche and his wife were meditating in a cave near Beding. After two days, the couple made a pact to rid the valley of evil. They stormed out and waged war against the demons.

Wings and scales were stripped like husks. Limbs were twisted; fangs, extracted. The demons rallied and tried to blot out the sun, stirring up dust to choke the gods. Guru Rinpoche summoned support, instructing his troops to gouge out their enemies' eyes. Crippled demons, swooping blindly, plunged into the Rolwaling River. Some of them sank. Guru Rinpoche waded in after the others, forcing their heads beneath the surface. Those who wiggled free of his grasp retreated to clefts in the rocks.

In the end, almost all of the demons were killed or tamed, but the war had taken a toll on the land. Features of Rolwaling's landscape—a massive rock on a level plain, a deep pit in the hills, a crack cleaving a boulder in two—attest to the battle. Afterward, the gods retired to the mountains, and Guru Rinpoche and his wife conceived five children, who became the genesis of all others. A few stayed. Most left the valley and became corrupt. That's the rest of us.

These days, the gods are impatient with the world outside Rolwaling. The elders predict that these gods will wipe out civilization fairly soon, maybe tomorrow, sparing only those who live in the valley. They frown upon anyone leaving. Deserters will be butchered along with everyone else.

The younger generation is less concerned. They say the apocalyptic legend is a scare tactic their grandparents use to get them to visit more often. In the standard Buddhist version of the founding myth, Guru Rinpoche traveled across the Himalaya like a sacred bounty hunter, tracking down demons and proselytizing them without the use of force. At that time, five sisters inhabited the crags in Rolwaling. Predating Buddhism by centuries, they were goddesses of an ancient Tibetan sect that demanded blood sacrifice.

As Guru Rinpoche entered the valley, chalk-faced Tseringma, the eldest, sent a snow leopard in pursuit. The guru charmed the cat until it purred and spoke of Buddhism, without pausing to eat or sleep, until Tseringma reformed.

Tseringma ascended a nearby mountain that now bears her name—but known to Hindus as Gauri Shankar—and renounced her diet of human flesh. Tseringma, the goddess of longevity, still lives on the 23,405-foot peak above Beding. Snowmelt from her glacier surges into the Rolwaling River, and its properties are miraculous. Some elders claim to be 120 years old, thanks to the water's effects.

After Guru Rinpoche subdued Tseringma, he pursued her four younger sisters. One by one, they repented and became Buddhist deities, moving to mountains of their own. Miyolangsangma patrols the summit of Everest on the back of a tigress. Now the goddess of prosperity, her face shines like 24-carat gold. Thingi Shalsangma, her body a pale shade of blue, became the goddess of healing after galloping on a zebra to the top of Shishapangma, a 26,289-foot peak in Tibet. Chopi Drinsangma, with a face in perpetual blush, became the goddess of attraction. She chose a deer instead of a zebra and settled on Kanchenjunga, a 28,169-foot peak in Nepal.

The final sister—Takar Dolsangma, the youngest, with a green face—was a hard case. She mounted a turquoise dragon and fled northward to the land of three borders. In the modern Rolwaling folklore, this is Pakistan. Guru Rinpoche chased after her and eventually cornered her on a glacier called the Chogo Lungma. Takar Dolsangma appeared remorseful and, spurring her dragon, ascended K2, accepting a new position as the goddess of security. Although Guru Rinpoche never doubted her sincerity, maybe he should have: Takar Dolsangma, it seems, still enjoys the taste of human flesh.

▲ ▲ ▲

Rolwaling is a *beyul*, a frontier community that granted amnesty to refugees. It was thought to be guarded by a powerful mountain goddess. By the mid-nineteenth century, the valley was a popular destination for debtors and thugs to settle down and become pious. At first, famine limited population growth. In the 1880s, the introduction of the potato provided a measure of food security, and the population quadrupled to about two hundred.

The next significant incursion, after the potato, was Edmund Hillary. Two years before he achieved the first ascent of Everest in 1953, Hillary trekked through Rolwaling with a British reconnaissance team, searching for the best route to Everest. The British ultimately chose a different approach, through the Khumbu Valley to the east, but some Rolwaling Sherpas were offered jobs, including Hrita Sherpa, who broke trail for Tenzing Norgay and Hillary days before their first ascent.

Rolwaling never underwent development like the Khumbu, where Everest-bound tourists injected money and jobs and Hillary built schools, a hospital, and an airstrip. During Chhiring's childhood in the 1970s, Rolwaling was the "most isolated, traditional and economically backward of all the Sherpa communities in Nepal."

Traders seldom passed through, and beasts of burden could barely scramble up the banks of scree. The Sherpas relied on local materials and their own labor to feed and clothe themselves. No one owned a cotton T-shirt; yak wool was woven into cloth. Chhiring's father dressed in a *chuba*, a wool robe secured by a sash over his trousers. In the winter, he wore buffalo leather boots that were padded with dried moss. His mother wore an *ungi*, a sleeveless tunic draped with a blue-striped apron that covered her front and back. To signify her unmarried status, Chhiring's younger sister wore an apron only on her back.

Chhiring was born in 1974 on the floor of a room that served as his family's kitchen, barn, and bedroom. The boy—said Chhiring's father, aunt, and uncle—was a slacker who loved to sneak away and explore the mountains. His relatives still tell the story of his gravest transgression: the time when, as an eight-year-old playing with fire, Chhiring set the hills ablaze. The flames burned the winter reserves of feed, and the animals went hungry. Chhiring's father beat him with a stick, and, twenty-six years later, still hadn't forgiven him.

It was a childhood disrupted by death. Chhiring's younger sister returned from the fields one afternoon with red blisters crawling up her skin. As the pustules clustered on her tongue, she suffocated. Another sister was carrying water from the river when a rock dropped off a cliff and crushed her internal organs. No one could figure out what happened to Chhiring's two-year-old brother. Perhaps he ate something toxic. One day, his gut inflated. With his stomach painfully distended, the child soon died. A third sister's birth left Chhiring's mother, Lakpa Futi, hemorrhaging. Mother and infant died.

Chhiring watched the *lama* perform the death rites on his mother, yanking her hair to let her spirit leave through the head, whispering into her ear advice about the afterlife. Chhiring tried not to cry, believing it could cause a veil of blood to cover her eyes and obscure her way into the next life. He was too young to go up the hill for the cremation, so he sat in the room where he was born and watched his mother's smoke lift into the sky. His father, Ngawang Thundu Sherpa, returned home and collapsed.

From then on, Ngawang passed out several times a day. Villagers suspected that a demon possessed him. As the fainting became more frequent, Chhiring's father stopped caring for the four remaining children. He fell mute and forgot to eat and bathe. When he slept, he woke crying, and sobbed until he fainted again.

The fields withered, the animals strayed, and the house fell into disrepair. The family ran low on food. The children's shoes and clothing wore out. No matter how hard he tried, Ngawang could not motivate himself to work. When able to rouse himself, he spent all his effort praying, trying to appease the gods. "I didn't understand what I had done to make them punish me," he recalled.

Chhiring, then twelve years old, became head of the household. He sold off livestock and bartered for food to feed his siblings but soon ran out of things to trade. In exchange for potatoes, he worked for other families, fetching water, gathering firewood, and sweeping. His sister, Nima, cared for their father and the two youngest children.

Chhiring didn't make enough to afford shoes, but he and his family didn't starve, and relatives helped when they became desperate.

Around the time he turned fourteen, Chhiring's aunts and uncles told him he had no choice: He was a man now, old enough to marry, and he had to find a faster way to pay off his father's debts. Some suggested he leave the village to carry fuel and equipment for European climbers and trekkers. Chhiring was reluctant. He had never wandered far from the sacred valley. At that time, few Sherpas had left Rolwaling, and those who had entered the climbing industry described it as miserable and speculative. "Chhiring seemed too young to be a porter, too small to carry loads for foreigners," recalled his uncle, Ang Tenzing Sherpa. "I told him it was a bad idea."

Furthermore, Chhiring worried about the deities who lived on the mountains; the glaciers were their embodiment. Climbing the spine of a goddess or trespassing into her home amounted to insolence, even blasphemy. Chhiring's grandfather, Pem Phutar, had carried loads for a 1955 British expedition to Gauri Shankar, the sacred peak where Tseringma resides, but the family rarely spoke of it. Many villagers looked down on mountaineers and told disparaging stories about them.

These tales had the same theme and usually ended with a broken man from Germany. Fifteen sherpas were infamously killed on German expeditions to Nanga Parbat in 1934 and 1937. Even Hitler's *Reichssportführer* had condemned two members of the 1934 expedition who abandoned their team in a storm, and a strange stereotype evidently developed among the Sherpas. For example, villagers in Beding spoke of a once-successful German businessman who tried to climb Gauri Shankar. He failed, of course, and the mountain goddess punished him. Within a year, the German lost his teeth, contracted leprosy, and was robbed of everything but his wife. When she left him, he died of despair.

Although that story must be apocryphal, another one isn't. In 1979, American mountaineer John Roskelley decided to conquer Gauri Shankar. Pitch after pitch, conditions on the peak were so frustrating that Roskelley found the experience vaguely erotic. The "goddess of love," he surmised, wanted to "remain a virgin." Approaching the summit, he had nearly seduced her when his climbing partner—"a young and upcoming Sherpa 'tiger'" named Dorje—begged him to stop. Roskelley, nonetheless, "hugged [the peak] like a fat lady's bottom and shimmied up," Dorje in tow. "Gauri Shankar was ours," he gloated. "We were the first non-deities to reach its 23,405-foot summit."

Although Roskelley didn't suffer any ill effects from the climb, residents of Rolwaling believe they did. Soon after Roskelley's summit, a glacial lake on the flanks of Gauri Shankar burst through a natural dam, triggering a flash flood. Icemelt and debris submerged three women working at a water-powered gristmill. Two were fished out alive. The third died.

Chhiring didn't want to end up like the German or cause a flash flood as John Roskelley had. He considered it risky even to speak to mountaineers and figured they all were crackpots. Why would anyone spend so much money to climb without any practical purpose? And why weren't they strong enough to carry their own food and gear, as the rest of the world did?

But necessity and curiosity got the best of him. His family needed money, and Chhiring couldn't make enough gathering firewood. His uncle Sonam Tsering, a mountaineer, told him that portering was the solution. The gods would overlook the offense, given his circumstances, and Chhiring could return home rich. So at the age of fourteen, Chhiring left for the city, walking most of the way.

When he arrived in Kathmandu, Chhiring discovered that the elders weren't exaggerating. The apocalypse, predicted to occur outside Rolwaling, was known to the general public. Even the U.S. Embassy was issuing survival kits. The capital was doomed.

▲ ▲ ▲

Kathmandu is still waiting for the Big One, an earthquake that could flatten the city. The tremors of 1253, 1259, 1407, 1680, 1810, 1833, 1860, and 1934 knocked down temples and killed tens of thousands. The next quake will be worse. Kathmandu has swelled to a million residents, and most of them live in brick warrens tottering atop shallow foundations. Assessing the risk, the United Nations has waged a campaign to promote earthquake preparedness, but nobody seems flustered. Fatalism is part of Kathmandu's character.

If driving rules exist in the city, they're Darwinian. A green light means full speed ahead; a yellow light means full speed ahead; a red light means full speed ahead and honk. Traffic spills into a medieval grid too narrow for the modern world, and no meaningful lines are painted on the road. Seat belts are a novelty, and drivers and pedestrians go wherever they dare, braving a crush of buses, bicycles, cows, chickens, children, dogs, food carts, lepers, motorbikes, peddlers, pilgrims, protesters, rats, rickshaws, sewage, strollers, taxis, trucks, and trash.

A moonscape of brick factories rings the city, and soot thickens the air and congeals in the slits between the tenements. The smog, cupped inside an amphitheater of mountains, rarely disperses from Kathmandu, even at night. The particulate matter in the air almost always exceeds World Health Organization standards, and pedestrians wear surgical masks so they can breathe through the grit that settles in the lungs.

Paradoxically, this polluted city started with a shade tree. According to legend, the Hindu god Gorakhnath, like many modern commuters, didn't respect the right of way. Racing to a festival, he plowed into a chariot processional, and, to avoid embarrassment, tried to impersonate a human. Fortunately, a responsible bystander made a citizen's arrest. To post bail, Gorakhnath planted a seed in the mud. It sprouted into a sal tree that grew tall enough to scrape the firmament. A monk felled the tree and used the wood to build Kasthamandap, a three-tiered pavilion. Still standing, it's one of the world's oldest wooden structures. Kasthamandap is Kathmandu's namesake.

In the 1950s, Kathmandu became a launching pad for mountaineering expeditions. Hippies followed in the 1960s, and Freak Street, acrid with incense, remains an asylum for the New Age movement. Tourism makes up a large percentage of Nepal's economy, and Kathmandu depends on it. Tour guides, prostitutes, drug dealers, and self-appointed messiahs hustle near the city's Durbar Square seven days a week.

When Chhiring arrived in Kathmandu for the first time, he had never switched on a lightbulb. The teenager settled in Little Tibet, a community of Buddhist refugees who had fled the Chinese invasion in the 1950s. Chhiring's neighbors helped him adapt to city life, and the nearby Boudhanath *stupa* gave him a sense of permanence. Considered one of the holiest Buddhist sites in Nepal, Boudhanath is a reliquary buried beneath an enormous mound of soil. The *stupa*'s shape symbolizes Mount Meru, the center of the Buddhist cosmos, with its summit in the heavens and its bedrock in hell. As soon as he arrived in Little Tibet, Chhiring joined the crowd of worshippers, pacing clockwise around the *stupa* in prayer. He repeated the ritual each morning until his uncle found him a portering job that paid $3 a day.

For that job, Chhiring spent a month hauling seventy pounds of kerosene, stoves, and climbing gear to Island Peak, near the base of Everest. The Japanese clients were surprised that a teenager could lug so much up steep trails without complaining, and they praised his upbeat attitude. To Chhiring, these trekkers seemed normal enough—and by the end of the month he had earned $90. Never had he seen so much money.

He spent half his wages on food, shoes, and clothes, which he took to his family in Beding. He returned to Kathmandu a few weeks later to find another job. It wasn't long before Chhiring was spending six months of the year outside Rolwaling, accepting one portering job after another. The work fit his talents. He befriended clients and picked up their languages, becoming a leader among the porters because he could serve as an interpreter. Around the time he turned sixteen, a women's team, impressed with Chhiring's endurance and command of English, invited him to carry loads on Everest. Chhiring had never climbed on a glacier but agreed to do it.

Western climbers spend years preparing for Everest; for many Sherpas, it's their training ground. During their first week on the job, some Sherpas who have never climbed will be breaking trail, hauling gear, and establishing camps for professional guides and their clients. It makes a certain kind of sense on Everest. Thousands of people have summited it. The routes are well established, the climbing is nontechnical, and the wage for each support climber is substantial— about $3,000 plus a bonus for each client who tops out. Sherpas from mountain villages are better acclimatized than their clients and often have superior strength and balance at high altitude. On Everest, these abilities can compensate for inexperience.

Sherpas begin with Everest for another reason too. Most believe the mountain can be climbed without retribution. Miyolangsangma, the goddess who resides on Everest, only occasionally punishes trespassers. If she dislikes being climbed, pragmatism offsets her displeasure. The goddess of prosperity loves to see Sherpas make money. "As long as you treat Miyolangsangma with respect, ask forgiveness and get paid well, she'll tolerate the climb," said Ngawang Oser Sherpa, the head *lama* of Rolwaling. "You shouldn't do it, but she is the most forgiving of the five sisters."

Chhiring went up Everest for the first time in 1991. In the beginning, the climb was straightforward. He didn't have much gear or formal training, but other Sherpas showed him how to strap on crampons and grip an ice axe, and he carried seventy pounds of bottled oxygen to the South Col at 26,200 feet. On his way down, however, a storm rolled in. The temperature dropped and Chhiring's fingers turned gray. As everyone rushed to camp, Chhiring tried to catch up, but he stepped on a smooth plate of ice. It gave way under him like a trapdoor. Chhiring sank down to his shoulders. He clawed at snow, but his fingers were too stiff to grab hold, and he slid deeper. Waiting, he hung, his feet dangling in space.

It seemed as though hours had passed, and he was nearly unconscious when another climber, also named Chhiring Sherpa, pulled him out by the collar. The older Chhiring was furious. He scolded the teenager. You're too young to be on Everest, he said. Nobody your age should be up this high.

The warning had an unintended effect. It humiliated Chhiring and made him want to climb even more. Something about failing, knowing he might have reached the top of the world if he'd worn thicker gloves and boots, made him want the summit. He decided he would learn to climb better than the Sherpa who had saved him—or anyone else. Money was another incentive. He made 35,000 rupees, or about $450, from his first Everest climb. Although it wasn't a fifth of what experienced climbers were receiving, it was more than the average Nepali made in a year, and he had earned it in a month.

For the next two years, Chhiring continued to work on high mountains, to seek advice and help from his uncle Sonam. Then, in 1993, Sonam left on an expedition that would be his last. Sonam, with four Everest summits to his credit, was joining Pasang Lahmu, a friend aiming to become the first Nepali woman on the summit of Everest. The duo topped out on April 22.

Sonam may have prayed to Miyolangsangma, the goddess of Everest, and apologized for violating her sacred space. Nevertheless, as he and Pasang Lahmu descended toward the South Col, an upturned bowl of swirling clouds coalesced around the summit. The lenticular formation meant brutal weather blowing in. With no time to strategize, Pasang and Sonam joined three teammates in a forced bivouac. Huddling together in the open, they braced against raging winds.

Miyolangsangma refused to intercede. The gale pounded them, and, after two days, they were presumed dead. Sonam may have forced himself to stagger several hundred meters before he fell. Climbers discovered his pack below Pasang Lahmu's body.

As confirmation of Sonam's death spread to Kathmandu, Chhiring couldn't accept it. He remembered how Sonam had assured him that Everest could be climbed without consequence. "I saw he was mistaken about that," Chhiring said. "My head was telling me to quit and go home." Yet when he returned to Beding, Chhiring saw the power of money. His six-year-old brother Ngawang was plump and wore new shoes. His father had installed a corrugated tin roof. His sister was learning to read. Although the family mourned Sonam, none of Chhiring's siblings were asking him to quit. "And I couldn't," he said. "I didn't want to."

The following year, Chhiring was back on Everest with a Norwegian team. Climbers recognized his endurance at altitude and recruited him to work for them on subsequent expeditions. Soon Chhiring had joined teams from Belgium, England, France, Germany, India, Japan, Norway, Russia, Switzerland, and the United States.

As Chhiring landed more jobs, he became more ambitious. When clients asked him to carry a forty-five-pound load, he hauled ninety. Instead of simply carrying, he volunteered to fix ropes, break trails, lead pitches, organize expeditions. He stopped using bottled oxygen, which purists regard as doping. He worked Everest as a yearly routine, reaching the summit ten times, and broke an endurance record for topping out three times in two weeks.

Family members saw him change. He became wealthy by Nepali standards and seemed indifferent to the elders' prophecy. Sometimes he climbed not for the money but for the exhilaration. His *lama* warned that it was only a matter of time before he'd be cursed. Chhiring's father, now healthy, decided that his son had gone mad. Villagers were afraid Chhiring's riches would tempt the younger generation to leave.

They were right. When Chhiring returned to Rolwaling during the off-season, he wore La Sportiva boots and a North Face jacket. He brought provisions for the village—fuel, rice, socks, wool sweaters—and described urban novelties, such as motorcycles and televisions. The teenagers were awed. Mountaineering may be a sin, but it sure made you rich. Villagers flocked to Kathmandu.

Chhiring gave them a place to stay, found them jobs, and started an expedition company, Rolwaling Excursion. The elders appreciated the clothing he brought back, and their opposition softened, even as Beding's population crashed to twenty-three permanent residents.

Chhiring's accomplishments impressed his peers, but critics dismissed his achievements because they were on Everest. Anyone can climb Everest over and over, they argued, even a *Playboy* centerfold. The mountain has fixed lines strung from nearly start to finish. Everest is commercial, more a jungle gym for tourists than one of the great climbing challenges. Although this guy may hold an endurance record, it's from high camp, not Base Camp. Real climbers take on real mountains, like K2. Chhiring craved the chance to prove himself, but getting to K2 cost money, and he was about to settle down.

At sixteen, Chhiring had fallen for Dawa Sherpani, a girl he'd seen herding yaks. Dawa hadn't taken him seriously then. Now she owned a teashop near Boudhanath, and Chhiring was a regular. He'd sit at a corner table, swilling black tea, and jump up, making his presence felt, if a male patron paid Dawa too much attention. Dawa wasn't impressed, but Chhiring had learned to move fast. He persuaded Dawa to consult his *lama* to see whether their horoscopes were compatible. It was a perfect match.

They skipped the traditional three-day ceremony, exchanged vows in an hour, and went to his place. Their daughter, Tshering Namdu Sherpa, arrived in the spring. Four years later, Dawa gave birth to a second daughter, Tensing Futi Sherpa. The family, along with Chhiring's brothers and sisters and Dolkar, a white spaniel, moved into a cream-colored townhouse that resembled a four-tier wedding cake. It had more than just running water and electricity; Chhiring's home had a television, a microwave oven, an office, a prayer room, two computers, and four bathtubs—luxuries he'd never dreamed of as a child.

Compared to Beding, this was easy living. Chhiring's expedition company boomed, nearly doubling in size every year. Chhiring began organizing climbs with dozens of employees, many from his village. By now a major patron of Rolwaling's monastery, Chhiring finally had won approval from the elders. He held platinum elite status at the Mount Everest Summiters Club. His daughters were becoming fluent in English and attended a private prep school. Only his wife seemed worried.

"So many people relied on him," Dawa said. "If he got killed in the mountains, Chhiring wouldn't just be hurting himself. He'd be hurting me and the children. I didn't know what we'd do if he died."

2

Doorway to Heaven

K2 was born during a period of mass extinction. Sixty-five million years ago, as dinosaurs were dying off, the Indian continental plate sped north at six inches a year, a reckless pace in geological time. It plowed into Eurasia, wedging itself under the larger continent, and K2, like Everest, rose from the sea. Still rising, the Karakorum is earth's youngest mountain range, with jagged edges unfiled by the elements.

The word *Karakorum* stems from several languages in the Altaic linguistic family of Central Asia: *kara* means "black" and *kor'um* means "gravel" or "rock." The city of Karakorum was Genghis Khan's opulent capital in thirteenth-century Mongolia, and traders used *karakorum* to describe the highest pass along the way. The British explorer William Moorcroft climbed the Karakorum Pass in the 1820s and applied the name to the mountains around it. In the 1930s, the Royal Geographical Society affirmed the title.

The range extends southeast through Kashmir, along the borders of Pakistan and China, and latches into the Himalaya. The Karakorum has the world's largest concentration of peaks more than five miles high. Harsher than the Himalaya, it is the most glaciated place outside the polar regions—so remote that Western explorers hadn't mapped it until the mid-nineteenth century.

The mountain now called K2 entered surveyors' books in 1856. The Great Trigonometric Survey of India had ordered British lieutenant Thomas Montgomerie to map Kashmir as part of an empire-wide effort to determine the exact shape of the earth. With help from Kashmiri porters, Montgomerie spent four days towing a plane table, heliostat, and brass theodolite up Mount Haramukh in the Himalayan foothills. The climb rewarded him with a panorama of spires. Two peaks 130 miles northeast jutted from the range's spine, towering above the rest. Montgomerie peered through the theodolite, took the mountains' bearings, and inked their outlines in his field book.

The closest peak, a hexagon with two summits, appeared taller to him. He labeled it K1. *K* stood for "Karakorum"; the numeral signified that it was the first peak in his survey. He marked the glistening pyramid farther away as K2 and later logged more mountains, all the way to K32. Along with the other peaks, K1 reverted to its local name, *Masherbrum*, or "mountain of fire" in Balti, the local language. K2's designation stuck. Mapmakers knew its local name, *Chogori*, was a cursory description the Baltis used to signify a great peak. Linguists now claim that *Chogori* is a Tibetan word that means "doorway to heaven." The Buddhist ancestors of the Baltis named the mountain soon after they migrated from Tibet.

Montgomerie's visual estimate was off by 2,592 feet. K2 towers over Masherbrum. Straddling the borders of China and Pakistan, the peak looms above the Karakorum, soaring 28,251 feet, making it the second-tallest mountain on earth. Everest stands just 778 feet higher. From a distance, K2 resembles a prehistoric shark tooth. Closer in,

Thomas Montgomerie's Sketch of K2: A British lieutenant sketched the mountain's profile in his field book and labeled it K, for the Karakorum mountain range, and 2, for the second mountain in the survey. To locals, K2 is *Chogori*, or "doorway to heaven" in Tibetan. Mountaineers often refer to it as the Savage Mountain.

you can see its striated gneissic rock, encased in ice. On clear mornings, the summit floats imperiously above the clouds and the sun bathes its glaciers with golden light.

K2 lacks the mass of Everest, but it's sleeker—and meaner. Climbers call it "The Savage Mountain." The peak has all the obstacles of Everest, and more. K2's glaciers are riddled with fissures concealed by layers of snow; climbers step on these crevasses, punch through, and, if unroped, disappear. Blocks of ice cleave off overhanging glaciers; avalanches roar down icy flanks. And then there's the altitude. No human, plant, or animal can tolerate such harsh conditions for more than a few days. With each lungful of air, climbers on the summit suck in only a third of the oxygen they breathe at sea level. Oxygen deprivation saps their strength and compromises their judgment. Altitude illness breaks them, giving some the coordination of toddlers.

As if these difficulties weren't enough, storms are harsher on K2. It stands 882 miles northwest of Everest, and, being farther from the equator, is more vulnerable to extratropical cyclones and their accompanying jet streams. Everest at least follows a reliable weather pattern: Water evaporates from the Bay of Bengal east of India, forming cloud banks; they float northward over the Himalaya, nudging the jet stream off the summit, in advance of the monsoon. In May, relatively windless weather graces Everest for as long as two weeks. In contrast, K2's weather window is a crapshoot. Climbers don't know when the window will open—or whether it will open at all.

All this makes for dismal statistics. Before 2008, only 278 people had stood on K2's summit. Everest's summit roll was 4,115, and its fatality rate—the percentage of climbers who went above Base Camp and died—had averaged 0.7 for the previous decade. Although the Himalayan Database crunches the numbers for Everest, no accurate statistics exist for K2. Climbers of the Savage Mountain can't reliably approximate their chances of survival and don't want to. In 2008, the fatality rate of those leaving Base Camp for a summit bid was 30.5 percent, higher than the casualty rate at Omaha Beach on D-day. Among high-altitude climbers if not statisticians, there's no comparison: K2 is more lethal than Everest.

It took a century of alpinism before a mortal stood on K2's summit. One early attempt involved "The Wickedest Man on Earth." Mountaineer, author, pornographer, and occultist, Aleister Crowley had eclectic passions, attracting admirers long after his death. The Beatles featured him on the album jacket of *Sgt. Pepper's Lonely Hearts Club Band* just as prominently as Karl Marx and Marilyn Monroe. In 1902, Crowley and his friend Oscar Eckenstein decided to climb K2.

On the way to the mountain, Eckenstein was arrested for espionage. Crowley, meanwhile, loaded the packs with tomes by Milton and whipped the porters. Some of these porters deserted, stealing Crowley's clothes.

As Crowley and his teammates negotiated K2's Northeast Ridge, weather pushed him back five times. One man's lungs filled with fluid, and Crowley was hallucinating from a combination of altitude and opium. At high camp, Crowley pulled out a revolver and tried to discipline a teammate, who knocked the gun away and socked him in the gut. Crowley accused another climber of hoarding food and going mad. He booted the hungry man off the team.

After nine weeks and five summit bids, they failed to reach the top, but Crowley's expedition achieved a measure of success. They spent a record amount of time at high altitude—more than two months—and climbed to a respectable 21,400 feet, a record on K2 that stood for decades.

If Crowley embodies the climbing nut, the leader of the next major expedition epitomizes the climbing aristocrat. Luigi Amedeo Giuseppe Maria Ferdinando Francesco di Savoia-Aosta, more concisely known as the Duke of the Abruzzi, was a veteran explorer who had lost four fingertips trying to reach the North Pole. Fleeing a scandalous romance in 1909, he decided to head for the hills. The duke failed to get permission to scale Everest, so he christened K2 as the Third Pole and left his *palazzo* to climb it.

Abruzzi departed Europe on the steamer *Oceana*, laden with 10,454 pounds of luggage, including a brass bedstead, feather pillows, and sleeping bags layered with four types of animal hides. Trekking through the princely states of Kashmir, he was slowed by banquets, polo matches, and gift-giving ceremonies. Runners brought in daily mail and newspapers, and one of the duke's early concerns was, to quote the expedition diary, "the smell of the natives," who were "unbearable, even in open air."

But even as Abruzzi pressed a scented handkerchief to his nostrils, he took in a majestic vista. K2 was "the indisputable sovereign of the region, gigantic and solitary, hidden from human sight in innumerable ranges, jealously defended by a vast throng of vassal peaks, protected from invasion by miles and miles of glaciers." The landscape impressed him enough to bestow his own name on its features. Some of these names, such as K2's Abruzzi Spur and the nearby Savoia Glacier, are still used today.

The duke spent six weeks trying one route after another, surveying and posing for photographs. He never made it above 20,500 feet. "If anyone does get to the top," he later informed the Italian Alpine Club, "it will be a pilot, not a mountaineer."

▲ ▲ ▲

The duke's prediction held for nearly half a century, but two men almost disproved it in 1939 during what became "the most bizarre tragedy in the history of Himalayan mountaineering."

Fritz Wiessner—"Baby Face" to his friends—had the dimples of a cherub and the charm of a hornet. Famous for first ascents on monoliths such as Devils Tower in Wyoming, he had hired eight Sherpas to help him bag K2. On the evening of July 19, one of them, Pasang Dawa Lama, had him on belay 750 feet below the summit. As the sun dipped, trailed by a sliver of moon, Pasang heard a rustle. Blue scales flared in the dusk.

According to *lamas* who mythologize the climb, Pasang was familiar with the goddess of K2 and her appetite for human flesh. He watched in horror as Takar Dolsangma dismounted her dragon, hitched the beast to the slope by its tongue, and sniffed the air. It had been 1,122 years since her last meal.

Pasang "was so afraid," recounted Wiessner. Oblivious of the danger, he shouted for more slack.

"No, sahib," Pasang responded, gripping the rope. "Tomorrow."

Incredulous, Wiessner turned back. The retreat, however, did not appease the goddess. As Pasang rappelled down the ice, she gripped the dragon's withers and soared into the sky. Spiraling toward Pasang, the dragon grazed his pack, knocking two pairs of crampons down the slope. Attempting the summit was now hopeless, and Pasang began strategizing about how to get down.

His first challenge was Wiessner, who was bent on topping out. The next day, as the men recuperated at high camp, Pasang watched for dragons, and Wiessner sunbathed nude. "Since the day before, [Pasang Lama] had no longer been his old self," Wiessner recounted. "[H]e had been living in great fear of the evil spirits, constantly murmuring prayers, and had lost his appetite."

At dawn, the men climbed to the Bottleneck and examined the ice. "With crampons, we could have practically run up," Wiessner puffed, but without crampons there was no choice. They turned around for the last time.

On descent, Pasang relaxed. The camps below would be stocked with supplies and armed with Sherpa support. He had provoked Takar Dolsangma yet somehow survived.

But she hadn't forgiven him. On an icy slope above Camp 8, Pasang's body lurched forward, as if jabbed by an invisible elbow. His throat let loose "a funny little noise" as he began to slide. Wiessner knew what to do. "I put myself in position, dug in as much as possible, and held him on the rope." Pasang regained balance, but what he encountered in the next camp shook him more than the fall. There was nothing: no additional supplies and no one except a dehydrated straggler, American millionaire Dudley Wolfe, who was slurping snowmelt from the folds of a tent.

Wolfe joined the rope team, and the trio descended through the fog until the goddess evidently tripped Wolfe. The line pulled taut and jerked all the men off their feet. They barreled toward a 600-story drop, gear spilling from their packs. "All I was thinking was, how stupid this has to happen like this," Wiessner recounted. About 20 yards before the cliff, he flipped onto his stomach, swung his axe, and broke the fall. All skulls were intact, but only one sleeping bag had survived. The men would have to share it.

In the next camp, it appeared as though a dragon-size raccoon had rummaged through the tents—shredding the fabric, sampling the food, and scattering trash. The air mattresses and sleeping bags had vanished. "I could hardly speak," Wiessner recalled. "We almost knew that we had been sabotaged." The men dug out a tent, pulled the remaining sleeping bag across their chests, and shivered through the night.

In the morning, Wolfe could barely stand. Pasang and Wiessner left to look for help but found camp after camp had been emptied. The reason for this became clear when they finally stumbled into Base Camp: Pasang, Wiessner, and Wolfe had been presumed dead.

The Sherpas mobilized to rescue Wolfe, but by the time they reached him, critical days had been lost. Wolfe, too debilitated to crawl outside, was using his tent as a latrine. The Sherpas pulled him out of the sewage, poured tea down his gullet, and descended to thicker air, aiming to haul him down the next morning.

A storm grounded the rescue for another day. Then, as the skies cleared on July 31, three rescuers—Kikuli, Kitar, and Phinsoo—went up to fetch Wolfe. They never returned. The slope, packed with fresh snow, avalanched, likely burying them alive. Wolfe presumably died in his tent. The Savage Mountain had claimed its first four victims.

Wiessner trudged home defensive: "On big mountains, as in war," he told the media, "one must expect casualties." He, like the Sherpas, developed a mythological version of the events. As the years passed, he began to claim that a nearly full moon had illuminated the sky on the night of his summit bid. This fostered a myth that Wiessner might have pioneered the first ascent of K2 if a superstitious Sherpa hadn't held him back. But lunar charts show that July 19 was three days past a new moon, and, as seen from K2, that moon was a useless sliver that stayed visible only three hours after dark. Pasang and Wiessner had confronted a bigger problem than a turquoise dragon: Headlamps wouldn't be invented for another thirty-three years, and they faced pitch-blackness. In the gathering dusk, Pasang's insistence on turning around probably saved Wiessner's life.

▲ ▲ ▲

Nobody attempted K2 during World War II. In the aftermath, the British relinquished their Indian empire, which split into two independent nations: Pakistan and India. Suddenly K2 had changed hands, ending up in Pakistan-administered Kashmir, a territory claimed by both countries.

The 1947 Partition of British India led to one of the largest and bloodiest exoduses in modern history. Religious persecution took the form of mob violence as fourteen million people dispersed to their respective nations: Hindus fleeing from Pakistan to India and many Muslims flowing in reverse. Their desperate caravans were ambushed by fanatics of the opposing faith. Refugees were butchered on the railway, and train cars stuffed with mutilated corpses had to be hosed out when they reached their destinations. One million were killed, and the new governments of India and Pakistan blamed each other. There has been constant hostility around K2 ever since.

Nevertheless, mountaineering revived, and the Karakorum reopened for business. A group of Americans cinched a permit for K2 in 1953, and their expedition came to define decency on a mountain.

As the team left for the Karakorum, Art Gilkey, a twenty-seven-year-old geologist, learned that Everest had just been conquered. Gilkey had hoped this would be his lucky summer, too, but eight weeks later he found himself dying at 25,500 feet. He was suffering from what felt like a charley horse in his left calf. He couldn't walk it off, and the leg kept swelling. A storm blew in, stranding Gilkey and several teammates. The gale pounded their tent for five days. When the wind slowed, Gilkey crawled outside and tried to stand. He collapsed.

A doctor named Charlie Houston examined Gilkey and diagnosed thrombophlebitis, or potentially lethal blood clots that can form when a climber is dehydrated, oxygen-deprived, and immobile for too long. Unwilling to let him die, the team tried to bring Gilkey down. Winds blasted them back, foiling their first evacuation attempt and trapping them inside the tents for another three days. Gilkey's cough became an incessant hack. As is often the case with thrombophlebitis, the clots had probably broken off and barged through Gilkey's main pulmonary artery, clogging his lungs. The resulting embolism would have impaired Gilkey's breathing and circulation.

After a break in the weather, the men decided to try again. They zipped Gilkey into a sleeping bag, wrapped a tent around his torso, stuffed his feet into a pack, and bound him with ropes. They dragged the improvised gurney through the snow with towlines, lowering him through the steepest sections.

When rescuers fanned out to scout the route ahead, one man, roped to a second, lost his balance and slid, yanking his partner and trolling him down the slope. Gaining speed, the pair clotheslined another two. This tangle of four snagged the rope connected to a fifth and to Gilkey. All six men flailed down the mountain, about to launch off a 7,000-foot drop. "This is it!" thought Bob Bates, one of the climbers. "There was nothing I could do now."

Above them was Pete Schoening, a twenty-six-year-old from Seattle. He leaped up and grabbed a rope attached to Gilkey, who—through a series of towlines, tangles, and tie-offs—was also connected to the five tumbling climbers. Schoening wound the line around his shoulders and anchored the wooden shaft of his axe behind a rock.

The line yanked Schoening, but he held the axe and simultaneously clenched the rope. Somehow, it didn't snap, and Schoening checked the momentum of five falling men while also bearing the weight of Gilkey's gurney. Mountaineers call this feat the Miracle Belay.

Almost as miraculously, the injuries were manageable. One man lost his mittens, pack, and glasses; another lost his short-term memory. Two were ensnared around a third, who was partially sliced by the rope. But one by one, they untangled themselves and got to their feet. The rescuers re-anchored Gilkey's gurney and went ahead to scout a route and pitch camp.

Some of them heard the muffled shout. The climbers returned to where Gilkey had been tied and saw freshly plowed snow. Charlie Houston later speculated that Gilkey "wiggled himself loose from the line" so his teammates wouldn't have to risk their lives to save him. It's more likely that an avalanche swept him off the slope. Whatever the truth, Gilkey was gone. His friends limped down the mountain, devastated but alive. Near Base Camp, their porters piled up stones, creating a memorial cairn that remains today. Although the team had lost Gilkey and the summit, their expedition was hailed as a high point in alpinism. The team had banded together, and no one had sacrificed his humanity for self-preservation.

▲ ▲ ▲

After Gilkey's death, the Savage Mountain became an object of desire for Italians. Robert Peary had touched the North Pole; Roald Amundsen had tagged the South; Tenzing Norgay and Edmund Hillary had summited Everest—but no one could conquer K2. Now the highest untouched summit, it was the hardest place to reach above sea level.

Still demoralized by World War II, the Italians pursued the mountain to restore national pride. Expedition leader Ardito Desio secured a permit for 1954 and made sure his climbers understood the stakes: "If you succeed in scaling the peak, as I am confident you will, the entire world will hail you as champions of your race long after you are dead." The Italian expedition was to become K2's most controversial, triggering fifty years of polemic—all over the disappearance of a tent.

The climb began with six hundred Pakistani porters carrying thirteen tons of gear to Base Camp, including 230 vermilion oxygen cylinders, but by late July, only four men were in serious contention for the summit. The strongest of them, twenty-four-year-old Walter Bonatti, had been relegated to the B-Team.

Two days before the summit bid, Bonatti was ordered to lug eighty pounds of oxygen cylinders to the two members of the A-Team. To manage it, Bonatti wanted to enlist help from Amir Mehdi, a Pakistani high-altitude porter who had carried Austrian mountaineer Hermann Buhl down Nanga Parbat the year before. Mehdi wanted the summit for himself, so Bonatti cut him a deal: If Mehdi delivered the oxygen to high camp, he could sleep in the A-Team's tent and join their summit bid. Mehdi agreed, and the next day he and Bonatti left for the drop-off point at 26,600 feet.

But when they arrived that evening, the A-Team had disappeared, along with their tent. Bonatti scoured the slopes for shelter, shouting for the missing climbers. At one point, Bonatti heard someone hollering instructions—"Leave the oxygen and descend." Mehdi, meanwhile, was pacing and kicking the snow "like an unchained force of nature . . . yelling crazily," as Bonatti recounted. Mehdi's toes were cramped inside Italian army boots two sizes too small.

Bonatti decided it was insane to descend in the dark with a screaming man who couldn't feel his feet, so he gave up looking for the tent and stomped out a platform in the ice. He and Mehdi huddled together chewing caramels, expecting to die. Frostbite consumed all of Mehdi's toes and about a third of one foot. In 1954, it was the highest open bivouac in history.

Meanwhile, Achille Compagnoni, the captain of the A-Team, was resting in his tent, quietly sipping chamomile and clutching a typed memorandum stating that he was in charge. But a soggy paper has no authority in the Death Zone, so Compagnoni had taken another precaution: He'd moved his tent to an unstable traverse so Bonatti couldn't supplant him on summit day.

At first light, Bonatti and Mehdi left the oxygen cylinders and descended. Only then did Compagnoni and his climbing partner, Lino Lacedelli, crawl out of their tent to retrieve the oxygen. They avoided the Bottleneck, but the rocks below the southeast face were no easier. The oxygen allegedly ran out, and the men staggered and slipped. Hallucinating, Lacedelli saw his fiancée tailing him. Compagnoni met the ghost of a teammate who had died in June. Their Due Lupe gloves became soaked and froze over their thumbs. Finally, at dusk on July 31, 1954, the A-Team planted the Italian flag on the summit. They descended in darkness, resting to take a swig of brandy, and reached their tent late that night.

Once at Base Camp, Compagnoni was unapologetic about hiding the tent and demanded to know why his oxygen cylinders had run dry, but euphoria soon smothered all argument. Steaming home on the *Asia*, a luxury cruise ship, the climbers presented a united front. No one disclosed the details of the forced bivouac. Radio and TV stations broadcast Italy's triumph worldwide; the Italian and Pakistani governments decorated the climbers; Pope Pius XII offered blessings. Compagnoni and Lacedelli's ascent was commemorated on postage stamps and cigarette cartons. As mountaineer Reinhold Messner later put it, the victory on K2 helped bring a "psychological reconstruction of Italians" after the trauma of fascism and war.

But a decade later, bizarre allegations emerged. Through a journalist, Compagnoni accused Bonatti of siphoning oxygen from his bottles, even though the mask and tubing had been inside Compagnoni's own tent. Furious, Bonatti successfully sued for libel. "Like an elephant," he never forgot the sins of the A-Team, and neither did anyone else. When Compagnoni died fifty-four years after the climb, his obituary in the *New York Times* focused on his choice to move the tent. A snap decision on K2 had cemented his reputation as the Judas of mountaineering.

Mehdi, after the amputation of his toes, returned home to Hunza and left his ice axe in the garden shed. Gradually, he learned to walk on his stumps. He was informed by mail that the Italian government had awarded him Cavaliere status, the equivalent of knighthood. Compagnoni sent him dozens of letters over the years, but Mehdi never had them translated.

▲ ▲ ▲

After the operatics of 1954, the Savage Mountain permitted no summits for twenty-two years. A Japanese team finally succeeded in 1977, with help from an army of 1,500 porters. In the late 1970s, Pakistan, which had limited the number of K2 expeditions to one a year, began allowing many more. Overcrowding contributed to the death toll, which spiked in 1986 when thirteen climbers perished in a single summer.

At the same time, the spirit of the sport was changing. The first generation of high-altitude mountaineers were the proud "Conquistadors of the Useless," pioneering first ascents. But what was left once all the major peaks had been conquered? Mountaineers scrambled for ways to distinguish themselves. Competing for media attention and corporate sponsorship, they took on more daring routes under ever-more-harrowing conditions. Reaching the top wasn't enough. Climbers had to ascend without bottled oxygen; claw up hypertechnical routes; race up two mountains, one right after the other; climb during the Himalayan winter; bag every summit higher than 8,000 meters. And all of this had to be documented, on camera, for the Discovery Channel.

Technology improved. GPS guided climbers through whiteouts;

satellite phones buzzed; supercomputers predicted storms; crampons grew front points; DryLoft replaced reindeer skin. As new tools and equipment allowed the sport to become more extreme, they simultaneously made it more accessible. Western guide companies such as Peak Freaks and Mountain Madness appeared in the 1990s. For popular destinations like Everest, these companies organized all the logistics, obtained permits, hired staff, fixed routes, and charged $30,000 to $120,000 a head.

Crowds packed the mountain. Amateurs who had trained on sea-level StepMills arrived at Everest, clipped their ascenders onto a fixed line, and winched their way through the clouds. Most Sherpas, grateful for the work, recognized that clients sometimes lacked technical expertise, but their dependence could be managed. They instructed weak climbers to avoid overexerting themselves and focus on their health. "We climb Everest twice," Chhiring explained. "First, Sherpas go up to set the ropes and camps, then we go down to collect our clients and take them to the top." A headline in *The Guardian* summarized the phenomenon: "Mount Everest: a not so novel feat." The subhead observed: "So many people, and celebrities, are conquering Everest that it's more resort than wilderness." Sherpas did the heavy lifting, and thousands of happy amateurs joined the Mount Everest summit roll.

The inadequacies of commercial climbing hit the spotlight in 1996 when fifteen climbers lost their lives on Everest, eight in a single day. Jon Krakauer's memoir about the tragedy, *Into Thin Air*, sold four million copies and became a finalist for the Pulitzer Prize. The book should have scared rational creatures away from the sport; instead, the "Krakauer effect" galvanized commercial mountaineering. Most newcomers arrived at Base Camp with the requisite experience, but a few imagined that their $65,000 expedition fee was a chairlift to the top, weather and ability be damned. Forced to turn back for their own safety, they sued for breach of contract. Even Sir Edmund Hillary worried that dilettantes were "engendering disrespect for the mountain."

The death of David Sharp in 2006 epitomized this decline. A thirty-four-year-old math teacher, Sharp was descending from the summit of Everest when he collapsed, still clipped to the fixed line, fewer than 800 feet above the highest camp. Over the next twelve hours, as many as forty summit-hungry climbers reportedly passed him as he lay dying. Some witnesses said they thought Sharp was merely resting. Others said he was in obvious distress and could have been rescued if anyone else had agreed to help. Nobody made an effort until they were descending from the summit, but by then it was too late. Sharp had been left to die; summit fever had trumped common humanity.

As an Everest conquest lost its purity and prestige, professional climbers and avid amateurs defected to K2. Its difficulty resisted commercialization. A successful ascent without bottled oxygen was a shortcut to media attention, fame, and sponsorship. The Savage Mountain got a second moniker—The Mountaineer's Mountain—and Sherpas wanted to bag it, too. Sherpas were the strongest on Everest. They held the records for the first, fastest, and greatest number of summits, and it was getting hard for them to distinguish themselves there. Hundreds of Sherpas had climbed Everest, but only two had succeeded on K2 without using bottled oxygen.

Chhiring intended to be the third, but his wife, Dawa, thought his ambitions were perverse. Now in his midthirties, Chhiring had a family, a house, a business, and a potbelly. By 2007, Dawa thought she'd persuaded him to give up on K2. "He had become more sensible," Dawa said. "K2 was a fantasy. And even if he got the chance, I knew I could stop him." But in his mind, Chhiring never relinquished the mountain. He kept looking for a way. After a decade of dreaming, he found a solution: a man named Eric Meyer.

▲ ▲ ▲

An anesthesiologist from Colorado, Eric Meyer had lived in a decompression chamber for six weeks in the mid-1980s. Researchers for Operation Everest II, a study on oxygen deprivation, barraged him with fitness tests to analyze how hypoxia had withered his body. They drilled cores out of his legs to determine how his muscles atrophied under high-altitude conditions. They forced tubes up his arteries to examine how his heart deteriorated. In exchange, Eric earned $4,000. He spent it on a climbing trip.

The ultra runner and triathlete tested his limits, cultivating his mind and body in tandem. He practiced yoga every morning for an hour, studied martial arts in Asia, and stocked his Sub-Zero refrigerator with green smoothies made of puréed algae, broccoli juice, and barley grass. These efforts cast an enchantment over his appearance. His skin was so smooth it seemed varnished. His hair was so radiant it practically glowed in the dark. He had virtually no body fat. Graceful and relaxed, he spoke with the mellow authority of a meditation guru.

In 2004, recovering from a divorce, Eric spotted Chhiring when climbing Everest. While everyone else at Advanced Base Camp seemed wasted, Chhiring bristled with energy. The Sherpa had arms thicker than most climbers' thighs. He pitched tents and set ropes faster than anyone. His five-foot-nine frame supported outrageous, unbelievable loads. "I'd never seen anyone so strong," Eric recalled. "I had to get to know him. We started talking, and we bonded instantly. I knew I'd made a friend for life."

Chhiring told Eric about his dream of climbing K2, his daughters, his village, and his mother dying in childbirth; Eric told Chhiring about his volunteer work to improve health care and reduce infant mortality in the developing world. Chhiring and Eric shared meals of rice and dal. They swapped stories and traded tips on climbing technique. They meditated. "He didn't treat me like a sherpa," Chhiring said. "To Eric, I was an equal. We became brothers." After climbing to the top of Everest, Eric asked Chhiring to visit him in Colorado.

In the summer of 2007, Chhiring and Dawa arrived in Steamboat Springs, a ski town known for its powder. In Steamboat, delis name their sandwiches after explorers, and toddlers learn to slalom almost as soon as they can walk. Chhiring fit right in. He and Eric pedaled up mountain trails and scaled crags. They carbo-loaded on noodles Dawa cooked in Eric's kitchen and ran marathons. Chhiring learned to drive a pickup along the back roads and laid cement foundations to stay in shape. "He never seemed to get tired of carrying bags of concrete," observed Eric's friend Dana Tredway. It was the perfect vacation until K2 got in the way.

Eric told Chhiring he planned to quit his job, secure a permit from Pakistan, and climb the Savage Mountain. Maybe Chhiring could join him—not as a support climber but as a full-fledged team member? Five friends were already planning to join up: three Americans, a Swede, and an Australian. Sponsors such as Warid Telecom would defray the cost, so Chhiring would only need to cover $3,000. As a team member rather than staff, Chhiring wouldn't have to babysit anyone. He could focus on reaching the summit. The team would follow the Abruzzi Spur, K2's southeast flank, the sanest way up. They wouldn't dope on bottled oxygen. Chhiring would join the ranks of the most elite climbers.

Chhiring didn't need convincing. Dawa did. "And I didn't want to step in the middle of it," Eric recalled. "There are plenty of reasons not to climb K2. I couldn't promise her he'd come back."

Dawa couldn't speak English as well as her husband, and she was oblivious to the plans that he and Eric were hatching. Chhiring tried to ease her into them before the end of summer. During the final week of their vacation, he sat her down on Eric's couch, slid a disk into the DVD player, and punched some buttons on the remote. A six-inch gorilla in a red Hawaiian shirt appeared on the flat screen. The puppet assumed a Kermit-the-Frog twang: "I'm Murph. I may not look like much, but I get around."

Murph Goes to K2, a hokey documentary for children, explained to Dawa how a puppet safely ascended the world's deadliest peak. When the screen went black, Dawa turned to her husband in disbelief. Now she understood what Eric and Chhiring had been talking about in English. Did Chhiring actually think he was going to climb K2 like a stupid puppet?

She wanted to leave Eric's home and walk the three miles to the airport. Instead, Dawa forced a smile and sat quietly for two hours as her husband and Eric joked in a language she couldn't understand.

When Chhiring and Dawa returned to their A-frame guesthouse for the night, Chhiring acted as though everything had gone well. He took off his shoes, sat cross-legged on the floor, and began the evening prayer. Facing the Rockies, he gripped his *mala* rosary and repeated a mantra: *Om mani padme um*. The rite, which Chhiring performed twice a day, is meant to invoke compassion. Dawa usually joined him in prayer, but she'd been compassionate enough that evening. Now it was her turn to talk. "You offend the gods," she said.

Chhiring kept repeating the mantra.

"Did you hear me, Chhiring? Climbing K2 is a sin."

Chhiring recited *Om mani padme um* for ten more minutes. Once he stopped, he got up and slinked into the bedroom, avoiding eye contact with Dawa.

Dawa watched him leave and took a moment to collect herself. She wouldn't call him a bad father, a bad husband, a bad brother, a bad son. Chhiring was none of those things, but she would tell him what he was. Dawa opened the bedroom door. "You're an addict," she said.

Chhiring, sprawled on the mattress, turned his head to the wall.

Later that night, Dawa lay beside him and waited for sleep to come. An hour passed. She listened to her husband's breathing. She knew he was still awake, so she decided to speak her mind. "If you go to that mountain," Dawa told him, "I will leave."

She'd never said that to him before, and even this was a bluff. A woman with two young children seldom divorces her husband in Nepal. Social mores are against it. So is the legal system. "But what else could I do?" Dawa recalled. "I could beg, I could cry, I could tell him why he shouldn't go, but he's a man. And in Nepal, men decide everything."

Dawa cried anyway. After a moment, Chhiring told her what she wanted to hear. Nobody should climb K2. Not a Buddhist. Not a parent. Not when it costs as much as a house. Chhiring couldn't justify gambling his life to stand on top of a mountain. K2 had worse odds of survival than Russian roulette. It didn't make sense.

But people don't climb because it makes sense. You can come up with reasons—it gives direction to the lost, friends to the loner, honor to the reprobate, thrills to the bored—but, ultimately, the quest for a summit defies logic. So does passion. So does a trip to the moon. There are better things to do. Safer, cheaper, more practical. That's not the point.

The next morning, when Eric asked Chhiring whether he really wanted to climb K2, Chhiring didn't look into his wife's face. He didn't pause. He didn't explain himself or describe the sacrifices his family would have to make. He had known the answer for twenty years, and his response was immediate.

Yes.

The Prince and the Porter

Narayanhity Royal Palace, Kathmandu, Nepal
Evening, June 1, 2001

Two hours before he murdered them, Crown Prince Dipendra tried to get his family to relax. He started a billiards game, poured drinks, and joked about turning thirty. The Tarantino-style bloodbath that followed inflamed a civil war that displaced 150,000 Nepalis, including a potato farmer named Pasang Lama.

Pasang's trajectory toward K2 started around 8 p.m. on June 1, 2001, as two dozen members of Nepal's royalty strolled into Kathmandu's Narayanhity Palace, a bubblegum-pink sprawl guarded by soldiers, high gates, and mildew-streaked walls. Together, the family formed the last of the Shah dynasty, the absolute rulers of Nepal since 1768.

The crown prince, a stocky playboy who went by the nickname Dippy, was a practiced host. Educated at Eton, a prestigious English boarding school, he held a black belt in karate and had enjoyed weaponry ever since he received his first pistol at the age of eight. Dippy was also in love with the wrong woman—or at least that's what his family thought.

She was on his mind that night. Watching the billiards game, he downed several shots of Famous Grouse whisky and smoked a joint laced with a black substance, probably opium. As the drug took effect, Dipendra swayed, unable to hold himself upright. He stammered and banged into furniture. Four relatives dragged him to his bedroom.

Sobbing, the prince called his girlfriend, Devyani Rana, who was of lower social standing. Dippy had been ordered to break up with her. He'd have to marry a woman his mother would select or be stripped of royal status. The prince's words to Devyani were slurred. He hung up, dialed, and hung up again.

Devyani Rana called back, reaching his aides, and warned them that Dipendra might injure himself. The aides rushed to the bedroom and found the prince on the floor, squirming and tearing at his clothes. They propped him up and helped him to the bathroom, where he vomited. They splashed cold water on his face and got him into bed.

Alone, the prince called his girlfriend again. He told Devyani he loved her and would try to sleep. Instead, he donned combat boots, black leather gloves, and a camouflage jacket and vest. Then he assembled his weapons: a 9 mm Glock pistol; a modified 9 mm MP-5K submachine gun; a Colt M16 assault rifle, with light and scope attached; and an SPAS 12-gauge pump-action shotgun. Carrying at least two of these guns, he stumbled toward the billiards room.

Almost the entire royal family was crowded inside. Among them was King Birendra Bir Bikram Shah, a soft-spoken grandfather with wide amber spectacles. By Hindu tradition, King Birendra was considered a demigod, an incarnation of Vishnu. He stood near the east end of the billiards table, sipping cognac and discussing the risks of high cholesterol.

When his son entered the room in combat fatigues, gripping a shotgun and a submachine gun, King Birendra didn't seem alarmed. The king, perhaps thinking Dipendra had come to show weapons from the royal arsenal, stepped forward. "Isn't the Crown Prince a bit old to be dressing like this?" remarked an aunt.

Then, as the guests watched, the prince pulled the trigger. Two bullets from the submachine gun tore into his father's side. King Birendra crumpled to the ground, blood soaking his dress shirt. "What have you done?" were his last words, according to official reports.

With a gun in each hand, Dipendra couldn't control the recoil. Bullets sprayed into the ceiling and the west wall. Two relatives lunged toward the king and tried to stanch the bleeding. His rounds spent, Dipendra threw down the machine gun and darted out of the room. "There was some screaming initially, but after that everyone was just looking around," recalled Dipendra's brother-in-law, Gorakh Rana.

Seconds later, Dipendra returned with the M16 in his right hand, the pistol in his left. He fired another shot at the king at point-blank range. Diprendra "really looked exactly like the Terminator 2, expressionless but very concentrated," recalled his aunt, Princess Ketaki Chester.

His favorite uncle, Dhirendra, raised his hands, trying to soothe the homicidal prince. "That's enough, Babu," he said. Without answering, Dipendra fired a burst of bullets that tore through his uncle's chest. He shot more rounds at the men applying pressure to the king's wounds. The prince left the room once again, retreating onto the veranda.

Then, as though he had forgotten something, Dipendra returned. Spraying bullets wildly, he kicked bodies to determine who was dead. Finally, the family panicked. Some shrieked and leaped behind a sofa. Others dashed down the hallway and into the botanical garden. Dipendra jogged out the door toward the royal apartments and dove up a stairway.

His brother, Prince Nirajan, raced after him, trailed by their mother, Queen Aishwarya, and from the landing, Dipendra took aim. His brother dropped.

The queen surrendered. "You've killed your father, you've killed your brother. Kill me too."

Dipendra shot her in the face. Aishwarya's body slid down the stairs, coming to rest on the seventh step.

The top royalty were now dead or dying, so the prince wandered through the gardens. It was a muggy night, thick with cicadas. Bats hung from the trees, and condensation dripped from the panes of the greenhouse. Quietly, Dipendra stumbled toward a bridge over the royal frog pond. He raised a gun to his temple and pulled the trigger. A single bullet tore through his head, just behind his left ear, and out the other side of his skull. He was found on the grass, near a statue of Buddha. In less than five minutes, Dipendra had shot himself and fourteen members of his family.

Early the next morning, doctors at a nearby military hospital declared nine of Nepal's top royalty dead. Prince Dipendra, in a coma, lived on. As funerals were arranged, an official spokesman released a statement that the "accidental firing of an automatic weapon" was responsible for killing several family members. Dipendra wasn't named as a suspect.

It was a clumsy cover-up. Nepalis didn't know exactly what had happened, but they had conspiracy theories. Some believed that Indian spies had framed Dipendra and orchestrated the massacre in an effort to install a puppet regime.

Others had supernatural explanations, stemming from a well-known prophecy. The legend held that the Shahs would soon fall because the dynasty's first king, Prithvi Narayan, had angered the god Gorakhnath. About two centuries earlier, the king had offered an ascetic a bowl of rancid curd. The holy man swallowed it and vomited; then, unexpectedly, scooping up the mess, he ordered the king to eat the curd himself. Repulsed, Prithvi Narayan flung the vomit in the man's face. It was the wrong move. Shielding himself with his hands, the ascetic revealed himself to be a god and cursed the Shahs.

Their dynasty, he said, would be limited to ten generations, one for each of his sticky fingers. Ten generations later, "I had known something was coming," said Dr. Raghunath Aryal, the royal astrologer. "But how do you tell your boss that his son is about to commit mass murder?"

Sixteen hours after the massacre, an eleventh-generation member of the dynasty was crowned. The comatose Dipendra ruled for two days. When he was removed from life support, the monarchy was returned to the tenth generation as his uncle Gyanendra became king.

Rioters stormed the streets because they considered Gyanendra a bad seed. Propaganda described how royal astrologers had examined Gyanendra at birth and declared him unfit to rule. The boy, nevertheless, had been king briefly, at age four, when his grandfather Tribhuvan was forced into exile, along with most of the family. When the Shahs returned, little Gyanendra lost his crown. The boy grew up with a scowl; in his second coronation portrait, he is scowling still. Even loyal subjects found him suspicious. Why had Gyanendra's own children been spared? Had the massacre been a plot by Dipendra's uncle?

After investigators had released the crime scene, Gyanendra razed the billiards room, the site of the massacre. By the time the first comprehensive investigation reports were released that summer, the Shahs had lost their credibility, and Maoist rebels were capitalizing on their weakness.

At the time of Gyanendra's succession, the Shahs embodied all that had gone wrong with the Nepali feudal system. The dynasty during its 239-year rule had produced a series of temperamental royals. In the eighteenth century, for instance, Prithvi Narayan had sliced off the lips of his opponents; in the nineteenth, Surendra had dropped his subjects down wells; in the twenty-first, Paras allegedly had run over a musician with his Mitsubishi Pajero because the man wouldn't play his request. Yet the Shahs remained constitutionally immune from prosecution, and the family enjoyed an extravagant and much-resented lifestyle.

The Communists promised to empower the populace, redistribute land, grant women equal rights, and eliminate the caste system. A coalition of Communist parties nearly secured a plurality of seats in the 1991 parliamentary election, and, five years later, the Maoists declared "The People's War" to extinguish the monarchy and bring about a secular republic. Over the next decade they accomplished little, but they had gained strength by recruiting troops, looting police stations for weapons, and hoarding homemade explosives. When the unpopular Gyanendra succeeded the beloved King Birendra, the Maoists knew it was time to strike.

The Maoists invaded remote villages unprotected by the royal army. They burst into classrooms, shot teachers, and abducted the pupils, forcing them to join their ranks as child soldiers. The troops tortured their opponents and displayed their mutilated bodies. They blockaded Kathmandu and gained control of the provinces.

In response, Parliament passed the Terrorist and Destructive Activities Act, allowing ninety-day detentions and aggressive interrogation of Maoists. King Gyanendra suspended the elected government and instituted martial law, assuming command over the military and the press. He censored criticism of his government, imprisoned journalists, and executed suspected terrorists. "Nepal has been experiencing a grave human rights crisis," declared a report from the United Nations General Assembly. Amnesty International and Human Rights Watch condemned the abuse, recording gruesome cases of electrocution, beating, assassination, kidnapping, public execution, and sexual humiliation. Until 2006, civil war raged. The government controlled Kathmandu, but Maoists penetrated nearly every village. More than 12,800 people were killed, and about 150,000 were forced to flee their homes. Unemployment soared to around 50 percent.

The Maoists finally got their way, in part. In July 2008, the monarchy was abolished and Nepal was declared a federal republic. Elections placed the Communists in power periodically, but protests and violence continued.

During the height of the civil war, Pasang Lama was living in Kathmandu in a one-room flat with seven others. His village in eastern Nepal was a war zone: The king's army, trying to root out Maoists, was arresting and shooting young men his age. Pasang couldn't go back home, and his family of refugees needed money.

Despite the violence, die-hard mountaineers kept climbing in Nepal, paying porters about $3 a day to carry loads to Himalayan base camps. The job required little skill beyond brute strength, making it one of the few options for men like Pasang. Cornered by war in a riot-torn city, living under curfew and fear of bombs, the seventeen-year-old potato farmer became a porter.

▲ ▲ ▲

Pasang Lama used a mnemonic to teach English speakers how to pronounce his name. "It's Pah-SONG," he would say, "because I'm always singing." While trekking, Pasang skipped down dirt trails, clapping rocks together and crooning a Nepali tune resembling "Take Me Out to the Ball Game." His high notes even made the *dzos* stop chewing the cud and pay attention.

A sticker on his helmet labeled him "The Joker," and Pasang lived up to it. He smuggled rocks into friends' sleeping bags, pillows, and packs. He wrapped pebbles in Tootsie Roll wrappers and handed them to children begging for candy. At night, he festooned tents with branch-and-trash towers. When the tents' occupants crawled out in the morning and the scaffolds crashed down, Pasang threw back his head, cackling, and galloped off in search of the next victim.

When he wasn't trekking or climbing, Pasang turned into someone else. In Kathmandu, he seldom sang or joked, cloaking his happy-go-lucky personality in an armor of shyness and caution. Men like Chhiring bounded up to newcomers with the enthusiasm of a Labrador, no matter the setting. In Kathmandu, Pasang couldn't do that. He hung back, keeping a safe distance. When acquaintances opened their arms for a hug, they received a handshake. While eating dinner with a group of new clients in Kathmandu, Pasang's body was at the table but his eyes were patrolling the room, ready to alert him of danger. It often took him several hours to crack a smile for a stranger, but when he allowed one, his grin was sincere.

Compact, stretching just shy of five-foot-two, Pasang had hands as rough as a cat's tongue. When he was twenty-four years old, he looked fifteen and accepted his nickname: "Little Pasang." Clients occasionally doubted that he was an adult and asked for "another sherpa with more experience than this baby." To age himself, Pasang rarely shaved, but it made no difference. His chin refused to grow a beard.

Pasang's village, Hungung, lies on the Tibetan border in the Upper Arun Valley along the watershed of 27,765-foot Makalu, the world's fifth-highest peak. For decades, Nepal's government has restricted anthropologists, journalists, and some relief organizations from entering this sensitive border area. But it's easy enough to sneak in. To get to Hungung from the nearest airstrip in the village at Tumlingtar, visitors have to ride for a day in a jeep and then undertake a ten-day trek.

The trails leading into the village fork around rod-shaped mounds of limestone. By custom, all travelers must pass by the mounds on their left; even Hungung's Tibetan mastiffs follow this rule. The residents live in rock-and-mud homes that roost among terraced hillsides, and black pigs dominate the pens. A stream trickles through the center of the village, providing running water of sorts, and rooftop solar panels, installed by a long-forgotten NGO, generate electricity. A health post is stocked with antibiotics, but no doctors.

About 250 people live in the region. It was once the hub of a medicinal plant trade; now a general store deals in flashlights, lollipops, Neosporin, and Communist manifestos that, curiously, are available only in French. The residents speak Ajak Bhote, an endangered language derived from Tibetan, and believe they descend from the Ajak, an ancient priestly class once charged with protecting Tibetan royalty. Most villagers are Buddhists who work as farmers, herders, or blacksmiths.

Growing up in Hungung, the oldest of four children, Pasang was reared without a father. Phurbu Ridar Bhote, a mountaineer, moved to Kathmandu to find work when his son was six. Phurbu visited his family every two or three years. Sometimes Pasang dreamed that an avalanche had buried Phurbu, but Hungung's *lama* reassured the boy. Using clairvoyance, the *lama* updated Pasang on his father's whereabouts—whether Phurbu was bound for Everest or K2 that year—and delivered messages Phurbu sent in prayer. The *lama* told Pasang that his father wanted him to apply himself and study mathematics. Pasang read whatever books he could find and attended school as often as he could, but living was usually hand to mouth. He sowed the millet and barley fields and dug potato tubers. He gathered firewood and swept the homes of wealthier villagers in exchange for rice or a few coins.

When Pasang was fifteen, he received word from his father to join him in Kathmandu. After a decade of saving and a stint on K2, Phurbu had amassed the equivalent of $1,000, plenty to send his son to prep school and university. "I wanted him to stay as far away from mountains as possible," Phurbu said. "Who would climb if he had a choice? It's only a matter of time before you're killed. I didn't want my first-born son to die before I did. He needed to get an education. I climbed mountains so he wouldn't have to."

Before leaving for Kathmandu, Pasang changed his surname from Bhote to Lama because he didn't want his heritage to hold him back.

Pasang is Bhote, a Tibetan ethnicity culturally distinct from Sherpa. Although the two groups have related beliefs and share many rituals, Bhotes frequently face discrimination. Like an immigrant taking the surname Rockefeller, Pasang chose Lama, the highest Sherpa caste, so no one in the city would look down on him.

With a new name and a new life ahead of him, Pasang Lama left for Kathmandu. During the ten-day trek to the nearest road, he planned his future. First he'd earn a degree that would lead to a safe and respectable job. Next he'd get so rich he would send his siblings to prep school in the city. Then he'd buy solar panels for his mother. Maybe he'd build her a new house. By the time Pasang reached the highway and saw a metal creature rumbling toward him, he had convinced himself that anything was possible. The teenager had never seen a bus before, but he confidently climbed inside and left his old life behind.

For several days, as the wheeled machine bounced down the road, Pasang watched a ghastly world appear. Kathmandu's pollution and bustle rattled him. How could a million people cram into such an intolerably tight space? As the bus kept plowing through traffic, he missed Hungung's expansive skies. Finally the vehicle delivered him to Balaju, a densely populated area northwest of the city center. Pasang joined his father and six other relatives in a one-room rental. At night, they all piled onto the same mattress. During the day, they tipped it upward to allow living space. The toilet was a hole dug in the courtyard.

Soon after arriving, Pasang started eleventh grade at British Gurkha Academy, studying commerce. His classmates taunted him. "They pointed at me and shouted, 'Bhote, Bhote, Bhote!'" Pasang recalled. "They were calling me a stupid villager." The teenager struggled to keep pace, unaccustomed to schoolwork in Nepali, a foreign language to him. He flunked the first year, costing his family precious tuition money. Demoralized, Pasang went back to Hungung for a season to harvest the potato crop. He then returned to Kathmandu in September 2000 to give school another shot. This time he was on track to finish, but in June the royal massacre disrupted exams. Kathmandu went into lockdown.

Hungung was worse. The Royal Nepalese Army invaded during a festival, publicly killing three suspected terrorists who were about Pasang's age. Fighting flared. Pasang's mother, sisters, aunts, uncles, cousins, nephews, and nieces fled.

"It wasn't safe to stay, especially as a woman alone with children," said Pasang's mother, Phurbu Chejik Bhoteni. Bus tickets were too expensive. Carrying two toddlers and whatever else she could strap on her back, Phurbu walked the entire way to Kathmandu on a fractured leg. The journey took more than a month. Exhausted and hungry, she and the children arrived in the spring of 2002 at Pasang's one-room flat.

They couldn't all fit inside, so Pasang, his mother, his father, his two younger sisters, his younger brother, and a fluctuating number of desperate relatives moved into a separate room that cost more than they could afford. Food and rent became higher priorities than education. Pasang had to find a job.

Competition was cutthroat. Refugees were flooding the job market. Destitute, they accepted any employment they could get. Wages fell; unemployment rose. After three months, Pasang found work, but it was humble. He received an offer to earn $3 a day carrying pots and pans to Gosaikunda, a holy lake north of the city.

Grateful for this first portering job, Pasang shouldered loads over the undulating terrain between Kathmandu and the lake. Afterward, with one trip on his résumé, it was easier to find the next job, and the next. An American trekker befriended him and offered to pay his tuition, so Pasang attended classes during the slow season between expeditions, but he no longer considered himself a commerce student. School could not support his family; portering could.

Still, he disliked it. Pasang didn't speak the same language as many of the other porters, and he hadn't learned their protocol. One misunderstanding nearly cost him his job. In 2004, Pasang carried a pack stuffed with tinned fruit, Clif bars, freeze-dried soup, and kerosene to the Base Camp of Annapurna, a mountain whose name means "full of food." Pasang had brought nothing of his own to eat, expecting his employers to feed him. They didn't. Pasang scrounged for handouts from kitchen hands, gathered scraps from his clients' plates before washing them, and bartered clothing for rations. When the clients extended the trip, supplies dwindled further. Pasang's peers had no more food to share. Feeling sorry for him, the cook brewed him stew from roots found around camp and offered him three days' worth of lemon-lime Tang. When the Tang ran out, Pasang reeled from hunger.

As he lugged his eighty-pound load, all he could think of was food, food, food. His muscles jittered. His feet kept missing the places he intended to step. "I was going to pass out unless I found something to eat," Pasang recalled. He didn't consider asking the Western climbers for help. "You just don't do that," he said. "Porters aren't hired to beg for things or complain." If he had, other staff would have alerted the expedition outfitter, who'd blacklist him.

Stealing seemed safer. After four days without food, Pasang staggered off the path and hid behind a boulder. Setting down his load, he rummaged through it and pulled out a tin of mandarin oranges and hammered it against a rock. The metal burst and the edge sliced deep into his middle and index fingers. Blood smeared over the can, but Pasang was smiling. He jimmied back the lid, slurped the sweet syrup, and dropped the delicate wedges into his mouth. Sugar coursed through his body. Revitalized, Pasang shouldered his load and tied a rag around his bleeding right hand.

On the trail that day, Pasang had visions of mandarin oranges— luscious wedges, dripping in syrup, melting in his mouth. He craved other tins inside the pack but resisted the urge until that evening, when he stole a can of tuna. If the other porters suspected, they stayed quiet. The thefts continued until his job finished three days later. "Annapurna was the first and last time I was a thief," he said.

After Annapurna, jobs poured in. Clients called him a porter, but Pasang—who eventually was setting ropes, pitching tents, and hauling gear up rock and ice—saw himself as something better. By the time he reached the summit of Everest in the spring of 2006, he was unquestionably a mountaineer. The civil war and its bombing and maiming had slowed that year, and the Maoists called a truce in November, but Pasang's mother doubted the fighting would stop. Refusing to return to Hungung, Phurbu Chejik said she'd seen enough violence. She and the children would stay in Kathmandu. Pasang continued to support them with the wages of what he considered to be a temporary career.

A proposal in May 2008 raised the stakes. Pasang was ushering a South Korean woman named Go Mi-sun up Lhotse, the world's fourth-highest peak. On their return from the summit, "Ms. Go" told Pasang about her ambitions. There are fourteen mountains taller than 8,000 meters, she explained. She intended to be the first woman to climb them all—and to do it faster than anyone else had. With five down and nine to go, K2 was next. Would Pasang help?

He was more than a little infatuated with Ms. Go, who laughed with him, joined him for meals in the kitchen tent, shared her energy bars, and asked whether he had a girlfriend. When her climbing partner, "Mr. Kim"—Kim Jae-soo—lost his cool, Ms. Go smoothed things over. To Pasang, she was angelic, and she had his trust.

Once in Kathmandu, Pasang had only had a few days to decide whether he'd join her. He scoured the Internet to learn more about Ms. Go. She was Asia's sweetheart. After a 200-foot fall shattered her backbone, she'd made a comeback as a star of the Asian X-Games. Go was backed by Kolon Sport, the Nike of Korea, and adored by her fan club.

But critics called her "a woman on the Go." They dismissed her as reckless, swept up in a publicity stunt. Only a handful of mountaineers had managed to climb every 8,000-meter peak, and it had taken Reinhold Messner, widely considered the greatest of all, more than sixteen years to do it. Kolon Sport couldn't wait that long, so the sportswear giant paid Go to replicate the feat in a quarter of the time. Unlike Messner, however, she was using support climbers and bottled oxygen—and simultaneously modeling a clothing line.

Setting aside his crush on Ms. Go, Pasang tried to evaluate a K2 attempt on its own merits. He sought out his father for advice. To Pasang's surprise, Phurbu Ridar saw the climb as a lucky break. True, Pasang could be killed, but Phurbu thought that was unlikely, especially if a beautiful woman were involved. And how could Pasang go into commerce when the Maoists were still halting commerce? If mountaineering was to be his career, he should make it his career, especially while he had no wife or children to hold him back. Pasang should not only load-carry on K2, Phurbu advised, but also shoot for the summit. When Phurbu had attempted K2's North Ridge in 1994, he'd put his clients' success above his own, staying in camp and boiling water as other men climbed to the top. He regretted being passed over. Pasang should have no regrets. A K2 conquest would make the family proud, and it would pay the bills for a year.

Furthermore, Phurbu noted, four of Pasang's cousins would be on the Korean team. Tsering Lama was like Pasang—in his twenties and unmarried. His other cousins were leaving families behind. Jumik Bhote had a wife who was eight months pregnant and expecting to give birth while he was away. "Big" Pasang Bhote had two toddlers. Ngawang Bhote, the team cook, also had a wife and daughter, but K2 was too profitable for any of them to pass up.

Nearly convinced, Pasang went to Big Pasang's house to see what his older cousin had to say. Big Pasang endorsed the expedition, reminding Pasang that K2 meant $3,000 for each of them, plus tips and a summit bonus. As Big Pasang spoke, his wife Lahmu boiled tea. She remained quiet but kept glancing up at the summit certificates proudly fastened above the rice sacks in the kitchen. Mountaineering had provided her children with a good home. Its walls were plywood and the floor was dirt, but a tarp and corrugated tin roof kept rain out, and her toddlers, Dawa and Nima Yangzom, always had enough to eat. Pasang could tell she was supportive of the plan.

He found himself nodding in support of it, too. "Everyone was saying I should go," Pasang recalled. "They said I'd lose my chance, and it meant so much money."

If Pasang doubted whether he had made the right choice, his concerns evaporated when he and his cousins met the rest of the Korean team in the lobby of the five-star Hotel de l'Annapurna in Kathmandu. The hotel features a massage parlor, four restaurants, a casino, and an underground shopping center. It promises in its brochure to "treat guests like gods."

Shy and unsure what to say, Pasang shook hands with the two Koreans he knew, Ms. Go and Mr. Kim. He nodded to other team members and slumped down on a leather couch. He filled out forms, including an insurance document from Highland Sherpa Trekking that amortized his life at $7,500. Ms. Go passed out team bumper stickers. For reasons no one explained, the Koreans called their expedition The Flying Jump.

As the Koreans talked among themselves, Pasang wasn't sure what they were saying, but he liked sitting among such affluent foreigners. The hotel's opulence impressed him. Globes dangled from the ceiling, emanating rose-colored light. Orchids in water bowls purged cigar smoke from the air. Buddhist *tangkas* adorned the walls. Mesmerized by their maze of red and gold paint, Pasang daydreamed until a waiter interrupted him. The man bowed and poured him a glass of chilled mango juice.

When the Korean team dismissed Pasang, he headed toward the glass door. It swung open spontaneously, before he could touch the massive brass handle. Pasang stepped into a wall of noise and traffic. Beside him, a doorman bowed. "*Namaste*," he said, as he did to all the guests, and offered to carry Pasang's duffel to a taxi.

Is he talking to me? It was beyond confusing. All his life, Pasang had been the one to bow, pour tea, open doors, lift bags. That's what people known as sherpas were expected to do, he thought: Serve. Hotel de l'Annapurna, the most luxurious place he had ever entered, showed him another kind of life. Yes, Pasang decided, his father was right. K2 was a golden opportunity. He couldn't overlook the prospect of earning $3,000 in eight weeks, but K2 could give him something he valued more. Respect.

Once he conquered the Savage Mountain, Pasang thought, nobody would consider him a stupid villager. Nobody would think of him as a baggage handler. Maybe he would have the chance to spend more time with powerful people like the Koreans. Maybe he'd drink mango juice again in places like the Hotel de l'Annapurna. Maybe the world would treat him as kindly as the doorman had.

In the driveway, Pasang turned around. He wanted to thank the doorman, but the words would not come out. He was too stunned to speak. Feeling like a prince, he strode out of the five-star hotel and into the chaos of the city.

"After K2, I thought, I'll no longer be treated like a Bhote."

4

The Celebrity Ethnicity

Mountaineers use *sherpa*, with a lowercase *S*, to describe a high-altitude load carrier, and the word is often applied commercially to anything that helps people get around. Haul your terrier in the Sherpa Dog Carrier. Brace your belly with a Baby Sherpa Maternity Belt. Stow your bibs and burp cloths in the award-winning Alpha Sherpa™ or Short Haul Sherpa® diaperbag. "It's no mystery how this pack got its name," reads the promotional website for the Evo-Sport Sherpa Rucksack. "The Sherpa is built to carry all your gear, and you won't feel a thing."

Many ethnic Sherpas tolerate the stereotype because it promotes their skill and unique genetic advantage. The people of the Tibetan Plateau, including Sherpas, have lived at high altitude for at least eleven thousand years, and physiological evidence suggests that they are well adapted to oxygen deprivation. Compared with other groups studied, often acclimatized Caucasian men, Sherpas are more resistant to illnesses and brain damage exacerbated by the thin air, and they sleep more soundly and demonstrate remarkable endurance at high altitude.

What explains their advantage? Contrary to one popular theory, it's not a high red-blood-cell count. Compared with Caucasians, Sherpas actually have fewer red blood cells per liter of blood. Nor is the difference explained by diet, acclimatization, metabolism, iron-deficiency, or environmental factors. At sea level, Sherpas have such a low red-blood-cell count that they are technically anemic, but, curiously, they don't show symptoms. Overall, Sherpas require as much oxygen as anybody else, but they have less of it dissolved in their blood.

Scientists initially found this puzzling. Red blood cells ferry oxygen around the body, and other populations well adapted to altitude, such as the Quechua and the Aymara of the Andean highlands, have veins teeming with red blood cells. How do Sherpas manage with less at a much higher altitude than the Andes?

Probably by circulating blood faster. Sherpas have wider blood vessels. They breathe more often when at rest, providing their blood with more oxygen to absorb, and they exhale more nitric oxide, a marker of efficient lung circulation. There is also a genetic explanation. Sherpas' red-blood-cell count stays low because of Hypoxia Inducible Factor 2-alpha, a gene that regulates response to low oxygen and turns on other genes. In addition, Sherpas have inherited a dominant genetic trait that improves hemoglobin saturation, allowing their red blood cells to soak up more oxygen. Sherpas' thin blood, in turn, may prevent the sort of clotting that crippled Art Gilkey on K2.

This genetic advantage only enhances the Sherpa mystique. Lowlanders clutching the Lonely Planet guide are convinced they want to hire "a sherpa," even if they don't know what a Sherpa is, and, after three generations of gathering tourist dollars, Sherpas now rank among the richest and most visible of Nepal's fifty or so ethnicities. They didn't start out that way.

Ancestors of the oldest Sherpa clans originated in the Kham region of Tibet. In the thirteenth century, Mongols, with their catapults and fast-riding archers, conquered much of Central Asia, and besieged Khampas fled to the Tibetan interior. In the sixteenth century, Muslims from Kashgar invaded Tibet from the west, displacing the Khampas again. Fleeing on foot, they migrated across the Himalaya to a region south of Everest known as the Khumbu. During the journey, they began to call themselves *sharpa* (people from the east), and their new Nepali homeland became *Shar Khombo*. Several immigrant waves followed. Some were driven from Tibet by famine, disease, and war; others moved to establish trading outposts. These newcomers, from various regions and social classes, assimilated into existing settlements or built their own, creating more clans. Steep passes isolated the villages, and unique cultures evolved. With language, for instance, dialects varied by as much as 30 percent—enough to produce misunderstandings and jokes, but not enough to qualify as separate tongues.

Despite the harsh geography, Sherpas from different clans traded and intermarried. The naming system they developed still causes mass confusion. According to custom, an individual's primary name is one of seven weekdays. Boys and girls born on Monday go by *Dawa*; Tuesday babies are *Mingma*; for Wednesday, it's *Lhakpa*; Thursday, *Phurbu*; Friday, *Pasang*; Saturday, *Pemba*; Sunday, *Nima*. Surnames aren't used, and phonetic transcriptions to English vary. When filling out legal forms, most Sherpas put their weekday as their first name and *Sherpa* (or the female version, *Sherpani*) as their last. Occasionally the clan name—such as *Chiawa*, *Lama*, or *Lhukpa*—substitutes for *Sherpa*.

The system works in a close-knit village. In a city, it's dysfunctional. Thousands of Sherpas in Kathmandu have identical names. Phonebooks are useless, and it's impossible to find someone by casually asking around. Gossipers must provide elaborate descriptions of the person they wish to malign. Nicknames abound, but they're inconsistent. A growing number of Sherpa parents are giving their children individualized names, but the naming convention may never resemble anything as varied as the Western system.

Making matters more confusing, primary names can be altered or scrapped based on events in a child's life. If a baby falls ill, the parents may change his name to *Chhiring* (long life), to confound the evil spirits. If a child dies, the parents may switch a sibling's name to something inconspicuous like *Kikuli* (puppy), so evil spirits will overlook her. Parents might also turn to a Buddhist *lama* for a new name provided by divine inspiration. Long before he conquered Everest, Tenzing Norgay went by Namgyal Wangdi, but the *rinpoche* of Rongbuk Monastery determined that the child was the reincarnation of a rich and devout man. The *rinpoche* thus renamed him "wealthy follower of religion." Chhiring received *Dorje* (lightning bolt) as his second name. It must have seemed appropriate for a child who set the hills ablaze.

Sherpas can receive virtue names as well, often those of saints. They combine with the primary name to bestow special attributes. Chhiring's wife, Dawa, received *Da Futi* (blessings to conceive a son). Pasang's cousin received *Lahmu* (a protector of temple gates). Virtue names also describe an individual. To distinguish a daughter from a mother with the same name, the child might acquire *Ang* (young). A Sherpa who gave a rousing speech might become *Lhakhpa Gyalgin* (courageous orator). Sometimes the same Sherpa goes by different names depending on context. When addressed by his *lama*, Chhiring goes by *Dorje*. When pronouncing his name for Tibetans, he says *Tsering*.

Sherpas also identify with one of roughly twenty clans that reflect ancestry. Children receive their father's clan name. Sherpas are supposed to avoid romantic entanglements with members of the same clan or anyone from their mother's clan going back three generations. And just as names such as Rockefeller have cachet in the West, some Sherpa clans, such as Lama, are top drawer. Others, such as the Bhote clans, are considered alien and second class—impostors who aren't ethnic Sherpas at all.

So what defines a Sherpa? When Europeans first encountered them in the nineteenth century, the Sherpas introduced themselves as *sharpa*, which was interpreted as *Sherpa*. The word resurfaced in the 1901 Darjeeling census, which classified Sherpas as one of four types of Bhotias, or Tibetans. Nepal's most recent census considers Sherpas to be a self-reported ethnicity, so anyone can claim to be one.

Sherpas from the oldest and wealthiest clans, living near Everest, would prefer a narrower definition. Just as colonial families who arrived on the *Mayflower* claim some special distinction, many old-clan Sherpas claim to be the only authentic members of the ethnicity. Tibetans, they argue, whether living in Tibet proper or in villages in Nepal, do not deserve the Sherpa identity, nor do those who have recently assimilated into Sherpa villages. Pemba Gyalje, a member of the Dutch K2 team, hails from the Solukhumbu region settled by the earliest immigrants. As he put it, "We are true Sherpas."

Chhiring prefers a broader definition. He belongs to the Kyirong clan, which suggests that his father's ancestors were part of a later immigration wave from the village of Kyirong in Tibet. His village of Beding hosts a mix of clans ranging from ancient to upstart. A Sherpa, he says, is anyone who can convince the established Sherpas that he deserves to be one. Good faith is cultivated by living in Rolwaling, adopting a clan name, following the clan-marriage rules, and speaking Rolwaling Sherpi tamgney language.

Pasang, from the Upper Arun Valley, uses the most inclusive definition, which disregards ethnicity. *Sherpa* is a job description, he maintains, so anyone who works on a mountain qualifies. He may favor this interpretation because old-clan Sherpas would never recognize Pasang as part of their ethnicity. To them, he is a Bhote, now and forever.

Bhote, pronounced BOE-tay, stems from *Bhot* (Sanskrit for

"Tibet"), and the Bhotes in Hungung observe many Tibetan customs. With marriage, for instance, the Bhotes of the Upper Arun Valley, like other Tibetan tribal groups, traditionally practice bride abduction. When Pasang's cousin Lahmu Bhoteni was fourteen, the groom's brothers secured permission from her father, seized her in the night, and dragged her to the wedding. This break from her paternal household may have been ritualized, but it was hard on the bride. "I was miserable for years," Lahmu said. It took a long time for her resentment to wear off. "When I was twenty-three," she added, "I finally realized I loved my husband." Sherpa marriage rites, by contrast, are public-relations campaigns. Before betrothal, a Sherpa couple consults all stakeholders—families and gods—and gets a horoscope cross-check. Sherpas widely consider the Bhote approach, which is less common nowadays, a brutal and primitive practice.

Another breach, according to Sherpas, is the Bhote practice of blood sacrifice. Bhotes of the Upper Arun occasionally stray from Buddhist precepts and slaughter animals as large as yaks, pulling out entrails to read divinations. In Pasang's village, the carcass is offered to Surra, a deity who occupies Makalu's eastern spur. God by day, demon by night, Surra charges through the Arun Valley on a black horse and drags a banner jangling with human hearts. Local Buddhist *lamas* have been unable to tame him. Sherpas say he causes epidemics, but Bhotes believe the opposite—that Surra heals the sick—so they make sure he gets all the offal he can eat.

Citing this sacrificial slaughter, some Sherpas describe Bhotes as bloodthirsty barbarians. Sherpas, competing with Bhotes for mountaineering jobs, popularized the use of the term *Bhote* for "yokel" in Nepali slang. According to a popular saying in the Sherpa villages near Everest, every Bhote "has two knives: one in his boot, which he can draw quickly to stab you in the stomach, and another in his waistband to stab you in the back when you embrace him."

But the sharpest knives are reserved for foreigners. Both Bhotes and Sherpas hate how they used to be described by outsiders, and the terms are still politically charged. Well into the twentieth century, Western mountaineers were calling both groups *coolies*, an offensive word that means "unskilled laborer" and, in some contexts, "slave." Now Western mountaineers use *sherpa* or *Sherpa-climber*, which conflates a job description with an ethnicity, frustrating ethnic Sherpas who want to distinguish themselves from Bhote competitors. Pakistanis use *high-altitude porter*, or *HAP*, but sherpas working in the Karakorum reject that term because it includes the word *porter*, and in Nepal, porters don't climb. Nepal's government now promotes the term *high-altitude worker*.

Despite these ethnic and linguistic tensions, coexistence is the norm among high-altitude workers. As Sherpas and Bhotes vie for the same jobs, they still befriend each other, worship the same gods, and intermarry. The life of Tenzing Norgay illustrates this duality: The man who made the Sherpas famous wasn't one, at first.

▲ ▲ ▲

One of *Time* magazine's most influential people of the twentieth century was born in a yak-herder's tent in Tsechu, a pilgrimage site in the Kharta region of Tibet—a three-day walk from Pasang's birthplace. Tenzing Norgay was the eleventh of fourteen children, one of only six who survived infancy. His parents, Kinzom and Mingma, subsistence herders of Ghang La, sent Tenzing to a monastery so he could learn to read, but monasticism didn't suit the boy. When a Buddhist *lama* beat him with a stick, Tenzing quit.

At age seven, Tenzing got a glimpse of his future. In the spring of 1921, the legendary British mountaineer George Mallory pitched several camps in the Kharta region to explore Everest's north side. During his four-month reconnaissance, Mallory spent a halcyon month in the grazing lands of Ghang La. Spreading money around, he hired local scouts and bought yak butter and cream from herders at Ghang La and Dangsar, where Tenzing's family stayed. Mallory would die three years later below the summit of Everest, but Tenzing never forgot the hobnailed boots that his expedition left behind.

Mountaineering was the least of Tenzing's concerns in the 1920s. His family leased the herd they cared for, and one day the yaks erupted in lesions and died, likely during the 1928 pandemic of rinderpest disease. Tenzing's father couldn't repay his debts or support his six children in Kharta, so the family migrated across the border, possibly to Thame or Khumjung, villages in the Sherpa heartland of the Khumbu.

The Sherpas in the Khumbu were relatively affluent, enjoying a monopoly on regional trade. For centuries, Tibetan salt and wool had been carried over the Nangpa La Pass into Nepal and exchanged for lowland products such as bamboo, medicinal plants, paper, rice, and soot-based ink. Tenzing labored as an indentured servant for a more solvent family, and, as a Tibetan among the Sherpas, suffered from ethnic discrimination. Inevitably, he fell in love with a beautiful Sherpani whose family disapproved of him. Tenzing, then seventeen, proposed eloping, and the girl, Dawa Phuti, agreed. The couple left the Khumbu, heading to a new life at the Indian hill station of Darjeeling.

Nepal, then an insular kingdom, forbade foreign mountaineering expeditions, so Darjeeling, with its hot baths and billiards, became the recruitment hub for Everest. When the couple arrived, Englishman Hugh Ruttledge was recruiting porters for his 1933 Everest expedition. "They wanted only Sherpas," Tenzing recalled. As a Bhote, he was turned away. "And you go away wondering if you will never get a job in your life." For two years, expeditions continued to reject him because of his ethnicity.

In the early 1930s, Sherpa mountaineers deployed aggressive tactics to force Tibetans out of the profession. Instead of merely staging strikes when they had to work alongside Tibetans, Sherpas on a 1931 German expedition even threatened to sue their paymaster, Paul Bauer, for refusing to hire and compensate Sherpas preferentially. Most expeditions, including Bauer's, caved. Sherpas dominated the local workforce, and they could halt expeditions that failed to meet their demands. To avoid delays and ethnic conflicts, some expeditions hired Sherpas exclusively, and only local climbers who passed as Sherpa were able to accumulate experience.

In 1935, Tenzing was still in Darjeeling, jockeying for a mountaineering job. Determined to hold out, he milked cows, set mortar, and read Darjeeling's eponymous tea leaves. He finally got a break. A mountaineer named Eric Shipton was about to leave for Everest as part of a British reconnaissance when he made a last-minute decision to hire more men.

At that point, pickings were slim: The most-experienced Sherpas had been killed the year before on Nanga Parbat. In a rush, Shipton decided to broaden his search and encourage Tibetans to apply. Tenzing darted up to the veranda of Darjeeling's Planters Club, where Shipton was inspecting a throng of candidates. "[T]here was one Tibetan lad of nineteen, a newcomer, chosen largely because of his attractive grin," Shipton later wrote. "His name was Tensing Norkay—or Tensing Bhotia, as he was generally called." Tenzing was finally on his way to Everest.

En route, the Sherpas staged a strike, refusing to carry loads, so Shipton had mules and Tibetan porters such as Tenzing lug the gear instead. Later, in a village called Sar, the Sherpas got into a drunken brawl with the Tibetans. Tenzing kept out of it, carried whatever weight he was given, accepted coworkers of any ethnicity, and kept on grinning until the reconnaissance ended with the approach of the monsoon.

Tenzing returned from Everest with new boots, snow goggles, and a recommendation from Shipton. His obsession with the summit may have started then, but the deaths of his wife and son may explain the determination he showed in the years to come. Climbing gave him solace and, with his reputation established, work became easier to find. Eventually, he married again. His new wife was Ang Lhamu, a Sherpani who helped him gain acceptance within her community, something he'd never had with Dawa Phuti.

By 1953, Tenzing had clocked more time on Everest than any mortal, and the British offered him an opportunity he couldn't refuse. During their Everest expedition, Tenzing would work as *sirdar*—chief of the mountain workers—and climb as a full team member, a status the British had never before afforded an indigenous climber. Tenzing quit smoking and started carrying around a rock-filled pack. This would be his seventh Everest expedition, and he was destined for the summit.

Early in the climb, Tenzing became fast friends with Edmund Hillary, a beekeeper from New Zealand. Hillary had tried to jump a crevasse but landed short, breaking off a cornice. He slid with the ice sheet into the chasm. As Hillary grasped for the sides, Tenzing snagged the trailing line, flicked it around his axe, and planted the axe into the mountain. The rope yanked tight. Hillary's ice axe and a single crampon dropped into the fissure. Tenzing, "after position-ing himself to gain some leverage, was able to gradually haul Hillary up to the edge of the crevasse, with some help from Hillary's sin-gle cramponed foot," wrote Tenzing's son and biographer, Jamling Tenzing Norgay. The rescue forged a friendship that led Hillary and Tenzing to the roof of the world.

During the summit bid, it was Hillary's turn to help Tenzing. Tenzing belayed Hillary as he cut steps toward their final obstacle, a 40-foot protrusion of near-vertical rock now named the Hillary Step. Sherpas call it Tenzing's Back, but, in fact, it was Hillary who led the section, "[t]aking advantage of every little rock hold and all the force of knee, shoulder and arms. . . ." As Hillary "heaved hard on the rope," Tenzing stemmed up a crack in the rock face and "finally collapsed exhausted at the top, like a giant fish when it has been hauled from the sea after a terrible struggle." Hillary was just as tired, but from the top of the Step, the route was straightforward: "A few more whacks of the ice axe in the firm snow, a few very weary steps," Hillary recounted, "and we were on the summit."

It was 11:30 a.m., May 29, 1953, when they became the first mountaineers to reach the highest point on earth. Tenzing felt "[a]t that great moment for which I had waited all my life, my mountain did not seem to me a lifeless thing of rock and ice, but warm and friendly and living. She was a mother hen, and the other mountains were chicks under her wings." Hillary felt emotional too, but expressed it differently: "We knocked the bastard off."

Tenzing left an offering of chocolates in the snow and tried to take a photo of Hillary but didn't know how to operate the camera. So he passed it to Hillary, who snapped Britain's iconic victory image: A Tibetan hoisting an axe strung with a flapping Union Jack, the most visible of his four flags. The men basked in the achievement for fifteen minutes before descending to an alien world.

The sudden stardom that followed caught Tenzing by surprise. "I appeared on television, before I had ever even seen a set." Queen Elizabeth got word of the triumph and invited Tenzing to receive the King George Medal. King Tribhuvan awarded him the Most Refulgent Order of the Star of Nepal, the Shah dynasty's highest civilian award. Mickey Mantle sent a signed baseball bat and cheers from the New York Yankees. Not to be outdone, India's prime minister, Jawaharlal Nehru, offered Tenzing a passport and suits from his own closet.

In the Kathmandu Valley, fans mobbed Tenzing, chanting his name and hoisting him aloft on their shoulders. Rumors swirled that Tenzing had three lungs. He and Hillary rode in the Shahs' gilded chariot and tried to ignore the banners overhead: An artist had depicted Everest with a brown man on the summit and a white stick figure sprawled

below. Autograph seekers muscled in, and Tenzing, who could neither read nor write, accepted their outstretched pens and scrawled his
mark. Far removed from his life in Tibet, he was visibly dazed.

Such wild, postcolonial display unsettled his teammates, and the
impropriety intensified when one of Tenzing's autographs suddenly
became front-page news. Tenzing had unwittingly signed a statement
declaring himself to be the first to summit Everest. Hillary did not
want to comment, so the British mobilized. Colonel John Hunt, the
expedition leader, called a press conference to deflate the native son.
Tenzing Norgay isn't a mountaineer of Hillary's caliber, Hunt proclaimed, and he lacked the technical skill to lead the climb. A Sherpa
wasn't first on the summit of Everest; that distinction belongs to a
citizen of the Commonwealth.

The backlash in Kathmandu was brutal. Tenzing's supporters
smeared Hillary as a buffoon carried to the summit in a sedan chair.
Hunt apologized and retracted his statement. Hillary drafted one of
his own, declaring that he and Tenzing had climbed to the summit
"almost together." The summiters signed it and released it to the press,
but they failed to bury the controversy.

"Why Hillary added 'almost,' I have no idea," Tenzing's son Jamling later said. "Ever since that day, my father and Hillary have maintained that they climbed together and reached the summit together.
People still ask who was first, and it doesn't matter."

Between Sherpas and Tibetans, another dispute arose. Which ethnicity could claim Tenzing as their own? Various Bhotia groups in
India and Nepal, including those claiming to be Tenzing's own relatives from Tibet, noted that Tenzing was born in Tibet and spent his
youth there. The Sherpas made their own case. Tenzing had married
Sherpanis, spent his adult life in villages with sizable Sherpa populations, and reared his children in the Sherpa language and culture.
"Many see my father as the godfather of Sherpas because he was the
one who brought the ethnicity into the limelight," Jamling said. "If

my father had said 'I am a Tibetan' then there would have been no Sherpas" as the West knows them. The Bhotias of Ghang La in Tibet would be the celebrity ethnicity.

In his autobiography, Tenzing chose to describe himself as a Sherpa from the Khumbu, and that's what the media continued to report. In a passage deleted from the book, he went further, distancing himself from Tibetans: Tibetans "would often pretend they were Sherpas so as to get jobs," he explained, and they would become "very quarrelsome and often draw their knives."

Tenzing also had an exigent reason to identify himself as Sherpa in the 1950s. China had invaded his Tibetan homeland, seizing a cornucopia of mineral wealth. Mao Zedong's Red Army, at the crest of the Cultural Revolution, consigned roughly one-sixth of ethnic Tibetans to prisons, labor camps, and starvation. Tenzing's spiritual leaders were under siege. The Dalai Lama fled to India.

If Tenzing had publicly declared himself Tibetan, China would have claimed him as one of the "Chinese" ethnicities and used the first ascent of Everest in its propaganda—something Tenzing would have deplored. Coming out as Tibetan, as biographer Ed Webster put it, "would only have magnified his nationality problems."

Tenzing had fully assimilated by then. He was the world's most prominent Sherpa. But in his heart he was neither Sherpa nor Tibetan, exclusively; he was both. After Everest, Tenzing honored his complex heritage by founding the Himalayan Mountaineering Institute in Darjeeling, which trains indigenous mountaineers of many ethnicities, including Sherpas and Bhotes. Since 1954, the school has trained more than 100,000 students, excelling in its mission to "produce a thousand Tenzings."

5

Insha'Allah

Shimshal, Pakistan
10,500 feet above sea level

Shaheen Baig warned his son and daughter to look before flopping into bed. A dormouse the size of an apricot pit lived between the cushions where the family slept, and Shaheen refused to trap it. With winter approaching, "the creature has no time to make another burrow," he said, "and if we turn him out, he'll freeze in half an hour."

For an entire winter, his family shared their bed and bread with the rodent. "Shaheen may be the toughest mountaineer in Pakistan, but he can't get rid of a mouse," said his wife, Khanda. "He hates to see anything suffer."

With humans, Shaheen was even worse. Working as a guide, he fretted over clients' headaches, tracked how much they ate and drank, checked and rechecked their harnesses, and filed their crampons with a nursemaid's anxiety. The thirty-nine-year-old had tapered brows that emphasized his constant concern. He had already summited K2 in 2004 without bottled oxygen, and when he returned four years later, many climbers recognized his familiar frown. They turned to him for advice, let him negotiate their labor disputes, and put him in

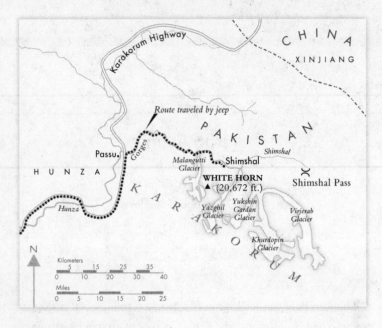

Shimshal Valley, Pakistan Shaheen Baig, one of Pakistan's best mountaineers, grew up in Shimshal and taught two local men, Jehan Baig and Karim Meherban, how to climb. All three Shimshalis worked as high-altitude porters on K2; Shaheen was at one point a leader of the climb.

charge of rope placement on the Bottleneck. Shaheen knew the terrain better than anyone.

"He was an ace," said Wilco van Rooijen of the Dutch team. "I trusted that guy completely. If he had been at the Bottleneck as planned, nothing would have gone wrong on summit day."

▲ ▲ ▲

Shaheen was born in Shimshal, a mountain village in the Hunza region of Pakistan, 76 miles northwest of K2. Shimshal lies beyond a snow-choked gorge that's impassable from November to March.

Nine peaks, each rising higher than the tallest mountain in North America, flank the village; to the east over a pass, the Silk Road meanders through Xinjiang, China. Shimshalis make up the majority of Pakistan's K2 summiters, and three Shimshalis were at the epicenter of the 2008 disaster.

Shimshalis have long been soldiers of fortune. Their ancestors, by some accounts, deserted Alexander the Great as he drove his army through the area in 372 BC on a campaign to conquer the world. Three shield bearers named Titan, Khuro, and Gayar wanted to find a strange creature described by the Greek historian Herodotus. "Northward of all the rest of the Indians," he wrote, live "the great sand ants, in size somewhat less than dogs, but bigger than foxes . . . and very much resembling Greek ants in shape." These ants excavated a deep tunnel network, and "the sand that they threw up was full of gold." Modern scholars suspect that Herodotus mistranslated the Persian word for marmots; the legendary ants were probably the whistling ground squirrels that burrow above Pakistan's Indus River, tossing up gold dust.

Disappointed, the prospectors abandoned their quest and settled in a hundred-mile-long valley that would be claimed by the Kingdom of Hunza. They worshipped their hometown gods at first, but around 150 BC Zeus gave way to Buddha, who was displaced, in turn, by Allah. In 711 AD, General Muhammad bin Qasim invaded the Indus Valley with "the Bride," a stone-launching precursor of the artillery gun. He sheltered those who submitted, disemboweled those who didn't, and introduced Islam. Qasim's faith spread, but not immediately throughout Hunza, which remained predominantly Buddhist and animist until the sixteenth century.

Around the time of the Islamic conversion, Shaheen's village was founded in a remote valley of the kingdom. According to legend, a herder and his wife wandered into the Shimshal Valley and tripped over a slab of slate. As they dusted themselves off, the wife noticed that the slab was vibrating. Curious, she flipped it aside. Water spurted from a hole underneath, soaking the couple, filling the gorge that led out of the valley, and creating the Shimshal River. The couple grabbed their bedraggled sheep and waded to shore. Unable to leave the flooded valley, they collected driftwood to build a hut and waited for the waters to drain. They planted apricot orchards along the river-bank and watched their sheep grow fat in the high grass.

The ewes and rams multiplied each spring, but the herder's family did not grow. The couple lived alone, praying for children but unable to conceive. One morning, when they had become infirm and too weak to feed themselves, the river abruptly receded, revealing a waterlogged saint named Shams. The herder and his wife were over-joyed to see someone after so many years of living in solitude. They offered Shams dry clothes and what little food remained.

Shams appreciated their kindness and took pity on them. He fished deep within his pockets and pulled out a pot and a stick that transmuted water into cream. Shams instructed the herder's wife to drink twelve drafts a day. She had to be strong, he said, if she wanted to start a village. Miraculously, the woman's belly swelled, and, forty-eight hours later, she gave birth painlessly to a son named Sher. Less than a few minutes old, the infant stood up, introduced himself to his parents, bathed, folded the laundry, and cooked breakfast. Sher had many talents, among them an ability to understand the speech of animals.

As Sher grew, he explored beyond the valley and discovered that Chinese merchants from Xinjiang had claimed his father's territory as their own. To settle the land dispute, Sher challenged the merchants to a game of polo, using the entire valley as a playing field. The Chinese told Sher he'd lose. After all, the boy rode a miniature yak against a team of expert horsemen. But Sher was resourceful. He discussed game strategy with his yak and carried the saint's stick as his mallet.

When the match started, the Chinese charged down the field in control of the ball, but Sher's yak knew the stakes and pushed himself to keep up. When one merchant tried to hit the ball forward, Sher hooked his mallet to block the swing and whacked the ball across the glaciers, winning single-handedly. Shimshalis trace their ancestry back fifteen generations to this original champion.

If Sher did live for two centuries, as the legend claims, he'd have seen Shimshal's population grow from three to 150, but this increase had more to do with sinners than saints. The Mir, Hunza's ruler, was sending his best thieves to Shimshal. He ordered them to scale the Shimshal Pass into Xinjiang and pillage camel caravans that were plying the Silk Road between the oases of Leh and Yarkand. Successful raids yielded bullion, cannabis, coral, felt, indigo, opium, pashmina, sugar, silk, slaves, and tea bricks, all of which were taken to the Mir. He either rewarded the raiders or, if dissatisfied, dropped their broken bodies into a pit beneath his stronghold, the Baltit Fort.

Faced with this choice—climb and steal or be killed—Shimshalis learned to climb and steal. In the eyes of the British, they served their master too well: slaughtering and enslaving, disrupting British trade, and exposing holes in British defenses. Intelligence officers were alarmed. The British had assumed that Hunza's peaks buffered their Indian empire from Russian invasion, but now raiders were punching through, using a previously unknown pass to slink in and out. Could the Russians use the same breach to launch an attack? The Shimshal Pass, the British determined, had to be secured.

They sent out their smoothest spy to find it. His mission ultimately positioned Shimshalis to become pioneers of Karakorum mountaineering.

▲ ▲ ▲

Francis Younghusband was a nineteenth-century James Bond. With a walrus mustache and hair slick with pomade, he considered marriage "coercive" and could talk himself out of danger in a dozen languages. In 1889, the twenty-six-year-old joined six Gurkhas—elite soldiers from Nepal—and left in search of Shimshal. From the stories traders told him, Shimshalis moved like snow leopards, silently stalking and devouring their prey, then vanishing into the Karakorum. Intrigued, Younghusband trekked in the direction of the raids. Within a month, he had found the Shimshal Pass and, below it, a den of thieves. Younghusband scrambled up the cliff to the raiders' fort, peered inside the wide-open gate, and waved a greeting.

The gate slammed shut. Instantly, "the wall was manned by wild-looking Kanjutis, shouting . . . and pointing their matchlocks" at him. The spy waited, "expect[ing] at any moment to have bullets and stones whizzing about [his] ears," until two henchmen emerged from the gate, sized him up, and left.

Younghusband returned that afternoon on horseback. This time, when he approached the gate, it swung open. Leaving his Gurkha soldiers behind, he trotted inside the fort. Before his eyes could adjust to the darkness, a man sprang from the shadows and yanked the horse's bridle. The startled animal reared, nearly bucking Younghusband off the saddle. In the commotion, the Gurkhas charged, ready to defend horse and rider, but Younghusband kept his cool. He dismounted as though he'd just arrived at a stable, and the Shimshalis burst out laughing. As the spy had guessed, this mock ambush had been their way of testing his mettle. He had passed.

The raiders welcomed him, offered him tea and dope, and showed off their matchlocks, which fired the only slugs available: garnets gouged from the hillsides. When conversation turned to the caravan raids, the Shimshalis said they couldn't negotiate; Younghusband would have to speak to their employer, Mir Safdar Ali. They agreed to escort him to Baltit, the Mir's stronghold down the valley.

Younghusband scaled the Shimshal Pass to map it and continued his reconnaissance. En route, he encountered his archrival, Bronislav Gromchevsky, a spy for the Russians. Although adversaries in the diplomatic duel known as The Great Game, Younghusband and Gromchevsky considered themselves gentlemen, so they shared vodka and brandy, debated imperial policy, and gossiped about the Mir, whom Gromchevsky knew by reputation. Mir Safdar Ali, Younghusband learned, claimed descent from Alexander the Great and a promiscuous fairy. Safdar had ascended the throne by chucking one brother off a cliff, beheading a second, dismembering a third, poisoning his mother, and garroting his father, who had murdered his own father by sending him a smallpox-laced robe. "Patricide and fratricide may be said to be hereditary failings of the royal families of Hunza," contemporary historian E. F. Knight once noted. The Mir, "whose cruelty was unrelieved by any redeeming feature," took personal and military advice from a drum pounded by invisible hands, audible only to him. Younghusband must have wondered how he could negotiate with such a psychopath.

When Younghusband arrived in Hunza, he buttoned up his scarlet Dragoon Guards uniform and, flanked by Gurkhas, strode into the Mir's ceremonial tent. The throne of absolute power resembled a wooden lounge chair, and, when Younghusband glanced around for a place to sit, the Mir motioned for him to kneel in the dust.

Younghusband suspended negotiations. The next day, the Mir visited Younghusband's tent and proposed a compromise. Raids through Shimshal were a legitimate source of income, Safdar declared, and would stop only if Britain provided a bribe.

But "the Queen is not in the habit of paying blackmail," Younghusband replied, balancing on the folding chair his aides had found. He switched tactics and tried intimidation, ordering his six Gurkhas to point their rifles out the tent flap and shoot a rock far down the valley. Every bullet struck the target. But when Safdar told the Gurkhas to shoot an innocent bystander scrambling along a path, they refused. Seeing this as a weakness, the Mir pressed for more money—and "some soap for his wives."

So Younghusband picked up his chair and left. The Mir "was a poor creature," he wrote, "and unworthy of ruling so fine a race as the people of Hunza." Younghusband returned to his handlers, recommended that the British seize Hunza, and in 1891, a thousand soldiers invaded under the command of Algernon Durand.

As the British colonel marched toward the kingdom, the Mir bombarded his enemy with maniacal letters. In them, Safdar promised to defend Hunza "with bullets of gold"; he considered one seized fort "more precious than the strings of our wives' pajamas"; he threatened to hack off Durand's head and serve it on a platter. Nonetheless, Durand kept advancing, snatched the fortress at Nilt, and seized Baltit Fort.

When Durand's troops blasted apart the gate of the Mir's stronghold, they stormed into empty rooms. Instead of exotic concubines, a search of the harem revealed "artificial flowers, scissors . . . toothpowder, boxes of rouge, pots of pomade and cosmetics." Safdar and his wives were gone, enjoying a comfortable exile in China. On Durand's orders, the soldiers dumped Safdar's wooden throne over the embankment, installed the Mir's half-brother as the new ruler, and set up a garrison in the valley.

The new ruler, Mir Muhammad Nazim Khan, kept his pledge to monitor the Shimshal Pass for the British. Shimshalis turned to herding, and the surrounding kingdom of Hunza became a vacation destination. Bestselling 1930s novelist James Hilton modeled his Shangri-la after the region; pseudoscientists claimed that the local apricots helped residents live to 160; *Life* magazine called the kingdom "Happy Land," a utopia "where the ruler sows gold dust with the year's first millet seeds, and where mothers-in-law go along on honeymoons in order to school their newlyweds in the intimate art of marriage." During the turbulent years of Partition, the Mir was so intent on maintaining stability that he refused to take sides with India or Pakistan. He asked to join the United States. Pakistan ultimately administered the region—first called the Northern Areas, sometimes considered part of Kashmir, and now governed by elected leaders as part of Gilgit-Baltistan.

▲ ▲ ▲

The next foreign invasion was by mountaineers. In 1953, Hermann Buhl and the Austrian Embassy sent a telegram to the Mir, asking him to recruit high-altitude porters for Buhl's expedition to Nanga Parbat. Buhl offered to pay the men 20 rupees, or $6 a month, to carry loads.

Aspirants, many of them Shimshali, packed the Durbar, a dusty courtyard below the Mir's Baltit Fort. Wearing a black velvet robe embroidered with gold sequins, the Mir rejected the weak and sent the strongest to a German doctor in the town of Gilgit. With a magnifying glass, the physician examined each patient's chest, mouth, and teeth, and then "he smelled us to see how we would do in altitude," recalled Haji Baig, one of the high-altitude porters selected for Buhl's expedition.

With men like Haji and Amir Mehdi, the sniff test proved accurate. When Buhl struggled down from the summit with frostbitten feet, Haji and Mehdi alternated carrying him on their backs. Impressed, Buhl spread the word about his Pakistani high-altitude porters, and the Italians recruited the same men the following year for the first ascent of K2. This success established a warrior class known as the Hunza Tigers, mountaineers whose political influence grew to rival the Mir's.

One of these Hunza Tigers, Nazir Sabir, later overthrew the Mirs' 950-year rule. Walking to elementary school one morning on the way to Baltit, a holy man waved him down and presented the young Nazir with a pebble of rock salt. Lick this once a day until it is dissolved, the holy man told the eight-year-old, and you will bring fame to these valleys.

The boy finished the rock salt and, decades later, pioneered a new line up K2's treacherous West Ridge with a Japanese expedition. Without using bottled oxygen, he survived a forced bivouac in the Death Zone, four days without sleep and two days without food or water. After K2, Nazir focused his legendary toughness on politics.

In 1994, Nazir ran against Crown Prince Ghazanfar Ali Khan, the hereditary Mir of Hunza, for a seat in the local legislature. With mountaineers as his supporters, Nazir trounced the monarchists, becoming the first commoner to lead Hunza in almost a millennium. Once forced to steal and kill to satisfy their Mir's greed, climbers now controlled Hunza politics. As the region's most powerful leader, Nazir fought corruption and built schools and roads, including a jeep track to Shimshal. He mentored Shimshali climbers and employed them on K2 with his expedition company.

Nazir Sabir Expeditions organized the 2008 Serbian K2 Expedition, and Nazir hired Shaheen Baig as the team's leader. "He's the safest climber around," Nazir said, "one of the best in Pakistan." Nazir breaks down when he thinks of what happened to Shaheen and the other two Shimshalis. "That village will never be the same."

▲ ▲ ▲

Despite the new jeep track, Shimshal seems inviolate. The six hundred residents farm barley and herd goats, which they carry in their arms to the grazing lands to avoid setting off landslides. In spring, Shimshal's apricot orchards explode in a pastel flurry; in winter, snow leopards pad along the riverbank, leaving prints in the frost. After dark, Shimshalis tell mountaineering stories while huddled around yak-tallow candles in a central hall where ancient beams, carved with stars, frame a skylight to the heavens. The village has one satellite phone, which is almost always switched off.

Shimshalis speak Wakhi, a rare language related to Persian. Many of their climbing tales feature Shaheen, but not everyone enjoys them. "These are ghost stories of living men," said Shaheen's wife, Khanda. "I leave the room." She tolerates only one: her husband's failure on Broad Peak. "It gives me confidence that he has the sense to stay alive."

Broad Peak, or K3, juts out of the Karakorum like a giant incisor. A moderate 8000er compared to its neighbor, K2, Broad Peak turns brutal in December. Winds pummel the slopes at up to 130 miles per hour, gouging out tents, shredding ropes, and shooting hail like rounds from a machine gun. No climber had yet managed a winter ascent. Only a few were daring enough to try.

On Broad Peak in the winter of 2007, Shaheen started each day with a clean shave, although it was *haraam*, forbidden by Quranic law. The Prophet directed Muslim men to grow beards as a visible sign of their faith, but a temperature of minus 49 degrees Fahrenheit made Shaheen a pragmatist. His whiskers created air pockets between his cheeks and his neoprene mask. At cold enough temperatures, those humid pockets could freeze the mask to his face.

After shaving, Shaheen and his Italian climbing partner, Simone Moro, left for the summit around 6:30 a.m. They made each other a promise: No matter how close they were to the top, they'd turn around at 2 p.m. That way, they'd avoid descending in darkness.

Shaheen felt strong, and at 2 p.m., he could taste the summit. It was perhaps an hour away. Winds were low. Shaheen understood the temptation to continue. If he topped out, the winter ascent would go down as one of the most extreme in mountaineering history, and he would become internationally famous.

"But you can't think clearly in the Death Zone," he said. "You have to do it before you get there, when you have judgment. Climbers die when they ignore a set turnaround time." So he and Simone turned back, reaching their tent before temperatures plunged further at sunset. By getting so close, yet respecting the turnaround time, Shaheen earned his reputation as one of the sanest of the madmen who take on winter ascents. Shimshalis respected his judgment, and if a local carpenter or a shepherd wanted to become a mountaineer, Shaheen was the man to talk to.

In 2001, two such men had approached Shaheen for climbing instruction. Twenty-four-year-old Karim Meherban and twenty-five-year-old Jehan Baig had been scrambling up mountainsides since they were boys, using hemp rope and ibex-horn anchors to reach the grazing lands. Now the two shepherds wanted to earn climbers' salaries.

"Karim and Jehan became my little brothers," said Shaheen. "I set technical routes on the White Horn and made them climb the ice, over and over, until I knew they had the skills."

Shaheen's students proved not only strong but lucky, with Jehan cheating death more than once. When Jehan was crossing an icy pass near Shimshal, the slope slithered beneath his boots as though the mountain were shedding its skin. He couldn't sprint faster than the tons of sliding snow, so he waded to a boulder, wrapped his arms around the granite, and hugged. The rock shielded Jehan, and the flow rumbled around him, leaving him unharmed.

Another avalanche brought Jehan recognition. On July 18, 2007, on K4, or Gasherbrum II, a German pulling fixed lines out of the snow triggered a slide. It partially buried Japanese mountaineer Hirotaka Takeuchi, crushing his rib cage and collapsing a lung. Jehan grabbed a shovel and sprinted more than 600 feet across the wash of the avalanche and made it to Hirotaka. Jehan dug him out of the snow and lowered him down to camp. Hirotaka survived, and Jehan won acclaim and gratitude. He'd seen enough to know that fortunes reverse in a split second on mountains. Now thirty-two, his experience made him seem much older than his friend Karim, whom clients called "Karim the Dream."

Unlike mountaineers who seldom look up from their boots, Karim reveled in the views and seemed unable to conceive of anything going wrong. It never did. In 2005 on Nanga Parbat, sometimes called "The Killer Mountain," Karim reached the summit and earned a hefty tip from his French client, an aristocratic insurance salesman named Hugues Jean-Louis Marie d'Aubarède. Karim returned to Shimshal and told his two children about the climb; his youngest, a three-year-old named Abrar, begged to hear what had happened on the summit. Had Karim entered the magical crystal palace of Nanga Parbat? Was it true that mischievous fairies buzz around the mountaintop, dining at translucent tables and kicking off avalanches for fun?

Karim shook his head. He'd seen nothing supernatural on Nanga Parbat, but he promised to pay better attention on the next climb. That peak, he announced, would be K2. His French client had hired him again for the following summer.

Karim's children cheered and hugged their father; his wife, Parveen, picked at the tablecloth. She asked her husband for more details about this plan. Wasn't his client pushing sixty? Could Hugues handle the climb? Was the money worth the risk?

Hugues brokers insurance, Karim replied. He is too sensible to sell our lives cheaply.

Comforted by Karim's confidence, Parveen congratulated her husband on getting the job and joined the rest of the family in celebration.

Karim guided Hugues on K2 in 2006 and 2007 and returned home both times with a stack of rupees but no summit. In 2008, Hugues hired him again, and Karim told his wife that he'd reach the summit this time. After all, Karim now had experience from two previous attempts, and this summer he'd be climbing alongside his friends, Shaheen and Jehan. The Shimshalis had been hired by different teams—Karim by the French, Shaheen by the Serbians, Jehan by the Singaporeans—but they planned to help each other on the mountain. Maybe they'd even stand together on the top. "Everything seemed so perfect," recalled Shaheen, echoing Karim's sentiments. "We were all so young and strong. I never thought there would be an accident."

Parveen was more realistic. In late May, as her husband prepared to leave for his third attempt of K2, she made a last-ditch effort to stop him. She told Karim that they didn't need the money; she could support him with her general store. Shimshal's most successful female entrepreneur, Parveen had invested her husband's mountaineering earnings in a one-room shop that sold soap, pens, children's shoes, embroidery, and nail polish. The family no longer needed to rely on Karim's dangerous career. "I asked him to stay in Shimshal," Parveen said. "Then I begged."

Karim embraced his wife and his children, grabbed his pack, and left the house he'd built. He walked down the irrigation channel, crossing barley fields cloaked in *waki sholm wush*, a yellow wildflower. Karim's father, Shadi, met him by the jeep track that runs through the village. Shadi also tried to convince Karim to stay.

No Shimshali has ever died on K2, Karim replied. Then, to make the assurance ironclad, he added, "Father, I'm going with Shaheen."

As he listened to his son, Shadi stared at the riverbed and remembered how three glaciers—the Khurdopin, the Virjerab, and the Yukshin—had once conspired to exterminate the village. Slow-flowing rivers of ice, the glaciers drain their summer meltwater through a subterranean channel. A natural ice dam constricts the flow, blocking a torrent. In 1964, the dam broke. Snowmelt gushed down, and the river rose 90 feet. It uprooted apricot orchards, hurled homes down the valley, and washed away half the settlement. Villagers scrambled to higher ground. The water tore through the gorge that leads out of Shimshal and demolished the village of Passu 40 miles downstream. Nature had devastated Shadi's family once. He knew it could happen again.

Shadi looked back at his son and tried to reason with him. "I said, 'You don't need to climb K2 again. What about carpentry?' But Karim smiled and told me: 'Father, I can't stop yet. Just this one summit, then maybe.'"

When Karim left that afternoon, Shadi watched the jeep disappear down the river basin, kicking up sand. He stayed fixed on the spot long after his son was gone.

"Insha'Allah," he prayed—if God wills it.

PART II

CONQUEST

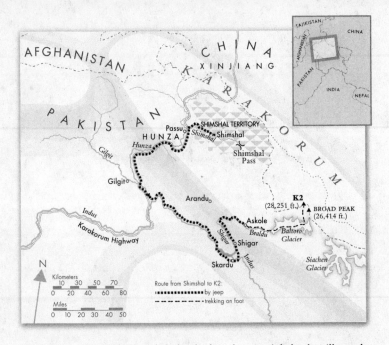

Shimshal to K2: From Shimshal, the climbers drove to Askole, the village where the trail to K2 begins. This trekking path is too treacherous for jeeps, so climbers employ hundreds of low-altitude porters, who ferry food and supplies to Base Camp.

6

The Approach

The Karakorum Highway, barely two lanes wide, rolls through the intersection of the Karakorum, Himalaya, and Hindu Kush. The builders of the original road faced tribesmen who stalled construction by "rolling down avalanches of rocks upon them." Blasting a modern highway from the cliffs was nearly as treacherous. It took twenty years and cost nine hundred lives—about a life a week. Today, jeeps bumping down the highway dodge pits and boulders, swerve around hairpin turns, and squeeze between trucks tricked out like pinball machines.

In June 2008, Karim Meherban left Hunza in a baby-blue Jeep Scrambler and jostled down the Karakorum Highway. He passed miners scraping rubies from the hillsides, children panning for gold along the river, and guards flaunting Kalashnikovs at military checkpoints. Near the town of Skardu, he passed an airfield and military compound best known as the home of the Fearless Five. Its hangar was emblazoned with a snarling snow leopard and a pentagram, signifying the squadron's five tenets: sacrifice, courage, devotion, pride, and honor. The Fearless Five command a fleet of helicopters used to defend Pakistan's borders and to airlift injured soldiers and avalanche survivors. Karim hoped he'd never need them.

Splashing through the milky-green water of the Shigar River basin, his Jeep then moved onto a rutted track, joining vehicles from other expeditions. Eight hours after leaving Skardu, Karim stopped at a dirt patch in Askole, the village at the end of the road. As the driver switched off the engine, local men mobbed the vehicle. Shouting welcomes and stirring a dust storm with their feet, they pulled supplies to the ground, unloading the cargo into snaking rows of stoves, tables, lawn chairs, blue plastic barrels, and duffels crammed with mountaineering gear.

These laborers are called *low-altitude porters*, or *LAPs*. Less expensive than mules, they ferry supplies across terrain too treacherous for jeeps. Pakistan's Ministry of Tourism estimated that, in 2008, low-altitude porters were hired to carry 5,600 loads from Askole to peaks such as K2, Broad Peak, Trango Towers, and Gasherbrums I and II. A seven-member expedition to K2 might hire 120 LAPs a season, spending $10,000. Low-altitude porters "are your umbilical cord during a climb," said Rehmat Ali, a porter coordinator for Nazir Sabir Expeditions. "Mountaineers don't have a shot at the summit without them."

In 2008, the low-altitude porters carried all kinds of things to K2: ropes, tents, orthopedic pillows, Cajun popcorn, chickens, skin mags, hand warmers, raspberry liqueur—whatever their clients paid for. The Flying Jump had its porters bring in a jug of pickled seaweed; Nick Rice, a climber from California, had porters shoulder a seventy-pound generator so he could power his laptop and access his blog—which, by the end of the climb, would receive two million hits. The porters weighed the loads on a hand scale and, when possible, divided them into fifty-four-pound piles, the limit established by their union.

With strips of fabric, they bound the loads onto wooden frames and hoisted them onto their backs, beginning the sixty-mile slog to K2.

As the low-altitude porters weighed in and left, the climbers exchanged satellite-phone numbers and audited each other, counting the peaks they'd bagged and the friends they'd lost. They told each other to quit climbing, but not yet. Some Serbians who had been soldiers compared leaving Askole with marching off to war. Beyond this outpost, there would be no more orchards, no more children, no more laws.

The hundreds of porters, trudging one behind the other, formed human trains stretching for miles. At noon, nearly everyone stopped while the Muslims dropped their packs to perform *salat*. Turning southwest toward Mecca, they pressed their foreheads to cloth laid on the scree, bowing to praise Allah. Then the work continued.

Thrashing through an undergrowth of scrub and wild rose, the porters brushed against spines as long as sewing needles. When temperatures scorched to 115 degrees, the men doused their heads in the side creeks and balanced along tracks cut in the cliffs. After two days, the poplars vanished, then the grass. The Baltoro Glacier, a thirty-five-mile tongue of ancient ice, rippled ahead. To the north stood the earth's tallest rock walls, the Trango Towers. Beneath the ice, a rush of subglacial melt could be heard, feeding the Braldu River. Sometimes the sun punched through the clouds, and from a single point in the sky, amber beams radiated downward in columns.

Within a week, the climbers had reached Concordia, where the Baltoro Glacier collides with the smaller Godwin-Austen Glacier. As the buckling ice cracked like rifle shots, K2 stood before them, a dusty carpet of ice and scree rolling off its slopes. Framed by lesser peaks, the pyramid seemed to prop up the weight of the sky.

On this, his third attempt of the mountain, Karim must have

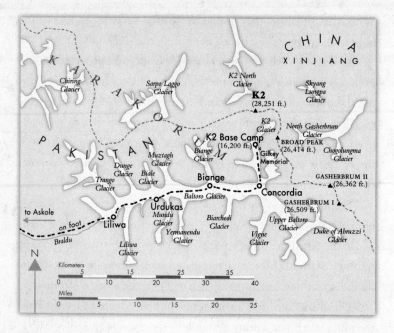

The Approach to K2: The week-long trek from Askole to K2 runs up the icy tongue of the Baltoro Glacier. Near Base Camp, 18,000 feet above sea level, a makeshift cairn known as the Gilkey Memorial commemorates those claimed by the mountain.

admired K2's symmetry and dreamed of the summit. At Concordia, still a day and a half's walk from K2, he pitched his tent next to the Sherpas'. Buddhist chanting was audible. As an Ismaili Muslim who believed in no god but Allah, Karim would never have prayed to a vacant mountaintop. To him, K2 wasn't a goddess—just a vicious piece of rock.

▲ ▲ ▲

The low-altitude porters and the foreign climbers spent a week together but kept their lives segregated. "I don't remember any of their names," said Marco Confortola, a climber from Italy. It was a challenge even to discuss practical issues with them, such as work he wanted done. Most porters spoke uncommon languages, such as Balti, Khowar, Wakhi, Shina, and Burushaski. Marco spoke Italian. Cultural barriers, such as Marco's appreciation of salami, made matters worse. Keeping *halal* according to Quranic dietary rules, the porters avoided pork and its by-products. As Muslims, some considered it immodest when Western women wore shorts and were disconcerted when the climbers showed a gay romance on DVD. "*Brokeback Mountain* shocked me," said Yaqub, a twenty-seven-year-old porter from Gulapur. He watched it anyway.

Like most of his peers, Yaqub ate and socialized away from his clients and slept out in the open. The porters even had their own latrines. "It felt a lot like separate but equal," recalled Nick Rice, "but I preferred the porter toilets. The white guys got sick and made a mess in theirs."

Low- and high-altitude porters found the cultural exchange educational and downplayed their employers' transgressions. "I was amused," said Shah Jehan, a fifty-three-year-old from the village of Kuardo. He had overheard a couple from the Flying Jump having noisy sex in their tent. "We don't encounter that kind of thing in Pakistan, but why should I mind? That's how they do it in Korea."

The expedition was also paying him good money. The average Pakistani worker earns $2.81 a day; Shah Jehan and other low-altitude porters made $9 a day, or about 90 cents an hour, assuming that every day they crossed two camps and worked ten hours. The porters could earn even more by pocketing a cash allowance for boots, socks, and shades. Expedition companies used to provide their porters with this crucial equipment, but many porters resold it the same day. "If you don't scratch the sunglasses, you can get 100 rupees [$1.20] for them at the bazaar in Skardu," said Shujaat Shigri, a thirty-six-year-old low-altitude porter from Gulapur. "That's a lot of money."

Now all porters receive the equivalent of a signing bonus intended for gear. Some buy adequate equipment. Some buy the minimum. Some buy nothing at all. Porters often walk barefoot or use cheap flip-flops to preserve the soles of their better shoes. Others wear mismatched sneakers discarded by former clients. When snowstorms hit, expeditions hand out charity supplies on a last-minute, as-needed basis, but there's never enough, and some porters would rather suffer and resell the gear than actually use it. Toes freeze and eyeballs, seared by ultraviolet rays bouncing off the snow, flush to the color of pomegranates.

Low-altitude porters can earn more by moving quickly. If they're fast and the weather cooperates, they can manage five or six round trips to K2 in a season. "If I carry three loads, I can earn enough to last the whole year," said Zaman Ali, a nineteen-year-old low-altitude porter from Tisar village, where he farms barley, peas, and wheat. Some loads, he explained, are better than others. "Tents and pots are the most prestigious" because they are needed throughout the trek in, he said. He carried the mess tent for the Serbian team in 2008. If he had carried rice, it might have been consumed en route, and he would have been sent back early and earned less.

Although porter strikes used to be routine, they were rare in 2008, because "all the expeditions agreed to our pay scale and standards," said Jaffer Wazir, president of the porters' union, Khurpa Care. To discourage expeditions from renegotiating these terms, porters carried laminated Khurpa Care ID cards and brochures that explained their civil rights.

Nonetheless, two-thirds of the porters heading to K2 were uninsured, despite Pakistani regulations that say expedition outfitters must insure them all, said Syed Amir Raza, general manager of Islamabad's Alpha Insurance, the only company that insures Pakistan's porters. The policy costs the equivalent of $1.75 per month and pays out $1,200 for deaths due to "visible accidents." If no one witnesses the death—as commonly happens when porters are spread out or lost in a crevasse—

the policy is void. On average, two insured porters die a qualifying death every year. Nobody tracks the deaths of the uninsured.

The foreign climbers also had to take their chances: Their lives were uninsurable. Even specialized insurers, such as Patriot Extreme, decline to extend coverage to climbers for accidents and deaths above 14,760 feet. That's lower than K2 Base Camp.

Medical evacuations for the critically injured aren't automatic, either. Pakistan used to provide emergency airlifts for the injured whenever Fearless Five pilots could land, but nobody reimbursed the army for these trips. It cost Pakistani taxpayers an arm and a leg so foreigners might save a toe, said Brigadier M. Bashir Baz, chief executive of Askari Aviation, which dispatches the choppers. Now the government requires every mountaineering expedition to register with Askari and to deposit a $6,000 refundable bond, but only three-quarters of the 2008 expeditions did this, he said. "And if you don't pay the deposit in advance," he said, "we won't pick you up."

In his office in Islamabad, Brigadier Baz displays a bumper sticker beneath the glass on his desk and directs climbers to read it: "Good judgment comes from experience, and experience comes from bad judgment." When climbers refuse to pay, he shakes his head in disgust, visualizing the quixotic legions, unbonded and uninsured, marching toward the Savage Mountain.

▲ ▲ ▲

The 2008 expeditions pitched Base Camp on a rocky glacier two miles from the foot of K2, a safe distance from avalanches. Green and yellow domes sprouted from the ice like mushrooms, sponsorship banners flanking their sides. By late June, Base Camp had swelled into a multicultural tent city, population 120. Laughter and rock music piped out of the tent flaps. Generators whirred amid snarls of power cables. Damp socks steamed in the sun. Solar panels baked.

Many found it a cheerful place, but Chhiring Dorje's first impression was the stench. It wafted over from a communal grave to the south, on a rise between the Savoia and Godwin-Austen Glaciers. The Gilkey Memorial, a cairn of rocks piled eight feet high, is K2's Tomb of the Unknown Soldier. Family photos and unread letters feather the monument. Threadbare scarves wrap around its base like the bindings of a mummy. These scarves, Buddhist offerings called *katas*, beat in the wind, petitioning the gods. On hot days, the cairn stews with the scent of defrosting flesh, and the odor clings to mourners' hair and clothing. Tin plates, fastened to the rocks, glint in the sunlight. Engraved with names of K2's victims, they display dates from 1939 onward, June to August, the climbing season.

The Gilkey Memorial is a grisly necessity because corpses rarely make it down the mountain in one piece. For Everest losses, families sometimes send a recovery team. This doesn't happen on K2. The Savage Mountain devours its victims during the long winter between climbing seasons. It encases the torsos in ice and grates them against the rocks, only to spit out the digested remains decades later, scattering limbs among avalanche debris.

When Art Gilkey's team gathered stones to honor their friend in 1953, they started a morbid tradition. To keep their campsites sanitary, climbers began using the memorial as a place to dispose of the fingers, pelvic bones, arms, heads, and legs found in the glacial melt. Burying these scraps under the Gilkey Memorial felt more respectful than leaving them to the ravens. For more than half a century, the memorial has been a place to caution the living and consecrate the dead. Mountaineers attempting K2 visit the site to remind themselves of what they are getting into.

Chhiring considered the memorial a travesty. In 2008, he was among the first to arrive at Base Camp for the season, and he felt sick sleeping and eating so close to corpses. Why, he wondered, would anyone pin these people under rocks? All they do is freeze at night, defrost in the morning, simmer in the day, then freeze all over again. Such mistreatment, he worried, trapped the souls inside the bodies when they were suffering for release. He assumed that the mountain goddess suffered along with them. "I would not go near the memorial," he said. He urged his friend Eric Meyer to stay away from it, too.

Chhiring believed the bodies deserved better. Sherpas and many other Buddhists prefer to cremate the dead. The smoke carries the spirit to the sacred realm above, as it did with Chhiring's mother. When someone dies above the timberline and it's hard to find firewood, a sky burial substitutes for cremation. Although outsiders consider sky burials barbaric—China outlawed the practice in Tibet from the 1960s to the 1980s—to Chhiring this was the sacred way to free the soul. During a sky burial, Buddhist *lamas* or others with religious authority carry the body to a platform on a hill. While burning incense and reciting mantras, they hack the corpse into chunks and slices. They pound the bones with a rock or hammer, beating the flesh into a pulp and mixing in tea, butter, and milk. The preparation attracts vultures, and the birds consume the carcass, carrying the spirit aloft and burying it in the sky, where it belongs. Souls inside the Gilkey Memorial receive neither cremation nor sky burial, and this troubled Chhiring.

He decided to find out more about the temperament of K2's goddess, so he approached another Sherpa to discuss it—Pemba Gyalje, a devout Buddhist on the Dutch team. Pemba belonged to the Paldorje, an ancient Sherpa clan of the Solukhumbu. At the top of the ethnic pecking order, Pemba had also summited Everest six times and trained at the prestigious Ecole Nationale de Ski et d'Alpinisme in Chamonix, France. Like Chhiring, he was a Sherpa climbing as an equal member of a Western team. They were natural allies but had opposite personalities. Pemba usually observed discussions in silence, offered some austere logic, then withdrew into silence again. That style put Chhiring on edge, so he ended up consulting someone else. He called his *lama* on speed dial from his $2-per-minute Thuraya satellite phone.

Ngawang Oser Sherpa picked up on the eighth or ninth ring. The *lama* told Chhiring he was praying at the Boudhanath *stupa* in Kathmandu. "I can't gauge Takar Dolsangma's mood long distance," he said. He advised Chhiring to perform a *puja* ceremony and pay attention to the mountain's reaction. "And don't climb on Tuesday," he added. "It's an inauspicious day for you."

Chhiring switched off the phone and began hauling rocks to the center of camp, building a *chorten*, a sacred mound to honor the goddess. He attached a string of Buddhist prayer flags to it. The red, blue, white, and yellow squares of calico, stamped with sacred verses and strung along a line, were his *Lung Ta*, Tibetan for "wind horse." Eric and other mountaineers joined him at the *puja* ceremony as the breeze picked up. The flags whipped, purifying the air and spreading blessings around camp. Chhiring knew Takar Dolsangma was present. Mindful, he recited mantras, asking the goddess for counsel and forgiveness. He leaned his ice axe and crampons against the *chorten*, balancing a plate of rice beside it and hoping she would accept the offering, bless his equipment, and forgive the injury they were about to cause her. Burning incense, Chhiring dusted the faces of his friends with flour to signify that he wished them to live until they were old and gray. Finally, he asked the goddess for permission to climb.

The ceremony failed. The goddess was still restive. Avalanches roared down her slopes that night, and the jet stream scoured the summit. For a week, she hid behind the clouds. When the Flying Jump arrived in Base Camp on June 15, Chhiring recognized the problem: Pasang Lama's boss.

Others saw Mr. Kim as an omen, too. "I was also praying the mountain wouldn't recognize Mr. Kim," said Ngawang Bhote, the Korean team's cook.

Although Kim had made sure the Flying Jump was one of the best equipped teams at Base Camp, he hadn't been welcome among the Sherpas since a scuffle at Everest in 2007. That year, a member of Mr. Kim's team discovered a quartz rock with the Korean symbol for Everest naturally ingrained in the crystal. According to the expedition organizer, Mr. Kim had declared the stone holy, and his team erected an altar in the kitchen tent. They believed the quartz would protect them as they climbed Everest's Tibetan flank.

But the stone disappeared and the Flying Jump panicked. For four days, the Koreans suspended climbing operations, combing Base Camp for their talisman. On the fifth day, the Chinese liaison officer—Base Camp's equivalent of a sheriff—arrived to investigate allegations that a Korean climber had assaulted a Sherpa for misplacing the rock. Jamie McGuinness, a New Zealander who had organized Kim's expedition, got into a shouting match with his client.

"I told Kim I'd pull his entire Sherpa staff if they were going to clobber someone over a missing rock," recalled Jamie, who consulted with the liaison officer about revoking the Korean team's permit.

Mr. Kim apologized and successfully climbed Everest with his teammates and Pasang's cousin Jumik Bhote. After Everest, Jumik joked privately that working for the Flying Jump was like jumping off a cliff and expecting to fly. On K2, the Koreans boasted to Chhiring and Eric that the Flying Jump "had sponsors to impress and would reach the summit, whatever the cost."

Chhiring stayed away from the Flying Jump just as he kept away from the Gilkey Memorial. Still, Mr. Kim's presence weighed on him. A few months earlier, Chhiring had been consumed with K2, but now he was beginning to think his wife may have been right; maybe K2 wasn't worth the risk. He spoke with Eric about going home. He asked Pemba for his opinion. He called his *lama* again by satellite phone and asked him to perform another *puja* ceremony at Boudhanath. For a week, Chhiring kept hauling rocks to his *chorten,* which grew seven feet tall, becoming the largest in camp. Climbing the mountain still felt wrong. Ngawang Bhote also sensed it. "I could feel the weather change every time Nadir Ali"—the Pakistani cook for the Serbs—"butchered an animal and served its ground flesh," he said. Chhiring agreed and stuck to rice and noodles.

Most of the others in camp ignored the goddess. They scarfed down Nadir's cheeseburgers, played poker, hoarded porn, licked Nutella from the jar, debated the Bonatti Bivouac, updated their blogs, complained about the weather. Chhiring saw that the young man hired by the Flying Jump, Pasang Lama, wasn't praying much, either. He was too busy leveling tent platforms and digging holes for the Flying Jump's latrine. Concerned, Chhiring watched him closely. Pasang worked hard and lacked fancy gear. That meant he needed this job and was ready to do whatever the Flying Jump asked of him, no matter the danger. Pasang reminded Chhiring of himself when he started out: eager but oblivious.

Chhiring hoped Pasang would acknowledge Takar Dolsangma soon. If Pasang was going to be on K2 with the Flying Jump, he would need her. Chhiring also recognized something Pasang didn't: Pasang and his cousins hadn't landed their jobs because of superior luck, strength, or skill. The Bhotes were climbing K2 because ethnic Sherpas did not want to work for the Flying Jump.

One evening, just before the weather cleared and the teams began their assault on the mountain, Chhiring saw Pasang kneeling next to the *chorten*. Chhiring hadn't spoken with him yet but decided to join him in prayer. He bent his knees, pressed his hands together, and leaned forward. Instead of directing his prayer toward the goddess or his wife and children, he prayed for Pasang, asking the mountain to protect him.

When he opened his eyes, Chhiring looked up and scanned the horizon. Hidden behind storms for weeks, K2's summit materialized and seemed to swallow the sky.

7

Weather Gods

Rawalpindi, Pakistan

On June 2, 2008, the day Shaheen's clients arrived in Pakistan, a white Corolla packed with sixty-five pounds of fertilizer, diesel, and TNT rolled through a security checkpoint in Sector F-6/1, near Islamabad's diplomatic enclave. The driver, an eighteen-year-old jihadi named Kamal Saleem, turned left at Street 21 and parked in front of the Danish Embassy. At 12:10 p.m., Kamal's car exploded.

The bomb blasted a four-foot crater into the road, incinerated Kamal, flipped the Corolla, caved in the embassy's metal gates, pulverized most of the embassy's front wall, blew out the windows, and punched through a quarter of the building next door. Dozens of cars shot off the road and rubble blanketed Sector F-6. "Bodies are littered all over the place," Al Jazeera reported. "The blast could be heard all over the city, and it has literally taken the leaves off the trees." Eight people died, including an unidentified child, and twenty-seven were wounded.

Al-Qaeda called the attack retaliation. Danish newspapers had published a series of cartoons satirizing Islam. One ridiculed the

Prophet by depicting a bomb concealed in his turban. After the explosion, journalists made it sound as though jihadis were on the verge of taking over Pakistan, seizing its nuclear arsenal, and annihilating civilization. But foreigners heading to K2 considered it a routine delay. As Serbian climber Hoselito Bite put it: "In Islamabad, Armageddon is nothing special."

Shaheen Baig, however, took the bombing personally. Waiting for his clients' cargo, he questioned the sanity of the world outside Shimshal. Al-Qaeda was slaughtering children over a cartoon. He instructed the Serbian team to stay inside the hotel. "I will show you the real Pakistan," he told them. The country Shaheen knew was peaceful, most of the time, and he wanted foreigners to see past the threat of terrorism and behold Pakistan's beauty.

So did the mountaineering industry. To persuade skittish tourists, the Alpine Club of Pakistan had successfully lobbied for climber-friendly incentives. By 2008, the Ministry of Tourism, using a sliding scale based on altitude and season, had slashed fees for 8,000-meter peaks to half their pre-9/11 rates. Some lesser peaks were on sale at 95 percent off. A K2 permit was $12,000, while Everest cost seven times more. At the same time, the ministry stopped enforcing caps on the number of expeditions to K2 and other peaks. In practice, anyone with ready cash could attempt any Pakistani mountain, at any time, by any route.

Most mountaineers appreciated the reduced fees and climber-friendly deregulation. " 'Pay to play' is how we want it," said the Alpine Club president, Nazir Sabir. "The government has no business deciding who can or can't climb." Nepal has policies similar to those of Pakistan. The United States is more restrictive. Although the summit of North America's highest peak barely reaches the altitude of K2's first mountain camp, climbers heading to Denali in Alaska must submit a climbing résumé before securing a permit. If prospective mountaineers don't appear to have enough experience, "I'll call them and say, 'I see you've been on Grasshopper Glacier for a few days, but Denali is different," said Joe Reichert, a National Park Service ranger. "We'll try to talk them out of it, tell them it's too dangerous."

The Park Service can't turn away mountaineers from public lands, but it reviews applications sixty days in advance and requires climbers to attend a PowerPoint presentation about avalanche risk, crevasse rescue, environmental impact, fixed-line etiquette, and sanitation. The Park Service installs and maintains fixed lines on Denali, and U.S. taxpayers pay for helicopter rescues. Injured climbers are airlifted to hospitals regardless of whether they can pay.

In the Karakorum, the bargain price for climbing has had the intended effect. After the September 11 attacks, tourists and mountaineers avoided Pakistan; in 2008, more than seventy foreign mountaineers arrived to climb K2, although half would be culled by illness before a summit bid. Hundreds more were attempting nearby peaks. Instead of cancellations, K2 had a crowd.

Shaheen wanted to give the climbers a good impression of his religion and his country, and when he arrived at Base Camp with the Serbian team, he tried to be an ambassador. "Part of my job is to keep harmony," he said. Still, diplomacy was tough when expeditions made unreasonable demands. The Singaporean team, for instance, ordered Jehan Baig, their Shimshali high-altitude porter, to carry loads through what Jehan believed to be an avalanche zone. Jehan balked. The team fired him.

Afterward, Shaheen found Jehan another job. Jehan's new employer, Hugues d'Aubarède, the sixty-one-year-old French insurance salesman, paid well, and he had already hired another Shimshali, Karim. But Shaheen soon had misgivings about Hugues. Hiking along the moraine near Base Camp, he and Karim had spotted Hugues crouched down as though tying a shoelace. On the rocks in front of him lay a gray forearm, chopped at the elbow, fingernails intact enough for a manicure. The empty shoulder socket was fringed in tendon. Hugues snapped several photos, aiming his lens at the man's desiccated lips.

Shaheen and Karim were sickened. Muslims consider the mouth, which recites the Qur'an, to be the holiest part of the body. Upon death, as Allah sends an angel to coax the soul from its body, Muslims traditionally close a corpse's mouth, shut its eyelids, and comb its hair. The body is bathed in scented water, shrouded in clean sheets, and lowered into the earth on the right side, facing Mecca—all before night falls on the day of death.

Shaheen gestured toward the dead man. "That could be any of us," he told Karim.

Karim asked what they should do.

"Let me handle this," Shaheen replied.

Several hours later in Base Camp, Shaheen intercepted Hugues. "What do you plan to do with those pictures?" he asked.

"Nothing," Hugues replied. Plenty of climbers photograph human remains along the glacier, he said. When Hugues climbed Everest, he had nearly tripped over a frozen cadaver. Death is part of this sport, Hugues noted, and he was simply "documenting it, as usual."

Shaheen knew what that meant: "Are you going to post those photos on the Internet?"

No, absolutely not, Hugues said. He vowed to keep the images to himself. "Exposing a body like that would be obscene. The dead man's family might even recognize him online."

Shaheen left satisfied. On July 11, he invited the Frenchman to a party. The celebration was in honor of the fifty-first anniversary of the Aga Khan's coronation, a day of solidarity for Ismaili Muslims who accept this direct descendant of Muhammad as their spiritual leader. Nadir, the Serbian team's cook, slaughtered a goat, set up a line of tables in the sunlight, and spread out a buffet of almond cakes and meat skewers. Shaheen, meanwhile, corralled guests into a circle, clapping his hands as Karim and Jehan sang in Wakhi. A dance

Chhiring Dorje Sherpa (left) became one of the most respected Sherpa mountaineers. A trekker passing through the village of Na in 1980 took the only known photograph of him during his childhood. (*credit Dr. Klaus Dierks*)

A decade later, Chhiring had begun working as a porter. In 1991, at the time this photograph was taken, he was sixteen years old, carrying loads for a French Everest expedition. (*credit Jean-Michel Asselin*)

To many devout Buddhists in Rolwaling, mountaineering is an offense to the gods. Chhiring's grandfather, Pem Phutar, carried loads for a British expedition to Gauri Shankar but never spoke about it. Although he received a recommendation letter from the expedition, he hid it from his family. (*Courtesy of Chhiring Dorje Sherpa*)

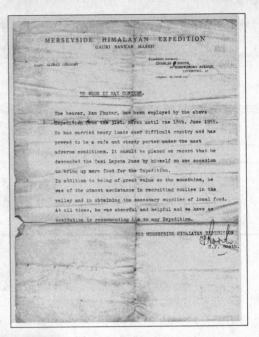

Phurbu Ridar Bhote (left), a mountaineer, left Hungung to find work when his son, Pasang, was six. When he had saved enough money from expeditions, he sent for Pasang to attend school in Kathmandu. (*Courtesy of Pasang Lama*)

Pasang's brother, Dawa, and sister, Lahmu, in front of the house that their father built with his mountaineering wages. Climbing was more lucrative than farming; most families in Hungung couldn't afford a corrugated tin roof. (*Courtesy of Pasang Lama*)

During school vacations, Pasang sometimes returned to Hungung from Kathmandu to help out at the house and with the potato harvest. (*Courtesy of Pasang Lama*)

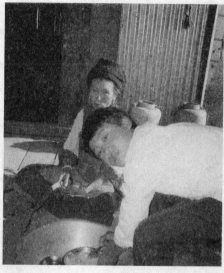

Serbian climber Dren Mandić shoulders the load of a low-altitude porter. Depending on the weather, the 96-mile slog to K2 Base Camp might take a week. The climbers and their low-altitude porters must carry all necessary food and equipment over the Baltoro Glacier. (*credit Iso Planić / Predrag Zagorac*)

Many mountaineers got their first glimpse of K2 from Concordia, a camp en route to the mountain where three glaciers meet. (*credit Lars Flato Nessa*)

Although paying mountaineers and the low-altitude porters rarely hang out together, Serbian climber Hoselito Bite made a point of getting to know the men he'd hired. (*Courtesy of Hoselito Bite*)

Pakistani high-altitude porter Karim Meherban (top) shears Serbian climber Iso Planić. Although the weather was often clear in Base Camp, the jet stream was pounding K2's summit, making it impossible to climb to the upper reaches of the mountain. (*credit Qudrat Ali*)

For twenty-seven days, the climbers waited in Base Camp for the weather to improve. To pass the time, Cecilie Skog knitted a cap for her husband. She and Rolf Bae (right) had been married just a year. (*credit Lars Flato Nessa*)

French climber Hugues d'Aubarède (right) hired Pakistani high-altitude porter Jehan Baig (left) after another team fired Jehan for refusing to carry loads through an avalanche zone. Here they display one of Hugues's gourmet dinners, freeze-dried chicken breast. (*credit Nick Rice*)

Pakistani high-altitude porter Karim Meherban guided Hugues on K2 in 2006 and 2007. In 2008, Hugues hired him again, and Karim believed they would reach the summit that time. "I can't stop yet," Karim told his father before leaving for the mountain. "Just this one summit, then maybe." (*credit Qudrat Ali*)

Shaheen Baig, who had previously summited K2, was appointed leader of the advance team. "We were all so young and strong," he recalled. "I never thought there would be an accident." (*credit Simone Moro*)

During the final logistics meeting at Base Camp, Muhammad Hussein wrote up the list of the lead team members who would break trail and place ropes through the Bottleneck. Only Pakistani and Nepali climbers were to lead; the Korean climbers volunteered to play an administrative role. (*Courtesy of Hoselito Bite*)

Muhammad Khan (left) and "Little" Muhammad Hussein worked as high-altitude porters for the Serbian team. They had previously summited K2 in 2004. (*credit Peter Zuckerman*)

Before their summit bid, the mountaineers took a group photo. Dren Mandić, Eric Meyer, and Chhiring Dorje Sherpa are in the second row, second, third, and fourth from the left. The French climber Hugues d'Aubarède leans forward directly above them, with Pemba Gyalje and Marco Confortola to his left. Standing in the front row is Korean leader Mr. Kim. Kneeling in the front row, third and fourth from the left, are Ms. Go and Karim Meherban. Kneeling front and center, with blond hair, is Dutchman Wilco van Rooijen. (*credit Hoselito Bite*)

Seracs loom above the Bottleneck, the deadliest stretch of K2. Giant blocks of ice routinely calve from the sheer ice wall. (*credit Iso Planić / Predrag Zagorac*)

The Bottleneck, a thirty-story ascent, is only wide enough for a single-file line of climbers. (*credit Lars Flato Nessa*)

Climbers want to move quickly through the Bottleneck and the Traverse to reduce the amount of time they spend below the seracs. Unfortunately, the line moves only as fast as the slowest mountaineer. (*credit Chris Klinke*)

Basque climber Alberto Zerain made it up through the Bottleneck before everyone else and topped out at 3 p.m., hours ahead of the other climbers. Chhiring took this photo of Alberto descending as seventeen climbers were still going up. (*credit Chhiring Dorje Sherpa*)

Upon reaching the summit of K2, Chhiring unfurled Nepal's double-pennant flag in celebration. He topped out at 6:37 p.m., too late to avoid heading back in the darkness and cold of night. (*credit Pemba Gyalje Sherpa*)

From the summit, the climbers surveyed the entire Karakorum range.
(*credit Lars Flato Nessa*)

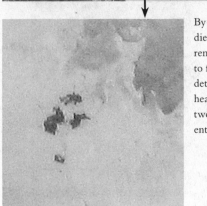

By 9:58 the next morning, at least five men had died. Marco Confortola and Ger McDonnell remained with three distressed climbers, trying to free them from a tangle of fixed lines. The detail shows Marco leaning over Jumik Bhote's head as Ger kneels beside him. Above them lie two members of the Korean team, hopelessly entangled. (*credit Pemba Gyalje Sherpa*)

Marco Confortola (center), the last survivor to return to Base Camp, had feet consumed with frostbite. Chhiring (right) helped treat him in a tent converted to a field hospital. (*credit Roberto Manni*)

The survivors mourned the dead by incising their names on metal dinner plates and placing them around a cairn known as the Gilkey Memorial. This plate, for Jehan Baig and Karim Meherban, notes that the men were HAPs—high-altitude porters—from Pakistan. (*credit Hoselito Bite*)

Some of the injured survivors were airlifted to Skardu's Combined Military Hospital, where the mortuary overlooks the children's park and helipad. (*credit Amanda Padoan*)

Dawa Sangmu, the widow of high-altitude porter Jumik Bhote, holds Jen Jen, the son Jumik never met. Behind them, rolled inside a duffel, is the Kolon Sport sleeping bag that Jumik used on K2. (*credit Amanda Padoan*)

Nazib, the mother of high-altitude porter Jehan Baig, holds a photo of her deceased son and his family. Without his wages and mourning their loss, Jehan's family in Shimshal struggled to make ends meet. (*credit Amanda Padoan*)

Karim Meherban's father, Shadi, and four-year-old son, Rahmin, in Shimshal. Rahmin still believes his father will return from K2. (*credit Amanda Padoan*)

pit formed and Hugues boogied into the center. Dressed in slacks, a button-down shirt, a sportsman's cap, and a cashmere sweater, he hopped and flopped his arms to the music like an injured seagull. The crowd adored him. Amid catcalls, Hugues ceded the dance floor to Karim. "I've got rheumatism," Hugues announced. Laughing, Shaheen decided he'd misjudged the good-natured Frenchman. He hadn't. Shortly after their conversation on the glacier, Hugues had downloaded the images onto a laptop. He composed an entry for his blog, speculating about the identity of the pieces. Then he tapped *SEND*.

▲ ▲ ▲

In many ways, the climbing community is like high school. The number of high-altitude mountaineers is small enough that almost everyone knows one another. With the added stress of death and dismemberment, cliques form and peer pressure builds. Mountaineers swap allies, trash-talk, tussle, hook up, and show off. In the weeks before the tragedy, some even squabbled like tweens.

Dutch expedition leader Wilco van Rooijen, for example, "did this, like, 13-year-old-girl thing to me," recalled Nick Rice, the climber from California. "Cold shoulder, completely bitchy, he wouldn't say 'hi' if I said 'hi.'"

"Because I couldn't believe what he was wearing!" Wilco explained. Nick wore only a lightweight Petzl Meteor helmet, too flimsy for K2. "A plastic bicycle helmet."

"Wilco just hates me," Nick said. "I don't know why."

"And he didn't bring his own rope," Wilco continued.

"The American team brought my rope."

"He surfed the 'net all day and mostly brought petrol so he could run his generator."

"Wilco had generator envy."

Such spats ranged from essential to existential, and when Chhiring overheard them, he drew into himself. Compared with those who climbed Everest, the K2 mountaineers more blatantly blurred the line between crazy and courageous. Many were hoping to bag all the 8000ers—the fourteen peaks taller than 8,000 meters—and their swagger sometimes overshot their skill. The strong resented the weak, the weak resented being discounted, and the arrogance unsettled Chhiring. Anticipating that they'd all have to work together, he sized up the most ambitious of the group.

Chhiring found the Basque climber Alberto Zerain astonishing; he had never seen a European who could climb like a Sherpa. Alberto had struck a deal with Shaheen, agreeing to work as a high-altitude porter in exchange for a tent spot.

In addition to Alberto and Shaheen, Chhiring considered Wilco among the most capable mountaineers at Base Camp. A knight of the chivalric Order of Orange-Nassau, Wilco was on his third crusade. He had attempted the Savage Mountain twice before and failed. In 1995, a rock smashed his arm "so the bone was jutting out through the skin." During the 2006 season, bad weather had beaten him back.

This time, Wilco was the first to arrive at K2, setting 3,000 meters of rope along the Cesen route. But when the knight abandoned chivalry and tried to charge the customary toll for use of these lines, his popularity tanked. On most days, he wanted to go home and see his wife and seven-month-old son. "I wanted to feel love," he recalled. "I was crying inside my tent, thinking, 'I'm done with this mountain.'"

Chhiring recognized Wilco's homesickness, but he rarely spoke to him. He preferred the company of Wilco's Irish teammate, Gerard McDonnell, who got along with everyone. A musician and engineer, Ger had acquired the nickname "Jesus" because of his messianic beard and his role as the camp peacemaker. He had also experienced a resurrection of sorts and had a dent in his head to prove it.

In 2006, climbing K2 with Wilco, Ger was at about 23,000 feet when a rock slide hissed down the slope. As Ger ducked behind a boulder to shield himself, a gneiss hockey puck spun at him and smashed into the left side of his Kevlar helmet. Climbers use Kevlar because it is tough—it's a common component of bullet-blocking body armor. Nevertheless, the helmet dented, and the impact chipped off a shard of Ger's skull, exposing his brain.

Ger's climbing partner, Banjo Bannon, tore a wool sock from his pack and wadded it over the peephole. Delirious and losing blood, Ger stumbled down the mountain. After several desperate hours, he staggered into Base Camp and passed out. Storms kept the helicopter from landing that afternoon. The next day, Ger was airlifted to Skardu's Combined Military Hospital.

Chhiring would have retired if he had a hole in his head, but this was a minority view. Base Camp was crawling with adrenaline junkies. Extreme skier Marco Confortola was in the vanguard, amusing his friends with videos of himself zipping down vertical drops in an aerodynamic catsuit. A tattoo of gothic script scrawled across the back of his neck cautioning, *Selvadek* (Wild Thing). His right bicep sprouted a row of edelweiss tattoos, each one signifying an 8000er that he had climbed. A Buddhist mantra was etched into the flesh of his wrist: *Om mani padme um*, a meditation for benevolent attention. The thirty-seven-year-old Italian lived with his mother. When anyone asked about his long-term plans, Marco said he refused to be tied down: "I am married to the mountains." K2, however, wasn't his type. "She is not a lady like Everest," he said. "K2 is a surly and disagreeable man." Marco was positive about the mountain's gender because women coddled him, and no female, not even a goddess, could reject him the way the Savage Mountain had. In 2004, a windstorm on K2 had slapped Marco's tent off the slope, taking his gear with it. Determined to succeed this time, Marco paraded around Base Camp wearing a patchwork of corporate logos and pumping hands with anyone he came across.

In contrast to the voluble Italian, Serbian mountaineer Dren Mandić spent his free time away from the crowd. Chhiring often watched him pacing the moraine, photographing birds or stooping to admire a clump of moss. At home in Serbia, Dren volunteered at an orphanage, and over the years he'd cared for a menagerie of strays and pets, including dogs, fish, geese, a goat, hamsters, parrots, pigeons, a squirrel, snakes, spiders, and turtles. As a child, Dren even refused to step on the grass. "How would you feel if someone stomped on your neck?" he had told grown-ups. Named after a medicinal tree whose sharpened sticks are used to lance boils, Dren was now thirty-two and in love with a woman who worked at the zoo.

Chhiring sometimes wandered the moraine as Dren did, but when he needed a retreat, Chhiring usually sought out the happiest people around, the newlyweds Cecilie Skog and Rolf Bae. They invited Chhiring to lounge on their inflatable IKEA couch and watch the comedy *Borat: Cultural Learnings of America for Make Benefit Glorious Nation of Kazakhstan*. The lack of oxygen made the film's antihero more hysterical than he might normally have been, and they played and replayed it.

Cecilie, who had once called climbing a "male-dominated affair," was the first woman to complete the Explorer's Grand Slam, reaching the top of the tallest mountain on every continent—the Seven Summits—and the North and South Poles. K2 was a kind of honeymoon for her and Rolf. They had been married only a year. After K2, they were planning a more conventional adventure: They wanted to have a baby.

Chhiring admired the newlyweds, and seeing them made him miss Dawa. He sometimes felt alone in a swarm of strangers. His friend Eric helped him practice reading English, and Chhiring helped Eric dispense medicine to the sick. They treated everything from bronchitis to appendicitis, stocked camps, and waited for the weather to improve.

For twenty-seven days, storms prevented anyone from going far. Shaheen flexed his diplomacy, Nick stoked his generator, Wilco cried in his tent, Ger told cautionary tales, Marco flashed his tats, Dren studied moss and birds, Rolf and Cecilie watched *Borat*, and Pasang set ropes for the Flying Jump. The jet stream battered the mountain, and snow flurries buried the camps. Until the weather cleared, the climbers could only wait.

▲ ▲ ▲

Around the planet churns an invisible sea of waves, swells, and currents. Alfred Russel Wallace, codiscoverer of evolution by natural selection, called it "The Great Aerial Ocean." Gas expands and contracts, rises and falls, warms and cools. Solar rays zip through atmospheric layers and strike the land, transforming into heat. Jet streams, cyclones, and ocean currents traffic the earth's energy.

Stuck in Base Camp, the teams monitored a raucous layer of atmosphere called the troposphere. The stakes were sky-high: Windless days deliver the summit; unpredicted storms kill. As Buddhists perform *pujas* and Muslims kneel in *salat*, all denominations worship the meteorologist. Well-funded expeditions engage one for the entire season at $500 per day.

Nothing predicts weather with absolute precision, but infrared photos, satellite images, weather-station data, and an ensemble of statistical models run through supercomputers can foretell the future up to ten days in advance. For most of the year, the models predict the same thing for K2. Week after week, the jet stream blasts the summit. Yet, in summer, for a few hallowed days every few years, the winds die. This weather window is brief and precious. Until it opens, climbers acclimatize so they can bolt up the mountain when the forecaster calls.

Acclimatization hinges on genetics. Some mountaineers can

adjust to altitude in two weeks; others will never get used to it. No matter how much they train, they can't climb high mountains without bottled oxygen. These different physical responses help explain why climbing is rife with theories about how best to acclimatize. Climbers will tell you to eat bananas, meditate, practice yoga, sleep on your left side, swallow Diamox, or avoid it and instead chew *yarsagumba*, a mummified caterpillar with a mushroom spore shooting from its brain.

Almost all altitude-adjustment routines involve climbing in order to stock camps, followed by a period of recovery at lower altitude—ideally, below 18,000 feet. Mountaineers ascend in the morning and descend before nightfall. Doing this seems to jolt the body into faster adjustment until about 27,000 feet.

Above that is the Death Zone. Nobody can adjust to it. At this extreme altitude, the percentage of oxygen in the air is the same as at sea level, but the air pressure is much lower—the same volume of gas has fewer molecules in it. As a result, the body can't extract enough oxygen from the air. The more time spent in the Death Zone, the weaker and sicker a climber becomes. The digestive system fails and the body devours its own muscle tissue. "It's living hell. You feel your body deteriorating," said Wilco. "Ever tried to run up a staircase while breathing through a straw?"

Acclimatization increases the amount of time climbers can survive in the Death Zone. During acclimatization, the kidneys excrete more bicarbonate ions, acidifying the blood, which quickens respiration. The bone marrow revs up red-cell production so the blood can transport more oxygen. Blood flow surges in the brain and lungs. Without acclimatization to altitude, someone dropped off at the summit of K2 would black out within minutes. Those who have acclimatized can last several days.

These adjustments nevertheless come with dangers. A higher concentration of red blood cells thickens the blood. Clots form more easily and the heart has to pump harder. In the deep veins, clots travel up the legs and eventually clog the pulmonary artery, causing hypoxia, shock, or sudden death. Other clots forming in arteries cut off oxygen supply to the brain, causing stroke, or block the coronary arteries, leading to heart attack. There is also the specter of edema, or fluid buildup. Desperate for more oxygen, the body's cells release nitric oxide and other chemical signals to the capillaries, directing them to accept more blood. As the capillaries expand, they expose themselves to higher blood pressure and tear. Fluid leaks, pooling in places it shouldn't.

Capillaries in the eyes explode like fireworks, and this hemorrhaging blurs vision in severe cases. When the fluid collects in the lungs, which have the body's greatest concentration of capillaries, climbers suffer from high-altitude pulmonary edema. Instead of breathing normally, victims of high-altitude pulmonary edema can only pant. The cough resembles the bark of a sea lion. The pulse races. Lungs cannot deliver oxygen. Death comes within hours unless the climber descends fast or is entombed within an inflatable pressure bag.

Like the lungs, the brain, which draws in an enormous supply of blood, can also leak fluid. When this happens, it's called high-altitude cerebral edema. Its first symptoms are often mild; they may be what causes acute mountain sickness. However, victims can deteriorate fast. The headache feels as though a sadist is testing a jackhammer on your cranium. Balance wavers and speech slurs—almost as though you've downed ten martinis. Half the body may go numb. Unreal smells, sounds, tastes, and visions appear. During an altitude-induced hallucination on the 1954 K2 expedition, "I found myself inside an ice cream parlor in Padova," recalled Italian scientist Bruno Zanettin. "I told myself, 'This can't be real. I'm alone inside a tent in Pakistan,' but I could still taste the flavor of the ice cream."

It's hard to predict whom these afflictions will strike. They can break even the best climbers, ones who have always excelled in thin air. Bizarrely, the dying commonly fail to notice how sick they are.

And even those handling the altitude well or breathing bottled oxygen can feel the drain. Viagra can help. The drug relaxes the vessel tone of the pulmonary arteries and can increase exercise tolerance, so mountaineers commonly take it.

Experts debate whether altitude causes permanent brain damage, but oxygen deprivation certainly impairs judgment. In 2008, for example, Roeland van Oss of the Dutch team nearly gassed himself. On July 1, at 23,000 feet, he was melting a pot of ice inside his tent without adequate ventilation. "On the burner there's a big sticker: 'Only use this outside,'" explained Wilco. Carbon monoxide filled the tent, and Roeland fell flat. He would have died if his teammate, Court Haegens, hadn't immediately dragged him into the open air. Although Roeland's mistake was just an oversight, the Savage Mountain had nearly claimed the first victim of the summer.

▲ ▲ ▲

Climbers call him "The Weather God," but meteorologist Yan Giezendanner is an atheist—"to the point of eating priests." Multiple sclerosis consigns him to a wheelchair, but his reach extends six miles into the troposphere. From his ground-floor apartment in Chamonix, Yan was responsible for choreographing the movements of Hugues, Karim, and Jehan.

On July 22, Yan studied two screens streaked with yellow slashes and green waves superimposed on the contours of Kazakhstan. A cyclonic circulation was blowing east. As the eye moved into China, a ridge of high pressure developed over the Karakorum on the cyclone's west side. In this ridge, right over K2, winds would become preternaturally calm for three to four days. "In ten years, I had never seen such a beautiful window," Yan recalled. He didn't pick up the phone right away. "I sat in my kitchen, stalling. I knew August 1 would

be perfect. I also knew my prediction might cause a friend to die."
Reluctantly, he dialed Hugues's number. When the Frenchman's satellite phone chirped at Base Camp, Hugues, Karim, and Jehan were
packing to go home. Hugues had no sponsors to impress. After four
dreary weeks stuck in Base Camp, he could catch a flight to Paris
without disappointing anyone but his dentist, who wanted a photo of
Hugues's teeth gleaming from the summit.

But once he heard the news about the weather window, Hugues
resolved to stay, and so did many others. That day, Thuraya phones all
over camp were bleating, and ecstatic climbers were zipping from one
tent to the next. "Base Camp turned upside down," said expedition
manager Maarten van Eck, who had received an earlier forecast from
the Dutch weather god. Although they still had nine days before the
window opened, climbers lined their axes, ropes, and pickets across
the moraine like butchers primed to gut a hog. They huddled around
laptops. They filed their crampons. And soon the problem became
obvious: With so many mountaineers planning to climb the mountain at once, crowds would pack the slopes. Nobody wanted to miss
this one chance, and forecasters had only predicted four days of good
weather. The teams decided to work together.

Four days after the news came in, about two dozen mountaineers crowded into the Serbian mess tent for the last logistical meeting
of the summer. A jaundiced light filtered through the nylon fabric.
A Warhol-style collage of food labels hung from a string overhead.
Climbers drinking sugar-laced tea fidgeted as though waiting to be
strapped inside a roller coaster. They discussed the siege of the Savage
Mountain. Teams would advance along two routes, the Abruzzi and
the Cesen, which converge at high camp, or Camp 4. Twenty-six
climbers had claimed the Abruzzi; ten had chosen the Cesen.

▲ ▲ ▲

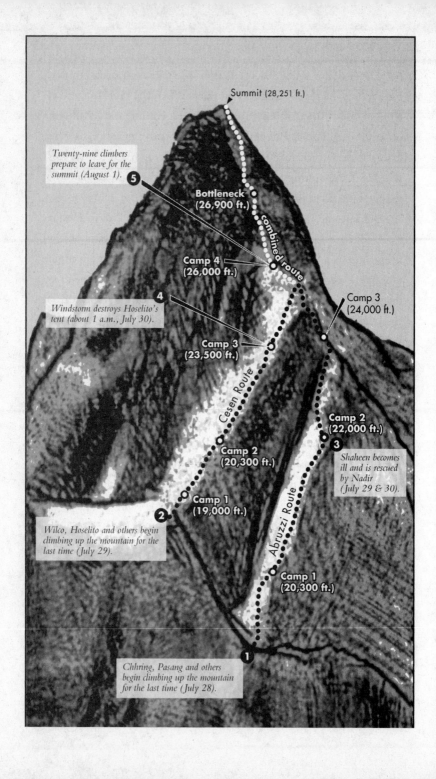

Summit (28,251 ft.)

Twenty-nine climbers prepare to leave for the summit (August 1). **5**

Bottleneck (26,900 ft.)

combined route

Camp 4 (26,000 ft.)

Camp 3 (24,000 ft.)

4

Windstorm destroys Hoselito's tent (about 1 a.m., July 30).

Camp 3 (23,500 ft.)

Cesen Route

Camp 2 (22,000 ft.)

Camp 2 (20,300 ft.)

3

Shaheen becomes ill and is rescued by Nadir (July 29 & 30).

2

Camp 1 (19,000 ft.)

Abruzzi Route

Wilco, Hoselito and others begin climbing up the mountain for the last time (July 29).

Camp 1 (20,300 ft.)

1

Chhring, Pasang and others begin climbing up the mountain for the last time (July 28).

The Abruzzi, the most popular route, traces the mountain's southeast spur. It has four camps: at 20,300 feet, 22,000 feet, 24,000 feet, and 26,000 feet. Past Camp 1, a 45-degree slope rains rocks. This stretch almost killed Wilco in 1995 and Ger in 2006. Climbers must clear it in the early morning when the ice is firm. Next, they face House's Chimney. Free-climbing this rock flue with a pack is impractical, so mountaineers ascend using a rickety ladder and a loom of fixed lines. Camp 2, above, is a wind-scoured platform that backs into a headwall. The route then claws toward the Black Pyramid, a 2,000-foot wall of granite-gneiss, with Camp 3 perched on top. Approaching the Death Zone, the route flattens onto the Shoulder, a glacial saddle reserved for high camp.

The Cesen route is longer and more technical but safer. It avoids some rockfall areas. From Base Camp, the Cesen follows a ridgeline that initially seems as gentle as a ski slope. The first camp, at about 19,000 feet, is jammed behind a butterfly-shaped outcropping. From there, a rock wall at 20,300 feet shelters Camp 2 from wind and avalanches. Snaking around the wall, the route plows upward, fanning into a monotonous incline called the White Desert. Camp 3 is pitched above a hump of gneiss at 23,500 feet. A steep ice field and a rock spire are the last obstacles before the Cesen joins the Abruzzi.

From Camp 4, the common camp on the Shoulder, the combined routes approach the Bottleneck. Seracs hulk above this channel like prows of tanker ships. Lines of climbers crowd the narrow passage. Once through the Bottleneck, the route swerves diagonally across K2's southeast face along the Traverse. A massive lump of ice called the Snow Dome bridges the Traverse with a crevassed snowfield. From there, a ridge leads to the summit.

Abruzzi and Cesen Routes (*opposite*): The weather on K2 allowed a climbing window of just three days, forcing a crowd of mountaineers to try for the summit at once. They took one of two routes, which converged at Camp 4.

During the logistical meeting, the group chose Shaheen Baig to supervise the men who would break trail and fix ropes through the Bottleneck. Each large team contributed support climbers. The Koreans volunteered Pasang Lama and Jumik Bhote. The Serbians assigned two Balti high-altitude porters, Muhammad Hussein and Muhammad Khan. Chhiring Dorje represented the American team; Pemba Gyalje represented the Dutch. This advance team of Pakistani and Nepali climbers would start from Camp 4 at midnight and scale the Bottleneck before dawn.

A second wave of climbers planned to set off an hour behind the lead team. If all went well, the fixed lines would be in place by the time they reached the Bottleneck. Another six hours of breaking trail and they'd be on the summit. "We should turn around by 2 p.m.," Shaheen said. If deep snow clogged the Bottleneck, the climbers might take an extra hour, "but no one should continue up after 3."

Everyone would set their radios to frequency 145.140 MHz. The teams agreed to share willow wands used to mark the route, as well as rope, ice screws, and pickets. Mr. Kim anointed his teammate, Park Kyeong-hyo, as equipment manager. He would check in with each team and confirm that they had brought the necessary gear. "Everything was decided in a systematic way, every small detail," recalled Pemba Gyalje. He felt confident about the plan.

Few recognized the cultural crevasse beneath the slick organizational surface. The advance team was dangerously diverse: Shaheen spoke Wakhi; the two Muhammads, Balti. These Pakistanis communicated in Urdu, a third language, which Shaheen translated into English for the Nepalis to understand. The Nepalis, in turn, played their own linguistic hopscotch. Pasang and Jumik's first language was Ajak Bhote; Chhiring's was Rolwaling Sherpi tamgney; Pemba Gyalje's was Shar-Khumbu tamgney. They used Nepali to communicate among themselves. Information could easily become garbled as it passed through four linguistic layers, not to mention the crackle of a radio. Furthermore, only Jumik could communicate with Park, the equipment manager, who spoke Korean. If one link in the linguistic chain broke—Shaheen, for instance—the Pakistanis would be completely unable to talk to the Nepalis.

The liaison officer of the Serbian team, Captain Sabir Ali, recognized the potential for breakdown. He made a list of the equipment the teams promised to carry and proposed a contract, insisting that each leader sign his name on the paper. But even after that, several climbers were still unsure of the particulars.

"I speak Tarzan English," Marco said to Shaheen after signing. "I hope I understood."

Shaheen shrugged.

Wilco soon regretted the decision to join ranks with all the other climbers. "I signed for it," he recalled, "but I should have said, 'I've never climbed with any of you. Why should I trust you based on nothing but your blue eyes?'" He didn't voice this concern at the time. No one did. The summit was waiting, and the teams felt ready. As the meeting broke up, Ger switched on a boombox. It blasted Biffy Clyro's rock ballad *Mountains* into the clearing sky.

8

Ghost Winds

Base Camp to Camp 4
Up the Abruzzi. Up the Cesen
17,388 feet to 25,800 feet
July 28 to July 31

Two hours before he left Base Camp, Chhiring blessed his ropes, smoking them with incense. He stuffed the coils in his pack below a cylinder of oxygen, stashed for emergencies. He placed a *mala* rosary of 108 gnarled bodhi seeds in his jacket. He'd use them for meditation at high camp. Beside the beads he put a Ziploc bag of *tsampa*, barley flour that his *lama* had blessed. He planned to scatter grain through the Bottleneck as an offering to the goddess.

Deep in his pack, beneath strata of energy powder and butane canisters, he carried an envelope of rock salt. His *lama* had told him to sprinkle it on his last meal before the summit—it would give him strength. Around his neck he wore a crimson thread called a *bhuti*. A gift from his *lama*, the *bhuti* had three charms attached. The most potent, a silver amulet, concealed a mantra stamped on rice paper. Lama Ngawang Oser Sherpa had forbidden Chhiring to open the amulet's casing and examine the mantra inside. If exposed, the mantra's power would evaporate, reversing Chhiring's fortune. The *bhuti*'s second charm, an oblong bead cocooned in black electrical tape, prevented cerebral and pulmonary edema. The third, a cluster of knots, halted avalanches and deflected falling rocks. Chhiring tucked the *bhuti* and its charms under his Capilene shirt, next to his heart.

Like Chhiring, other climbers deliberated over what to carry. Provisions supplied warmth, orientation, and motivation, but everything added weight, so they packed needful things first: altimeters, batteries, cameras, candy, crampons, downsuits, duct tape, goggles, headlamps, helmets, ice screws, ice axes, lighters, nose guards, radios, ropes, sleeping bags, stakes, stoves, sunscreen, tents, toothpaste, and satellite phones. But everyone had different ideas of what was essential.

The Nepalis wore *bhuti*s similar to Chhiring's, but charms differed. Pasang's older cousin, Big Pasang Bhote, wore a pendant of red coral, symbolizing eternal life. He hoped it would relieve him of his recurrent nightmare in which a horned demon came to gore him in the stomach. Pasang's other cousin, Jumik, wore a *bhuti* with a special weave to protect his teenage wife, Dawa Sangmu. Their baby was two weeks overdue.

Pasang usually kept two *bhuti*s: one to wear around his neck and another to slip beneath his pillow to dissolve nightmares. But as he left Base Camp, Pasang realized that he'd forgotten them both. At least he remembered the lucky ring. Its soft gold, soldered into a snake, coiled up his middle finger. The ring belonged to his mother, Phurbu Chejik Bhoteni, who lent it on the condition that Pasang return it to her in person.

Many climbers brought reminders of people they loved and hoped to return to. Serbian climber Hoselito Bite carried a photo of his four-year-old daughter, Maya. "I've grown a lot in two months," she had told him via satellite phone before he left for the summit bid. "When you come back, you won't recognize me." Hoselito kept her photo in a locket wrapped in waterproof tape.

Marco kept his grandmother's rosary inside the top lid of his pack. It was a peculiar inheritance. She had died when Marco was a child, and, on the day of her funeral, Marco had tiptoed to where her body lay. "The rosary was laced between her fingers," he explained, "and I stole it."

Dren carried a miniature Snoopy that his girlfriend, Mirjana, had given him at the airport in Belgrade. He bound the doll to the right strap of his pack. It reminded him of his pretty zookeeper and their home filled with reptile tanks.

Rolf wore a blue-gray cap his wife had knitted at Base Camp. His bride, Cecilie, wore her wedding ring on a chain, so she wouldn't have cold metal around her finger, increasing the chance of frostbite. It was a replacement for the first ring Rolf had given her. En route to the South Pole, Rolf had removed his skis, knelt in the snow, and presented her with a ring fashioned of steel wire from a repair kit. With tears freezing on her face, Cecilie had agreed to marry him. She had worn the ring, which dug into her finger, until they returned to Norway, where Rolf replaced it with a white-gold band.

Nick, the climber from California, brought an iPod filled with a motivational mix of Coldplay, Radiohead, and The White Stripes. He liked to lip-synch, infuriating Wilco. Wilco carried a Thuraya satellite phone with fresh batteries and raised buttons that he could punch even if he were snow-blind.

Others carried intangibles. Hugues climbed with faith in Yan, his weather god; Hugues's high-altitude porters, Karim and Jehan, who believed "no atom's weight in earth or heaven escapes Allah," both shouldered seventy-pound packs filled with Hugues's food and bottled oxygen. Hugues's dehydrated meals were not *halal* by Islamic dietary law but luxurious by mountaineering standards. The most appetizing was a silver packet of freeze-dried Bumble Bee chicken. With boiling water, it would swell into a juicy fillet.

At least one climber, Mr. Kim, itemized his gear with military precision, rejecting all items of superstition except for a single object. The leader of the Flying Jump was rumored to be carrying the lost quartz, the same rock that had caused a scuffle with the crew on Everest.

Chhiring's friend Eric packed a portable pharmacopoeia. Aside from diuretics, steroids, antibiotics, and antivirals, the anesthesiologist carried several doses of alteplase, a clot-busting tissue plasminogen activator, designed to reverse severe frostbite. Each 50 milligram shot cost $1,375. The doctor wore a Capilene undershirt silk-screened with the motto: "K2: A Little Shorter/A Lot Harder." A climber who asked not to be named brought JWH-018, a synthetic marijuana with ten times the punch of THC. The drug's street name was "K2."

Irish climber Ger McDonnell carried a crucifix, his grandfather's pocket watch, an eighty-five-year-old whistle that had called four generations of McDonnells to the dinner table, and a vial of holy water mixed from Lourdes, Knock, and St. Bridget's. Just before he departed, Ger assured his mother in a final blog entry that he had not misplaced the holy water, adding in Gaelic: "*Tá an t-am ag teacht*"— The time is coming.

▲ ▲ ▲

Climbing an 8,000-meter peak resembles a siege, and over the years, two campaign strategies have emerged: expedition style and alpine style.

Expedition-style climbing is akin to trench warfare. High-altitude workers scout the route, break trail, fix lines, and establish fixed camps, each higher than the last. Returning to Base Camp, they scoop up supplies and climb the mountain again, stocking the tents with food and fuel. Then, on the summit push, they climb to the camps again, escorting the clients through crevasse fields and up the slopes. With expedition-style climbs, clients frequently use oxygen during the long and expensive assault on the mountain, and many have no compunction about taking drugs to aid acclimatization.

Alpine-style climbing is like a blitz. Elite teams with as few as two people sprint up and down the mountain as fast as their bodies allow; speed is safety. They pack light, only the bare essentials, and carry their tent between camps. They also adhere to a protocol called "fair means," which rejects acclimatization drugs, high-altitude porters, and bottled oxygen. Alpine-style climbers who adhere to fair means are the real rock stars of mountaineering. They generally are highly skilled and experienced, and they attract considerably more attention and respect than expedition-style climbers.

True alpine style forgoes fixed lines, but hardly anyone attempts the purest form on K2. Mountaineers on K2, regardless of style, need to fix ropes. To do this, a lead climber, with a rope attached to his harness, starts up a pitch and creates a protection by driving in a snow picket, twisting in an ice screw, hammering in a piton, or looping a sling over a solid rock. Then the climber clips the rope through the protection, continues up, and adds more hardware as required by the terrain.

A well-placed anchor should hold on rock, but snow and ice are harder to predict. If the lead slips and the anchor holds, the belayer can quickly brake the rope, and his partner will only fall twice as far as the last anchor. To absorb some of the shock of a fall, ropes are designed to stretch, but that's not always enough to avoid pulling out an anchor. The astute belayer knows whether to stop a fall instantly or to slow it more gradually, thus reducing the yank on the line.

With alpine-style climbing, the leader climbs to a suitable spot, puts in a solid anchor or two, and prepares to stand nearby to belay. The second climber then ascends. With expedition-style climbing, the ropes stay in place. The followers clip onto the fixed ropes with a jumar—a D-shaped device that bites the rope like a ratchet, sliding up but not down—and winch their way along the lines. If a climber slips, the jumar, leashed to the harness, stops the fall immediately. On descent, fixed ropes serve as a convenient hand line, and, on steep terrain, they provide an easy way to rappel down.

Expedition-style climbing might appear safer, but it isn't necessarily. Hanging from knots that strangers have tied, many commercial expeditions' clients don't have lead-climbing experience or a clear understanding of climbing mechanics. Faster clients get caught behind slower ones, or climbers set out in groups, placing the weight of several bodies on a single anchor, which "increases the chance that somebody is going to blow up the whole thing," as Wilco put it. Overloaded anchors pull out and then everyone goes down, initiating a death train. In 2008, all the climbers approached K2 in expedition style, but each team imposed its own ethos. The Flying Jump relied heavily on fixed lines, support staff, and bottled oxygen; the Dutch team abstemiously followed the fair-means rules of engagement.

▲ ▲ ▲

Early on the morning of July 28, Chhiring, Pasang, and Shaheen left Base Camp as part of the lead team on the Abruzzi route. The snow was pitted and pocked, Chhiring recalled, "as though the goddess had swung a hammer" along the route. Ice screws had melted out or vanished. Fresh snow slides covered the bamboo stakes that marked supply caches, and sections of fixed lines, now buried, had become useless. Pulling them out could trigger avalanches. The climbers strung new ropes.

Pasang, breaking trail, stomped out bucket steps for the climbers to follow, testing for hidden crevasses and marking weak snow bridges with purple flags. When he reached camp, he realized that the jet stream had sent some tents sailing, leaving lonely platforms. So he pitched new tents.

Once the lines were reset, the rest of the climbers followed, using jumars attached by a line to each climber's harness. The followers stepped in the lead climbers' tracks to reduce the chance of setting off an avalanche or dropping down a crevasse. "You take a step. You breathe. You take another step. You breathe again," explained Wilco. "Your whole mind is occupied with taking each individual step." Using just an ice axe or a ski pole to balance, they climbed a distance roughly the equivalent of three Empire State Buildings on the first day.

To overcome the exertion, mountaineers use several tricks to stay strong at altitude. One method is to inhale deeply, pursing one's lips and exhaling forcefully, as if blowing up a balloon. This is known as pressure breathing; physicians call it positive end expiratory pressure, or PEEP. Patients with emphysema or other breathing difficulties use this technique reflexively, and research shows that it improves gas exchange and prevents fluid buildup in the lungs. The pursed lips and forceful exhalation increase air pressure, which resuscitates the lungs' air sacs, or alveoli, so they can expand, absorb more oxygen, and expel more carbon dioxide.

Many climbers also take rest steps, a gait with a momentary pause and knee lock. Greater weight rests on the leg when locked, not bent, and spares the calf and thigh muscles. The gait looks stiff, as though the climber were wearing stilts, but it postpones "Elvis leg," or uncontrollable muscle twitching.

Some members of the teams were professional guides who knew the safest and most efficient ways to climb; others floundered, wasting energy. Based on how they moved, "it became clear that not everyone was as skilled at mountaineering as they had made out," recalled Marco, who had been a mountain guide for eighteen years. This worried him and many others. "Some of them were ignorant of basic safety," recalled Fredrik Sträng, a Swedish mountaineer on the American team. "Kicking off rocks [that could hit climbers below], stepping on ropes with crampons, yanking fixed lines, clipping six people to a rope that should only hold two. When I saw the crowd climbing, I thought, 'What the hell? They're going to get us killed.'" Fredrik was so frustrated he started climbing at night to avoid the crowds. He hoped that by the time the two major routes converged at Camp 4, exhaustion and altitude would have culled the weak, forcing many to turn back.

Alberto Zerain sometimes avoided fixed lines altogether. He took the advice a friend had given him after attending an organizational meeting at Base Camp. "K2 is set for tragedy," Jorge Egocheaga had told Alberto, suggesting he avoid "the circus" and climb the mountain independently. With this in mind, Alberto broke a trail of his own, hauling everything he needed on his own back. He pulled ahead of the crowds, caught up with Shaheen, and helped him break trail to Camp 2.

For safety, if not comfort, mountain camps are often wedged underneath rock outcroppings, away from avalanche trajectories. These few protected spots are usually cramped and crowded, as was the case with Camp 2. "Tents were on top of each other," recalled Eric. By the evening, "more than 30 people were there, and it was just too dangerous to go far to take a crap, so the space between the tents turned into a sewage canal." When melting snow for dinner, the mountaineers scooped up the whitest stuff they could find in the darkness, dropping iodine tablets into the pot. Many smeared their fingers with Purell before handling food. But it takes just a speck of stool to infect climbers with campylobacteriosis, or some other digestive illness.

In Camp 2, Shaheen drank two cups of Balti milk tea and fell asleep. A few hours later, he doubled over at the threshold of his tent, vomiting uncontrollably. "It was clearly bacterial gastroenteritus from contaminated water," recalled Eric, who treated Shaheen. "He could have gotten it from the tea"—as Shaheen suspected—"but might have picked it up even earlier than Camp 2." Eric gave Shaheen six gray-green tablets of Compazine, which reduces vomiting and nausea, and six chalky pills of Cipro, an antibiotic. He advised Shaheen to descend in the morning.

Shaheen had no intention of going down. He'd never left his team midclimb and wasn't going to start on K2. He willed himself to feel better by daybreak and retreated into his tent. Tossing, he tried to sleep but spent the night heaving, trying to vomit out his empty stomach.

In the morning, something else was wrong: his lungs gurgled. As other climbers prepared to leave, Shaheen managed to yank on his boots. He weaved 10 feet across camp to where Alberto was about to strike his tent. "Leave your tent up and use mine in Camp 3," Shaheen said. He handed Alberto dried apricots, about 40 yards of lightweight rope, three ice screws, and a Ziploc bag of oatmeal.

"Can you get down?" Alberto asked him.

Shaheen waved off discussion. He needed Alberto to forget about him. Describing the precise location of his tent in the two highest camps of the Abruzzi, he instructed Alberto to take his place on summit day and supervise placing ropes through the Bottleneck.

Alberto stuffed Shaheen's vital gear into his pack and left to face the Black Pyramid.

"We shook hands, said good luck," Alberto recalled. "He said goodbye to his friends, and that was it."

As Camp 2 began to empty, Shaheen heard Iso Planić of the Serbian team radio Base Camp. "Shaheen Baig needs an evac on the Abruzzi," Iso said. Shaheen interrupted on the same frequency. "I am fine," he insisted. Iso left camp, and soon Shaheen was alone.

Furious with himself, Shaheen decided to rest for an hour and catch up to the others once his health improved. As the hours passed, his stomach burned and kept trying to empty itself. He spat pink froth into his glove. His wheezing became shallower, and he coughed so hard he expected to crack a rib. Shaheen could ignore the nausea, but not the telltale gurgle in his lungs. Pulmonary edema had set in, and he'd drown in his own fluids if he didn't drop altitude fast.

He sat there thinking about it for the rest of the day. As the sun sank behind Broad Peak, Shaheen realized it was too late. Getting down on his own felt impossible. He could barely move. He refused to radio the climbers higher up the mountain, which would jeopardize their summit bids, and he couldn't imagine that anyone left in Base Camp could reach Camp 2 in time to save him.

Sullenly, he picked up the radio and called Nadir Ali Shah, the Base Camp cook for the Serbian team. "Shaheen asked to be left on the mountain," Nadir recalled. "He didn't want anyone to risk dragging down a dead body."

▲ ▲ ▲

Around the same time, Wilco sat inside a tent anchored to a pinnacle at 23,600 feet. Unaware that Shaheen had fallen ill, the leader of the Dutch team was on a different part of the mountain, the Cesen route.

Wilco was having a bad day. Most of his frustrations came from things he couldn't control. For example, he had just missed a $500 shipment of Mars candy bars, ferried by nationalistic Dutch trekkers. The sixty pounds of chocolate, intended to power him to the summit, sat melting in Base Camp. His main gripe, however, was Serbian climber Hoselito Bite. Wilco couldn't shake him. "I was telling him straight," recalled Wilco. "I said, 'Hoselito, we want to be friends with you, but you can't climb with us. You're too slow. . . . You are not going with us to the summit because you are not capable of it.'"

Wilco disliked being K2's bouncer, but someone had to do it. The altitude had debilitated Hoselito, who had spilled a can of sardines in one of the tents, saturating the fabric with fish oil. The close quarters of the tent now carried the stench of low tide. What would happen if Hoselito failed to buckle his harness or crampon correctly? Wilco wanted him to turn back before he hurt himself and needed an evac, endangering his rescuers and costing them the summit.

But Hoselito pushed himself to keep going. He told Wilco he was feeling fine and would soon be climbing faster. He had oxygen cylinders in his pack, and he'd start using gas at Camp 4. "I have my daughter to return to," Hoselito told him. "I'm not going to get killed."

▲ ▲ ▲

When the radio crackled at Base Camp, Nadir Ali was in the Serbian mess tent, scrubbing dishes in a tub of glacial melt. The static made it hard to hear the details, but Nadir understood enough.

"It had something to do with Shaheen's lungs, and he was in Camp 2," along the Abruzzi route, Nadir recalled. "He didn't want a rescue, but he needed one, and I knew he was too proud to ask. I figured he'd be conscious if I got there fast enough."

Nadir, a thirty-three-year-old with a pompadour of black hair, usually fried cheeseburgers at the Chancery Guest House in Islamabad, chatting with tourists. He had little formal training as a mountaineer but aspired to be a climbing guide, and Shaheen had helped him break into the business, finding him work as a cook and, occasionally, as a high-altitude porter on mountains lower than K2. A devout Muslim, Nadir believed that he had an obligation to help those in need and that Allah had meant him to hear the radio call. "We couldn't let Shaheen stay at that altitude with a lung problem," he said. "You can die overnight."

Others in Base Camp apparently didn't see it that way. Nadir sought help, but no one would take the risk. Mountaineers higher up the mountain said they never heard a call come through, and those remaining in Base Camp told Nadir he was overreacting. With the wind picking up, a late-night rescue two camps up the mountain began looking more and more irrational.

Still resolute, Nadir didn't have much climbing gear of his own, so he scrounged for a parka, an axe, and whatever else other climbers would donate. It took two hours to gather the equipment. Most climbers refused to part with their gear and discouraged Nadir from going up. There was nothing he could do, they said, especially with what looked like an incoming storm. Nadir managed to get through on the radio to Eric, who was near Camp 3. Eric offered his extra gear and told Nadir which drugs and shots to grab from his medical kit.

Around midnight, wearing mismatched socks, Nadir left Base Camp alone to rescue Shaheen. Before starting, he radioed up to inform Shaheen he was coming. The only response was static.

"I figured he had passed out," Nadir recalled. He knew this meant he had to climb fast with the drugs. A few minutes could make the difference between life and death.

With no stops for meals, Nadir chewed tea leaves and chocolate, pulling himself up the fixed lines. He passed three Western climbers who politely declined to assist. Nadir justified their refusal by assuming that these climbers probably lacked the energy to help and were descending with ailments of their own.

Would they have helped if Shaheen were, say, Australian, not Pakistani? "I don't want to answer that out loud," Nadir said later. "They don't work for us. We work for them, and I want to keep working for them. They pay good salaries. Most of them are good people, and we need them to keep coming back to Pakistan, so please don't make them look bad in your book." It's unfair to judge people when they're oxygen-deprived and exhausted, he said.

When Nadir got to Camp 1, he tried to contact Shaheen again on the radio. No answer. Was he alive? Nadir knew that if he sat down to rest and think about it, he might quit. He kept heading up, praying to Allah for strength as he slid his jumar up the ropes, ignoring the quiver and burn in his calves and the pain in his throat from the dry air. Around noon, after twelve hours of frantic climbing, Nadir arrived at Camp 2.

It was deserted. Sun soaked the scrim like bleach, blazing the landscape ultrawhite and blistering his face. He called out for Shaheen. Nothing.

Where was he? Nadir shook one of the tents, unzipped a flap, and leaned inside. All he saw were empty sleeping bags. He eyed one of them and considered collapsing into the soft down. Even if he found Shaheen now, how would they descend? Nadir couldn't carry him—Shaheen was almost a foot taller and forty pounds heavier—and, in his condition, the sick man wouldn't be able to do more than slither.

Nadir sat down to collect himself. About to shut his eyes, he spotted a lump between the tents. It was Shaheen, curled up in a fetal position on the snow and surrounded by "something that looked like Pepsi."

▲ ▲ ▲

At Camp 2 along the Cesen route, Wilco and Hoselito waited out a blustery day in their tents. Hugues, with his high-altitude porters, Karim and Jehan, kept moving up. Hugues's weather god in Chamonix had predicted windless days ahead, and the Frenchman wanted to position himself for the summit.

Yan's forecast was right—at first. The weather stayed calm on July 29, and the men arrived at Camp 3 that evening. At sunrise, they continued up, enjoying the fine weather, but by late afternoon, winds began shrieking down K2's Shoulder. Karim and Jehan worked fast, stomping out a platform and staking the tent. Cramming inside with Hugues and Nick Rice, they heard the rising growl of the wind. As gusts buffeted the tent, they supported the poles by pressing their shoulders against the fabric dome.

The Shimshalis, who had less faith in Yan's statistical model, tried to rest as Hugues grabbed a sat phone and punched in the thirteen numerals for Yan's home in Chamonix. Shouting above the wind, he kept asking the voice at the other end of the line to repeat the message.

"The winds don't exist," Yan said.

"What?"

"I said, 'They don't exist.'"

"What do you mean they don't exist?"

Yan explained that he was at his desk, studying two monitors that undulated with waves and darts. They showed a gentle breeze blowing across K2's Shoulder. That meant the seventy-mile-an-hour wind blasts pummeling Hugues, Karim, and Jehan were katabatic, ghost winds that the supercomputers of Météo-France could not see. Katabatic windstorms form when air at higher altitude cools, becoming more dense, Yan explained. Pulled by gravity and a lower pressure gradient, the air pours down the mountain like water.

These ghost winds were dangerous, but they materialize and vanish so suddenly that they only terrorize climbers for brief periods. Yan told Hugues that if the three of them would sit tight, the gusts should stop within an hour or two.

Straining to catch the words, Hugues listened without saying much. "OK," he screamed into the receiver. "You have my trust."

▲ ▲ ▲

Lower down on the Cesen route, Wilco was having another bad day. He'd been enjoying the view in Camp 3 until he saw Hoselito trudge in, his six-foot, three-inch frame bent over in exhaustion. Hoselito pitched a flimsy tent beside Wilco's. "It looked like a doghouse," Wilco decided, "and I doubt he even anchored it."

But Wilco decided against lecturing Hoselito about the tent. He couldn't force Hoselito to stop climbing. If Hoselito wanted to risk being blown away inside a poorly secured tent, that was his problem. Wilco had already been explicit enough—he would not babysit a straggler. Those who were weak needed to climb down; those who were strong needed to conserve energy. Wilco ducked into his sturdy North Face VE 25 tent, anchored with aluminum snow pickets, and went to sleep.

He woke a few hours later to the sound of howling. The ghost winds from the Shoulder had sheared down the Cesen route to Camp 3, scouring snow and plastering the sides of Wilco's tent. The gusts were threatening to turn his tent into a kite.

Huddled in his tent, Wilco pulled out his satellite phone and called the *Archimedes*, a canal barge docked in Utrecht. On the other end of the line, he heard the voice of Maarten van Eck, the liaison for Ab Maas, a forecaster at the Royal Netherlands Meteorological Institute. Wilco demanded a scientific explanation for the weather and listened as van Eck assured him that the satellite and infrared photos all showed that the jet stream had pulled off K2. The weather would soon improve, Maarten said.

"Fuck you and your predictions!" Wilco shouted into the receiver.

Maarten told Wilco to put on his downsuit and be prepared to descend. "If your tent rips, that's your only option," he said, "but I promise you, tomorrow morning will be gorgeous."

▲ ▲ ▲

"It's something inside me," Shaheen said between gasps and coughs that sounded like gravel in a garbage disposal.

Nadir knelt down. He pulled Shaheen out of the pool of dark vomit, propped him against his pack, and fished for a brown glass vial. He cracked open the sterile seal and poured the liquid into a syringe. Stabbing the tip into Shaheen's deltoid, he pushed the plunger until it hit the number 3 on the barrel, just as Eric had explained. Nadir hoped this injectable steroid, Dexamethasone, would help Shaheen.

He pushed three Tic Tac–shaped antibiotics into Shaheen's mouth, tipped back his jaw, and dribbled some tea onto his tongue, forcing him to swallow.

All this movement was too much. Shaheen vomited and passed out.

"You must get up," Nadir said. He shook Shaheen's shoulders, slapped his cheeks. No response.

At least Shaheen was still breathing. Nadir searched the camp for stragglers but found no one. Radioing down to Base Camp, Nadir reported Shaheen's status to the Pakistani liaison officer, Captain Sabir Ali. "I need help," Nadir said. Shaheen couldn't walk and was too big to carry.

Nadir was on his own. Most climbers were higher up the mountain, and nobody lower down seemed eager to help. Fortunately, the ghost winds over the Cesen ridge stayed off the Abruzzi. Nadir wasn't about to blow away, and the steroid seemed to be working. Shaheen recognized Nadir, said he was feeling better, and tried to stand.

Although Shaheen could walk, he needed help clipping onto the fixed line and barely had the dexterity to use the simple Figure 8 rappel device. After rappelling a steep section and reaching more level ground, Shaheen collapsed. "I tried to motivate him," Nadir recalled. "I told him his clients wouldn't be mad if he made it back alive."

That failed to get Shaheen moving. Praying to Allah, Nadir attached a rope to Shaheen and dragged his body across the snow as though the man were a sled. It was slow going, and, after perhaps an hour, Shaheen awoke. He tried to stand but toppled over, so he inched down the slope on his rear.

When they reached an icy gutter that didn't have a fixed line, Nadir attached a rope to Shaheen, paying it out as Shaheen slid. As the slope steepened more and that tactic became too dangerous, Nadir pounded a snow picket into the slope and lowered Shaheen down.

Shaheen passed out so many times he barely remembered the descent, and Nadir described it as a blur. Nadir's focus was so intense and the exhaustion so pronounced that hours went by like minutes. He refused to let himself rest because he knew he'd never get going again. When he considered how much his legs burned and how far they had to go, he prayed and once again was able to focus.

At one point, Shaheen begged him to quit. The pain was too much, and he was tired of being swung around like a gunnysack. He asked Nadir to leave him. Then, passing out, Shaheen went limp.

Nadir prayed to Allah, injected the last of the steroid into the meat of Shaheen's shoulder, and kept pulling. Shaheen's body scraped against rocks, and he eventually woke again and stood, teetering.

The two were on their own until they reached Advanced Base Camp at the foot of the mountain. By then, Nadir had been awake for more than thirty hours. He collapsed inside an empty tent beside his friend, choked down an energy bar, and passed out. He was too exhausted to check whether or not Shaheen was even alive.

▲ ▲ ▲

Leaving a tent during a gale is generally a bad idea. Mountaineers don't even step outside to relieve themselves—it's too easy for the tent or the climber to get blown away. But Hoselito had no choice. Around 1 a.m. in Camp 2 on the Cesen route, a ferocious blast peeled his "doghouse" from the ice. Hoselito spread his arms and legs against the tent's sides to keep the walls from collapsing. This worked, but not for long. Another gust snapped the poles, and the fabric ripped. All his gear—burner, down jacket, food, fuel, and helmet—flew away. Hoselito squirmed out from the ruins, hunching against the wind. Despite the snow and darkness, he managed to get his bearings and weave a few yards to the nearest tent, a three-person heavy-duty dome staked onto relatively level ground. The wind blasted it and the poles shuddered, but this tent stayed secured.

Hoselito shook the dome, hugging it for balance. He felt for the entrance, unzipped the flap, and craned his neck in. Frigid air and snow spat in behind him. Inside, he saw two men, Wilco and his climbing partner Cas van de Gevel. They were doing their best to sleep. "I knew Wilco disliked me, but even a half-human would let me inside," recalled Hoselito. "I was going to die."

The circumstances did not allow for much conversation. If they had, Hoselito might have heard Wilco explain himself. Wilco might have noted how his tent clung to a platform that barely supported two bodies, that he'd been straightforward about what help he could offer, and that he had wanted Hoselito to turn around for his own safety. Instead, as flurries swept through the open flap, Wilco got right to the point: Get out.

"Of course, I would have helped him if he had no alternative, but for me it was too easy to say, 'Of course, my dear Hoselito, you can sleep with us.' . . . I had warned him before."

Hoselito crawled backward, zipping the flap behind him. He felt his way above Wilco's tent to another staked above it. When Hoselito unzipped the flap and stuck his head in, he saw three men crammed inside: Irishman Ger McDonnell, Sherpa Pemba Gyalje, and Dutch-man Jelle Staleman. The men pulled Hoselito's shivering body inside, knowing they'd all have to sleep sitting up.

"He was blue, so we made him tea, and he relaxed," Pemba recalled. Nobody slept much that night.

Through the Bottleneck

Shoulder to Summit
26,000 feet to 28,251 feet
Evening of July 31 to August 1

Planets blinked on one by one. The night before the summit bid was moonless and cloudless, with constellations sprinkled across the sky like loose gems over pitch. Most of the mountaineers were too miserable to notice.

More than thirty men and women had pitched their tents on K2's Shoulder, the frost-tipped saddle of ice where the Abruzzi and Cesen routes converge. Camp 4, the final camp, offered space to spread gear, scoop fresh snow, and shovel platforms, but the altitude was agony. Burning more oxygen than their lungs could draw in, the climbers felt hung over and strung out. Nobody spoke or moved more than necessary.

Crowd control had failed. Delayed by windstorms, most mountaineers now planned to summit in one wave instead of two. If they deferred, the weather window might close, ruining the chance of a lifetime. Twenty-nine people were now aiming for an August 1 summit. Only a handful of climbers had decided to hold back. Among those who remained in the thicker air of Camp 3 were Pasang Lama's cousins, Big Pasang Bhote and Tsering Bhote, and several Koreans.

With crowding came disorganization. Crucial gear had been left behind, including the Italian team's 100-meter rope. When questioned at Camp 4, the Italians' high-altitude porters said they'd misunderstood instructions to carry the coil up. Others besides the Italian team had also failed to bring the supplies they'd promised to carry, but exactly who was responsible and what they'd left behind was unclear. Park Kyeong-hyo had agreed to lead an inventory once everyone arrived at the Shoulder, but he fell asleep instead.

"Rope was missing, ice screws were missing, and I was thinking, 'What the fuck? We're at 8,000 meters' [about 27,000 feet] but we don't even have the essentials," recalled Swedish climber Fredrik Sträng, who had come to make a documentary. With the summit bid due to start at midnight, nothing could be done anyway, so Fredrik tinkered with his video camera. "It was a beautiful night. We were a big team, and I thought, 'We can probably do this. We can probably do anything.'"

Pasang spent the evening preparing oxygen canisters, which were carrot-colored and had the Russian word *poisk* (search) scribbled across the side. Each three-liter aluminum cylinder contained 720 liters of oxygen, weighed five pounds, and cost $385. When turned on, the odorless gas hisses out of the can, past a regulator, and into a face mask originally designed for fighter pilots. Pasang set the flow rate to one liter a minute. He rubbed moisturizer on his clients' cheeks and fitted the masks onto their faces. That night, as his clients sucked bottled oxygen, every inhale and exhale sounded mechanical, a Darth Vader-ish *pwuh-kwah*. Pasang told his clients to turn up the flow from one to two liters per minute when they started climbing in the morning, and each planned to consume three bottles during the twenty-hour trip to and from the summit.

Chhiring wasn't using bottled oxygen, which made his summit gear simpler. In his tent, he slurped two liters of tea and sprinkled sacred salt in his soup. The excitement quivered to his fingertips. With a grin, he asked Eric whether he was ready for the Bottleneck. Sure, Eric replied.

As Eric nodded off to sleep, Chhiring remained awake, anxious, as though he'd never climbed a mountain before. He leaned to his side and cupped his *mala* prayer beads. Blowing on them, rolling them in his palms, he tried to interpret the mood of the goddess. If all went well, he would reach the Bottleneck before sunrise, tag the summit before 2 p.m.—Shaheen's suggested turnaround time—and return to his tent in Camp 4 before dark. Chhiring recited a mantra under his breath. The Death Zone distorted his sense of time, and it seemed as though only minutes had passed when his Suunto wrist altimeter glowed a quarter past midnight. Time to move.

With a rustle, he slid out from the warmth of his sleeping bag and, sloughing off the ice crystals, zipped up his downsuit. Stomping his feet into the heels of his boots, he scooted toward the tent flap, stuck out his legs, and strapped on his crampons. Hoisting his pack, he left to find the rest of the lead team.

They were waiting: Pasang and Jumik of the Korean team; Pemba Gyalje of the Dutch; Muhammad Hussein and Muhammad Khan of the Serbian team; and someone else, a Basque climber Chhiring didn't recognize. Who was this stranger, and where was Shaheen, who had promised to supervise rope placement through the Bottleneck?

The stranger introduced himself as Alberto and explained that he had climbed from Camp 3 in the night. "Shaheen is sick," he said. "He won't be coming."

Chhiring was indignant. "Right when we needed him, Shaheen was gone," he recalled. "We did not like [Shaheen]. All the sherpas were saying things about him that we probably should not have said." Their voices brittle in the dry air, they wondered whether Shaheen had feigned illness to avoid the toughest climbing. They questioned whether the truant had actually summited K2 before.

Even though the Pakistanis didn't speak Nepali, they understood enough from the conversation's tone and a few familiar words: The Nepalis were ridiculing them. "It was unjust," recalled Muhammad Hussein. "K2 is our mountain, and Shaheen is our brother, the greatest climber in the region. He taught us to show respect to Buddhists and other foreigners, but the sherpas didn't respect me." Nobody bothered to ask him, but Muhammad had summited K2 in 2004 and was familiar with the route and the rope-setting in the Bottleneck. "They assumed I didn't know where I was going," he said, "and dismissed what I had to say."

Or they would have, if they understood him at all. With Shaheen gone, nobody could translate from Urdu to English. Discussion was disjointed, split between Nepali and Pakistani factions, and when Alberto tried to take charge, he was not recognized as their leader.

Resentment, language barriers, and oxygen deprivation all contributed to the flawed decision-making that followed. The lead team members carried willow wands, but nobody used them to mark the trail. Worse, the lead team squandered rope. Jumik directed the Pakistanis to set lines along moderate terrain, where climbers could use their ice axes to arrest a fall. Unaware of the rope shortage, the Bhotes were accustomed to the procedure on Everest, where, on the north side, new rope is laterally fixed from the bottom of the North Col to the summit, with only a single break at Camp 1. Jumik probably didn't realize that trying to set rope all the way up to K2's summit was a mistake.

Muhammad Hussein did. "Save the rope for the bad places," he tried to tell Jumik. But nobody could translate his warning, and "nobody cared until our situation was obvious," Muhammad recalled. The lead team didn't have much line to begin with, and soon it was gone.

"All of a sudden we were asking each other, 'Do you have any more rope?'" recalled Pasang. "We did not understand. How could we run out? Where had it all gone?" They checked their packs, argued, and backtracked, plucking out line already set and anchoring it higher up. They'd hoped to reach the Bottleneck before sunrise. When the barbed horizon flushed red, the lead team was still climbing along the Shoulder.

Back at high camp, the mountaineers tracked the progress of the lead team with binoculars and radio calls. The climbers had planned to leave camp before dawn, but, seeing that the lead team was off to a bad start, several delayed their departure. By sunrise, Nick Rice still hadn't left his tent. He had spilled a pot of snowmelt on his gear and was drying a soggy sock over a burner. By the time he had finished, Nick decided that August 1 wasn't going to be the day he would reach the summit of K2. He'd lost too much time. The mountain would still be there next season. "I wanted to make sure I would be, too," he recalled. A simple mistake—sloshing a pot of water—probably saved his life.

▲ ▲ ▲

Above the Bottleneck of K2, a restless glacier appears to be lunging off a cliff. For centuries it has inched forward, midleap, creating formations known as *seracs*, massive hunks of ice that frequently calve. The mountaineers had been training their binoculars on these seracs for weeks, evaluating the gutter below.

American mountaineer Ed Viesturs calls this section The Motivator, because the seracs overhanging the gutter inspire climbers to get the hell out of there. Nazir Sabir, who pioneered K2's West-Southwest Ridge, calls the channel below the seracs Death Throat, because it resembles a giant's gullet. Most people call this narrow passage the Bottleneck. The Bottleneck is not the end of danger. Above it, the route turns left onto the Traverse, a steep, exposed slog up K2's southeast face. But the Bottleneck's nearly vertical, 30-story rise is the

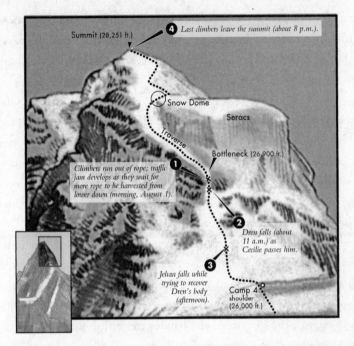

Summit (28,251 ft.)

4 *Last climbers leave the summit (about 8 p.m.).*

Snow Dome

Seracs

Traverse

Bottleneck (26,900 ft.)

1 *Climbers run out of rope; traffic jam develops as they wait for more rope to be harvested from lower down (morning, August 1).*

2 *Dren falls (about 11 a.m.) as Cecilie passes him.*

3 *Jehan falls while trying to recover Dren's body (afternoon).*

Camp 4 shoulder (26,000 ft.)

Camp 4 to Summit: A lead team of Balti, Bhote, Sherpa, and Shimshali climbers broke trail and set ropes toward the summit. Language gaps and miscommunication led to problems with the ropes, which caused a deadly delay in the Bottleneck.

most stomach-churning section of the climb. Falling ice and traffic are the killers. The Bottleneck only lets climbers squeeze through one at a time, in a queue that moves only as fast as the slowest legs will allow.

By the time the lead team had reached the Bottleneck, an impatient, single-file line had formed behind them. "I was waiting and waiting, and everybody was waiting," Wilco said. "And the Bottleneck is not the place where you want to wait."

▲ ▲ ▲

Several stories above Wilco, Alberto stood near the front of the line; around 9 a.m., he pulled ahead of the pack. Hard, blue ice, its air bubbles expelled by compression, rejected his pick, and loose snow balled beneath his crampons, but Alberto advanced up the Bottleneck, twisting in ice screws and tying in rope until he had climbed so high he vanished from view.

Skeptical about clipping onto the lines Alberto had set, the Sherpas on the lead team hung back. They were accustomed to the thicker lines for the Everest crowd. Alberto's Endura five-millimeter seemed recklessly thin, unable to support the weight of several bodies and unsuitable for jumars rated for eight-millimeter rope. Chhiring decided to set a secondary rope. He placed it parallel to the Endura but ran out after about 50 yards.

So Chhiring backtracked, weaving through the line of climbers and once again plucking out rope from lower slopes. He waved to some stragglers on the Korean team. They were squatting in the snow, unclipped, observing his gyrations. Chhiring then made his way up, past the spectators, and handed the coil to Jumik. This line went another 75 feet, more than halfway, but another 100 feet would be needed to reach safer ground.

Chhiring turned back to collect more rope, but when he looked down, he saw that fifteen climbers had clipped onto the lines directly below him. They were advancing through the steepest area of the Bottleneck, forming a head-to-toe snarl. Chhiring wasn't sure why they were advancing. Without fixed lines, they wouldn't be able to get far.

Chhiring knew they shouldn't all be weighing on the same anchor. One falling block could bowl everyone over. He stepped to the side, twisted in an ice screw, and clipped himself onto it, hanging to the right of the oncoming train. Others saw Chhiring's logic. Pasang, Wilco, and three others followed, unclipping from the main line and free-climbing toward a rock ramp.

The climbers waited, hanging in place. More rope was needed, but nobody seemed to know who might pass it forward, and the lead climbers couldn't navigate the gridlock below. As the sun beat down, the men peeled their jackets to their waists. They praised the weather gods for bringing such a glorious day and whined about the holdup. The men sucked in the moistureless air and changed their oxygen cylinders. Those climbing without oxygen tried to ignore the drumming inside their skulls. Every once in a while, an ice chunk fell from the seracs and bounced down the slope.

Eric had turned around hours earlier, giving up on the mountain and his dream of reaching the summit. Without his friend, Chhiring became restless. "Instead of sweating, I started to shiver," he recalled. It felt as though the goddess were breathing down his neck. He had to get moving, but where? About to free-climb, he noticed that Wilco was already giving it a try.

The Dutchman soon slipped, and he whisked toward Chhiring. "I didn't have time to blink," Chhiring recalled. His left hand shot out to grab Wilco's harness. His right hand seized the collar of Wilco's downsuit. Then, out of hands, Chhiring body-slammed him, pressing Wilco into the ice.

Wilco slid only six feet. His right crampon nicked Chhiring's side. The left ripped into Iso Planić, a Serb below them, and released a flurry of feathers from Iso's down jacket.

Swiveling, Wilco heaved his axe into the ice. The pick sank in and held. Wilco clenched the axe and leaned hard, pulling himself to a stop. Winded, the men could only nod. The slide had been harmless.

The next one wouldn't be. Below them, the newlyweds, Cecilie and Rolf, were maneuvering around the clog of climbers, carrying about 50 yards of rope harvested from the lower slopes. Cecilie, pushing herself up the Bottleneck, passed Chhiring, Wilco, and Iso to her right. Continuing, she reached Dren Mandić, who unclipped. "He was being a gentleman," said Hoselito, Dren's friend, who thought he'd unclipped to let Cecilie pass. If so, it was a fatal courtesy.

Cecilie asked Dren to stow the loose rope in the top of her pack.

She ducked down and around; he pivoted up and over. This choreography jerked the fixed line, according to Chhiring and Muhammad Hussein, who were a few yards away. The rope slapped into Dren, pushing him off-balance. He lost his footing, then his grip. Both he and Cecilie plunged.

Cecilie shrieked. Her jumar caught, and she fell only a few feet. Dren, with no rope to stop him, tried to bear-hug her. Unable to hold onto her, he dropped, feet first on his stomach, his face raking the Bottleneck. Frantic, he flailed at the snow with his arms, trying to self-arrest.

For two stories, Dren slid. Then his crampons snagged a rock and spun him around like the second hand of a clock. When he had turned a full 180 degrees on his stomach, his leg released and he took a nose-dive down the Bottleneck. His helmeted head crunched into a rock ramp, launching him into the air. Somersaulting, he plunged another 10 stories and smacked into a spongy mound of snow, off-route.

Above him, the mountaineers froze. It happened so fast that some barely saw it. Stunned, Chhiring watched Dren's legs squirm, sticking out of the snow.

Chhiring had never seen anyone die on a mountain before. Dren had to live, Chhiring rationalized. A week earlier, he'd watched this man kneel on the moraine to admire tiny flowers sprouting from a clump of moss. The goddess would never exact revenge from a sentient being who appreciated even the smallest life, a man with Snoopy strapped to his pack.

Chhiring radioed Eric in Camp 4, telling him an injured man needed a doctor. After the call, he shut his eyes and looked away from the mound where Dren lay. Chhiring visualized Dawa and his daughters and thought of Dren's family somewhere, not yet knowing. It was past 11 a.m., and Chhiring knew he'd have to climb well past the planned turnaround time. Contemplating his options, he gazed at the seracs above, "softening like yak butter in the sun."

▲ ▲ ▲

Acoustics distorted Cecilie's scream into a maniacal wail that echoed off the Shoulder. The noise startled Fredrik in Camp 4. Clutching his thirteen-pound Sony video camera, the Swedish filmmaker opened his tent flap and peered through the zoom lens, using it as a telescope. Focusing on the Bottleneck, he could see the line of climbers proceeding, one by one, like an ant army. Fixing the coil of line that Cecilie had delivered, they were "continuing on as if nothing had happened," he recalled. Fredrik scanned for something crumpled in the bright snow and shouted to Eric, who was on the radio with Chhiring.

"I grabbed an oxygen set, water, and a survival bag," along with the video camera to shoot footage, Fredrik recalled. Eric took a medical kit. Only midway up the slope did they confirm the fallen man's identity over the radio. "Dren was my friend in Base Camp," Fredrik recalled. "We were always laughing, cracking jokes." Fredrik climbed faster, pulling ahead. "I wanted to see my friend alive."

After climbing for about ninety minutes, Fredrik saw two Serbs, Iso Planić and Pedja Zagorac, dragging a body in a red bivy sack. "You don't want to know what his face looked like," Fredrik recalled.

Iso and Pedja explained what had happened. It had taken them fifteen minutes to climb down to Dren. By the time they'd reached him, he was no longer breathing. Iso had pumped Dren's chest and forced air into his mouth, but CPR couldn't revive him. Dren's pulse was now long gone. The least they could do was take his body back to his mother in Serbia.

Fredrik, pressing a finger to Dren's carotid artery, confirmed that his friend was dead. "I was mad as hell. I was going to bring him back alive. I was committed to that. It was a perfect day, and I was staring up at that blue sky thinking this should not be happening on a day like this."

Iso and Pedja wrapped the Serbian flag, intended for the summit photo, around Dren's battered head. "I was aware that it would be way better if someone cold-blooded took over the recovery," Iso recalled. "We were in shock. Fredrik had experience in rescues. He was fresh and rested." The Serbians wanted his help.

Fredrik wavered. "I do not support the idea of trying to recover a body from the Death Zone," he said. Transporting the dead puts the living at risk. Still, Dren deserved a dignified burial, and it was hard to say no to that. "I was asked to help to bring down my friend to Camp 4, and I agreed."

He stowed his camera in his pack, leaving the audio on, and bound Dren's ankles. He coiled more line around Dren's torso like a corset. From this makeshift harness, he tied two towlines, which radiated from Dren's body in a *V*. Pulling these leashes, the men sledded Dren's body along the ice toward the Shoulder.

As they inched the bundle forward, they spotted Jehan Baig rappelling toward them. The Pakistani "seemed disoriented," recalled Fredrik. He moved like a man in a squall, stumbling but somehow staying on his feet.

Jehan shook his head when he caught up with the others and extended a hand, grabbing the towline. He joined Fredrik to pull the front line; Iso and Pedja pulled the back.

Soon they reached an icy slope that might have been a blue-square ski run, except that it flattened before a sheer cliff. Fixed lines had been strung through this stretch in the early morning. Now, the ropes were gone, removed for use in the Bottleneck.

Trying to lower Dren's body and simultaneously keep it on the route, the men payed out rope a few feet at a time. The corpse had made it roughly halfway down the slope when several things happened at once.

Jehan lost his footing and crashed into Fredrik's right side, knocking him off-balance. Without saying anything, Jehan slid down the slope on his rear and hooked an arm around Dren's body, holding fast.

Meanwhile, Fredrik tipped forward, and his shin slapped into the rope as though it were a tripwire. He flipped, face first. Fredrik righted himself and dug in his crampons to gain purchase on the ice. It worked—Fredrik didn't slide—but the twist of his body wound the rope around his right calf, cinching it like a butcher's wire.

Fredrik clawed the slope. He couldn't hold the position. The rope sawed into his leg as the combined weight of Dren and Jehan pulled down on him.

"Release the rope!" Fredrik yelled.

Jehan said nothing.

"Release the rope!"

Jehan kept silent.

"We're screaming at the Pakistani in three different languages— Swedish, English, Serbian—and I'm panicking," recalled Fredrik. "If [Jehan] had let go, all he would have to do was use his ice axe to self-arrest, but he wouldn't let go."

After roughly one minute, Jehan finally did as he was told. He released his grip around Dren's body and started to slide, as still as a corpse.

Limp and silent, Jehan gained speed until his crampons caught, and, in a sickening reprise of Dren's choreography, he spun around headfirst. He began to slow down as the slope flattened, and it looked as though he might stop on his own before the edge.

Eric and Muhammad Hussein, who had arrived to help, shouted at Jehan, ordering him to wake up and save himself. All he had to do was fan out his body. But still he crept forward. "Maybe it was a heart attack," recalled Muhammad. "Jehan had placed himself in God's hands."

The rink at the bottom was slick. Jehan had just enough momentum when he reached it to go sliding across the ice, barely moving forward. His head went over the ledge first. As his legs followed, he seemed to wake from his trance. He kicked and yelped, disappearing over the precipice.

The men kept shouting after he was gone, and the screams captured on Fredrik's tape suggest that they had trouble believing what had just happened. "What the hell is this?" Fredrik cried. "I came up here to help you guys." Unable to see where Jehan had landed, they knew the drop was about 1,000 feet. Trying to recover one corpse had already produced a second. Stupefied, Iso and Pedja swaddled Dren in extra clothes. Fredrik pounded a stake into the slope and tied the towlines to it. Dren's body was left to hang there until the mountain claimed it.

Returning to the Shoulder in the direction of camp, the men broke down, sobbing in the snow. "The summit wasn't worth it anymore," Iso said. "Everything seemed so senseless."

▲ ▲ ▲

At 2:21 p.m., the moon, cruising through space, barged between the earth and the sun. Its dusty body whittled daylight into a crescent. Jehan's mother, Nazib, was in Shimshal. Around the time of her son's death, a symbol of her faith was branded on the sun. The horizon glowed tangerine. Far to the north, a perfect corona gave the illusion of a hole in the sky.

Above K2, the eclipse wasn't total. A small slice of sun darkened for 121 minutes. Some mountaineers, still in the Bottleneck, wore yellow-tinted goggles and missed the change in light. "A solar eclipse is an omen," said Chhiring, "but I didn't see this one." Most were unaware that K2 had claimed a second victim. They only knew that their pace was too slow. To reach the summit, they would need to descend in darkness. Nonetheless, the nineteen climbers in the Bottleneck continued upward.

Each came up with tactical reasons for disregarding the 2 p.m. turnaround time. Marco, the Italian, mentally compiled a list of mountaineers who had gotten away with a late summit, including K2's original Italian conquerors, Achille Compagnoni and Lino Lacedelli. He considered how his mentor, Agostino da Polenza, had survived an overnight bivouac in the Death Zone. Sure, some of these legendary mountaineers had lost digits, but all had survived, and Marco was convinced that he, too, could make it down in one piece.

Wilco used applied physics to justify his decision. Descending at night, he concluded, would actually be safer—the sun wouldn't be heating the seracs and causing them to calve. "It seemed almost illogical that ice chunks would cleave off [at night] when the temperature was decreasing." He'd spent years preparing for K2, had done everything he could to reduce the risk, and wasn't going to turn around just because the weak were holding him back. "I knew I'd regret it if I came home without a successful climb."

Chhiring felt comforted by the crowd. If scores of less able climbers were heading to the summit, why shouldn't he? The weather was stable. The fixed lines would guide him down in the dark. "I'll never get another shot at K2," he told himself. But Dren's death had persuaded him that the mountain goddess was no ally. He tried to ignore the queasiness that radiated down his throat and pooled in his stomach.

Thinking about the goddess reminded him of the rice and barley in his pocket. Still suspended from an ice screw beside the Bottleneck, he removed the Ziploc bag and flung the contents into the air. They shimmered in space. Suddenly a gust of wind grabbed the grains and spat them back in his face. The offering had been rejected.

▲ ▲ ▲

It took until 2 p.m.—the planned turnaround time—for the members of the Flying Jump to break through the Bottleneck. "We were too slow," Pasang recalled, "and we were burning through our oxygen too fast." But he didn't raise these concerns with his boss. Mr. Kim had already been clear enough: Pasang wasn't hired to retreat; he was hired to lead. In this spirit, Pasang, now in front of the pack, blazed the trail above the Bottleneck. Seventeen people followed him.

Trying to make up for lost time, Pasang pushed himself but struggled with the terrain. He was now on the Traverse, the steep, exposed ridge that cuts under the seracs, tracing the mountain's southeast face. As he climbed, his crampons scraped and clicked against the granite. To maintain purchase, Pasang had to deliberate over each step. "I told myself concentrate, concentrate, concentrate. Only think about the next step."

About two hours later, he reached the Snow Dome, the lump of ice that bridges into snowfield below the summit. Pasang waded in and sank to his hips. Plowing forward, he checked his oxygen pressure gauge and turned the flow to low, below one liter a minute. He climbed faster, probing for weak snow bridges. It was 4 p.m.

His legs pumped forward, making a deep furrow in the snow, but he wasn't on solid ground. One of Pasang's boots punched through the crust, the ice around the ankle broke away, and his leg dropped into a crevasse.

His reactions were quick. As he sank, Pasang fanned out his elbows, spreading his weight. He dropped slowly, and by the time he stopped sinking, he'd been swallowed only to the waist. One boot dangled into space. Keeping his weight on his arms, Pasang wriggled left and right, flipped his knees to his chest, and belly-flopped over the lip of the crevasse. He clawed himself out and away.

Once standing, he patted his body to see if he'd lost any gear. It was all there, but his thoughts were scattered. The dip into the crevasse had left him shaken. If the crust he'd stepped on had been any thinner, he'd have fallen inside a splinter of ice and shattered his limbs. Unable to clamber up or make himself heard, he might have waited in the stillness to die.

Pasang wanted to ensure that this didn't happen to anyone, so he pulled out a wand with a flag, marking the snow bridge he had broken. Before starting the climb again, he scanned his surroundings. Ahead of him, a solitary red suit was tromping down the mountain. Pasang recognized Alberto Zerain, the Basque climber on the lead team who had surged ahead of everyone at the Bottleneck. Alberto flashed a zinc-oxide–streaked grin, and Pasang recognized the look: summit glow. "I was thinking, 'How is this possible?'" Pasang recalled. Alberto had soloed up the rest of K2, topping out at 3 p.m., hours ahead of everyone else. Now he was on his way down. "That guy made K2 look easy."

Alberto dug his heels into the slope, advancing on Pasang, but he was approaching a crevasse. "I tried to get his attention," Pasang recalled. "I waved my hands and yelled, 'Not this side! Crevasses! Not this side!'"

Alberto waved back but also stepped forward. The buttress beneath the snow bridge gave under his weight, and he lurched in. Unfazed, he wriggled out like a worm, and, a moment later, was descending again, digging his heels into the slope just as before.

When the two men met, Pasang shook Alberto's hand, congratulating him for a successful summit. Although there had been radio chatter, Pasang didn't brief him about the deaths in the Bottleneck. It would have ruined the moment. "If I had witnessed those falls, I wouldn't have cared about the mountain anymore," Alberto later said. "I'd have lost the pleasure." Both men were in a hurry, and they went in opposite directions.

Pasang envied Alberto, who was heading down to hot soup and a sleeping bag. Pasang watched him weave through the pack of climbers. As Alberto passed, several Flying Jump members motioned to him as if asking directions on a motorway. They wanted to know how many more hours to the top. Alberto shrugged, barely slowing. "I wasn't going to try to predict how long it would take them to reach the summit," he recalled. Climbers move at different speeds. Alberto assessed their pace and wanted to suggest a U-turn, but he hesitated. Turning around was a personal decision, he decided, between a mountaineer and his maker.

It was 4:45 p.m., and Pasang realized he was wasting time watching Alberto. Annoyed with himself, he turned away and resumed kicking steps. The summit reared ahead of him like a cobra's hood. Sundown would bring a temperature plunge that wouldn't stop until dawn. Pasang was late, at a time when every second counted. The slower he went, the deeper he would climb into the night.

▲ ▲ ▲

After so much fantasy and anticipation, the summit was unglamorous. When he summited at 5:30 p.m., Pasang stood atop the pinnacle of a 100-foot snow ramp, with a ditch to the west where exhausted climbers had defecated. That was it. Unlike the summit of Everest, no prayer flags lay in weathered clumps. The snow beneath his boots looked like any other snow. Nevertheless, Pasang recalled, "it was the most perfect place."

Stepping to the highest point of the ridge, he slung off his pack, crowed and whooped. For an instant, exhaustion evaporated. The panorama dizzied him. The sun was slipping like a brass coin into a pocket behind K2, which cast a triangular shadow into the dark hills of Asia. A dusky band of purple swept around the horizon, and shadows snuffed out the lacy cornices of Chogolisa and Masherbrum. Down the Baltoro Glacier, the scree-paved glaciers at Concordia merged like a freeway interchange. At his back was China; to his face,

Pakistan; and above, infinity. At 28,251 feet, Pasang was the highest human on earth.

He pulled a Sony camcorder from his pack and switched it on. He panned over the violet shoal of clouds and peaks and focused on the climbers marching up the summit ridge: his cousin Jumik; his boss, Mr. Kim; and the rest of the Flying Jump: Ms. Go, Park Kyeong-hyo, Hwang Dong-jin, and Kim Hyo-gyeong. Just ahead of the Flying Jump were two Norwegians, Lars Nessa and Cecilie, who had climbed the last stretch without her husband. In all, eighteen people topped out on August 1. As the sun set, the celebrations continued for as long as ninety minutes.

Wilco, the irritable Dutchman, replaced his pout with a beatific grin. He bear-hugged his teammate Ger, who howled: "We are on the summit of Kay-Toooo!"

Mr. Kim lit a cigarette, took a drag, and passed it to Jumik. Lars put on bunny ears and hopped. Karim prayed, taking in the divine sweep of earth and sky.

"I'll never leave you again," said Hugues, into a satellite phone. His girlfriend was listening. "I'm finished now. This time next year, our family will be at the beach!" He trained a camera on his teeth to satisfy the dentist in Lyon. Both Karim and Hugues were losing it. "They had used up their bottled oxygen and barely responded to our congratulations," Wilco recalled.

Coughing and crying, the climbers yanked pageantry from their packs. Ger, the first Irishman to summit K2, dropped on one knee and hoisted Ireland's tricolor flag in triumph. Chhiring, who summited at 6:37 p.m., unfurled his flag, kneeling with the double pennant before him like an apron.

Last on the summit, Marco waved a ski pole strung with the flags of Italy and Pakistan, plus two pennants representing his sponsors, the Métis temp agency and Credito Valtellinese bank. In the weak light,

Marco removed the shell of his glove and punched twelve numerals into his sat-phone keypad. Battery life was short, so he kept it brief as he told his banker, Miro Fiordi, general director of Credito Valtellinese, the news. The bank's sponsorship investment had paid off.

Like Marco, others felt similar obligations to sponsors who had subsidized their climb. Mr. Kim and Ms. Go modeled Kolon Sport, high fashion for 28,251 feet; Chhiring promoted ColdAvenger face masks; Wilco's mango-colored downsuit displayed the triangular logo of Norit Group, a water filtration company that had provided a healthy six-figure contribution. Nearly every summit photo contained a logo or product placement. These mountaineers documented their triumph not only for posterity but also for publicity. The photos advertised their businesses, their skills, and their sponsors.

Fredrik, part of the team sponsored by ColdAvenger, had once estimated how much summits could be worth. On his website—under the heading "The Value to You!"—he explained to potential sponsors that a $120,000 investment could generate a $4.3 million public-relations value and brand recognition. "We can guarantee a PR ratio of 10 times the invested money," he wrote, basing his estimate on the value of the resulting advertising. Corporate interests had been speculating on a K2 summit. On August 1, they hit pay dirt.

The high-altitude porters and the sherpas also cashed in when their clients topped out. For each mountaineer they ushered up, they earned a bonus of $1,000 or more. This money encouraged them to push clients who were unfit to continue. "When your family needs that money," Pasang acknowledged, "sometimes you don't insist a weak climber turn back."

But summits also have a cost, and by 7:45 p.m. on August 1, the human price was becoming apparent. The Flying Jump started lurching down the mountain like lushes leaving a bar—reveling, swearing, and puking on their boots. The summit party was over. Now they needed to find the way home.

PART III

DESCENT

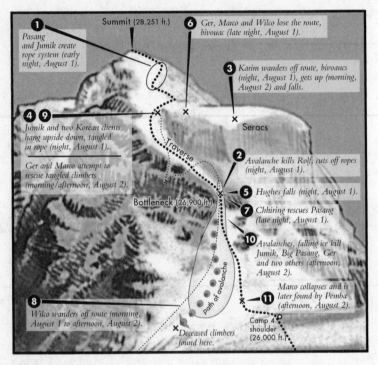

1 Pasang and Jumik create rope system (early night, August 1).

Summit (28,251 ft.)

6 Ger, Marco and Wilco lose the route, bivouac (late night, August 1).

3 Karim wanders off route, bivoucs (night, August 1), gets up (morning, August 2) and falls.

4 9 Jumik and two Korean clients hang upside down, tangled in rope (night, August 1).

Ger and Marco attempt to rescue tangled climbers (morning/afternoon, August 2).

Traverse

Bottleneck (26,900 ft.)

Seracs

2 Avalanche kills Rolf, cuts off ropes (night, August 1).

5 Hughes falls (night, August 1).

7 Chhiring rescues Pasang (late night, August 1).

10 Avalanches, falling ice kill Jumik, Big Pasang, Ger and two others (afternoon, August 2).

Marco collapses and is later found by Pemba (afternoon, August 2).

11

8 Wilco wanders off route (morning, August 1 to afternoon, August 2).

path of avalanche

× Deceased climbers found here.

Camp 4 shoulder (26,000 ft.)

Summit to Camp 4: As the climbers descended in the gathering darkness, an avalanche severed the ropes through the Bottleneck. Some climbers tried to make it down without the fixed lines; others spent the night in the Death Zone.

10

Escape from the Summit

As Pasang left the summit, his head throbbed so relentlessly he could hear his pulse in his ears. Ahead of him, Mr. Kim squatted in the snow, waving his arms like a wizard casting spells. He had run out of oxygen.

Going off the bottle is harder than never having been on it at all. In the best case, you're slammed by extreme exhaustion. The thin air can knock you out, just as it does to a fighter pilot with a failing oxygen mask. Cerebral or pulmonary edema can set in, filling the brain and lungs with fluid. In a worst case, the body revolts with acute vasospasm as arteries constrict, cutting blood supply to the organs. Within three minutes of acute vasospasm, cells wither in the heart, lungs, kidneys, liver, and brain. Within twenty minutes, the organs degrade to medical waste, and the climber does too.

Pasang could see headlamps fanning out below. Sucking a guilty breath from his regulator, he trudged forward and crouched beside Mr. Kim. Pasang's boss was too tired to waste words. Kim tapped the side of his oxygen canister and pointed to the gauge, which registered empty. Pasang understood what was expected. He gestured for Mr. Kim to hold still. Kneeling down, he detached Kim's empty cylinder and swapped it with his own.

His oxygen now gone, Pasang braced for the shock. It hit, but he remained functional, still able to climb and think. It may have helped that he was Bhote—a carrier of genotypic variants for NOS3, a gene that codes for an enzyme that helps modulate blood flow to the lungs—and was perhaps less susceptible to acute vasospasm. His clients, however, were at higher risk.

He and the rest of the Flying Jump had at least three hours to go before reaching the fixed lines on the Traverse, so Pasang decided to take a shortcut. He descended in a straight shot toward the Snow Dome, the massive lump that signaled the start of the Traverse and the fixed lines. The new route allowed the climbers to bypass the summit ridge, but the Snow Dome also had a sheer drop on one side. With no moonlight or stakes for direction, there was no discernible path. Climbers scattered in the darkness.

Pasang spotted a man veering left above the Snow Dome. It was Karim. He never turned around. Now heading away from the Traverse, he would end up on top of the seracs; instead of descending toward the Bottleneck, he'd climb high above it.

If the descent continued like this, Pasang knew delirium would pull his team apart. He herded the Flying Jump together and devised a plan to keep them from stumbling and falling. Pasang tied a Figure-8-on-a-bight, the first climbing knot he'd ever learned, and looped it over his axe. Plunging his axe into the snow, he handed the rest of the rope to Jumik, who uncoiled it while descending ahead of the group. When the line payed out, Jumik tied it to his axe, anchored in the snow. The rope, now strung between two axes, resembled a clothesline.

It led in the direction of the Traverse. The climbers gravitated toward this rope, clipping in and clutching on. Once they'd reached Jumik's end of the clothesline, Pasang pulled out his axe, coiled the slack around his elbow, and raced ahead of the pack. Pasang and Jumik created and re-created this rope system about a dozen times, lower and lower toward the Snow Dome.

It served to guide the group, more or less. The rope caught the climbers when they slipped and kept them from making the disastrous left turn that had led Karim to the crown of the seracs. "It was saving lives," said Chhiring, who used it. But the system was slow. After each step, men slumped over their ice axes or ski poles to rest and shivered for warmth. By sea-level standards, the night was frigid, about minus four degrees Fahrenheit; by K2 standards, it was moderate. On an ordinary evening, the jet stream would have tossed them to China, but August 1 was relatively windless, so the cold merely seared exposed flesh.

As Pasang anchored the last stretch of rope, he thought about his axe. More climbers, all clearly in need, had attached their Figure 8s to the line dangling from it. Pasang couldn't recover his axe without dismantling a rope system that was serving as a lifeline.

Shivering, he waited, punching his fists out for warmth. More figures materialized in the darkness and attached to the line. Occasionally one climber stalled, forcing those behind him to wait. Pasang's headlamp dimmed, and he was no closer to getting his axe back. "I had to make the decision: Take the axe or leave it." He radioed his boss for approval to ditch the axe and descend.

Mr. Kim agreed that the axe wasn't crucial: With fixed lines through the diagonal ridge, the Traverse, and the Bottleneck, Pasang could manage without one. Pasang started down and soon overtook Jumik, leaving him behind with several clients. Descending without an axe would be tough, Pasang thought, but not deadly.

▲ ▲ ▲

Rolf was shivering uncontrollably when his wife reached him, but he smiled when he saw her. Debilitated by altitude, he had waited 300 vertical feet below the summit as Cecilie reached the top at 5:45 p.m. Now, about an hour later, the newlyweds were reunited. Lars, the third member of the Norwegian team, videotaped their exchange, one of their last:

"Are you freezing?" Cecilie asked.

"Not especially," her husband replied.

Lars had removed the bunny ears he'd worn on the summit. He zoomed in on Rolf's face. "Long day?" he asked.

They'd been climbing for seventeen hours, but Rolf's tone sounded as though he were denouncing a desk job: "More than average." With shaking fingers, he manipulated a chalky tablet of Dexamethasone, trying to bring the steroid to his lips. He dropped it, and the tablet hit the ice. "Oh, hell," he said, "it broke."

The newlyweds were the first to start down after Alberto. Behind them, Hugues seemed to be applying risk assessment: Out of oxygen, in pursuit of thicker air, he was moving down rapidly. Next in line was Cas van de Gevel, of the Dutch team, who, climbing even faster, caught up with Hugues along the Traverse. "It never occurred to me to ask Hugues, 'Where's your porter? Where's Karim?'" Cas recalled. "When you see two people climbing together, then one is descending alone. . . . I would have known to ask if we'd been at sea level." But the problem eluded him in the rarefied air.

Hugues stepped aside. "You are quicker," he said. "You go first."

Cas nodded, slid around Hugues, and resumed his descent.

When Cas arrived at the mouth of the Bottleneck, he was 30 feet in front of the Frenchman. That's when he heard a noise—a scratching, like a rat in a wall. Cas looked back. Hugues, who had probably snagged a crampon, shot toward him. "I couldn't see his face at such high speed," Cas recalled. He only recognized the yellow-orange blur of Hugues's downsuit whizzing past within an arm's length. The insurance salesman with dazzling teeth was gone.

▲ ▲ ▲

Just as a sealed glass jar full of water shatters when left in a freezer, refreezing meltwater in the seracs' fissures was expanding, wedging apart the glacier's interior cracks. As the pressure built, the seracs let off slow, elastic, electrified *zoings*. A percussion of pops, snaps, creaks, and booms accompanied the breaking ice. These sounds—high and low, short and long, soft and loud—overlapped in rhythm.

Pasang's cousin Jumik was tied to two exhausted clients, wading through snowdrifts. As he approached the Traverse, the seracs hulked above him. As the *zoings* amplified, Jumik would have moved as fast as possible, frantically dragging his clients along, urging them to rush. But the two Koreans with Jumik could barely walk. Speed wouldn't have mattered much, anyway. To avoid the falling ice, the three men needed a miracle.

The mountain announced its intentions with a drum roll: *Crrrrrk-crrrrk-crrrk-crrk-crk-ck*. The men would have looked up as the seracs crumbled, dropping chunks large enough to transform the terrain. One of these chunks sped toward Jumik, gouging out fixed lines. The three men, still attached to these fixed lines, were yanked downward.

Jumik's boot tore off. His gloves flew away. One Korean's German Rollei camera split open and his skull crunched. Down jackets ripped open, snowing feathers. Jumik may have thought he was going to die and been surprised when he didn't. One of the anchors above him held. The rope cinched tight. The three men jerked to a standstill, coming to rest on a precipitous snow slope.

Dangling from the line's end, Jumik hung upside down, blood pooling in his lungs and head. The rope had wound around Jumik's trunk, binding him, and he was too tangled to adjust his clothing or cover his bare hands. Squirming free would have been impossible, and he would have only been able to see the ice two inches in front of his face.

▲ ▲ ▲

At 9 p.m., about 50 yards from the Bottleneck, Rolf was hit by a serac fall. As chunks of hard ice sailed over the Traverse, one came so fast he had no chance to shout. It must have hit him head-on, severing the rope and burying him under tons of ice.

Twenty yards behind him, the tremor knocked his wife flat. Cecilie slid several feet, but the fixed line caught her. As she scrambled to stand again, the batteries shot out of her headlamp. Cecilie clutched the rope with a gloved hand, felt the limp end, and realized it no longer linked her to her husband. She scanned the slope for the glow of his headlamp. It had disappeared.

Cecilie was stunned, too horrified to move. This was supposed to be her honeymoon. From behind, Lars touched her shoulder. Cecilie stayed frozen. Lars said something as he stepped around her, but Cecilie heard him as though she were underwater. Dazed, she watched him shuffle in front. Lars examined the cord cut by the ice fall, pulled a 50-meter coil of thin rope from his pack, and secured it to one of the surviving ice screws. Then he rappelled down until his headlamp dimmed to a pinpoint.

Cecilie remained fixed in place. Without Lars's light, darkness enveloped her. The ice creaked and the breeze whistled. She wondered why she was there. "I hadn't seriously prepared myself for coming home alone without Rolf," she recalled. "It was not something I could have prepared for. It's a pain you can't simulate." She couldn't climb—she didn't want to. The desolation was complete and unbearable.

Lars's voice jolted her out of contemplation. "Come here!" his cheerful tenor exclaimed from below. Had he found Rolf? Cecilie knew that climbers had survived worse falls. Maybe her husband had landed relatively unharmed.

"Rolf?" she yelled. "Rolf!" Her hope revived, she rappelled down the Bottleneck, repeating her husband's name and shouting at Lars to tell her more. When the rope ended, Cecilie focused on climbing so she could reach her husband sooner. Axe, front point, front point. Axe, front point, front point. *Chuck, shink, shink. Chuck, shink, shink.*

She couldn't see her boots without the headlamp. Slipping once, she heaved her weight onto the axe and stopped herself. As she got closer to Lars, he shined his headlamp to guide her down. Finally, she could see Lars's face. He looked crushed.

"Where's Rolf?" she asked him, out of breath.

Lars wouldn't lie to her now. "Rolf is gone."

Despite the pain, Cecilie appreciated what her friend had done: "He had tricked me into descending." Still, she held out hope that Lars was mistaken. Maybe Rolf was alive, somewhere below the Bottleneck. She kept calling for him and hoping, praying that he might be limping to camp on his own.

Shattered blocks of ice littered the mountain, and the trail made earlier that day had been obliterated, but she saw a red strobe blinking in Camp 4, far below. Lars took a compass bearing in case they lost the beacon, and he and Cecilie continued toward the Shoulder.

When Cecilie reached camp at 11 p.m., she went directly to her tent. Crawling inside, she hoped to see her husband. His sleeping bag was empty.

"It was quiet," she later wrote. "No wind. Just stars and loneliness."

▲ ▲ ▲

Pasang Lama squinted into the darkness as three lights streaked down like shooting stars. What had happened to the headlamps behind him? They had turned a corner or dipped below a rise, he told himself. Pasang waited for the lights to reappear, but they didn't. "I knew what it was, but I didn't want to know," Pasang recalled. Too tired for analysis, he suppressed the thought of an avalanche. He told himself he was losing his mind, and for a time he found that idea reassuring. Perhaps the streaks of lights were a hallucination of his oxygen-starved brain? Trying to ignore the loose ice, scuttling like insects, he waded blindly toward the Traverse.

Soon Pasang felt his boots breaking fresh powder. The terrain, once so familiar, now seemed alien. K2 was another mountain. The route to the Bottleneck had disappeared, along with every landmark. Cursing under his breath, he concluded that he'd missed a turn, just as Karim had, and strayed into China. Disoriented, Pasang backtracked, miserably plodding over the steps he'd just made. Pasang recognized nothing around him.

Finally, he squatted in exhaustion and studied his tracks. The ruts were too deep, the steps too varied, to have been trod by his boots alone; obviously others had climbed along the same route. Pasang decided he had been following the path to the Traverse all along. This meant that fixed lines were nearby. He patted the slope above the track, dug around, and felt something snaking through the ice: ropes, dusted in snow. He excavated them and attached his Figure 8, sliding along a diagonal ridge leading into the Traverse.

As the slope steepened, Pasang rappelled down and across slick ice. Then, unexpectedly, the rope frayed and stopped short.

This seemed inconceivable. The fixed line shouldn't end here. Pasang stared at the tattered end. Confounded, he dropped the rope and glanced around for another section. To his right, he spotted a slender line dangling from an ice screw. The original fixed lines had run horizontally; this one dropped vertically. Pasang didn't know where this strange rope led or how it had gotten here, but he loved the sight of it. Relieved, he threaded his Figure 8 through and rappelled down another 50 yards into the mouth of the Bottleneck.

This rope stopped short too, delivering Pasang to a landing no wider than a shoebox. Once again, his intuition rebelled against the reality. Where was the rest of the rope? Why did the lines keep vanishing?

As he sifted through his thoughts, the rope above him whipped to the side. Another headlamp was making its way down, smoothly and quickly. The glow approached. Beneath a halo of light Pasang could see the silhouette of Pemba Gyalje, the Sherpa on the Dutch team. Pemba stopped beside Pasang on the shelf.

Above, stars dappled the sky but offered only faint light. Shining their headlamps in wide sweeps, Pasang and Pemba hunted for the next section of line. To Pasang, the channel below seemed to extend infinitely. Ice cubes rained down on him, dinging his head harmlessly. Like the plucks of a rubber band, the seracs above chirped and *zoinged*. Soon they would calve blocks the size of Buicks.

Pemba seemed calm, but fear gripped Pasang's chest and gummed inside his throat. He looked below. Mist glided off like fingers goading him to jump. Pasang would have to free-climb the Bottleneck without an axe, which he knew was nearly impossible.

Nonetheless, Pasang tried, clawing and pounding the ice to create holds. He hooked his fingers in and shifted his weight, kicking his front points into the slope. He could barely grip the wall, and as he started to step down, his hands skittered across the wall's surface, searching for soft spots. The ice was as hard as a skating rink.

Shaking, he shuffled back to the ledge and grabbed hold of the rope's end. Pasang was stranded. He tried to say something to Pemba, but his throat, like a corroded pipe, only sputtered. The glacier responded in a cacophony of creaks and *zoings*.

Pasang had no hope. An avalanche or falling ice would certainly kill him before sunrise. Neither Pemba nor anyone else could help him unless that savior carried extra rope. Pasang thought this unlikely—he was certain that all available rope had been located and requisitioned for the fixed lines in the Bottleneck.

"It's over," Pasang told himself. His time to die had come. Trying not to move, he swore and prayed that his next life would be better.

▲ ▲ ▲

Following the freshly excavated line along the Traverse, Chhiring recognized his wife's face. The visitation came on gradually and intensified as he approached the Bottleneck. Dawa appeared to him as he'd first seen her, a teenager driving yaks toward a stream in the Khumbu. Clucking and prodding her animals to drink, she paced the bank.

Suspended between dream and memory, Chhiring felt this stream swell into the river that flows below Beding, the village where he was born. Chhiring's father, Ngawang Thundu, flickered on. With fingers gnarled from years of gripping a plow, he pointed to a boulder, smoothed by millennia in the rapids. He pressed a bony shoulder against its side and rolled the stone homeward to shore up a collapsed wall.

Chhiring's visions continued like a series of celluloid clips: his older daughter, Tshering Namdu, at the family altar, filling copper bowls to the rim with water; his younger daughter, Tensing Futi, emptying them into a flowerpot; his brother, Ngawang, singeing juniper branches at a rooftop *puja*; Ngawang Oser, his *lama*, blessing the charms on his *bhuti*.

Of all the faces he needed, his mother's was the one Chhiring couldn't summon. All he could see were her ashes, billowing in the sky. Chhiring imagined that Lakpa Futi was speaking, but he couldn't make out her words. He squatted, nodding off in the snow, but woke when he understood her. "She was telling me I had to live."

Chhiring focused his attention on the mountain. Studying the plowed ice, he realized what Pasang had not: The seracs had calved, transforming the icescape. "The goddess had timed it for maximum impact," Chhiring recalled.

He slid down the rope in small hops, and, when the first line ended, he quickly spotted the auxiliary rope that Lars had secured to the slope. Chhiring peered down the Bottleneck, wondering how far this slender line would go. Clipping on, he heard a weak cry. A headlamp switched on. Someone was below him. Chhiring rappelled down 50 yards and maneuvered himself next to two men, one of whom clung to the line's end like fish bait. Chhiring shone his headlamp into their faces.

Pemba looked worried. Pasang, his cheeks raw from cold and tears, looked defeated. "No axe," he said.

Chhiring had no idea how to respond. As the three climbers huddled together to speak, their breaths sent puffs of condensation into the air, giving the impression of a smoky backroom. Discussion was stilted. Pemba shaded his headlamp with a finger so it wouldn't shine in the others' faces. After a pause, he excused himself. "I'm going to look for some rope," he said. Old lines might still be strung to the slope. Pemba hacked his axe into the ice, and his headlamp dropped into the murk.

"What do you see?" Chhiring yelled after him.

Pemba kept descending.

"Any rope?" Pasang called down.

If Pemba responded, Chhiring and Pasang couldn't hear him.

"He went fast, and I couldn't blame him," Chhiring recalled. Pemba had a wife and a three-year-old daughter waiting for him, and he'd been climbing for twenty-four hours. Pemba's headlamp disappeared.

Pasang turned to Chhiring and spoke without emotion. "You can go, too," he said.

Chhiring considered it. Taking responsibility for Pasang—stranded without an axe, on the deadliest pitch of K2, on a moonless night, without a rope, beneath crumbling seracs—wasn't rational. But Chhiring never doubted that it was the right thing to do. *Sonam*, the Buddhist concept of virtue, is nonnegotiable, particularly on K2, so near a goddess who could influence his next reincarnation. She was watching and expected him to show compassion. He expected it of himself.

The seracs creaked.

"It's better if the mountain only takes one of us," Pasang continued. "Go."

Chhiring clipped his safety tether onto Pasang's harness and sank his axe into the ice. "If we die," he said, "we die together."

Sonam

Chhiring felt the weight of the life attached to him. His limbs operated on their own.

Chuck. His axe sunk into the ice.

Shink. Shink. His crampons pierced the slope.

He descended five feet and then braced himself, poised against the wall like a gecko.

Pasang, to his right, mimicked Chhiring's movements as best he could. He clenched his fist and punched it into rotten ice, but his hands didn't sink in like the pick of an axe. So he grasped Chhiring's outstretched arm and leaned against him. Intent on maintaining balance, Pasang stepped down, kicking in with his front points: *shink*.

They relied on instinct to read each other as the dance repeated—one man still as the other stepped, partners communicating with nods and grunts. The tether connecting them provided enough slack to maneuver, but they were all too aware that one false move could plunge both of them into the abyss.

Their headlamps formed a cocoon of light, and a hail of icy golf balls pierced through it, bouncing off their helmets. As the night wore on, the hailstones became bowling balls too heavy to ignore. Pelted by ice, Chhiring dodged the larger pieces, knowing he had to hurry. Soon the mountain might release something so big it would flatten them both.

Fortunately, "K2 sounds a warning before she tries to kill you," Chhiring later said. He listened for the telltale sound, and, midway down the Bottleneck, heard it: a prehistoric groan. Above, hurling at him, bashing and cartwheeling, was an ice boulder.

Chhiring tried to determine the mass's trajectory. "But I didn't know which way it was coming or the direction I should go," Chhiring recalled. "It was fifty-fifty," whether to duck left or duck right.

He guessed left. With barely time to shout, he plunged his ice axe to the side and lunged.

Simultaneously, Pasang let go, sliding on his stomach. He shuffled left, dangling off Chhiring's harness, which bore almost his entire weight.

Swooooof.

The block swished past and tumbled into black space. As it slammed into the slope, a gust of powder shot up from below.

The men drew deep breaths. "You OK?" Chhiring hollered.

Pasang, staring at the column of powder, didn't respond. "I thought I was already dead," he recalled.

After a pause, they resumed inching downward over alternating bands of hard blue ice and frost. To navigate these lips, holes, and bulges, they climbed side by side, holding hands. Sometimes Pasang clung to the tether between them as Chhiring supported the weight of his body.

Pasang wasn't sure what went wrong midway down the Bottleneck. Ice hit his helmet, and he could no longer hold on. All of a sudden he was falling—and so was Chhiring. Their bodies whisked down the Bottleneck. Their noses and chins raked the ice.

Chhiring hacked at the channel.

The blade sank in but did not catch.

Chhiring tried again, plunging in his axe. This time, granite repelled it, nearly flicking the tool from his hand.

Gaining speed, falling faster, they dropped another story. Another two. Another four.

Pasang clawed the mountain and banged it with his knee. Nothing slowed them.

"We were going too fast to survive," Chhiring recalled. "If I had seen someone survive this in a movie, I would have laughed."

But somehow their skulls missed the rocks that should have knocked them out. Their bodies missed the ice ramps that should have launched them into space. The tether between them held.

They'd fallen at least nine stories when Chhiring skimmed over the perfect patch of ice. The pick of his axe dug in, and, despite their speed, Chhiring held on. He gripped the shaft of the axe with his right hand, clamping it diagonally across his chest. At the same time, he angled the adze of his axe with his other hand, grinding the pick into the ice, squeezing in his elbows, and splaying out his knees. The axe dragged down the slope and his body slowed. Choking on ice chips, Chhiring flutter-kicked with both crampons. He stopped.

Chhiring was leaning hard against the ice axe, unable to see below. Shaking, he took a moment to listen to his heart beating. His calves and forearms burned, but he liked this pain. It reminded him that he was still alive.

Below, Pasang was panting and hacking. So we're both still here, Chhiring realized. They hadn't even dislocated their shoulders or broken their wrists.

"Keep going," came Pasang's rasp. The seracs were growling again, and fragments rained down. They needed to move. Fast.

Chhiring followed Pasang's bidding. It was miraculous that they'd survived the fall, and it saved them a tremendous amount of effort by depositing them near the Shoulder. With a *chuck,* a *shink,* and a *shink,* Chhiring stabbed his axe and his crampons into the slope and turned, grateful to see that the gradient had become less sheer. Pasang could move largely on his own now. Still, their progress seemed too slow. "I didn't know how long our luck would hold," Pasang recalled. As he continued downward, he counted the seconds like a mantra.

When they neared the end of the Bottleneck, climbing with barely any slack in the tether between them, Chhiring sensed something drop from above. It flew softly, without a rumble, an errant slab of granite aiming for their skulls. Chhiring and Pasang were exposed, in a channel with no room to maneuver.

Chhiring could do nothing. He exhaled, flattening his torso into a depression in the ice.

Pasang hunched, expecting his helmet to crumple like a can of Coke.

The block hit.

Chhiring tensed.

Pasang shrieked.

The blow never came.

The slab touched Chhiring's helmet and pulverized into crystalline dust. In the darkness, the layer had looked like rock, but it was only a sheet of sticky powder. Chhiring's *bhuti* was working.

He and Pasang continued downward until the slope merged into the Shoulder. Mist was thickening the air, and, in the distance, around a bend, a strobe light flashed.

▲ ▲ ▲

When Pasang staggered into Camp 4 at midnight, mist clung to the tents like cobwebs, too dense for him to see his boots. All around him, nervous climbers clutched radios and shone headlamps into the murk. Pasang avoided them. He couldn't bear to hear the death toll and hadn't the will to announce, "I'm alive."

His crampons crunched on the ice as he reached the ledge where he'd pitched his tent. Crouching down, he doubled over and vomited. Then he rose slowly to steady himself and wandered a few steps, bumping into a fabric dome. Groping for the tent's flap, he tore open the zipper, unstrapped his crampons, and flopped inside. Wrapping himself in a sleeping bag, he tried to switch off his mind and go to sleep, but his eyelids wouldn't stay closed. His thoughts raced, replaying the descent. Questions flooded in. Where was Jumik? Why was he late? Who would be dead in the morning?

Cold air suddenly gripped him, squeezing his chest. Pasang had visions of a tidal wave of snow sweeping over him and interring his body. His head pounded and his lungs constricted. He was suffocating.

Frantic and gasping for air, he thrashed, kicking off his sleeping bag. The tent spun. He rolled over and patted the ground, feeling for Jumik. Stop, he told himself. You're hyperventilating. Get back in the bag and calm down.

He sucked in a lungful of air and reassured himself. Jumik was a strong climber, and he'd be back before dawn. Now Pasang needed to stay warm and recover. He closed his eyes.

Whumpt.

A gloved fist slammed into the top of the tent. Pasang bolted upright as the fist continued to hammer. His hypoxic brain told him that less than a minute had passed since he'd entered the tent, but the light filtering through the fabric meant he'd been there for hours. The *whumpt*s came faster.

Woozy, Pasang turned on his side and let darkness envelop him. He felt Jumik roll in the sleeping bag beside him and heard his cousin's steady breathing. Pasang paced his breathing to match.

Deep sleep at this altitude was impossible, but this time, when Pasang closed his eyes, they stayed shut. Shrouded in a sleeping bag, he felt better—not safe, but contained.

▲ ▲ ▲

Some mountaineers consider a stove a crucial piece of safety equipment. A burner and a canister of propane can weigh less than a beer bottle, but if you find yourself without shelter in the Death Zone, that weight can save your life. A stove melts snow, and the drinking water prevents dehydration, which aggravates hypothermia and frostbite.

Those trapped above the Bottleneck on August 1, 2008, took a different approach. Although they had space in their packs for banners, cameras, camcorders, and flags, not one of them had carried a stove. They didn't even have emergency bivy sacks—wind-breaking, heat-reflecting shells that weigh less than a pound.

"No alpinist goes for the summit of an 8,000-meter peak with useless weight like a stove," explained Marco Confortola. "You don't go for the summit thinking you're going to bivouac." He had planned to make it to the top and back all in one day and wasn't going to be weighed down by safety equipment he'd never use.

But in the early hours of August 2, the Italian was wishing he had carried one. After posing for pictures and calling his sponsor from the summit, Marco had spent half the night pacing the slope above the Snow Dome—searching for the fixed line, the route to the Traverse, or anything at all that looked familiar. He backtracked, gesticulated, reviewed where he had gone, scouted, and returned to where he'd started. The icescape had changed, and Marco was lost.

As the temperature hovered at minus four degrees Fahrenheit, the Italian dug out a perch to rest on, planning to get up at dawn. Ger McDonnell, his messianic beard dripping icicles, joined him. Shivering, they slumped down within shouting distance of Wilco, who was pacing in the darkness.

Marco had enough juice in his sat phone to make a call, and he knew whom he wanted to reach: Agostino da Polenza. His mentor, who affectionately calls Marco "Stupido" behind his back, had also spent a night near K2's summit without a stove. Agostino had made it down despite losing the insoles of his boots, which blew away while he was rubbing his feet. Marco wanted to know how Agostino had survived.

After a few rings, Agostino picked up. He got right to the point: "Fall asleep and you'll die," Marco heard him say matter-of-factly. And when you get up in the morning, rub and extend your legs before you stand. "If you don't warm up your muscles, you'll fall."

Saving battery life, Marco ended the call. Without betraying emotion, he stood up again and paced alongside Wilco, searching futilely for the fixed lines. Ger rose and stared into the dome of the sky. "The stars were so dense," Marco recalled. "They pressed down on us like a blanket, trying to keep us warm." Nonetheless, he was shaking like a windup toy.

Around 1:30 a.m., they finally quit the search for a route and returned to their perches. Ger and Marco stayed together, and Wilco sat 15 yards away. To keep each other awake, Marco and Ger got creative. They clapped. They rubbed each other's legs. They beat their arms. They forced themselves to shiver even harder for heat. They sang a folk song that Marco's *papà*, Fonzi, had taught him for passing the time while herding goats. "La Montanara," a hymn of the Alps, describes the mountains as "sweet little dwelling-place of Soreghina, daughter of the sun." Ger must have appreciated the irony, Marco recalls, because the Irishman substituted Gaelic lyrics from the Irish band Kila: "Don't fail, don't fall, don't slip, don't wreck . . . do what you want, but be sure that's what you want to do."

This was not what they wanted to be doing. Marco fixated on a better place. He concentrated on the spores of light below—Camp 4 at 25,800 feet—a Shangri-la of stoves, tents, and the promise of survival.

▲ ▲ ▲

On the crown of the seracs, another man was crouched in the snow, trying to survive. It's hard to know how cold Karim Meherban became after taking a wrong turn, but he certainly suffered.

Hypothermia was unavoidable. As he shivered, Karim's blood would have shunted away from his fingers, toes, and skin, gathering around his vital organs. If his body temperature fell to 96 degrees Fahrenheit, amnesia and disorientation would have dulled his pain and fear. At 86 degrees, he would have passed out. At 79 degrees, Karim's heart and lungs would have stopped, but this is a reversible death. If rewarmed slowly at a hospital, a hypothermia victim can be resurrected hours after breathing stops, because the heart and brain require less oxygen when chilled. They don't usually degrade much, despite the loss of circulation, and they can start up again once body temperature rises.

Along with hypothermia, Karim surely suffered from frostbite, which tends to strike the fingers, toes, ears, nose, and other extremities farthest from the heart. Ice crystals crowd around the cells, causing them to burst from the pressure. This makes the extremities itch. The itch progressively evolves into a deep, dull pain, similar to that of pressure on a bruise. As his nerves, muscles, blood vessels, and tendons froze, the pain would have subsided as Karim's skin blanched to a waxy-white and then darkened to blue-gray.

But the cold didn't kill him. With the heat at sunrise, his veins would have dilated slightly, sending blood coursing through some of his thawing tissues and causing a throbbing pain far worse than what he would have felt before. His digits probably stayed frozen and wooden, making it difficult to clench an ice axe tightly. Nevertheless, a photo taken at 9:58 a.m. on August 2 shows a climber—almost certainly Karim—standing on top of the seracs, to the east of the summit.

A photo of the same spot taken nine hours later shows a skid mark. Karim, perhaps unable to warm his muscles properly before he stood, must have slipped, his body carving through soft snow or powder. Just before the lip of the overhanging glacier, the track stops. Next to it is a horizontal trail of boot tracks. The bootprints lead toward the junction above the Snow Dome.

▲ ▲ ▲

Battered and weary, Chhiring had thought of nothing but sleep as he trailed Pasang into Camp 4. When he found his tent, the flap opened and the arms of his friend yanked him inside. Eric Meyer locked him in a bear hug.

"Is it bad?" Chhiring asked.

Eric nodded. Eight sleeping bags were empty. He held out a Nalgene bottle of scalding Powerade, and Chhiring, his throat too tight to gulp, took small sips. He crawled into a sleeping bag but felt little warmth. Drifting in and out of sleep, he listened to the commotion outside the tent.

Sometime after daybreak, Chhiring overheard two raised voices. Eric, now outside the tent, and Pemba Gyalje, the Sherpa on the Dutch team, were debating what to do.

"The visibility is terrible right now," Eric said. The American team must descend, he continued, and so should you.

Pemba was crying, barely able to respond. "He was determined to recover what was left of his team," Eric recalled. Pemba's teammates, Wilco and Ger, were still lost somewhere on the mountain. "So I gave Pemba something that might help."

Chhiring rolled over in his sleeping bag and listened to the pills being administered. Pemba swallowed 30 milligrams of dextroamphetamine, a psychostimulant to keep him awake; 10 milligrams of Modafinil, another drug for workers on a graveyard shift; and 10 milligrams of Dexamethasone, to stall the onset of cerebral edema. No stigma attaches to mountaineers who take drugs in exigent circumstances, and Eric gave Pemba the medicine bottles in case he needed more.

When Eric ducked into the tent, Chhiring immediately pulled on his boots. Eric shot him a look that said, You want to die, too?

12

Survival

As night fell on summit day, Pasang's cousins, Tsering and Big Pasang Bhote, were deciphering fragments of radio chatter. Conflicting reports in a babel of languages told of confusion and death. Ten o'clock passed. "Our team should have been back by then," Tsering recalled. Another hour passed. And another. None of the seven summiters from the Flying Jump had returned.

Tsering and Big Pasang had moved up to Camp 4 to guide a second wave of Korean clients to the summit. "But no one was thinking of summits anymore," Tsering recalled. Worried, he and Big Pasang filled their bottles with juice and left to find their missing teammates.

Along the Shoulder, they spotted Mr. Kim. Skin chapped from exposure, eyes bleary with exhaustion, he looked tired but defiant, strong enough to make it back to camp on his own. He spoke to the Bhote cousins in a stammer, explaining that his climbing partner Ms. Go had lagged behind. "Serve her tea and help her down." Tsering pressed his boss to drink some juice himself. After reassuring Kim that he'd find Ms. Go and bring her back safely, he and Big Pasang continued up the Shoulder.

As they climbed, mist coalesced around them, obscuring the slope. Without fixed lines to guide them, the Bhote cousins often squatted and scrutinized the contours of the snow, searching for boot tracks. They took turns calling for Ms. Go, shouting the honorific "Didi" (Elder Sister), and listening for a response. After about two hours, their voices were spent and they still hadn't found her.

In the distance, Tsering saw something that made him think that Ms. Go was gone. High on a ridge, a dot of light plunged downward. A moment later, a second light mimicked the first. Although it was too dark to tell, Tsering feared that one of those climbers was Ms. Go. "It was a terrible thing to see," he recalled. He and Big Pasang climbed in the direction of the falling light. They kept calling, but their voices had lowered to croaks.

Finally, on a slope east of the Shoulder, the cousins heard a wail. The men hollered again. A woman's voice responded. Ms. Go hadn't fallen after all. As in a game of Marco Polo, the Bhote cousins exchanged shouts with her, blindly guessing where she stood in the mist. Sometimes it seemed as though she were only a few steps away; at other times, she sounded much farther off. Climbing toward the sound, Big Pasang spotted a flash. Ms. Go was clinging to an exposed band of granite on the unstable slope, blinking her LED headlamp off and on, off and on. One of her boots was jammed in a crack in the rocks, trapping her, but she smiled through gritted teeth.

Big Pasang climbed down and jimmied out her leg. Leashing her to his harness, he helped her plod toward Tsering. "We didn't talk with Ms. Go," Tsering recalled. "She was not in a state where she was able to communicate." Sandwiching Ms. Go between them and carrying her pack, they marched her back to Camp 4, arriving around 4:30 a.m.

Sobbing men mobbed Ms. Go as she arrived, smothering her in

hugs. An American with swollen eyes brought her a steaming mug of Powerade and announced into a radio: "She's alive and kicking." Tsering escorted her to her tent and filled up a water bottle, tucking it in her sleeping bag so it wouldn't freeze. He unstrapped her crampons, pulled off her boots. She was as comfortable as one can be at 25,800 feet. As Ms. Go shivered in her sleeping bag, Tsering crouched nearby, melting snow on the burner and worrying about Jumik.

About ten minutes later, Kim opened the tent flap and waved, signaling for Tsering to speak with him out of earshot of Go. "We were all so relieved to have found Ms. Go, and I thought Mr. Kim wanted to tell me how much he appreciated the rescue," Tsering recalled. "I was hoping he had good news about the others."

But Mr. Kim wasn't ready to give thanks yet. He gave his high-altitude porter the update. Pasang Lama, he said, was passed out in his tent. Jumik and three other members of the Flying Jump—Hwang Dong-jin, Kim Hyo-gyeong, and Park Kyeong-hyo—were still missing, probably somewhere above the Bottleneck. The radios weren't getting through to them. The weather, Mr. Kim feared, was deteriorating. You and Big Pasang, he told Tsering, need to head up immediately and bring the four missing climbers down to camp.

Tsering nodded but decided to consult with Pemba Gyalje of the Dutch team. Pemba had overheard the discussion. "It's too dangerous," he said. Pemba, like Chhiring and Eric, had assessed the lack of visibility, the potential avalanche conditions, and his own level of exhaustion. He'd determined that a rescue attempt at this time would cause more deaths, not fewer. Pemba was waiting to launch a search-and-rescue after the sun rose and visibility improved. "Don't go yet," he advised.

Tsering doubted he had a choice. Mr. Kim had hired him to help the Flying Jump immediately, not to wait. He found Mr. Kim again. As they were talking, Big Pasang joined them and listened, his face hardening. "Maybe he was thinking of Jumik's baby," Tsering recalled. "Jumik was my brother and his cousin, after all." Whatever the reason, Big Pasang was ready to go. He had already grabbed two oxygen cylinders, snapped fresh batteries into the radio, and filled several bottles with boiling water. Neither Big Pasang nor Tsering challenged Mr. Kim. "He had paid us some money," Tsering recalled, "so we acted as though he owned our lives."

▲ ▲ ▲

At 5 o'clock the morning after summit day, Wilco took an inventory. Frostbite had consumed his toes, but his friends were still there: Marco and Ger were dozing on a perch, three yards above him. The Dutchman approached their predicament as a mathematical equation, considering the variables: "I kept telling myself there has got to be a solution." He remembered the night well enough. He'd made it to the summit. The fixed lines had vanished. He had searched for two hours. Then the night had never seemed to pass. From 1:30 to 5 a.m., Wilco had sat apart from his friends. "I don't know why I didn't go over and sit next to them," he recalled. Too numb to feel lonely, "I just sat there by myself and waited for the sun to rise."

Now, with the sun blazing in front of him, he roused Ger and Marco with a loud croak. Marco barely looked up. He began rubbing Ger's thighs and forearms. Wilco, meanwhile, fantasized about water. It had been twenty-two hours since he'd drained his bottle below the summit, and the snow around him looked tantalizing. He wanted to scoop up a handful and melt it in his mouth. But he fought the urge. The slush would lower his body temperature and sap more energy than the hydration was worth. Trying to distract himself from the thirst, Wilco scanned the slope and wondered where the fixed lines were hidden. When he stood up, the crust beneath his boots squeaked, splintering under his weight. "It's unbelievable there wasn't an avalanche right then," he recalled. "The snow was so tense."

Once they had warmed their muscles, Ger and Marco rose, too, and the men fanned out, hunting for the fixed lines.

As Wilco searched, he removed his glacier glasses and rubbed his eyes. A breeze wafted across his face, and, gradually, his corneas began to freeze. It took him some time to notice it. At first, the faces of his friends became milky, and, blinking hard, Wilco strained to focus. An hour later, he was peering through a fogged-up windshield. "And I was thinking, 'I am so fucking fucked I don't know how to unfuck myself.' I couldn't see anymore and had to take action."

He turned to the others and told them he was going blind. "I said to Ger, 'Listen, I'm not going to discuss this. I'm going down. Directly down. It doesn't matter if I'm going in the right direction or not.'"

Wilco gripped his axe, plunged the heel of his boot into the snow, and headed straight down, dropping into a soup of white. "It was pure focus," Wilco recalled. Although he suspected that the path he was on led toward China, not Pakistan, Wilco was actually descending below the Snow Dome.

After about 200 feet, he heard a whimper. Confounded by the noise, he moved toward it and, a moment later, nearly bumped into something that made him gasp. As his mind processed the sounds and shapes, Wilco realized he was staring at a writhing knot of climbers. They were suspended upside down, hanging from the missing fixed lines, bound together in a snarl of secondary rope. The climbers were members of the Flying Jump—Pasang's cousin Jumik and two of his Korean clients.

The man at the top was hanging headfirst, his harness at his shins. About 10 yards below him, another Korean was curled on the ice, his face swollen, slashed, and bruised. He didn't respond to Wilco's voice. Below him hung Jumik. His eyes were glazed and his cheeks were covered in a gray crust, but he was alert enough to ask for gloves.

Wilco pulled out his spare pair, tugged them over Jumik's bare hands, and tried to understand why the men were tangled in so much rope. When the serac fall had cut the fixed line, the men had been attached to it by a safety leash and roped up to each other with a separate line. Falling, they must have somersaulted over each other. The two lines would have wound around them, twisting and cinching.

Wilco didn't want to imagine the horror of hanging upside down all night in the freezing cold. He moved Jumik into a more upright position and offered help, although he had no idea what he could do.

Jumik told him that help was on the way, and, after ten minutes, Wilco decided to leave. He descended toward a band of rocks. He tried to put the hanging men out of his mind. "They were trying to survive," he recalled, "but I had to survive, too."

Beyond the band of rocks was a sheer drop. Wilco turned back, "hanging over my ice axe, almost dead," he recalled, "and progressing centimeter by centimeter." He saw that Ger and Marco were far above him, kneeling beside Jumik.

"Where do I go?" Wilco shouted. He got no response. Too exhausted to climb up, he trudged forward, beneath the overhanging serac and saw a fragment of rope, his team's own five-millimeter Endura. It lay in the snow like a gift.

▲ ▲ ▲

By noon, Wilco was lost, wandering south of the Cesen route. He had made it through the Bottleneck with help from the rope but veered right, dropping off the Shoulder. "I really had no clue where I was," the Dutchman recalled. He hadn't recovered his sight, but even with perfect corneas, he wouldn't have seen much. A cloud bank obscured the slopes. Wilco went in the one direction he was certain of: down.

Pursing his lips to preserve moisture, he counted his steps. "I was busy with only one thing," he recalled. "Survival." Aiming to keep three limbs touching the mountain at all times, he backtracked when crevasses blocked his way. At one point, he saw more survivors, waved, and climbed toward them. The survivors ignored him, and, when Wilco finally reached them, they all turned out to be rocks. Defeated, he squatted in the snow. "I couldn't move any farther," he recalled. "I couldn't go to the left, I couldn't go to the right. I couldn't go down, I couldn't go up. I had no more strength. I was really trapped. That's when I was thinking I should make a phone call."

He pulled out his Thuraya sat phone. The keypad looked like pudding, and his mind was washed of all numbers except one. He felt out a familiar combination, and, at 9:30 a.m. Pakistan time, he heard the phone ring as it tried to connect to Utrecht.

A soft hello—the voice of his wife, Heleen—jolted Wilco. "I'm alive," he told her. Wilco tried to sound confident and paused, squinting. "I think I see people ahead."

Heleen sounded simultaneously shaken and relieved. "Are they moving?"

Wilco thought so. Switching off the Thuraya, he sculled forward, anxious to greet his rescuers. Again disappointed, he encountered more freestanding rocks.

The hours compounded. "I didn't have the guts to look at my watch," Wilco recalled. "I got frustrated at how slowly time was passing." He couldn't remember whether he slept. Sometimes his legs wobbled and tried to collapse. His eyes stung. He willed himself to keep going and to think of home. He began to regret the brusque call to Heleen. "Did I tell her I loved her?" Wilco couldn't remember. Squatting in the snow, he once again fished for the Thuraya in his pack and dialed.

This time, Heleen tried to orient him. "Do you see Broad Peak?" she asked.

"Of course I see Broad Peak," Wilco fumed. Why was she asking about the view? He was too unhinged to realize the significance of the question. Only climbers on the Pakistan side of K2 can see Broad Peak.

A few minutes later, Wilco hung up. The call reminded him of another he'd made four years earlier, and the memory buoyed him. From the summit of Everest in 2004, he had dialed Heleen and, shouting above the wind, asked her to marry him. Even then, Heleen had tried to orient him. "Just forget about this," she had said. "Get down safely. Then we can talk about it." That's probably how she felt now, Wilco realized. She wanted him to focus on climbing and survive so their toddler might have a father.

Each step was punishing on his frostbitten feet. The thirst was just as severe. As the day wore on, he wondered whether a swan dive was the solution. Everything looked milky, and he had no idea where he'd land, but a leap of faith seemed simple, even sensible—he'd certainly get down at breakneck speed. What remained of his reason fought against this idea. "If I landed in a crevasse," he considered, "nobody would ever find me."

Lights floated around him, burst apart, and dissolved. Deep in his pack, the Thuraya remained on, losing its charge. The sky darkened, and he readied himself for a second night in the Death Zone.

As he traversed toward a rock outcropping, Wilco spotted something yellow—another mountaineer—and climbed toward him. This man, Wilco was sure, had to be real. He was huddled in a sunbleached parka, and a rope led from his harness to another man, who seemed asleep on his belly.

Wilco introduced himself, but the strangers, long frozen, had nothing to say. Wilco wondered how long they'd been waiting for him. Lonely and lost, he stomped out a pit in the snow and sat out the night in the company of the dead.

13

Buried in the Sky

Snow Dome to Bottleneck

Once they had warmed their muscles, Marco and Ger rose from their perches and started down the mountain after Wilco. Around 8 a.m., they too encountered the three desperate men tangled in ropes. Marco couldn't tell whether they were alive until he noticed their shallow breathing. The sight was surreal, he recalled. "Maybe it was useless. Maybe they would die anyway, but we couldn't abandon them."

The slope was slick, and he and Ger moved like crabs. First, they tried to revive the men. Marco noticed that Jumik had lost a boot, so he took off his glove and pulled it over Jumik's exposed foot. Rooting through Jumik's pack, he found an oxygen cylinder, but the regulator was missing, making it useless. In the snow, Marco discovered a radio with live batteries. He called several frequencies for help. Someone answered. Marco asked for backup, and, in response, he heard a few words punctuated by static.

Ger, meanwhile, approached Jumik and raised his head to help him breathe. Then he tried to rotate the hanging man above him.

"They were like puppets on a string," Marco recalled. One would straighten and another would bend back. To help get the man upright, Marco wedged a ski pole under his armpit.

Sometime after 9:58 a.m., Ger turned and, without a word, climbed up the slope. Marco shouted after him, using his messianic nickname: " 'Jesus,' I cried. 'What the hell are you doing?' No answer. He didn't even turn around. . . . Nothing. He continued toward the top of the serac."

Marco continued with the rescue effort. He hammered his axe into the snow and attached the fixed line, creating a backup anchor so the chain of climbers wouldn't slide. He spent more time trying to free them—maybe an hour, but the passage of time was hard to calculate—and eventually he could do no more. He left. With only a ski pole for balance, he climbed along the Traverse and descended into the Bottleneck without an axe. "I clawed down by my fingernails," he recalled.

By the time he made it through the Bottleneck, Marco could barely walk. After that, he crawled, "moving with his hands and legs like a horse," recalled Tsering Bhote, who encountered Marco below the Bottleneck. "He had his buttocks up in the air. Sometimes, he slipped and crawled with the help of his hands."

Tsering and Big Pasang offered Marco oxygen. Gesturing, Marco indicated that he would never touch the stuff. Before he continued down, the Italian took a chocolate bar from his jacket and handed it to Big Pasang. "It was nice of him, but weird," Tsering recalled.

As Marco crawled toward the Shoulder, his mind, like his body, began to fail. The Death Zone does that to everyone. Scientists suspect it's the lower pressure that makes blood vessels leak, causing the brain to swell. Brain cells receive less oxygen and short-circuit. Neurons misfire. Climbers see and hear things. Marco heard an avalanche roar. A man wearing yellow La Sportiva boots surfed past him. Before he lost consciousness, Marco saw the man's blue eye pop from its socket. It rolled into his palm like a gumball, and Marco was certain it belonged to Ger.

▲ ▲ ▲

Ger kept his eyes and his wits. At Camp 4, two digital cameras were zoomed in on the upper slopes. Although observers couldn't see his rescue effort by naked eye, their memory cards capture some of what happened.

Evidence suggests that Jumik was freed. A photo taken at 9:58 a.m. shows a figure in a lime downsuit—Marco—and another in a red downsuit—Ger—working on the ropes binding Jumik. Another photo taken later shows the ropes, but Jumik is gone. Two eyewitnesses, Tsering and Big Pasang, spotted him near the Bottleneck around 3 p.m., and a photo from 3:10 p.m. shows Jumik, dead, below the Bottleneck.

Jumik couldn't have slid out of the rope tangle and down to the location where his body was found; he would have had to traverse 300 yards to get even near that trajectory. And Jumik was too entangled to have rescued himself. Clearly, Ger, the only able-bodied person in the vicinity after Marco left, helped him. Here's how it could have been done.

Sometime after about 9:58 a.m., Ger lumbered up the 50-degree slope, leaving Marco and the three tangled men below. Ger probably couldn't hear Marco shouting at him. Snow muffles sound; down hoods block it. Ger, according to Marco, continued up without turning around, climbing in the direction of the anchor point of the fixed line.

The upward slog would have been long, perhaps a hundred yards, and, given Ger's condition, might have taken him an hour. At least one ice screw had been gouged out by the falling serac, and Ger went up high enough to disappear from Marco's view. Trudging up the mountain, Ger would have paused to pressure-breathe, resting every few steps.

Many rescue techniques require a climber to reach the anchor point of the rope, and Ger had practiced rescues of this kind in the mountains of Alaska. Once at the anchor point, he would have studied the ice screw to assess how well it was holding. Depending on what he saw, he might have jammed it deeper into the ice, the goal being to establish a stable rope system that releases tension on the main line.

Unlike rescues dramatized by Hollywood, actual mountain rescues are slow-paced, technical affairs that prioritize risk management over speed. They commonly involve tying a complex series of knots. Ger's hands would have been clumsy from the cold as he tied and retied knots he knew by rote.

Matt Szundy, founder of the Ascending Path guide service in Alaska, taught and tested Ger on rescue techniques. He speculated that Ger "rigged a secondary anchor near the first, using an ice screw in his pack." Then, using a Prusik hitch and a Munter hitch, Ger would have created a series of pulleylike knots and loops that, thanks to friction and leverage, provided some slack and a strong backup anchor so that when he freed the tangled men, their bodies wouldn't go sledding down the mountain.

After creating the rope system, Ger descended toward the men. Now that he had enough slack to work with, he would have begun untying the climbers and equipping the people he freed. Jumik was missing a boot. Ger might have yanked a boot off another man and given it to him. Photos suggest Jumik was eventually worked free and able to stand.

Ger could do nothing for the man at the top of the tangle. He couldn't be revived, according to Marco and Wilco, the last living witnesses to see him. A grainy photo taken at 7:16 p.m. shows his body splayed in the same orientation as it appears in the morning photos.

But Ger may have rescued the man in the middle of the knot. The evidence is inconclusive. In the three grainy photographs of the rescue site—taken at 8:06 a.m., 9:58 a.m., and 7:16 p.m.—the man's position appears unchanged. But two eyewitnesses believe they saw him that afternoon with Jumik and Ger on the Traverse. Perhaps the shape in some of the photos is something other than a body, such as a pile of discarded rope.

Although the Korean was injured and weak, it is possible that he revived enough to climb. Mountaineers have gone from comatose to ambulatory under similar circumstances, as Texas mountaineer Beck Weathers did in 1996. Beck was in the upper reaches of Everest when a blizzard engulfed him in 80-mile-an-hour winds. His friends had left him in a hypothermic coma, assuming he would never wake. But, sometime the next morning, Beck opened his eyes, struggled to his feet, and began climbing toward camp. "I am neither churchly nor a particularly spiritual person," he later wrote, "but I can tell you that some force within me rejected death at the last moment and then guided me, blind and stumbling—quite literally a dead man walking." The Korean was injured and Jumik's foot was severely frostbitten, frozen to the ankle, but the two men may have felt the same way that Weathers had as they climbed up to the Traverse with Ger.

Somewhere along the way, a fourth man joined them, according to Big Pasang's radio calls. Who was he? It's hard to rule out a third Korean who hadn't been seen since the night before, but it is also possible the man was Pakistani high-altitude porter Karim Meherban. Photos suggest that Karim, after spending the night alone in the cold, slid down the crown of the serac, self-arrested, and managed to retrace his steps to the junction at the Snow Dome. There he could have met Jumik, Ger, and the Korean climber before they reached the Bottleneck.

Whoever they were—Jumik and Ger were among them, but it's impossible to identify the others with any certainty—four men were hobbling along the Traverse, driven by a force that rejects death.

▲ ▲ ▲

After accepting Marco's chocolate bar, the Bhote cousins resumed climbing toward the Bottleneck in search of survivors. By 3 p.m., Big Pasang had pulled ahead of Tsering by 900 feet. He looked up ahead and jubilantly reported on the radio what he saw: "Jumik is alive," he exclaimed, "and behind him are three men in red downsuits." He couldn't tell who they were.

Stowing the radio, Big Pasang may have waved and shouted at the men coming toward him and must have been overcome with relief. As Big Pasang approached the climbers, he may have heard a crack as an ice block fell. It bludgeoned one man—probably Ger, based on Big Pasang's description on the radio—and knocked him off the Traverse. "One man in a red suit with black patches was hit by falling ice," Big Pasang shouted over the radio to Pemba Gyalje and Tsering. "Now there are only three men descending."

Big Pasang probably tried to pick up the pace, eager to lead the three survivors out of the fall zone. Jumik was in front, so Big Pasang would have reached him first. Maybe the cousins embraced. Perhaps Big Pasang offered him some of the contents of his pack: water, bottled oxygen, and juice. He definitely attached Jumik to a rope.

As the two other climbers in red suits approached him, Big Pasang might have yelled up, reassuring them. All his effort was in vain. A thunderous boom ricocheted off the mountain.

▲ ▲ ▲

Contrary to legend, you can't start an avalanche by yelling or yodeling, but almost anything that deforms the snow can set one off: falling rocks, melting ice, rain, hail, an earthquake, a footstep. In nine out of ten cases, victims trigger the avalanche that kills them.

Avalanches can take various forms—ice, loose powder, heavy wet snow, rock and glacial flows—but the terrain the climbers traversed on the morning of August 2 was ripe for a dry-slab avalanche. Climbers on the mountain reported that each time they stepped on the snow, they heard a distinctive creak, and cracks shot across the snow's surface. They were climbing down a slope of about 40 degrees, an angle well within the 25- to 45-degree range that's common with dry slabs. Snow had been piling up for weeks, and the temperature had spiked over the previous few days, helping loosen layers of snow.

Skilled climbers will notice these danger signs, but predicting avalanches is imprecise even with the most sophisticated equipment. The chances of a flow depend on the snow's stickiness, the size and density of the ice crystals, how well those crystals are bonded, the steepness of the slope, the shape of the terrain, the temperature, the humidity, the location and force of the trigger. In broad terms, a slab avalanche occurs when a top layer of snow slips over a lower layer. Anything that makes the space between the two layers more slick (such as watery or ball-bearing ice crystals), or anything that adds pressure on the top layer (such as more snow) increases the likelihood of an avalanche.

Many people imagine an avalanche as being a lot of loose snow and ice tumbling down the mountain like a bunch of BBs rolling down a slide. When an avalanche starts, it's more like a plate sliding off a table. At first, a slab of snow breaks free from the mountain and moves down the slope. As it picks up speed, the slab shatters, breaking into increasingly smaller pieces that eventually become so tiny they flow like water. The material at the bottom of an avalanche is as fine as powdered sugar. Most avalanches flow at around 70 miles per hour; the big ones can reach 200 miles per hour and flow on for miles, washing up and down hills and valleys and striking with enough power to take out trees, houses, and entire towns.

The last, deadly avalanche of the day began all at once, with an enormous, thundering crack. Karim would have known what the sound meant. The men had about a second and a half to get off the snow slab. That wasn't enough time.

A moment after the crack, the slab slid out from under them. Within a second, the snow would have been moving at about 10 miles per hour, breaking into giant pieces. Two seconds later, the avalanche would have been sliding between 10 and 30 miles per hour, with chunks further fragmenting. Faster-moving snow at the surface of an avalanche carries more force than the slower-moving snow below it, causing a tumbling motion. For the next five seconds, the slide accelerated, the snow churning like the surf after a wave breaks. At this point, the men would no longer have known which way was up. When this happens in water, surfers sometimes call the condition "being washing-machined."

The snow, mixing with air, packed into the climbers' lungs and plugged their mouths, ears, and noses. Their goggles, hats, and mittens were ripped off. Big Pasang and Jumik were short-roped together. They spooled and threaded around each other, becoming tangled ever more tightly. This apparently broke their necks. Around 3 p.m., Pemba saw Big Pasang and Jumik tumble past him. They were dead at 3:10 p.m. when he photographed their bodies, tightly wound together in ropes. The snow around them was streaked with blood and tissue.

The flow would have reached its maximum speed, somewhere between 40 and 80 miles per hour, after roughly eight seconds. And then it would have begun to slow. Once it did, it probably took less than a few seconds to stop. The other two climbers were never found, suggesting that the avalanche sucked them down and buried them.

The snow probably would have cushioned them so that they remained conscious.

A trained climber would have tried to clear a space around his face, creating an air pocket before the slide halted completely. Then he'd have flailed out his arms and legs so his body would be easier to find.

Once the flow stopped, the snow would have compacted so tightly around him that he couldn't move even his fingers. Spitting to see which direction was up wouldn't have helped. The snow feels like concrete, too hard to dig without a shovel. In that situation, all a climber can do is wait, hope, and cough out the snow in the lungs, trying to relax and consume less oxygen.

More than enough air can diffuse through densely packed snow to keep a human alive, but warm breath causes the snow around the face to melt. Inevitably, that melting snow refreezes. This forms a capsule of ice around the climber's head, preventing fresh air from cycling through. As a result, he is forced to inhale and exhale the same air, with increasingly lower concentrations of oxygen. The climber, buried alive, slowly asphyxiates.

During asphyxiation, the heart initially beats faster. Breathing speeds up. People revived from this state commonly recall seeing a ray or tunnel of light. Many consider it a religious experience. Scientists have an explanation as well, but it hasn't been tested in a laboratory: Oxygen deprivation causes peripheral vision to decline, narrowing the field of view and giving the illusion of an ever-contracting tunnel of light. Survivors have described it as heavenly.

After about four minutes of asphyxiation, the brain goes into a manic version of REM sleep. Some researchers believe that this brain-wave pattern delays damage to neurons. Victims revived from these moments often remember seeing their entire lives flash before their eyes. They report feeling relaxed, falling into a Zen-like trance that has been known to turn atheists into believers.

After that, the heart, starved of oxygen, slows; the pulse drops to roughly thirty beats a minute. Then the heart beats erratically and soon stops completely, quivering in place, jellylike. Breathing slows, then ceases. The body cools. Electrical activity in the brain diminishes and the central nervous system gradually shuts down.

If the climbers buried by the avalanche didn't form an air pocket in front of their mouths, they died within thirty-five minutes. With an air pocket, death could have taken about ninety-five minutes. If their bodies cooled quickly, they might have survived for hours in a state of suspension between life and death; hearts stopped, brains partially on, they could be summoned back. Doctors at a state-of-the-art hospital might have been able to revive them.

But the men buried by the avalanche on August 2 were never found. Their bodies stayed interred, cooling beneath the snow.

▲ ▲ ▲

When Tsering Bhote, climbing 900 feet below Big Pasang, saw the avalanche sliding toward him, he darted to the nearest rock, wrapped his arms around it, closed his eyes, ducked his head, and prayed. The snow hit the rock and parted, roaring past him on both sides, shooting over him. The noise resembled a jet engine at takeoff. Grains of ice sprayed him, blasting him with powder. He screamed but couldn't hear his own voice. Snow particles gusted into his mouth and nose.

As the roar continued downslope, gradually subsiding, Tsering opened his eyes and wiped them with his glove. All he saw was snow emulsified in air. Again he yelled, but the whiteness swallowed the sound, creating a hollow silence. He sucked in to breathe and felt the suspended ice crystals cake his throat. He coughed and snorted, panting. Still hugging the rock, he braced for more.

The powder around him drifted down and the sun tunneled through the dense white. As his ears stopped ringing, Tsering shook his head to dislodge the ice coating his hair. He relaxed his grip on the boulder and looked around, seeing only raked snow, bleak and featureless. Far below, a field of debris fanned into an embankment. Tsering recognized the contours of a mass grave. He hunted for a red splotch, something to signify a downsuit. He saw only chunks of ice and snow, no hint of where the men were buried. He yelled out for the other climbers, calling Jumik and Big Pasang by name, but "the goddess had hidden them well." So he moved downward, mindlessly placing one boot in front of the other, not caring what came next. He barely noticed Pasang Lama climbing toward him. When the two men met, Pasang was breathless. He explained that he and Pemba had ascended from Camp 4 as swiftly as they could to help the survivors. "What survivors?" Tsering replied. Unwilling to describe what he'd seen, Tsering turned away and traversed the slope to a rock outcropping and slumped down, shaking.

Pasang followed, crouched next to him, and held out a water bottle. Tsering refused the liquid and stared into the reef of clouds, contemplating the sky above and the sky below. "I didn't think I would lose my family," he said. "Somewhere in my heart I felt I would meet them below."

14

The Fearless Five

Soon after giving the Bhote cousins chocolate, Marco collapsed. Exhaustion had beaten him, and now, splayed out below the Bottleneck, he rested his head in the snow. An avalanche could have barreled down the slope at any moment and swallowed him alive, but he slept on, wavering in and out of consciousness.

Around 3 p.m., a hiss jolted him awake. Something dark glommed onto his nose and mouth like a slug. He knew instinctively to yank it off. Coughing, he tossed and turned his head and tore at the slug's rubbery hide. Unable to pull it from his face, he pried his fingers beneath its lip. The thing came loose, finally, releasing the suction around his cheeks, but then an oblong shape—a wrist—pressed it back into place. Marco tried slapping and pinching, but now the thing wouldn't budge. The hiss amplified to a wheeze, and dry air blew into Marco's throat and down his windpipe, inflating his lungs.

He reluctantly inhaled lungful after lungful of the gas. As he breathed, his vision sharpened and his mind rebelled. He realized that an oxygen mask was on his face. The wrist pressing it on him belonged to the Sherpa on the Dutch team, Pemba Gyalje. The hiss came from the regulator attached to the bottle. "Marco," said Pemba's soothing voice. "Marco. Marco. Marco. I'm trying to help you."

But Marco didn't want this kind of help. He had suffered plenty to avoid the bottle. Now, with each breath, he was ruining his record of climbing without supplemental oxygen. Why now, so close to high camp, should he surrender? To satisfy the recordkeepers, he'd have to climb the Savage Mountain all over again. Meanwhile, the Italian media might dig up an old taunt from 2004 when he had climbed Everest on the bottle: They'd call him *il bombolaro*, the bottle guy. Marco tore off the gas mask. Using it was exactly what he hadn't wanted. Pemba extended an arm and Marco, infuriated, grabbed it, pulling himself to his feet.

They had barely begun descending when something—Marco thought it was an oxygen cylinder, Pemba thought it was a rock— bounced down the incline and bludgeoned Marco in the nape, knocking him to his knees. Blood trickled from the puncture on his neck, and a dying avalanche, which had propelled the missile, flowed hard against him, threatening to whisk him away. Within seconds, Marco felt as though he were levitating.

Pemba grabbed him by the scruff, "like a lioness protecting her cub," and towed him to the side, out of the slow-moving flow. The avalanche slid past, blasting powder into the air and carrying the entangled bodies of Big Pasang and Jumik. Sickened, Marco shut his eyes, and Pemba, with the equanimity of a coroner, snapped photos.

To their far left, the man who had eaten Marco's chocolate bar came to rest. Ropes bound Big Pasang's corpse to Jumik; the Bhote cousins were aligned head-to-toe. Marco sucked in and looked away, contemplating something far worse than his tarnished record as Pemba photographed the streaks of gore in the snow.

Clouds moved in, "as if trying to hide the disaster," Marco recalled. He got moving, climbing side by side with Pemba, heading down the 50-degree slope toward the Shoulder. The nightmare was too real to talk about, so they made their way back to Camp 4 in silence.

▲ ▲ ▲

Locating Wilco the next day became a collaboration that stretched around the globe and into space.

As he wandered down the mountain, lost, GPS satellites installed by the U.S. military were orbiting 12,000 miles overhead, spitting signals to Earth. Wilco's phone grabbed several GPS signals. Using an algorithm based on the time the signals were sent and the satellites' positions, his phone calculated its latitude and longitude.

Every time Wilco called his wife, his 7.5-ounce phone quietly tossed its GPS coordinates to a Thuraya communications satellite floating 22,000 miles above equatorial Africa. This satellite then volleyed the data to Thuraya's computer server in Dubai.

The data sat there for a day, idling on the server. Thuraya's United Arab Emirates office refused to release any information about Wilco's location. Company policy promises its customers uncompromising confidentiality. The U.S. military uses Thuraya phones; so do spies, pimps, and politicians. Thuraya's policy protects its clientele from assassins who could use GPS coordinates to hone in on targets. Disclosing Wilco's location, the company feared, could put him in danger. Thuraya needed permission from the man himself.

Unfortunately, the subscriber was rather hard to reach. Tom Sjogren, Wilco's expedition tech provider, tried to reason with Thuraya and assure the company that he was telling the truth. "We had to convince them that a customer lost at 26,000 feet on K2 had other concerns than being ransomed by terrorists." It took several hours of verification, but Sjogren eventually prevailed. On the afternoon of August 2, he secured the data from Thuraya and plotted Wilco's rough location on a three-dimensional map of K2, e-mailing the information to Maarten van Eck, Wilco's expedition manager.

Aboard the *Archimedes* canal boat in Utrecht, Maarten further manipulated the data, factoring in his knowledge of Wilco's last-known location, photos of the mountain, and details about the routes. What he found surprised him. Everyone had thought Wilco would be somewhere above Camp 4, and climbers had spent hours scanning those slopes with binoculars. Maarten discovered that they were looking in the wrong place. Wilco was below Camp 4, at about 24,000 feet, south of the Cesen route. Maarten relayed this information to K2 Base Camp.

In Base Camp, a crowd of mourners lifted their binoculars and scoured the area Maarten had described. Even Hoselito Bite, the Serb whom Wilco had evicted during a windstorm, pitched in to help. "I'd have even climbed up to help that asshole," Hoselito recalled. "This was no time to nurse resentment." But no one spotted Wilco, even with clues to his location. Fog obscured Camps 3 and 4, and the prevailing opinion was that Wilco was tough but K2 was tougher.

Nadir, the cook for the Serbs, disagreed. "Wilco wasn't the type of man to give up," he said. After rescuing Shaheen from Camp 2, Nadir was back in the kitchen, wishing he could do more than prepare lunch. He didn't really expect to find Wilco, but he figured that if nobody had spotted him yet, he should leave the grill. "Everyone had lost their appetite anyway," he recalled. Long after others had quit, Nadir continued to scan the slope in a grid pattern, even when all he could see were clouds.

Around 3 p.m., the fog lifted, and Nadir spotted a dot south of the Cesen, above Camp 3, just where the GPS geometry had predicted. At first, the dot appeared to be a rock, but, after studying it, Nadir decided that the object was unquestionably orange—and moving. "This had to be Wilco," who had been wearing a mango-colored North Face downsuit. But a moment later, fog rolled in and others couldn't see the spot.

Three and a half hours later, the fog burned off, and Chris Klinke, an American, sighted the orange dot. It was definitely a survivor. Chris became ecstatic and alerted others. Base Camp radioed Wilco's teammate, Cas van de Gevel, near Camp 4.

Guided by bearings radioed from Base Camp, Cas descended toward the dot. As the sky darkened, he switched on his headlamp, but soon it went out. Cas crouched, trying to swap dead batteries with live ones. His fingers were stiff with cold, and all the batteries dropped from his grasp and slid down the slope. Forced to stop, Cas pulled a sleeping bag from his pack, wrapped it over his head like a shroud, and waited. He spent the night less than 700 yards from Wilco. At first light on August 3, he intercepted the last survivor near Camp 3.

Wilco could march, but his gait was robotic. His face resembled a barbecued bell pepper, and his lower lip was swollen, ready to pop. His eyes were poached. Cas had known him for twenty-five years, and when he grabbed his friend in a bear hug, both men began to cry. "I thought I'd never see you again," Cas said. Unable to speak at first, Wilco accepted a liter of water and downed it. His throat now wet, Wilco rasped something to his friend, but it took a few tries before he could be understood. Cas was anxious to hear what he had to say.

"I'm fine," said Wilco. "I'm feeling good."

▲ ▲ ▲

At Base Camp, the vacant tents unsettled everyone, but the dome of the first victim was the strangest. As the glacier melted around its perimeter, Dren Mandić's red-and-blue tent appeared to rise. On a four-foot pedestal, too prominent to avoid, it resembled a *stupa*. "I tried not to look at it," Pasang recalled.

Entering his own tent was intolerable enough. Inside, his cousins' sleeping bags were rolled in the corner. Jumik's socks were paired on top of each other. Big Pasang's wallet was wedged inside a shoe. The neatness of the space repulsed Pasang and made him imagine his cousins, entombed in the glacier, being ground into scrap.

He was unsure what to do with their gear. The various equipment—down gloves, glacier glasses, parkas, sleeping bags—were valuable. The Flying Jump had provided it all, but Pasang doubted that his family would accept anything with Kolon Sport's twin-tree logo. He left the tent and asked another cousin, the team cook, what to do.

Take whatever you want, Ngawang Bhote replied. "You're a stranger to them. A few weeks from now, Mr. Kim won't remember your name."

Pasang didn't care. He didn't want to remember his name either.

Pasang heaved, crying, and Ngawang gripped him by the shoulders. "I have good news," he said. On the day before the summit bid, Ngawang had received a call from Kathmandu. Jumik's wife, Dawa Sangmu, had given birth to a son on July 29. Ngawang had tried to radio high camp to surprise the new father, but terrain blocked reception. And then Jumik had died. Ever since, Ngawang had been burdened with good news. Now, he told Pasang everything he knew about the baby, a healthy boy named Jen Jen.

The birth of a baby buoyed some survivors, and Ms. Go went around to the occupied tents to announce it. In the Serbian tent, Nadir, the team's cook, listened to her and wondered what would happen to the fatherless child. He tapped a stubby metal pick with a mallet, incising letters on an aluminum dinner plate; then he took out a semipermanent Magic Marker. On the surface of the plate, he glossed over the name Karim Meherban and added *HAP PAK* to identify him as a high-altitude porter from Pakistan.

Carrying several of these memorial plates, Nadir and a kitchen hand named Nisar Ali hiked to the Gilkey Memorial, the putrid burial cairn beyond Base Camp. With fishing line, Nadir strung the shiny plates around the rocks, and Nisar Ali found and buffed an old, oxidized platter engraved with the name of his father, Lashkar Khan, a high-altitude porter who died on a 1979 French expedition. In all, eleven new names were added to the memorial in 2008.

Miraculously, neither a twelfth nor a thirteenth plate was added. Wilco and Marco limped into Base Camp, skeletal but alive. Eric Meyer turned the Dutch mess tent into a field hospital, propping the two men against the soap-suds pattern of Cecilie's inflatable IKEA sofa. Most of the survivors he had treated needed food, water, and sleep, or blisters disinfected and dressed. Wilco and Marco, however, were living cadavers. After enduring three days in the Death Zone, Wilco had lost twenty-two pounds. Frostbite had tinted his feet violet, and much of his skin had the consistency of cheese. Marco had similarly severe frostbite, plus a concussion.

It was hard to tell how deep the frostbite had penetrated. To treat the patients, Eric soaked their feet in warm water. He injected Wilco with the clot-busting drug alteplase and the anticoagulant heparin. As the pain intensified, he offered morphine and Valium. Chhiring worked as the physician's assistant. He fetched supplies for Eric, monitored the IVs, maintained the temperature of the tubs, and served tea, bread, and Powerade. On breaks, he walked over to his *chorten* in the center of camp and prayed, thanking the goddess for his deliverance.

Across camp, the Flying Jump survivors were arranging a deliverance of their own. Askari Aviation had quoted a price of $60,000 to dispatch the Fearless Five pilots. It was an expensive and unnecessary chopper ride, but Pasang and the Koreans were going to fly back to town. When Eric learned of this, he thought of the dead sherpas' children in Kathmandu and Shimshal. "If the Flying Jump saved the 60 grand and trekked out like the rest of us," he told Chhiring, "they could have set up those kids for life."

▲ ▲ ▲

The Fearless Five provide a peculiar taxi service. The elite Pakistani military unit is stationed in Skardu to defend a frozen wasteland called the Siachen. The glacier, fifty miles southeast of K2, has little strategic importance, but, at an altitude of 21,000 feet, it is the world's highest battleground, occupying disputed ice between India and Pakistan. The two countries disagree where their border should be drawn, and they've fought for control of the glacier since 1984. The war has cost more than four thousand lives, mostly due to cerebral and pulmonary edema. A ceasefire has held since 2002, but the Fearless Five are constantly training for a flare-up.

During the first days of August, K2 upstaged India. Foreign nationals needed help and Pakistan's oft-maligned military seized the opportunity to score a public relations coup. As the tragedy unfolded, the Fearless Five pilots were in the mess hall, standing around a flat-screen TV. Soft leather sofas faced the screen, but the men never considered sitting. "We were ready to move," said Major Aamir Masood, who had been trained to suit up and get airborne within two minutes. Conversing with his colleagues in clipped British English, he felt restless. "I dislike the wait before a rescue mission," he said, noting that the tenets of the Fearless Five—sacrifice, courage, devotion, pride, and honor—do not include patience.

At first, Masood could only watch the reports on the Geo Television Network. Wilco and the Flying Jump had been evacuated days before, but Marco still needed an airlift on August 6. Wind gusts were stalling takeoff.

At lower altitudes and better conditions, you have a margin of error," said Major Suleman Al Faisal, one of the pilots. "We don't have any margin in the Karakorum. Every mission is high risk." Altitude makes flying a helicopter formidably complicated. The downwash generated by the main rotor blades depends on air density, and the thinner the air, the harder the rotors have to work to produce the same amount of lift. Fuel also burns less efficiently in thin air, so pilots must keep flights short or they'll run out of gas. The Karakorum's unpredictable winds, inconsistent visibility, and uneven terrain magnify the danger. Fortunately for the men being rescued, the Fearless Five are among the best high-altitude aviators in the world. Selected from a pool of combat pilots, they undergo years of specialized training to fly rescue missions in the Karakorum.

Masood, whose jet-black beard matched the shade of his aviator sunglasses, waited, monitoring the weather, until finally, at 12:30 p.m., his team received clearance. Within 120 seconds, Masood's team conducted about two hundred mechanical checks—a list they'd committed to memory—and buckled themselves inside the chopper's slanted seats. Masood trusted his machine absolutely. The green Ecureuil B3 Mystery, with a single rotor, had a sister that touched the summit of Everest in 2005, and Masood loved its power at altitude. The rotors whirled, the skids lifted, and the Mystery was soon flying east, followed by a second, the backup helicopter that wouldn't land unless Masood's mission failed. The two choppers, noses angled downward, cruised over the Baltoro Glacier toward K2.

Fifty-five minutes later, the chopper was circling Base Camp. Winds were gusting at a relatively calm 20 miles per hour, and Masood could see that the climbers had tied socks to their ice axes to signal a wind change. As the Mystery sank toward the glacier, grit shot into the air. "It's like being in a blender," said Masood. "You can't see a thing."

As the helicopter touched the ice, Rinjing Sherpa, a mountaineer from the Makalu region, raced toward the fuselage with Marco riding piggyback. Rinjing dumped the Italian into the chopper's open door and jogged backward, his head held low to avoid flying debris.

The Mystery lifted off. Marco, cradling a liter of Coke, pointed to Masood's camcorder and signaled for him to pass it over. Marco trained the lens on a freewheeling blur of glaciers below. As the camera quivered, K2 receded from sight.

▲ ▲ ▲

When Shaheen heard the *whup-whup-whup* of rotor blades beating overhead, he was strapped to a mule, plodding slowly back to town, still recovering from the illness that had nearly killed him. For days, with each passing helicopter, his mind spun. At first, he told himself that the helicopters were a sign of homesickness encouraged by a liberal insurance policy, but as more choppers crossed the Baltoro, he knew something had gone wrong. He spurred the mule.

Reaching the village of Askole in the heat of the day, he didn't bother to have his lungs checked at the local clinic. He only wanted the names, and they were easy to come by. News had already filtered in from Skardu, and it was even worse than Shaheen had imagined. Eleven were dead on K2, among them two Shimshalis, Karim Meherban and Jehan Baig.

"I took it like a knife in the gut," Shaheen recalled. He tried to think straight, but his thoughts circled, emphasizing every mistake he might have prevented if he had led the climb as planned. He never would have sanctioned the recovery of Dren's body. He would have tried to dissuade anyone who wanted to climb past the 2 p.m. turnaround time. So many lives—including Jehan's and Karim's—might have been spared if only he hadn't fallen ill.

Shaheen prayed that word hadn't yet reached Shimshal. He felt that he needed to be the one to deliver it. "I loved Karim and Jehan like brothers," he explained. "I led them to K2. I was the only man who should face their families." So he calculated: How fast was this information moving? How fast could he move himself? If he were lucky, he could get to Shimshal within a day or two. If the village's one satellite phone, used for natural disasters, were switched off, he might arrive in time. He hitched a ride to Skardu, and, on the main drag at College Road, found a truck bound for Hunza.

But in Shimshal, the phone had already rung. Shaheen had been too late even before he'd heard the first rotor blades above the Baltoro. Jehan's death had been reported to his mother, Nazib, on August 3, and, later that evening, another call had come in. By daybreak, nearly everyone in the village knew that Karim had died—everyone, it seemed, except Karim's wife, Parveen. No one had had the stomach to tell her about the second call confirming her husband's death, so Parveen assumed that Karim had survived. "After hearing what had happened to Jehan, I felt I had to see Karim right away," she recalled. So Parveen had decided to leave Shimshal and meet Karim along the Karakorum Highway. "That way, I could see my husband a day sooner."

At 7 a.m. on August 4, she waited on the mud stoop next to her general store, desperate to catch a lift. The bus, a battered military jeep, came on time, but the driver, Merza Aman, told Parveen he wasn't driving through the gorge until 11 a.m. "It was the lie of a good man," Parveen recalled. "Merza wanted to save me the trip." At 10:45 a.m., Parveen returned to the bus stop, unaware that Merza had left at 8 a.m. with his passengers.

Another hour passed. Those who saw her waiting wouldn't make eye contact, and Parveen began to understand. Finally, Didar Ali, a farmer, came to the stoop and told her the truth: Karim had never returned to high camp.

Parveen's first instinct was to reach her children, Umbreen, Abrar, and Rahmin. She ran to their elementary school. When she walked into the classroom, Parveen didn't have to ask whether her children had been told the news by classmates. Their faces said it all.

▲ ▲ ▲

At the Fearless Five base, Marco was lifted from Masood's chopper into the backseat of a military van. The Italian nodded off, unsure of his surroundings, until he woke in front of a dusty playground with swings and a canary-yellow seesaw. Squat buildings on the periphery resembled concession stands at a fairground. Painted in candy-apple red, the sign on one building read MORTUARY. Another cautioned: OPERATING THEATRE. NO ENTRY. VISITORS NOT ALLOWED. This was the Combined Military Hospital in Skardu.

Nurses helped Marco out, lowered him into a wheelchair, and pushed him into the operating theatre. The bright room smelled rancid, a mixture of renal failure and nail-polish remover. Following faded instructions taped to the wall, the nurses lowered Marco's feet into tubs of lukewarm salt water and told him the pain would get worse.

Within an hour, reporters from the local stations, now working as correspondents for international media, had pushed past the NO VISITORS sign on the swinging door. They fended off doctors ordering them to leave and mobbed Marco's cot, shoving microphones under his chin. The reporters tossed Marco questions, snapped photos of his feet, and videotaped his grimaces. Marco, communicating in rudimentary English, was so exhausted he could barely make sense. But he was photogenic enough for the Associated Press, and his sentence fragments, strung together by reporters, managed to offend and enthrall. "I was surprised by his interview," South Korean climber Go Mi-sun later wrote in an e-mail to Ger's family. "Marco had a mental breakdown."

Media outlets around the world picked up the story. Many romanticized the horror and misrepresented important details. It was widely reported, for instance, that Pasang's cousin Jumik had learned of his son's birth during a satellite phone call from the summit. That is fiction, according to Jumik's wife. In the *New York Times*, a front-page article about the disaster displayed a photo of Gasherbrum IV—the wrong mountain. *ExplorersWeb*, the insiders' website for mountaineering news, ran a column titled "K2's Double Tragedy," castigating Base Camp bloggers for releasing premature casualty lists that traumatized some victims' families.

The disaster captured the attention of viewers around the world. In London, Jerry del Missier, the president of Barclays Capital, was engineering the "Deal of the Century," the acquisition of Lehman Brothers, involving $47.4 billion in securities and $45.5 billion in trading liabilities. He took a break to send worried e-mails to Kathmandu. Jumik Bhote was his friend and had climbed with him. In Dublin, President Mary McAleese, a fan of Ger's, released a statement consoling his family: "Following so closely on their righteous pride, and that of the country, at Gerard becoming the first Irish person to scale K2, it is truly heartbreaking that they must now contemplate the loss of a beloved son and brother." She dispatched a diplomat from Tehran to meet Ger's family in Pakistan. In Islamabad, Vincenzo Prati, Italy's ambassador to Pakistan, prepared a note for Marco: "Hoping you've unwound from your tremendous efforts on K2." The note included an invoice for $10,614, the cost of Marco's airlift.

The press, meanwhile, vied for the chance to interview Wilco. Inside the lobby of Islamabad's Regency Hotel, the Dutchman hunkered below a crystal chandelier and rested his bandaged feet on a Louis Quatorze chair. He tried to be polite as reporters swarmed over him, but his mind was still on the mountain. *What do these people know about fighting for your life?* he thought, while the cameras flashed. He held up his bandaged hands, as requested. "I guess it's showtime," he said.

15

The Next Life

As the survivors returned to Islamabad, Pakistan's Ministry of Tourism invited them to the Committee Room of the Green Trust Tower. A press release stated that government officials were hosting a "tea party" on August 8 to "pay tribute to the heroes who took part in this noble rescue that saved human lives."

At 4 p.m., sixteen guests crammed around a rectangular conference table on the twelfth floor. Fans sliced the air as condensation pooled in the window frames. A bureaucrat passed around crackers and bottled water, and, despite the swelter, poured steaming tea. He gave the climbers gifts: lapel pins enameled with Pakistan's flag and picture books of alpine flora.

The room hushed as Dr. Shahzad Qaiser, secretary of the Ministry of Tourism, slid behind a makeshift podium. Sweating in a suit and tie, Qaiser read from prepared remarks. He commended the rescuers for their courage, thanked the people of Pakistan for their hospitality, and apologized as though K2's seracs had fallen in violation of ministry protocol. He and everyone else around the table had a patchy understanding of the events and limited insight from the Pakistani mountaineers, who were not present to explain what they had done. Of the lead team, only Pasang Lama and Pemba Gyalje attended the tea party.

As Qaiser spoke, Nazir Sabir—the Hunza mountaineer and president of the Alpine Club of Pakistan—sat at the opposite end of the room, wishing the tourism secretary would make it fast. Nazir had a headache from arguing with Alpha Insurance agents about Jehan Baig's policy. His printer had run out of ink, so he couldn't produce the summit certificates that the climbers wanted to frame. Everyone knew our party was a farce, he recalled. The ministry couldn't smooth over the loss of eleven lives by serving tea and cookies. When Dr. Qaiser finished speaking and sat down, nobody clapped.

When it was Wilco's turn to speak, he didn't try to stand on his frostbitten feet. His cheeks, crusted over from exposure, had sunk inward, and his fingertips were starting to swell into purple grapes. He waved a bandaged hand at Nazir. "You need to train your high-altitude porters," he snapped.

Wilco was among several survivors who felt that the Pakistanis had failed him. Some blamed Shaheen Baig, accusing him of feigning his illness. As more facts surfaced, Wilco came to a better understanding, but his perspective at that moment reflected a widespread stereotype. "Pakistani high-altitude porters are not the right kind of climbers for K2," he said. "They are just too lazy to do the work."

Nazir tried to keep the tone civil: "Some of our high-altitude porters aren't as trained as Sherpas, but we are not ashamed of them," he said. "They are not expected to do everything, and you cannot blame them for every problem." No one had debriefed the Pakistanis yet, he reminded his guests, and speculation was fueling a blame game.

Sitting to the right of Nazir, Brigadier M. Bashir Baz, the head of Askari Aviation, chimed in. "Pakistan treated you well," he shouted at the Europeans. "Some of you did not pay for evacuations, but we picked you all up. Your mistakes cost Pakistan a great deal of money."

Disgusted, Nazir forgot Wilco and turned on Baz. How could Askari Aviation lecture his distraught guests about the bill? Nazir got in his face, and the two men shouted at each other in Urdu. Someone restrained Nazir, yanking him away from the brigadier. Sixty-five-year-old Ashraf Aman, the first Pakistani to summit K2, then sprang out of his seat like a jack-in-the-box. He shouldered his way toward the brigadier. "This is a tea party," he pleaded.

Someone threw a punch, and Ashraf tackled the brigadier. Ministry bureaucrats dove between the two and pried them apart. Unexpectedly, Mr. Kim kicked back his chair and lunged at Wilco. You maligned me to the Korean media, he charged. Wilco had done no such thing. Ministry bureaucrats pulled Kim off the bewildered Dutchman.

By then, Nazir had seen enough. He stormed into the hallway. Mr. Kim followed and jumped in front of him, blocking his way and stuttering something in Korean. You don't understand what we're going through, Kim's expression seemed to say.

Nazir said nothing. His brother had been buried by an avalanche on Mount Diran, a peak he could see every morning from his driveway. I've lost fifty-eight close friends and a brother to the mountains, Nazir thought to himself. He shoved past Kim and stomped down twelve flights of stairs. The tea party was over.

▲ ▲ ▲

Chhiring avoided the receptions. After trekking back from K2, he picked up his summit certificate and boarded an empty flight to Kathmandu. Loneliness pressed in on him. To distract himself, he stared out the window of the plane. In the valley below, the smoke from the brick factories undulated in the air currents like strands of seaweed. When the plane jolted to a stop on the runway, Chhiring grabbed his pack and stepped out into a sheet of rain.

He had not spoken with his wife since leaving for K2, and he prayed Dawa would be waiting inside the terminal. He scanned the corridors of Tribhuvan International, trying to spot her—or anyone he knew. Stray cats swatted dung beetles across the pink marble floors. Bug-eyed TV monitors flickered with snow and cryptic numerals, informing travelers that they had missed the last flight.

Chhiring switched on his cell phone, but the network was over-loaded as usual. Taking a bus to Boudhanath, he trudged home through leech-infested mud, rehearsing what he'd tell his wife. K2 had never been worth it, he planned to tell Dawa. I've always loved you more than any mountain.

When he unlocked the front gate of his house, his white span-iel, Dolkar, whipped his tail so fast it nearly tipped him off-balance. Chhiring gave the dog a pat and, climbing up the stairwell, found his brother, Ngawang, in the rooftop prayer room. But his little brother and the dog were not the ones Chhiring wanted to see most. He wandered down the hallway, through the kitchen, and into the bedroom. His wife was gone.

▲ ▲ ▲

As August wore on and the monsoon moved northward, Big Pasang's widow felt as though she were sinking. On September 6, when a doorman led her into the Hotel de l'Annapurna, Lahmu considered turning around. Inside the hotel's opulent lobby, she felt tense, perched on the edge of a leather couch in front of a man who was blaming himself for the death of her husband.

Mr. Kim was in Kathmandu, preparing to leave for Manaslu,

another 8,000-meter peak. He looked weary. His eyes teared as he provided life-insurance paperwork and helped Lahmu fill it out. Kim, speaking through the interpreter, told Lahmu about the perils of climbing. He told her that he was the president of a mattress company and could not offer much money or ask his sponsor, Kolon Sport, for further support. He handed her a thick envelope with Big Pasang's earnings and a donation from the survivors of the Flying Jump, a sum of about $5,000.

After Lahmu accepted the envelope, Kim appeared to relax. He ordered tea. The interpreter ordered a soda. Kim offered to take Lahmu to a restaurant where the entrées cost more than her month's rent. But Lahmu doubted that her young daughter would accept the breast of the woman caring for her while she was away. Kim shook her hand and left. Lahmu didn't expect to hear from him again.

She didn't hear much from Pasang Lama, either. He had become a pariah in the Bhote family. When Pasang returned from K2, Jumik's older brother, Pemba Jeba, was unsparing. You abandoned my brother to save yourself, he told Pasang. Jumik and Big Pasang are dead, and you're alive. How could you have let this happen?

Pasang avoided his relatives, but he asked himself Pemba Jeba's question, again and again. How could I have let this happen?

"I hate climbing," he told anyone who would listen. He found himself in a bar drinking *chang* so cheap it didn't have a name. It tasted like lye, and he liked it that way; that's what he thought he deserved. A greasy wad of rupees was all he had left over from the climb, and he spent the money as fast as he could, draining jug after jug until he passed out. He woke up in a gutter one morning, filthy and lost, not knowing where he was or where to go. Pasang was convinced he never wanted to see another mountain again.

Two weeks later, he took a job with the Flying Jump and left for Manaslu, the world's eighth-highest peak.

▲ ▲ ▲

Pushing a cart of duffels through Los Angeles International Airport, Nick Rice was just bones wrapped in cellophane. One blogger dubbed him "Freddy Krueger's cousin." Nick's life had been saved by a soggy pair of socks. Now he wanted to gulp down a life-affirming Starbucks Frappuccino, lock his bedroom door, and hide. Hobbling on a bandaged right foot, he plowed through a wall of video cameras and microphones. "Twenty-seven interviews so far," he said in response to a question from TMZ, adding that he intended to return to K2 whenever he could find a sponsor.

Many climbers faced a similar spectacle—so much so that, in Holland, Cas van de Gevel had to plan an escape. "Wilco, good luck with all this media shit," he told his friend before flying south to meet his girlfriend in Málaga. "I hope they never find me."

Cecilie, devastated by the death of her husband, had difficulty getting out of bed. When she could, she paced the beach near Stavanger, Norway, and watched waves beat the shore. "The pain was physical, too," she explained. "Every part of me hurt, every muscle." Gradually, she started to run on the sand, "so I didn't have to think." Each day, she ran farther and faster. Eighteen months later, she had completed the first unsupported, unassisted crossing of Antarctica.

Marco adapted to fame better than the others. As Italian journalists reported his amputations—"my little pedicure," as he put it—his cell phone twitched with texts and his inbox filled with fan mail. He moved out of his mother's place and purchased a hot tub with rotating jets and a bed with a mirror on the canopy. The media attention turned him into a toeless sex symbol. His story was covered in newspaper articles, television specials, talk-show appearances, two book deals, and a five-page spread in *Vanity Fair*, which featured Marco performing planche push-ups over a lead pipe. The Italian Olympic athletes association awarded him a medal for heroism. Dolce & Gabbana inquired whether he would model underwear; Italian housewives nearly swooned in anticipation.

But Marco had alienated Pemba Gyalje, the Sherpa who had saved his life. In Marco's memoir, he characterized Pemba as a porter, not an equal, and misidentified him as "Pemba Girgi." Scrutiny intensified when Pemba complained to Shaheen Baig's climbing partner, Simone Moro, in a searing four-hour interview. Moro, in turn, dissected Marco's errors on K2 for the newspaper *Corriere della Sera*.

Pemba's interview with Simone "made my mama cry," Marco recalled. He considered himself "persecuted like Bonatti," the Italian martyr of K2—until he flew to Kathmandu to visit Jumik Bhote's mother. Gamu Bhoteni met him beside a frog pond at the Hotel Mala. With her was Jen Jen, her grandson. Marco was moved. "Holding Jumik's baby was one of the great privileges of my life," he said. "I told Jen Jen, 'I wish I'd been strong enough to bring your papa home.'"

Gamu asked to see Marco's stubs, and he unlaced his sneakers. She examined the amputations briefly, then waited for him to pull on his socks. "You are fortunate, sir," she said. "You can conceal your sorrow inside your shoes."

Marco nodded and pressed her hand. "K2 was good to me."

Across town, Pemba Gyalje must have felt the same. His double rescue had attracted fame, and visitors to his home in Kathmandu could squish down on the living room sofa and stare up at an effigy of their host: a five-foot-by-three-foot poster of Pemba Gyalje's face on the cover of *National Geographic Adventure*. The magazine had christened him "The Savior."

▲ ▲ ▲

By helping Pasang down the Bottleneck, Chhiring had pulled off one of the most heroic rescues in K2 history; by sacrificing his ice axe and anchoring it to a rope system, Pasang had anonymously prevented many climbers from wandering off-route to their deaths. Both men had played crucial roles in leading the climb and keeping others alive, but hardly anyone knew it.

"The mainstream media focused on the rescues of August second and third," Pemba noted. Those rescues involved Western lives. But the cameras eventually reached the Bhotes in Kathmandu. In January 2009, Pemba Gyalje's agent, Pat Falvey, arrived at the Hotel Marshyangdi with a film crew. Pat was producing a documentary about the tragedy, and Pemba had agreed to conduct the interviews in Nepali. Pat met with the Bhotes, introducing himself as a ragpicker-turned-millionaire.

"I owe Ger this film," Pat told Pasang Lama. Four years earlier, Ger had found Pat dying on Everest and short-roped him down the mountain, saving his life. Now Pat wanted to ensure that Ger received credit for his heroism on K2.

Pat offered to fly the Bhotes to Switzerland to shoot a reenactment on the Eiger. They would wear the same Kolon Sport suits used on K2. Pasang liked the idea and agreed to share his summit footage, but his cousin Pemba Jeba objected. Pemba Jeba didn't know the photo of Jumik's corpse was already making the rounds in one climber's slideshow, but he'd seen enough Hollywood films to fear that Jumik would be depicted by a test dummy leaking red dye and corn syrup. "What do you know about survival?" Pemba Jeba implored Pasang. Gamu, Jumik's mother, had burned her forearms and chest in grief. His widow, Dawa Sangmu, had spent her nights inside the same Kolon Sport sleeping bag that Jumik had taken to K2. Their infant, Jen Jen, would never know his father.

Pemba Jeba snatched the summit footage. "I am saving this video for Jen Jen," he said.

Pasang didn't try to justify himself. "My life didn't make sense anymore," he recalled. He had survived K2 but wasn't sure he could survive now. The crime of survival weighed upon him. It was the guilt of breathing when other men—better ones, he felt—no longer could.

During the filming, Pasang met Chhiring for the first time since August. He thanked him, but the pain was transparent. Pasang's spirit seemed to be cannibalizing his body. He smelled sour, of beer and sweat, and spoke in monosyllables. Chhiring, unsure what to say, invited him to go climbing.

▲ ▲ ▲

Under the skylight of the great hall, Parveen, Karim's widow, served Nazir Sabir tea and *chilpindok,* a flatbread soaked in melted goat cheese. As they waited for Jehan's mother to join them, Nazir thanked her. "I wanted to come to Shimshal to pay my respects to you," said the Alpine Club president. The house filled with mourners; soon it was standing room only. Finally, Nazir broke the silence. He asked how the families were doing.

For a time, no one spoke. Then Karim's father, Shadi, broke down. "I've been cut in half," he said. "I hide my grief in front of my grandchildren, but they see it. They feel it."

Karim's four-year-old, Rahmin Ullah, skimmed the air with a toy Pan Am jet, as his grandfather spoke. "He still believes his father will return from K2," Shadi explained.

Children are the most affected when their fathers leave for the mountains, Muhammad Raza, the local schoolteacher, told Nazir. The students become distracted in class and silent during recess. They spend too much time alone. As climbing season ends, they start to laugh again, and they listen for the rumble of jeeps along the riverbed. Once their fathers are safely home, he said, "The children become themselves again."

For the children whose fathers would not return, it was different. Jehan's son, Asam, had borrowed a cassette player. The boy spent hours alone, listening to a tape he had made. "Long live my father," the tape repeated. "Long live brave Jehan." The ten-year-old had become withdrawn, said Nazib, his grandmother.

Jehan's youngest son, eight-year-old Zehan, had grown to resent Western expeditions that employ Shimshalis. When his grandmother was discussing the downturn in tourism, the boy had blurted out: "I hate foreigners. Why do they come to climb mountains and kill our fathers?"

The elders worried for the children but had no solution except the passage of time. No one had dealt with deaths like these. Karim and Jehan were the first Shimshalis to die in modern mountaineering. The community had banded together to help the widows, but for some, it was hard even to look at the White Horn, where Karim and Jehan had learned to climb. Shaheen Baig found the memories so unbearable that he had quit mountaineering for a time and left Shimshal to work as an oil prospector in the Taliban-occupied North-West Frontier Province.

Nazir nodded, knowing he could do little else but listen. And even that felt inadequate, for soon the families had nothing more to say. The great hall became quiet. Nazir cupped his hands, lifting them toward the skylight. He tried to compose himself, but soon he wept openly with Shadi. Struggling to keep his voice steady, he twice recited the Surah Ikhlas, a Quranic verse, for the lost men:

> Say: He is Allah, the One and Only.
> God, the Eternal, Absolute.
> He begets not, nor is He begotten.
> And there is none like Him.

After the prayer, almost all the men were sobbing. Grief made it hard for Shadi to stand. Nazir supported him, helping him rise. Out-

side, the sun tinted White Horn's glacier a brassy gold. Nazir realized
he'd have to leave soon or navigate the Shimshal gorge in the dark.
Shadi led him down the irrigation channel, along the jeep track, to
the place he'd last seen his son.

▲ ▲ ▲

As the disaster on K2 was unfolding, Dawa tried to follow the online
reports. Sometimes Chhiring's wife asked tourists at Internet cafés to
decipher the news. Otherwise, she had to guess what *ExplorersWeb*
was reporting in a foreign language she couldn't read. Kathmandu's
electrical grid fizzled daily, for eight hours at a time, so Dawa often
went without any news at all. She had to go on instinct and tended to
imagine the worst.

The stress of the expedition had been too much. She'd needed to
get her mind off K2, so she had stayed with German friends while her
daughters attended summer school. But in the first days of August,
even fast Wi-Fi couldn't confirm whether Chhiring was among the
living. Newspapers listed sherpa fatalities but typically failed to provide names.

"The only time I didn't suffer was when I was asleep," she said.
She tried calling Chhiring's brother Ngawang, to see whether he'd
heard anything, but the circuits were overloaded. In early August, still
unsure what had happened and unable to reach anyone who could tell
her, Dawa summoned her courage and headed home.

As she opened the gate, Dolkar the spaniel yelped and spun in
circles, charging ahead to alert his master. Moments later, Dawa was
reunited with her husband. She wanted to reproach Chhiring for
going to K2 against her wishes, but she couldn't do it. She was too
grateful to see him alive. As Chhiring told her a sanitized version of
the climb, Ngawang gathered up relatives and neighbors, and soon a

dozen people had arrived. Instead of debating love and death, Dawa found herself snatching fermenting socks off the rug, chopping vegetables, and scrambling to host a party. Things were back to normal.

But not everything was the same. Chhiring now considered mortality when he deliberated about future expeditions. As anticipated, his ascent of K2 netted a sponsorship offer to climb another deadly peak, Nanga Parbat. Chhiring declined it. Instead, he decided to spend the summer with his family and climb Makalu, a statistically safer mountain, with two Swedes. Dawa appreciated the compromise and set forth her terms: "Stay away from Annapurna, K2, and Nanga Parbat"—the most dangerous mountains—"and you may climb Everest and the others."

Chhiring agreed. Survival had given him strong resolve to hold onto Dawa and the rest of his family and friends. Perhaps this was why, for a second time, Chhiring couldn't leave Pasang Lama behind. He was taking him along to Makalu. Dawa considered it a good partnership, and when Chhiring and Pasang left for the mountain, she gave them a tepid blessing.

▲ ▲ ▲

At Makalu Base Camp, everything reminded Pasang of his cousins. The village where they were born was nearby, two days on foot. While dicing potatoes for dinner, Pasang had a dim memory of Jumik hiding boiled potatoes from his mother; while exploring the foothills, Pasang thought of a hot spring where the cousins used to bathe; while preparing gear for the summit assault, he remembered how Big Pasang first showed him an artificial claw he dubbed "the crampon."

One afternoon before the Makalu summit bid, Pasang and Chhiring huddled around a stove, heating beer in a pot. Pasang spoke of his most recent climb with the Flying Jump on Manaslu. His family had called him a collaborator. "They tried to stop me from working for the Flying Jump again, but I didn't listen," he told Chhiring. The money was good, and there was a fair chance of getting killed, which seemed attractive at the time. Chhiring asked him if he still felt that way. Pasang put down the mug and, unwilling to say more, studied a rising cloud bank.

The despair that haunted Pasang also unsettled Chhiring. He usually slept soundly at altitude, but that night Pasang heard him tossing. They didn't speak much while climbing to the summit on May 2, and they could barely grin for their clients' victory photos. Pasang turned to Chhiring and tried to point out his village, but Hungung remained smothered in low-lying clouds.

The sky above was a bright celestial blue. As Pasang stalked the summit plateau, he lost a crampon and slipped. Chhiring shot out a hand to grab him, but Pasang slid from his grasp.

Plunging down on his back, Pasang felt more freedom than fear. He gripped his axe and, for a split second, still had a choice. What he chose surprised him. "I decided I didn't want to miss this life," he recalled. "Would the next be any better?" He wasn't ready to find out, so, twisting onto his stomach, he hacked his axe into the slope. His body fishtailed and skidded to a halt. Choked on adrenaline, Pasang stood up and smiled. The rush had cleared his head, and, on his way down from the summit, he had an idea. "I need to climb every 8,000-meter peak," Pasang confided to Chhiring.

"Don't get married," his friend advised, "until you've bagged all fourteen."

On the descent, their Swedish clients had a crazy inspiration, too: take a hot shower in town, then go for a second 8000er. Soon, Chhiring, Pasang, and the Swedes were making a beeline for Lhotse, Everest's conjoined twin. Eighteen days later, all four were on the top, completing the fastest doubleheader of the season.

From the summit of Lhotse, Chhiring pointed southwest to Rol-waling, the place where his mother had died and his father had gone mad, the valley he'd left to become a porter. He told Pasang what the elders used to say: The world began in Rolwaling, and it would end there. Then it would begin again.

Acknowledgments

This tragic climb impacted many lives, and we owe a special debt to the survivors who shared their experiences, as well as those family members who spoke about the loved ones claimed by K2. Patient with our questions and generous with their time, they helped us understand a more complete story. Heartfelt thanks to:

Qudrat Ali, Guldana Baig, Khanda Baig, Nazib Baig, Shaheen Baig, Ngawang Bhote, Pemba Jeba Bhote, Phurbu Bhote, Dawa Sangmu Bhoteni, Gamu Bhoteni, Lahmu Bhoteni, Phurbu Chejik Bhoteni, Hoselito Bite, Marco Confortola, Muhammad Hussein, Chris Klinke, Pasang Lama, Tsering Lama (Chhiring Bhote), Nela Mandić, Gisela Mandić, Roberto Manni, J. J. McDonnell, Margaret McDonnell, Parveen Meherban, Shadi Meherban, Eric Meyer, Lars Nessa, Damien O'Brien, Denise O'Brien, Iso Planić, Nick Rice, Nadir Ali Shah, Chhiring Dorje Sherpa, Ngawang Sherpa, Ngawang Thundu Sherpa, Pemba Gyalje Sherpa, Dawa Sherpani, Cecilie Skog, Annie Starkey, Fredrik Sträng, Cas van de Gevel, Wilco van Rooijen, Pedja Zagorac, and Alberto Zerain.

Mountaineering historians Jim Curran, Ed Douglas, Jennifer Jordan, and Ed Webster offered insightful comments and corrections to the manuscript. It was a privilege to get to know some of the primary sources and their family members from historic K2 climbs, including Erich Abram, Liaquat Ali, Sultan Ali, Zulfiqar Ali, Ashraf Aman,

Haji Baig, Lino Lacedelli, Jamling Tenzing Norgay, Leonardo Pagani, Tony Streather, and Bruno Zanettin.

We couldn't have understood many important sources without a team of excellent translators. Thank you to Rehmat Ali, Ragnhild Amble, Aleksandra Basa, Hussn Bibi, Erik Brakstad, Snighda Dhungel, Oddvar and Anne Hoidal, Paola Meggiolaro, Paolo Padoan, Aava Shrestha, Gava Shrestha, and Ester Speggiorin.

For providing us with important information and helping us out, we'd especially like to thank: Suleman Al Faisal, Ahmad Ali, Qudrat Ali, Zaman Ali, Ashraf Aman, Dee Armstrong, Judy Aull, Raj Bajgain, Banjo Bannon, M. Bashir Baz, Seanan Brennan, Joëlle Brupbacher, Eddie Burgess, Dana Comella, Marty Davis, Jerry del Missier, Karen Dierks, George Dijmarescu, Fred Espenak, Pat Falvey, Yan Giezendanner, Asif Hayat, Soukat Hayat, Brian Hogan, Lance Hogan, Shah Jehan, Katie Keifer, David Kelly, Sher Khan, Sultan Khan, Gourish Kharel, Richard Klein, Sonia Knapp, Dorie Krahulik, Joe Krahulik, Ab Maas, Caroline Martin, Major Aamir Masood, Dan Mazur, Dean Miller, Simone Moro, Colm Ó Snodaigh, Rónán Ó Snodaigh, Rossa Ó Snodaigh, Dr. Simon Outhwaite, Mario and Rosina Padoan, Dan Possumato, Nathaniel Praska, Jake Preston, Ronnie Raymar, Muhammad Raza, Syed Amir Raza, Joe Reichert, Rebecca Rice, David Roberts, Alexander Rokoff, John Roskelley, Richard Salisbury, Araceli Segarra, Janmu Sherpa, Jigmeet Diki Sherpa, Ngawang Oser Sherpa, Pasang Sherpa, Tshering Mingma Sherpa, Shujaat Shigri, Tina Sjogren, Tom Sjogren, Ryan Smith, Sam Speedie, Jelle Staleman, Matt Szundy, Hirotaka Takeuchi, Dana Tredway, Mueen Uddin, Maarten van Eck, Jaffer Wazir, Freddie Wilkinson, Yaqub, Ellen Zuckerman, and Katie Zuckerman.

Special thanks to: University of Maryland professor of anthropology Janice Sacherer, an authority on Rolwaling, for reviewing the book for accuracy and sharing with us her original research, which will be published as an academic ethnography; Cambridge University professor Hildegard Diemberger, for discussions about Buddhist religion and mythology and the Bhote culture; Professor Cynthia Beall of Case Western Reserve University, for discussions of her genetics studies; the late Dr. Klaus Dierks, for his photographs of Rolwaling; Jean-Michel Asselin, for his photographs of Chhiring during his first Everest expedition; Kunda Dixit, editor of the *Nepali Times*, for sharing his knowledge of Nepal's political history; Dr. Michael Su, for answering our medical questions; mountaineer Jamie McGuinness, for reviewing the manuscript many times and improving accuracy throughout; Nazir Sabir, for insightful analysis and for facilitating our interviews in Pakistan; documentary filmmaker Nick Ryan, for his tireless collaboration; Wilco van Rooijen and Lars Nessa, for reading the manuscript in advance of publication; Kelly McBride, a journalism ethics expert at the Poynter Institute, for providing advice on how to make the best writing and reporting decisions; the Multnomah County Library and the American Alpine Club reference librarians, for helping track down obscure books and articles; Brian Wannamaker and the Falcon Art Community, for providing Peter with a work space and a fun, supportive environment in which to write; the Corporation of Yaddo, for granting Amanda a residency and providing her with a sanctuary to write; Adrian Kitzinger, for creating our maps; and Kathleen Brandes, for fearlessly copyediting our manuscript.

Our agents, Stephen Barr and Dan Conaway, picked forty pages out of the slush pile at Writers House and brought this book to life. Their guidance has been invaluable. Our editor, Tom Mayer, steered us with insight and good sense. His dedication to our book brings to mind Saint Jerome.

Our writing process involves a degree of self-mortification as we rewrite each other. This would not have been possible without the majesty of Google Docs, which allowed us to collaborate closely even when we were thousands of miles apart.

Peter's partner, Sam Adams; Amanda's husband, Paolo; and Amanda's sons, Eli and Matteo, all deserve special recognition. Their love and patience were unwavering.

Background Notes

The notes below provide additional background information about this book and our research. When multiple versions of a story existed—as they frequently did—we chose the interpretations that best fit the verifiable facts. For the folklore based on historical events, we checked known facts but related the storytellers' perspective as well. We hope that we have made clear, within the text itself, when we are speculating and what supports that speculation. We maintained editorial control, but K2 survivors Wilco van Rooijen and Lars Nessa reviewed the manuscript for accuracy. Others—such as anthropologists Cynthia Beall and Janice Sacherer; alpine historians Ed Douglas, Jennifer Jordan, and Jamling Tenzing Norgay; *Nepali Times* editor Kunda Dixit; and mountaineer Jamie McGuinness—scrutinized specific sections pertaining to their areas of expertise and, in some instances, reviewed the book in its entirety. After the manuscript was completed, we returned to Nepal with interpreters and reviewed it with Chhiring and Pasang for accuracy.

Just as climbers have conflicts of interest, writers do, too. Before the disaster, Amanda knew several characters, including Marco and Karim, who was her high-altitude porter on Broad Peak in 2004.

Peter quickly found out that being an effective journalist in Nepal and Pakistan is far more complicated than practicing traditional newspaper journalism in the United States. Although reporters are generally expected to avoid getting involved with a story, Peter lived with Chhiring and Pasang and spent about two months trekking with them to their villages, interviewing their friends and families, and gathering information while hiking, hanging out, and learning the art of mountaineering.

Some of the characters went out of their way to help us gather information. Nazir Sabir arranged interviews, and we hired his trekking company to help us get around Pakistan. Damien O'Brien, Gerard McDonnell's brother-in-law, became our friend, and he shared photographs and recordings from the expedition and his original research. Chhiring and Pasang put their lives on hold so Peter could go with them to their villages. Shaheen Baig did the same for Amanda in Shimshal. We agreed to reimburse them for their time and expenses, based on the equivalent rates set by trekking companies, so we could spend as much time with them as necessary during the three years it has taken to complete this book. We did not ask for exclusivity to their story. After completing most major interviews, we wanted to help the families and communities of those who were lost on the mountain. We discussed how to do so with Chhiring and Pasang and decided to donate a part of the proceeds of this book to the Gerard McDonnell Memorial Fund, a trust directed by the McDonnell family for the education of the Bhote, Meherban, and Baig children, and, through other charities, help the communities of Chhiring and Pasang.

We relied on photos, videos, and site visits for location descriptions. When we couldn't reach a certain place, such as the Bottleneck of K2, we had the characters take us to locations with a similar look and feel. In some instances, we asked interviewees to reenact what happened. We also observed several reenactments on the Eiger by Chhiring, Pasang, Tsering Bhote, and Pemba Gyalje while Nick Ryan's documentary was being filmed. For the descriptions of the trek to K2, Amanda had trekked this route in 2004. We relied on her recollections, in addition to interviews and photos. Sound descriptions are based on what characters remembered hearing or recordings from the actual events.

We adapted some words to English phonetics. For consistency and readability, we refer to the same person by the same name throughout the book, even when that name sometimes changed because of the cultural context. In a few instances, we use sources' nicknames or alternative spellings because their first and last names were identical to those of other characters. Many places above 8,000 feet in Nepal have both Tibetan and Nepali names. When there were multiple names for a place, we applied the name used locally.

For biographical research, we received help from photojournalists who captured images of Chhiring's childhood and teen years. These images from Jean-Michel Asselin and the late Dr. Klaus Dierks complemented the anthropological research of University of Maryland professor Janice Sacherer, who studied Rolwaling during the period of Chhiring's childhood, and the mythology studies of University of Cambridge professor Hildegard Diemberger, who studied the cultures of the Upper Arun Valley during the period of Pasang's childhood.

For the action sequences and dialogue exchanges, we relied on interviews conducted with witnesses separately and, when possible, together, asking them what they said and did. When film footage of the incidents was available, we used their recorded words. The majority of the interviews were conducted in the sources' native languages. We relied on interpreters and, for ease of reading, all the quotes were translated into English.

PROLOGUE: THE DEATH ZONE

The descriptions of the climb down the Bottleneck in this chapter (and in chapters 11 and 12) come from the recollections of Chhiring, Pasang, and Pemba. We also viewed photographs and videos of this location.

5 **"at the beach"** Mine Dumas, quoted in Hugues's memorial blog.

1: SUMMIT FEVER

The descriptions of Beding and Chhiring's childhood are from interviews with him and his family during Zuckerman's three-week trek to Rolwaling in 2009 and subsequent interviews with the authors in Kathmandu in 2009 and 2010. The standard version of Beding's history, and much of the Rolwaling history, comes from correspondence with Professor Janice Sacherer and her writings.

12 **"like a yam between two boulders"** According to King Prithvi Narayan Shah, founder of the Shah dynasty in Nepal.

13 **job description** According to the common usage, *sherpa* means a high-altitude mountain worker of any ethnicity, and the word is spelled with a lowercase *S* to distinguish it from the ethnicity, which is spelled with an uppercase *S*.

13 **150,000 Sherpas** Government of Nepal Central Bureau of Statistics. *2001 Nepal Census, Population by Caste/Ethnic Groups.* The most recent ethnic-group–specific census was conducted in 2001, when the Sherpa population was 125,738 and .64 percent of the total population; 150,000 is an estimate for 2008.

13 **Rolwaling Sherpi tamgney** See Janice Sacherer, "Sherpa Kinship and Its Wider Implications," in *Han Language Research—34th Session of the International Han Ji-no-kura Language and Linguistics Conference Proceedings* (Beijing: Zhaojia Wen Feng Shi National Press, 2006), pp. 450–57.

14 **astonishing amounts of potatoes** In 1977, Sacherer did a study in which she calculated that an average Rolwaling family who ate nothing but potatoes most days of the year would consume approximately twelve pounds a day, for a diet of 6,000 calories. The potato represented a revolution in food security with three times the calorific value of barley, the Sherpas' alternative crop.

14 **giant horse and plow** This is according to Rolwaling's oral tradition, dating back to 1870. See Janice Sacherer, "Rolwaling: A Sacred Buddhist Valley in Nepal," in Rana P. B. Singh, ed., *Sacredscapes and Pilgrimage Systems* (New Delhi: Shubhi Publications, 2010), pp. 153–74. The written tradition differs. Tibetan texts of the thirteenth century describe *beyuls* as always present on earth but rendered invisible by Guru Rinpoche's powers of meditation to preserve them until sanctuary was needed.

14 **center of the universe** This is based on the version told by Ngawang Thundu Sherpa, Chhiring's father. As he recounted the legend, relatives and friends interjected with elaborations. Some parts of this story are based on these elaborations.

16 120 years old The actual mortality rate in Rolwaling was much starker during Chhiring's childhood. According to a 1973 survey of Beding, preadolescent mortality was 28 percent, and hardly anyone lived past seventy. Death in childbirth, disease, hunger, and nutritional deficiency were commonplace. See Ove Skjerven, "A Demographic and Nutritional Survey of Two Villages in the Upper Rolwaling Valley," *Kailash: Journal of Himalayan Studies* (Kathmandu) 3, no. 3 (1975).

16 land of three borders The Buddhist text, *Tseringmi Kangsu*, makes reference to Takar Dolsangma's flight to a mountain in a northern region that straddles three borders. Rolwaling *lama* Ngawang Oser Sherpa believes this mountain to be K2. The Tibetan translation of Chogori (possibly *Chomo go ri*), as well as the nearby Chogo Lungma (*Chomogori lungma*) Glacier, invokes five mountain deities, likely the Tseringma sisters.

17 Hrita Sherpa This is based on Sacherer's research.

17 "most isolated, traditional and economically backward" Janice Sacherer, "The Recent Social and Economic Impact of Tourism in a Remote Sherpa Community," in Christoph von Fürer-Haimendorf, ed., *Asian Highland Societies: An Anthropological Perspective* (New Delhi: Sterling, 1981), pp. 157–67. Sacherer gives a comprehensive description of the local economic forces.

19 Pem Phutar See photo included in this book. Chhiring's paternal grandfather had been a porter for the Merseyside Himalayan Expedition in 1955. After this service, Pem received a commendation letter, which he kept inside a box at his home in Rolwaling. This family history came as a surprise to Chhiring, who discovered the letter in 2011. Pem had never told his son—Chhiring's father—about his experience as a porter. Of Pem, expedition leader C. P. Booth wrote: "He has carried heavy loads over difficult country and has proved to be a safe and steady porter under the most adverse conditions."

19 two members of the 1934 expedition The men who abandoned the Sherpas on Nanga Parbat were actually Austrian but their German-run expedition was blamed. The tales of unlucky Germans appear to have surfaced in modern Sherpa folklore during the late 1930s.

20 "remain a virgin" John Roskelley, *Last Days* (Mechanicsburg, PA: Stackpole Books, 1991). Roskelley actually had more than one goddess to contend with. The mountain is shared by up to five Buddhist goddesses, one on each of the five summits seen from Beding, as well as two Hindu gods, as evidenced by the two summits seen from Kathmandu. Shiva, also known as Shankar, resides on the highest summit, sharing it with Tseringma. Parvati (Gauri), Shiva's consort, occupies the second highest summit with one of Tseringma's sisters. Roskelley trampled on the highest summit, presumably offending the two most powerful deities—Shiva and Tseringma.

20 ill effects from the climb John Roskelley was unaware that his climbing partner, Dorje, had objected for religious reasons. He believes his conquest of Gauri Shankar and the subsequent flash flood were unrelated.

20 **The third died** Personal correspondence, Professor Janice Sacherer, October 2011. See also "Tsho Rolpa, GLOFS, and the Sherpas of Rolwaling Valley: A Brief Anthropological Perspective," Mountain Hazards, Mountain Tourism e-conference, 2006.

21 **If driving rules exist** See "Traffic Fatalities in Nepal," *Journal of the American Medical Association* 291, no. 21 (June 2, 2004).

21 **World Health Organization standards** See Sumit Pokhrel, "Climatology of Air Pollution in Kathmandu Valley, Nepal" (master's thesis, Southern Illinois University Edwardsville, May 2002).

24 **up this high** This encounter is based on Chhiring's recollection.

26 **twenty-three permanent residents** This was the population of Beding when Zuckerman visited in spring 2009 during the trekking season. The population is higher at other times of the year.

26 *Playboy* **centerfold** In 2006, Playmate Martyna Wojciechowska summited Everest.

2: DOORWAY TO HEAVEN

This version of the 1939 Fritz Wiessner expedition was interpreted by elders in Rolwaling, but we supplemented the story with details from Wiessner's writings and accounts of alpine historians, including Maurice Isserman, Jennifer Jordan, Andrew Kauffman, William Putnam, and David Roberts. The actions of the climbers are consistent in both accounts. Although Pasang told Wiessner that he saw a supernatural being, historians rarely attribute the problems of the climb to Takar Dolsangma, as Buddhists in Rolwaling do. For information on the 1954 Italian expedition, we interviewed Lino Lacedelli, Erich Abram, and Bruno Zanettin of the 1954 expedition on K2; Leonardo Pagani (son of Guido Pagani of the 1954 expedition); Sultan Ali, Liaquat Ali, and Zulfiqar Ali (son and grandsons of Amir Mehdi of the 1954 expedition); and Haji Baig (friend of Amir Mehdi during their 1953 Nanga Parbat expedition). The description of Chhiring and Dawa's argument comes from several interviews with them in Kathmandu during 2009. The sequence of quotes is from Dawa's recollection, and each quote is what the speaker remembers saying. We also visited the house in Colorado where the argument took place.

28 **highest pass** The Karakorum Pass is 18,290 feet, or 5,575 meters.

28 **affirmed the title** Charles Close et al., "Nomenclature in the Karakoram," *The Geographical Journal* 76, no. 2 (August 1930), pp. 148–58.

29 *Chogori* Correspondence with Sacherer. *Chogo* means "great" and *ri* means "peak" in both Balti and Tibetan. Sacherer proposed another interpretation of *chogo*. In Tibetan, *cho* means "god" and *go* means "door." Balti is a form of archaic Tibetan once written in Tibetan script. Persian script was imposed during the Islamic conversion of Baltistan in the sixteenth century.

31 **averaged 0.7 for the previous decade** The Himalayan Database calculates

the rate based on all those who attempt the peak, not just those who succeed. Although it is common practice, calculating the death rate based on the number of summiters is misleading: "This is sort of like calculating auto death rates by using only the number of drivers and ignoring all the passengers," explains Richard Salisbury of the Himalayan Database. "Death Analysis" in *The Himalaya by the Numbers*.

33 **"most bizarre tragedy"** See Galen Rowell, *In the Throne Room of the Mountain Gods* (San Francisco: Sierra Club Books, 1977). See also Jennifer Jordan, *The Last Man on the Mountain* (New York: W. W. Norton, 2011).

33 **heard a rustle** According to *lamas* who interpret this incident from a Buddhist perspective. Wiessner did not report seeing or hearing a goddess.

33 **"No, sahib"** This is what Wiessner heard Pasang say. Correspondence with David Roberts, who got the quote from his interview with Fritz Wiessner in 1984. The quote also appears in Roberts's *Moments of Doubt and Other Mountaineering Writings* (Seattle: The Mountaineers Books, 1986).

34 **sunbathed nude** Wiessner was sunbathing in the threshold of his tent. It's likely he became sunburned, which would have severely sapped his strength, making the climb the next day all the more grueling. See Jordan, *The Last Man on the Mountain*, pp. 190–91.

34 **"fear of the evil spirits"** Fritz Wiessner, "The K2 Expedition of 1939," *Appalachia* (June 1956).

34 **They turned around** Wiessner left his sleeping bag in camp, intending to use one he thought had been left for him lower down the mountain.

34 **"a funny little noise"** Fritz Wiessner, interview with David Roberts, 1984.

34 **"dug in"** Wiessner interview with Roberts, 1984.

34 **"how stupid"** Wiessner interview with Roberts, 1984.

35 **"sabotaged"** Ed Webster, "A Man for All Mountains: The Life and Climbs of Fritz Wiessner," *Climbing* (December 1988), quoting Wiessner interview.

35 **three rescuers** The fourth member of the rescue team, Tensing Norbu, stayed behind in a lower camp. When the rest of the team never returned, he went down to Base Camp and told others what had happened.

35 **nearly full moon** Wiessner interview with Roberts, 1984.

35 **lunar charts** "Planet Notes for July and August, 1939," *Popular Astronomy* 47 (July 1939), pp. 314–15. (Data courtesy of Maria Mitchell Observatory, Harvard; provided online by NASA Astrophysics Data System.)

35 **bigger problem than a turquoise dragon** Headlamps were invented in 1972 by Petzl. The handheld bulbs that Wiessner and Pasang would have used to light their high camps were too dim for effective night climbing.

37 **"This is it!"** See Maurice Isserman and Stewart Weaver, *Fallen Giants* (New Haven, CT: Yale University Press, 2010), p. 313.

38 **"wiggled himself loose"** Charles Houston interview with Bill Moyers, 2004.

39 fifty years of polemic See Lino Lacedelli and Giovanni Cenacchi. *K2: Il prezzo della conquista* (Milan: Mondadori, 2004).

39 Amir Mehdi He is also sometimes referred to as Amir Mahdi or Mehdi Khan.

39 join their summit bid This is the account Amir Mehdi gave his family when he returned to Hassanabad, Hunza. Interview by the authors, 2009, in Hassanabad, Hunza, with Mehdi's son, Sultan Ali, and grandsons Liaquat Ali and Zulfiqar Ali, and the recollections of Mehdi's friend and fellow porter on Nanga Parbat in 1953, Haji Baig, in Gilgit (interview with Zuckerman, 2009). Bonatti acknowledged that he offered Mehdi a shot at the summit but says this was a trick to motivate him to carry the oxygen bottles.

39 "yelling crazily" Bonatti interview with David Roberts, 2003. Bonatti declined the authors' request for an interview. "I'm 80 years old," he replied, "and tired of talking about the bivouac!" He died in 2011.

39 two sizes too small The Italians had provided army boots for their high-altitude porters, but Mehdi's feet were too big for any of them. The Italians wanted to stretch and cut the boots to fit, but Mehdi objected, fearing this would slash their resale value.

39 sipping chamomile Compagnoni said that he wanted to pitch the tent out of the fall-line of the seracs. Although this sounds plausible, he chose an inconvenient location that was exposed to rockfall.

40 oxygen allegedly ran out See Robert Marshall, *K2: Lies and Treachery* (Herefordshire, UK: Carreg Ltd., 2009). The summit photo shows that the oxygen systems had been carried to the summit. If the bottles had been empty, they would have been discarded as unnecessary weight. The frost on Lacedelli's beard corresponds to the shape of an oxygen mask.

40 "Like an elephant" Erich Abram interview with Paolo Padoan, November 2009.

41 a single summer See Jim Curran, *K2: Triumph and Tragedy* (Boston: Houghton Mifflin Harcourt, 1989). For a survivor's account, see Kurt Diemberger, *The Endless Knot: K2, Mountain of Dreams and Destiny* (Seattle: The Mountaineers Books, 1991).

41 "Conquistadors of the Useless" Lionel Terray used this term for his autobiography, *Conquistadors of the Useless: From the Alps to Annapurna* (Seattle: The Mountaineers Books, 2008, reprint).

42 "more resort than wilderness" See Ed Douglas, "Mount Everest: a not so novel feat," *The Guardian*, May 19, 2010.

43 forty summit-hungry climbers Estimates of the number of summiters who passed Sharp vary.

45 "treat me like a sherpa" Chhiring is using the term *sherpa* (with a lowercase *S*) to mean any high-altitude mountain worker.

3: THE PRINCE AND THE PORTER

The description of the massacre is from the official reports issued by the government of Nepal during the summer of 2001. The initial June 14 report, by a two-member panel of Supreme Court Chief Justice Keshav Prasad Upadhyaya and House Speaker Taranth Ranabha, compiles the testimony of crime-scene investigators and all surviving witnesses. We supplemented our account with a visit to the palace and the massacre memorial site, photos of the crime scene, discussions with Kunda Dixit of the *Nepali Times*, and interviews with Dr. Raghunath Aryal, the royal astrologer who knew many of the victims and was familiar with the locations. We also corroborated these accounts with the BBC Panorama documentary about the massacre, *Murder Most Royal*, and Jonathan Gregson's book, *Massacre at the Palace: The Doomed Royal Dynasty of Nepal* (Talk Miramax, 2002). The quotes are what witnesses heard, and Ketaki Chester's interviews with Kunda Dixit and the BBC were a major source for these quotes. The descriptions of Pasang's childhood are based on interviews with him during Zuckerman's trek to Hungung and the Upper Arun Valley in 2009, and from interviews with his friends, family, and neighbors. The interactions with Ms. Go are based on Pasang's recollections. The description of the Hotel de l'Annapurna is from the authors' observations of the hotel and Pasang's recollection. The authors interviewed Pasang, Ngawang Bhote, and Tsering Bhote about this meeting at the hotel.

48 bloodbath See Jonathan Gregson, *Massacre at the Palace: The Doomed Royal Dynasty of Nepal* (Talk Miramax, 2002). See also *Murder Most Royal*, a BBC Panorama documentary (2002).

49 probably opium According to official investigation reports, Dippy was smoking "a special kind of cigarette prepared with a mixture of hashish and another unnamed black substance." The description and effects match those for "black hash," an opium-and-hashish mixture that the prince liked to smoke. No one tested the exact composition of the joint.

49 lower social standing Not by much. Devyani's mother is a member of the royal family of Gwalior state in India. Queen Aishwarya nevertheless considered the maharajahs of Gwalior to be beneath the royalty of Nepal.

49 stripped of royal status Despite the laws of succession set forth in the constitution, Queen Aishwarya could have "excommunicated" Crown Prince Dipendra just as his uncle, Prince Dhirendra, once had been.

49 high cholesterol King Birendra's last conversation with his wife, Queen Aishwarya, concerned his family's predisposition to high cholesterol.

50 an aunt Princess Ketaki Chester interview with the BBC in 2002. Information from the official report is supplemented by Ketaki Chester's June 2011 interview with Kunda Dixit of the *Nepali Times*.

50 last words "*Ke gareko?*" in Nepali. This is according to official reports and subsequent interviews with witnesses, including Ketaki Chester's 2011 interview with Kunda Dixit.

50 Two relatives Gorakh Rana, the husband of Dipendra's sister, Princess Shruti, and Dr. Rajiv Raj Shahi, the king's nephew, sprang forward to help.

50 "That's enough" "*Pugyo Babu*" in Nepali. *Babu* is a term of endearment for younger brothers, sons, and grandsons in Nepal.

50 from the landing This comes from Ketaki Chester's interview with Kunda Dixit, 2011. It is also possible that Dipendra shot his brother from a position in the garden beside the stairs, according to the official investigation report.

51 surrendered From Ketaki Chester's 2011 interview with Kunda Dixit.

51 shot her in the face Queen Aishwarya's face was so mutilated that a porcelain mask, painted to resemble her, was used during her funeral.

51 released a statement The statement may have been mistranslated or misreported at the time. See Gregson, *Massacre at the Palace*, p. 214.

51 clumsy cover-up See Ketaki Chester's interview with Kunda Dixit. Prime Minister Girija Prasad Koirala consulted with Queen Mother Ratna, who asked that he provide full disclosure to the public. Her instructions were not followed, and the ensuing media blackout allowed conspiracy theories to flourish.

52 "how do you tell your boss" Dr. Raghunath Aryal interview with Padoan in Kathmandu, 2009.

53 "grave human rights crisis" See *Report of the U.N. High Commissioner for Human Rights,* U.N. GAOR, 60th Sess., UN Doc. A/60/359 (2005), available at www.nepal.ohchr.org. See also *Nepal: Heads of Three Human Rights Organizations Call for Targeted Sanctions*, The International Commission of Jurists (April 18, 2006).

53 forced to flee The estimated number of refugees varies from 100,000 to 150,000, according to UNHCR, Human Rights Watch, and Amnesty International.

55 sneak in Interviews in Hungung were conducted by Zuckerman in 2009. As a journalist, he was not permitted in the region, so he snuck in.

56 250 people This estimate is based on Zuckerman's observation during the height of the tourist season in 2009. Others have given different estimates, ranging from fifty to several hundred. The discrepancies may be a result of migration during the tourist season as well as the various meanings of *Hungung*, which, depending on context, can refer to an individual village, a collection of villages, or a region of the Upper Arun Valley.

58 "wasn't safe to stay" This is based on interviews with Pasang's parents in Kathmandu and his relatives and friends in Hungung. The village is now peaceful.

61 publicity stunt Most pundits were other climbers, interviewed by the authors in Kathmandu. Ms. Go was not overtly criticized in mainstream climbing blogs, such as *ExplorersWeb* and *Everest News*. Pasang had a vague understanding of the

244 ▲ BACKGROUND NOTES

controversy surrounding Go, based on his online research and conversations with others, but it's unlikely he knew the level of detail as described here.

62 kept rain out Lahmu Bhoteni, 2009 interview with Padoan at the home Lahmu shared with Big Pasang in Kathmandu.

4: THE CELEBRITY ETHNICITY

For the details on Sherpa genetics, we examined more than twenty studies. Cynthia Beall, professor of anthropology at Case Western Reserve University and an authority on Tibetan genetics, compiled much of the data. Although Beall's research focuses on Tibetan highlanders, she said her research is generalizable to Sherpas. Evolutionarily speaking, Sherpas split from Tibetan highlanders very recently. To make this section easier to understand, we use the term *Sherpa* when, in many instances, the researchers studied Tibetan highlanders. We also interviewed Beall, and this section includes information from ongoing research. For the ethnicity details, we drew extensively from interviews and correspondence with Professor Sacherer and Professor Diemberger. The biography of Tenzing is based on an interview with his son, Jamling Tenzing Norgay, visiting Tenzing's private museum at his home (Ghang La in Darjeeling), viewing his mountaineering gear at the Himalayan Mountaineering Institute Museum in Darjeeling, and library research, with *Tiger of the Snows* by Tenzing Norgay (with James Ramsey Ullman) serving as a primary source and Ed Douglas's *Tenzing: Hero of Everest* serving as our main secondary source.

64 Sherpa® diaperbag These are all real products, and the Sherpa trademark signs are part of the product names as advertised.

65 red-blood-cell count One of the best overviews of the research on this topic is C. M. Beall, "Adaptations to Altitude: A Current Assessment," *Annual Review of Anthropology* 30 (2001), pp. 423–46.

65 populations well adapted to altitude In extreme altitudes, Sherpas' bodies will ramp up red-blood-cell production, but not nearly as much as the bodies of other populations do.

65 dominant genetic trait Researchers have yet to identify the location of this gene, and the Sherpa red blood cells affected by this gene have yet to be compared with red blood cells in other populations.

66 oldest Sherpa clans See Michael Oppitz, "Myths and Facts: Reconsidering Some Data Concerning the Clan History of the Sherpa," *Kailash* 2 (1974), pp. 121–31. When Oppitz wrote the clan history, he used the term *Khamba* throughout. At the time of his paper's publication, he was unaware of the linguistic distinction between *Khampa*, meaning someone from Kham in eastern Tibet, and *Khamba*, meaning a poor, landless wanderer. The latter can be a derogatory term.

66 as much as 30 percent Interview and correspondence with Sacherer, October 2010.

66 naming system The naming system varies among villages and families. The version here is based on the system in Rolwaling.

67 roughly twenty clans The number of clans that are Sherpa is disputed. This number reflects an inclusive definition of the ethnicity. By the narrowest definition, there are only four clans plus a handful of subclans.

68 one of four types of Bhotias See Ed Douglas, *Tenzing: Hero of Everest* (Washington, DC: National Geographic, 2003), p. 6. The four Bhotia ethnic groups are Sikkimese, Sherpas, Drukpas, and Tibetans.

68 the *Mayflower* Sacherer provided this analogy.

68 Good faith Communication with Sacherer based on an unpublished manuscript, "The Sherpas of Nepal: Using Anthropology to Reconstruct History."

69 bloodthirsty barbarians Zuckerman interview with Professor Hildegard Diemberger, University of Cambridge, 2010. Buddhists are not vegetarian, per se. No sin attaches to consuming the flesh of an animal that has died of natural causes. Slaughter, however, is a sin. And, as sin goes, there are varying degrees. Diemberger emphasizes the distinction between slaughter for consumption and sacrificial slaughter. Tibetan Buddhists, including Sherpas, do eat meat of slaughtered animals for essential nutrition, although they feel guilty about it and try to avoid direct responsibility by nudging the animal off a cliff or buying their steak from a Muslim butcher. Slaughter for consumption can be justified from the Buddhist perspective because it provides nourishment for the body, fueling it to perform good deeds. But Sherpas draw the line at sacrificial slaughter, which they regard as a gratuitous waste of life.

69 "stab you in the back" See Douglas, *Tenzing: Hero of Everest*, p. 11.

70 Tsechu, a pilgrimage site The name of the birthplace of Tenzing Norgay has been subject to half a century of translation error. *Tshe-chu*, which means "long-life water" in Tibetan, is a well-known pilgrimage site in the Kharta region. In some biographies of Tenzing Norgay, Tshe-chu was replaced by the word *Cha-chu*, which means "hot mineral springs" in Tibetan. See Ed Webster, *Snow in the Kingdom* (Eldorado Springs, CO: Mountain Imagery, 2000).

71 recruitment hub In the 1930s, Everest was attempted from the north side in Tibet, and the expeditions were exclusively British. Britain had a choke hold on Everest permits thanks to its influence with the Tibetan government.

71 "never get a job" Tenzing Norgay (with James Ramsey Ullman), *Tiger of the Snows* (New York: Putnam, 1955), p. 30.

72 compensate Sherpas preferentially See Douglas, *Tenzing: Hero of Everest*, p. 12.

72 "his attractive grin" See Eric Shipton, *That Untravelled World* (London: Hodder & Stoughton, 1969), p. 97.

73 any mortal Tenzing had also come very close to the summit in 1952 with Swiss partner Raymond Lambert. The duo had reached 28,215 feet, just 813 feet shy of the summit.

73 "single cramponed foot" Jamling Tenzing Norgay and Broughton Coburn, *Touching My Father's Soul* (Harper San Francisco, 2001), p. 93. Other books give slightly different versions of this incident.

74 "like a giant fish" John Hunt, *The Ascent of Everest* (London: Hodder & Stoughton, 1953), p. 209.

74 "A few more whacks" Edmund Hillary, *High Adventure: The True Story of the First Ascent of Everest* (Oxford: Oxford University Press, 2003, anniversary edition), p. 226.

74 "under her wings" We used the version that appeared in the *New York Times*. Tenzing's choice of metaphor also belies his origins. His biographer, Ed Douglas, learned that "hen" is the local name for Everest in the Kharta region.

74 Union Jack Tenzing held up four flags strung in the following order: the United Nations, the United Kingdom, Nepal, and India. The Union Jack is the most visible in the photograph. Tenzing's face was obscured by the oxygen mask. Ed Douglas wrote that this anonymity allowed every nation to project its dreams onto this iconic image.

74 "on television" See Tenzing Norgay, *Tiger of the Snows*, p. 272.

75 press conference. This version of the press conference is from Jamling Tenzing Norgay's recollection of how his father, Tenzing, described it. Contemporary British sources describe Hunt's press conference less critically. Hunt's comments were based, in part, on Hillary's account of having to drag Tenzing up the Hillary Step. No known transcripts exist.

75 "it doesn't matter" Hillary did eventually say that he was first on the summit, but he waited to do so until after Tenzing's death.

76 "draw their knives" See Douglas, *Tenzing: Hero of Everest*, p. 11. James Ramsey Ullman's notes for *Tiger of the Snows* are in the Princeton University Library. Although anthropologists sometimes use the term *Bhotia* to mean a larger grouping of which Sherpas and Tibetans are part, Tenzing is using the term *Bhotia* interchangeably with Tibetan.

5: INSHA'ALLAH

Both authors visited Shimshal in April 2009, and Padoan traveled with Shaheen Baig through northern Pakistan in June 2009. The authors interviewed Shaheen's wife, Khanda, his children, his parents, his close friend Qudrat Ali, his climbing partner Simone Moro, and his employer, Nazir Sabir, as well as the families of Karim and Jehan. The folklore of the region is from stories locals told Zuckerman and Padoan, supplemented with academic studies and Pam Henson's *Shimshal* (Obisan Press, 2006) and *The Women of Shimshal* (Shimshal Publishing, 2010). Many of the details relating to the Baltit Fort are based on the authors' visit to it and interviews with Soukat Hayat of the Baltit Heritage Trust. For descriptions of Younghusband's exploits, we relied on his own accounts in *Wonders of the Hima-*

laya (John Murray, 1924) and *The Heart of a Continent* (John Murray, 1896), as well as Peter Hopkirk's *The Great Game* (John Murray, 1990). We supplemented the research with Patrick French's biography *Younghusband: The Last Imperial Adventurer* (HarperCollins UK, 2004), and *Where Three Empires Meet* (Longmans, Green, 1918) by contemporary historian E. F. Knight. Knight was present during the siege of Hunza as a reporter for British newspapers. Some of the details about the Mir are also from R. C. F. Schomberg, who wrote *Between the Oxus and the Indus* (Lahore: al-Biruni, 1935) and befriended Safdar Ali in exile. For the campaign to defeat the Mir, we also drew from Algernon Durand's *The Making of the Frontier* (London: Thomas Nelson & Sons, 1899). The quotes and details, such as the Mir's conversations with Younghusband, appear in several of these accounts and are based largely on Younghusband's own writings. The physical descriptions are from photographs and the contemporary accounts. For the details of the porter selection process, we interviewed Haji Baig, the only living high-altitude porter of the 1953 Nanga Parbat expedition, and we visited the Durbar below the Baltit Fort where the selection took place. The Mir's ceremonial coat is on display at the Darbar Hunza Hotel. As mentioned above, Padoan climbed with Karim on Broad Peak in 2004, so some of the observations about him are from their interactions. The descriptions of Karim's interactions with his family and his departure for K2 are based on interviews with his wife, Parveen, and his father, Shadi.

79 **a strange creature** For further reading, see Michel Peissel, *The Ants' Gold* (New York: HarperCollins, 1984), in which the author sets out to solve this mystery posed by Herodotus. The legend of the gold-digging ants was popular with Alexander and his troops.

79 **"bigger than foxes"** Herodotus, *The Histories*, 3.102–5.

79 **marmots** Marlise Simons, "Himalayas Offer Clue to Legend of Gold-Digging 'Ants,'" *New York Times*, November 25, 1996.

79 **"the Bride"** Iftikhar Haider Malik, *The History of Pakistan* (Westport, CT: Greenwood Press, 2008).

81 **had to be secured** For further reading, see Peter Hopkirk, *The Great Game* (London: John Murray, 1990).

81 **considered marriage "coercive"** For more details, see Patrick French, *Younghusband: The Last Great Imperial Adventurer* (HarperCollins UK, 2004), p. 283.

82 **"bullets and stones whizzing"** Francis Younghusband, *The Heart of a Continent* (London: John Murray, 1896), p. 228.

83 **vodka and brandy** See Francis Younghusband, *Wonders of the Himalaya* (London: John Murray, 1924), p. 183.

83 **"hereditary failings"** E. F. Knight, *Where Three Empires Meet* (London: Longmans, Green, 1918), p. 350. Knight portrayed Safdar Ali in harsh terms, but the Mir eventually found his apologist. Colonel R. C. F. Schomberg, who befriended Safdar Ali during his exile in Yarkand, claims that at least one instance of fratri-

cide (the killing of a fourth brother in Shimshal) was "self-defense." Schomberg could find no excuse, however, for the other killings. See R. C. F. Schomberg, *Between the Oxus and the Indus* (Lahore: al-Biruni, 1935), p. 153.

83 **"redeeming feature"** Algernon Durand, *The Making of a Frontier* (London: Thomas Nelson & Sons, 1899), p. 230.

83 **"paying blackmail"** Younghusband, *Wonders of the Himalaya*, p. 199.

84 **"soap for his wives"** Younghusband, *Wonders of the Himalaya*, p. 201.

84 **"poor creature"** Younghusband, *Wonders of the Himalaya*, p. 202.

84 **on a platter** Knight, *Where Three Empires Meet*, p. 361.

84 **"pomade and cosmetics"** Knight, *Where Three Empires Meet,* p. 487.

84 **pseudoscientists** See, for example, Ralph Bircher, *The Hunzas: A People without Illness* (Bern: Huber, 1936).

85 **20 rupees** In 1953, the exchange rate for one U.S. dollar was 3.3 Pakistani rupees.

86 **hereditary Mir** Crown Prince Ghazanfar Ali Khan would have ascended the throne in 1976 if Pakistan had not disbanded the kingdom two years earlier and stripped his father of royal status. The Mir's family continues to wield significant political power in the elected government. As a show of respect, the crown prince is called "Mir" by foreign dignitaries.

87 **Wakhi** Wakhi-speaking people of Shimshal are considered a distinct ethnic group from the Hunzas. During the Great Game era, many Hunza raiders employed by the Mir assimilated into Wakhi villages.

87 **taste the summit** Simone Moro was even closer to the summit when he turned around at 2 p.m. In 2011, Moro would pioneer the first winter ascent in the Karakorum on Gasherbrum II.

89 **crystal palace** The mythical palace is translucent with gaudy pearl and coral decor. Gottlieb W. Leitner, *The Hunza and Nagyr Handbook* (Calcutta: Superintendent of Government Printing, 1889), p. 6.

91 **"What about carpentry?"** This conversation is based on Shadi's recollection.

6: THE APPROACH

We rode a jeep along the same route that Karim took. We based these descriptions of the ride to Askole on that road trip. Further descriptions of Askole are from Padoan's trek to K2 as well as from videos and conversations with climbers about what they were doing during their trek to Base Camp in 2008. Because of political instability, many of the LAPs interviewed for this section were interviewed not in their villages but rather in Skardu or Machulu. (They were compensated for their three days of travel expenses.) The description of K2 Base Camp is from photos, videos, and interviews, as well as from Padoan's visit to the Gilkey Memorial in 2004. The descriptions of what the porters carried are from interviews with the climbers. Chhiring described sky burials, but his description was supplemented with the writings of anthropologist Sherry Ortner. The incident involving Mr. Kim and the quartz rock was described by several sherpas as well as by Jamie McGuinness.

95 **"rolling down avalanches"** See E. F. Knight, *Where Three Empires Meet* (London: Longmans, Green, 1918), p. 359.

96 *LAPs* In Balti, low-altitude porters are called *khurpas.* For clarity and consistency, we use the term *low-altitude porters,* even in translations where the speaker used the word *khurpas.*

99 **Yaqub** As a LAP, Yaqub was responsible for bringing his own food. The expedition kitchen crew is responsible only for feeding the HAPs and the clients. (As with many other porters, Yaqub doesn't use a last name.)

101 **the uninsured** Although expeditions could buy more extended coverage for their porters, Raza said he'd never heard of that happening in his thirty-four years with the company.

101 **uninsurable** Of course, you can insure anything if you're willing to pay a high enough premium. Celebrities often insure such body parts as legs, faces, buttocks, and breasts, for exorbitant premiums, but this hasn't caught on with the 8000er set.

103 **sky burial** The practice differs throughout Tibet and Nepal, depending on the materials available.

7: WEATHER GODS

The discussion of the attack on the Danish Embassy is based on news reports from Al Jazeera and videos. Pakistan's Ministry of Tourism and Alpine Club president Nazir Sabir provided details of the climbing rates and the reasons behind the changes. Shaheen described his encounter with Hugues, and photos on Hugues's blog corroborated many of the details. The description of Ger's injury is from interviews with friends and family, including Annie Starkey, Banjo Bannon, and Joëlle Brupbacher. The description of Roeland van Oss's near-death experience is based on interviews with Jelle Staleman and Wilco. The description of Yan Giezendanner's workstation is from Padoan's visit to his home in Chamonix. The description of the final team meeting is from interviews with several of the men who were present, as well as from video footage.

108 **seven times more** A permit to climb Everest from the south side in Nepal was $70,000. As with K2, up to seven mountaineers are included in the price of the permit.

110 **"would be obscene"** This is what Shaheen heard Hugues say. The photographs of the corpse appeared on Hugues's blog on July 9, 2008.

111 **"completely bitchy"** This dialogue did not occur between Nick and Wilco.

They were interviewed separately about their feelings toward each other and their quotes were spliced.

112 **customary toll** The Dutch team brought 4,000 meters of new lightweight Endura rope, which cost $5,500, and they fixed the route along the Cesen to Camp 4. A donation to the team that brings the rope and fixes it is customary on 8,000-meter peaks. Wilco was asking for $450, a reasonable sum under the circumstances.

116 **ideally, below 18,000 feet** This is equivalent to 5,484 meters; the benchmark many climbers use is 5,600 meters.

118 **"'Only use this outside'"** Mountaineers have to settle for an open tent flap.

118 **"eating priests"** Correspondence with Yan Giezendanner, December 2009.

119 **Dutch weather god** Ab Maas of the Royal Netherlands Meteorological Institute was the first to report the weather window to the mountaineers at Base Camp. His prediction was ten days in advance of the window.

121 **four camps** Camp 1 is usually at 6,200 meters; Camp 2 is at 6,700 meters; Camp 3 is at 7,300 meters; Camp 4 (the Shoulder) is a large site where tents can be pitched at heights between 7,700 and 7,900 meters.

121 **about 19,000 feet** Wilco's Camp 1 on the Cesen route was at 5,800 meters.

121 **20,300 feet** Wilco's Camp 2 on the Cesen was at 6,200 meters.

121 **about 23,500 feet** Wilco's Camp 3 on the Cesen was at 7,150 meters.

122 **Muhammad Hussein** He was also known as "Little Hussein."

122 **Muhammad Khan** He is also listed as Muhammad Sanap Akam on summit records.

122 **rope, ice screws, and pickets** The rope supply consisted of 400 meters from the Dutch team and 200 meters from the Italian team.

8: GHOST WINDS

The rescue of Shaheen is based on interviews with Shaheen and Nadir. Yan's discussions with Hugues are from Yan's recollection, and all of Hugues's quotes are also from Yan's recollection. Wilco's discussions with Maarten are from both men's recollections. Hoselito's discussion with Wilco about the tent is based on interviews with both men and corroborated by Pemba. All quotes in the conversation between Hoselito and Wilco are from our interviews with the men who said them and as reviewed by Wilco and Hoselito.

127 **"K2: A Little Shorter/A Lot Harder"** Mike Farris of the American K2 International Expedition created this motto.

9: THROUGH THE BOTTLENECK

The scenic descriptions of the mountain are based on interviews with the climbers, their photographs, and video footage. The descriptions of the conflicts in the lead team are from interviews with all surviving members. The descriptions of the traffic jam in the Bottleneck come from about a dozen of the mountaineers who were there, plus several photos. We based the description of Cecilie's encounter with Dren Mandić on her memoir and interviews with her. Cecilie's account was corroborated by Chhiring, Pasang, and Lars. The descriptions of the attempted recovery of Dren's body come from interviews with Fredrik, Muhammad Hussein, Iso, and Pedja, plus footage from Fredrik's documentary *K2: A Cry from the Top of the World*. The description of Jehan's slide down the mountain is based primarily on the versions told by Muhammad Hussein and Iso, who had unobstructed views. Dr. Fred Espenak of NASA's Goddard Space Flight Center provided information about the eclipse above K2. Pasang's encounter with Alberto comes from interviews with both men. The scene on the summit is from interviews with the people described and from photographs. The detail about Kim and Jumik playfully smoking a cigarette is from Pasang.

143 **"the essentials"** The Italians still had a second coil of 100 meters, and the Dutch team had brought 400 meters of rope. This would have been enough if the fixed lines had been set in the appropriate locations.

143 **$385** This is based on 2008 prices. Zuckerman examined and tried on some of the oxygen cylinders that Pasang used, and Pasang demonstrated how he prepared them.

143 **turn up the flow** The maximum is four liters a minute.

144 **Sure, Eric replied** This conversation is based on Chhiring's recollection. (Eric had only a vague recollection of their exchange, which is why his words aren't in quotation marks here.)

144 **"He won't be coming"** Paolo Padoan interviewed Alberto in Vitoria-Gasteiz, Spain, in 2009.

145 **Muhammad Hussein** Zuckerman interviewed Muhammad in his village of Machulu in 2009.

145 **procedure on Everest** On Everest, an army of sherpas fixes lines systematically, and every team contributes with supplies, porters, or payment. The Bhotes tried to deliver extensive fixed lines on K2, but, given the time frame of the project—a few hours' lead time before the main group—this was unrealistic.

149 **"being a gentleman"** Hoselito, who didn't see the fall, bases this theory on Dren's personality.

154 **a perfect corona** A total eclipse of the sun was visible in areas of China, far to the north of Shimshal.

155 years preparing Wilco also remembered the summit time of the 1995 K2 expedition in which he took part. The team reached the summit at 6 p.m. and descended safely to Camp 4 by midnight.

159 "at the beach!" This was the August 4 entry on Hugues d'Aubarède's memorial blog by his girlfriend, Mine Dumas.

10: ESCAPE FROM THE SUMMIT

The encounter with Mr. Kim is from Pasang's recollection, as are most of Pasang's encounters with Kim, who declined to be interviewed. To understand Kim's perspective, the authors reviewed transcripts of Kim's interviews with Fredrik Sträng, who filmed him throughout the climb for the documentary *K2: A Cry from the Top of the World*. We also reviewed transcripts from Kim's interviews with Ryu Dong-il on behalf of author Freddie Wilkinson for his book *One Mountain Thousand Summits*. Several climbers described the rope system, including Chhiring and Pasang. Cas van de Gevel described the death of Hugues. The sounds are based on climbers' descriptions. For Jumik's fall, we do not know the precise time this serac calved, but it was a separate serac fall from the one that killed Rolf at 9 p.m. The descriptions of Rolf's death come from interviews with Cecilie and Lars, as well as from Cecilie's memoir, translated from Norwegian by Erik Brakstad, and their video footage, translated by Ragnhild Amble and Oddvar and Anne Hoidal.

164 stumbling and falling Between 1953 and 2008, twenty-four of the sixty-six deaths on K2 occurred during descent from the summit.

166 "You go first" This quote is according to Cas's recollection.

167 two Koreans with Jumik Neither Marco nor Wilco could positively identify the two Korean climbers tied to Jumik.

169 "Where's Rolf?" This quote is what Cecilie remembers saying; the quote after it is how Lars remembers responding.

169 "stars and loneliness" See Cecilie Skog, *Til Rolf: Tusen fine turer og en trist* (Oslo: Gyldendal Norsk Forlag AS, 2009). Excerpts translated by Erik Brakstad.

170 streaked down The next morning, Jumik was found hanging about 70 vertical meters (230 feet) below the Snow Dome.

172 all available rope Lars carried 50 meters of rope for emergencies. After the serac fall, this coil would be the key to survival for those trapped above the Bottleneck.

172 The visitation This is based on interviews with Chhiring.

173 "No axe" The quotes from exchanges with Pasang and Chhiring are from interviews with both men.

11: SONAM

Pasang's encounter with the specter of Mr. Kim is based on interviews with Pasang. The description of the bivouac is from interviews with Marco and Wilco; from Marco's memoir, *Giorni di Ghiaccio* (*Days of Ice*, 2009); and from Wilco's memoir, *Surviving K2* (2010). The specific lyrics that Ger substituted during the singing served as his climbing mantra. They were written by the Irish band Kila. Dr. Michael Su provided details about what would have happened when Karim became hypothermic. Eric provided information about what drugs were given to Pemba. Go Mi-sun died on Nanga Parbat in July 2009, three weeks before our scheduled interview with her. We did, however, obtain copies of e-mails she sent about the K2 climb, and we talked to other climbers about what she told them had happened.

180 **when Pasang closed his eyes** Pasang originally arrived at Camp 4 around noon on July 31, and it was now roughly 6 a.m. on August 2.

180 **"useless weight"** There are some celebrated exceptions. Dan Mazur and Jonathan Pratt survived a bivouac on K2 at 28,000 feet and kept their fingers and toes, thanks in part to a lightweight stove.

180 **minus four degrees Fahrenheit** This figure (equivalent to -20°C) is Marco's estimate.

183 **skid mark** This photo was taken from Camp 4 by Pemba at 7:16 p.m.

183 **"Is it bad?"** This exchange (and the one between Pemba and Eric) is from Chhiring's recollection but corroborated by Pemba and Eric.

12: SURVIVAL

The accounts involving Tsering, Big Pasang, and Go are from interviews with Tsering. Padoan and Zuckerman both interviewed Tsering on separate occasions in Kathmandu in 2009. Zuckerman did a followup interview with him in Grindelwald, Switzerland, in 2010. Tsering's conversation with Kim is told from Tsering's perspective but corroborated by Pemba, Eric, and Chhiring. Wilco's assertion that Jumik said help was coming is corroborated by the conversation between Lars and Go in Base Camp. The details of Wilco's descent are from interviews with him and from his memoir.

185 **Tsering** Tsering Lama was more commonly known as Chhiring Lama, reflecting the Nepali pronunciation of his Tibetan name. We refer to him by his Tibetan name to avoid confusion. He also sometimes goes by Chhiring Bhote in other books and articles.

189 **corneas began to freeze** Even a slight breeze at this altitude can begin to freeze the corneas when a wind shield (such as goggles) is removed. Vision gradually becomes cloudy, and it takes at least six hours to recover sight. To avoid this,

high-altitude mountaineers keep their eyes closed for five to ten seconds at a time and roll their eyeballs around on every third or fourth breath.

189 **After about 200 feet** Wilco estimates that Jumik and his two Korean clients were hanging 50 to 70 vertical meters (164 to 230 feet) below his bivouac site.

190 **twisting and cinching** This is what Wilco and others later figured must have happened.

190 **help was on the way** When Ms. Go left Jumik the night before, she promised to send help, according to Lars, who spoke with Go at Base Camp on August 4 or 5.

190 **"I had to survive, too"** This quote is from a 2009 interview with Wilco at his home in Voorst, Holland.

190 **Wilco was lost** See Wilco van Rooijen, *Surviving K2* (2010), p. 127.

190 **three limbs** Or two limbs and an ice axe, maintaining three points of contact.

191 **familiar combination** The number was also on speed dial, but the phone's memory failed. Wilco had to dial by "feel."

191 **"I'm alive"** Wilco's conversations with Heleen are from his recollection.

13: BURIED IN THE SKY

The descriptions of the entangled men are from interviews with Marco and Wilco and from photographs taken by Pemba and Lars. The description of Big Pasang's radio calls comes from interviews with Pemba. The description of the avalanche assumes a dry-slab avalanche because that is consistent with the conditions described by Tsering and what photos suggest. Several books provided details of what happens and what to do during an avalanche. *The Avalanche Handbook*, by David McClung and Peter Schaerer (Seattle: The Mountaineers Books, 2006), was an especially good source. Dr. Michael Su provided many of the details about asphyxiation and dying. The interaction between Tsering and Pasang is based primarily on interviews with Tsering but supplemented by interviews with Pasang and with Jumik's mother, Gamu.

193 **Around 8 a.m.** A photo by Lars, taken from Camp 4 at 8:06 a.m., shows Marco and Ger first encountering the tangle of men and Wilco descending below them.

194 **after 9:58 a.m.** Pemba's 9:58 a.m. photo taken from Camp 4 shows Marco leaning over Jumik's head as Ger kneels beside him.

194 **"nice of him, but weird"** Marco doesn't recall giving any chocolate to Tsering and Big Pasang.

194 **an avalanche roar** Marco does not believe what he experienced was a hallucination. During a 2010 interview with documentary filmmaker Nick Ryan, Marco acknowledged that the body could have been anyone wearing yellow La Sportiva Olympus Mons Evo boots and a red downsuit. Ger and Karim both wore that gear.

195 taken at 9:58 a.m. This photo was taken by Pemba from Camp 4.

195 Jumik is gone Pemba took this photo at 7:16 p.m. from Camp 4.

195 photo from 3:10 p.m. Pemba photographed the corpses of Jumik and Big Pasang at 3:10 p.m. from a few feet away.

195 rescued himself This is the assessment of Wilco and Marco, the last surviving witnesses to see Jumik alive.

196 sledding down Or Ger may have used a simpler system. He might have rigged up a second rope that he had attached to the two living climbers and then cut the first rope.

197 two eyewitnesses They were Big Pasang and Tsering, as described later in this chapter.

197 "dead man walking" See Beck Weathers with Stephen G. Michaud, *Left for Dead: My Journey Home from Everest* (New York: Villard Books, 2000), p. 7.

198 four men Big Pasang and Tsering counted four men, and Big Pasang reported this over the radio.

198 reported on the radio Pemba received this radio call while he was trying to revive Marco.

198 thunderous boom Tsering heard it.

202 death What's considered the moment of "death" varies among doctors, cultures, and jurisdictions. We define it here as the moment when breathing and circulation stopped.

203 "lose my family" This quote is from an interview with Tsering and corroborated by Pasang.

14: THE FEARLESS FIVE

The description of Marco's rescue is from interviews with Pemba and Marco, supplemented by Marco's memoir. The descriptions of Wilco's descent are based on interviews with Wilco, Cas, Pemba, Nadir, Tom, Maarten, Hoselito, Chhiring, and Chris. The description of Pasang's return to Base Camp is from interviews with Pasang and Ngawang Bhote. The field hospital description is based on photographs and on interviews with Eric and Chhiring. We also discussed the treatment with Wilco and Marco. The scene at the Gilkey Memorial is from interviews with Nadir, supplemented by photos of the memorial and interviews with Hoselito, who was nearby. The authors visited the Fearless Five at the military base in April 2009, including the mess hall and barracks. The landing at Base Camp and Marco's airlift were videotaped by the military. We reviewed this footage and interviewed the pilots involved in the rescues. Shaheen's return comes from interviews with him. Zuckerman and Padoan visited the hospital rooms used by Marco and Wilco and interviewed the medical personnel who treated them. We also relied on information broadcast by media outlets. Details about personal responses to the disaster stem primarily from news reports but also from interviews with Dawa Sherpa and Jumik's friends with Internet access, Judy Aull and Jerry del Missier.

205 **might dig up** And they did. See Cristina Marrone, "Confortola scalerà da solo «È un campione ma antipatico»," *Corriere della Sera*, February 7, 2010.

205 **"like a lioness"** See Marco Confortola, *Giorni di Ghiaccio* (Milan: Baldini Castoldi Dalai Editore, 2009), p. 128.

206 **afternoon of August 2** All times refer to the local time on K2. Utrecht, Holland, was four hours behind K2. Denver, Colorado, was eleven hours behind K2.

207 **Maarten** Padoan interviewed Maarten van Eck in Utrecht, Holland, in October 2009.

208 **the orange dot** Zuckerman interviewed Chris by telephone. Chris was credited in the media as the first person to spot Wilco, but he does not dispute Nadir's earlier sighting.

208 **near Camp 3** Strictly speaking, Wilco was not rescued. He had located Camp 3 on the Cesen route and was approaching it on his own. Cas climbed toward Wilco, meeting him about 100 meters from camp, while Pemba remained in Camp 3, standing in front of his tent.

209 **"a stranger to them"** Ngawang Bhote interview in Kathmandu (2010) with Snighda Dhungel, Padoan's translator.

210 **$60,000** This is based on Eric Meyer's recollection of his discussion with English-speaking members of the Flying Jump as they arranged their evacuation from Base Camp. The average cost for an airlift is $6,000 per person, and approximately ten members flew out, so this estimate is reasonable. Askari Aviation told the authors that the Flying Jump's airlift cost a total of $13,000, but mountaineers said these figures were inaccurate.

211 **Siachen** The name of this wasteland means "place of many roses" in Balti.

212 **Ecureuil B3 Mystery** Didier Delsalle landed an Ecureuil/AStar AS 350 B3 on the summit of Everest on May 14, 2005, for two minutes.

212 **Rinjing Sherpa** In addition to carrying Marco to the chopper, Rinjing, along with his brother-in-law, George Dijmarescu, and Mingma Sherpa, intercepted Marco above Camp 2 and helped him descend to Base Camp.

15: THE NEXT LIFE

For the description of the tea party, Zuckerman visited the room where the meeting took place and spoke to members of the Ministry of Tourism about it. The quotes are from interviews with Nazir and Wilco. The meeting between Lahmu and Mr. Kim is from interviews with Lahmu and a visit to the hotel where the discussion took place. The description of Nick Rice's return is from interviews with him and his sister, Rebecca Rice, and video footage. For the scenes with Nazir

Sabir, we joined him on his drive to Shimshal and attended the meeting with the families of Karim and Jehan. The quotes come from followup interviews with those who spoke; it would have been insensitive to have our interpreter translating during a memorial service. The quotes of Jehan's children were reported by their grandmother, Nazib. Chhiring's return home is based on interviews with him, Dawa, and Ngawang. Pasang's return is based on interviews with Pasang, Pemba Jeba, Tsering, Dawa Sangmu, Lahmu, and Gamu. The descriptions of the doubleheader climbs are from interviews with Chhiring and Pasang.

218 Jehan Baig's policy Alpha Insurance eventually compensated Jehan's family.

218 "the right kind of climbers" This quote is from interviews after the tea party when Wilco, Nazir, and others recalled what they were saying and thinking at the time. Unfortunately, the party was not taped by the ministry, and Geo TV and Dawn TV had lost their tapes of the meeting.

222 unsupported, unassisted Cecilie, with American Ryan Waters, crossed Antarctica using strictly their own muscle power. For previous crossings of Antarctica, skiers had used wind for propulsion.

223 "Pemba Girgi" Marco Confortola, *Giorni di Ghiaccio* (Milan: Baldini Castoldi Dalai Editore, 2009), p. 102.

223 Jumik Bhote's mother This visit was in April 2010. Padoan and Joëlle Brupbacher were present with translator Snighda Dhungel.

223 *National Geographic Adventure* See "The Savior and the Storm on K2," *National Geographic Adventure* (December 2008/January 2009).

224 "focused on the rescues" Pemba Gyalje interview with Padoan, Nick Ryan, and Pat Falvey at Pemba's home in Kathmandu, January 2009.

224 rescues involved Western lives Freddie Wilkinson was a notable exception to the media focus on Westerners. By November 2008, Wilkinson had broken the story, investigating and writing the first article about Chhiring's rescue of Pasang. See "Heroes in Fine Print," *The Huffington Post*, November 12, 2008. Wilkinson followed the article with a longer piece: "Perfect Chaos," *Rock and Ice*, December 2008. He also wrote the first book about the tragedy from the Sherpa perspective: *One Mountain Thousand Summits* (New York: New American Library, 2010).

226 little else but listen That is only true of this particular meeting. Nazir continued to do a great deal for the families. He coordinated a fundraising effort for the support of the families, contributing his own money, and ensured that they were treated fairly by insurance companies.

Selected Bibliography

BOOKS

Biddulph, John. *Tribes of the Hindoo Koosh*. Calcutta: Superintendent of Government Printing, 1880.

Bonatti, Walter. *The Mountains of My Life*. New York: Modern Library, 2001.

Bowley, Graham. *No Way Down: Life and Death on K2*. New York: HarperCollins, 2010.

Clark, John. *Hunza: Lost Kingdom of the Himalayas*. New York: Funk & Wagnalls, 1956.

Confortola, Marco. *Giorni di Ghiaccio*. Milan: Baldini Castoldi Dalai Editore, 2009.

Curran, Jim. *K2: The Story of the Savage Mountain*. London: Hodder & Stoughton, 1995.

Douglas, Ed. *Tenzing: Hero of Everest*. Washington, DC: National Geographic, 2003.

French, Patrick. *Younghusband: The Last Great Imperial Adventurer*. Hammersmith: HarperCollins UK, 2004.

Gregson, Jonathan. *Massacre at the Palace: The Doomed Royal Dynasty of Nepal*. New York: Talk Miramax, 2002.

Hopkirk, Peter. *The Great Game: On Secret Service in High Asia*. London: John Murray, 1990.

Houston, Charles S., and Robert H. Bates. *K2, The Savage Mountain*. New York: McGraw-Hill, 1954.

Hunt, John. *The Ascent of Everest*. London: Hodder & Stoughton, 1953.

Isserman, Maurice, and Stewart Weaver. *Fallen Giants: A History of Himalayan Mountaineering from the Age of Empire to the Age of Extremes*. New Haven, CT: Yale University Press, 2010.

Jordan, Jennifer. *The Last Man on the Mountain: The Death of an American Adventurer on K2*. New York: W. W. Norton, 2010.

Kauffman, Andrew J., and William L. Putnam. *K2: The 1939 Tragedy*. Seattle: The Mountaineers Books, 1992.

Knight, E. F. *Where Three Empires Meet*. London: Longmans, Green, 1918.

Lacedelli, Lino, and Giovanni Cenacchi. *K2: Il prezzo della conquista*. Milan: Mondadori, 2004.

Leitner, Gottlieb. *The Hunza and Nagyr Handbook*. Calcutta: Superintendent of Government Printing, 1889.

Norgay, Jamling Tenzing (with Broughton Coburn). *Touching My Father's Soul: A Sherpa's Journey to the Top of Everest*. San Francisco: Harper San Francisco, 2001.

Norgay, Tenzing (with James Ramsey Ullman). *Tiger of the Snows: The Autobiography of Tenzing of Everest*. New York: Putnam, 1955.

Ortner, Sherry B. *Sherpas Through Their Rituals*. Cambridge, UK: Cambridge University Press, 1978.

———. *Life and Death on Mount Everest: Sherpas and Himalayan Mountaineering*. Princeton, NJ: Princeton University Press, 1999.

Peissel, Michel. *The Ants' Gold*. New York: HarperCollins, 1984.

Schomberg, R. C. F. *Between the Oxus and the Indus*. Lahore: al-Biruni, 1935.

Skog, Cecilie. *Og De Tre Polene*. Stavanger, Norway: Wigestrand, 2006.

Tenderini, Mirella, and Michael Shandrick. *The Duke of the Abruzzi: An Explorer's Life*. Seattle: The Mountaineers Books, 1997.

Tenzing, Tashi. *Tenzing Norgay and the Sherpas of Everest*. New York: Ragged Mountain Press, 2001.

van Rooijen, Wilco. *Overleven op de K2*. National Geographic, 2009. (Published in English as *Surviving K2*. Diemen, Netherlands: G+J Publishing, 2010.)

Viesturs, Ed, and David Roberts. *K2: Life and Death on the World's Most Dangerous Mountain*. New York: Broadway Books, 2009.

Webster, Ed. *Snow in the Kingdom: My Storm Years on Everest*. Eldorado Springs, CO: Mountain Imagery, 2000.

Wilkinson, Freddie. *One Mountain Thousand Summits: The Untold Story of Tragedy and True Heroism on K2*. New York: New American Library, 2010.

Younghusband, Francis. *The Heart of a Continent*. London: John Murray, 1896.

———. *Wonders of the Himalaya*. London: John Murray, 1924.

PERIODICALS

DeBenedetti, Christian. "The Savior and the Storm on K2," *National Geographic Adventure* (December 2008/January 2009).

Kodas, Michael. "A Few False Moves," *Outside* (September 2008).

Power, Matthew. "K2: The Killing Peak," *Men's Journal* (November 2008).

Sabir, Nazir. "K2: A Letter from Nazir Sabir," *The Alpinist* (August 2008).

Wilkinson, Freddie. "Perfect Chaos," *Rock and Ice* (December 2008).

FILMS

Disaster on K2 (The Discovery Channel, March 2009).

Hillary and Tenzing: Climbing to the Roof of the World (PBS, 1996).

K2: A Cry from the Top of the World (Mastiff AB, Stockholm, Sweden, 2010).

Murder Most Royal (BBC Panorama, 2002).

Index

Page numbers in *italics* refer to maps.

• A *New York Times* Culture Bestseller • An *Entertainment weekly* Best
Pop Culture Book of 2015 • A *Booklist* Top Ten Arts Book of 2015 •

"Even the brightest star is occasionally eclipsed by a moon. Sue Mengers was a moon. . . . Kellow is the first to pull back the caftan, to consider what really made Mengers Mengers. He has made a specialty of forceful showbiz women—previous subjects include Pauline Kael and Ethel Merman—and she fits easily into that pantheon. . . . [Mengers] came of age as the moving pictures, and seemingly the world, burst into Technicolor, Kellow vividly renders this time of alliterative rat-a-tat names begat of the typewriter—Boaty Boatwright, Freddie Fields, Lionel Larner, Maynard Morris—and restaurants that treated regulars like family: Downey's and Lindy's and Sardi's. . . . [A] reflective and soulful book."   —Alexandra Jacobs, *The New York Times Book Review*

"To call Sue Mengers a 'character' is an understatement, unless the word is written in all-caps, followed by an exclamation point and modified by an expletive. And based on Brian Kellow's assessment in his thoroughly researched *Can I Go Now?* even that description may be playing down her personality a bit. Gutsy, pushy, and savvy, Mengers was the take-no-b.s. power agent for many of Hollywood's boldest bold-faced names in the late 1960s and the '70s. . . . *Can I Go Now?*—a title inspired by something Mengers often said to cut short conversations—offers plenty of dishy, inside-'70s-Hollywood stories, including tales from those soirees at her Beverly Hills home. . . . Kellow doesn't shy away from highlighting her negative traits as well, qualities that often worked at odds with her strongest attributes."

—Jen Chaney, *The Washington Post*

"Picture Joan Rivers with less of a filter, bulldozer-setting ramped up to 12, shpritzing venom alongside comic abuse. Imagine that, and you'll start to get a vague idea of the lioness named Sue Mengers. . . . [Kellow's] book is immensely readable and full of dish."   —Scott Eyman, *The Wall Street Journal*

"A minor masterpiece of Hollywood history in its most exciting, glamorous, and gossip-wise period."   —Liz Smith, *New York Social Diary*

"Superagent Sue Mengers handled some of the hottest stars in Hollywood. . . . Brian Kellow's new biography, *Can I Go Now?*, derives its title from one of her favorite ways to end a phone call. As one of the most powerful agents in Holly-wood for two decades—*Time* magazine described her as a 'cross between Mama Cass and Mack the Knife'—Mengers was uncensored. She also was a skilled negotiator. And a trailblazer for women in the male-dominated field."

—Susan King, *Los Angeles Times*

"*Can I Go Now?* offers as much authoritative information about '70s filmmaking as it does about Mengers. . . . [Kellow] captures his subject . . . and more impor-tant, he captures a crucial era in American filmmaking. At the end of the book . . . you'll be convinced of her importance, her drive, and the significance of what she accomplished."   —David Wiegand, *San Francisco Chronicle*

"Mengers was the first woman to amass the sort of power she did, representing Barbra Streisand, Gene Hackman, Michael Caine, Candice Bergen, Ryan O'Neal, Mike Nichols, and so many more. But Mengers, as this insightful, of-ten hilarious, and celebrity-filled book relates, was a mass of contradictions."

—Larry Getlen, *New York Post*

"[Kellow] brings her rollicking personality to life with outrageous anecdotes while pointing out the behaviors that doomed her . . . In the 1990s, she walked into a party, looked around, and muttered to her companions, 'Schindler's B-list.' Her biography, however, is A-list all the way."   —Paul Teetor, *LA Weekly*

"'Colorful' is the kind of code word one uses when actual examples can't be published in a review. Kellow fills his lively book *Can I Go Now?* with enough ribald tales of Mengers being 'colorful' to fill a crayon box. That she could be endearing as well as rude and insulting to the people she represented is surprising—and just one aspect of a fascinating personality Kellow places squarely in the context of the way the movie business worked at that time. . . . Kellow give[s] Mengers the place in Hollywood history that she deserves."

—Douglass K. Daniel, Associated Press

"Before there was Ovitz or Ari, there was Sue Mengers. During the peak of her clout in the 1970s, the brash barrier-breaker helped popularize the idea of the Hollywood superagent. The media lapped up her comic crudity. . . . Her leg-endary dinner parties attracted Tinseltown's A-list, and *60 Minutes* came calling to do a lengthy interview that captured Mengers dishing and deal-making. . . . She didn't believe in gussying up hard truths and could be brutally candid with her clients. That lost her some accounts . . . but it also earned her respect. 'Everyone prized her honesty,' Kellow said. 'In a town like Hollywood, that's hard to come by. . . . She was a scrutinizing, tough Jewish mama.'"

—Brent Lang, *Variety*

"An absorbing read."   —Clark Collis, *Entertainment Weekly*

"With his new book *Can I Go Now?*, Brian Kellow follows up his 2011 biography of film critic iconoclast Pauline Kael by telling the story of Sue Mengers, 'the first enormously successful female agent in the movie industry.' As the representative for many of the major players of the day . . . Mengers helped to define a new concept of Hollywood stardom for a new, post–studio system era. Mengers also set a new standard for female power in the workplace, with a brash, inimitable style that mixed sweet talk and harassment, employing 'feminine wiles' more often than not as a weapon. . . . The story of how a strong woman steamrolled through the Hollywood glass ceiling is an important one, but what makes *Can I Go Now?* worth reading is its careful chronicling of what happens after the glass shatters, and that woman has to figure out how to stay on top without revealing her wounds."   —Karina Longworth, *Slate*

"Mengers was a complicated, powerful trailblazer, one who barged down doors for women and changed the nature of the talent-agent business. Kellow's absorbing biography not only peels back the layers to reveal the true nature of this fascinating individual but also delves deeply into the film industry in the latter half of the twentieth century."   —*Booklist* (starred review)

"Effortlessly readable, especially for *Vanity Fair* enthusiasts and film buffs."

—*Library Journal*

"From the 1950s through the 1980s, Sue Mengers represented some of the most famous names in show business. . . . [The agent's] coveted gatherings, her bawdy appearances at premieres and nightclubs, and a profile in *Vanity Fair* made her as recognizable as her glamorous roster of actors, and she worked tirelessly to promote them—not just to get them parts, but also higher and higher salaries. . . . Kellow, an admirer of Mengers's spunk and achievements, serves her well in this deft, entertaining biography."   —*Kirkus Reviews*

Brian Kellow is the author of *Pauline Kael: A Life in the Dark*, which was a 2011 *New York Times* Notable Book of the Year and also appeared on the Best of the Year lists of *Entertainment Weekly*, *The New Yorker*, and the *Chicago Tribune*. He is also the author of *Ethel Merman: A Life* and *The Bennetts: An Acting Family* and the coauthor of *Can't Help Singing: The Life of Eileen Farrell*. Kellow's articles have appeared in *Vanity Fair*, *The Wall Street Journal*, *The New York Observer*, *Opera*, and other publications. He lives in New York City.

Can I Go Now?

THE LIFE OF SUE MENGERS, HOLLYWOOD'S FIRST SUPERAGENT

Brian Kellow

PENGUIN BOOKS

PENGUIN BOOKS
An imprint of Penguin Random House LLC
375 Hudson Street
New York, New York 10014
penguin.com

First published in the United States of America by Viking,
an imprint of Penguin Random House LLC, 2015
Published in Penguin Books 2016

PHOTOGRAPH CREDITS

Courtesy of Joanna Poitier: pages 1 (top, bottom), 2 (top, center, bottom), 3 (center),
7 (top)

Courtesy of Leo Sender: page 3 (top)

Courtesy of Boaty Boatwright: pages 3 (bottom), 7 (bottom), 8 (bottom)

© Gary Lewis/mptvimages.com: pages 4 (Streisand), 5 (MacGraw/Evans)

Author's Collection: pages 4 (all except Streisand), 5 (all except MacGraw/Evans),
6 (bottom)

Universal Pictures/Photofest: page 6 (top)

Courtesy of Toni Howard: page 8 (top)

ISBN 9780670015405 (hc.)
ISBN 9780143108870 (pbk.)

Printed in the United States of America
1   3   5   7   9   10   8   6   4   2

Set in Bodoni Std Book
Designed by Francesca Belanger

For Scott Barnes,

who shows me what it means to be Two for the Road

Introduction

It is difficult to believe that in the late 1950s or early 1960s, even in the hard-boiled, wised-up, seen-it-all world of show business, there were many secretaries like Sue Mengers. The era of Helen Gurley Brown's *Sex and the Single Girl* had not yet arrived—not quite. Perhaps Rona Jaffe described this period most succinctly in the opening of her best-selling novel of 1958, *The Best of Everything*:

> You see them every morning at a quarter to nine, rushing out of the maw of the subway tunnel, filing out of Grand Central Station, crossing Lexington and Park and Madison and Fifth avenues, the hundreds and hundreds of girls. Some of them look eager and some look resentful, and some of them look as if they haven't left their beds yet. Some of them have been up since six-thirty in the morning, the ones who commute from Brooklyn and Yonkers and New Jersey and Staten Island and Connecticut. They carry the morning newspapers and overstuffed handbags. Some of them are wearing pink or chartreuse fuzzy overcoats and five-year-old ankle-strap shoes and have their hair up in pin curls underneath kerchiefs. Some of them are wearing chic black suits (maybe last year's but who can tell?) and kid gloves and are carrying their lunches in violet-sprigged Bonwit Teller paper bags. None of them has enough money.

The Best of Everything is set in the world of book publishing, but in the world of Hollywood and the world of the New York theater—in virtually any field in the arts at that time—women in subordinate positions were expected to behave in a fairly regimented way. Show up on time. Never complain about having to work after hours or on weekends. Never complain at all, in fact. Pay for your own taxi home. Treat your boss as if he were the center of the universe.

Sue Mengers did not come close to fitting into this rigid concept of a woman in the workplace during the Eisenhower and Kennedy years. "I was a little pisher, a little nothing, making $135 a week as a secretary for the William Morris Agency in New York," she told Mike Wallace in her famous 1975 interview for a segment of CBS's *60 Minutes*. "Well, I looked around and I admired the Morris office and their executives, and I thought, Gee, what they do isn't that hard, you know. And I like the way they live, and I like those expense accounts, and I like the cars. . . . And I suddenly thought: That beats typing."

There is an Elizabethan term, "self-panicker," meaning someone whose behavior is funniest of all to herself, and thus persuades everyone around her that she is the funniest person in their sphere. Sue Mengers might be called the ultimate "self-panicker." Her rise through the ranks of the secretarial pool took place before the eras of Helen Gurley Brown, Rona Jaffe, Jacqueline Susann, Marlo Thomas as Ann Marie in *That Girl*, and Mary Tyler Moore as Mary Richards. Lionel Larner, who worked with Mengers at the agency Baum & Newborn in the early 1960s, remembered that on Monday mornings she would walk in, toss her purse down, throw her feet up on her desk, and proclaim, once she was sure she had the attention of the entire office, "Sue had a tough weekend. Sue's *thingy* hurts."

Sue Mengers, from the start, showed a remarkable gift for leveling with the actors and directors with whom she crossed paths. "I remember coming into the offices of Baum & Newborn to get the sides for a new play," recalled actress Phyllis Newman. "She was beyond fresh mouthed. *Beyond!* It was a tiny office and she was the 'everything' girl. And I was up for some part and so was another client of Baum & Newborn. Sue said, 'Don't even bother going. She's *schtupping* the director!' I wasn't a prude at all, but it made me scream with laughter, even then! And she liked to get in those Rosalind Russell poses, with the leg up on the desk."

Unlike many women who learned to play the game as they advanced in the workplace, Sue Mengers, the first enormously successful female agent in the movie industry, remained throughout her career very much the woman she had always been. Her refusal to rein in her behavior became a kind of calling card; it made people sit up and take notice of her. She gave every appearance of being as shrewd, as cunning, as confident, as any of the most powerful people on the screen—and more so than many of them.

When one takes into account her rocky early years—what used to be described in fan-magazine articles as "humble beginnings," it might make a very tidy argument that Sue Mengers's outward bravado was a mask for a deep-seated insecurity, a hidden belief that she did not really belong in the elite Hollywood circles that she so masterfully orchestrated. But those who knew her well do not feel that her blazing confidence was a mask or pose. The truth is somewhat simpler: she was a woman who prized a finite number of things—proven talent, success and the ability to achieve it, wit, brains, wealth, social position, grit, integrity, beauty—and something that used to be called moxie. She believed in these qualities so completely that she was generally dismissive of anyone who didn't possess them. The world according to Sue Mengers was divided into winners and losers, A-lists and B-lists. She devoted herself to being an A-list winner. She pulled no punches and made no apologies for the life she lived. Many years after she had cemented her reputation as the most colorful agent and most exclusive hostess in Hollywood, she commented on the glittering parties she threw, which were among the most coveted invitations in town. "I never invited anyone who wasn't successful . . . I was ruthless about it. It was all stars. I would look around my living room at all of them and even I'd be impressed with myself."

And yet as much as Sue Mengers threw a grenade into the conventional boundaries for women in show business, she was also, in certain ways, defined by that early *Best of Everything* view of women in the workplace. She believed that men were objects of sexual and financial gratification and that it was a woman's place to master that particular dance to the best of her satisfaction. She believed that men were by nature feckless and undependable and that women needed to embrace that fact; it was up to women to figure out how best to manipulate them, to turn the automatic advantage men were born with—the lust for power and drive for financial success, the natural aggressiveness and competitiveness—to women's advantage.

Although she certainly resented the way that powerful men exploited her, she did not at any point define herself as a feminist. Sue Mengers wanted to make it—pure and simple. She wanted money and security and power. She was sure these were the things that everyone wanted, if only they would be honest enough to admit it. And, apart from the occasional lie she believed was necessary in order to stay afloat in a cutthroat business, she was consistently, often shockingly, honest. In the end, her honesty was the most valuable tool in her arsenal. It was also the quality—however much it may have hurt her, however much it may have hurt her clients and colleagues—that made her a Hollywood legend. She became one of the power players in one of the greatest creative periods in Hollywood history, the 1970s, and her reputation outlived those of many of the biggest stars whose careers she helped mold. She was as far from being a little pisher, a little nothing, as she could ever have imagined.

CHAPTER ONE

1901–1946

"My mother, the Gorgon."

No matter how famous and successful Sue Mengers became, her mother was both her quickest point of reference and the last subject on which she would yield any detailed information. For her daughter, Ruth Mengers was paradoxically easy to dismiss and impossible to shake off, the source of so much anger and the wellspring of her determination to succeed. This potent dual role that Ruth played for decades gave Sue all the more reason to resent her. "The Gorgon" was one of the kinder appellations Sue assigned to her. During her peak years as an agent, and throughout her prolonged retirement, Sue frequently expressed the belief that she had been cruelly cheated out of the upbringing she felt she deserved. "I should have been *you*," she frequently complained to her most celebrated friends and clients. Sometimes it sounded almost like an accusation: "Why couldn't I have been *you*?" The memory that Sue most wanted to erase—more than the memory of the father who abandoned her, or the nasty, depressing apartments that she lived in as a girl, or the popular students who snubbed her in grammar school—was the memory of her mother. She felt that, by rights, someone of her drive and taste and native intelligence should have been the daughter of a dignified show-business aristocrat, someone like her client Candice Bergen's mother, Frances, a beautiful, elegant woman widely respected by Hollywood's old guard. Or even someone like comedienne Kathy Griffin's mother, a tough-talking but ultimately supportive Irish Catholic lady of the old school.

The film producer Lili Zanuck, for years part of a close circle of successful and well-connected Hollywood women friends Sue jokingly dubbed "the Dyke-ettes," believed that one reason the members of the group meshed so well was that many of them knew what it was like to have an unyielding, hypercritical mother. Another member of Sue's sorority, Sherry Lansing, felt that most of the successful businesswomen she knew in

Hollywood had mothers who never stopped pointing out their flaws and weaknesses.

Some of the world's worst snobs are the ones born into miserable circumstances. For Sue, once she had attained immense success, almost any reminder of her impoverished early years was to be avoided, buried, and recalled only to remind herself of how far she'd come.

During her adult life, Sue did not often acknowledge, even slightly, her German Jewish background, which is easy enough to understand; even before the outbreak of World War II, there was a long history of potent anti-German sentiment in the United States. During World War I and in the years immediately following, there were countless examples of hostility toward U.S. citizens who were guilty only of having a German surname. Eudora Welty's classic story "June Recital" tells of a German-born piano teacher, Miss Eckhart, who gives music lessons to the children in the fictional town of Morgana, Mississippi. With the eruption of World War I, Miss Eckhart comes to be regarded with hostility by the locals. She cooks foreign food, like cabbage sautéed in wine, and the smell of it cooking "was wrong, as the pitch of a note could be wrong. It was the smell of food nobody else had ever tasted." Later in her story, Welty wrote, "The war came, and all through it and even after 1918 people said Miss Eckhart was a German and still wanted the Kaiser to win." All across the United States there were ugly incidents, in both major metropolitan areas and backwater towns, in which people with German names were made to drop to their hands and knees and kiss the ground.

Practically none of Sue's close friends can ever recall her speaking German, which she knew how to speak quite well. She felt her German past was nothing more than an accident of birth—which probably took place on September 2, 1932, or possibly on September 2, 1931, in Hamburg. (The exact date is difficult to determine, since many birth certificates from the early 1930s in Germany are hard to obtain.)

Sue's father, Georg Mengers, was born in Hamburg on December 27, 1906, the son of Carl Mengers and Mary Goldsmith Mengers. Her mother, Ruth, was born on January 28, 1909. Georg was a rather slight man, who went bald prematurely; Ruth was short and plump, and her daughter would grow up to favor her in that respect. Both Georg and Ruth came from slightly elevated stock; Sue often told friends that her mother's family owned a medium-sized department store in Hamburg, roughly comparable to Loehmann's or Alexander's in New York City during the first half of the twentieth century. Dr. Mark Elias, whose parents were close to the Mengers family in the 1930s, recalled that Georg Mengers's mother, Mary, was a highly social individual who maintained a regular salon in her home, inviting the most talented local young musicians and writers to perform or read from their work. The Eliases themselves were a well-established couple in Hamburg. Moritz Elias was a successful M.D., a general practitioner, and his wife, Else, was a homemaker; both had come from rather primitive little villages in the interior of Germany and were happy to be settled in the comparatively cosmopolitan Hamburg.

About her early years in Hamburg, Sue remained mostly silent throughout her life. Occasionally, to a close friend who kept pressing her with questions, she intimated that she did indeed remember living in Germany but felt it had nothing to do with her adult life and did not particularly care to discuss it. In 1993, Patrick Baker, the son of Sue's close friend Boaty Boatwright, a top agent at International Creative Management (ICM), escorted Sue to a showing of Steven Spielberg's Holocaust drama, *Schindler's List*, at a movie theater on the Upper East Side of Manhattan. Only a short while into Spielberg's graphic film, Sue leaned over, kissed Baker on the cheek, and whispered that she had to leave. Assuming that the movie was too upsetting for her, Baker followed her out and asked her if she would like him to take her home.

Sue grabbed Baker's hand lovingly. "I'll call you in the morning," she said.

The next day she telephoned Baker at his mother's apartment. Without skipping a beat Sue said, "*Aaach!* If I have to see any more Jews in pajamas, I'm going to kill myself." Years later, Spielberg's film would inspire one of her most famous quips. As she walked into a crowded L.A. party, she looked around the room and murmured, "Schindler's B-list."

Once, when Patrick Baker introduced Sue to his close friend Chris Pilaro, Sue asked Pilaro what he did.

"I'm an outdoor educator," Pilaro replied.

Sue looked at him blankly.

"I'm an Alpinist," Pilaro explained. "I've climbed a lot of mountains."

Sue pondered this for a moment, then replied, "You know what? Jews own banks. We *don't* climb."

In the strictest sense, she was embellishing her own personal history. Sue's father never accomplished anything remotely close to owning a bank. "Sue's father was not well enough off," remembered Mark Elias. "He wasn't a good provider."

The Elias and Mengers families kept up a steady friendship in Hamburg, but in 1935, as the Nazi presence intensified, Moritz and Else Elias made the decision to emigrate to the United States. Else had an older sister who had married an American and settled in Baltimore. In the 1930s, both the United Kingdom and the United States demanded that refugees from Europe provide proof of sponsorship, since it was widely feared that the thousands of refugees would wind up on the public dole. Else Elias's sister provided an affidavit for her younger sibling and her family, and in mid-1935, the Eliases arrived in New York. For a short time, they resided in Baltimore with Mrs. Elias's sister and her husband. Soon Dr. Elias was delighted to learn that the state of New York would recognize his German medical license and diploma. After passing a basic English-language requirement test, Moritz Elias took over a family practice in New York Mills, New York, a textile-manufacturing town in Oneida County, two hours northwest of Albany and four hours northwest of New York City. The Eliases settled into their new life, keeping in touch with the Mengerses, sending encouraging news of the possibilities that existed in the States, and eventually becoming the sponsors for the Mengers family to enter the United States.

On August 15, 1938, Georg, Ruth, and Susanne sailed from Antwerp on the SS *Koenigstein*, arriving in New York City on August 25, 1938. The ship's passenger roll lists Georg as a thirty-one-year-old "merchant," Ruth as twenty-nine, and their young daughter, Susanne, as five years and ten months—not an exact match for the birthdate Sue generally gave of September 2, 1932, but close.

The Eliases had plenty of space—their house in New York Mills had fourteen rooms—so the two families were never in danger of crowding each other to any serious degree. But Mark Elias sensed, from his child's perspective, that the marriage of George (as he now called himself) and Ruth Mengers was not a happy one. Ruth was a particularly volatile personality. "What I remember about her is that my parents had to be very careful not to offend her," recalled Elias, "because she was rather easily offended. You didn't want to pay a social slight to her."

More than anything, George and Ruth Mengers wanted to move into their own home, which, after a few months of living with the Eliases, they did, renting a modest apartment in a four-story building at 1104 Steuben Street in Utica, New York—the city that bordered New York Mills. Settled in 1786, Utica had become a city in 1832; one century later, it was home to over 103,000 people. Like New York Mills, Utica's commercial life was centered on textile production, and while it was anything but glamorous, it was at the time a rather bustling small city in the Rust Belt. It had a thriving business center, a healthy local tool-manufacturing industry, many knitting mills, and numerous brickyards and railway yards. Dorothy Goodale, who moved to Utica from rural western Pennsylvania in the early 1940s, recalled that Utica struck her at the time as a booming metropolis.

The Jewish presence in Utica had grown steadily from the mid-nineteenth century, when the first immigrants, most of them peddlers, had settled in the area. Early on, according to local historian S. Joshua Kohn, many of them were not even registered in city directories because they were on the road selling. By the mid-1930s, the Jewish Community Council had been established in response to the rise of Hitler in Europe. The Mengers apartment on Steuben Street was in Lower Cornhill, an area inhabited by many Jewish refugees. It was a lower-middle-class neighborhood, dingy and undistinguished; Dorothy Goodale remembered that there was "a bar on practically every corner" in Lower Cornhill. West Utica was predominantly Polish, while East Utica was mostly Italian; these neighborhoods were primarily populated by the workers employed in the textile mills.

In Germany, George Mengers had already been a habitual gambler, and despite his reduced circumstances in the United States, he brought his bad habit with him. He was always making bets, not very successfully, and from the fairly early days of his arrival in his new home, he was often in some degree of debt. He got a job as a salesman for the American Furniture Company in downtown Utica. With its headquarters in Wilkes-Barre, Pennsylvania, the company employed a fleet of door-to-door salesmen. Despite the fact that his heavy German accent might have put off some potential customers, George was a competent salesman. On Saturdays, the Utica branch office conducted merchandising inventory, and Susi would join her father there, sitting quietly and reading a book or drawing with pencil and paper while George went about his duties.

The American Furniture Company had many country accounts, and

George was constantly on the road, selling pots and pans and blankets and dish towels to rural housewives for one dollar down and one dollar a week. Being away from home for stretches of time only exacerbated George's itch to gamble. His job didn't pay much, so Ruth took a position as a sales clerk at the Boston Store. Located on one of the city's most traveled streets, at the northeast corner of Genesee and Bleecker, it was the biggest department store in Utica. It was a sleek, modern emporium with elegant elevators, selling clothes, home furnishings, and toiletries, with a top floor devoted to toys that was a favorite destination for the children of Utica.

Although Ruth enjoyed her job and was proud to be contributing something to the household income, she never warmed to life in Utica and was deeply resentful that the family had been forced to leave Germany. She also detested Utica's long winters. "You rounded the corner," Dorothy Goodale remembered, "and the snow would be up to your shoulder. They had a ski tow in town, and lots of people could go skiing right there. It always seemed like the spring came sometime around July Fourth!"

At the time the family was getting settled in Utica, Susi Mengers spoke only a little English, in a thick German accent. She was, remembered her childhood friend Arthur Segaul, exceptionally shy. "Because her mother was working, I used to take her home from school for lunch," he recalled. "Everyone walked to school in town. I took her to my house for lunch every day until I finished third grade and went to another school."

Her parents were very concerned that Susi rid herself of her German accent, since it was hardly an advantage in most medium-sized and small towns in America during World War II. Susi began taking after-school elocution lessons, and in only a short while after entering Kemble Street Elementary School at age seven, she was speaking mostly unaccented English. Her closest friends included other girls who attended her school—Adele Marsh, Rosalind Slakter, Lucille Kall. "When she started speaking without an accent, she had the most beautiful diction," remembered Arthur Segaul. "And she became outspoken. It really changed her personality."

Mark Elias recalled the young Susi as being very much a blueprint of the brash, outspoken woman she would eventually become. "She had a flair for the dramatic," remembered Elias. "She was funny. She was sort of stagestruck."

In fact, she was *deeply* stagestruck. Even as a small child, she went to the movies obsessively. The Stanley Theater, a grand Mexican Baroque picture palace, was the best place in Utica to see the new films out of Hollywood. From the late 1930s on, she loved going to see Judy Garland, Bette Davis, Katharine Hepburn, Joan Fontaine, Rita Hayworth, and her favorite, Ingrid Bergman—all for a dime a throw. If you were a girl becoming entranced with the glamour of Hollywood, Utica was the kind of place that was bound to flood you with an anywhere-but-here feeling. It was an isolated pocket full of families who had lived there for generations, most of whom had very little curiosity about life elsewhere. Many of the people Susi knew growing up had boasted about never having visited New York City, and having gone as far as Syracuse only when circumstances demanded.

In 1943 the Mengers family moved to a new flat, still in the Lower Cornhill neighborhood, in a four-story apartment house at 1121 Summit Place. The following year, on April 5, 1944, both George and Ruth became fully naturalized citizens of the United States.

While they lived in Utica, the Mengers family regularly attended services at the Temple Beth El Synagogue on Genesee Street. Each spring one of the temple's chief cultural events for the town's young people was the Hattie Levine Goldbas speaking competition, sponsored by the Utica section of the National Council of Jewish Women. In the spring of 1944 Susi won the contest's first prize—five dollars. She would claim the top prize again in April 1945, choosing as her topic "Penrod, the Little Gentleman," and again in May 1946, for reciting one of Katherine's speeches from *The Taming of the Shrew*. That year, amidst advertisements for Freezone Corn Remedy (twenty-one cents), Veto Cream Deodorant (fifty-nine cents), and Cashmere Bouquet soap (three bars for twenty-seven cents), the *Utica Observer-Dispatch* ran a small story about Susi, accompanied by a photograph of her. The article pointed out that only seven and a half years earlier she had not spoken a word of English, and that she donated her five-dollar prize to the United Jewish Appeal. By this time she was in demand locally for readings and recitations at various churches, clubs, and Parent-Teacher Association meetings, but George and Ruth were careful to restrict her appearances to once a week. Susi loved these moments in the spotlight and would have been eager to appear as often as she was asked, but Ruth, in

particular, cautioned her against becoming conceited. Lucille Kall, who
had taken elocution lessons alongside Susi and also participated in some of
the speech competitions, remembered, "I couldn't speak. I was always
afraid, but Sue wasn't. She was absolutely terrific—very dramatic."

While she was growing up, Susi spent several summers at Camp Kron-
gold, a bucolic retreat in Holland Patent, just north of Utica. The camp,
which had the backing of the National Council of Jewish Women, was a
departure for her. Cows routinely tromped through its grounds; there was a
terrific swimming hole in a nearby creek and a gazebo for late-night assig-
nations. Lucille Kall attended, too, and remembered being on the receiving
end of Susi's teasing. "At camp," said Kall, "I had a sister who wet the bed,
and every day I had to change the sheets. Susi laughed at me every day!"
Susi got leading roles in most of the plays that were done there, including
H.M.S. Pinafore.

Her schoolmate Rosalind Slakter Fisher remembered that everyone at
Kemble Street Elementary School was well aware that Susi had her heart
set on becoming an actress. When Bette Midler portrayed Sue in John Logan's 2013 hit Broadway play *I'll Eat You Last,* she employed a recurring
mannerism of using one hand to rearrange her hair. Seeing the play, Rosalind Fisher experienced a potent sense memory of seeing Susi push back
her hair behind one ear in just that way as a child. "She was chutzpah personified," said Fisher. "She was very nervy in school. And she wanted to be
an actress very badly. She wanted to emulate Ingrid Bergman. She was her
idol at the time." She spent whatever spare change she might have on movie
magazines and talked endlessly of going to Hollywood, doing her best every
day to keep the dream alive—which in Utica was far from easy.

As she moved through her teens, she left "Susi" behind and became
"Sue." She got along well with her father, who enjoyed having her on his
weekly visits to the American Furniture Company offices. But even this
early on, Sue was often battling her mother. Her friends who visited the
house on Summit Place do not recall having much sense of a warm or cohe-
sive family life. Ruth impressed Sue's classmates as strong willed and
brusque, and George was not much in evidence. By now Utica had developed quite a reputation for crime and for gambling; many of the local men
were continually betting on college football games or the horse races.
George frequented several of the corner bars, where the local bookies hung

out. "My dad had a dry goods/furniture store in the Italian section of Utica," remembered another of Sue's schoolmates, Adele Rosen, "and on the corner there was a café. As a kid, I would be the runner for the bets. My dad would bet on numbers, and I would take the money down to the café where there was this bookie, and deliver it!"

George Mengers was no more successful as a gambler than he was in any other dimension of his life. Most of the time he suffered losses that could not be offset by his salary or Ruth's, and he was perpetually scrambling for ways to settle his debts. Unfortunately this usually involved approaching a friend or business acquaintance for a loan, and the atmosphere in the apartment on Summit Place steadily deteriorated. Ruth constantly complained that George didn't make a bigger salary, railed against their lower-middle-class existence in an unfashionable neighborhood, and never let George forget that their life in Germany had been altogether superior to the one they were leading now. In the midst of all this, Sue's dreams of a Hollywood acting career intensified.

In early September 1946, as Sue was getting ready to enter high school at Utica Free Academy, George was growing more and more depressed and was deeper in debt than ever. Having tapped out his usual sources, he went to see Oscar Dale, a well-established furrier who operated a business in nearby Rome, New York, and asked him for a loan. Dale turned down George's request. A few days later, having exhausted all other possibilities, George left Utica, supposedly on a sales trip.

He went to New York City, where he checked into the Times Square Hotel at Forty-third Street and Eighth Avenue under the name Oscar Dale. He swallowed a bottle of pills and was found dead of barbiturate poisoning on September 21, 1946. George's body was identified by a cousin who lived in Manhattan.

The suicide of a parent is the rejection that can never be rationalized completely, the ultimate and most agonizing abandonment. George's suicide had an enormous effect on Sue's already aggressive personality, on the confidence she had shown from childhood: it triggered in her an unexamined, and at times sadistic, anger. For the rest of her life she would often astonish friends and colleagues with the intensity of her prejudice and intolerance. From now on, sometimes consciously, often not, she used anger as her own personal weapon, her own defense. She was going to create the kind of life for herself that she wanted, and she was not about to apologize for her single-minded pursuit of it.

George Mengers's life had been marked by failure, and so, literally, was his death. He was buried along the outside parameters of the Temple Beth El cemetery in Whitesboro, New York, near the fence where those who died by suicide were relegated.

CHAPTER TWO

1946–1950

Ruth and Sue struggled on alone in the apartment on Summit Place. It might have proven reassuring to those around them if they had forged some kind of truce, however uneasy, in the wake of George's death, but that didn't happen. Their mutual antagonism continued as each pondered her future; since George had committed suicide there would be no payment of life insurance. In the decades to come, Sue would continually brand him as a loser, a failure who succumbed to his own weaknesses. George's worst sin, Sue would tell friends for the rest of her life, was that he had left her alone with Ruth. More than ever, Sue was determined to get out of Utica as fast as possible.

She didn't have to wait long. Ruth remained in Utica for a little more than a year after George died, but it was clear that her meager salary at the Boston Store would not do to support herself and her daughter. Now that she had a few years of solid business experience, she saw no reason why she would not be able to find a better-paying job elsewhere. In 1948, as Sue was finishing up tenth grade at UFA, mother and daughter departed Summit Place and headed for New York City. Before leaving, Sue gave her good friend Rosalind Slakter a black-and-white photograph of herself and wrote across the back of it: "To Rozy—the girl with the big heart from one who'll always remember it."

Ruth found an apartment in the Bronx, in a heavily Jewish neighborhood. In the early 1930s, the Bronx's population was estimated at nearly 50 percent Jewish; by the end of the war, that figure had declined significantly, to about 37 percent, and it would continue to decline over the next decade as more Jewish families moved to the suburbs of Long Island, Westchester, and New Jersey. In the booming postwar atmosphere of New York, jobs were plentiful, and Ruth soon landed a position as a bookkeeper. Rather than attending high school in the Bronx, Sue enrolled at George

Washington High School in Washington Heights, at the northern tip of Manhattan.

At the time, Harlem, immediately to the south of Washington Heights, had not yet begun the staggering decline that would overtake it in the late 1950s and '60s. Washington Heights was a drab but reasonably safe part of New York City. At the close of the nineteenth and beginning of the twentieth century, Washington Heights had experienced an enormous influx of Irish immigrants, but in the decades to follow, thousands of Russian, Polish, and German Jews had made their way there, triggering a significant rise in the number of local synagogues.

For Sue, both Washington Heights and her Bronx neighborhood were a depressingly long distance from the exciting world of Manhattan show business she had dreamed of for years, but she soon found ways to bring it a bit closer. George Washington High School had a thriving drama department, and Sue was active in several of the productions there. During her senior year she was accepted into the All City Radio Workshop, a group composed of students drawn from each of New York City's five boroughs who acted in radio plays broadcast by WNYE, the New York City Board of Education's designated radio station. Sue got course credit for participating, and she loved being able to skip classes in the afternoon to head over to WNYE and go to work as an actress. She also made a move that was, in its way, fairly remarkable: she became an acting student of the well-known Betty Cashman, who maintained a studio at Carnegie Hall.

By 1950, Cashman was in her early forties and had begun to crest as a New York City drama coach of flair and imagination. She had started coaching young fashion models registered with Ford Models, the top agency owned by Eileen Ford; with television just getting off the ground, there was a demand for beautiful young women to perform in commercials. She was also working with Jack Palance, who later in 1950 would break through as an exciting and original screen personality in Elia Kazan's *Panic in the Streets* and would quickly earn a pair of Academy Award nominations for his work in David Miller's *Sudden Fear* (1952) and George Stevens's *Shane* (1953). Cashman would later also help groom Tony Curtis for movie stardom.

Betty Cashman was a striking woman with a dynamic, authoritative presence. "It was almost as if there was a force field around her when she came into the room," recalled Seymour Kover, who began studying with her in 1956. Cashman had jet-black hair, her makeup was always carefully done, and she favored expertly tailored suits; Kover remembered her as "not Rita Hayworth attractive but Joan Bennett attractive, Paulette Goddard attractive." She didn't present her students in full productions, but concentrated on intensive and detailed scene work. Although she discussed Lee Strasberg and the Actors Studio Method in her classes, she believed it was not the actor's job to come up with motivations rooted in his personal past. Cashman was a strict mistress of re-creation, who believed that the playwright had given the actor the reason for every move he made, and it was up to the actor to discover what it was. Before studying with Cashman, most young actors worked with one of her assistants on articulating and projecting their lines. Once they had passed that test, they were moved on to Cashman's beginning-level class. "Betty taught us to have a certain accent—close to Midwestern, white-bread," recalled Kover. "She called it a 'silver cup' accent. She wanted us to get rid of our New York sound."

Cashman had strong ties to the Bronx; Tony Curtis had been born Bernie Schwartz there. Several of Cashman's students found out about her by hanging around Schneider's candy store on 174th Street and Bryant Avenue, and it seems likely that this is where Sue learned about her. In later years she told Hollywood friends about a particular candy store in the Bronx that had been a favorite haunt of hers as a high school student.

Cashman generally wouldn't accept high school students, preferring to work with young actors who could devote themselves to their craft full time, with no other distractions. When Sue began studying with her in 1950, she was a bit intimidated by the older woman's cosmopolitan manner. But she liked the fact that everything in Cashman's studio reeked of authority and class. Cashman sat at her desk, in front of the window, while the students seated themselves on couches lined up around the walls, waiting to get up and do their scenes and monologues. Sue responded well to Cashman's rigorous coachings on various accents, and she loved the improvisatory exercises that the students were called upon to do whenever Cashman threw out a title or a subject. "We were challenged to be creative," said Kover. "Maybe we would take the scene from *Julius Caesar* where Mark Antony is screaming after Caesar is assassinated. She would ask us to throw a couple of nuances in, making it a little bit different. Maybe you'd do it like you were a gangster in New York, or a Frenchman."

After her stifling years with George and Ruth, Sue seems to have relished the opportunity to let her imagination fly. She also knew that Cashman was connected with casting directors at several of the major Hollywood studios, most of whom maintained corporate offices in New York. To get a "New York test" was a coveted opportunity for any young acting student, and Sue hoped that she would be one of the lucky ones called. Her biggest problem was her weight, which she constantly struggled to keep down. She was not helped in this battle by Ruth, who, upon leaving for work each morning, left Sue a muffin and a glass of milk on the kitchen countertop. Decades later Sue would tell journalist Marie Brenner that the sight of that muffin and glass of milk came to symbolize for her the squalor that she longed to escape.

By now Sue was a very pretty blue-eyed blonde, with thick, lustrous hair and luminescent skin. But try as she might to glamorize herself, she could not conform to Hollywood standards of beauty; she was simply a bit too zaftig to prolong the fantasy of becoming a leading lady. Given her sharp wit and sense of the absurd, she might have done very well as a brassy, hard-edged character actress—someone along the lines of Barbara Nichols, who worked steadily throughout the 1950s. But being a young edition of a Glenda Farrell or Joan Blondell—the heroine's sharp-tongued girlfriend—wasn't an avenue she cared to explore. Even at this early age she had her heart set on becoming an above-the-line star in some field, although her sense of how to accomplish it was amorphous. Ruth considered her daughter's ideas of Hollywood fame to be zany, and she was routinely dismissive of the idea, urging Sue instead to find a good, steady job as a secretary—an existence that sounded poisonous to Sue.

At home the tension between Ruth and Sue continued to escalate. For many Jewish families at this time, it was a strange thing to have a daughter who was bursting to go out and conquer the world. Sons were encouraged to achieve, to make money, but daughters were generally expected to make a solid marriage and raise a family. Ruth's resistance to her daughter's yearnings for fame are understandable; after what she had endured, she was no doubt genuinely frightened of the unknown. (Sue's close friend Sherry Lansing, whose mother also escaped Nazi Germany, observed, "What happens to someone who is a happy-go-lucky person filled with love, and all of a sudden they slap an armband on you and you can't go into this building, and you have to escape, and you don't speak the language in the new country? How guarded do you become?") Ruth also possessed the classic Germanic pursuit of perfection, hence her incessant criticism of Sue. There may have been another side to her disparagement of her daughter as well. "German Jews think if they say anything good, God will curse them," said Lansing. "Don't praise the ones you love, or bad things will happen."

Much insight into the struggles of Jewish refugee families can be found in *A Bintel Brief*, a collection of letters to the advice columnist of the *Jewish Daily Forward*, compiled and edited by Isaac Metzker. These letters, revealing the experience of Jewish immigrants of George and Ruth Mengers's generation and their thoroughly Americanized children, are funny, moving, outrageous, and frustrating, in fairly equal parts. A woman writes to ask if she should forgive her daughter for once having married a Gentile because the daughter is now about to marry again, to a Jewish man. A man complains that his wife is addicted to playing Bingo, which she justifies on the grounds that she doesn't drink and smoke as other women do. A woman who divorced her first husband decades ago has discovered that he has since become very wealthy and wants to know, even though she has remarried, if it is all right to approach Husband No. 1 about money. A man who married for a second time is devastated to learn that his new wife has secretly been saving money in a separate bank account. The shadow behind these letters, of course, is the arduous transition to life in America that took years to make, the longing for security that, for many, the passage of years did nothing to diminish.

Sue continued to develop the formidable survival tool of her sharp wit. During the end of her high school years, she mailed a black-and-white snapshot of herself, provocatively hiking up her skirts with her thumbs, to Roz Slakter back in Utica. "Dear Roz," Sue wrote, "Don't you dare hang this up in your bathroom. I'll haunt you if you do. How about one of you? We're running out of toilet paper."

CHAPTER THREE

1950–1957

On March 11, 1950, Ruth remarried, becoming Mrs. Eugene Sender. Her new husband was also a German émigré, who had come to New York from Wittberg, where he had operated a shoe store. Ruth's second marriage was by all accounts far happier than her first. Eugene saw to it that they all moved out of the Bronx and into an apartment in a far better neighborhood, at 108-50 Austin Street in Rego Park, Queens. It was another heavily populated Jewish neighborhood, and Ruth had no trouble making friends; soon, she was part of a regular group of ladies who played mah-jongg. The friction between mother and daughter only increased with the addition of Sender to the household, since Sue and Eugene were never very fond of each other. "I always thought that Ruth and Sue didn't get along because they were so much alike," remembered Barbara Sender, who married Eugene's nephew, Leo Sender. "Ruth had a sharp wit, and a lot of those staid German people didn't appreciate it. She was not a typical German wife and mother. I think Sue had a lot of her mother's qualities. And Eugene had never been married before, and suddenly there is this bombshell of a daughter in the house. I don't think he knew how to deal with that."

After graduating from George Washington High School in 1950, Sue pursued work as a radio actress in New York, but the glory that the medium had once represented was fading fast in light of television's enormous popularity. She still indulged herself by idly dreaming of Hollywood fame, but in the end her strong sense of pragmatism trumped her ability to keep the dream alive. For Sue, Hollywood represented the kind of drop-dead glamour she would experience in movies like *How to Marry a Millionaire*. She might dream about living a life designed by Travilla and Charles LeMaire, but it must have been difficult to keep believing in the fantasies of Sue Mengers, struggling actress from the Bronx, when she was being confronted with so much evidence that she might never be invited to the parties she desperately longed to attend.

Was there ever a better time than the mid-1950s to be living in New York City? Even though World War II had ended ten years earlier, there was still an almost palpable feeling of confidence and excitement that it was over and that life was now, it seemed, better than ever could have been imagined. In her book *Manhattan '45,* Jan Morris memorably caught the spirit of the times when she described the arrival of the *Queen Mary* into New York Harbor on June 20, 1945, carrying over fourteen thousand American servicemen and women returning home a little more than one month after V-E Day. The ship, Morris wrote, "was welcomed like a promise of great times." Those times weren't long in arriving: the lean, claustrophobic atmosphere of the war years, with everyone weighed down by shortages and self-sacrifice, had receded. In fields ranging from big business to the arts, Americans believed they could accomplish practically anything.

In 1955, Broadway was still in the midst of a very rich period, with hits like *Cat on a Hot Tin Roof, Bus Stop, The Diary of Anne Frank, Janus,* and *The Matchmaker* pulling in the crowds. The nightlife was intoxicating: clubs like the Copacabana, the Latin Quarter, and the Bon Soir frequently didn't close their doors until 4 A.M. or later.

On a daily basis Sue was pressing her nose against the glass, scrutinizing any one of a number of young New York women she considered far more fortunate than herself—the women in their Ceil Chapman "New Look" dresses, with nipped-in waists and full skirts, and elbow-length evening gloves, daintily carrying evening bags—women who were continually turning up at New York's top nightspots on the arm of handsome and eligible men.

At Six East Fifty-eighth Street, just off Fifth Avenue, was a restaurant called Reuben's. It was an all-night place famous for being home to the Reuben sandwich, and it was frequented by nightclub singers coming in after they finished their 2 A.M. shows, by Catskills comics, and by Broadway performers who liked to drop by for a bite after their shows had let out. After Sue and her friends attended a Broadway play or a late movie, they went to Reuben's, where they were inevitably made to stand in line, the smell of corned beef and pastrami wafting out of the kitchen, and wait for quite some time for a table in Siberia to be made available to them.

While she was waiting, Sue often saw Judy Balaban, a young woman she was always reading about in Cholly Knickerbocker's and Walter Winchell's columns, saunter in the front door, looking like Sue's vision of Daisy

Buchanan in *The Great Gatsby*. As the daughter of Paramount Pictures president Barney Balaban, Judy was part of the Hollywood elite, one of Grace Kelly's closest friends, and eventually one of the star's bridesmaids at her wedding to Prince Rainier of Monaco. Balaban would walk into Reuben's with some attractive man, and Sue would watch forlornly while the maître d' snapped into action and secured Balaban the best table possible. Years later, when Sue confessed to Judy how envious she had been, Balaban explained it all to her: "I was Patsy Reuben's best friend, and Patsy was the stepdaughter of Arnie Reuben, the owner. When I walked in, anyone in the place knew me as Patsy's best friend!"

Sue had dropped her studies with Betty Cashman, but if she had to join the masses of working girls whom Rona Jaffe described as streaming in and out of the subways, at least maybe she could find a job in a reasonably glamorous environment. One day in 1955, she answered a newspaper advertisement for a receptionist at the Music Corporation of America, the monolithic talent agency headed by Jules Stein and Lew Wasserman. Her typing and steno skills were only fair, but she landed the job anyway.

In that year MCA was approaching its zenith as the most powerful agency in the country. While agents had been a regular presence in New York from the nineteenth century, talent agencies in their modern definition—organizations that set out to find work for their clients under the best possible financial and creative terms—hadn't really sprung up in the movie business until the late 1920s. In his fine history of the birth of the agency business, *Hidden Talent: The Emergence of Hollywood Agents*, Tom Kemper states that by the early 1930s there was a total of four firms representing the lion's share of members of the Academy of Motion Picture Arts and Sciences. In a few years that number would balloon, but during the 1930s, the field of agenting was dominated by a handful of tough-minded, imaginative, and forward-thinking individuals like Myron Selznick and Charles Feldman. William Morris and MCA, which both got their start as bookers of vaudeville and variety talent, didn't get into the movie business in a major way until the 1940s.

Founded in 1924 by Jules Stein and William R. Goodheart, Jr., MCA had established itself by booking swing bands and singers; for more than two decades, the agency's Bands & Acts Department had a powerful lock on placing talent at nightclubs, speakeasies, and dance halls throughout the country. In 1936, Stein hired twenty-three-year-old Lew Wasserman, a move that would have a sweeping effect on both MCA's future and the future of show business at large. Knowing that any agency's power depended on the level of talent it had to sell, Wasserman eventually persuaded Stein that the company's real future lay in representing top Hollywood actors. MCA moved swiftly and surely, raiding clients of other agents by promising them that their careers would be in better hands than they could ever have imagined. Within a few years it had swept past William Morris to become the most powerful and star-laden agency in the country. James Stewart became a client, as did Bette Davis, Joan Crawford, Kirk Douglas, Jack Benny, and dozens of others.

Wasserman was a hardheaded executive and a lethal adversary. He confounded studio heads by demanding duplicate copies of the scripts being offered to his clients and often sharply contradicting the studio bosses with his own views on how a picture should be cast or rewritten—or whether it should be made at all. Jack L. Warner, the pugnacious head of production at Warner Bros., had a particular antipathy for Wasserman; among other things, he held him responsible for the decline in Bette Davis's career after World War II, claiming that she relied too heavily on Wasserman's script judgment. (The real culprit here was the succession of second-rate vehicles that Warner Bros. saddled Davis with after 1945.)

Wasserman was also enormously self-protective, and could not be counted on to stand by one of his clients in time of trouble. In the 1940s, Nancy Coleman was a gifted, rising Warner Bros. contract actress, whose strong performances in movies such as *Kings Row* (1942) and *Edge of Darkness* (1943) seemed to destine her for stardom. Wasserman took charge of all facets of her career and even helped her pick out a house. But after Coleman displeased the studio bosses by marrying Warner Bros. publicist Whitney Bolton, Wasserman refused to come to her aid when she was abruptly dropped from the company roster and found herself a Hollywood has-been. In the end, Wasserman was not the kind of agent who could lend a steadying, helpful hand to an actor's artistic growth; like most agents of the time, he was out to make money, first, last, and always.

Wasserman's fame and power outlasted that of many of his famous clients. By 1955, when Sue came to work at MCA, the agency had gotten itself into the business of television production, a move that was supposed to be unlawful. The period had seen a great deal of antitrust legislation. The crucial moment for the entertainment industry was the decision in *United States v. Paramount Pictures, Inc.* of 1948, which led to the separation of the studios' production and exhibition enterprises; in order to remain in business, the studios had to divest themselves of the chains of theaters into which they had booked their own movies for years. Similarly, supplying talent and producing the entertainment in which to cast that talent was defined by the government as a monopoly. No agency was supposed to be able to get away with it. Just how Wasserman *did* get away with it owed a great deal to his brilliant instinct for recognizing and taking advantage of a critical turning point in Hollywood history. Audiences were rapidly withdrawing from the movie culture that had been so strong from the 1930s through World War II and immediately after; by the 1950s, Americans were trying to knit their lives back together after the disruption of the war years, and many were far happier to stay at home playing regular Thursday night canasta or watching *I Married Joan* and *Dragnet* than they were to get dressed up and go out to the movies. In their CinemaScope splendor, *The Robe* and *Three Coins in the Fountain* might individually clean up at the box office, but they didn't do anything to halt the trend of declining movie revenues. With the studios in retrenchment mode, making fewer films and canceling actors' contracts left and right, Wasserman put his energies behind television as a lucrative source of potential employment that could provide a haven for newly out-of-work movie stars. One of Wasserman's clients—not a particularly successful one in recent years—was actor Ronald Reagan, who had become president of the Screen Actors Guild in 1947. Wasserman assured SAG that he would provide actors with desperately needed job opportunities through TV work, and Reagan saw to it that SAG granted MCA a special waiver to go into TV production. Through its home company, Revue Studios, MCA began the march on monopoly that would eventually land it in trouble with the U.S. government.

As a TV producer, Wasserman employed the same bullying tactics that had marked his career as an agent. Performers who objected to his mafioso tactics and wanted to leave MCA were threatened with being blackballed in the industry. As the big studios were cutting back production and selling off their back lots, the balance of power was shifting to the agents—most of all, to Wasserman.

According to Wasserman's biographer Kathleen Sharp, so many MCA stars were appearing on Revue TV programs that a dispiriting sameness had spread across the networks, much to the consternation of many network television executives. If a TV host or producer objected to the fee the agency demanded for a guest appearance by one of MCA's clients, Wasserman might vindictively jack up the price another notch or two. MCA did some pioneering deal making in the early days of television. In the early 1950s, one of Wasserman's top executives, Taft Schreiber, met with William Paley, chairman of CBS Television, to tell him that he was planning to move three immensely popular radio acts—George Burns and Gracie Allen, Jack Benny, and Edgar Bergen and Charlie McCarthy—into television. Schreiber offered Paley a deal in which the stars would own the negatives. "Who ever heard of an entertainer being owner of his material?" recalled George Burns's longtime MCA agent, Jerry Zeitman. "NBC Radio had owned everything and that's the way it worked! So we ended up making that deal and George ended up owning 240 episodes of *The George Burns and Gracie Allen Show.*"

During Hollywood's Golden Age of the 1930s and '40s, most actors—even huge stars like MGM's Clark Gable—had simply collected their salaries and done as they were told. Occasionally a savvy star such as Claudette Colbert would land an outside picture deal with profit participation. In 1950, Wasserman cut a deal that would signal an enormous shift in actors' dealings with studios. James Stewart had signed to make the Western *Winchester '73* for Universal Pictures. Wasserman, sensing that the picture might net more money for Stewart and MCA on a straight percentage basis, cut a deal with the studio in which Stewart waived his salary in return for 50 percent of the profits. The film was a smash, and Stewart went from being a highly paid actor to being a wealthy man; it was estimated that he made $1 million on the deal, and that MCA's take was $100,000.

As the 1950s progressed, with the studio system steadily collapsing, more and more actors and their agents began getting rich on percentage deals and by founding their own production companies. By the time the veteran multiple Academy Award–winning director Frank Capra was setting up his final movie, *Pocketful of Miracles*, in 1960, the demands from actors and their agents, attorneys, and business managers were so complicated that he began to wonder why he had ever bothered to come back to make the picture; simply casting the leading male role demanded a level of deal making unknown to Capra during his salad days in the 1930s.

But for every star like Cary Grant and Tony Curtis who worked out advantageous percentage deals, there were plenty of actors stuck with contracts that were not bringing them serious money. Major 1950s stars like Grace Kelly, who had a multiple-picture deal at MGM, and Marilyn Monroe, under a long-term contract to Twentieth Century Fox, did not make huge salaries, even though many of their pictures were top grossers. "Most of the pictures Grace did away from MGM were on loan-out to Paramount for not much money," remembered Kelly's MCA agent, Jay Kanter, "and usually if they loaned somebody, the studios would charge them double as to what the actors were actually getting from their contract. From time to time, on some of those pictures, Grace would get a bonus." Kelly did better on *High Society*, the 1956 Cole Porter musical she made with Frank Sinatra and Bing Crosby. "She sang a few lines on the record that Crosby did of 'True Love,'" Kanter recalled, "and because the record became a huge success, and because he had a very lucrative recording deal, Grace made more on those two or three lines she sang than she did on the picture." Marilyn Monroe, for her part, didn't earn a salary that could be called truly substantial until her own production company made the 1957 romantic comedy *The Prince and the Showgirl*, costarring Laurence Olivier, and she commanded $250,000.

Obviously, it was heady stuff for an agent to line up a lucrative deal for a star client, but the MCA bosses did have some concern about their responsibility to the film industry at large. While Wasserman encouraged his agents to work the best deal possible, there was an understanding that they were to operate within certain basic parameters and not demand anything that the industry couldn't support in the long run. Kanter recalled that Marlon Brando's salary for his Oscar-winning role in *On the Waterfront* (1954) was $125,000. Brando was famous for not wanting to go to work, but after an unpleasant and financially draining divorce from his wife, Anna Kashfi, in 1959, he was in need of quick cash. Kanter made a deal for him to do *The Fugitive Kind* for $1 million for United Artists. When the studio boss, Arthur Krim, called Wasserman to complain about Brando's salary, Wasserman came into Kanter's office to warn him, "Jay, you're going to ruin this business." During the 1950s, stars were not making $1 million salaries, or anything close to it. Kanter recalled that John Wayne had gotten "a deal at Fox for two or three pictures for $750,000 each. That was top money then."

Looking at the run of movie premieres, the casual observer might easily assume that films were more in demand than ever—big-budget, color, wide-screen pictures like *Love Is a Many-Splendored Thing*, *Picnic*, and *Demetrius and the Gladiators* were box-office successes. But partly because of escalating production costs since the end of the war, the number of movies being made was declining rapidly. Universal Pictures slid from producing thirty-three pictures in 1953 to eleven in 1959, Paramount Pictures from twenty-five to seventeen, MGM from thirty-four to twenty-two. (Columbia Pictures was one of the only studios to hold steady, going from thirty-three productions in 1953 to thirty in 1959.) This period saw a particularly marked decrease in the number of the black-and-white "B" pictures that had been the mainstay of the studios for so long. These films, often released on the bottom half of double bills, were cheap to make and more often than not posted a decent profit. But from the mid-1950s on, the studios would favor fewer and bigger pictures. It would become harder to make second features like *Ma and Pa Kettle at Waikiki* or *Abbott and Costello Meet the Mummy* or even a classic little noir thriller like *The Narrow Margin* when the studios were eager to provide glossier fare.

When Sue reported to work at MCA's offices at 598 Madison Avenue, on the corner of Fifty-seventh Street, the atmosphere was very buttoned-down. The agents, under Wasserman's orders, wore crisp black and charcoal suits and starched white shirts with black ties; "Dress British, think Yiddish" was one of Wasserman's dictums. There was little room for personal flamboyance or individuality in Wasserman's formal corporate atmosphere. Most employees waited for him to address them instead of saying good morning and asking how he was today; it was made clear that one did not shoot the breeze with Lew Wasserman. There was also a strict policy against personal publicity for agents. "I always turned down being interviewed," said Jerry Zeitman. "We were not allowed to talk about ourselves. If a reporter wanted to interview us, we would talk about our clients."

As Jules and Doris Stein were both serious collectors of eighteenth-century English furniture, the New York offices of MCA, as well as those in Los Angeles, were showrooms that displayed the bounty from their frequent

antique-hunting trips to England. The Steins believed that since the employees spent more time in the workplace than they did in their homes, the
offices ought to be furnished as attractively as possible, and they leased
the antiques to MCA. (They were smart businesspeople, too. Office furniture
only declines in value, while antiques appreciate.) "They did insist on one
thing," remembered Jay Kanter. "Your office had to be spotless. Not a piece of
paper on the desk. And at the time there was a lot of smoking going on, and
they had these beautiful antique ashtrays in every office, but you could
never leave your office with a speck of ash or cigarette in them. And they
would go through the offices at night, making sure that everybody kept the
place as it if was their own home."

Sue's first post at MCA was as a general receptionist, but after several
months she became Jay Kanter's secretary. She loved taking calls from
Kanter's clients—Marlon Brando, Grace Kelly, Marilyn Monroe. Kanter recalled her as efficient and cheerful throughout the time she worked for him.
She was bright, and most of the people at MCA were quite taken with her
quick, sharp wit.

In December 1955, MCA threw its annual Christmas celebration for its
employees. Sue was the life of the party, sipping champagne and moving
from one conversation to the next. As the party wound down, Kanter thought
that things were too pleasant to break up, and he telephoned his wife, Judy
Balaban, at their apartment at Two Sutton Place South. The Kanters were
planning to entertain some friends with a rather elaborate after-theater
party in their home the following evening, and Judy Balaban had spent two
days readying the apartment, setting up the cocktail glasses on the table in
the foyer, stocking the bar, arranging the dining room table, and ordering
flowers for the living room. She was still applying the finishing touches
when Kanter telephoned to say he was bringing home several people from
the office party. It had all been Sue's idea. "She had somehow negotiated
that a whole group of affable folk would accompany Jay back to our apartment," recalled Balaban. "There, they promptly drank all the booze, used
all the plates for whatever food I had in the house, dirtied all the ashtrays.
Whatever it was—gone! But Sue was very sweet with me, and the only thing
that bothered me was that I had to get it all together again between then
and the next night at ten o'clock!" Decades later Balaban remembered that
it was the first time that Sue's assertive personality revealed itself to her.

But when evenings like this ended, Sue still had to get herself on the subway, back to her unglamorous existence. It must have given her cold comfort to think how far she had come from the days when she lived in Utica, not speaking more than a few words of English. She was still the little pisher from the Bronx, still the girl standing on the outside.

One of her good friends around this time was Joan Fisher, who worked as secretary to former MCA agent Johnny Greenhut. "We became friends on the phone," said Fisher. "We had lunch all the time at Reuben's. We would have tongue sandwiches and corned beef sandwiches, and she always had cheesecake for dessert, and she would put it on her bill. She talked a lot about her mother. I think in a way that she felt her mother was holding her back. She saw the end of the tunnel, and she didn't want anything in her way."

With movie and television stars constantly dropping by, the office was a great escape for Sue, but even there she was constantly being reminded of her third-class citizenship. After her stint in Jay Kanter's office, she went to work for Maynard Morris, whose MCA clients included Tyrone Power. Once she was asked to drop a film script off at Power's apartment. She was thrilled with the assignment, hoping to have a few words with the handsome star of *In Old Chicago, The Razor's Edge,* and *Nightmare Alley.* When she arrived at 760 Park Avenue, though, she got a frosty greeting from a doorman, who took the script from her and sent her on her way. Years later, after she had become a successful agent, she would make a point of telling reporters how lowly and insignificant the episode had made her feel.

CHAPTER FOUR

1957–1959

In 1957, Sue left MCA. She always claimed that she had been fired because of an unpleasant episode with Maynard Morris. As she told it, one day Morris was expecting a call from Tyrone Power to confirm a tentative dinner date. The day went by, and Power didn't telephone. Finally, around five in the afternoon, Morris had to use the bathroom and told Sue that, if Power called, she wasn't to say anything other than "Mr. Power, I will get him on the phone." She was then to knock on the men's room door and alert Morris. Sue always remembered that Power's call came through just after Morris went to the men's room, and before she could ask him to hold, Power told her to inform Morris that he couldn't have dinner that night after all, and hung up. According to Sue, Morris was enraged by her ineptitude and fired her immediately.

When another secretarial post opened up at a smaller concern, the Baum & Newborn Agency, she grabbed the opportunity, even though she still wasn't very good at shorthand. Her new place of employment was not even ten years old; her bosses, Martin Baum and Abe Newborn, had gone into business together in 1948, just a few years after Baum returned from World War II service. During its early years Baum & Newborn specialized in representing actors and directors in the New York theater. Their offices were originally located at 743 Fifth Avenue, just across the street from Bergdorf Goodman department store. The two partners seemed, on the surface, to have entirely different styles. The rather taciturn Abe Newborn cut corners any way he could, ordering second-rate delicatessen food to be brought in for client meetings and using the cardboard cutouts that came in dry-cleaner shirt boxes for place mats. Martin Baum was a pugnacious man who believed in doing business in a first-class way, and whatever touch of refinement the office possessed was due to him. Baum lived in tony Brookville, Long Island, and made sure that his wife's jewelry came from Cartier, so she always looked her best.

Acting teacher Wynn Handman, a Baum & Newborn client at the time, remembered that no one in the office used an intercom; the staff communicated by shouting from one room to the other. When it came to theatrical excess, it often seemed that the employees rivaled the clients. One of the agency's top stars at the time was Red Buttons, and as he became more and more popular in the 1950s, Handman became his clearinghouse for dramatic scripts. "If I said, 'Red, this is junk,' it would naturally bother Martin Baum, because he was making a commission," Handman recalled. "One time, Martin was on the phone, shouting and all of that, and he sees me come in. A script for Red was on the desk, and he's shouting and shouting, and then he looks at me and immediately starts crying: 'Just read the last page! It's so *moving*!'"

Actress Sylvia Miles, who signed with Baum & Newborn in the mid-1950s, remembered that the agency was considered "small potatoes. Not classy. It was a place you went on your way to somewhere bigger. Abe Newborn didn't have any class. He was like a Dead End Kid. Marty Baum, though, was different—he was someone who was destined to be big in Hollywood. And he trained a lot of people."

Not long after Sue's arrival, the second secretary's position at Baum & Newborn was filled by a dapper young Englishman named Lionel Larner, who, coming from a rather formal background, behaved very appropriately, turning up each day well before the office opened at ten, neatly dressed in a jacket and tie. Sometime around ten fifteen, Sue would stroll in, her hair still in curlers—just like many of the girls Rona Jaffe described in *The Best of Everything*. In the years since she had given up her acting ambitions, she had gained weight. Her seams might not be exactly straight, and she would have deli coffee in a cardboard cup as she sat down at her desk to begin opening submissions from actors. Larner recalled that Sue would slit open the envelopes, pull out the 8 x 10 glossies, and say, "Oh, honey, *you're* never going to make it. Oh, you poor thing!" and toss the photos into the wastebasket.

Larner had never experienced anyone remotely like Sue. At the time, it was unusual for any woman in business to use rough language in the workplace, but Sue unleashed a shower of four-letter words on a daily basis— one of the many things she did that provoked Martin Baum's anger. She tried his patience so much that he fired her on several occasions, only to hire her back quickly.

One major blunder involved Red Buttons, who during Sue's first year in the office would win an Academy Award for Best Actor in a Supporting Role for his performance in Joshua Logan's *Sayonara*. Buttons was doing a nightclub act in Las Vegas that had opened to dreadful reviews. Baum had commissioned some new material for Buttons to liven up the act and handed the pages to Sue to send by express mail. Instead, she sent it by regular mail. When Baum found out, he was furious and fired her on the spot. As Larner recalled, "She went down to the mailbox and waited for the postal worker and desperately tried to persuade him to give the envelope back to her. And he said, 'Lady, it's against the law. I can't do it!' She pleaded and cajoled and simply wouldn't let it go. She said, 'My mother's dying, and I need this job to pay her hospital expenses,' and she cried and carried on. She got the envelope back."

Another time a call came in to the agency with a job for actress Sarah Marshall. It required a fast commitment, and Sue wasn't able to reach Marshall by phone. Baum screamed at her to use her brains and try to figure out where Marshall might be. Sue turned to Larner and cooed, in the third-person baby talk she now often used when referring to herself, "Baby Sue's smart. Baby Sue goes to Sardi's and Lindy's and Downey's, and Baby Sue knows what's going on. Baby Sue knows that Sarah Marshall is *doing it* with Conrad Janis. Just watch this." Certain that Marshall must be at Janis's apartment at that very moment, she picked up the phone, dialed a number, and said, "Sarah—you sneaky, sneaky thing. Hold on for Marty Baum." The woman who answered the phone was Conrad Janis's wife. Baum sacked Sue once again.

Somehow Sue always found her way back into Baum's good graces, however briefly. As his constant rehiring of Sue reflects, Baum was not unreasonable or intractable, though he did demand a great deal of his employees, all of whom had to be on call seven days a week. All of them had to subscribe to an answering service so Baum would know exactly where they were at all times. "Once I had to go out to Fire Island to find some actor for Marty," Larner remembered. "I had no idea, really, where Fire Island was, and I said, 'How can I find him?' Marty said, '*Fire Island is Fire Island*. Everyone knows everybody else. Just go out there and do it. Don't come back until you've found him.' I was quite terrified, but I had to do it."

Even in the chaotic atmosphere of Baum & Newborn, Sue's behavior stood out. She had carried into adulthood her childlike way of spitting out scalding opinions simply for shock value, and it had the intended effect: to make people notice her. Ruth frequently called the office, and when Larner would tell Sue that her mother was on the phone, she would often say, in mock incredulity, "Mother? *Mother?*" Then she would pick up the phone and shout, for dramatic effect, "Mother, what do you want *this* time?"

Her sharpness also took on a racist edge at times. In Sue's case it was done chiefly for comic effect, to put people off guard. She would open envelopes containing 8 x 10s of African-American actors and laugh that the photos looked like negatives. In 1959, Baum & Newborn represented Sidney Poitier and Claudia McNeil, who were starring in Lorraine Hansberry's new Broadway play *A Raisin in the Sun*, about a struggling black family in Chicago; the office also represented the play's director, Lloyd Richards. On opening night the staff was getting changed in the office to go to the opening. When Larner returned to his desk after putting on his suit in the men's room, another secretary, Sandy Newman, asked Sue if she thought they were overdressed.

"Are you kidding?" she replied. "Wait till you see what those *schwartzes* are wearing!"

The tough-talking Sue and the buttoned-down Lionel Larner might not have seemed destined to be friends, and at first they maintained a cool distance. Martin Baum and Abe Newborn usually weren't in the office before eleven, and frequently, Sue and the other staff members ignored the rule that the office open for business at ten, choosing to roll in around ten thirty. One day Baum summoned Larner and demanded an accounting of the exact times that people showed up at the office. Larner equivocated. Baum called in the staff and ordered them to tell him what time they reported to work, adding that Larner had had the decency not to snitch on them. Later Sue piped up, "You know, when Lionel came here, we didn't like him. But he's a great guy." They were good friends from that point on.

Sue worked hard but maintained a clear sense of independence as well. Sandy Newman was always staying late or coming in on weekends to catch up with the filing.

"Well, some girls go on dates," Sue would say, "and some girls do the filing."

Sue went on plenty of dates. Now in her mid-twenties, she made sure

34 Can I Go Now?

that men knew she was interested and available. But she was very skilled at manipulating them. Through her work at Baum & Newborn, Sue got to know the famous theatrical producer and songwriter Billy Rose, who by the late 1950s was well past his peak years. Rose was a coarse-looking man, far from handsome, and he was more than thirty years her senior, but Sue found his reputation quite seductive, and Rose became one of her first big affairs. When she met him, she didn't want to tell him she was a secretary, so she fibbed harmlessly and said she was an agent with Baum & Newborn. The next day Rose telephoned the office, and Sue answered his call.

"This is Billy Rose calling for Sue Mengers."

There was a long pause. "Just one moment, please."

Then she came back to the phone using an entirely different voice.

"Miss Mengers's office."

"Is Miss Mengers in?"

"Who's calling?"

"Billy Rose."

Another long pause. Another change of voice.

"Hello, *darling*!"

At the time, Sue was living in a rooming house for older Jewish ladies at 269 West Seventy-second Street, on an undistinguished block just east of West End Avenue. After the war, many German refugees had settled in the neighborhood, and there was a gym in the basement of the Ansonia Hotel on Broadway with a staff of European masseuses catering to women who had enjoyed a certain social standing in their home country. Many of these ladies would go for an afternoon massage, then stroll up Broadway or Columbus Avenue and drop in at one of the specialty shops that sold apple strudel and linzer tortes. Billy Rose would leave messages with Sue's answering service asking to take her out to dinner or the theater, and Sue would call him back and tell him to pick her up at the elegant Hampshire House on Central Park South, where she said she had an apartment. She warned him not to call her there, because the girls on the switchboard listened in, and they would both wind up in the columns—and they didn't want that, did they?

Sue's determination to reinvent herself was seen by many people as charming and admirable, and they were willing to do whatever they could to help her along with her schemes. Others, however, were annoyed by her envy of people from superior backgrounds and her head-on determination to become someone she wasn't. Sylvia Miles had grown up in a fairly prosperous family at the Osborne, a fashionable apartment house on West Fifty-seventh Street, where successful actresses such as Shirley Booth and Paula Laurence lived. Miles recalled that whenever she came into the Baum & Newborn office, Sue was never particularly friendly toward her.

During Sue's Baum & Newborn years, she became friendly with Jerry Herman, a young composer/lyricist a few years away from his first Broadway success, *Milk and Honey* (1961). They went to the theater together constantly, and Sue would make note of performers that Baum & Newborn might represent. She was enamored of many of the great stage actors of the period, and Herman remembered in particular her fondness for Geraldine Page. Sue took him to see Tennessee Williams's 1959 hit *Sweet Bird of Youth*, and Herman recalled that Page's performance as on-the-skids actress Alexandra del Lago "took our breath away."

Herman had a house on Fire Island, at the corner of Oak and Ocean, and in the summer Sue often came for weekend visits. Herman relished her spirit and wit and flouting of convention—such as not wearing clothes. He also loved her ability to tell stories on herself, such as the one about getting locked out of her West Side apartment while taking out the trash. She had been stark naked at the time, and there was nothing for her to do except take the elevator down to the lobby, casually stroll over to the man on the front desk, and ask for her apartment key.

One story of Sue in the raw struck closer to Herman's own home. Sue made no secret of her ambition to become a prominent woman agent in the theater, the equal of powerhouse Flora Roberts, the colorful, bourbon-voiced agent to Ira Levin, Stephen Sondheim, and a number of other up-and-coming talents in the theater. Once, in the summer of 1961, when Sue was visiting Herman at the Fire Island house, he and the other guests decided to go down to the beach for a swim. Sue was skinny-dipping in the pool when she heard someone pull up in the driveway, followed by footsteps coming around the back. It was director Jules Dassin and his lover, Melina Mercouri, who just the year before had scored an enormous hit with the Greek comedy *Never on Sunday*. Sue floated in the water for a moment, debating what to do, then emerged naked and dripping wet, strode over to

Dassin and Mercouri, stuck out her hand, and said, "Hi, I'm Flora Roberts." "Melina Mercouri and Jules Dassin were never the wiser," said Jerry Herman. "And that made it even funnier."

In her eagerness to present herself as someone more important than she really was, Sue frequently stepped out of line with the agency's clients, much to Martin Baum's annoyance. One of the big Broadway hits of the fall of 1960 was David Merrick's production of Jean Anouilh's *Becket*, starring Laurence Olivier as Thomas Becket and Anthony Quinn as King Henry II, directed by Peter Glenville. After a few months the play was being transferred from the St. James to the Royale Theatre. Baum booked an audition for the elderly character actor Joseph Sweeney, a veteran of decades' worth of stage and film productions. Sweeney's last notable Broadway role had been in Arthur Miller's *The Crucible* in 1953. When Sue telephoned the actor with the news, he replied coolly, "Joe Sweeney doesn't read."

"I don't think you understand me," said Sue. "This is Sue Mengers, and I have made an appointment for you to read for Peter Glenville in *Becket*, which is starting in mid-December at the Royale Theatre."

"And I told you, Joe Sweeney doesn't read."

"Joe Sweeney doesn't read," answered Sue, "and Joe Sweeney doesn't *work*."

The talent agencies of that period were almost entirely a man's world, though there were a few women agents in the theater—Flora Roberts and the even more prominent Audrey Wood, who represented some of the theater's leading playwrights, including Tennessee Williams, William Inge, Robert Anderson, and Carson McCullers. As the head, with her husband, William Liebling, of the Liebling-Wood Agency (which had been purchased by Sue's former employer, MCA, in 1954), Wood boasted many reasons for her enormous success in the theater: an editor's eye, a keen imagination, extreme patience while waiting for a client's script to take shape, and an ability to identify a play that had both artistic merit and commercial potential. Although she had begun her career with a hit farce, John Murray and Allen Boretz's *Room Service* in 1937, Wood's taste generally did not run toward musicals or boulevard comedies. (She did advise DuBose Heyward to sell the musical rights of his novel *Porgy* to George Gershwin rather than to Al Jolson, famously observing, "Jolson had the dough but Gershwin had the dream.")

Wood embraced scripts that were groundbreaking or experimental in nature, and she had an instinct for matching a playwright with a producer. Under her guidance playwrights like Williams, Inge, and Anderson became both rich and famous. "The theater today is wide open," she told a reporter in 1958. "There's a tremendous need for new talent. If you have any kind of talent at all, it sticks out—it cries out to be helped. But a play has to be good to succeed now. There is room only for quality now."

Wood was a woman with a distinctive personal style as well. Blue-eyed and auburn haired, she was small and dainty in stature and manners. She conducted her business wearing sensible suits and crisp little hats—a style that some of her colleagues believed harkened back to a time when female shopkeepers wore hats to distinguish them from the salesgirls. She was firm and decisive while maintaining an every-inch-a-lady demeanor, despite her disconcerting habit of hanging up the telephone without saying good-bye. She didn't yell and scream, partly because she didn't have to—in Williams, Anderson, and Inge, she had three of America's leading playwrights under her wing, and she had negotiated royalty agreements and movie sales for them that brought in enormous sums of money.

But Wood and Roberts were exceptions, as many actors of the time simply couldn't conceive of putting their business affairs in the hands of a woman. As a result, Sue's ambition, for the time being, remained latent, and she was content to impress people with her brightness and outrageous wit and fresh mouth. She would later look back at this time and dismiss it as her "Tillie the Toiler" era.

Still, she was a perpetual student, snaring tickets to as many plays as she could and studying the scripts, the actors, the set design, the lighting— trying hard to immerse herself in every aspect of the theater from the audience's point of view. She continued to frequent Downey's and Lindy's and Sardi's and to share whatever information she picked up there with her bosses.

She also made the rounds, as much as she was able, with actors and directors. This was near the end of the era when many young women in the workforce still believed that "nice girls didn't." Apart from the low-level salary, she loved the life of a working girl in show business in the late 1950s and early '60s—the invitations to parties and Broadway and nightclub openings, the proximity to celebrities, the nightlife, and the easy access to men. She believed that it was a woman's job to flatter a man, to make him think he had the ability to achieve immense power and financial success. She felt that men were essentially testosterone driven and faithless and that women should accept it and not expect them to be anything else. "They used to call her the Fucker to the Stars," said her friend Joan Fisher. "She knew it, too, and I don't think she cared. At this point, I don't think she was interested in anything but her career."

While she was still working for Baum & Newborn, Sue had an affair with a client of the agency, a low-level director, and underwent an abortion. (In her later years, she would tell some of her friends that she had had three.) She quietly shopped around for a doctor who could perform the surgery in clean, safe circumstances, and she had a quick recovery. She seldom indicated that the termination had cost her much emotionally. Clearly she was not in a position to raise a child, even had she wanted to—and she didn't. For all her life, she would almost always consider children—even if they belonged to her star clients—a nuisance, a bore, a waste of time. Sue believed that her friends' children should be kept away from her until they were eighteen and old enough to hold up their end of the conversation. Only *then* would they be worth her attention.

Sue agreed with Sylvia Miles's assessment of Baum & Newborn as "small potatoes." She could tell that if she was a good, complacent girl and stayed in one place for too long, she would be dead-ended. And when another secretarial job came up at the William Morris Agency, she took it.

CHAPTER FIVE

1959–1963

Sue's new post was as secretary to Charles Baker, head of the theater department at the William Morris Agency. This was the job she held when she undertook the first major transition of her professional life—when she began to think of herself as capable of doing something bigger than typing and making appointments for actors.

In his 1984 Broadway play, *End of the World,* Arthur Kopit made a character of his own agent, Audrey Wood, who occasionally steps forward to address the audience. In one of these asides, Wood (played by Linda Hunt) observes, *"What does an agent do? (pause)* This is a question I am asked all the time." On many evenings during the play's run, this line drew an enormous laugh from the in-the-know New York audience, who understood the implied complexity of the show business agent-client relationship, and how many actors and directors complained that their agents weren't working hard enough for them and that their career difficulties would be fixed if only they had the right representation.

Often those actors and directors were right, and often the situation was far more complicated than they would admit. In Kopit's play Wood goes on to answer her own question, "In *theory,* an agent is supposed to find her client *work.*" As she learned the ropes of the business during her years at William Morris and beyond, Sue would no doubt have defined the agent's task this cleanly and directly. But her time at William Morris led her to a deeper understanding of the business. She began to study the techniques and tactics of her bosses and to learn more about the history of the business she had only superficially grasped up until now.

The William Morris Agency had been incorporated in 1918 and flourished as the most popular form of American entertainment segued from vaudeville to silent movies. Because Broadway productions were so plentiful in the early part of the century—the number of New York plays produced annually hit its peak in 1928, with 224 productions, and off Broadway did

not really exist until decades later—there were many agents available to
deal with the enormous overflow of actors and directors. All day long actors
traipsed up and down the stairs to the agents' and producers' offices in
Times Square, going through a series of mostly fruitless interviews in an
attempt to get someone to sign them. Even by the 1950s, this was largely
how work in the theater was found. Actress Barbara Barrie remembered, "I
got my first Broadway job by making the rounds, by going into an office and
saying, 'I want to be in this play.'"

The first Hollywood talent agency is generally acknowledged to have
been Joyce-Selznick, Ltd., whose cofounder Myron Selznick, brother of titan producer David O. Selznick, is often said to have essentially invented
the role of the movie agent as an act of vengeance for the way the boys' father, Lewis J. Selznick, was treated by studio heads when his production
company went bankrupt in 1925. The relationship between film companies
and agents was an ever-fluctuating power play in which one side was up one
year, down the next. Myron Selznick was a gutsy gambler who delighted in
dangling a client before the studio heads and then mercilessly driving up
the price for her services. He was one of several agents viewed as the enemy
by major studios, thanks to his practice of inflating actors' salaries. In the
1930s, his star clients included Katharine Hepburn, Fredric March, Gary
Cooper, William Powell, Carole Lombard, and Kay Francis, as well as directors such as Lewis Milestone, William Wellman, and George Cukor. His
bullheaded approach was often stunningly successful; in 1931 Warner
Bros. was desperate for stars, and Selznick, according to film historian
Tom Kemper, persuaded the studio to pay $8,000 a week for Ruth Chatter-
ton, a popular and respected leading lady but never a top moneymaking
star. (The Chatterton deal is all the more striking when one takes into account that Bette Davis, who was a top box-office attraction, was making
only $7,000 a week at the peak of her fame in the mid-1940s—but then,
she didn't have Myron Selznick for an agent.) Also in 1931, Selznick worked
out a spectacular deal at Warner Bros. for Constance Bennett: $30,000 a
week for appearing in a middling soaper, *Bought!*, a deal that fell outside
her regular RKO contract. Selznick had a major advantage over many
of Hollywood's other agents: thanks to his status as a Selznick, he had
A-list social connections in Hollywood that permitted him easy access to

the top brass at the studios, no matter how much some of them cursed him behind his back.

Among the other prominent agents in Hollywood during the 1930s was Zeppo Marx, who figured out that no one really cared if he dropped out of his brothers' comedy team and went on to represent Clark Gable, Jean Harlow, Lana Turner, and Joan Fontaine. Then there was Charles Feldman, agent to Claudette Colbert, Irene Dunne, Charles Boyer, and Ann Sothern. Feldman's true distinction as an agent was his imaginative way of maneuvering around the strictures of the standard seven-year studio contract, which normally allowed only for fixed escalations of salary year by year. Feldman constantly explored nonexclusive arrangements with studios, and lucrative independent and one-picture deals that vastly multiplied the amount of money put in his clients' pockets—and his own. Feldman, Tom Kemper wrote, "banked on the general uncertainty surrounding movie productions, the need to guarantee some sort of return on the investment in production. The age-old belief in Hollywood was that stars offered such certainty." This would become one of Sue's own maxims throughout her agenting career; she believed that studio executives almost never really knew when a movie would hit or miss and that pushing stars at them was the quickest way to win their confidence and their dependency.

Unlike such powerful figures as Selznick and Feldman, the average contract player didn't have a great deal of leverage, simply because the studio was in full charge, with contract options drawn up that were almost entirely in its favor. Jane Powell recalled that her first agent at William Morris was more of a formality than a prime mover in her career. "The studio handled everything," Powell said. "I didn't know the workings of studio politics, and I felt I was an employee; I did what they told me to do. The agent didn't have to do much, because I was always working."

During the studio era, agents came in all stripes and temperaments. Anne Jeffreys, a contract player at RKO in the 1940s, recalled how reckless agents of the time could be with their clients' futures. Jeffreys was filming a small role in MGM's *I Married a Witch*, and the studio was debating whether to put her under contract. While she was taking a lesson with MGM drama coach Lillian Burns, Jeffreys's agent, Mitch Gertz, burst in, demanding to know when the studio was planning on offering his client a contract. An unholy argument broke out, and Gertz bet Burns a hundred dollars that he could get Jeffreys a contract that very afternoon. He drove Jeffreys across town and auditioned her, and on the spot a contract was offered—at lowbrow Republic Studios. "I was heartbroken," remembered Jeffreys, "because I was planning on going to Metro. But at least Mitch instigated a start for me. I found that most agents didn't do much. The job came up, and the agent took the percentage. Louis Schurr was my agent for a time; he would court you and buy you a mink coat, and then later, he would demand that you give him back the mink coat!"

If the structure of the motion picture and television industries in the 1940s and '50s meant that the average agent's job was far less complicated than it would later become, it was still often an emotionally wrenching process for clients to move to new representation. There was virtually no way to disguise the process as anything but a slap in the face, a statement of dissatisfaction with whatever agent had previously represented them. The smartest agents realized that business was business and took such defections in stride, but many—perhaps most—interpreted the loss of a client as the most painful sort of rejection. Barbara Hale, who had long-term contracts with RKO and Columbia during the 1940s and '50s, never forgot the day that she left her longtime agent, Mel Sher. Hale had been cast as private secretary Della Street in CBS's *Perry Mason* TV series, which would become a huge hit, running for nine seasons. At the time she joined the show, her costar, Raymond Burr, suggested that it might prove advantageous to sign with Lester Salko, the agent who represented Burr and all the other members of *Perry Mason*'s cast of regulars. "I figured I might as well be with the rest of the folks," Hale recalled. "So I said all right. But I told Mr. Salko that I wouldn't leave Mel unless he was paid something. So Mr. Salko took five percent of my salary and gave five percent to Mel, and Mel and I still cried and cried. He'd been family to me."

The New York offices of William Morris occupied the twentieth and twenty-first floors at 1740 Broadway. The various entertainment divisions were laid out in a sort of square, with the variety department, run by the Kalcheim brothers, Nat and Harry, coming first. It was not unusual to see showbusiness legends like Milton Berle and Sophie Tucker floating out of the Kalcheims' offices. This area was followed by the press department, where ticket orders for house seats were taken, and then by the "legit" department, headed by Martin Jurow, which represented hundreds of Broadway's leading dramatic artists, from Katharine Hepburn to Elia Kazan to Shirley MacLaine to Ben Gazzara. Within the legit division, Nathan Beers was in charge of performers off Broadway, an area that was then blossoming, fueled by the success of José Quintero's 1952 Circle in the Square production of Tennessee Williams's *Summer and Smoke*, starring Geraldine Page.

The William Morris offices were much less grand than those of MCA; Morris favored a basic, sleek, 1950s advertising agency look, with a glass door leading to the secretaries' desks and frosted glass on each agent's office door. Each week a regular meeting of the legit staff was scheduled in the executive boardroom on the twentieth floor, at which every agent was expected to give a full accounting of all the work he had lined up for his clients during the previous week, while the secretaries, Sue among them, dutifully scribbled notes on their shorthand pads. Martin Jurow would grill Charlie Baker and all the other agents under his supervision to find out why they hadn't gotten more work for Celeste Holm or tell them they had to start thinking more aggressively about how to employ Eva Marie Saint. The agency was intensively competitive with MCA. In 1951 WMA agent Bruce Savan had attended a performance of George Kelly's *The Torch-Bearers* at the Bucks County Playhouse, where a beautiful unknown actress named Grace Kelly (the playwright's niece) had caught his attention. Knowing star quality when he saw it, Savan raced backstage to try to sign her to a contract, only to find that MCA's Maynard Morris had seen the play the week before and already signed Kelly.

By the time Sue arrived at William Morris, its ultimate center of power was still the tireless Abe Lastfogel, who had joined the agency as an office boy in 1912 and in the 1930s had expanded the roster of screen stars to such a degree that in a few short years annual client income had risen from well under $1 million to $15 million. Lastfogel was now in his mid-sixties and lived in Los Angeles, where he had moved in the mid-1930s to lead the company's West Coast division. But he was still a formidable presence during his frequent visits to the New York offices.

"I used to sharpen Abe Lastfogel's pencils," remembered Robert Schear, who started at William Morris in the mailroom in the mid-1950s. "They had to be exactly three inches long, because he was a tiny man, and you would take those big pencils and have to sharpen them until they were a certain length. When you got about twenty-five of them, you brought them into his office. He was very pleasant, but it was like going to God." Every now and then one of the secretaries would have to trek all the way out to Coney Island to get one of Lastfogel's favorite lunches—Nathan's hot dogs and French fries. "It had to be Nathan's," said Schear. "Nothing else would do."

William Morris's New York office wasn't as buttoned-down as MCA was under the stern eye of Lew Wasserman. At Morris, flamboyant characters abounded; it almost could have been a rehearsal for George Kaufman and Moss Hart's showbiz farce *Once in a Lifetime*. Ed Bondy, one of many who had worked their way up from mailroom boy to agent, was a big, expansive personality who seldom missed a chance to grope any of the young men in the office, gay or straight. Bondy could be alarmingly blunt. Barbara Barrie remembered that once, after she had auditioned for a live television drama, she phoned Bondy to find out what the producers' verdict had been. "Oh, darling," Bondy said cheerily, "they just *hated* you."

In 1960, Bondy submitted his client Jennie Goldstein for a role in a new Broadway play. Goldstein had been a prominent figure in the great days of the Yiddish theater; her most recent Broadway appearance had been in Tennessee Williams's *Camino Real* in 1953. Bondy told the producers that Goldstein was perfect for the part but would not agree to a reading, and the producers approved her. Only when Bondy sat down to negotiate the contract did he realize that Goldstein had died a few months earlier.

Sue's boss was Charlie Baker, a silver-haired dandy reminiscent of Clifton Webb, right down to his waxed moustache, cape, and walking stick. Baker's right hand was a tough, fire engine–voiced woman named Phyllis Rabb, who was often in watchdog mode where Baker was concerned. "Sorry, he's not going to be able to see you today, and that's *final!*" Rabb would rasp over the phone to a client. "Phyllis was a powerhouse," said Barrie, who was a client of Charlie Baker's at the time. "She wanted me to feel that she was looking after my interests. She wasn't. She had bigger fish to fry than me." Another prominent agent in the office was Biff Liff, a pleasant, low-keyed man who maintained his diplomatic poise even in the most tense situations.

Sue fit into this wild mix of personalities without much difficulty. Both coworkers and clients remember her as being funny and fairly aggressive, but

smart enough to know when not to cross someone; she was particularly careful to stay out of Phyllis Rabb's way. Often she would join some of the other
Morris secretaries and assistants for lunch at the Stage Deli or House of
Chan, where she could order a full Chinese meal for seventy cents, or at Frances Bell, a long, railroad-style restaurant named for its tough-talking owner,
whose first question was always a surly "Didja call for a table?" Sue also took
advantage of the pay raise she received at WMA to move to a slightly better
apartment in the same neighborhood, at 226 West Seventy-second Street.

Despite the fact that she was still a secretary, Sue continued to take great
pains to pass herself off to the outside world as someone who was in the know
about all aspects of the theater world. Once Lionel Larner accompanied her to
Henry Miller's Theatre for a performance of the romantic comedy *Under the
Yum-Yum Tree*. The play's leading lady, Sandra Church, was fresh from her triumph in the title role of Jule Styne and Stephen Sondheim's *Gypsy*, and had had
an affair with Styne during the run, much to the annoyance of the show's star,
Ethel Merman. Midway through the performance of *Under the Yum-Yum Tree*,
Church's character had a line about never loving a man until she was twenty-
one. Sue called out from the audience, "AND THEN IT WAS JULE STYNE!"

Sue was also building her reputation as an important source of information for the various people around the business. "All the big guys had a
secretary, and you had to cultivate them," remembered veteran press agent
David Rothenberg. "You didn't call Brooks Atkinson—you called Clara
Rotter at the *New York Times*. Sue was ubiquitous—fun and bright and certainly efficient. I remember her at an opening-night party at the Rainbow
Room. She could work the room. I saw the baby cub at work." She became
a favorite of the press agents, tipping them off when an actor was about to
be signed for a new show; the press agents could then plant an item about it
in their columns.

She was at the theater night after night, often making note of talented
actors and passing her thoughts on to Charlie Baker and Phyllis Rabb. One
performer she saw around this time did not make a positive impression. In
October 1961, she attended the Gramercy Arts Theatre in the East Twenties for a performance of a revue called *Another Evening with Harry
Stoones*. Word of mouth had been good—it was reported as being a sharp-
edged and irreverent comedy show, just Sue's style, and it featured future
star comedian Dom DeLuise. Also in the cast was an ambitious, gifted

young actress-singer who had been taking various acting classes around town but had yet to make any kind of mark in the theater. Nineteen-year-old Barbra Streisand had several sketches in *Another Evening with Harry Stoones*, but Sue couldn't see that she had much to offer. "She thought I was nothing, which she told me later," Streisand said, laughing. "She didn't get my drift." *Another Evening with Harry Stoones* turned out to be only a minor footnote in the Streisand career, running for nine previews and one performance.

Sue made a point of walking into Jim Downey's Steak House on Forty-eighth Street and Eighth Avenue, carrying the latest best-selling novel with the cover facing out for all to see, or strolling into Sardi's on a busy night holding a *Playbill* from the hit Broadway show she had just attended. Vincent Sardi, the restaurant's owner, was amused by her chutzpah and always found a seat for her somewhere so she could scrutinize the parade of Broadway personalities and maybe get her hands on some worthwhile information to take back to Charlie Baker's office.

It was at Sardi's that Sue met Alice Lee "Boaty" Boatwright, a young casting director at Universal who had recently completed her first big job: finding the child actors for Alan J. Pakula's forthcoming film of *To Kill a Mockingbird*. Boatwright was sitting with her friend Roddy McDowall, and Sue strolled in on the arm of William Morris agent Hillard "Hillie" Elkins. The two women were introduced.

"Oh, I know who *you* are!" Sue said. "You and I are sleeping with the same guy!"

Boatwright, who came from a proper Southern background, was stunned by Sue's direct hit. "We are?" she asked, incredulous.

"Marty Balsam!" Sue announced.

"No, he hasn't slept with me yet," said Boatwright.

"Well, he has with *me*!" Sue crowed.

The next day Sue telephoned Boatwright, and they got together. Although they might have seemed an odd pair, they had a tremendous amount in common: a quick wit, healthy ambition, a strong belief in their own abilities, and a love of good-looking men of talent and accomplishment. Boatwright would become one of Sue's closest friends for decades and would introduce her to many people she knew in the business, with Sue returning the favor.

Although Sue was fascinated by all of the talent that had emerged from the Actors Studio in the 1940s and '50s, she had never had the opportunity to meet Studio director Lee Strasberg. Once, Boatwright took her to a Christmas Eve party at the Strasbergs', where Sue followed the young Stephen Sondheim around all night. At this point in his career he had written the lyrics for *West Side Story* and *Gypsy*, but had yet to compose both the music and lyrics for a show. Sue was stunned by his brilliance and wandered around the party all night saying, "Sue Sondheim . . . Sue Sondheim . . . ," just to see how it sounded.

One of the friends Sue made through Boaty was Gore Vidal, who was among the star writers represented by Charlie Baker. The two women initially met Vidal through his partner, Howard Austen, who became a regular after-theater pal of theirs at Downey's. In 1948, Vidal had made literary history with his powerful novel of gay life, *The City and the Pillar*. He had enjoyed some success as a screenwriter, and his 1957 Broadway hit *Visit to a Small Planet* had recently been turned into a movie vehicle for Jerry Lewis.

Sue was naturally drawn to Vidal's uncompromising dissections of the people he knew in the world of entertainment. From a distance she heard him hold forth to Charlie Baker about a man who was considered to be a major talent but whom Vidal regarded as a worthless hack. She loved it when Vidal would come into the office, though at first he didn't appear to take much notice of her. That changed soon enough. One day, while Vidal was having a closed-door meeting with Baker, the author suddenly jumped up to keep an appointment and pushed open the door to discover that Sue was eavesdropping. Years later in an interview, Vidal recalled "nearly putting her eye out as she was down peeping through the keyhole, or with her ear to the keyhole—I could never get her to admit which it was."

It was the beginning of a friendship that would endure, with frequent flare-ups and cooling-off periods, for decades. It might seem odd that Gore Vidal would take an interest in his agent's secretary. Since the publication of his first book in 1946, Vidal had enjoyed an astonishing degree of early success and the benefits that success brought—including the opportunity to mix with other celebrated people. For Vidal, mingling with the famous was nothing new: he was the son of Eugene Luther Vidal, a member of Franklin D. Roosevelt's administration and later a powerful airline magnate, and socialite Nina Gore. Growing up in Washington, D.C., Vidal had entrée to many of the leading politicians and thinkers of the day. But his love of celebrity was not limited to the world of politics and the Social Register; he also delighted in the company of movie stars and became close friends with many of them, including Paul Newman and Joanne Woodward. He was fond of quoting what he referred to as "Vidal's Theory": that everyone famous in the world knows everyone else who is famous.

"I knew Gore initially as a social friend," observed Judy Balaban. "Did we laugh together, and did I have a reasonable amount of intelligence? Sure. But I think it was really that I was Judy Balaban!" Vidal also had an uncanny gift for recognizing talent and beauty and simultaneously critically dismantling them—and this was something that he shared with the young Sue Mengers. One of Vidal's gifts as a high-level celebrity hound was the ability to divine who was on the rise and about to break through as an important figure in the world of arts and show business. From the beginning Vidal perceived that quality in Sue, and he delighted in her raunchy wit and outrageous comments about people they knew.

In 1962, William Morris's longtime rivalry with MCA came to an end. Four years earlier MCA had made its most daring move yet toward total monopoly by purchasing the Universal Studios lot, which became the base of operations for MCA's television production company, Revue; the company leased part of the property back to Universal Pictures for its use at a rate of $1 million a year. That year Lew Wasserman fulfilled his longtime dream of buying Universal Pictures outright, but this proved a step too far for U.S. attorney general Robert F. Kennedy, who had been monitoring Wasserman's movements for some time. Kennedy's Justice Department declared that MCA was in complete violation of antitrust laws—it was not fair play to operate both as a studio and as an agency feeding talent to that studio— and ordered the company to shut down its agency business altogether. On July 12, 1962, Wasserman called his officers and staff members into the company's theater and announced that they were effectively out of business. The employees, who had thought the gravy train would go on forever, were stunned and began scrambling to find work elsewhere.

As she sat at her desk studying the maneuvers and triumphs and slipups of the various agents at William Morris, Sue had plenty of time to ponder her own position in the scheme of things. One of the people who had been watching Sue's progress at William Morris was Tom Korman, who had worked under Martin Baum and Abe Newborn during Sue's years with their agency and had plenty of opportunity to observe her in action. A fast-talking, Brown University–educated, red-haired, freckled-faced native New Yorker with a hustler's instincts, Korman was leaving Baum & Newborn to start his own agency, and he thought it might be a smart move to hire a shrewd, driven young woman who would balance him and potentially appeal to a wider cross section of clients. He offered Sue a position as a full-fledged agent, and in doing so, he moved her career out of first gear.

CHAPTER SIX

1963–1966

Korman Associates opened shop in an undistinguished office at 225 West Fifty-seventh Street. The business was bankrolled by Korman's father, who ran a Manhattan dress shop. (The new agency's telephone cards had "Korman's Wraps" printed on them.) Korman didn't have much of a client list. In fact, there were only three: Claudia McNeil, the African-American actress who starred in the stage and screen versions of *A Raisin in the Sun*; Lillian Roth, an old-time singer whose best-selling memoir about her decline into alcoholism, *I'll Cry Tomorrow*, had been made into a popular movie starring Susan Hayward; and Joan Bennett, the glamorous star of classic films such as *The Woman in the Window* and *The Macomber Affair*, but a back number in Hollywood by the 1960s. It was not exactly a roster that would guarantee that Korman's phone calls would be quickly returned, but he was sure that Sue could be an asset in bringing the agency to a higher level. From the beginning, she was. "Sue went over to work for Tom," recalled Lionel Larner. "They were everywhere together. They went to all the opening nights. She had the balls, and she had the taste." Joan Bennett, for one, was never quite sure about Tom Korman, but she told her daughter, Stephanie Wanger Guest, that she was sure Sue was the one in the office destined for big things.

At Korman Associates the staff plunged into work, trying to find job opportunities for the agency's handful of clients. For several years Joan Bennett's employment had mostly been confined to appearances on the summer-theater circuit; the Korman office negotiated a number of episodic TV roles for the actress and an offer for her to make her London debut at the Prince of Wales Theatre in Sumner Arthur Long's comedy *Never Too Late* in September of 1963. Later Korman would provide Bennett's fading career with a boost when he got her a leading part on the ABC-TV daytime series *Dark Shadows*, which became a big hit. "I don't think he did very well for my mother," recalled Guest. "He was not a trusted

adviser. But Sue was extraordinarily smart and hid her smarts under a ve-
neer of being coquettish. Also, she knew how to give a comfort level to people, and that's what they like. After a little while with her, people thought
they were her best friends."

Korman client Lillian Roth had recently landed a job that would figure
indirectly yet crucially in Sue's career. In March 1962, Roth had opened in
the new Harold Rome musical *I Can Get It for You Wholesale*, which had a
modestly successful run of three hundred performances. Barbra Streisand,
who had failed to impress Sue in *Another Evening with Harry Stoones* two
years earlier, scored an enormous hit as the love-starved secretary, Miss
Marmelstein, and during the run had begun a romance with the show's
leading man, Elliott Gould, cast as unscrupulous garment industry rat
Harry Bogen. *Wholesale* didn't do as much for Gould as it did for Streisand,
but he did receive a fair amount of attention and soon became a client of
Korman Associates. While many agents employed a strict policy of their
clients being represented by one staff member only, Korman was rather
loose about how he dealt with the talent on his roster; sometimes he would
attend to them, and sometimes Sue or someone else in the office would step
in. Thus, Sue often found herself acting on Elliott Gould's behalf. In the
summer of 1963 Gould married Barbra Streisand, and Sue was frequently
in their company. Soon she had landed Gould his first movie, a low-budget
independent film called *The Confession*, starring veterans Ginger Rogers
and Ray Milland. Gould played a deaf mute who at the end of the film suddenly gains the power of speech. The movie languished unreleased for several years. "I came up zero on the Richter scale," said Gould, "but it was
my first film experience, and Sue booked it."

Sue's chief interest in Gould was no doubt his proximity to Streisand,
whose talent she now recognized. Streisand recalled that she first met Sue
when she visited Charlie Baker's office; Sue cracked that because Streisand
was from Brooklyn, Baker would probably have the office fumigated after
she left. Sue understood that many people might object to Streisand's eccentric way of dressing herself in thrift-shop chic, or her way of chatting on
talk shows that seemed alternately brash and funny, but she agreed with the
many who believed that Streisand possessed the great voice of her generation. She had an uncanny way of digging into music, displaying electrifying
bravado one minute, close-up intimacy the next, and often she showed both

qualities in the same instant. For all her powerhouse vocalism, it sometimes seemed that her singing was utterly spontaneous, as if she were making up the lyrics and the dramatic situations as she went along. When Sue began to hear her in New York's more popular nightclubs, such as the Blue Angel, and on recordings, it marked the birth of a lifelong obsession with Streisand's talent.

If might have been best if her fascination with Streisand had stopped there. But Sue, from the beginning, viewed Streisand as kindred. Both had grown up in marginal circumstances, Streisand in Brooklyn, Sue in Utica and the Bronx. Both had lost their fathers early on. They had frequent conversations about the grief and anxiety and anger that their fathers' deaths had instilled in them, and that anger, in both their cases, was directed mostly at their respective mothers. Diana Streisand Kind was no more supportive of Barbra than Ruth Mengers had been of her daughter. Both women were too often critical, derisive, skeptical that their daughters could ever really achieve anything close to their dreams.

But the greatest connection that Streisand and Sue had was a positive one: each possessed an overpowering urge to do something distinctive and important. As time went on, Sue would become more and more certain that, singing and acting talent aside, she was Streisand's alter ego.

For several years, producer David Merrick had been talking to producer Ray Stark about a Broadway musical based on the life of Stark's mother-in-law, the brilliant Jewish comedienne and singer Fanny Brice. The prolonged efforts to fashion a script and find the right actress to play the role have been detailed, often inaccurately, in various histories and biographies. In his richly detailed (though unauthorized) 2012 book *Hello, Gorgeous: Becoming Barbra Streisand*, biographer William J. Mann gives the most complete and persuasive account yet of this quest. Among Mann's other accomplishments in the book is his dismantling of the often-repeated myth that Ray Stark didn't want Streisand to play Fanny; in fact, both Stark and Jule Styne, the composer of the show that eventually became *Funny Girl*, favored her, prevailing over the objections of Merrick and lyricist Bob Merrill. After much speculation in the press over who would play Fanny—Carol Burnett and Anne Bancroft were also front-runners—it was announced in July 1963, one full year after her first audition, that Streisand had the role.

When the play went into rehearsal at the Winter Garden Theatre six months later, Sue had legitimate reason to be loitering backstage. Character actress Kay Medford, a client of Korman Associates, had been cast as Fanny's mother, Rose Brice, and Sue often stopped by the theater to meet with her. Quickly, however, Streisand became the real reason for Sue's frequent visits to the Winter Garden. By now Streisand was the biggest female recording star in the country, with one album of pop standards after another topping the charts, and Sue was mesmerized by her talent. She would sit in the back rows of the Winter Garden, watching in amazement as Streisand inhabited every moment of the songs and the book scenes with a spark and immediacy that seemed superhuman. She studied each scene carefully as the show gradually evolved, despite the inattention of director Garson Kanin, who was desperate for a hit but increasingly unsure of how to shape the material. *Funny Girl* went to Boston and Philadelphia for tryouts, where it underwent constant polishing and cutting. When it opened on Broadway on March 26, 1964, it was clear that all the care and persistence in casting had paid off: Streisand was hailed as the star of the decade, the hottest theater performer in years. Sue became an unapologetic Streisand groupie, turning up at the Winter Garden night after night. Once, at the end of a performance, while Kay Medford was removing her makeup in her dressing room, she heard Sue's gutsy laugh floating down the hallway. Medford cracked her door, stuck her head out, and said, "Sue? It's Kay. Come on in."

On her way to Streisand's dressing room, Sue called back, "Kay? Kay *who*?"

Tom Korman was keen to make his business succeed, and the immediate goal at his fledgling agency was to get as many new clients as possible. There were certain unspoken rules in the agency business about not raiding competitors. But Tom Korman wasn't one for paying attention to unspoken rules. Why insist on treating agenting as a gentleman's business when everyone knew that it was really every man for himself and about maximizing reputations and profits? He was pleased to learn that his instincts about Sue had been correct; she was relentless when it came to pursuing new talent, and her audacity and drive were starting to be talked about around town—mostly favorably. One incident became part of her own personal show-business legend: during an evening at Sardi's, she spotted actor Tom Ewell sitting at a table. She marched over and dropped her business card in the bowl of soup he was eating. He soon became a Korman client.

She also began to see a lot of Paul Newman and Joanne Woodward, who were represented by John Foreman of the Creative Management Agency. Newman's film career was flourishing—he had recently had enormous successes with *The Hustler* (1961) and *Hud* (1963), but the pictures in which he costarred with his wife, *Paris Blues* (1961) and *A New Kind of Love* (1963), had been unmemorable. He had agreed to make the latter simply because Woodward had pressed him to costar with her; she was tired of her routine as a housewife and mother.

The Newmans liked Sue. They were considered two of show business's class acts, but they were also down-to-earth and unpretentious, and Sue's high-low style, her combination of brains and bawdiness, appealed to them. The couple talked to her about their love of the theater, where both their careers had begun, and Sue began to hammer away at this vulnerable spot, urging them to talk Tennessee Williams or Arthur Miller or William Inge into writing a play for the two of them. This rankled Foreman, who felt he was more than capable of providing the Newmans with career advice. Around this time, Sue claimed to have had a one-night stand with Newman. She would tell her friends that it wasn't intercourse, just a blow job—but it still counted, because it was Paul Newman.

If the Newmans eluded Sue's grasp—she never signed them as clients—her pushy yet charming style was helping her up the ladder elsewhere, both professionally and socially. She had left Seventy-second Street for a better apartment at 120 West Fifty-eighth Street, and by the mid-1960s she and Boaty Boatwright were often spending weekends at the Hyde Park house that Gore Vidal shared with Howard Austen. While Vidal and Boatwright had a great deal in common, including their Southern roots, Vidal and Sue continued to strike some as strange bedfellows. But they relished each other's company, even when they did battle, which was a fair amount of the time. Often they would end up hitting New York's gay bars with their mutual friend English interior designer Nicky Haslam. "I think Sue and Gore thought very much the same way," observed Haslam. "They had . . . more than curiosity about people. They made topping jokes, topping remarks. They wouldn't exactly put people down; they would just react to what people said with much funnier lines."

Sue became deeply devoted to Howard Austen, often telling people that he was a far more loving and genuine friend than Vidal could ever hope to be. While Vidal would drink long into the night, gossiping about various people they knew in common, Sue could have serious, profound conversations with Austen. "I think that Howard was able, in a way that even I wasn't, to tell her to be open and honest with people," observed Boatwright. "I know they explored a lot with each other." In the summer of 1964, Sue and Boaty were invited onto Gore Vidal's boat for a trip through the Greek islands. At one point they were in a bar, where Vidal struck up a conversation with a handsome young sailor. When Vidal got up to use the bathroom, Sue took matters in hand, advising the sailor, "Gore wants to fuck you— and if you're smart, you'll let him." Sue and Boaty had their own fun with men on the trip, and Sue often used to threaten to tell Boaty's current beau (and future husband), Terence Baker, about her "swinging all through Greece."

Her assertiveness also led to a number of noteworthy signings at Korman Associates. Anthony Newley, the star and co-composer (with Leslie Bricusse) of the hit musical *Stop the World—I Want to Get Off*, became a Korman client at Sue's urging. She also spruced up Korman's list when she snared one of the most respected actresses in the American theater, Julie Harris, who was impressed with Sue's drive and decided to take a chance on her. At the agency, Harris's relationship was exclusively with Sue, not with Korman, whose brash New York manner didn't mesh well with the star's quiet elegance. While Sue was equally brash, she knew how to channel her assertiveness into a style that the client would find palatable, even endearingly eccentric. She was perpetually giving Korman lessons in professional etiquette. One day when Harris was coming in to the office, Sue reminded Korman that the star was one of the leading lights of the New York stage, not a cheap chorus girl—he was to call her "Miss Harris," not "Julie."

Korman and Sue fought constantly—loud, dramatic fights that resembled excised scenes from an Edward Albee play. On several occasions, Korman swept his arm across her desk, wiping everything off it; she would respond by screaming at him that he was a loser. Unlike Marty Baum, however, Korman never seriously entertained the idea of firing her; he knew how valuable she was. For one thing, she had forged a close working relationship with Broadway's most powerful producer, David Merrick, and to some hinted strongly that she had slept with him. One of the legendary stories that quickly sprang up about her was that when she rushed at Tom Ewell in Sardi's, he asked her what she could do for him that his current agent, Abe Lastfogel, couldn't, and she answered him in a shot, "Fuck David Merrick!"

Perhaps she did have an affair with Merrick. It was how the era of *Sex and the Single Girl*, Helen Gurley Brown's 1962 bestseller, became a Bible of sorts for Sue since it advocated educating yourself as well as possible, dressing as well as you could within your budget, and keeping up with current events, all in order to attract the most desirable men possible. Sue may not have followed the book's advice to the letter (e.g., brushing her teeth with baking soda to save money on toothpaste), but she told her friends that the spirit of the book captured her imagination. Because of his stature on Broadway, Merrick would have fit nicely into Sue's quest to sleep with the most powerful and successful men she could get her hands on. Also, Merrick was a rule breaker, a devil, and Sue was bound to respond to his aggressive way of doing business—such as the famous prank he pulled on the opening-night critics who reviewed (mostly unfavorably) his 1964 musical *Subways Are for Sleeping*. Merrick had his staff go through the New York City telephone directories, track down the numbers of ordinary citizens who happened to have the same names as the leading drama critics, and invite them to attend the show as his guests. Then Merrick printed their comments in the advertising: thus Howard Taubman, Walter Kerr, John Chapman, Richard Watts, and several of the other leading New York critics all saw themselves quoted in a full-page ad in the *New York Herald Tribune*, all raving about *Subways Are for Sleeping*. It was the brand of chutzpah Sue loved.

When Carol Channing was nearing the end of her commitment to star in the enormous Broadway hit *Hello, Dolly!* (in which she defeated Barbra Streisand for the Tony Award for Best Actress in a Musical), it seemed the show might be stumbling toward its closing. But Merrick hit on the idea of prolonging the run by substituting a string of celebrated female stars to take over the title role. Sue always claimed that Channing's first replacement, Ginger Rogers, was her idea. Rogers was between agents at the time, and Sue went to see her in New York to try to get the star to allow her to negotiate the contract for her. As Sue told *Vanity Fair*'s Peter Biskind years later, "I thought I would faint on the way up to her suite in the elevator. And there she was, sitting behind a tray, sipping coffee, and she never even offered me a cup. She made me feel—ugh."

But the Rogers snub was nothing compared to the insult she received from another once-great movie star, Constance Bennett. The older sister of Joan Bennett, Constance had joined the Korman roster a decade after her last appearance in a feature film. In recent years, she had been doing summer-stock tours of comedies and musicals, but suddenly in the fall of 1964, a movie role came up that seemed ideal for Bennett: Estelle Anderson, the evil mother-in-law in Ross Hunter's Technicolor remake of the old soap opera *Madame X,* to be released by Universal Pictures. Hunter, who had a great allegiance to the golden age of Hollywood, wanted a big old-time star to play Estelle, and he was making the rounds of veteran actresses. Because Sue had an "in"—Boaty Boatwright was working in casting at Universal—she began calling Hunter's office on a daily basis to persuade him that Constance Bennett was ideal for the part. Eventually, Hunter gave in and cast her.

Although she was delighted to be returning to films in such a glossy production, Bennett was also a supreme narcissist who made trouble on the set by refusing to wear any makeup or costumes that would make her look like an old lady. As a result, Lana Turner, who played the title role in the film, wound up looking more like Bennett's slightly younger sister than her daughter-in-law. Bennett was also peeved by her featured billing and wanted a box around her name to set it off from the rest of the supporting players. Sue offered to do what she could, but Hunter would not comply. When Bennett learned that Sue had failed to get her what she wanted, she refused to pay her agent's commission.

In July 1965, Constance Bennett suffered a cerebral hemorrhage and died.

Sue immediately telephoned Ross Hunter: "I guess Constance finally got her box."

Stories like the one about Constance Bennett helped consolidate Sue's reputation around New York. She relished every moment of her rising stardom and was spending her weeks having dinner with Sal Mineo and Roddy McDowall, attending Harold and Judy Prince's wedding, going to parties given by Stephen Sondheim and Phyllis Newman and Adolph Green, and attending rehearsals of *Skyscraper*, the new Broadway musical starring Julie Harris, which had an undistinguished score that Sue feared (rightly) would doom it to failure. She was also spending a lot of time at rehearsals for Mary Drayton's drama *The Playroom*, a promising script about a group of privileged New York teenagers that Sue thought was wonderful, though she worried that the director, Joseph Anthony, wasn't up to the piece. The Korman office connection to *The Playroom* was that Marge Champion was playing the leading female role, though Champion was not an official agency client. At the time, many agents would phone an actor or director to let them know about a specific project and ask if they could represent them on it. Often the clients agreed, assuming nothing would come of it, but now and again, the tactic was successful. It was a practice—one that Korman loved to employ—that was also used to point the finger of blame at the actor's official agent, to reveal him as lazy and unimaginative, and not up to the job. In the case of Marge Champion, Sue was undoubtedly trying to snare the actor's husband, Gower Champion, as a Korman client, since he was at the time one of the hottest directors on Broadway, thanks to *Carnival* and *Hello, Dolly!* In the case of *The Playroom* and Marge Champion, no one benefited: the actress left the cast even before the play opened for what turned out to be a brief Broadway run.

Sue wrote of her fast-paced new life to Gore Vidal, who was abroad at the time. Her letter makes her sound like a cross between a Hollywood gossip columnist and eighteenth-century social arbiter Lady Mary Wortley Montagu:

Gore, dear:

I find myself thinking of you today because I am pregnant. Well, not really, but I am in just as bad a way, because today is the day I have started my diet. Trusty Dr. Scapone has decided to give me "cold turkey," and I am to subsist on nothing but vegetables for two days. It is now four o'clock in the afternoon, and I have just bitten my secretary (yes, she's a girl).

Our Boaty is leaving this Saturday, but thank God Princess Margaret will be arriving to soften the blow. Hal and Judy Prince are giving an enormous party in her honor. Can you imagine traveling all the way from London to be entertained by Hal Prince?

. . . Howard is desolate without you, and kvetches endlessly about the houses. You can take the boy out of the Bronx, but . . . Seriously, he has been in much better spirits, and I think he is now beginning to adjust to New York. I think he misses you—as do I—and if you would come back for a visit—I promise you excitement. How do you feel about an orgy with Tom Ewell and Julie Harris? . . . Lee Remick is having a dinner party tomorrow night, and the biggest name there is expected to be Phyllis Newman. Phyllis promised to show us pictures of she [sic] and Adolph [Green]'s wedding night. I think Lee and Steve Sondheim are madly in love, and do not quite no [sic] what to do about it. Of course, it must be difficult to think in terms of leaving the sparkling Bill Colleran?

Steve had the best party on Halloween that I have ever been to. Mary Rodgers, the John Barry Ryans' [sic], Roddy etc. We were divided into teams of five, and each team was escorted into a limousine with a map of New York City, and a clue. We then proceeded on a wild treasure hunt that took us everywhere from a beach on Forty-second Street, to Steve's analyst's apartment. It was mad and quite gay (if you'll pardon the expression). . . . Take care of yourself . . .

Love, Sue

CHAPTER SEVEN

1966–1968

After just a few short years working with Tom Korman, Sue realized that she was going to have to make a break if she wanted to crack into the big time. She had developed a nose for second-raters and small-timers, and Korman, for all his fast-talking charm, was one of them. It disturbed her that he couldn't be bothered to do the research and careful preparation that representing top-line clients required; she had him pegged as a spoiled child of privilege who wanted the financial gratification without doing the work. Korman's professional judgment was also at times highly questionable, and as time went on, Sue's arguments with him escalated to the point that she thought it best to distance herself from him.

Sue's progress in Korman's office had come to the attention of Freddie Fields and David Begelman, cofounders of the rapidly growing talent agency Creative Management Associates. Fields and Begelman had spent a number of years working for MCA, but feeling increasingly hamstrung and underappreciated, they left the company just two years before it was split up by the antitrust decision, incurring the enduring wrath of Lew Wasserman. Fields and Begelman took several important MCA clients with them, including Henry Fonda and Judy Garland. (They also gleefully transposed the initials of MCA into their new company's name, CMA.) Together Fields and Begelman had been responsible for jump-starting Garland's seesawing career in the early 1960s, most spectacularly with her 1961 Carnegie Hall concert. The pair were imaginative and fearless in their guidance of their stars' careers; Fields's then-wife, Polly Bergen, claimed that Fields had paid fifty individual audience members fifty dollars apiece to rush the stage at the end of Garland's Carnegie Hall concert. (Fields and Begelman would also, in later years, be accused of bilking Garland out of several hundred thousand dollars in concert earnings.)

Both men had reputations that rivaled the size of their egos. Fields was widely known as a ruthless, secretive executive who worshipped his most talented clients and fought hard for them. He also had a genuine gift for connecting with people and, subsequently, getting them top-paying jobs. His tactics were sometimes brutal. "People said he was sleazy, and I never saw it in all the years I was married to him," said Polly Bergen. "I'm sure he pulled some really sleazy deals to get some of those actors work over other actors. It's awfully hard to be an agent when there are twenty-five people who are perfect for one role. Who's going to get the part? The one with the agent who's willing to shit on everybody else in order to get it."

David Begelman was more complicated: a wily yet immensely charming and likable scoundrel who suffered the crippling weakness of being a compulsive liar. Among other things, he invented a tony Ivy League background that he didn't possess. In his attire and accent, he was a poseur and was often thought to be the model for the suave, womanizing lawyer Lyon Burke in Jacqueline Susann's best-selling showbiz novel *Valley of the Dolls*.

"Sue was going into a world of total sociopaths," observed veteran journalist Peter Bart. "Freddie and David would tell lies and they didn't even know they were lies. The moment they uttered it, they were convinced of its truthfulness. Sue could lie, but she did it with a wink. She had a beguiling sense of humor, and I think that sociopathy really disturbed her."

Most of Fields and Begelman's CMA clients were Broadway and musical artists; they were in the process of steadily moving toward a dominant share of Hollywood names, but by the mid-1960s they weren't quite there yet. This was a period when the American film industry was shedding its skin. While the old studio contract system had to a great extent faded out by the early part of the decade, the style of making films hadn't changed nearly as much as might have been expected. On one hand, the infamous Production Code, which exerted fierce control over what could and could not be depicted on-screen, had been relaxed in 1960, and the results were immediately evident: that year, many mainstream Hollywood productions such as *BUtterfield 8* and *The Apartment*—to say nothing of European imports like *Never on Sunday*, *Breathless*, and *La Dolce Vita*—sported an adult tone and subject matter that would have been unheard-of only a few years earlier. Audiences must have been stunned to see Janet Leigh and John Gavin making love on a hotel bed in the opening sequence of *Psycho*, and to hear

Shirley Jones boasting about Burt Lancaster ramming the fear of God into her in *Elmer Gantry*.

Despite that loosening of standards, glossy, old-fashioned movies continued to retain a foothold with audiences. Expensive, elephantine roadshow movie musicals, spurred on by the success of *My Fair Lady* and *The Sound of Music*, would continue being made until 1970, and Ross Hunter would keep turning out new movies for old audiences until about the same time. The ripple effect created by the daring Nouvelle Vague (New Wave) films coming out of France was being felt, but American moviemaking wouldn't really grow up until the end of the 1960s, when it would enter a glorious ten-year period of artistic fruition. New stars and directors were needed to lead audiences forward. On the business side, agents needed to have a firm grasp of the zeitgeist as well, and none understood it better than Sue Mengers.

Just exactly how she accomplished her move to CMA is something of a mystery. It has been reported, inaccurately, that Barbra Streisand engineered the move by appealing to her CMA agents, Fields and Begelman, who by now had had plenty of opportunity to observe Sue in action. "I thought David Begelman was so bright and talented," said Elliott Gould. "Marty Bregman [Gould's friend and business manager] and I were somewhat helpful in getting David to get Sue into Creative Management Associates." Whoever helped broker the move, Sue joined CMA in late 1966. She respected Fields and took great care during their years of working together not to anger him, but it was unquestionably Begelman to whom she felt closest.

Much of her time at CMA was spent reading scripts. This was a task, according to Polly Bergen, that Fields loathed, and Sue was happy to take it on. She had been a voracious reader for years—of newspapers, magazines, biographies, novels, and plays. It soon became clear that another big part of her job would be to go after clients whom Freddie Fields and David Begelman couldn't be bothered pursuing. Her bosses wanted an influx of new talent, but they were too busy negotiating deals either for established stars, such as Judy Garland and Barbra Streisand, or for the young Faye Dunaway, whom Fields had seen on the New York stage and vowed to make into the biggest star of her generation. Neither Fields nor Begelman had any interest in chasing after an underemployed actor who might prove useful in the future, which they knew was a perfect assignment for someone with Sue's natural assertiveness and energy.

Probably neither man was quite ready for the hurricane strength of Sue's presence in the office. By the mid-1960s, conditions were rapidly changing for women in the urban American workplace, but most female employees honored male expectations of the gentler sex and maintained reasonably composed, buttoned-down conduct at the office. Not Sue. "I remember walking into Sue's office a million times," said Polly Bergen, "and she would be sitting in her chair behind her desk with both legs on the desk spread apart, and these short miniskirts on. That's the way she did business. And she made people love her. 'Love' isn't the right word. She made people *fascinated* with her." A visitor to CMA, whether it was a Hollywood producer or a potential acting client, might initially be caught off guard by "Baby Sue's" routine. A combination of bawdy barmaid and precocious brat, Sue would call a client in Hollywood and bawl into the telephone, "Tell him Baby Sue is calling! Hi, honey! How are you doing? You gotten laid lately? Are you telling me you're *not* fucking so-and-so? Get *out!*"

When Sue left Korman Associates, she persuaded several of her clients to come with her, including Anthony Newley, for whom she landed movie roles in *Doctor Dolittle* with Rex Harrison and *Sweet November* with Sandy Dennis, though neither film did much for his career. Eventually Sue also got Julie Harris to follow her to CMA, after Harris and her husband, attorney Manning Gurian, had gotten fed up with Korman's haphazard handling of a television deal. By now Harris had earned two Best Actress Tony Awards and had been a frequent performer in dramas on live television, but her stage career had recently been in a slight slump and her appearances in movies and mainstream TV had been sporadic.

In August 1967, Sue wrote to Alfred Hitchcock, who was in the early stages of planning the thriller that eventually became his comeback film, *Frenzy.*

Dear Mr. Hitchcock,
    I did so enjoy talking with you the other day and have conveyed your regards to Tony Perkins.
    As we discussed over the phone, JULIE HARRIS is one of your most ardent admirers and would love to work with you. Julie is

forty-three years old and feels it is time for her to begin playing parts
that show her closer to her own age. Therefore, the idea of playing John
Philip [*sic*] Law's mother interests her enormously.

Julie recently finished co-starring with Elizabeth Taylor and
Marlon Brando in *Reflections in a Golden Eye* and perhaps you could
arrange to see it at your convenience. Meanwhile, many thanks for
your time and my warmest good wishes for your continued success.

Yours,
Sue Mengers

Frenzy would not be filmed until 1972. Neither Julie Harris nor John
Phillip Law was in the cast.

When Sue sat Harris down and asked her what sort of acting job she
would most like to get, the actress replied that she would love to guest star
in NBC's long-running Western *Bonanza*, which topped the Nielsen ratings
as the most watched TV series from 1964 to 1967. Sue called *Bonanza's*
producers, who were thrilled by the prospect of an artist of Harris's stature
appearing on the show. A script was written for her, and on the April 14,
1968, episode, "A Dream to Dream," Harris's wish came true. Sue went on
to obtain additional television work for the actress in an attempt to broaden
her popularity.

One of the out-of-work clients Sue had acquired while she was still at
Korman Associates was young Anthony Perkins. The actor had enjoyed
spectacular early success on Broadway, with *Tea and Sympathy* (1954) and
Look Homeward, Angel (1957), and in films, with William Wyler's *Friendly
Persuasion* (1956), which earned him an Academy Award nomination. In
1960, Alfred Hitchcock cast him as Norman Bates, the mama's-boy mur-
derer in *Psycho*. But the enormous success of that film seemed to close
more doors than it opened; Perkins effectively became Norman Bates to an
entire generation, and producers had to squint a little to see him as anything else. After some unsatisfying roles in Hollywood films post-*Psycho*,
Perkins traveled to Europe to make a few pictures. Sue was determined to
sign the actor and pursued him aggressively for the better part of a year
before he agreed to come to CMA as her client. Perkins had been unem-
ployed for some time and was vulnerable to Sue's campaign.

Her immediate goal was to restore Perkins to some of his earlier stature as a Hollywood star. Otto Preminger was casting a Southern racial drama, *Hurry Sundown*, based on a novel by K. B. Gilden, and Fields had gotten his new star-in-the-making, Faye Dunaway, a prominent part in it. When Sue got hold of the script, she thought there was a role that was perfect for Perkins, but when she pressed Preminger on the issue, the director told her casting Perkins couldn't possibly work because everyone knew he was gay. "Oh, Otto," said Sue. "He's *not* gay. I know. I fucked him!" Perkins wasn't ultimately cast, but he was well out of *Hurry Sundown*, which turned out to be one of Preminger's many late-career failures.

Sue also ran into trouble trying to get Perkins cast in Jerry Schatzberg's offbeat drama *Puzzle of a Downfall Child*, about a fashion model (Faye Dunaway) examining where it all went wrong. There was a role of a fashion photographer, which Schatzberg admitted was largely based on himself. Every time Schatzberg ran into Sue she would push Anthony Perkins for the role. "Sue, can you see Anthony Perkins as a New York Jewish photographer?" Schatzberg would ask. And Sue always snapped, "He's an *actor*, isn't he?" Schatzberg still refused to cast him, and although Sue wasn't happy about his decision, the director remembered that she was always cordial. "After all, who knew? I might turn out to be a moneymaking director!"

Eventually Sue succeeded in putting Perkins together with Noel Black, who was casting a low-budget thriller set in a small New England town. The part for which Black interviewed Perkins had some faint echoes of Norman Bates: a twisted young man who passes himself off as a CIA operative in order to impress a young girl (Tuesday Weld) he meets; it soon becomes apparent that she is even loonier than he is, and together they embark on a casual murder spree. *Pretty Poison* was scheduled to be shot on location in Great Barrington, Massachusetts, in the summer of 1967. Noel Black was in his mid-twenties and still looked like the disheveled UCLA film student he had been only a few years earlier, but Sue was quick to recognize that he had the kind of new-generation sensibility that might well catch on with audiences. *Pretty Poison* was something of a scrappy cousin to Arthur Penn's *Bonnie and Clyde*, which would be released in the late summer of 1967 and, after a slow start, would explode like the first shot in a civil war—in this case, a revolution of new talent taking aim at Hollywood's stodgy, antiquated way of cranking out movies and coddling the audience. It would also accomplish what Fields had vowed to do—make a star out of Faye Dunaway.

When *Pretty Poison* opened in the fall of 1968, Twentieth Century Fox essentially sneaked it out, and it was about to be pulled from release when a few notable critics, such as Pauline Kael and Joseph Morgenstern, got firmly behind it. In *New York Magazine* Judith Crist called it a "small, deft, beautifully performed thriller." *Pretty Poison* was handicapped by some shoddy, TV-style production values and a tacked-on ending that wasn't nearly as dark as Black's original had been; because of the recent assassination of Robert F. Kennedy, early audiences reacted badly to the darkness of the ending, so a new, slightly moralistic one was substituted. Perkins was paid only $75,000 for his work on the picture, but Sue had landed him in a film that spoke to the youth culture, putting the actor precisely where he needed to be. Perkins hadn't really been conventional leading-man material since *Tall Story* in 1960, and in the years to come he would continue to be cast most often in eccentric roles. But he was to remain one of Sue's favorite clients and one she would consider a true, close friend. "She was there all the time," said the actor's son Osgood Perkins. "Every birthday party, every Christmas—Sue was always there."

The major motion-picture event at CMA in 1967 was Columbia Pictures' big-budget screen version of *Funny Girl*. Ray Stark had Barbra Streisand under contract to his production company, Rastar, whose first picture was the Fanny Brice musical. Sidney Lumet had been set to direct, but he was eventually replaced by the celebrated William Wyler, who had guided *Mrs. Miniver, The Best Years of Our Lives*, and *Ben-Hur* to Academy Award–winning status.

There was considerable anxiety once *Funny Girl* went into preproduction in May 1967. How much to emphasize the story's Jewish content had always been a serious consideration, for fear that it would not appeal to a wide enough audience. (As early as 1959, Judy Holliday had been considered for a film biography of Fanny Brice, with Stark producing and Richard Quine directing—Holliday being viewed as a safe choice who didn't read "Jewish.") The question of ethnicity in casting *Funny Girl* had been a matter of some debate as well: Harold J. Stone, Robert H. Harris, and Luther

Adler were all contenders for the part of Florenz Ziegfeld, but in the end they lost out to the eminently Anglo-Saxon Walter Pidgeon. Names mentioned for the role of Fanny's mother, Rose, included Ruth Gordon, Ethel Merman, Shirley Booth, Kathleen Freeman, and Eileen Heckart, the part finally going to Sue's client Kay Medford, repeating her Broadway characterization. The casting of Fanny's husband, the suave, sexy gambler Nick Arnstein, went on for months, with George Segal, David Janssen, Gene Barry, Mike Connors, Craig Stevens, Cliff Robertson, and Dirk Bogarde all emerging as possibilities; Omar Sharif was ultimately signed to play the role. Sharif had enjoyed enormous success in David Lean's *Lawrence of Arabia* and *Doctor Zhivago*, but once the Six-Day War between Israel and Egypt erupted in June 1967, his casting was greeted angrily by many Jewish civic and women's groups around the country. General outrage over an Egyptian actor playing a Jew led to threats to boycott the movie once it was released, but eventually the furor died away.

In the screen version of *Funny Girl*, nearly everything would be riding on Streisand, just as it had on Broadway. David Begelman and Freddie Fields had worked out very good terms for her: she was to be paid a flat fee of $200,000 for seventeen weeks' work, plus ten weeks free—a sweet deal for an untried movie star. While this was not nearly as much as some of the top male stars of the era were earning for a single picture, it was a remarkable salary for a film debut. It was also far above what the other actors were being paid: Sharif was to receive $50,000 for sixteen weeks' work, Walter Pidgeon $40,000 for ten weeks (plus special billing "as Florenz Ziegfeld"), Kay Medford $25,000 for ten weeks, and Anne Francis, cast as Fanny Brice's hard-boiled showgirl friend Georgia, $1,785.72 per week with a fourteen-week guarantee—all for a part that would be substantially cut from the final print. Begelman and Fields also negotiated Streisand's right to have one of her personal representatives on the set at all times. The contract further stipulated that in foreign prints of the film, Streisand's speaking voice could be dubbed but her singing voice could not.

Sue saw as much of Streisand as she could during some of the location shooting in the East, such as the sequence in the abandoned New Jersey train station that figures in the "Don't Rain on My Parade" number. The two were becoming closer, and Streisand delighted in her friend's barbed

wit and ruthless honesty. In the wake of the record-breaking success of
The Sound of Music, movie musicals were still big business; *Thoroughly
Modern Millie*, starring Julie Andrews, had opened in March 1967 to huge
box-office returns. Sue was certain that her friend's enormous success as
a stage actress and recording artist was going to translate into big movie
stardom.

Well aware that many show-business marriages broke up when the
wife's career left the husband's in the dust, Sue also began doing whatever
she could to promote Elliott Gould as a potential film star. She was always
keeping an eye on the career moves of young directors, among them William
Friedkin, who had distinguished himself with several hard-hitting
television documentaries and was now beginning to work in features, though
as yet not too successfully. When Sue discovered that Friedkin was preparing
a nostalgic comedy-drama called *The Night They Raided Minsky's* for
United Artists, she got hold of a script. She phoned Friedkin daily, nagging
him that Gould would be ideal casting as young Billy Minsky, the overseer
of the burlesque dynasty. Friedkin had never before encountered an agent
this aggressive, and when Sue began to hammer at him to drive to a summer
theater in upstate New York to catch Gould appearing opposite Shelley
Winters in a production of Murray Schisgal's play *Luv*, the director balked.
Finally Sue told him that David Begelman had offered to lend them his
chauffeured limousine for the evening. "You're going to love Elliott Gould,"
she insisted. "He's going to be a huge star."

Eventually Friedkin relented, and agreed that Gould was indeed impressive
in the play. But on the way back to Manhattan, Begelman's limousine
driver, who had gotten drunk while Friedkin and Sue were attending
the play, began running stop signs and railroad lights. "I was sort of new to
living in New York," said Friedkin, "and this guy is driving erratically—
crazily. I yelled, 'STOP THE CAR!' I grabbed him by the neck and threw
him aside, and I got in the car and drove it back. I did not know where we
were going. I had to stop at gas stations and follow signs and misdirections.
It must have taken us four hours to get back to Manhattan. I dropped Sue at
her apartment, and I went home to the apartment I was renting on Park Avenue.
I parked Begelman's limousine in front of the apartment, and the next
morning I get a phone call from Begelman asking, 'Where the fuck is my

car?' I said, 'Fuck you and your car. I left the car in the street. I don't know if they impounded it or not, but you sent a drunk to take us upstate. No thanks to you, but I am going to hire your client." With *The Night They Raided Minsky's*, Gould's movie career was launched. Sue had won—and there was even a good story to go along with it.

CHAPTER EIGHT

1968–1969

By 1968, it was clear to Fields and Begelman that the future of their business was in Los Angeles, not New York. They were keen to keep discovering the actors who were going to make up the new wave of movie stars in the 1970s, and Fields made plans to reshape the company as a management firm, moving the bulk of operations to company headquarters in Los Angeles, at 9255 Sunset Boulevard. After talking it over, Fields and Begelman decided to send Sue to Los Angeles as well, with Begelman remaining in the New York office for the time being. A large part of the motivation for moving Sue to L.A. was to have her step in and perform the hostess duties that Polly Bergen had previously handled. At this point, Bergen was involved with numerous entrepreneurial ventures and charities and no longer had the time to do the lavish entertaining she had done in the past. With her gift for charming people and making anywhere she went seem like a party, Sue seemed the natural choice to take over this role for CMA.

Sue had always had difficulty in adapting to major changes and she admitted to many friends that she was apprehensive about the move to California. "She was still in New York," said David Yarnell, who had known her since her Fire Island days, "and she said to me in her baby voice, 'Oh, David, they want to send me to Hollywood. I'm so scared. What do you think? Should I go?'"

When she got to Los Angeles, she discovered she was happy to be there, happy to say good-bye to the cramped, expensive apartments, mean streets, long, bitter winters, and miserable, suffocating summers that were all an integral part of life in New York. Sue often said that during her first week in L.A. she was driving around when she spotted Fred Astaire walking down the street in Beverly Hills and felt instantly that she had made the right decision.

For a brief time she rented a house in Hollywood, at 3913 Fountain Avenue—not a particularly fashionable area. Given Fields and Bergen's plan to have her assume the role of official hostess, however, it was imperative that she find a proper place for entertaining as soon as possible. Eventually, she found one, at 1354 Dawnridge Drive in Beverly Hills. It was a rental, the guesthouse at the home of the famous designer Tony Duquette. It was a small, pink house, with an elaborate jumble of flowers in the back. When she moved in, Sue hardly did a thing to it; she couldn't have had less interest in interior decorating. But as a cozy, intimate setting for organizing social evenings that were really all about work, it would do nicely. There were gold and green tapestries thrown around, and with all the pot being smoked at the parties, the house reminded some friends of a seraglio. Sue claimed never to have heard of Tony Duquette, but she later told friends that she was perpetually annoyed to see "an irritating little faggot wandering around the property."

It was during this period that she began to cultivate the women who would, with various changes and additions, make up her inner circle for the rest of her life. Boaty Boatwright had been first, and Sue would always have a special feeling about the history they had shared. She still loved to tweak Boaty for her Southern manners, and for not sharing Sue's new passion for smoking pot. By the time Sue moved to Los Angeles, Boaty was living in London, where she was now working for Columbia Pictures, married to agent Terence Baker, and expecting their first child, Kara. At some point in 1968, Boaty wrote Sue a letter telling her how excited she was about the baby. Sue responded with a telegram that read:

YOU SWORE TO ME YOU'D NEVER LET HIM TOUCH YOU

There was also Toni Howard, just starting out in the business as Freddie Fields's secretary, but who would in time become a top Hollywood agent. Ordinarily Sue wouldn't have paid much attention to anyone on a lower professional level, but she liked Howard, who was funny and sexy and hard-edged, and over the years they grew closer. But she was in no way the younger woman's mentor. The rising buzz of the feminist movement in the 1960s bored Sue, who regarded it mostly as a lot of strident noise, and she was at this point uninterested in acting as adviser to talented women who might be on the way up. When she met young Marlo Thomas, who was having an immense success with ABC's sitcom hit *That Girl*—one of the first TV series about an independent woman on her own—she didn't view her as any kind of emblem of feminism, but simply as a hot young TV star she admired and wanted to get to know.

Some of the women she met around this time wouldn't become closer friends until later. Marcia Murphey, soon to be the wife of Neil Diamond, was dining with her younger brother in a popular Los Angeles restaurant in mid-1968; seated at the next table were Elliott Gould and a pretty, zaftig blonde. Diamond ordered a slice of chocolate supreme cake. When the waiter brought it, the blonde leaned over, fork in hand.

"I hope you don't mind," Sue said. "Just one bite," and she jabbed her fork into Diamond's dessert. "She would get away with this kind of thing anywhere," said Diamond.

There was also Joanna Shimkus, a stunning young model who had attracted attention in a number of French films during the mid-1960s and who would make her first English-language screen appearance in 1968's *Boom!*, starring Elizabeth Taylor, Richard Burton, and Noël Coward. Shimkus, a client of Freddie Fields's, knew Sue from the CMA office. One night Fields and Polly Bergen threw a party at their Beverly Hills home, and while Shimkus was sitting at the bar, Neil Simon came over and sat down next to her. Simon's wife, Joan Baim, had recently been diagnosed with cancer, and Shimkus provided a sympathetic ear. At the end of the evening, Simon asked her if she would like to go to the Factory, the hot new disco in town. Shimkus agreed, and Simon asked if she minded if Sue came along. "It turned out that he was her date that night, and he paid no attention to her. He was with me the whole evening. I didn't find this out until she was sort of sulking all the way through the Factory. A couple of days later, I went into the office, and Sue didn't even talk to me, she was so upset. I sent her some flowers and apologized. But there was nothing to it—it wasn't as if I dated him. Still, she always talked about it until the day she died: 'I could have been Mrs. Neil Simon if it wasn't for that *bitch!*'"

It was a classic, confrontational way for Sue to become close to someone—and keep her. She could say terrible things to her best friends, reasoning that they were living in Hollywood, where everyone was being scrutinized constantly; what she said to them was simply for their own good. It didn't seem to occur to her that she was duplicating her mother's intensely critical attitude toward her. Most of the women in her inner circle absorbed the abuse without harboring any real ill will. Joanna Shimkus, who later married Sidney Poitier, observed, "She would say, 'Oh, your hair looks awful. What the hell did you do with your face? Did you gain weight?' She criticized you a lot, but if she loved you, she loved you unconditionally." Boaty Boatwright put it neatly: "Even the people who got angry with her needed to be around her."

Shortly after her arrival in Los Angeles, Sue took care to consolidate several friendships that would be important to her in the years ahead. Perhaps the most significant one was with Robert Evans. A perpetually suntanned go-getter, Evans had spent several years as an energetic promoter of his brother's fashion business, Evan-Picone, and had an unsatisfying stint as an actor—his portrayal of the oily playboy Dexter Key in *The Best of Everything* was a classic study in lounge lizardry. By this time, many of the old studios had passed into the hands of conglomerates, among them an ailing Paramount Pictures, which was purchased by Gulf & Western in 1966. The head of Gulf & Western, Charles Bluhdorn, was impressed by Evans's savvy when he snared the movie production rights for the best-selling novel *The Detective.* In 1968, Bluhdorn installed Evans as Paramount's production chief.

Sue often said that her friendship with Evans had been practically preordained. They each possessed a deadly wit and very little capacity for suffering fools. In the cotton-candy, kiss-kiss world of Hollywood social life and industry politics, they shared a New York kid's street smarts and tough edge. During their early morning phone calls and frequent dinners, they reveled in each other's scalding candor: Sue called Evans "Prick" and Evans called her "Mengela," and being nicknamed for one of the Nazi regime's most notorious criminals delighted her. Sue was one of Evans's greatest champions in the business, as she quickly recognized that this was the man to wipe out the memory of Paramount's creaky leadership and yank the company into the changing entertainment world of the 1970s. He had gotten off to a spectacular start with two vivid evocations of modern New York life, *The Odd Couple* and *Rosemary's Baby.* Evans was a man of the moment, with a strong connection to the new movie audience, and he was the kind of young Hollywood player with whom she wanted to be associated. She was no longer concerned with trying to get Tom Ewell a guest shot on *Adam-12* or *The F.B.I.*

It was Evans who fostered Sue's friendship with Joyce Haber, one of the

most powerful journalists in Hollywood; Haber's syndicated gossip column
in the *Los Angeles Times* was widely and enthusiastically read. Sue and
Haber quickly developed a dynamic of trading material that would benefit
them both—in much the same way that Tony Curtis's Sidney Falco played
Walter Winchell–style columnist J. J. Hunsecker in the classic 1957 movie
Sweet Smell of Success. "Sue was a master at getting things presented to
Hollywood through Joyce's column in the way she wanted—with her own
spin," said Haber's former husband, Douglas Cramer. "This was in return
for giving Joyce other sort of quiet, off-the-record tips." Haber immediately
recognized that Sue had a keen instinct for personalities and what would
work well on film, and the two women formed a close bond that was nonetheless tinted with a certain wariness and suspicion. "Joyce knew when she
was in trouble," said Cramer, "and hadn't had any real news for a couple of
days. She would call Sue, and Sue would give her a lot."

But Sue took care not to make Haber part of her close circle. While Sue
was never much of a drinker, apart from the occasional glass of wine or
champagne, pot was now her drug of choice, and it was always in strong
supply at her parties at Dawnridge Drive. Inviting Haber to her biggest parties was out of the question: she was too smart to bring a powerful member
of the press into her home when there were bowls of joints scattered around.
Eventually Sue would wind up being mentioned prominently in Haber's
1975 Hollywood potboiler *The Users.*

During her first year in L.A., Sue had a quick fling with pop singer Trini
Lopez, whose recording of "Lemon Tree" had been a hit single. She went to
hear Lopez perform at the Beverly Hills nightspot the Little Club. "Sue
liked me," said Lopez, "and wanted me to come and see her at her beautiful
home in Beverly Hills. She told me she was representing Barbra Streisand.
She never did anything for me careerwise, but I dated her two or three
times." Years later Warren Beatty would corner Sue at one of her parties
and tell her he heard she gave great blow jobs.

"Who told you?" Sue demanded.

"Trini Lopez," said Beatty.

"*Trini Lopez!*" Sue shrieked. "I don't want reviews from *Trini Lopez!*"

From the time she arrived in town, Sue scoured Hollywood for new clients. One actor she had her eye on was Oskar Werner, who had appeared to
great effect in *Ship of Fools* and *Fahrenheit 451.* She invited Werner and

his girlfriend, Diana Anderson, to a party at Dawnridge Drive. At one point in the evening she cornered Anderson.

"How do I sign Oskar?" Sue pressed.

"You don't," replied Anderson.

"What do you mean?" Sue asked.

"Oskar doesn't have an agent and doesn't want one," said Anderson. It was the last time the couple was invited to Sue's.

Much of mid-1968 was spent in visits to the set of *Hello, Dolly!*, which Barbra Streisand was filming at Twentieth Century Fox. Fields and Begelman had renegotiated Streisand's contract with Ray Stark so that she would be permitted to do a number of outside pictures, and for *Hello, Dolly!*, an expensive prestige production, she was being paid $750,000—a substantial raise from her *Funny Girl* salary. There was resentment in certain quarters that Carol Channing was not being allowed to repeat her Broadway triumph on film, especially after she had earned an Oscar nomination for her work in *Thoroughly Modern Millie*. Streisand told the press that when she saw the musical onstage, she had seen only Carol Channing. "I didn't see any character at all in Dolly Levi," she admitted. "But I saw Pearl Bailey and I loved her. She grasped something of the character plus using something of herself."

Despite her reputation as a control freak, Streisand saw herself as not maintaining an assertive enough approach to her career. "In fact, I'm too easy for my own good," she said in 1969. "When I should fight back, and say I don't want to do it . . . I do it." That's where Fields and Begelman, and to a certain extent Sue, came in. And already Sue was imagining the day when her bosses might be out of the picture and she would be Streisand's sole movie agent. Sue often told friends that she understood the star better than anyone.

The film version of *Funny Girl* had turned out magnificently—better even than Sue had imagined. In her big-screen debut, Streisand showed an extraordinary gift for operating on several levels at once. She made Fanny Brice's commonness and coarseness intriguingly sensual; in her scenes with Omar Sharif, she brilliantly conveyed both the fear of love and the overwhelming desire to have it. And musically she was stunning: in scene after scene she demonstrated the truth of what Fanny says to Florenz Ziegfeld: "A song, you know, it's a very, very intimate thing. I mean, it's really between me and the audience." She sang "I'm the Greatest Star" with an imagination and audacity that no one before her would have attempted.

When the picture opened in the fall of 1968, Streisand's reviews were lyric, and the film did enormous box-office business.

Early in 1969, Sue was assigned a task that she relished: accompanying Streisand to London for the Royal Film Performance of *Funny Girl*. Columbia Pictures was going all out for the occasion with various lavish events, including an enormous party at Claridge's. The studio's London publicity staff, which included Lionel Larner's nephew, Jeffrey Lane, had been thoroughly briefed for the occasion. When the plane landed, Streisand and Sue emerged, both clad in enormous mink coats, with a jumble of shopping bags and expensive luggage. "Sue was perfect, for what she was wearing," recalled Jeffrey Lane. "She was the pushy, fast-talking agent, pushing everyone around, organizing. She started playing the sergeant major, giving out orders, and Barbra was quite passive with her and allowed her to do all the pushing around. We had all been warned—we were petrified of this person coming in!"

Streisand and Sue stayed at the Dorchester hotel, where Sue complained loudly about the weak water pressure in her room. When the day of the premiere arrived, Streisand discovered that she was expected to wear opera-length white gloves, which she didn't have, so Sue pressed the Columbia publicists to go out and find some: Princess Margaret was going to be in attendance and wouldn't dream of shaking a naked, sweaty hand.

The film was shown—to a very enthusiastic audience response—and then it was on to the party at Claridge's. A member of Buckingham Palace's staff appeared in Streisand's green room and announced that Princess Margaret was preparing to make her entrance, and that Streisand and Sue should take their seats in the ballroom. "But Barbra's the star of the movie," Sue said, arguing that Streisand should arrive last because she would receive a standing ovation. The staff explained to Sue that people didn't stand for Princess Margaret—they simply applauded politely—and that if the two women didn't go in soon, the princess would depart for Annabel's or some other smart London club with her coterie of friends. ("Princess Margaret wasn't that crazy about ladies," Lane said. "It was more the men she enjoyed being with.") Once the finer points of royal protocol had been explained to Sue, she overcame her initial belligerence, and she and Streisand entered the ballroom to await Princess Margaret's arrival. When the princess finally appeared, she reserved most of her attention for Omar Sharif.

Sue's new job with CMA required her to make frequent business trips to New York. On one of these, she was walking up Sixth Avenue, headed toward Henri Bendel, when she suddenly spotted Jacqueline Onassis striding up the street in her mink coat. Sue walked up to her and said, "Excuse me, Mrs. Onassis—I just wanted to say that there are two reasons people look at you. They look at you first because you're beautiful, and second, because they recognize you."

Back in Los Angeles, Sue went about the business of further making her presence felt on the CMA staff. Begelman eventually left New York behind and joined his colleagues in Los Angeles, and Sue was happy to have him there; her relationship with him continued to be deeper and closer than the one she enjoyed with Freddie Fields. Begelman's longtime secretary, Constance Danielson, remembered occasionally hearing Sue's and David's voices raised, but never in outright animosity. They had a deep, mutual respect and loved combining their talents to try to solve various problems. "David had a keen mind that preferred to be active," said Danielson, "and I think Sue Mengers was one of the people who could keep him entertained and on his toes. She was often projecting a bigger-than-life public image, and David tended either to sit back and observe the performance, or jump into the fray with her. They were a spirited challenge for each other."

Sue stalked the hallways at CMA, chain-smoking and almost daring the junior agents and secretaries not to commit every move she made and word she said to memory. She was in an enviable position at the company. Many agents were assigned "coverage" of a given studio: A key part of their job was to know exactly which script at each studio was in what stage of development and to press the executives about which agency clients would be right for each project. They were then expected to give progress updates at the weekly all-agency meetings. Sue was not a covering agent, per se; her rank in the overall structure of CMA was higher, though her close friendship with Robert Evans meant that she always knew exactly what was going on at Paramount. In fact, as her CMA colleagues soon found out, she knew what was happening at all the major studios because she commanded a far greater web of connections, both professionally and socially, than most agents did, and the information dropped at her parties, after a few cocktails or a few hits of weed, proved invaluable to CMA.

Her work ethic was fierce. Unlike many agents who left the business behind at 5 P.M., Sue was always thinking about her job. Evenings and weekends were spent reading piles of scripts, trying to assess them to determine if there was a good part for one of her clients. She was always on the lookout for a role that was appealingly different from the sort of parts they usually played, because she knew that, John Wayne notwithstanding, repetition could spell death in a movie star's career. And she was forever worrying about her clients' financial status, trying to boost their salaries so they would be a little further down the road to personal security. It was the dawn of the young Hollywood set of the 1970s, and she knew that she was in a position to make a crucial difference in their lives—a responsibility she took with the utmost seriousness. "She didn't care who she stepped on if it meant a job for one of her actors," said veteran Hollywood gossip columnist Rona Barrett. "She put the actor first. She never seemed to remember that actors come and go for the most part, and the people who run the business stay forever."

One of Sue's chief responsibilities was to keep an eye out for properties for Streisand that could be produced by First Artists, a creation of Freddie Fields. The idea was to secure quality vehicles for the quartet of founding partners—Streisand, Paul Newman, Steve McQueen, and Sidney Poitier. First Artists was a subsidiary of Warner Bros., which would distribute the films while allowing greater than usual creative input from the partners. Under the agreement, each partner was contractually committed to make three pictures over the next ten years; if there were any films owed Warner Bros. by 1979, the studio could force the stars into any movie on their schedule. Streisand's first film under the agreement would be Irvin Kershner's offbeat 1972 fantasy *Up the Sandbox.*

Sue's position at CMA also brought her one of the great and enduring friendships of her life—with David Geffen. She had known him slightly when he was working in the mailroom at William Morris a few years earlier. He and Sue had an enormous amount in common, including a passionate love of the movies. As a child growing up in Brooklyn, Geffen attended double features on a weekly basis. The day he graduated from high school, he fulfilled his desperate dream to leave Brooklyn and head to California, where his brother was attending law school at UCLA. But he soon returned to New York and got the job at William Morris, where he learned the valuable trick of reading memos on executives' desks upside down. As Sue had done, Geffen took stock of the Morris offices and decided that becoming a big agent must not be all that difficult. He later recalled listening to the deal making over the phone as he delivered the mail and thinking, "like that song in *A Chorus Line*, 'I can do that.' They just bullshitted on the phone." He moved up fast, signing Laura Nyro, who he believed had the potential to become the greatest recording artist in the world. By the time Sue encountered him in California, he was also managing Crosby, Stills, Nash & Young. He made millions in a short time, often saying, "I'd rather die than fail."

There were other parallels in David Geffen's and Sue's backgrounds. His parents were also Jewish refugees, and he lost his father when he was eighteen. Like Sue, he was terrified of being trapped in an ordinary, routine life. Like Sue, he had a tough, scrutinizing mother. Like Sue, he had an astonishing gift for brutal honesty that could often seem like an assault. They did business together on a high level. Sue put Geffen together with Barbra Streisand, who was striving to create a more contemporary image as a recording artist. Soon Streisand was recording Nyro's songs "Hands Off the Man (Flim Flam Man)," "Time and Love," and her great rock hit single, "Stoney End."

It had not taken Sue long to realize that she had landed in the right job at precisely the right time—and one ideally suited to her personality. Fields and Begelman didn't encourage the kind of self-effacement for the good of the company that prevailed at other agencies; they were both indulgent of their agents' becoming stars in their own right. The Abe Lastfogel attitude that had prevailed at William Morris—no individual publicity for the agents, save it all for the stars—was nowhere to be found at CMA, where it was unwritten company policy to attract the most attention possible; Polly Bergen observed that Fields was delighted when his employees received the recognition he knew they deserved. And within a short time after she arrived in Los Angeles, no one was getting more recognition outside the agency than Sue: as her parties were reported in Joyce Haber's column and elsewhere, her reputation began to shoot up.

Sue's parties were simple affairs: Guests were served beef brisket and chicken potpie, and macaroni and cheese for the vegetarians. At the larger gatherings, there would be hors d'oeuvres and a buffet, but because of the scale of her house, Sue preferred sit-down dinners for a small group—it was easier to keep an eye on everyone, maintain some control over the flow of the conversation, and see to it that business got done. The guest list typically included a key producer, a name director, and a few of her star clients who were looking for work. Then she sat back and watched what happened.

In later years, Sue would complain that Fields and Begelman had never paid her what she was worth, but at the time she appreciated that they weren't mean about details and fringe benefits. While the top brass at William Morris were notoriously tightfisted, Fields, in particular, maintained a "What do you want? You got it" sort of attitude toward his employees—and as a result, many of them remained deeply loyal to him. Sue's expenses for entertaining were covered by the agency. Harry Ufland, an agent at CMA during the 1970s, recalled, "William Morris had a strict policy about your salary and what kind of car you would get. I'm negotiating with Freddie, and he said, 'What are you talking about? Have whatever kind of car you want!' He just didn't care about that."

Sue saved most of her charm for her bosses; she tried to impress them with her loyalty and hard work, just as she had during her Tillie the Toiler years. She didn't work nearly as hard to get along with the other agents or the support staff at CMA. Sue's outspokenness notwithstanding, she could be rather difficult to get to know. The louder and funnier she was, the more she smoked in the office and let fly with a stream of four-letter words, the more remote she could seem. In a sense, she had something in common with the great stand-up comedians she loved—so much was invested in the persona she created that it was often hard to get past it to the "real" her.

Sue never became close to Guy McElwaine, the polished, hard-drinking, much-married CMA agent who would move into film production and many other ventures over the years; there seems, from the beginning, to have been an elemental lack of trust between them. And she vexed many of her colleagues by not showing much interest in developing an unknown talent from the ground up; she was looking for someone who had already broken through, someone for whom she could achieve maximum financial results. When Harry Ufland discovered the young Martin Scorsese, fresh out of NYU film school, Sue was dismissive. "Why do you spend all this time on these guys?" she asked. "Why not steal someone else's client?" When Ufland responded that spotting unknown talent was what excited him more than anything else, Sue shook her head dismissively. "I think that's what made her a difficult part of the company," observed Ufland. "She wouldn't help younger agents who wanted to do that. The younger agents were kind of afraid of her. She would make their ideas look inconsequential, insignificant. She could be charming and funny and smart, but when you left the room, you learned that you didn't turn your back."

One person who learned that lesson well was Sam Cohn. Although the competition between one agency and another was becoming far more cutthroat, there was a general policy that an agent didn't undercut the business dealings of a colleague within the same company.

By 1967, negotiations were under way for CMA to merge with General Artists Corporation, a company that had been purchased by Herbert Siegel, president of Chris-Craft Industries, earlier in the decade. At the time, one of the key people who came on board at GAC was Cohn, a smart entertainment lawyer and former TV producer with a highly elevated level of taste in dramatic and literary material and a great passion for the arts. "Sam didn't care about money," said Toni Howard. "He just cared about getting the project done in the right way." Cohn was representing a young actor named Joel Grey, who had the good fortune to be in on the ground floor of a new musical drama by John Kander and Fred Ebb that Harold Prince was set to direct.

But the new show had rocky beginnings. Prince had hoped that this musical, based on Christopher Isherwood's *Goodbye to Berlin*, would be a dramatic step forward for him creatively. But he was not satisfied with the original script and original concept of the show. "I thought we were doing yet another Gwen Verdon show for someone dancing on tables and being charming, and I said, 'This is not what we should be doing,'" Prince recalled. Prince and his wife took a trip to Russia, where they attended a performance of a revue called *Ten Days That Shook the World*. The play resonated powerfully with Prince, and he began to think about transforming the troubled Kander and Ebb project into something that dug in deeper, something that expressed his own passions and convictions. "I went back to New York and said, 'I'm not interested in any of these people, really,'" said Prince. "'I'm interested in Germany, and Germany should be the star of our show.'" From this sprang his first groundbreaking success, *Cabaret*.

In *Cabaret*, the "voice" of Germany just before the triumph of the Nazis was personified by the character of a master of ceremonies in the sleazy Berlin nitery the Kit Kat Klub. Prince had a young friend who had been raised in the traditions of the Yiddish theater. "He was a real showbiz kid," said Prince, "the kind wearing dinner suits at six and singing 'My Yiddishe Momme.'" It was Sam Cohn's client Joel Grey, and he was always Prince's only serious choice for the role of the emcee.

Grey got the part, winning the Tony Award for Best Featured Actor. By the early 1970s, when ABC Pictures was planning the screen version of *Cabaret*, with Bob Fosse set to direct, Sue became obsessed with the idea that her client Anthony Newley should play the emcee. Despite the fact that Cohn was pushing Joel Grey to repeat his stage role, Sue campaigned for Newley behind Cohn's back. "What do you want to cast that little midget Joel Grey for?" she demanded of Fosse. "He's a *nothing*."

Both Sue and Cohn had their personal eccentricities: she loved to sit with her feet up on her desk so that her panties were showing, and Cohn manically chewed on pieces of Kleenex and paper napkins—a habit that unnerved many of the colleagues who sat next to him in staff meetings. But the two would never become close allies, and the Joel Grey–Anthony Newley incident marked the beginning of their circling each other warily for the next several years.

Yet her penchant for wildly outrageous remarks, her ability to explode tension in the room by voicing what everyone else was thinking, continued to endear her to many. The day after the murders of Sharon Tate and her friends at 10050 Cielo Drive in Beverly Hills, Anthony Newley and his wife, Joan Collins, received a call at their home on Summit Drive. The voice of "Baby Sue" floated over the phone lines.

"Oh, Susie's *scared*. She's scared they're going to murder her. Can Susie come over and stay with Joanie and Tony?"

"She was quite fearful," recalled Collins. "I think she stayed for one or two nights."

Her fear didn't prevent her, however, from ridiculing Streisand when she expressed the same concerns about her personal safety.

"Don't worry, honey," said Sue. "Stars aren't being murdered. Only featured players."

CHAPTER NINE

1970

Sue's rise into the ranks of Hollywood's major players began in 1970. The "New Hollywood" had "officially" been born with *Bonnie and Clyde*, but it was Peter Fonda's *Easy Rider* in 1969 that moved the era into high gear. It was now more important than ever for movies to grapple with the changes wrought by the tumultuous 1960s. The majority of new American films, both the good and the bad, strove to show both how the social fabric had been ripped to shreds, and the ways in which Americans were stumbling forward, trying to figure out how they fit into a dramatically changed country. Strangely, the Vietnam War seldom made its way to the screen in any direct way, and when it did, the results were usually negligible (such as 1969's *Hail, Hero!*). But the generational conflict that was dividing families was exploding on-screen, in movies that ranged from *Joe*, John G. Avildsen's overheated rednecks-versus-hippies, drama, to *Getting Straight*, Richard Rush's study of the price of nonconformity on a college campus, to Bob Rafelson's magnificently subtle meditation on a social dropout, *Five Easy Pieces*. The anxiety and uncertainty of the early 1970s was the screen's most frequently examined subject; if the general feeling of unrest and rebellion wasn't directly addressed by films such as *M*A*S*H* and *The Owl and the Pussycat*, it was certainly their subtext. When Jack Nicholson abandoned his girlfriend and hitched a ride with a trucker at the end of *Five Easy Pieces*, young audiences perceived the scene not so much as tragic but as an emblem of a new Lost Generation that didn't seem overly concerned with finding itself.

With his cynical, skeptical, coolly rebellious persona, Nicholson was the actor who seemed to fit most comfortably into the changing movie landscape of the early 1970s. Dustin Hoffman, for his part, supplanted Rod Steiger as the movies' most compelling star character actor, in idiosyncratic performances in *The Graduate*, *Midnight Cowboy*, and *Little Big*

Man. Sue met Nicholson on the set of *On a Clear Day You Can See Forever*, in which he supported Barbra Streisand. As the decade went on, Nicholson would become one of Sue's closest friends, and Hoffman would turn up at her house as a fairly regular party guest, though she never represented either actor.

Even though the women's movement had gained much momentum, actresses didn't command good roles nearly as often as the male stars did. Carrie Snodgress in *Diary of a Mad Housewife*, Candice Bergen in *T. R. Baskin*, and Jane Fonda in *Klute* were examples of performers having the opportunity to show the struggles of modern women, but the occasions were all too rare.

Sue was taking stock of the upheaval in the movie world and seeking out the talents that were most likely to hold sway with audiences. She was too smart and too observant not to recognize that she was in the middle of a thrilling, history-making creative period. While she had an enormous respect for golden-age Hollywood—when she first came to Los Angeles, she was obsessed with the idea of meeting Rita Hayworth—she was steadily gathering the core group of stars and directors that would put her at the center of the movie business for the next fifteen years. Her parties at Dawnridge Drive and her quotable wisecracks at movie premieres and nightspots had made her an increasingly recognizable name—and 1970 was the year that many elements of her legend-in-the-making fell neatly into place.

That June, Robert Evans invited Sue to be one of his guests on a private plane to San Diego to catch a major preview of Paramount's *On a Clear Day You Can See Forever*. The year before, Streisand had drawn very well with the gaudily overproduced *Hello, Dolly!*, though not well enough to cover the movie's astronomical $25 million cost. *On a Clear Day You Can See Forever* was her third big-budget musical in a row. The Burton Lane–Alan Jay Lerner show about a chain-smoking New York kook whose sessions with a psychiatrist (Yves Montand) reveal that she has lived a number of past lives might have clicked on-screen if it had been put in the hands of a young, hip filmmaker, but it was unfortunately entrusted to the once great but now floundering Vincente Minnelli.

When Sue boarded the plane to San Diego, decked out in a cinnamon-colored pantsuit, the person she was most eager to meet was the new woman in her friend Robert Evans's life: Ali MacGraw, who had recently wrapped *Love Story* and was hotly tipped to be the next big female star. MacGraw had made a virtually invisible screen debut in 1968's *A Lovely Way to Die*, starring Kirk Douglas. "I had one line," MacGraw remembered. "I yelled 'Come on, sweetheart!' to a racehorse in the opening credits. I did it three times, and the crew was saying, 'What is this person's problem? This jerk can't say three words!'" The following year, MacGraw scored a big success as the snotty Brenda Patimkin in the film version of Philip Roth's *Goodbye, Columbus*. Evans had a hunch that *Love Story* was going to hit big when it was released at the end of 1970. At the time, MacGraw was represented by Martin Davidson, who had gotten hold of the script for *Love Story*, about the doomed love of two Ivy League students, wealthy Oliver Barrett IV and working-class Jenny Cavalleri, which was initially being produced by United Artists. Although she was a stunningly attractive woman who had brightened the many magazine layouts in which she had appeared, Mac-Graw was both disarmingly honest and insecure about her abilities as an actress. She had no formal training at all, no technique to rely on, but in *Goodbye, Columbus* she had fit the part well, with a natural screen presence that earned her good reviews: the *New York Times*'s Vincent Canby called her "exactly the right mixture of innocence and guile," and the *Village Voice*'s Andrew Sarris wrote that she "makes up for all the fashion models over the years who have fizzled after their first fizz on the screen." She owed Paramount a movie and worried that the studio was going to force her to make something that might sink her promising career, so she asked Davidson to see if the studio might be persuaded to make *Love Story*. Davidson asked the producer Howard Minsky to take the script to Paramount, and Evans read it and soon purchased it from United Artists.

MacGraw remembered that when they met, Sue talked "a great big agent's game." "I fell in love with Sue in five seconds," said MacGraw. "It was as simple as that." Shortly before *Love Story* opened that December and became an enormous hit, Sue became MacGraw's agent, as well as her devoted friend. Their backgrounds could not have been more different—MacGraw came from a family of bohemian artists, had graduated from Wellesley, and had worked as a fashion stylist for Diana Vreeland—but she became one of the clients to whom Sue was most loyal.

This combination of business and friendship was in itself a tricky balancing act for most agents. "I do love my clients and many of them I consider family," said Risa Shapiro, who later became an agent with William Morris. "*But they are not your friends. They are your clients. Don't ever expect that it will be different from that. Protect yourself.*" For all of Sue's toughness, she also showed that she had a generous heart, and it came quite naturally for her to invest an enormous part of herself in the lives of the clients about whom she cared most deeply. She knew that a client's departure was an occupational hazard, but at this point she was hell-bent on keeping all of them.

In 1970, Sue also connected professionally with Ann-Margret. The Swedish-born actress had entered the movies with appealing performances in *Pocketful of Miracles* (1961) and *Bye Bye Birdie* (1963) and had become a popular star opposite Elvis Presley in *Viva Las Vegas* (1964). Throughout the 1960s, Ann-Margret was never associated with the decade's angst and striving for social change but instead embodied its Day-Glo glitz and cheap thrills: with her husky, come-hither voice that often seemed to be ventriloquial, she suggested the world of bubblegum rock records, *True Detective* magazines, and sexy, low-grade Matt Helm movies. By the end of the 1960s, her movie career had faded.

On-screen Ann-Margret may have personified va-va-va-voom, but in private she was a serious-minded, modest woman who wanted to do good work. For years she struggled to be taken seriously. In 1965, when she was cast opposite Steve McQueen in *The Cincinnati Kid*, the movie's original director, Sam Peckinpah, didn't want her. In the fall of 1964, Peckinpah wrote to the movie's producer, Martin Ransohoff, that he felt that the casting of both Ann-Margret and Tuesday Weld would give the picture the look of a sister act.

Sue saw immediately that Ann-Margret's sex-kitten image needed to be put behind her. Ann-Margret wanted to be given a chance to prove herself as an actress, and Sue helped land her a good part in Stanley Kramer's *R.P.M.*, but the movie made barely a ripple. Then came the lowbrow *C. C. & Company*, produced by Ann-Margret's manager Allan Carr in 1970, as an attempt to make a star out of the New York Jets' number 12, Joe Namath. Carr and Sue were friends, and because both were overweight—Carr far more than Sue—both dressed somewhat similarly, in large, flowing muumuus.

(Comedy writer Bruce Vilanch, remembering Carr and Sue together at parties, referred to them as "Battle of the Network Caftans.") *C. C. & Company* even contained a tribute to Sue: in a sequence set in Las Vegas, a theater marquee advertises "WAYNE COCHRANE AND HIS CC RIDERS," and billed underneath them, as the lounge act, is "SUE MENGERS."

Neither film advanced Ann-Margret's career in the way she had hoped. The star's husband, Roger Smith, who took an active role in managing her career, locked horns somewhat with Sue at this time, urging his wife not to settle for taking the first big commercial offer that came through. This was not in keeping with Sue's way of doing business; she believed that actors needed to keep working, even if a script was less than ideal. One day, while debating the issue with Smith, Sue snapped, "Look, Mike Nichols isn't exactly calling with an offer."

A week later Mike Nichols was doing just that. The director was preparing *Carnal Knowledge*, a drama about the sexual exploits and problems of two friends (Jack Nicholson and Art Garfunkel) over the course of more than twenty years. Just how Ann-Margret got cast in *Carnal Knowledge* is open to debate. In her memoir, Ann-Margret claims that Kathleen Tynan, wife of the noted English theater critic Kenneth Tynan, suggested her for the part of Bobbie, the big-breasted sexpot who moves in with randy-boy-who-never-grows-up Jonathan (Nicholson) and winds up an overweight, sniveling, neurotic mess. But Sue always insisted that Ann-Margret's casting stemmed from a party she threw at Dawnridge Drive, at which she had the foresight to seat the actress and the director next to each other. It seemed the unlikeliest combination: the thinking man's director whose work on both stage and screen had been greeted with ecstatic critical acclaim, and the likable yet vapid star of *Kitten with a Whip*. But the part of Bobbie was a good one, and after rejecting Nichols's original offer of $50,000, Sue got $75,000 for Ann-Margret's services. "I'm not a technical actress," Ann-Margret admitted in her memoir. "I'm all raw emotion and nerves." But when filming began in late 1970, she found that Mike Nichols showed her the respect as a performer that she had always craved.

Carnal Knowledge was intended to be biting and trenchant, but instead was sour, cynical, and extremely mannered, with a sleek production design that served only to alienate the audience. Still, the critics praised the film both for its adult content and for Ann-Margret's work as an actress: in

Newsweek Paul D. Zimmerman lauded her "quiet, soft, moving performance"; of the major critics only *The New Yorker*'s Pauline Kael dismissed the actress's contribution to the film, calling it "simp pathos." Ten years into her career, the role of Bobbie legitimized Ann-Margret as an actress, bringing her the Golden Globe Award and an Academy Award nomination for Best Supporting Actress.

The pairing of Mike Nichols and Ann-Margret became one of the celebrated anecdotes of Sue's career, Exhibit A in support of her reputation as one of the most resourceful of agents. It also helped make her at-home parties such a coveted invitation in Hollywood: turn up at Sue Mengers's house for dinner and you might come away with a career-making part in a movie. As it turned out, Sue was the power behind *Carnal Knowledge* in other ways, too. She had negotiated the deal for Candice Bergen to play the role of the proper college girl who has affairs with both Nicholson and Garfunkel. *Carnal Knowledge* marked a turning point in Bergen's career. Up until then she had approached acting as a dilettante at best, and her reviews for the most part reflected this. Always strikingly beautiful, she tended to come across on film as rather cold and disengaged. But in *Carnal Knowledge* Bergen fell under Nichols's sway and began to think herself capable of better things. "I was good in *Carnal Knowledge*," she wrote in her autobiography, "the best I'd ever been." Sue would serve as Bergen's agent throughout the actress's up-and-down career in the 1970s and would also eventually represent Mike Nichols throughout much of the decade.

In 1970, Sue also signed Kim Darby, the actress who had leaped to stardom the year before playing Mattie Ross, the stubborn teenaged girl bent on avenging her father's murder in Henry Hathaway's autumnal Western *True Grit*. Darby had had a tumultuous childhood; her parents were professional dancers, and she had been raised in Los Angeles by her grandparents. For someone so young, she was a remarkably serious-minded actress; she had been trained by Tony Barr at Desilu Studios and had begun acting professionally at fourteen. For much of the 1960s she distinguished herself in episodic television work. Casting for the part of Mattie in *True Grit* was a drawn-out process, but when Hathaway saw Darby in an episode of the popular suspense series *Run for Your Life*, he refused to settle for anyone else in the role. Darby had just had a baby and felt she was overweight and didn't look her best, but Hathaway hammered away at her, and after turning down the part six times, she finally agreed to do it. When the movie was released in the summer of 1969, with Darby in third-position star billing above the title, directly after John Wayne and Glen Campbell, it was a smash hit. Darby also received widespread acclaim as one of the most exciting discoveries in years, with one magazine referring to her as "the Doris Day of the Counter-Culture."

Her next career move would be crucial, and on the advice of her then-husband, William Tennant, she accepted the female lead opposite Glen Campbell in a meandering, picaresque comedy, *Norwood*; Tennant felt she should do it as a favor to the picture's producer, Hal Wallis, who had also produced *True Grit*. Once the Glen Campbell fans had shown up to see it, *Norwood* didn't do much at the box office. But by now Darby had lost her baby weight, and when she went to Dawnridge Drive, Sue was delighted with her appearance. "The first thing she said to me," Darby recalled, "was 'You're tiny! You're thin! How wonderful! We can do everything you want!'" Sue signed the actress and immediately demonstrated her worth: while Darby had received $150,000 for *True Grit*, Sue jacked her price up to $250,000 for *The Strawberry Statement*, based on James Simon Kunen's book about the student unrest that rocked Columbia University in 1968.

"In those days, when I had my day in the sun," said Darby, "I didn't read for a part. I just met. They didn't even read me for *True Grit*." This was the way the process often worked for a number of leading actors at the time; the ones who had to go through the paces of readings before casting directors were mostly second leads and supporting actors and bit players. If a part was prestigious enough, tests would still be run—a few years later, for *The Great Gatsby*, Robert Evans would make screen tests of six different actresses vying for the role of Daisy Buchanan—but for many pictures it was simply a matter of the producer and director wanting a certain star and making the pitch.

Darby was exceedingly in demand during the time Sue represented her. "Scripts were piled up in my house," she remembered—among them *Panic in Needle Park* and *Diary of a Mad Housewife*. In the end, her film career wouldn't fulfill its early promise, partly because she was distracted by a string of volatile, destructive relationships with men, including actors James Stacy and Pete Duel. But decades after they worked together, the actress's memories of Sue remained vivid and affectionate. "She was always on the

90

phone," Darby recalled. "I thought she was wonderful. And I know that I missed out on wonderful things by not staying with her longer."

Another actress who had broken through in 1970 was Dyan Cannon. The picture was Paul Mazursky's sophisticated marital comedy *Bob & Carol & Ted & Alice*, with Cannon playing opposite Sue's client Elliott Gould. The daughter of a Seattle insurance broker, Cannon studied acting with Sanford Meisner, toyed with being a concert pianist, toured in *How to Succeed in Business Without Really Trying*, and had a tumultuous four years as Mrs. Cary Grant. *Bob & Carol & Ted & Alice* made Cannon a star after years of struggle, and in 1970 the New York Film Critics named her Best Supporting Actress. Given her blind spot toward developing talents, Sue would not have bothered with Cannon prior to her breakthrough success, but now she pursued her avidly.

After *Bob & Carol & Ted & Alice*, Cannon had no shortage of offers. In fact, in the early 1970s, both Cannon and Gould were appearing in a remarkable number of films—many of them not any good. Cannon's output for 1971 included *Doctors' Wives*, *The Anderson Tapes*, *The Love Machine*, and *The Burglar*, all low-grade fare in which Cannon's crack timing and naughty-girl sexiness—she often came across like a teenager who had just pulled something rotten—were virtually the only redeeming features. (In *The Anderson Tapes* her role was so sketchily written and incidental to the action that it almost seemed an insult to her very potent abilities as an actress.) Then, in March 1971, she set her sights on one of the most coveted roles of the year: Julie Messinger in Paramount's *Such Good Friends*, directed by Otto Preminger. Based on a best-selling novel and inspired by the actual experiences of author Lois Gould, it concerned a woman who discovers, while her husband is dying in a New York hospital, that he has been serially unfaithful to her. After Cannon had devoured the book, she immediately telephoned Sue to ask who would be doing the movie. Sue, who had known Preminger for years, went to work, and Cannon landed the part. Principal photography began on location in New York in July 1971.

"Otto was famous for his control of the set," Cannon recalled. "When we were shooting, I woke up one morning with a fever and called right away. I was very sick. They were shooting that day in a hospital, and they were taking the intensive-care patients out of the unit and putting them upstairs. Otto's people said, 'We've only got the hospital for this one day.'" Bowing to the pressure that one of her big scenes in the picture had to be shot on that day or not at all, Cannon showed up for work. "It was an emotional scene I was to play," she said, "and I found it very easy on that particular day because I was vulnerable. The choice I made in the scene was to laugh instead of cry, and Otto was so angry he chased me down the hall and into a bathroom. I locked myself in; I never had this kind of thing with anyone I had worked with."

In an interview she gave around the time of the film's release, Cannon denounced Preminger: "You could not reason with him. His attitude toward you changed every day. It didn't matter *who* you were." (Many people on the set reported that Preminger had, in fact, met his temperamental match in Cannon.) When *Such Good Friends* was released in December 1971, it received mixed reviews, and did decent business at the box office, thanks to Cannon's marquee value and the book's popularity. But it never became the first-class film that Cannon had hoped it could be, and following its release the actress was off the screen for over a year—from Sue's point of view, a lifetime.

In 1966—a big year for British films and stars, including *Morgan!*, *Georgy Girl*, and *A Man for All Seasons*—Michael Caine had enjoyed an international success as the casually corrupt but immensely likable hero of *Alfie*, a kind of swinging update of John O'Hara's Pal Joey. *Alfie* was meant to explore the new restlessness of working-class '60s youth, and Caine's monologues, delivered straight to the camera in his engaging Cockney lilt, resonated with huge numbers of people.

Caine hadn't really had a worthy follow-up since then, and by 1970 he was in serious pursuit of a Hollywood career. "Sue took me on," Caine remembered. "I was her least known, least expensive actor. She had all these big stars—and me. It was wonderful to go to her house for dinner because I got to sit with all these big movie stars. I wasn't a big American star. I was British with a funny accent. She worked on me and really did a job on me."

When it came to mapping out Caine's career, Sue applied a more specific strategy than she often did. Her aim was to push Caine further into the American market, to put him more on a par with American male stars and steadily drive up his price. Caine recalled that she had a good eye for scripts, coupled with a hard-core pragmatism about what kind of material was available. "She would call me and say, 'You got a great review for that movie. . . . *Helloooo?*' If it was bad, she wouldn't say, '*Helloooo?*' She would often say, 'This isn't the best thing you're going to do but it's going to hold you until the other one comes out, the good one that you've already made.' You had to keep working. If you had a bad lot of scripts—you picked the best."

Shortly after Caine got settled in Hollywood, he was summoned to dinner at Dawnridge Drive. "I was putting sugar in my coffee and she said, 'Don't touch that. It's cocaine.' A bowl of cocaine—on the table! That's how it was then. She would have these evenings, and you would always have meatloaf or something like that because she couldn't be bothered to do anything else. Lots of big stars. And then she'd say something hospitable like 'You're finishing at ten thirty and you can all fuck off!'"

Caine did everything Sue told him to do. "No disagreements," he recalled. "It didn't always work out. I didn't care because we had timed it in such a way—we could take a chance if we thought we had a hit coming. She always said, 'You have to make money. I come from a poor family. I had to make some money as well.'"

On one of Caine's movies, *The Italian Job*, she also snared a job for Joan Collins, who was still married—just—to Sue's longtime client Anthony Newley. Collins remembered that Sue represented her only "vaguely." *The Italian Job* was being produced by Paramount, and Charles Bluhdorn fired Collins before filming began because he didn't believe she could handle an American accent. "Through Bob Evans, who was a good friend of hers, she got me $75,000 for this role," Collins said. "And after I was fired, she insisted that I get the $75,000."

Sue had known and admired Tuesday Weld from the time the actress had costarred with Anthony Perkins in *Pretty Poison*. Weld had been deprived of anything resembling a normal childhood: from age four, she was working as a child model to support her mother, brother, and sister, her father having died a year earlier. She began acting in films at twelve—the year, she recalled, of her first suicide attempt—in the lowbrow musical *Rock, Rock, Rock!*, did time in the TV sitcom *The Many Loves of Dobie Gillis*, and by the mid-1960s had already come through a period of heavy drinking and emerged as a strikingly natural and inventive actress in films such as *Soldier in the Rain*, *The Cincinnati Kid*, and *Lord Love a Duck*. She had the face of a watchful, wise child, and an ability to project amazing vulnerability, partly through her eloquent silences. Critic Tom Milne succinctly described her extraordinary talent in an essay he wrote in 1970. Weld, he wrote, "starts with the inestimable natural advantage of being able to suggest, at one and the same time, untroubled reserves of wide-eyed innocence and incalculable depths of depravity. She is also a brilliant comedienne, capable of exploiting both facets of her personality with the sort of delicate understatement which is rarely recognized as talent."

Weld's highly individual and complex gifts as an actress did not always lead to serenity on the set. She remembered *Pretty Poison* as a miserable experience because of her difficulties with director Noel Black. ("I don't care if the critics liked it; I hated it," she told interviewer Rex Reed in 1971.) And she chose parts because they interested her, not because of any particular commercial considerations. One of the scripts she rejected was *Bonnie and Clyde*, because she had just given birth to her daughter and didn't want to work, but also because she sensed it would be an enormous hit. She had turned down Paul Mazursky's *Bob & Carol & Ted & Alice* for similar reasons. "It reeked of success," she later said. "I may be self-destructive, but I like taking chances with movies." Weld seemed anything but the ideal client for an agent as commercially minded as Sue, but by 1970 the two of them were working together.

"She wanted me to work all the time," Weld recalled. "You can't have a huge hit every time, and you've got to work in between. I was always very picky about things, and I wanted to do small things rather than great big things. I didn't want Academy Awards. I didn't want people following me around. I didn't want to be her trophy actress. I think she was very disillusioned by that, because she took on the fame of all her clients; that just boosted her more. She bathed in their fame. And she should have. But she was disappointed with me."

Weld had not earned spectacular money for any of her recent films. For *The Cincinnati Kid*, she had been paid $75,000 for ten weeks' work (and gave the finest performance in the film). For *Lord Love a Duck* she made $40,000 for six weeks' work, plus $25,000 deferred from the first profits, in addition to 5 percent of the profits. For *Pretty Poison* she had gotten $75,000 for ten weeks' work, plus $500 in weekly expenses.

Columbia Pictures was casting *I Walk the Line*, a drama set in

small-town Tennessee, with Gregory Peck starring as an over-the-hill sheriff falling for a much younger woman, the daughter of a local moonshiner.
John Frankenheimer was set to direct, following a string of successes that
included *The Manchurian Candidate* and *The Train*. Carol Lynley, Ann-
Margret, Samantha Eggar, and Anjanette Comer were among the possibilities considered for the female lead, but Weld landed it, at a salary of
$100,000 for ten weeks, plus two weeks free, and $500 in weekly expenses.
When *I Walk the Line* was released in November 1970, Weld once more
drew excellent reviews, but Sue was not thrilled with the actress's next
choice of a project, *A Safe Place*, an offbeat drama that was decidedly out of
the mainstream.

Despite Weld's lack of career drive, Sue always felt an affection for the
actress—and it was returned: "I think one reason everybody could relate to
her was because she put everything out on the table most of the time. You
did see her raw ambition. You did see her anger, and her disappointment.
And her depression. But I think it was the fact that she voiced it. She would
tell you, 'I don't want to talk now.' I think that somehow kept her going, because things didn't fester in her."

For all the exciting new work being done in films like *Five Easy Pieces* and
Robert Altman's *M*A*S*H*, there were still a few reminders of the old studio system. For Universal's *Airport*, the first in a string of all-star disaster
movies that made big money throughout the decade, producer Ross Hunter
bought Arthur Hailey's best-selling suspense novel and cast the film version with bona fide movie stars (Burt Lancaster, Dean Martin), Broadway
legends (Helen Hayes, Maureen Stapleton), and "familiar faces" (Lloyd
Nolan, Barry Nelson). *Variety* was dead wrong when it predicted that it
was "doubtful there will be the kind of stampede necessary to bail out Universal's investment of around $10,000,000." *Airport* was a spectacular,
belated gasp from old Hollywood, outgrossing nearly every other picture
of 1970.

One new filmmaker was a striking combination of the old and the new:
Peter Bogdanovich, a prolific journalist and former actor whose first film,
Targets, had attracted some serious critical attention during its brief run in
1968. *Targets* was a violent, low-budget suspense drama about a young man
who slides over the edge mentally, wipes out his family, and goes on a

shooting spree at a local drive-in theater where a faded "B" horror-movie actor (Boris Karloff) is making a personal appearance. Sue saw *Targets* not long after arriving in Hollywood, and it grabbed her attention from the opening sequence.

In late September 1970, she met with Bogdanovich. "Sue Mengers, a big agent, I found out—came over and desperately wants to represent me," Bogdanovich wrote in his diary. "Had an hour of her on the subject—at first I didn't like her but came around. And I think I'll go with her. Polly thinks so too—after I got great recommendation for her from Tuesday. " ("Polly" was Polly Platt, the gifted production designer who at the time was Bogdanovich's wife; "Tuesday" was Tuesday Weld.)

Within weeks Sue was sending ideas to Bogdanovich in care of the Ramada Inn in Wichita Falls, Texas, where he was staying during the shooting of his new film, *The Last Picture Show*, based on Larry McMurtry's novel about angst and sexual frustration among the residents of a dying West Texas town in 1951. One of the properties Sue was trying to interest Bogdanovich in was Daniel Stern's *The Suicide Academy*. "We think an excellent film could be made from this novel, and if it interests you perhaps we could try to set it up with you co-authoring it with someone else," she wrote to him. She also tried peddling *The Looters*, a project that producer Walter Wanger had been developing and that had come Bogdanovich's way after Wanger's death in 1968. *The Suicide Academy* went nowhere, and *The Looters* eventually got made by Don Siegel as *Charley Varrick*, but Bogdanovich dispensed with his current agent, Lee Rosenberg of Adams, Ray & Rosenberg, and on December 15, 1970, signed a one-year contract with CMA, with Sue as his principal agent.

"Sue was sort of outrageous and pushy," said Bogdanovich. "She was putting down Adams, Ray & Rosenberg. 'You want to be with CMA,' she said. 'I will really work hard for you.'" Sue told everyone who would listen that she was certain that *The Last Picture Show* was going to be a major success for Bogdanovich.

Another client Sue snagged at this time who was on the way up was Gene Hackman, who had just made $35,000 for *The Hunting Party* when she signed him—and he proved an exception to her general rule of waiting until the actors had broken through to take over handling their careers. At Twentieth Century Fox, William Friedkin was preparing *The French*

Connection, with a script by Ernest Tidyman, based on a nonfiction book by Robin Moore about the biggest heroin bust in U.S. history. It was being shot on location in New York City and Marseille, and the budget wasn't large. Friedkin and his producer, Philip D'Antoni, thought that it had the potential to be a thrilling picture but were faced with an enormous casting obstacle: finding the right actor to portray the corrosively tough New York cop Jimmy "Popeye" Doyle.

After Paul Newman was ruled out as too expensive, the first name Friedkin mentioned to Fox's production chief, Richard Zanuck, was Jackie Gleason, who had recently wrapped up his popular comedy-variety series on CBS-TV. "Instantly, Dick Zanuck said, 'No way will I use Gleason,'" Friedkin recalled. "He was in a movie called *Gigot*, and Dick described it as the biggest disaster in the history of Fox. Our next choice was Peter Boyle, who had been in *Joe*, as the bigot with the baseball bat. He turned the picture down; he said, 'You know, I'd like to spend the rest of my life doing romantic comedies.' We were considering people like William Devane—guys who had limited careers but who we thought were much more spot on."

Richard Zanuck had assured Friedkin and D'Antoni that the picture didn't require a major star, simply the right actor. At this point Friedkin hit on the idea of using *New York Herald Tribune* journalist Jimmy Breslin. Despite initial resistance on Breslin's part, Friedkin rehearsed him for a week. "On the first day he was great," said Friedkin. "On the second day, he showed up drunk. On the third day, he showed up contrite because he had been drunk. On the fourth day, he showed up late. And on the fifth day, I fired him."

Throughout all this, Sue had been pushing Gene Hackman for the part, without stirring up any interest. Unbeknownst to Friedkin, on a trip to New York, Sue attended a dinner party given by producer Irwin Winkler and his wife, Margo, at which Breslin was also a guest. When Breslin asked her what she thought about the idea of his doing *The French Connection*, Sue replied, "You can't do this movie! Are you crazy? You're taking work from an actor. You're going to fail." As Friedkin observed, "She actually talked him out of it, which is why on the next to last day he came in late and was awful."

D'Antoni and Friedkin finally agreed to meet Hackman for lunch at the Oak Room in New York. "I almost fell asleep at the lunch," said Friedkin.

"Zanuck told us we'd better cast the part soon, because he was going to get fired by Fox, and he had $1.5 million set aside for the picture. Hackman was the last man standing."

In 1970, Hackman was anything but a household name. He was a respected young actor, with an Academy Award nomination for *Bonnie and Clyde* (and another one to come for 1970's *I Never Sang for My Father*). In 1969, he had earned $75,000 for nine weeks' work on *Downhill Racer*, in which he took second billing to Robert Redford.

Hackman had had a hectic, nomadic early life, including a stint in the Marines, before he came to New York to seek work as an actor. He had received some training at the Pasadena Playhouse, and one of his most appealing qualities was his authenticity. He never actually seemed young; he looked like a lot of other ordinary men who would sit next to you on the bus or the subway, but his ordinariness had an extraordinary quality, and he radiated a certain sexiness that didn't have anything to do with conventional handsomeness or virility.

He could also be difficult. Throughout his career, the majority of directors who worked with him would report that he was often highly argumentative on the set. His movie career had almost gotten grounded before it was off the runway. Hackman was a good friend of two other struggling and volatile New York actors, Robert Duvall and Dustin Hoffman, and had shared spartan lodgings with them at a cold-water flat on West 109th Street. In 1967, despite being only seven years older than Hoffman, he was cast as the father of Hoffman's Benjamin Braddock in Mike Nichols's *The Graduate*. The film had a two-week rehearsal period, and Nichols had ordered his cast to show up for it with their lines learned. This was not the way Hackman preferred to work—he liked to feel his way into his character intuitively once rehearsals began—and at the end of the two weeks, he still hadn't memorized his part. Nichols fired him, and that night Hackman sought solace in the company of the noted character actress Elizabeth Wilson, who had been cast as his wife in *The Graduate*. They went out for several drinks, and then Hackman drove Wilson back to her apartment at the Chateau Marmont, where they began to make out in the front seat of his car. Their heavy petting didn't go very far. "I went upstairs alone," said Wilson. "I just thought, well—I don't want to be with a *loser*."

Hackman failed to impress during the first day of filming on *The French*

Connection. "It was the scene where Hackman and Roy Scheider rough up this young African-American in a car," said William Friedkin. "I did thirty-six takes, and the African-American and Roy were great in every one, and Hackman was weak and insecure. I always show the actors the rushes. I printed thirty-six takes, which is completely off the wall and totally unproductive. And Gene quit the picture." When they were informed of what Hackman had done, Sue and the other officers at CMA collared him and told him that if he quit the movie, he'd have to pay for it, so Hackman returned to work. "He delivered a great performance," said Friedkin. "And Sue took a lot of credit for it."

Sue's shrewdest maneuvers in 1970 revolved around what became one of the year's box-office sensations as well as a commercial landmark in book publishing—*Love Story.* Once the movie's enormous grosses started rolling in—it would earn $136 million internationally—no two movie actors could ever have felt as thoroughly duped as Ryan O'Neal and Ali MacGraw must have felt. They had signed to do the picture for $25,000 and $20,000, respectively. This was the second film in MacGraw's two-picture deal with Paramount, and she had never imagined its making so much money. The part of Oliver proved difficult to cast, and Robert Evans received many turndowns from star actors. Ryan O'Neal was a friend of the screenplay's author, Erich Segal, who had written the script for the actor's previous picture, *The Games,* and Segal arranged a test for him at Paramount. O'Neal's agent at the time was Howard Rubin, who initially told Paramount that the offer was insulting. But O'Neal had a hunch about the picture, and despite the fact that he had recently commanded $125,000 for starring in *The Big Bounce,* he told Rubin to accept the offer and get him enough of a per diem to live in New York for twelve weeks during the filming.

O'Neal and MacGraw shot the picture and then waited about ten months for its release in December 1970. In the interim, Segal had, at Robert Evans's suggestion, turned his screenplay into a quick-and-dirty novel, which made a fortune, selling over four hundred thousand hardcover copies by the time of the film's release and eventually reaching paperback sales of over four million copies.

One fascinating thing about *Love Story*'s success was the way in which it compelled so many critics to rationalize precisely why they had been affected by its soap-opera plot. In the *Chicago Sun-Times*, Roger Ebert admitted that he had enjoyed it, adding, "If the formula of *Love Story* is not outdated, what formula is? And yet it is not out of date; wherever there is a market for *Romeo and Juliet*, there you will find it." In the *New York Times*, Vincent Canby posited that audiences were crying throughout the film because "they are crying for themselves, for all the blessed things—represented by the unblemished love of Jenny and Ollie—they themselves have been deprived of." The picture reversed Paramount's declining fortunes, earned Academy Award nominations for Best Picture and for both its stars, and landed Ali MacGraw on the cover of the January 11, 1971, issue of *Time*.

Shortly after the movie opened at Christmastime to astonishing grosses, O'Neal met Sue at a party at the home of producer Richard Shepherd. She walked past O'Neal and muttered, "Howard Rubin *sucks*." O'Neal, pondering the film's success, was already wondering about the deal he had accepted. "Sue didn't find people off the street," O'Neal said with a laugh years later. "She stole them from other agents. We sat down and started to talk, and she cracked me up. She was funny. Vulgar. No one I wanted to sleep with, but there was something intriguing about her. And she was now at this very big agency, run by Freddie Fields, who represented Leigh Taylor-Young, my bride. I thought, I just can't do this to Howard. I've been with him a few years. So I told Howard, 'You're now my manager.' I threw another ten percent of my earnings, which weren't much then, to Howard, so he couldn't be lost in the shuffle." As Robert Evans's wife, MacGraw eventually received additional compensation—a percentage of the German grosses—for her work in *Love Story*, but Evans declined to pay O'Neal anything extra, creating bad blood between the two men. Rather than waste time bludgeoning her friend Evans, Sue took over O'Neal's career, helping to propel him into the ranks of the most highly paid male stars of the 1970s.

CHAPTER TEN

1971–1972

In the early 1970s, most Hollywood movie stars were paid big money for the time, but it paled compared with the astronomical sums they would be able to command a decade later. For *The Hawaiians*, released in 1970, Charlton Heston received $250,000 against 10 percent of the gross profits. For playing the title role in *Patton*, which earned him the Academy Award for Best Actor of 1970, George C. Scott received $600,000 for twenty weeks' work, plus 5 percent of the gross after 2.6 percent. Generally speaking, male actors made far more than the women and got better material, too. For much of the decade, top-line actresses would have difficulty finding good, substantial parts, and Quigley Publishing's annual Top Ten Money-Making Stars Poll was dominated by men. In 1971, only one actress—Ali MacGraw—made the Top Ten, and in 1972, Barbra Streisand and Goldie Hawn were the only women listed.

For actors and directors, maintaining a certain salary level was crucial to surviving in Hollywood. Often a star might turn down a superior script because the production wasn't budgeted high enough to command his usual salary—and he was afraid that once his salary came down, word would get out and it would stay down. An agent, often in concert with an attorney, was expected to work out all the details in a star's contract: a schedule of payments (many actors had their salaries deferred to avoid being heavily taxed in a given year), the specific aspects of percentage agreements, the exact size and position of billing in relation to the point size of the title. For instance, Gregory Peck, Tuesday Weld's costar in *I Walk the Line*, received up-front payments of $45,000 weekly for four weeks, commencing with the start of shooting. The remainder of his salary was to be paid in installments of $95,000 annually each January for six consecutive years; in addition, he was to be paid 10 percent of the first $2.5 million of the gross after breakdown, escalating to 12 percent if the gross continued to rise.

Despite her obsessive concern for her clients' financial security, Sue was never much interested in the finer points of any particular deal and tended to leave the secondary details to lawyers or her colleagues at CMA. She saw herself as a top-level agent to top-level stars, and once the basic salary deal had been set, she didn't see why she needed to concern herself with anything else and made no apology for not thinking otherwise.

"The wonderful thing about Sue," recalled Kenneth Ziffren, a Los Angeles entertainment lawyer who represented some of her clients, including Ryan O'Neal, "was that she was absolutely straight with everyone, which is why they adored her. They always knew she wasn't bullshitting them." Her attitude toward the studio chiefs was amazingly fearless, but she knew something important that other agents either didn't know or didn't recognize: that studios were not so inundated with good material that they could afford to be dismissive of just about anything submitted to them. Their success, Sue believed, was more of a happy accident than the result of their high level of expertise about the workings of the movie business.

In meetings at CMA, she could be quite dismissive of her colleagues' concerns. Mike Medavoy, a top agent at CMA, did not share her feeling that stars should keep working no matter what; he was much more concerned with finding his clients just the right script. Medavoy remembered a rough encounter he had with Sue not long before he left CMA in 1972. "She said, 'I don't get why you need to handle Leslie Caron and some of the older stars,'" recalled Medavoy. "She said, 'You're better than that. You represent the younger guys, and they are the future.' I got angry at her and said, 'You fat cow, get out of my office, and I'll tell you when I'm ready to handle whoever I want to handle.'" Medavoy added that however hard she might have been on other people in the office—she could be particularly brutal to the support staff—she was too smart ever to cross Freddie Fields.

She was also erratic about attending major meetings, especially if they were scheduled for early morning. Richard Shepherd, the producer of *Breakfast at Tiffany's* and other films, who was a partner at ICM before becoming head of production at Warner Bros., recalled a memorable entrance Sue made shortly before he left the agency in 1970. "We set up this important meeting with the heads of all the studios and production companies, for eight thirty in the morning. And I said, 'Sue, for once in your life, would you please be on time?' On the day of the meeting, we were in the production marketing room with all these executives from the studios and production companies and individual producers. And at exactly eight thirty Sue walked in the door in her evening dress and said, 'Well—I'm here on time.'"

In the early 1970s, before becoming the chairman and chief executive officer of Paramount and Fox, Inc., Barry Diller was a high-ranking executive at ABC-TV, the man responsible for creating the inexpensively produced, ninety-minute made-for-television movie; his *ABC Movie of the Week*, starring big names from television and films, regularly ranked high in the ratings during the decade. "Sue was the greatest negative seller I've ever seen," said Diller. "If you were going with a nonclient for a role, she would tear that person down and give you all sorts of reasons of why it didn't make sense. I would listen and weaken under her great negative selling, although usually I hung up the phone and went back to what I was going to do anyway." Despite her general feeling that movie stars should only consider television as a last resort, Sue was a fan of the *ABC Movie of the Week*, partly because she considered that it provided an excellent training ground for future directors and writers. (Steven Spielberg and Lamont Johnson were among the series' notable graduates.) In fact, the first job she got for Ryan O'Neal after *Love Story*'s release was in *Love Hate Love*, a Movie of the Week costarring Lesley Ann Warren, made in 1971.

That was overall another big year for Sue, even though three of her clients were involved in a picture that never saw the light of day. *A Glimpse of Tiger* was a strange, bittersweet comedy-drama directed by Anthony Harvey and starring Elliott Gould as a crazy eccentric who knows a little bit about just about everything. The picture was very much a Sue Mengers project: playing opposite Gould was Kim Darby. With the success of *M*A*S*H*, Gould was listed as number five in the exhibitors' poll of top-ten box-office stars of 1970, four slots above Barbra Streisand. Gould had been making one failed picture after another, films like *Move* and *I Love My . . . Wife*. (This led Bob Hope to crack one year at the Academy Awards that it had been a very strange year—he had just seen a movie that didn't have Elliott Gould in it.)

There was a certain amount of friction between the two *Glimpse of Tiger* stars from the beginning. During rehearsals, Darby often found Gould unintelligible. One day on the set he strolled over to her and said, "I've just talked to my wife, and she doesn't think you're right for this picture. You're not interesting enough—that's what she said." But the real difficulties came from Gould's emotional outbursts, which many attributed to his abuse of LSD. Darby remembered that during a sequence being shot in the New York subway system, Gould showed up wearing a football helmet, with cotton balls pasted all over his face. On another occasion, he turned violent: Darby was sitting at a glass coffee table, and Gould, sucking a baby's pacifier, ran in and put his foot through the table. "He never laid hands on me, actually," said Darby. "But I was terrified. I jumped up and ran out. He was completely out of control."

Darby was not a client of Sue's for much longer. After *The Strawberry Statement* failed, Darby's next Sue-negotiated project, *The Grissom Gang*, posted a loss of over $3 million. Darby left but even years later regretted her decision, as her film career abruptly faded out.

"It was more than terrible on my part," said Gould of the *Glimpse of Tiger* debacle. "I did not know how to play the part. I had no perspective and no judgment." The resulting publicity from the incident, plus his rejection of the leads in both Robert Altman's *McCabe and Mrs. Miller* and Sam Peckinpah's *Straw Dogs*, put a temporary crimp in Gould's career—though he would come back magnificently in 1973 as detective Philip Marlowe in Altman's stunning *The Long Goodbye*. By mid-1971, Gould's marriage to Streisand, in trouble for several years, had essentially ended, and with it, Sue's involvement with his career. Sue was often dismissive of the actor, occasionally making a point of telling him that he was as nutty as a fruitcake. For years, if a guest at one of her parties was rattling on in a drug-induced stupor, Sue would cut him short by telling him that he sounded as crazy as Elliott Gould.

Immediately after Gould's episode on the set of *A Glimpse of Tiger*, the picture was shut down. Streisand, who had just done a brilliant comic turn in Herbert Ross's *The Owl and the Pussycat* and was looking for a drama, took an interest in *A Glimpse of Tiger* for a time. Eventually the script was passed on to Peter Bogdanovich, who didn't like it but began to imagine that it could be reworked as a very different kind of movie—a screwball comedy.

Sue's relationship with Robert Evans and Ali MacGraw grew closer each day. Every morning, while he and MacGraw were breakfasting in bed, the first person Evans spoke with on the telephone was Charles Bluhdorn—and

104

the second was Sue. "Prick" and "Mengela" laughed themselves sick over the latest disastrous love affairs or ill-fated casting ventures around Hollywood. "They both had a kind of irreverent sense of humor about show business, in its many facets," said Jack Nicholson. "And they rather enjoyed the times when they would outdo each other, and they told anecdotes about it. 'My love,' Sue always called Bob."

Occasionally they had a skirmish when she tried to sell him a client he didn't want. At the moment the project demanding most of Evans's attention was *The Godfather*, Francis Ford Coppola's screen version of the blockbuster novel by Mario Puzo. Evans had been *The Godfather*'s godfather from its inception. In 1968, Puzo, a gambling addict like Evans, needed a quick $10,000 to settle some debts, and Evans agreed to pay him $12,500 to back him during the writing of a novel the author called *Mafia*, with the movie rights automatically going to Paramount. Retitled *The Godfather*, Puzo's book became the bestseller sensation of 1970—a pulpy yet affecting and absorbing study of the brutal machinations and complicated relationships of an Italian mob family. Despite strong resistance from Paramount to making the film—there was plenty of evidence that movies about organized crime were no longer box office—Evans forged ahead, David O. Selznick style, obsessively putting the pieces together for his own *Gone with the Wind*. Sue didn't have any clients placed in *The Godfather*, though she had tried hard to interest Evans in casting Ryan O'Neal as the brooding Michael Corleone. Despite her daily harassing phone calls on the subject, Evans couldn't envision a fair-haired Irish boy as a Mafia prince and cast Al Pacino instead.

Sue remained a regular guest at Evans and MacGraw's home on weekends, for what Evans called "a film festival for the toughest audience in town"—among them Mike Nichols, Warren Beatty, Jack Nicholson, and Roman Polanski. It was her association with Evans and MacGraw that revealed her at her most vulnerable. Sue idealized them as a gilded couple, rich and beautiful, who had come together at a magical turning point in Hollywood history. She believed that they both had years of outstanding work and fame ahead of them; if they stayed together there was very little they couldn't accomplish. There was an almost adolescent naïveté about her romantic worship of the pair. "There was so much about the fairy-tale piece of Ali MacGraw and Bob Evans that was her dream scenario," said MacGraw.

After the success of *Love Story*, MacGraw received lots of offers, but there was only one picture she wanted to make: *The Great Gatsby*. MacGraw loved Fitzgerald's work and had hand-copied one of his short stories, "Winter Dreams," which had certain similarities to *Gatsby*, as a wedding present for Evans. *The Great Gatsby* is a richly interior story that had repeatedly resisted dramatization; although Paramount had tried twice, it had failed to make a satisfying film of the book. Few agreed with her, but MacGraw saw herself as ideal casting for Gatsby's fragile lost love, Daisy Buchanan, and she persisted in pitching the project to Evans until he agreed to make it for her. But there were numerous delays, including a screenplay by Truman Capote that turned out to be unusable.

In the meantime, Evans envisioned *The Getaway* as MacGraw's next film, costarring opposite one of the great sex symbols and box-office stars of the period, Steve McQueen. *The Getaway* was a heist-gone-wrong story, with a script by Walter Hill that Paramount's Peter Bart had developed and Peter Bogdanovich was set to direct. MacGraw, however, wanted nothing to do with *The Getaway*; she thought she would be completely out of her depth trying to play a white-trash Texas girl who goes on the lam with her burglar boyfriend. Bogdanovich agreed with her, and refused to go ahead with the project unless his girlfriend, Cybill Shepherd, who looked great in the rushes of *The Last Picture Show*, was cast in the project. Evans wouldn't back down, and kept badgering his wife to do *The Getaway*, telling her that she and McQueen would make the hottest box-office team imaginable. Eventually Sam Peckinpah signed on to direct the film.

McQueen wasn't sure MacGraw was right for *The Getaway*, either, but after meeting with her, he agreed that it could work. Sue was pressing MacGraw to commit to the picture as well, promising that this time around she would get her the real movie-star salary she deserved. Angrily, as Evans recalled in his memoir, MacGraw signed the contract for *The Getaway* in January 1972 and a few weeks later set off for the film's location in El Paso, Texas. Evans stayed behind in Los Angeles, too preoccupied with pulling *The Godfather* into shape to visit the set of *The Getaway*. Once in Texas, MacGraw began a torrid affair with McQueen, which she confessed one night to Sue on the telephone.

"She said, 'Oh, God. Oh, *God*,'" MacGraw remembered. "She was horrified. This was a pretty huge force of nature, Steve McQueen. He was somebody who walked into the room and had everybody, every woman, every man, staring at him. And this did not make Sue happy." During frequent phone calls to the Texas location and after MacGraw had returned to Los Angeles, Sue kept up a vigilant campaign for her to stay with Evans. This was risky, since McQueen was a CMA client, represented exclusively by Freddie Fields. But Sue delighted in telephoning Evans and telling him that McQueen had just left her office and slammed the door in her face, all because "I'm trying to convince Ali to stay with my Bobbie. It's a good thing I'm hot!"

But the golden aura of the Evans-MacGraw romance had been permanently dimmed, and Sue responded with a heavy heart, going into disappointed Jewish-mother mode. She simply could not understand, hormones aside, why her favorite magical couple could toss away their future together. The schism seemed to play into her deepest fears about her friends' and clients' security, their place in the grand scheme of things in Hollywood—and, by extension, her own fears for herself.

Many have intimated that there was great animosity between McQueen and Sue, though MacGraw has generally soft-pedaled the tension between them: "I think Sue was so angry and heartbroken about what I had done to my family. And Steve was tough. Selfish. It's so easy to make me the whitewashed virginal victim, but that's bullshit. Decades later I wish I had done what I did with so much more grace, because I loved Bob, and he was terrific to me. I've loved a few people in my life. That's just the way I am."

For Sue, the only positive result of the McQueen-MacGraw union was that *The Getaway* turned out to be a big hit when it was released in December 1972—the fourth picture under the First Artists agreement, but only the first one to make any real money.

In March 1971, along with David Dworsky and Ray Stark, Sue had attended a private screening of three reels of *The Last Picture Show*, which was still in the editing process. She was completely taken with the results: it was perhaps the most authentic portrayal of desperate small-town life the American screen had ever shown. Nothing was overdone; every connection seemed just right, and she reveled in Robert Surtees's evocative black-and-white photography and the castful of stunning performances. She told Peter Bogdanovich how proud she was of him, and also that she wanted to represent Cybill Shepherd, who seemed to have the makings of a big star. Candice Bergen later recalled the night that Bogdanovich brought Shepherd to Sue's house for the first time; she was wearing a powder blue sweater and matching pants and stunned everyone in the room with her beauty.

Warner Bros. was having the stymied *A Glimpse of Tiger* rewritten for a female character, and Barbra Streisand was set for the lead. Sue wanted Streisand and John Calley, the head of Warner Bros., to see *The Last Picture Show*, with an eye toward Bogdanovich's taking over the direction of *A Glimpse of Tiger*. Bert Schneider, *Picture Show*'s producer, was reluctant to let anyone else view it, but Sue prevailed and Schneider permitted Calley to see six reels and Streisand to see the entire film. Streisand loved the picture and was keen to work with Bogdanovich, but the director didn't like the script of *A Glimpse of Tiger*. "The only thing I liked," Bogdanovich remembered, "was the idea that this character knew something about everything."

Sue arranged a meeting between Calley and Bogdanovich, and when Calley asked him what kind of picture he would like to do with Streisand, Bogdanovich suggested a daffy comedy, something on the order of one of his favorites of the 1930s, Howard Hawks's *Bringing Up Baby*. Calley gave him the go-ahead to produce as well as direct, and verbal approval of then-hot screenwriters David Newman and Robert Benton to fashion a script. "I left the office producing and directing Barbra Streisand's next picture," remembered Bogdanovich. "I called Benton and Newman, and they said, 'Well, we've only got three weeks, because we're supposed to write another picture.' I said, 'If Ben Hecht and Howard Hawks can write *Scarface* in eleven days, I think we can do this in three weeks.' So they came out, and we holed up in the Sunset Tower, where I had an apartment with Cybill, and we knocked out a script, the three of us. David came up with the title— *What's Up, Doc?*"

During the rush job on the script, Sue called Bogdanovich and urged him to cast Ryan O'Neal as the male lead, the befuddled geologist Howard Bannister. Bogdanovich dismissed the idea, but Sue wouldn't relent. "Just go see *Love Story*, would you?" she begged. Bogdanovich and Cybill Shepherd finally went to see *Love Story* at a theater in Westwood, where they laughed all the way through it—though Bogdanovich did see some spark in O'Neal.

"Have lunch with him," Sue urged him. "Barbra really would like it if you used him in the picture." Bogdanovich remembered: "Barbra was having a thing with Ryan at the time. So I had lunch with Ryan, who in those days was very funny in life. He had a wise-ass kind of thing, and he was self-deprecating and charming. I liked him. I said, 'If you do this, I'm going to make fun of you. You have to shorten your hair and we will put you in a seersucker suit and glasses. You're really going to be square.' He loved the idea. So I said, 'Oh, fuck it.' So we got Ryan."

Bogdanovich and Calley both felt the script needed further work, and Buck Henry was engaged to do a rewrite. "You're going to hate me," said Henry when he read the Benton-Newman version, which depicted an epic mix-up over three identical overnight bags. "But I think it's not complicated enough." Henry added a fourth overnight bag. At the time, journalist Daniel Ellsberg was big news, having leaked the Pentagon Papers to the *New York Times*. So a character (played by Michael Murphy) carrying a bag with top-secret government documents was added, and this became the incident that triggered the screwball plot. Bogdanovich called Henry during his feverish rewriting and asked him how it was going. "I'm having a difficult time," said Henry. "I've lost one of the suitcases—I don't know where the fuck it is!" Henry and Bogdanovich had agreed that the plot should make sense—that there should be no loose ends when it came to the audience's ability to track the progress of each piece of identical luggage—and eventually Henry was able to work out the script to the last detail. Streisand, though, found the movement of the suitcases too confusing, and called Bogdanovich to tell him so. "*What's Up, Doc?*, you're calling it?" she said over the phone. "Barbra Streisand in *What's Up, Doc?*" But in her contract Streisand had agreed to something unusual: she had surrendered her script approval, and *What's Up, Doc?* proceeded, with Streisand set for a salary of $500,000 and O'Neal for $350,000—a spectacular jump from the $25,000 he had earned on *Love Story*.

O'Neal had never done a comedy before and was slightly apprehensive about the challenge. "Barbra was funny," the actor recalled. "Every other thing out of her mouth was hysterical. I had this tan—that's what I brought to the picture!" Shortly before filming began, Ryan O'Neal met Cary Grant on a yacht party. Since Grant had starred with Katharine Hepburn in *Bringing Up Baby*, the film that was the taking-off point for *What's Up, Doc?*, O'Neal asked Grant for any advice. "Have a good tan," Grant replied.

"That way you don't have to come in to make-up so early. You get an extra hour to sleep."

The filming, much of it on location in San Francisco with a huge team of stunt doubles, went well. Very few changes were made to Buck Henry's re-write. "Barbra is great," observed O'Neal. "But she's a strong woman." O'Neal, who at the time was still married to actress Leigh Taylor-Young, called Sue and complained, "'Listen—we're too close. There has to be breathing room.' She said, 'You have three more weeks to go. Stand up. Be a man. Treat her well.' That was my responsibility, so that's what I did."

Buck Henry became a regular guest at Sue's house. "She knew I was always on the prowl, like most every guy who was around," said Henry. "At one dinner she set me up with a really delectable actress from another country, who shall go nameless. She said, 'You'll probably have to take her home, and she lives in Malibu. But with a little luck. . . .' As we were about to leave, I was getting my car, and Sue said, 'Give it your best shot and call me right afterward. Call me if you fuck her.'"

While *What's Up, Doc?* was being readied for release, *The Last Picture Show* opened at the New York Film Festival in October 1971 to glorious reviews. In *Newsweek*, Paul D. Zimmerman opened his review: "*The Last Picture Show* is a masterpiece. It is not merely the best American movie of a rather dreary year; it is the most impressive work by a young American director since *Citizen Kane*." Bogdanovich not only was anointed as a major new directorial talent but did well financially: although his salary had been only $75,000, he received over 20 percent of the profits. On a budget of $1.3 million, *The Last Picture Show* went on to gross over $29 million— one of the best performances by a "small" picture in years.

Only a few months later Bogdanovich topped himself, at least commercially. In March 1972, *What's Up, Doc?* opened at Radio City Music Hall to excellent press and huge audiences. The *Hollywood Reporter* revealed that the picture had pulled in the biggest gross for a single day in the history of the Music Hall: $65,398. Bogdanovich's salary this time around was $150,000, plus a percentage of the profits, which were enormous: the pic-ture grossed in the neighborhood of $66 million. Shortly before *What's Up, Doc?*'s opening, *The Last Picture Show* received eight Academy Award nominations, including Best Picture and Best Director, and won two—for Best Supporting Actor (Ben Johnson) and Best Supporting Actress (Cloris

Leachman). In the space of a few months, Bogdanovich had become the hottest and most bankable director in Hollywood, the subject of dozens of newspaper and magazine stories.

In the long run, no one benefited from the success of *What's Up, Doc?* any more than Sue Mengers did. She had been the orchestrator behind the scenes, the godmother to the whole project. "Packaging" had been a concept that had been around the movie business for years, but with this film Sue became known as the most successful packager of the 1970s: she had put Bogdanovich, Streisand, and O'Neal together, and now her phone was ringing incessantly with calls from actors and directors and screenwriters, desperate for her to become their agent.

And Streisand was now her official property. Fields and Begelman, who were involved in higher-level production deals by this point, felt the time had come for Sue to take over exclusive representation of CMA's biggest star. "Before that, we were just good friends," said Streisand. "And somehow, Sue took over by default."

In April 1972, Gene Hackman's performance as Popeye Doyle in *The French Connection* earned him the Academy Award for Best Actor. In his acceptance speech, he thanked William Friedkin, Philip D'Antoni, his costar Roy Scheider, and his acting teacher, George Morrison, but never got around to mentioning Sue. (In fairness, at the time, Oscar winners did not thank their agents with the scrupulous regularity that they would years later.) Hackman was never one of Sue's favorite clients, and as the years went by, the Oscar speech snub would often be included in her litany of complaints about him.

In October, Universal released *Play It As It Lays*, the film version of Joan Didion's critically acclaimed bestseller about Maria Wyeth, a disillusioned, psychically wounded actress who spends most of her time roaming the Los Angeles freeways, pondering how her life went off the rails. The film was produced by Didion's brother-in-law, Dominick Dunne, and Sue scored a grand slam in her negotiations: her client Frank Perry was the director, Tuesday Weld got the coveted role of Maria, and Anthony Perkins was cast opposite her as her gay friend B. Z., whom Maria helps commit suicide. Didion's novel had been considered a definitive literary study of modern urban alienation, and there was much discussion of how it might be put on film. Perry claimed to have auditioned over a hundred actresses, always hoping that Weld would accept in the end. Weld, as she often did, took her time before agreeing to do the movie. She hated the endless delays involved in making a film, complaining that it was impossible even to focus on reading a book during the protracted camera setups because she needed to keep her mind on the scene. She was no more of a player of Hollywood politics than she had ever been, and Sue's working relationship with her remained contentious, with the two women often fighting over material. Weld was already famous for not wanting to commit to projects, and Sue kept the flame up under her, worrying that too much inactivity would lead audiences to forget about the actress. After the movie's release, Frank Perry observed to the press that Weld's "fear of total public acceptance as an actress is the prime cause of her run from Hollywood and her New York hibernation. She's been resisting the success she's having in this movie all her professional life, fighting against it tooth and nail. Why? To call it masochistic is too simple. There's a strong ambivalence there. Tuesday not only wants to bite the hand that feeds her but gnaw her way through its wrist." *Play It As It Lays* received some very good reviews, and Tuesday Weld did receive a Golden Globe nomination for Best Actress, but the film's tone of alienation proved too much for public appeal.

The costumes for *Play It As It Lays* were designed by Joel Schumacher, an acquaintance of Sue's from the 1960s in New York. A prizewinning graduate of the Parsons School of Design, Schumacher was friendly with Halston and got the designer to open his salon and lend him gorgeous sample clothes, so Schumacher was able to dress the cast elegantly and keep costs to a minimum. Sue began inviting Schumacher to her weekly parties. "It was great networking," said the designer. "I got jobs out of it and I made a lot of great friends out of it. I told her later, 'Sue, do you know what you did for me when I was a two-hundred-dollar-a-week costume designer?' She would say, 'I don't know what you're talking about. Why *wouldn't* I invite you?'"

Earlier in 1972, Sue had joined Ali MacGraw, Robert Evans, and some other friends for a dinner party at the home of socialite Charlotte Ford. Dinah Shore showed up with a date, a darkly handsome Belgian in his early forties named Jean-Claude Tramont. He was a charming man, and he and Sue connected in conversation right away. He was bright and witty and well read, an irreverent commentator on the world political scene. He loved Sue's own sharp wit and spent much of the evening talking to her. Since moving to Los Angeles, indulging in pot smoking and compulsive eating, and avoiding exercise whenever possible, she had put on a great deal of weight, which she tried to camouflage under the flowing caftans she favored. But her size was of no importance to Tramont; in fact, he loved zaftig women. Although Sue claimed to have enjoyed plenty of encounters with some of Hollywood's top leading men since coming to California—Ali MacGraw called it "a major above-the-title sex life"—she had never had an enduring relationship until Tramont entered her life.

Tramont had been born into show business; his father, Emile de Tramont, appeared on the stage throughout Europe and the United States, notably in the 1917 Broadway production of *Lilac Time*. Jean-Claude spent a great deal of time in Paris, where he enrolled at the Institute of Political Studies before deciding to pursue a career as a film director. He attended Paris's Institut des Hautes Études Cinématographiques and in May 1948 sailed to New York, where he eventually found work as a page at NBC television, later moving up to stage manager, assistant director, and director; his sparse directing credits included the 1958 live *NBC Opera Theatre* telecast of Gian Carlo Menotti's *Amahl and the Night Visitors*. Later he returned to France, where he worked in television and became a documentary director for the United Nations, and then moved to Los Angeles, burning to write and direct movies.

Sue's taste in men typically ran to more obviously virile types, but she now found herself confronted with a cultured, sophisticated European man who seemed plainly to adore her. "Jean-Claude was one of the most attractive men you'd ever meet," said Candice Bergen. "Dashing and elegant and intellectually her equal in every way." Sue threw a party at Dawnridge Drive to introduce Jean-Claude to her friends and clients. She did not have any domestic skills to speak of; since moving to the Duquette house, she had hired a housekeeper and seemed only vaguely aware of where the kitchen was. The day before the party, Jean-Claude asked her if they shouldn't go out and buy some proper cheeses. "She thought, what—Velveeta?" recalled Candice Bergen. "They went to a nice cheese shop in Beverly Hills and got an assortment of cheeses and other things." Jean-Claude's debut was successful: Ryan O'Neal was a guest, as was a new client, Jacqueline Bisset, who was translating all that went on for her date, François Truffaut.

At the beginning of their relationship, Sue often told friends, she worked overtime to make sure Jean-Claude would leave her; after all, none of the men she had been with previously had lasted for more than a handful of dates. Even with close friends, Sue would often find it easier to demonstrate than to receive affection; she was known to roll her eyes and pull back when anyone tried to kiss her at the end of one of her parties.

But Jean-Claude didn't leave. At first, Sue found it difficult to believe that he truly cared for her. After he told her that she snored, she taped herself one night and, horrified when she heard the playback, told friends that only someone who really loved her could put up with such a god-awful noise.

"I think Sue couldn't believe it when she met Jean-Claude," said Ali MacGraw. "I think she was stunned."

CHAPTER ELEVEN

1973–1974

As Sue solidified her position in Hollywood, she regularly kept in touch with her mother. Ruth was still settled in her apartment in Rego Park, happily married to Eugene Sender. She ran the household efficiently and enjoyed her weekly mah-jongg games with a group of Jewish ladies who lived in the neighborhood. Ruth was proud of Sue's accomplishments, and now that her daughter was becoming a celebrity in her own right, her activities regularly reported on in the Hollywood press and the New York gossip columns, Ruth made a point of clipping the articles and sharing them with her friends. But she missed having more contact with her only child, and during their phone conversations frequently asked Sue when she was planning to visit her in New York. Sue routinely brushed her off by insisting that she was far too busy to leave Los Angeles. If Ruth broached the subject of a visit to California, Sue claimed that her house on Dawnridge Drive was too small for overnight company and that, in any case, work would prevent her from spending any significant amount of time with her. Sometimes she didn't bother to see Ruth at all on her trips to New York.

But it would not be fair to say that her mother was never in her thoughts. Sue kept careful watch over Ruth via Joan Harris, CMA's special services administrator. It was Harris's job to attend to the executives' and clients' personal and entertainment needs, and because she was a woman of taste and discrimination who always delivered what was required, she quickly came to Sue's notice. Sue would call Joan and ask her to arrange theater tickets for her during one of her New York visits or pick up a gift of antique jewelry at James Robinson II for one of her clients. Once she told Boaty Boatwright, "If I ask Joan Harris for an elephant, and I tell her I need it right now, her reply would be, 'Plain color or polka dot?' and she would deliver it."

It soon became part of Harris's job to look in on Ruth on a regular basis, and Harris found her to be a sweet, likable woman who clearly missed her daughter. "I think she had the impression that Sue worked from nine to five," said Harris. "She would say, 'Why isn't she here? Why doesn't she call me more?'" Harris would assure Ruth that Sue was very busy, but was always thinking about her. Ruth appreciated Harris's solicitude, and each year sent her a Christmas stollen from one of the fine German bakeries in Rego Park. Sue expressed her gratitude, too, by sending Harris a five-hundred-dollar check at holiday time.

Joan Harris could not always he used as a go-between, however, and there were many times when Sue had to deal directly with her mother. Once, in the mid-1970s, while Ruth was making one of her rare visits to California, Sue arranged a lunch with a couple of her "twinklies"—her name for her star clients. She invited Ali MacGraw and Candice Bergen, and the choice of the two actresses was quite intentional: they were Sue's glamorous shiksa goddesses. "We were the kind of girls she wanted her mother to see were her really close friends," said MacGraw. "I thought the mother was a lumpy, poor soul. I saw this person that I couldn't really see being cruel—though she was probably on her best behavior." Bergen recalled the lunch as being rather fraught, and Ruth as "tiny and tough. But she was titillated by our presence, I think; she was sort of fluttery about it."

Ruth was often appalled by her daughter's foul language, and whenever Sue wanted to be sure of getting under her mother's skin, all she had to do was light up a joint. Ruth railed at her, warning her that she could be arrested and wind up with her name in the newspapers, but Sue merely shrugged and gleefully took another puff. She also chain-smoked Gauloises, often with a joint in the other hand. Ruth constantly lectured her that all of this was bad for her health, to no avail.

One decision Ruth did approve of was Sue's relationship with Jean-Claude. She was completely charmed by him, and Jean-Claude knew exactly how to treat her. Ruth was delighted when, on May 5, 1973—Jean-Claude's forty-third birthday—he and Sue were married in the chapel at the Highlands Inn in Carmel. The only friend in attendance was Barbra Streisand, her maid of honor. Sue and Jean-Claude then flew to Greece, where they spent their honeymoon as guests on John Calley's yacht; Calley later told *Vanity Fair* that bands of Greek men, who had a preference for zaftig women, pursued Sue all over the beaches of Greece, much to her delight.

Around Hollywood many who were not in Sue's camp wondered about her marriage. Some felt it seemed an act of desperation by a woman in her early forties, while others had Jean-Claude pegged as an operator who viewed a union with Hollywood's most celebrated agent as a chance to move his directing career into high gear. But Sue's closest friends believed that the marriage was founded on genuine mutual love. "He just was not the kind of guy who would have married her to get a director's career," said Ali MacGraw.

Where her parties were concerned, Sue had one rule that was known to all her friends: DO NOT BRING YOUR KIDS. One day Tuesday Weld was shooting a movie and had her young daughter on the set with her. Weld had been invited to Sue's house that night. At the time, the actress was living at the beach, and once she had finished the day's filming at the studio, it was inconvenient for her to take her daughter home and then go back to Sue's place. When Weld showed up with her daughter, Sue protested, but eventually said, "Oh, all right. Come in. But only if she stays in my bedroom upstairs." Years later, Weld laughed. "She gave my daughter a bowl of suger cubes to play with. I think Sue was unhappy with the outcome, because the suger cubes ended up all over her bedroom."

Sue had a gift for putting together unlikely combinations of guests and making the magic happen. She believed in the value of party giving, reasoning that it was much harder for stars to decline to take her phone calls after they had been guests in her home. The gatherings at Dawnridge Drive grew more star-studded each month, and more intimidating for some of the clients, among them MacGraw and Candice Bergen. The two actresses used to meet beforehand and work up their courage so they would be able to hold their own in a room full of top producers and studio executives, A-list movie stars like Jack Nicholson and Dustin Hoffman, living legends like Gregory Peck, Bette Davis, and Billy Wilder, and literary heavyweights like Gore Vidal, Norman Mailer (though never Vidal and Mailer on the same evening), Joan Didion, and John Gregory Dunne.

Jacqueline Bisset also found Sue's command performances challenging. "When you were there, you wanted to be attentive to her," said Bisset. "I'm not a competitive woman, and I do think she liked a degree of obeisance. There were rules, unspoken rules, about behavior, and she was a really good hostess." Bisset remembered that Sue never pressed her to do anything professionally on Jean-Claude's behalf. "I think it's difficult for someone in the business today to try to promote a lover or husband. It goes off wrong. People don't like it." Bisset frequently invited Sue and Jean-Claude to her own home in

Benedict Canyon for dinner, where she herself cooked simple French meals. Jean-Claude was always appreciative of Bisset's culinary skills and tried to persuade the actress to give Sue cooking lessons, but Sue jeered at the idea.

In 1973 Jean-Claude had another reason to celebrate, apart from his marriage to Sue: he had written a screenplay, *Ash Wednesday*, about a middle-aged wife who attempts to win back her husband's faded love for her by submitting to plastic surgery, and Sue had talked Robert Evans into putting it into production at Paramount. The movie was being directed by the talented Larry Peerce, whose credits included *One Potato, Two Potato* and *Goodbye, Columbus*, and it would star Elizabeth Taylor and Henry Fonda. Larry Turman, who had an office at Paramount, remembered that when he passed on producing the project, Sue, with whom he had always had friendly relations, abruptly shut him out.

A bit later Sue worked with Turman again when he was developing a thriller called *Burnt Offerings*, based on a novel by Robert Marasco. Turman described it as "a metaphysical mystery without a solution," and felt that it would be a great change of pace for Sue's new client Bob Fosse, who had just had an Oscar-winning triumph with *Cabaret*. Directors were generally tricky clients for Sue: while actors could work in three or four films a year, a director's intense, long-term involvement with a project restricted him to one life every fourteen or fifteen months. Turman, Fosse, and Sue worked on *Burnt Offerings* for a short-lived movie department started up by CBS Television, but the project was slow to come together and was ultimately dropped after CBS's movie division "died a-borning," in Turman's words. *Burnt Offerings* was later made into a dreary film with Oliver Reed, Karen Black, and Bette Davis. Fosse's relationship with Sue ended not long after.

Different agents used different methods to try to get their clients work in films, and the smartest producers and studio chiefs were clued in to each agent's individual style. Most filmmakers began with a short list of actors who might be acceptable for each of the leading parts in their upcoming project; the smaller roles were put into the hands of a casting director.

Many agents thought it best to apply a steady stream of gentle pressure— the better not to anger or upset the producer or director. When Fred Zinnemann was planning to film Frederick Forsyth's suspenseful novel *The Day of the Jackal* in 1971, agent Stephanie Phillips obtained an advance copy of the book and tried to sell Zinnemann on the idea of casting her client Robert Redford as the man who attempts to assassinate Charles de Gaulle. "I know no actor cooler, steelier or more detached than Robert Redford," Phillips wrote. "Please consider him." When Zinnemann politely vetoed the idea, saying that he wanted to cast an English actor, Phillips responded: "I have a conviction that Bob is as good an impersonator as anyone I know; I merely hope that one day you will share that conviction."

There was a time when Sue might have approached a casting issue with such diplomacy and tact, but as her success and confidence grew, she began more and more to resemble a Force-10 hurricane. When *The Thief Who Came to Dinner*, a 1973 comedy directed by Bud Yorkin, lost its leading lady, Charlotte Rampling, the part was offered to Jacqueline Bisset. Sue cornered the actress at a party and hounded her with phone calls, telling her she had no choice but to do the movie. "She said, 'You've got to do this film—your career will be ended if you don't do this,'" Bisset recalled. "For one thing, I didn't believe it. But then, as I thought about it, I wondered if it might not be true. She did that to people quite often." Bisset disliked the script and the role, but eventually capitulated in the face of Sue's relentlessness. Making *The Thief Who Came to Dinner* was not a happy experience: Bud Yorkin would give Bisset one piece of direction, production designer Polly Platt would offer another, and her costar Ryan O'Neal would then ask her at the end of a scene, "You're not going to do it like *that*, are you?" Bisset's instincts had been correct: in the end, *The Thief Who Came to Dinner* did nothing for her career. It did more for Ryan O'Neal's, at least in terms of his salary, which Sue had now boosted to $400,000.

Sue believed that one of the trickiest things for an agent to master was the gambler's instinct—the moment at which to insist on more money for a client. "See, I know what heat is," she told journalist Paul Rosenfield years later. "It's a killer instinct, to know that. . . . It's knowing the right price. And the right price is never an unfair price." Sometimes, of course, the high-pressure strategy failed her. In 1971, she had been pushing to get her client Rod Steiger the lead in United Artists' satiric, urban comedy-drama *The Hospital*. The script was by Paddy Chayefsky, who didn't want him, but Sue campaigned for Steiger with the author, director Arthur Hiller, and the UA top brass on a daily basis. Because they were running out of time, UA agreed to sign Steiger, but they were $50,000 under Sue's salary demand. Confident she could bluff them because of the deadline pressure, she held out for the extra money—on the same day that Chayefsky flew to Europe and persuaded George C. Scott to take the role. "If I had closed that day," she told Rosenfield, "Rod would have had the picture."

By now Sue was frequently being profiled by major newspapers and magazines. Although it has often been argued that such exposure ultimately hurt her in a profession in which agents are supposed to be effectively invisible, having such a colorful star on its payroll brought CMA valuable publicity, and as Sue herself later commented, her own fame never prevented big stars from signing with her: "They figure, 'If she's got Barbra Streisand, she must be O.K.'" She had become so well known that she began to appear in thinly disguised fictional or theatrical form in several films and books. Although it was not much discussed at the time, it seems likely that she helped to inspire the character of Ethel Evans, the chubby, ambitious, star-fucking press agent in Jacqueline Susann's 1969 best-selling novel about the television industry, *The Love Machine*. (Susann's close friend Rex Reed claims the character was actually an amalgam of Joyce Haber, Rona Barrett, and Toni Howard.) It seems even more likely that Gore Vidal used her as the inspiration for his cunning Hollywood agent Letitia Van Allen in *Myra Breckinridge*.

In June 1973, Sue received her biggest homage yet when Warner Bros. released a murder mystery set among the international movie crowd, *The Last of Sheila*. The screenplay was coauthored by Stephen Sondheim and her client Anthony Perkins, who turned it over to Sue and had her package it. Her new client Herbert Ross was the director, and three actors on her roster were in the cast—James Coburn, Richard Benjamin, and, as Christine, a fast-talking bulldozer Hollywood agent, Dyan Cannon. There was no question that Sondheim and Perkins had used Sue as the model for the character: Christine was a playful tease, quick-witted, sexually rapacious, a compulsive eater, and a perpetual name-dropper who signs off on phone calls with Sue's trademark "Kiss, kiss!" and categorizes everyone she knows as A-list or B-list. "Honey, shoot me down a Tab!" Christine calls to the ship steward while floating in the Mediterranean. "My mouth is so dry you could shoot *Lawrence of Arabia* in it." Sue told Herbert Ross that Cannon was the only one who could play the part, and Cannon promptly gained twenty pounds before filming began.

If there had been any question about the inspiration for the character, Dyan Cannon's performance clearly settled the matter. She was pure Sue, right down to her pink-tinted glasses: a Miss Full Charge who treats the whole Hollywood world as a game, laughing at it and herself every step of the way. Cannon differed from Sue in one significant detail only: her performance had a fast-paced, almost manic edge far removed from Sue's more languid style.

The shooting schedule for *The Last of Sheila* included nearly three months on Sam Spiegel's yacht on the French Riviera, during which time it rained incessantly. The unhappiest member of the cast was Raquel Welch, playing the glamorous movie star Alice, who at first didn't think the script was realistic enough. "Take the character Dyan plays, supposedly based on Sue Mengers," she told the press. "Now I barely know Sue, but I can't imagine but that maybe sometimes she has trouble with her man, as we all do, that sometimes she's lonely, cries, acts like a human being. She's not just a joke."

The Last of Sheila received generally favorable reviews, returning a respectable $2.2 million in North American rentals. But it was a bit too arch and sophisticated, too full of insider hints about Hollywood personalities and their sex lives, to become a significant hit. The cast tried hard, but the film never quite carried off the high style of a story about the rich and famous, instead playing as if Aaron Spelling had decided to do a TV-movie exposé of Hollywood's beautiful people. (Perkins and Sondheim had originally wanted Lee Remick and Ryan O'Neal for the roles played by Joan Hackett and Richard Benjamin because, according to Sondheim, they would be closer to an "open-faced, typical hero and heroine.")

The Last of Sheila did not help accelerate Cannon's career, and in 1974 Sue received a call from her friend the producer Howard Rosenman, who wanted the actress for a made-for-television movie he was preparing called *The Virginia Hill Story*. "You've got to help me," said Rosenman, and Sue promised, "I'm going to deliver the cunt for you." Rosenman remembered that Sue drove a hard bargain and got the actress a handsome salary by TV-movie standards. "And Dyan Cannon *was* a cunt, and she was a nightmare," said Rosenman. "But I remember Sue telling her, 'You're cold and you're over with. Unless you do this, you'll be doing nothing.'"

Rosenman's close friend Paul Jabara was one of many around this time becoming obsessed with the cult of Sue Mengers. Jabara often claimed that in the late 1960s he had set Sue up with a sexy Arab lover and watched from a nearby closet while she was in the heat of sexual passion. Jabara went on to write *Rachael Lily Rosenbloom (And Don't You Ever Forget It)*, a

Susi Mengers, as a child
in Hamburg.

Teenage Sue, just before leaving Utica, New York.

The fledgling actress who studied with Betty Cashman.

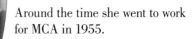

Around the time she went to work for MCA in 1955.

At the engagement party for
her cousin Leo Sender, 1958.

Mother and daughter:
Even when Sue was on her
way up in the 1960s, Ruth
Mengers Sender remained
hypercritical.

On the night before her friend
Boaty Boatwright's wedding
in North Carolina, with
Suzanne Pincus and Boaty's
fiancé, Terence Baker.

The jewel in Sue's crown of clients, Barbra Streisand; Sue always told people that she and Barbra were "sisters."

Michael Caine in 1969's *The Italian Job*; Sue wanted him to attain the stature of top American male stars.

Sue urged Candice Bergen to take a secondary role in *Starting Over* (1979), which established her as a deft comedienne.

Ann-Margret with Art Garfunkel in Mike Nichols's *Carnal Knowledge* (1971); the role of Bobbie was a big boost to Ann-Margret's acting career.

Dyan Cannon, who did a funny riff on Sue in *The Last of Sheila* (1973).

Gene Hackman won an Oscar after Sue pressed him on director William Friedkin for the lead in *The French Connection* (1971).

Tatum and Ryan O'Neal on the set of Peter Bogdanovich's *Nickelodeon* (1976).

Sue with her client Ali MacGraw and Ali's husband, Robert Evans; they were Sue's Hollywood dream couple.

Peter Bogdanovich directing Cybill Shepherd in her impressive screen debut in *The Last Picture Show* (1971).

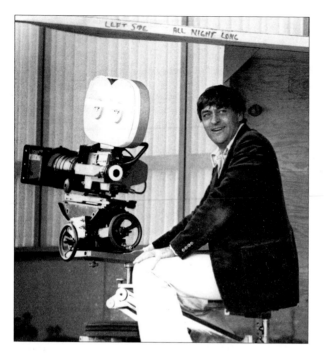

Sue's husband,
Jean-Claude
Tramont, on the
set of *All Night
Long* (1981).

Gene Hackman
and Barbra
Streisand in *All
Night Long*; the
film seriously
damaged Sue's
friendship with
the star.

Ruth and Sue with her stepfather, Eugene Sender, late 1970s.

Jean-Claude, Sue, Howard Austen, Boaty Boatwright, and Gore Vidal in Venice, mid-1990s.

Comedians' galop:
Back row: Jan Murray, Betsy Mazursky, Louis Nye, Anita Nye,
Juliet Hohnen, Buddy Hackett. Front row: Sue, Jean-Claude,
Paul Mazursky, Toni Howard, David Yarnell, and Toni Murray.

Jean-Claude; Boaty
Boatwright's daughter,
Kara Baker; Sue; and
Boaty's son, Patrick
Baker, at the Tramonts'
house on Lexington
Road.

musical based on her life. It starred the up-and-coming young actress Ellen Greene, and told of a savvy Brooklyn girl who rises from her lowly beginnings to become a powerful Hollywood columnist, adding the "a" to "Rachael" that was dropped from Barbra Streisand's first name. *Rachael Lily Rosenbloom* played several previews and closed in December 1973 without ever opening on Broadway.

Not long after *The Virginia Hill Story* aired, Dyan Cannon left Sue. Cannon had always liked her, and doubled over at the things that came out of her mouth at her dinner parties or on shopping trips through Beverly Hills. But the actress found her "a curious woman. So funny. But also rough and tough, and I guess that was the only way she knew how to be." Once, while Cannon was still under contract to CMA and living in the Malibu Colony, she received a message from her assistant telling her to phone Sue immediately.

"I just had a call from someone telling me that you are running on the beach in sweats," snapped Sue. "If you're going to run on the beach, you *don't wear sweats.*"

Cannon threatened to hang up on her, but Sue replied, "Just listen to me. I give you good advice."

When Cannon left CMA, Sue tried her best to dissuade her, though the actress assured her that they could be better friends if they weren't working together. But the end of her time with Sue was also the end of Cannon's peak years as a movie star. After *The Virginia Hill Story*, it would be two years before she appeared in another film.

From the time he signed for *The Last of Sheila*, Richard Benjamin and his wife, Paula Prentiss, became Sue's clients. It had taken Benjamin a bit of time to get a foothold as an actor; in the early days of their marriage, when Prentiss was making films steadily and he was out of work, he used to tell people he was a director, because "a director between jobs sounded more respectable than a jobless actor." Eventually he got a break, starring in the national company of Neil Simon's *Barefoot in the Park*, and went on to specialize in Simon for a time, touring in *The Odd Couple* with Dan Dailey and starring on Broadway in one of the playwright's lesser efforts, *The Star-Spangled Girl*. Beginning with *Goodbye, Columbus*, Benjamin specialized in playing uptight, neurotic urbanites, such as the social-climbing husband in *Diary of a Mad Housewife* and the coveted lead in *Portnoy's*

Complaint, which he landed over contenders such as Elliott Gould and Dustin Hoffman. With his knowing, smart, New York Jewish-boy brand of appeal, he was, along with Gould and Hoffman, a new kind of antihero star.

Prentiss had had a far easier path to success. A native of San Antonio, she studied drama at Northwestern University, where she met Benjamin. After graduating, she was signed to an MGM contract, appearing in lightweight 1960s fare such as *Where the Boys Are* and *Bachelor in Paradise*; soon critics were comparing her with the gifted British comedienne Kay Kendall. Prentiss had wanted the role Raquel Welch eventually got in *Sheila*, but Sue vetoed it, believing it would not do for a husband and wife to appear in the same film. The Benjamins were frequent guests at Dawnridge Drive. "The parties were totally constructed to try to get you work," said Benjamin. "We met Bette Davis at one of her parties. You would be astounded as you looked around, at who was there. But the focus on work was like a laser, and it also made you feel that you were in a show of some kind and you had to perform. Sue would come over and whisper something in your ear—'Oh, honeeey, such-and-such isn't cast yet.' And all of a sudden, you couldn't have the kind of spontaneous thing you would have at a party. You were working."

Benjamin did not partake of the pot and cocaine at Sue's parties, but decades later Paula Prentiss admitted with a laugh, "I was always interested! I was sort of in my drinking and drugging years, so it all seemed quite fine to me. I had obliterated myself from the room, so I just came in and had a nice time. I just took to the fun of it, frankly."

While *The Last of Sheila* was being filmed, Sue snared Prentiss a starring role in an *ABC Movie of the Week* called *The Couple Takes a Wife*. She also got Benjamin a job opposite Yul Brynner in Michael Crichton's futuristic movie thriller *Westworld*, which was a hit when it was released in November 1973. She talked Prentiss up to Alan Pakula when he was casting his political suspense drama *The Parallax View*, starring Warren Beatty. When Pakula agreed to interview Prentiss, Sue gave her a piece of advice: "'Sew your blue jeans to your panties. You want a crease in there.' That's all she told me," remembered Prentiss. "To hell with Sanford Meisner! Just sew your panties to your jeans." Sue pressured Pakula, and after several more meetings, Prentiss got the part. When Paramount released the film in the summer of 1974, it was modestly successful.

"Did she really read all of the scripts, or any of them?" wondered Benjamin. "Who knows? I never got from her, 'I know you only want to do good things, and good things will lead to good things.' Her idea was to work. And both things are kind of right. William Goldman, who wrote *Adventures in the Screen Trade*, said in big letters, 'NOBODY KNOWS ANYTHING.' And it's true. You don't know what's going to work and not work. And an actor is often left not wanting to turn down work, because he thinks it's not good enough—and yet, possibly some miracle will happen."

Certainly Sue continued to believe that there was a huge accidental component to Hollywood success—that the so-called trend makers seldom had any clue about what might hit big with the public. But she worked hard for the Benjamins, as she did for all her clients at this time. Once, when she was trying to get a certain part for him, Benjamin accompanied her to an intimate dinner for six or eight people at the Beverly Hills Hotel. The scuttlebutt around town was that her client Ryan O'Neal was the leading contender for the role. The dinner went on, and at a certain point, Sue drifted past Benjamin and whispered in his ear, "Ryan's *out*." "She kept right on going," said Benjamin. "So now I had information to deal with at this dinner, and it was no longer about socializing or food or anything."

Richard Benjamin and Prentiss jointly left Sue in late 1974; Benjamin signed with Bob Shapiro at the William Morris Agency and got one of his best roles, as Walter Matthau's harried nephew in Herbert Ross's film version of Neil Simon's *The Sunshine Boys*, which earned him a Golden Globe Award for Best Supporting Actor of 1975. Prentiss would go on to give one of her finest performances as the daffy, pent-up Bobbie Markowe, who gets turned into an automaton, in Bryan Forbes's *The Stepford Wives*. By the end of the 1970s, the couple's film careers had wound down; Benjamin would later move into directing, with fine films such as *Racing with the Moon* and *My Favorite Year*. But their memories of Sue remained happy ones. "There aren't too many people in your life who are such a force of nature," commented Benjamin.

Since *What's Up, Doc?*, Peter Bogdanovich had been developing a dream project: a large-scale Western for Warner Bros., written by Larry McMurtry and starring a big cast of old and new Hollywood actors: John Wayne, James Stewart, Henry Fonda, Ryan O'Neal, Cybill Shepherd, Ben Johnson, and

Cloris Leachman. During this time, Paramount asked Bogdanovich to direct a comedy based on Joe David Brown's novel *Addie Pray*, about a con man and a tough-minded little girl who meet up in Kansas during the Depression. Bogdanovich passed, and continued work on his Western, but then John Wayne withdrew from the project. "It's kind of an end-of-the-West Western, Pete," said Wayne, "and I'm not ready to hang up my spurs yet." (Bogdanovich later learned that John Ford had read the script and cautioned Wayne not to do it.) When Paramount heard the project was off, another offer for *Addie Pray* was extended. Bogdanovich read the script and perceived that it needed work, but there were many things about it he liked. *Addie Pray* would also solve a practical problem for the director. During the scripting of the Western, McMurtry had told Bogdanovich that he couldn't write the intended part for Ryan O'Neal. When O'Neal was informed that he was out, he was deeply hurt. Bogdanovich saw *Addie Pray* as a way of making it up to him and cast him as the con man, Moses Pray. Polly Platt, who was still working with Bogdanovich despite his romance with Cybill Shepherd, suggested that O'Neal's eight-year-old daughter, Tatum, might be ideal as the shrewd, poker-faced Addie, who becomes the con man's partner in crime. Tatum was delighted when she found out that appearing in the movie would get her sprung from her boarding school in Arizona, where she was constantly in trouble. Bogdanovich went to work on the script, which was retitled *Paper Moon*, and filming got under way, with Sue setting Bogdanovich's fee at $300,000, plus a nice cut of the profits. Like *The Last Picture Show*, *Paper Moon* was filmed in black and white, in keeping with the nostalgia craze that had been sweeping America for the past few years.

In the meantime, Charles Bluhdorn had proposed launching a kind of directors' cooperative, in which the participants would be Francis Ford Coppola, William Friedkin, and Bogdanovich, all riding high as the hottest directors of the period. The idea was to give them the right to direct any picture they wanted to do for a cost that would not exceed $3 million; they could also produce anything they didn't care to direct, for $1.5 million—all without having to get approval from the studio. The plan was that eventually the company would go public, and everyone would make a lot of money. Once the deal was closed and the Directors Company, as it was called, was launched, Bogdanovich, whose back-to-back successes had put him in a generous mood, agreed to throw in the profits for *Paper Moon*, even though it had not been initiated as a project for the Directors Company.

Ryan O'Neal was superb in *Paper Moon*. "Ryan has to be directed," said Bogdanovich, "but the thing he brought to *Paper Moon* was the cackle. That was the best performance, I think, of his career. He really identified with the guy, because the guy was a prick, and Ryan can be a bit of a prick." The surprise of the film was Tatum O'Neal. Although she frequently vexed both her director and her father by blowing take after take, she came through with an utterly natural, perfectly pitched performance as the smart-beyond-her-years Addie. When *Paper Moon* opened in May 1973, she received fine reviews: *Time*'s Jay Cocks, who disliked the film, called Tatum "peppy, coarse, funny, sort of a cyanide Shirley Temple." Andrew Sarris wrote in the *Village Voice* that the film was a tribute "to Bogdanovich's extraordinary flair with actors." It was the third consecutive smash for Bogdanovich, who earned a great deal from *Paper Moon*—as did Friedkin and Coppola, as partners in the Directors Company—but he remembered that Sue was only focused on the initial salary: "She didn't deal with the back end and all of that stuff." O'Neal did well, too, since Sue had negotiated a salary of $500,000, plus ten points of the gross after breakeven.

Tatum O'Neal won the Academy Award for Best Supporting Actress of 1973. With her father being paid such a hefty salary, she had earned a mere $8,000 for the film. Tatum, however, mistakenly thought the amount was $80,000, and began announcing her plans to buy a ranch and raise horses.

"What eighty thousand dollars?" Ryan O'Neal told her. "It's eight thousand."

"But I won the Academy Award," Tatum protested.

"Let me explain something, Tatum. It's not the first film you do in your life that gets you a good salary. It's the second film that can get you good money if the first film is good."

Tatum thought for a long moment and replied, "Maybe I'd better do another picture." Her father promised her he would look around for her, and soon Tatum, too, was a client of Sue's. "She never treated me as a child; she always treated me like I was an adult," Tatum said in an interview years later. "Sue didn't have maternal instincts, but she could be like a Jewish aunt to me. She wouldn't give advice—she would just scold me."

• • •

As driven as she was, Sue was quite realistic about the parameters of her job as agent to the stars. She never felt that it was simply her advice that led a client to decide whether or not to do a specific film. "Any agent who thinks that way is foolish," she told a journalist in the mid-1970s. "The creative person knows what they want to do. They'll listen to me, to their husband, or their wife, then they'll take all the input and make up their own mind."

The client who occupied the biggest amount of her time was Barbra Streisand. Even though Sue was not involved with the music end of Streisand's career, there were countless decisions to be made about the huge number of scripts being submitted, and hundreds of details to be worried about. As time went on, Jean-Claude would frequently become annoyed with the number of hours Sue devoted to Streisand. But Sue approached her job with complete discipline, working hard for all of her clients. Her life during the 1970s has often (wrongly) been portrayed as a time of constant partying, night after night. But in fact, most evenings, when not at a premiere or business dinner elsewhere, she was at home, making her way through scripts to see if there might be something in them for one of her clients.

By her own admission, Streisand was very careful about which projects she accepted and took a great deal of time to make up her mind about them; during the protracted decision-making process, Sue functioned as a sounding board, but the final yes or no always came from Streisand. Sue was a devoted friend and agent, and the two women shared many secrets with each other, notably about past love affairs, and about whose mother was a bigger cross to bear. But Sue was anything but subservient. She and Streisand bickered like sisters over all manner of things—often when Sue was trying to get her to accept an offer, and Streisand was vacillating. "She was totally obsessed with work, with career," said Streisand. "I was very different. She couldn't get me to work." Earlier, when she was still represented by Fields and Begelman, Streisand had turned down *They Shoot Horses, Don't They?* and *Klute*, because there was no director attached when they were offered to her. Both roles went to Jane Fonda, who succeeded brilliantly in them. (For years, Sue would pursue Fonda as a client, without success.)

When Sue pressured Streisand to accept a script, she could be as manipulative as she was with any of her clients. "Sue knew how to push your buttons," said Streisand. "She was very clever. She could make you feel very unworthy about your talent or your age: 'You're getting on. You'd better do this movie.'" Streisand was also learning that she needed to assert a greater degree of personal control over the details surrounding her films, and many of her conversations with Sue revolved around this issue. (One example: the actress was displeased with the ads for her 1972 film about the fantasy life of a New York City housewife, *Up the Sandbox*, a serious movie that featured a caricature of Streisand strapped to a baby bottle.) But Sue's focus remained on the salary, rather than on secondary particulars.

Streisand sometimes wondered about how deep Sue's loyalty ran. She would find herself in the offices of CMA, listening to Sue talking to one of her other clients on the phone. "Yes, darling," Sue would say. "Of course, darling." She would then hang up the phone and mutter, "Cunt." Streisand asked her from time to time if Sue spoke that way about her behind her back, but Sue always seemed horrified that Streisand might even suspect her capable of such professional disloyalty.

Streisand had two more films remaining under her personal contract with Ray Stark, and the fall of 1973 saw the release of one of the best pictures of her career, *The Way We Were*. Like Bogdanovich's films, *The Way We Were* reflected the continuing American fascination with nostalgia. The movie was a love story about the uneasy union of Hubbell Gardiner, a talented, conformist WASP writer who longs to sail through life, and Katie Morosky, a driven, uncompromising, politically angry Jewish woman who loves him deeply but is unable, to paraphrase William Congreve, to dwindle into a proper wife. It boasted an unusually perceptive and intelligent script by Arthur Laurents, drawn from his own background at Cornell University and as a Hollywood screenwriter during the McCarthy era.

Streisand seized on the role of Katie Morosky as the strongest acting opportunity she'd been given to date, and she was delighted when, after some prolonged negotiations, Robert Redford was cast as Hubbell Gardiner. One of Sue's frustrations, which she spoke about in an interview at the time, was the attitude of studio executives on the rare occasion when a script would turn up with equally strong starring roles for both an actor and an actress. "Great. We would agree to make the film with any one of twenty actresses, but with only one of the men. If you can't get one of those ten 'desirable' men, forget it," Sue complained. "*The man is the catalyst*." The short list of bankable actresses included Streisand, Ali MacGraw, Faye

Dunaway, Jane Fonda, and, for a brief time, Liza Minnelli. Sue admitted that while she didn't believe in crystal-ball gazing, "for the next one or two years, I'm discouraged about the prospect of good women's roles."

Despite some arguments between Arthur Laurents and director Sydney Pollack over cuts and story emphasis, *The Way We Were* turned out quite well. It was a lively reimagining of the screen personae of both Streisand and Redford, and a very important boost for her as an actress. The movie opened in October 1973, earned fine notices, and quickly made around $10 million in North American rentals, eventually earning about $45 million. Streisand received her second Academy Award nomination, but, in an upset, lost the Oscar to Glenda Jackson for the comedy *A Touch of Class*—which Sue took as a personal affront.

In 1973 Streisand solidified her reputation as the supreme combination of old-style/new-style star. Her LP *The Way We Were* included new hits such as the title cut and "All in Love Is Fair," plus brilliant reinterpretations of standards such as "My Buddy" and "How About Me?" In other words, Streisand was Sue's kind of show business.

Just a few weeks after the premiere of *The Way We Were*, Jean-Claude's debut as a screenwriter, *Ash Wednesday*, had its premiere in New York and Los Angeles. Since the film's producer, Dominick Dunne, had arrived in Hollywood in the 1950s at the invitation of his friend Humphrey Bogart, he had gone on to produce three big-screen movies: *The Boys in the Band*, *Panic in Needle Park*, and *Play It As It Lays*. The screenplays for the last two had been written by his brother, John Gregory Dunne, and sister-in-law, Joan Didion, who had also written the novel *Play It As It Lays*. None of the films had done much at the box office, but their tough subject matter gave them all a certain cachet with critics.

Unlike these films, *Ash Wednesday* was not remotely contemporary in feel; it was a dull story of a failing marriage, complete with a saccharine Maurice Jarre score that seemed out of another era. Jean-Claude's script moved at a glacial pace; the mood of the film was muted to the point of being somnolent; and the final confrontation, in which Elizabeth Taylor's character begs her husband to stay with her because she has gone to the trouble of restoring her former beauty via surgery, was almost repellent. The reviews were mixed, but by no means disastrous; one of the harshest comments was made by the *New York Times*'s Vincent Canby, who felt that it was "directed by Larry Peerce . . . and written by Jean-Claude Tramont with all the fearlessness and perception demanded in the boiling of an egg."

The trouble with *Ash Wednesday* had started much earlier, however. Dominick Dunne was in the midst of a period of heavy drinking, one that would eventually end with his exiling himself to rural Oregon at the end of the decade and embarking on his hugely successful writing career. Richard Burton skulked around the set, behaving rudely to nearly everyone who crossed his path. Location shooting in Cortina d'Ampezzo in the Veneto region of Italy went on for months, punctuated by a great deal of drinking and partying among the company—with the exception of Henry Fonda, who stayed aloof from all the carousing going on around him. "Instead of telling the actors to get to bed," recalled Griffin Dunne, Dominick's son, "Dad would be up partying with them. He was never really secure being in that position of 'Get the picture in under budget or I'm going to fucking fire you.'"

Keith Baxter, who played a supporting role as Taylor's friend in the film, recalled that Jean-Claude wandered around the set in the first days of shooting looking rather lost. "I liked him," said Baxter, "and felt rather sorry for him. He left me at reception a Penguin copy of T. S. Eliot poems with a bookmark for *Ash Wednesday*. There was a lot of rewriting on the set. People said it wasn't witty enough—not enough jokes. Burt Shevelove, who was a great friend of mine and Dominick's, came to Cortina to see me, and he wrote some funny lines, which were put in. There were rumors saying that Sue's closeness to Bobby Evans had made the film possible. But Jean-Claude seemed sad—a rather lowly figure."

There was another issue: when production started, Dominick Dunne told a number of people that he remembered meeting Jean-Claude years earlier. According to Dunne, Jean-Claude's real name was Jack Schwartz, and he had been a page at NBC when Dunne had been a stage manager for the network's anthology series *Robert Montgomery Presents*. Dunne was wrong: the ship's log from Jean-Claude's arrival in the United States in 1948 plainly shows that his name was indeed Jean-Claude Tramont, but that his mother's maiden name was Schwartz. If Dunne really did know him as Jack Schwartz, it was probably because Jean-Claude was trying to assimilate into American life as quickly as possible; he certainly did some directing at NBC under the name Jean-Claude Schwartz before returning to the name Tramont permanently in the 1960s.

One day, viewing the rushes of *Ash Wednesday* and recognizing that the picture was not going to turn out as he had hoped, Dunne, after several drinks, said, "This picture should be subtitled, 'What Happens When a Fat Girl Falls in Love.'" The remark was overheard by a journalist and a few days later found its way into print in the *Hollywood Reporter*.

When Robert Evans read it, he was enraged at the slight on his dear friend. He called Dunne and told him he had made a grave mistake in crossing the most powerful woman in Hollywood, and he hoped that Dunne knew that he would never produce another picture. Sue also knew that Dunne had been telling people that Jean-Claude's real name was not Tramont; she worked overtime calling in favors from the various studio heads, urging them to blackball Dunne. "In drinking and talking out of school, Dad was falling into a self-destruction that intersected with Sue," commented Griffin Dunne. "That happens, and you've got to pay for that."

Robert Evans was right: Dunne's film producing career ended with *Ash Wednesday*.

At home Sue was seldom not working. She absorbed all the information she could by reading Hollywood biographies, the trade papers, and every prominent news and cultural magazine she could lay her hands on. Often, if someone quoted an incident that had been recounted in a Hollywood biography, Sue would instantly correct him if he got so much as one minor detail wrong.

She also sniffed out news before anyone else had a chance to do so. In 1973, Joan Rivers wrote a television film, *The Girl Most Likely to . . .* , which aired as an *ABC Movie of the Week* that November, starring Stockard Channing. Early one morning, while Rivers was at the Fairmont Hotel in San Francisco, she received a call from Sue: "Congratulations on those wonderful numbers for your movie. I'd like to meet you when you come back to L.A." Rivers was impressed that Sue had gotten hold of the ratings before anyone else had. "I had dinner with Sue and Jean-Claude once or twice,"

Rivers recalled. "But the minute she found out I had an agent and was happy, I never heard from her again. It was obvious: 'I love you. You're wonderful. Oh. Well, fuck you!'"

In 1973, Fields's seemingly happy marriage to Polly Bergen had run aground when Bergen discovered he was having an affair with one of his clients, Samantha Eggar. Bergen recalled a very public scene in a Beverly Hills restaurant, when she clouted Eggar with a service tray. When Sue learned of the split, she sprang into action and invited Bergen to lunch at the Bistro Garden. Although the two of them had never been close, they had a healthy level of respect for each other. They sat down, and Sue delivered her opening argument:

"You cannot divorce Freddie."

"What are you talking about?" asked Bergen.

Sue went on to explain that she would be giving up everything—the money, her position as a Hollywood hostess, all that went with being Mrs. Freddie Fields. Bergen explained calmly that her husband had humiliated her before the international movie community and she was not about to take it. Sue insisted that men were wired to be unfaithful, and Bergen was foolish to expect that they would behave any differently; she should make her peace with it and stay where she was. Given the feminist spirit of the era, Sue's speech sounded almost antiquated—much like the one on the infidelity of husbands that Mrs. Morehead delivers to Mary Haines in Clare Boothe's *The Women*—and it ultimately did no good. Bergen and Fields divorced in 1973, and Bergen moved to New York.

A new client whom Sue did sign the following year was Faye Dunaway, whose career in films had been strangely stalled since Freddie Fields had launched her in the 1960s. Fields was increasingly involved in production matters by this time, and Sue inherited Dunaway, who came with a reputation for being highly difficult. In mid-1974, the actress had vexed director John Milius with her last-minute withdrawal from the $4-million epic *The Wind and the Lion*, which had an expensive and complicated production schedule in Spain. Sue saw to it that Dunaway was replaced by Candice Bergen.

Sue continued to pursue celebrities from the movies, literature, and the Social Register. She seemed unfazed by any level of personal fame, and only occasionally would she register the slightest social timidity. In the mid-1970s, writer Joan Juliet Buck was serving as the London correspondent for *Women's Wear Daily*, a job that frequently took her to Paris. One night she was in Régine's on the rue de Ponthieu with her new beau, Eric de Roth-schild, along with his uncle Edmond and aunt Nadine. Across the nightclub they spotted Woody Allen walking in with Sue and a few others. The Roth-schilds recognized him, and when Sue saw Buck, she waved them over to the table, and introductions were made. "Each side was as dazzled as the other," Buck remembered.

A few days later Sue invited Buck to lunch in the garden of the Plaza Athénée, where they were joined by Robert Evans, model Lisa Taylor, and Orson Welles. Sue kept telling Buck that she needed to talk to her privately, and after the meal the two women repaired to the bar at the Ritz, where Sue laid it out: "Now listen, Joanie—the Rothschilds ain't for the likes of you and me." Buck said, "I remember thinking, I know I'm not the most beauti-ful girl in the world, but I don't think we're the same person. She sort of identified with *any* woman. I was twenty-four or twenty-five, and here she was, taking my boyfriend away from me. I knew he was sleeping with eight other people. But 'ain't for the likes of you and me'? She had these kind of rules."

Robert Evans had been longing to make his own films for some time, and Charles Bluhdorn had worked out a deal for him to produce one movie a year for five years as head of Robert Evans Productions, while remaining at the head of Paramount. Robert Towne delivered an original script called *Chinatown*, a murky, complex thriller centered on civic corruption over wa-ter rights in 1930s Los Angeles. The script took some time to work out—Evans admitted that initially he didn't have a clue what it was really about—but Jack Nicholson was committed to star as a tough private eye. Sue had a running joke with Nicholson that she always tried to talk him out of doing all his major roles. "She always teased me about maneuvering me out of *The Great Gatsby*," Nicholson recalled. "Of course, I didn't want to do it. But she always said that she had advised me against my biggest successes. Early on she told me not to be so available in order to enhance the quality, the mystery, that's hard to maintain as a public figure. She would say, 'Jack, you would go to the opening of a supermarket if they would ask you.'"

For the mysterious female lead in *Chinatown*, a kind of cousin to Dashiell Hammett's duplicitous Brigid O'Shaughnessy, hopes were centered on Jane Fonda. But Fonda vacillated for weeks, and Sue began her promotion of Faye Dunaway. Finally, as the movie's start date drew nearer, she called Evans, telling him she needed an answer about Dunaway by the end of business Friday, because the actress had been offered a good role in Arthur Penn's *Night Moves*. In the meantime, Fonda passed. The budget for *Chinatown* wasn't high, and when Evans told Sue that all he could offer Dunaway was $50,000, she slammed down the phone on him. Later she called back, wheedling that the offer was so low that if she presented it to Dunaway, she'd be sure of losing her as a client, and again mentioned the Arthur Penn film. Evans pointed out that Dunaway needed a good part because she was "colder than Baskin-Robbins," but upped the offer to $75,000. Sue called back quickly to say that Dunaway had accepted, and then Evans persuaded the director, Roman Polanski, to assent to Dunaway. When he called Sue to tell her that Dunaway had the part, she burst out laughing.

"Bobbeee . . . I fibbed. There was no part in *Night Moves* for Faye."

At that point Evans told her that Fonda had already passed. Once again, Sue slammed down the phone. But she could never stay angry at a fellow cutthroat like Evans; she loved playing the game too much, especially when facing so evenly matched an opponent.

From the high point of *The Way We Were*, Barbra Streisand slid backward in 1974 with *For Pete's Sake*, a forced, manic comedy that was produced by Ray Stark's Rastar Productions for Columbia but was not part of her contract with Stark. Around this time, the actress met Jon Peters, a famous and ambitious Los Angeles hair stylist who used to brag that in his early days he had run a pussy and poodle parlor. "If I thought the pussy looked good in purple," he once told producer Lynda Obst, "I would dye it, and then dye the poodle purple to match." By the age of thirty he had already made a good deal of money by launching a string of high-end hair salons. (For his personal clients, he charged $100 a cut.) Being situated in Los Angeles, he harbored an overpowering lust to become a major player in the movie industry; he claimed to have wanted to make it in the movies ever since crossing the Red Sea as an extra in Cecil B. DeMille's *The Ten Commandments* back in 1956.

"Jon is a formidable figure and has a lot of influence on the people that he engages with," observed Lesley Ann Warren, who was briefly married to Peters. Warren was a one-time Walt Disney contract player who, prior to Ali MacGraw's discovery, had been cast as Brenda in Paramount's *Goodbye, Columbus*, only to drop out when she discovered she was pregnant. Warren had a shining, good-girl image, based on her work for Disney and in Rodgers & Hammerstein's TV musical *Cinderella*. "Jon urged me to explore other facets of my character and my young womanhood," she said. "He wanted me to drop the image of the sweet, innocent, virginal girl and explore other avenues of sexuality." Among other things, Peters insisted that Warren do a season of the hit television series *Mission: Impossible*, which was not a rewarding experience for the actress. The couple divorced in 1974—the same year that Gould and Streisand were divorced.

Peters was not intimidated by Streisand; he later remembered that at their first meeting, he was furious because she kept him waiting. Streisand was at a crucial juncture in her personal life, having one failed marriage to Elliott Gould and collapsed love affairs with Ryan O'Neal and Canadian prime minister Pierre Trudeau behind her, so she was vulnerable to Peters's bulldozing campaign for her attention. Peters began by obsessively telling Streisand what hairstyle to wear and how to dress; soon, despite his complete lack of experience in the business, he was advising her on which pictures to make.

When it came to the others involved in shaping Streisand's career, Peters, hell-bent on making his mark, responded neither to direct opposition nor to a Neville Chamberlain appeasement approach. He was very much in favor of Streisand's quest to contemporize her image. In 1974, Streisand was committed to make a sequel to *Funny Girl* for Ray Stark, and Peters thought it was a bad idea. Streisand also strongly resisted the project, but eventually gave in to Stark and made the film. Peters then became deeply involved in what would become Streisand's next picture—a rock-and-roll-themed remake of the classic Hollywood story *A Star Is Born*.

Six months after Peters and Streisand got together, Martin Erlichman dropped out as the star's manager. The two would remain professionally disconnected before joining forces once again in the 1980s; during this time, Sue's role in Streisand's career intensified. At first, Sue dismissed

Peters as a social-climbing hairdresser and did not perceive him as anything resembling a real threat. But his influence over Streisand would only escalate in the coming years, and Sue would find herself in direct conflict with him more often than not. Decades later Streisand said simply, "She hated Jon Peters."

CHAPTER TWELVE

1975–1976

On January 26, 1975, Sue's burgeoning status as a Hollywood legend was cemented when *60 Minutes*, CBS's highly rated Sunday night newsmagazine show, ran a segment called "Mengers' the Name . . . Hollywood's the Game," produced by Grace Diekhaus and hosted by the series' prickly anchorman, Mike Wallace. "What do these five famous names have in common? Barbra Streisand, Ryan O'Neal, Ali MacGraw, Gene Hackman, and Gore Vidal," began Wallace. "Well, besides fame and fortune, they have Sue Mengers, their talent agent. She is friend, adviser, psychologist, job-getter and job-turner-down for each of them, and she makes the deals that make them rich."

It was a generous, nearly ten-minute-long feature on a program that covered Hollywood only rarely, and Sue was delighted with the exposure. She sat for the interview with Wallace wearing her trademark pink-tinted glasses and perfectly manicured frosty-mauve nails, and chain-smoking. When Wallace asked her how she got clients, Sue giggled. "I thought you'd never ask. In the beginning, it was through aggression. Now it's through reputation. And a little aggression."

The segment went on to show her deal making over the phone with Ryan O'Neal, Mick Jagger (whom she was trying to help set up a movie deal), and Richard Zanuck, the head of Twentieth Century Fox, doing business from her bed. There was also a clip that featured her pestering Robert Evans, poolside, about a script called *The Bodyguard*, which she was pitching as a vehicle for O'Neal and another recent addition to her client roster, Diana Ross. When Wallace inquired about her script acumen, her response seemed to take him by surprise: "Of course, I don't know what a good script is. If I knew what a good script was, I'd be producing or I'd be directing. All I can do is give my opinion and try to be as objective in terms of my artists as I can be, and it would be pretentious of me to say, 'Peter Bogdanovich, I don't agree with you about that piece of material.' That's not my job!" Here she was being disingenuous. She often disagreed with clients over material, and Bogdanovich's new Cole Porter musical, *At Long Last Love*, for Twentieth Century Fox, was a case in point: according to Bogdanovich, she had been dubious about the project from the start. The segment showed her on the set of the film, where Sue took care to assure the director, "It's gonna pay off—it's really gonna pay off."

On the topic of her personal power, she said simply, "Golda Meir had power, Kissinger has power, Kay Graham has power. When I die, God forbid, I'm not really going to feel that I made any great contribution to the world and that I had power. My clients have power—power to get movies made, power to bring people in to see those movies. And I guess, by default, I get a little of that power."

At the end of the segment, Wallace asked her, "Do you ever pinch yourself and say, 'Why me?'"

"Oh, yeah," Sue replied. "A lot. And then I say, 'Who deserves it more?'"

Off camera she had asked Wallace not to mention the clients who had left her, but the interviewer, eager to provoke her, immediately brought up Dyan Cannon. "Oh," said Sue, who turned to the camera and uttered an expletive that was neatly edited out of the end result.

By now Sue and Jean-Claude had left Dawnridge Drive. The Tramonts had purchased an enormous 1926 French Normandy mansion, which had once belonged to Zsa Zsa Gabor, at 938 Bel Air Road. For many of their friends, the new house, despite its spaciousness, floods of light, and a total of four bedrooms and seven bathrooms, lacked the intimate charm of Dawnridge Drive. Sue and Jean-Claude engaged Garrett Lewis, the set decorator on many of Herbert Ross's pictures, to help them get the home in shape. Lewis bought a number of white sofas for the spacious living room, and there were always vases full of white orchids; a large anteroom known as the Moroccan Room had a banquette and lots of plush cushions. It was altogether more the type of classical Hollywood house that one might see featured in a magazine layout. For Sue, the Bel Air Road house symbolized life as she expected to live it—everything in its proper place, from the table settings and flower arrangements to the paintings on the walls. "It was cool and white and blue and beige and full of famous people sitting around," remembered Ali MacGraw. "But it wasn't that interesting. It lacked the soul of the Duquette house."

The house also had vast closet space, and Sue organized her clothes by season as well as by location—Los Angeles, New York, Europe. Her evening gowns and evening shoes were arranged with a fastidiousness Joan Crawford no doubt would have approved of, and she told the *New York Times* about her penchant for lining all her bureau drawers with a certain quilted fabric from Minka's Bath Shop in Beverly Hills; it served to protect articles of clothing against mildew.

In Hollywood, both her allies and enemies were abuzz over the visibility the *60 Minutes* appearance gave her. It was unheard-of for an agent, or for that matter, most studio executives, to be the subject of national television exposure. After the episode aired, there was an uptick in the number of major magazine and newspaper features being written about her—in *New York Magazine*, the *New York Times*, the *Hollywood Reporter*, *American Film*, *Cinema*, and elsewhere. The resulting publicity also helped fuel the rumors that Paramount was considering her as a possible successor to Evans, and that she was being pursued to be future production chief at Columbia. It seemed unthinkable to most people that only thirteen years earlier she had been a secretary.

There was some logic behind the speculation that she might move into the production end of filmmaking, because both Freddie Fields and David Begelman had been heading in that direction for some time. (The example of Lew Wasserman, who had moved from the agency business into running a studio, was still a potent and instructive one.) Begelman left CMA first, in late 1973, to become president of Columbia Pictures, which was floundering, thanks to too many box-office disappointments like *The King of Marvin Gardens*, *Images*, *Oklahoma Crude*, *40 Carats*, and Ross Hunter's disastrous $7 million *Lost Horizon*. Begelman brought a smart, contemporary outlook to his job, launching successful movies like 1975's *Shampoo* and *Tommy*, both of which helped accomplish a major makeover of the studio's image.

When both Twentieth Century Fox and Warner Bros. had purchased novels about a burning high-rise office building—one called *The Tower* and the other *The Glass Inferno*—it was Fields who had masterminded combining them into one spectacular disaster movie, *The Towering Inferno*, which featured almost as many stars as *Airport* and far more impressive special effects. It was a big hit when released at Christmas 1974, and soon it was announced that Fields would be heading up his own production company at Paramount, responsible for six movies a year. Soon afterward, Guy McElwaine, head of the motion picture department at CMA, decamped to become production chief at Warner Bros., which was riding high thanks to the record-shattering success of William Friedkin's *The Exorcist* in 1973. All of this undoubtedly looked attractive to Sue: producers stood to make far more money than most agents, and they would also be relieved of many of the unending, trivial details of servicing clients.

Instead of following her CMA comrades to the other side of the negotiating table, though, Sue reasoned that without them she could now be more influential than ever at the agency, and decided to stay. In late 1974 she reupped with CMA for $200,000, although that was not pure salary; stock options and an expense account were included in the total. Impressive as this sum of money was, it still wasn't close to what many of the most powerful men in the business were making. (One of Sue's professional eccentricities was that, while she could be incredibly tough when negotiating a deal for one of her star clients, she wasn't as cunning about money when it came to her own personal finances.)

Her timing turned out to be adroit. The industry trade papers had been hinting for some time that CMA might merge with another major agency, and on January 1, 1975, CMA joined with Marvin Josephson and Associates, owner of the respected and successful International Famous Agency. Letters were taken from each firm's initials to form ICM—International Creative Management—which would emerge immediately as one of the most powerful talent agencies in the world, guiding the careers of topflight actors, directors, writers, and classical musicians. Josephson was noted for being far more tightfisted than Fields had been; only a handful of his IFA agents had formal contracts. But Sue had shrewdly maneuvered herself into a strong position: she was a bona fide star, making as much as some studio chiefs.

Around this time, a much less commented-upon exodus took place over at CMA's principal competitor, the William Morris Agency. Phil Weltman, the tough, enterprising head of WMA's television department, had been unceremoniously retired from the company, and a group of his loyal followers—Michael Ovitz, Ronald Meyer, Rowland Perkins, Bill Haber, and Mike Rosenfeld—chose that moment to leave WMA and form their own agency, initially meeting in one another's homes and doing business across card tables. "We trusted Phil Weltman," said Ron Meyer. "He took care of us. If Phil had still been at William Morris, the five of us would never have left. We were energetic and new and hungry, and I think that all kinds of things set us apart—but that was probably the main thing. We were small and aggressive and unified." The new group christened itself the Creative Artists Agency, and part of its preliminary focus was putting actors together with screenwriters, though its impact wouldn't be felt until a few years later.

From mid-1973 into early 1974, many of CMA's clients had been working on major European productions, and Fields had taken Sue on a worldwide trip to help solidify the company's relations with some of the big stars. Ryan O'Neal was filming Stanley Kubrick's *Barry Lyndon* in Ireland, Candice Bergen was shooting *The Wind and the Lion* in Spain, Jacqueline Bisset was in England filming *Murder on the Orient Express* (directed by Sue's client Sidney Lumet, whom she had tried to dissuade from doing the project) and *The Spiral Staircase*. Many stars had "key man" clauses in their contracts, meaning that if their agents left the firm, they could also leave, with impunity. With Begelman now at Columbia, Fields wanted the stars performing in Europe to know that Sue was essentially the new David. With the merger, all the contracts had to be re-signed, and Ryan O'Neal remembered Sue tromping across a wet field in Ireland, where a scene for *Barry Lyndon* was being filmed. "Stanley Kubrick said, 'Who's that?'" said O'Neal. "He never let anyone on the set. I said, 'Here she comes—you're in trouble now, Stanley.' He hid behind one of the trucks as if Sue was the FBI."

Shortly after the merger, Sue met with young Paula Weinstein, who had previously been a junior agent at IFA. Referring to a job Weinstein had gotten for one of her clients, Sue derisively said, "You're going to represent someone who is going to be making fifty thousand dollars?" Weinstein, who was making only fifty thousand herself, was appalled. "It was one of my first moments of seeing how removed Hollywood was from the real world. She was horrified that there should be any riffraff around the fifty-thousand-dollar level. But she was very generous, and started to invite me to her parties, which was unusual, because I didn't know that many people."

Ali MacGraw re-signed with the new agency, but it was a slightly moot point. In 1973, she had married Steve McQueen, and her new husband didn't want her to work. Sue would frequently ask studio chiefs, "Do you have anything for my Ali?" in an attempt to persuade MacGraw to go back before the cameras. MacGraw, for whom movie stardom had been a happy accident to begin with, didn't object at first to being consigned to housewife duty.

There were times, however, when being out of the movie business made her feel like a second-class citizen. In the mid-1970s, Katharine Hepburn was peddling a script called *The Ultimate Solution of Grace Quigley*, a black comedy about an elderly woman who teams up with a down-on-his-luck younger man to do sick, old people a service by euthanizing them. Knowing that she could not hope to sell the script to a studio without a major male star attached, Hepburn called McQueen and asked to come out to his beach house and discuss the project with him.

On a hot summer day, MacGraw, clad in a bathing suit, was preparing a big salad for her husband's lunch with Hepburn, while her young son, Joshua Evans, and McQueen's son, Chad, tore around on the beach outside. Shortly before the actress was scheduled to appear, McQueen, nervous at the prospect of meeting the screen legend, took off on his motorcycle. Hepburn arrived punctually, and MacGraw apologized for McQueen's absence, asking her if she would like to wait a bit for her salad.

"But I'm hungry!" snapped Hepburn, and immediately began rooting through the cupboard, where she found a package of Knorr Onion Soup mix. As MacGraw looked on helplessly, Hepburn turned on the tap and made herself a saucepan of soup. "She looks at me like I'm some bimbo television wannabe," recalled MacGraw. "Then Steve comes in, and she turns on the charm. I served the salad, they had their little chat. And as she walks out the door, she said, 'By the way, that is the most *ghastly* soup I have ever eaten!'"

Sue would continue to inquire after scripts that might be suitable for MacGraw, even though she knew the actress didn't want to work. MacGraw's marriage was something of a conundrum for Sue: she wanted Ali to make money, but there was no denying that Steve McQueen was a powerful man in Hollywood—not as powerful as Robert Evans, but powerful enough.

"I don't think Sue ever gave a shit about feminism," said Boaty Boatwright. "She wanted women to be achievers, but she never thought a woman should leave a man because she was in love with someone else if the man happened to be rich. She said to Gloria Steinem, 'I'm a woman who always wants to go home with a man at the end of the party.'"

While MacGraw was serenely out of the business for the time being, Peter Bogdanovich was unexpectedly facing a rough patch in his career. After the consecutive successes of *The Last Picture Show*, *What's Up, Doc?*, and *Paper Moon*, the director had farther to fall than almost any of Sue's clients, and the first drop came with the Directors Company's *Daisy Miller*, based on Henry James's novella and released in the spring of 1974. Bogdanovich had by then developed a reputation around Hollywood for extreme hubris, and many both within and outside the industry were gunning for him to fail. *Daisy Miller* gave them what they wanted. The reviews of the film were unfairly dismissive; the adaptation by Frederic Raphael was intelligent, and it was magnificently photographed by Alberto Spagnoli and adroitly edited by Verna Fields. There was a fine supporting cast including Eileen Brennan, Cloris Leachman, and Mildred Natwick, but what sank the film was its two leads—Cybill Shepherd and Barry Brown. As Bogdanovich's girlfriend, Shepherd in particular had a target on her back, and critics rushed to point out her poor grasp of the part; she made Daisy's Yankee independence and naïveté about European mores irritating rather than endearing. Ultimately *Daisy Miller* did far more harm to Shepherd's reputation than to Bogdanovich's, and everyone waited to see what he would achieve with his next venture, *At Long Last Love*.

A musical tribute to the black-and-white Art Deco Ernst Lubitsch films that Paramount turned out in the 1930s, *At Long Last Love* was built around a string of great Cole Porter songs. The trouble arose, again, in the casting of the leads: Burt Reynolds and Cybill Shepherd, who were not anyone's idea of prime singing and dancing talent. Reynolds's presence in the film had been engineered by Sue, who had recently acquired him as a client. Initially, Bogdanovich wanted Elliott Gould—who did possess legitimate song-and-dance-man credits—for the lead in the film, but Sue had talked him out of it. "Sue called me one day and said, 'You don't want to use Elliott Gould. He's not a big name anymore,'" recalled Bogdanovich. "'Why don't you use Burt Reynolds?' I said, 'Can he sing and dance?' She said,

'*Anybody* can sing and dance. It's Burt Reynolds!' I met with Burt and liked him, and I had to let Elliott Gould go, which he never forgave me for. I don't blame him."

Burt Reynolds, as it turned out, could not sing and dance, and neither, really, could Shepherd (though she did eventually develop into a respectable cabaret artist). Years later Bogdanovich admitted that he had listened to the opinions of too many people, including Sue and the Twentieth Century Fox executives, as he was assembling the film, and wound up with a terribly compromised version that did not remotely represent his original vision. In particular, Sue urged him to cut Madeline Kahn's excellent opening number, "Down in the Depths on the Ninetieth Floor," and open with one of Cybill Shepherd's songs, which Bogdanovich later judged a big mistake. *At Long Last Love* had a disastrous screening in a cavernous Cinerama Dome in San Jose. "By the time the picture was over, everybody had left the theater except for the Fox people and Cybill and me," remembered Bogdanovich. "I made some cuts, and we previewed it in Denver, where it played well. Then I really fucked it up"—meaning that he again listened to too many outside opinions and rearranged the film. A *Newsweek* cover story on the director was subsequently killed. The movie opened at Radio City Music Hall in March 1975 and did well, but the reviews were so bad that it was barely screened elsewhere. In *The New Yorker*, Pauline Kael called it "a stillborn picture, without a whisper of a chance to recoup its six-and-a-half-million-dollar cost."

Around this time, Bogdanovich received a call from Cary Grant, who had noticed that it was impossible to open a newspaper or magazine without reading a mean crack aimed in Bogdanovich's and Shepherd's direction.

"Peter!" Grant barked. "Will you for Chrissake stop telling people you're happy? And stop telling them you're in love!" When Bogdanovich asked why, Grant answered, "Because they're *not* happy and they're *not* in love! Let me tell you something, Peter—people *do not like* beautiful people!"

The mid-1970s saw the start of a major escalation in star salaries. There had been $1 million salaries in the 1960s—Elizabeth Taylor for *Cleopatra* and Audrey Hepburn for *My Fair Lady*—but the real jump in Hollywood came when the English movie producer Lew Grade began overpaying for his projects, and stars' asking prices began steadily rising. In 1974, producer Alexander Salkind pulled off one of the fastest tricks in movie history with his production of *The Three Musketeers*, starring Michael York, Charlton Heston, Oliver Reed, Faye Dunaway, and Raquel Welch. The film's contracts made use of the seemingly innocuous phrase "a production of *The Three Musketeers*," whereas U.S. agreements would normally have stipulated the specific use of an actor's services "for the film *The Three Musketeers*." Salkind's ambiguous language went unnoticed by all of the top agents and entertainment attorneys in Hollywood, whose clients in the project were horrified when they showed up for the premiere and were greeted with the legend: "Coming soon . . . *The Further Adventures of The Three Musketeers*." The film's stars were enraged: they had effectively been duped into making two movies for the price of one. *The Four Musketeers* was released in 1975, and nobody got paid a second time.

For many actors, movie salaries had remained at a relatively modest level. By the mid-1970s, a good salary for a major star generally topped off somewhere around $200,000. Jeff Bridges, despite having been nominated for an Academy Award for *The Last Picture Show*, received a mere $87,000 for costarring with Clint Eastwood in 1974's *Thunderbolt and Lightfoot*. As time went on, however, actors began rebelling against the studio heads' custom of amassing huge amounts of money and refusing to share it.

Sue played a significant part in the rising tide of star salaries. In 1975, Stanley Donen was preparing to shoot the adventure comedy *Lucky Lady* in Mexico, with a cast headed by Liza Minnelli, Burt Reynolds, and George Segal. But Segal dropped out at the last minute, and the producers were desperate for a replacement. No one with marquee value was available, with the exception of Gene Hackman. His presence in the film would mean that the cast would include two Academy Award winners—Minnelli being the other—and the studio decided they had to have him. Sue conducted a tortuously prolonged negotiation until Twentieth Century Fox finally agreed to pay Hackman $1 million. Fox's then-head of creative affairs, Alan Ladd, Jr., remembered, "I never paid anybody in my lifetime one million dollars. But I was in a spot and I had nothing to do but finally agree to it. I needed a star and I had no time to run around looking for who else was available. Sue delivered him to the set the next Monday." Word got around town, and soon other leading men of Hackman's age began demanding the same salary of their agents. Many of Sue's peers around Hollywood began to grumble loudly that she was in danger of ruining the business—much as Lew Wasserman had warned Jay Kanter of doing back at MCA in 1960.

Sue appeared unconcerned in the face of such criticism. "If a couple of these studios would really take a stand," she told *American Film*, "I'd be delighted to say to my client, 'Hey, they just won't pay it.' But I'm not going to say anything if they're going to pay it to a rival's client. I just won't. As long as they're dumb enough to pay these prices, I'm willing to let them." (In Hackman's case, she also defended his decision to risk overexposure with four films released in 1975, because he felt he had waited for so long to become a big movie star.)

At ICM Sue continued to do business in her own singular, somewhat isolated style. Michael Black was a smart young New York attorney who had arrived at CMA in late 1973 to work in the business affairs department. He was eager to learn about the inner workings of entertainment law and figured that a short time at the agency would qualify him to return to New York to a top firm that specialized in it.

When he first came to work for CMA, Black considered Los Angeles to be about nothing more than organic food, astrology, and Charles Manson. It wasn't long before he understood that it was also about Sue Mengers. Sue had just returned from her around-the-world trip with Freddie Fields, and an important morning meeting had been called. Black, who had never dealt directly with Fields before, was sitting nervously with other staff members around the big black marble table in the conference room. Fields walked in and began the meeting. Ten minutes later, Sue sauntered in, wearing a muu-muu. Yanking her hair back into a ponytail and attempting to shove a tortoiseshell comb through it, she plopped herself down in a chair, perched on top of one foot. Black, who was sitting directly across from her, could plainly see that she wasn't wearing any underwear. While she was fiddling with her tortoiseshell comb, one of her false nails popped off and fell in front of her on the marble table. "Aaach," she muttered, "that fuckin' gook didn't do the paste right on my fuckin' nails." The comb then fell out of her hair and onto the ground, and when Sue bent over to pick it up, she exposed her bare bottom to the entire table full of employees. "I was like a kid in grade school," remembered Black, "when you are laughing and you make believe you're bending over to tie your shoes because you're gagging for air."

But Sue was far more than CMA's resident class clown. At the regular weekly staff meetings on Mondays, Wednesdays, and Fridays, when the air was blue with cigarette smoke and redolent of the aroma of coffee, she could be quite supportive of her colleagues. "You would say, 'I tried to get so-and-so on the phone and couldn't,'" remembered agent Jack Gilardi. "And she would say, 'Let me help you, darling.' She helped me a lot."

She could be quite kind and generous to many of her ICM coworkers. She would pad barefoot down the hall to the office of Elizabeth Gabler and ask if she had anything to eat, and what good scripts she had read lately. "I never felt she was condescending or disinterested in any way, no matter how junior I was," said Gabler. "Later on, a lot of women who were studio execu-tives and producers would yell and slam doors, because a lot of guys be-haved that way. It was a trend with a lot of women to behave like that. It was all, as I saw it, a misguided attempt to emulate Sue."

Gabler also remembered Sue's frequent lunches at the swank restaurant La Scala. There was no parking in front, but she would routinely park her Mercedes there anyway; frequently, the car would be towed, and one of her secretaries would be sent to retrieve it while another drove to La Scala to pick up Sue.

During this period, Fields had instituted something known as the CMA rider, which sharpened and specified all the details in the standard studio contract, including a clear definition of profits, much to the client's advan-tage. Once an agent set a deal with a studio, an internal booking report would be filled out that indicated the name of the movie, name of the studio, start date, billing position for the client, salary, degree of profit participa-tion (if any), living expenses, and transportation. Certain agents could be even more specific: net profits would be spelled out at a breakeven bonus, or a rolling breakeven; much later, stars would contractually receive a per-centage of gross at first dollar, but such a thing was unheard-of in the 1970s. In fact, only a handful of top-echelon actors received any kind of profit participation. The miscellaneous details in film contracts varied widely: when he arranged the deal for Steve McQueen's 1973 adventure film *Papil-lon*, Fields stipulated that the actor's weights would be housed in a separate trailer so he could work out whenever he liked, and that McQueen's per-sonal barber would be flown to the European location every few weeks.

As a member of the business affairs department, Michael Black was responsible for examining the booking reports and matching them against the deal memos submitted by the studio. Sue's booking reports were a study in vagueness. Under "Profit Participation" she might write simply "5," not indicating whether it was net or rolling breakeven. Under "Billing" she would write "STAR," without indicating whether it was first position, second position, or at the end of the credits with a box around the name. Black would invariably have to trek to her office to clarify the details—something he found more than worthwhile, because he got to overhear her bouncing between telephone calls and barking out orders to her secretaries.

"Get me Barbra. Then get me Warners. I want John Calley. And then call Columbia and get me fucking David Begelman. No, I can't come to the screening tonight. I want to know who's coming. Maybe I will be there after all."

When Black would attempt to question some of the individual points she had negotiated, she would ask, in her "Baby Sue" voice, "What is this 'rolling breakeven?' Rolling breakeven. It sounds like a bakery. Let me get David Begelman on the phone. David? It's Sue. I'm sitting here with an attorney from business affairs. He wants to know who gets first billing. I think my client should. Don't you think Jimmie Coburn should get first billing? I do. Not that fucking shriveled-up cunt you cast opposite him."

Eventually Michael Black did so well in the business affairs department that he was promoted to agent. His legal background stood him in good stead, since he could explain all the contract details to a client; there was no need for the client to engage a personal attorney. ICM's Marvin Josephson insisted that Black work closely with Sue, partly so that he could learn from her and partly so that he could sew up some of the business details with which she couldn't be bothered. And since Hollywood had entered the age of the summer blockbuster with the unexpected, history-making success of *Jaws* in 1975, those details would become increasingly complex in the years ahead.

The phenomenon of *Jaws* made Sue uneasy. She understood why so many regarded the film's success as a sign of a financially healthy industry, but fretted that studios were now going to commit to fewer and fewer projects. There were thousands of actors, writers, and directors scrambling for jobs, but Sue felt that "the pictures being done seem to be of a higher budget, a higher caliber and commerciality, but certainly they are not enough in my opinion and my projection of the next year or two to keep an active industry going."

While most of Sue's clients might have loved her, and many of her colleagues might have been amused by her, she was deeply resented by those people in the business for whom she made it clear she had little use. Sue was not a politician, and as her success grew, her focus became narrower, not wider. Only above-the-title Hollywood stardom was good enough for her. For the most part, she continued to require a certain glamour factor in order to accept a client, lest her A-list stature be affected. Thus, Burt Reynolds, who was enormously popular in the 1970s, was someone she was happy to snap up, but she had little interest in serious-minded character actresses like Ellen Burstyn or Cloris Leachman, despite the fact that both were Oscar winners. Her A-list/B-list obsession was often extended to others in the industry as well. She was not particularly kind to many of the studio employees she spoke with on the phone, and she made several tactical errors in this regard that would come back to haunt her later. By now she had acquired Sidney Lumet as a client, and at one point Ned Tanen, the head of Universal's film division, phoned about using Lumet for an upcoming movie. Sue offended Tanen deeply by asking if his was a solid offer, or if Universal president Sid Sheinberg should call her to confirm it. Tanen immediately got on the phone with Michael Black.

"This fuckin' cunt is trying to get Sid to call her to verify the deal?"

Whenever she was aware that she had misstepped, Sue always tried to rescue the situation with the same tactic: "Oh, dear. Baby Sue was wrong. Baby Sue made a *boo-boo*."

Still, she was now positioned as one of the top agents in the business, perhaps equaled only by Sam Cohn in New York and Stan Kamen, the buttoned-down gentleman agent who had brought greatness to the motion-picture division of the William Morris Agency. (Frank Rose, author of the fascinating history of WMA, *The Agency*, aptly contrasted Kamen's and Sue's divergent styles as premium vanilla and exploding passionfruit crush.) If Sue didn't quite command the respect that Kamen did, and if she didn't work in the deep, intellectual way that Cohn did—taking a New York play, developing it as a film project, and casting it with a brilliant up-and-coming actor who would become a major film star—she could easily have pointed

out that *60 Minutes* hadn't done a feature on either Kamen or Cohn. She
had become what she'd always wanted to be: a star.

The last film in Barbra Streisand's contract with Ray Stark had been
Funny Lady, and when it was released in the spring of 1975, it did enormous
box-office business. Despite a snappy collection of songs by John Kander
and Fred Ebb that revealed Streisand in great voice, however, the star's misgivings had been well founded: the movie itself was sluggish and labored.

Rex Reed remembered a phone call he received from Sue just before
the New York premiere of *Funny Lady*. Streisand, Sue told him, had been
upset by his stinging review of her 1974 comedy *For Pete's Sake*. Sue had
arranged for Streisand and Peters to go out on the town with her and Reed
while they were in New York. In "Baby Sue" mode, she cooed to Reed,
"Now, listen, Pussy, I will make this a magic intervention. . . ."

She was interrupted by a voice in the background. Making certain that
Reed heard her, she growled, "What *is* it, Barbra? Shut up! I'm talking to a
major critic." Then she reverted to Baby Sue: "Now, listen, Pussy . . ."

Reed and Sue had a pleasant evening in New York with Streisand and
Peters. At one point Sue whispered in Reed's ear, "This is a snap. She likes
you. You're her new best friend." Reed never saw Streisand again.

Streisand was eager to get her hands on some first-rate material like *The
Way We Were*, but her new project was proving to be problematic. The first
scripts of the remake of *A Star Is Born* were written by Joan Didion and
John Gregory Dunne, but after a year's work they withdrew. At one point
nineteen-year-old Jonathan Axelrod was brought in to work on the script; he
later remembered that a three-week rewrite stretched to nearly a year. Although Axelrod told Sue that he was not a talented writer, she simply replied, "Honeeey, keep that to yourself." Axelrod had admired the
Dunne-Didion script, but his own version was substantially different. Soon
after he submitted it, he was fired from the project. "I decided not to sue for
credit, much to everyone's chagrin, including Sue's," Axelrod remembered.
Soon after, he was offered a prominent job with ABC-TV and telephoned
Sue to ask what she thought. "Are you kidding?" she responded. "You're not
a very good writer." Axelrod protested that he had tried to tell her that all
along, and Sue's only advice to him was to get himself some decent suits so
he would look the part of an ABC executive.

A number of additional scripts were prepared, some with Streisand in the role of the alcoholic fading star that Fredric March and James Mason had played in the previous versions. Ultimately, however, she chose to play the star who rises, even though the part of the washed-up husband (eventually played by Kris Kristofferson) was unquestionably the better one.

Jerry Schatzberg was one of the directors approached about helming the film. He liked many things about the Dunnes' script, but wanted certain elements changed, which they resisted doing. He also found Peters a formidable challenge. "If I got a stereo to listen to music for the film, he would get a stereo," Schatzberg recalled. One day Peters brought Axelrod in without ever mentioning the matter to Schatzberg in advance and began pushing him as the person to rewrite the script. After much back-and-forth discussion, Axelrod finally said he thought it would be best if he left the room, and Schatzberg told Peters never to put him in that position again. Eventually, Schatzberg felt that he would have limited control over the film and withdrew from it.

The picture had become a Jon Peters project, and he got full producer's credit. Some of his decisions were good, such as the one to stage a rock concert in front of a real audience to give a greater feeling of veracity. But his inexperience showed in countless ways. For one thing, he possessed no real level of taste in the artistic side of movies; his ideas were utterly marketing driven. He was tactless and blunt, and Sue soon grew to despise him. Sue, of course, could be tactless and blunt as well, but she mitigated her abrasiveness with her immense charm. Peters was bossy and domineering, and he began to use the tactic of isolating Streisand from other people in her inner circle. And Streisand, who was relentlessly self-critical and eager to keep stretching herself artistically, had begun relying on him more and more as time went on. Sue saw that Peters was attempting to monopolize Streisand's decision making, and tried to hold her ground, taking him on directly. But it was becoming increasingly difficult, especially when *A Star Is Born* turned out to be an immense box-office hit, and Sue found Peters's behavior more insufferable than ever. In his diaries, Andy Warhol recorded that at the film's premiere in New York, Sue buzzed around the lobby, pressing everyone that they had to tell Streisand the picture was wonderful, or else she would be upset.

At ICM a great gulf of tension existed between the motion picture and television departments. The general feeling among the movie agents was that television represented the wrong side of the tracks. This attitude trickled down from the top: Freddie Fields was well known for regarding television as nothing more than a glorified night-light. Then, too, many of the big TV stars of the 1970s did not conform to most agents' concept of sexiness and glamour; it's difficult to imagine Sue having gotten excited about representing Carroll O'Connor, Jean Stapleton, William Conrad, Peter Falk, Carol Burnett, or Raymond Burr. On the occasions when someone tried to persuade her that a hot, young TV actor had movie potential, she usually couldn't see it: when John Travolta, then having a big success as Vinnie Barbarino on ABC's popular sitcom *Welcome Back, Kotter*, was called to her attention, she dismissed him as "that fucking sweathog."

"Rules are made to be broken," says Bette Davis as the elderly pearl thief Mrs. Van Schuyler in the 1978 murder mystery *Death on the Nile*. "At least mine are. By me." Sue might well have had those words embroidered on one of her sofa pillows. When ICM's Bob Bookman spotted Henry Winkler in a stage production at Yale University, he mentioned the young actor to Sue. "Bobbee." Sue sighed. "I need to get a job for Gene Hackman, a job for Ryan O'Neal. I don't need an up-and-coming actor."

In the winter of 1974, the nostalgic sitcom *Happy Days* premiered on ABC and jumped to the top of the ratings; a short time later Winkler was television's newest sensation. One day at the office, Sue purred, "Bobbee . . . are you still friendly with Henry Winkler?"

Another exception to her no-TV-stars rule came along in 1976. One of the major television events of the season was ABC's miniseries *Rich Man, Poor Man*, based on Irwin Shaw's novel. Lou Pitt, an ICM colleague of Sue's, represented the young Nick Nolte, who Pitt was certain was ideal for the role of the embattled Tom Jordache. After months of trying, he finally persuaded director Boris Sagal to give Nolte a test. The actor got the part, and when the series bowed on February 1, 1976, he received great acclaim for his performance. The night that the first installment aired, Sue was watching at home. The next day, at an ICM staff meeting, she said she had to meet Nolte.

Nolte wanted more than anything to be a movie star, and although Pitt worked principally in television, he soon got the actor a leading role in an adventure picture that became one of the big box-office hits of 1977, *The*

Deep. But Sue had kept her eye on Nolte, who was young and vital and represented the next generation. A little over a year later, he left Pitt and became part of her roster, starring in another big hit, *North Dallas Forty.* She continued to be a good colleague of Pitt's over the years, but she had made it clear that she wasn't interested in collaborating with anyone else in shaping Nolte's career.

By the mid-1970s, Sue's friendship with David Geffen had grown closer than ever. She delighted in watching as he moved from strength to strength, managing Jackson Browne, Joni Mitchell, Neil Young, and the Eagles, whose *Greatest Hits* album would become the best-selling rock album of that time. One key to Geffen's success was that he had signed up unknowns early on and helped build them into major stars. Geffen had launched an extraordinarily successful record label, Asylum, which recorded some of the top artists of the time. He sold Asylum in 1972 for $7 million—a decision he ultimately considered a profound error, because only a year later it was worth $50 million. But he reasoned that the sale gave him a net worth of $10 million total, which was the first time he felt his fear of poverty abate. "It's not about reality," he told *Playboy* in 1994. "It's about how you feel."

Geffen had always had difficulty embracing his sexuality—as if being gay did not mesh with his image of a financially successful man. He had an eighteen-month romance with Cher, which ended when she fell in love with rock musician Gregg Allman; later, he became romantically involved with Marlo Thomas. In the years that followed, there would be a string of men in Geffen's life, and Sue was known to be dismissive of several of them, always referring to herself as "Mrs. Geffen" in her customary self-mocking tone. Geffen recalled that when he was mistakenly diagnosed with bladder cancer in 1976, Sue was at his bedside, incessantly asking, "Am I in the will?"

In 1976, Sue made a significant addition to her roster of directors by signing Brian De Palma, who had recently received positive critical attention with two low-budget films, *Sisters* (1973) and *Phantom of the Paradise* (1974). *Obsession*, a 1976 homage to Alfred Hitchcock, performed only modestly, but De Palma had recently obtained some first-rate pulp material that would fuel his visual imagination: Stephen King's novel *Carrie*, the story of a girl with telekinetic powers who wreaks havoc on the high school classmates who torment her. Nancy Allen, who played Carrie's chief bully in the film, recalled that De Palma set up a series of private rehearsals at his home about a week before shooting began. "What he had us do were these theater games," Allen said. "We elected a class president, and each person had to make a plea for himself and campaign from the character's point of view. It was very useful—it really established those relationships, so when we came to the set, it was already there."

Carrie was shooting at MGM, where Daniel Melnick was head of production, and Sue and Bob Bookman visited De Palma on the set. Even though there was a no-parking rule in front of the Irving Thalberg Building, Sue left her car there. After the meeting ended, Sue and Bookman returned to find the vehicle surrounded by wood barriers. Sue backed over one of them, and as a guard came rushing over, she rolled down her window and purred, "Put it on Mr. Melnick's account."

As 1976 ended, Sue found herself more in demand than ever. She could never have given the proper attention to all the actors and directors who wanted to be represented by her, certain that their careers would flourish under her guidance. Given her outspoken nature and love of telling the unvarnished truth, she had lost surprisingly few clients, among them Richard Benjamin and Paula Prentiss, Dyan Cannon, and Rod Steiger.

But the most significant loss she suffered around this time was Mike Nichols, whose much anticipated comedy *The Fortune*, starring Warren Beatty and Jack Nicholson, had been released by Columbia in the spring of 1975. At the time, Ruth was visiting Los Angeles, and Sue arranged for a special screening of the film for her at the Beverly Hills Hotel. "This was all for her mother," remembered David Geffen. "And the next day, when I spoke to Sue, she said her mother was not impressed at all. She wanted to kill her mother. She always used to say, 'Sure—instead of being born to Princess Margaret, I got born to Ruth.' All of Sue's success meant nothing to her mother. I do recall Sue saying about her father, 'Who wouldn't commit suicide to get away from Ruth?'"

The Fortune received mostly negative reviews, and failed miserably at the box office. Nichols, who had triumphed so brilliantly in the 1960s with *Who's Afraid of Virginia Woolf?* and *The Graduate*, seemed unable to shake off the recent slump he had experienced with films like *Catch-22* and *The Day of the Dolphin*. His relationship with Sue had been prickly; they had never been particularly close, and to some he complained that Sue had been verbally abusive, and he saw no point in taking it anymore. Sue's brutal and sometimes cruel opinions were often absorbed by clients who were essentially insecure about their talent or their position in the Hollywood hierarchy. Nichols, for his part, did not lack confidence. For much of his career, he had enjoyed a tremendous string of successes and won many awards; he had a powerful belief in himself and his own talent.

Perhaps the real reason Nichols left Sue was that by this point he had developed an intense dislike of Hollywood. "Mike did not feel L.A. was a place he should be living," said Candice Bergen. "He felt it was too destructive there. Sue was very much a motivating factor, I think, of what to avoid in L.A."

Nichols returned to the New York stage and in 1977 made a magnificent comeback with a musical, *Annie*, and a play, *The Gin Game*, starring Hume Cronyn and Jessica Tandy, both of which enjoyed critical acclaim and long runs. He would not direct another film until 1983, under the guidance of Sam Cohn.

"Honeeey," Sue said once to Lou Pitt, "everybody leaves. Some just take longer than others." At that point in her career, however, it's doubtful that she actually believed it.

CHAPTER THIRTEEN

1977–1978

One client Sue was happy to see depart during this period was the trouble-some, temperamental Faye Dunaway. Sue's machinations to get Dunaway the part of Evelyn Cross Mulwray in *Chinatown* had turned out triumphantly: Dunaway had given her best screen performance to date. But there had been plenty of difficulty on the set of *The Disappearance of Aimee*, a made-for-television film, in which the star portrayed the charismatic evangelist Aimee Semple McPherson and found herself in perpetual conflict with director Anthony Harvey and costar Bette Davis. For many staff members at ICM, Dunaway was a problematic client. Joan Harris of the special services department remembered a time when Dunaway was planning a visit to New York and phoned Harris to ask her which exhibits were going to be on at the city's art museums. "I would be digging out the information for her," said Harris, "and she would say, 'Come on! Quick! *Quick!*' I said, 'Don't you ever snap your fingers at me again. You are being so rude to me, Faye.'" Dunaway apologized and the next day called Harris to say, "Hi, sweetie—how are you?"

Sue tired of Dunaway's temperamental outbursts fairly quickly. Some time after *Chinatown*'s release, Dunaway moved over to agent Joel Dean, who got her a high salary for a role in Stuart Rosenberg's *Voyage of the Damned*. Sue was pushing hard for Candice Bergen to play the monomaniacal television executive Diana Christensen in Sidney Lumet's satirical drama *Network*, which had a provocative script by Paddy Chayefsky and was predicted to be one of the big pictures of 1976. But MGM's Daniel Melnick didn't think Bergen was up to the part and was more interested in hiring Dunaway. "Every chance she would get," Joel Dean recalled, "Sue would badmouth Faye. But I won, and Faye got the part." On March 28, 1977, Dunaway's performance in *Network* brought her the Academy Award for Best Actress. Later, as Dunaway was standing outside the Beverly Hills Hotel, on her way to a victory party Lumet was throwing, Sue walked over to

Joel Dean and within Dunaway's earshot said, "Don't let this little trophy make Faye think she's a movie star. She's not. *The only movie star in the whole town is Barbra Streisand.* Don't let Faye get any fancy ideas that this Oscar means she's worth a million dollars a picture. She's not worth it." Dean suggested that Sue go over and tell Dunaway the same thing herself, and Sue shrugged and stalked into the hotel.

Having Lumet as one of her director clients helped make up for the disappointment of losing Peter Bogdanovich. One of the trickiest parts of Sue's job was to make a judgment on a script submitted to her by a producer that didn't yet have a home at a studio. She made her way through stacks of potential projects sent to her in the hope that one of her stars or directors might be attached, making for an easier studio sale. After the debacle of *At Long Last Love*, Bogdanovich was researching a script about the early days of moviemaking. One day Sue called him at home to tell him that Robert Chartoff and Irwin Winkler were producing a movie called *Starlight Parade* on that same subject. Sue liked the script by W. D. Richter and suggested that Bogdanovich simply film that one, rather than work on a competing picture. Bogdanovich insisted on doing a complete rewrite with Richter; the end result was over two hundred pages and had to be cut down considerably. "I always kind of regretted that I hadn't done the whole thing myself," said Bogdanovich. "I always felt this was not a good idea, but Sue was pressuring me. She kept saying, 'Arthur Penn is going to do this script if you don't do it.'" (Once again, Sue was throwing out Arthur Penn as a wild card to get her way.) The end result, *Nickelodeon*, would be released by Columbia, where Sue's close friend David Begelman was now studio boss.

The picture was cast largely from Sue's roster—Ryan O'Neal, Burt Reynolds, Tatum O'Neal—and although the leading female role had been written for Cybill Shepherd, right down to the character's streak of myopia, David Begelman refused to hire the actress for the part. The industry had placed much of the blame for the failures of *Daisy Miller* and *At Long Last Love* on Shepherd, and no amount of persuasion on Bogdanovich's part would change Begelman's mind.

W. D. Richter remembered that at this point, Bogdanovich, Shepherd, and Sue launched a bizarre scheme: they would stage a public breakup between the director and Shepherd so that Columbia couldn't object to

Bogdanovich's nepotism. "I was sitting in Peter's Bel Air office, talking about the script," said Richter, "and Sue and Cybill were talking about the strategy. I'm hearing out of my left ear this incredible conspiracy that is going to be sprung soon. I went to Irwin Winkler and said, 'I don't even know who should have my allegiance. I am so confused!'" Richter told Winkler about the plot, and the studio assured him that Shepherd had no chance of being cast in the film.

Columbia had, in fact, been planning to use Shepherd for a good secondary part in Martin Scorsese's *Taxi Driver*. Scorsese had been unable to find anyone he liked for the part, which he described as a Cybill Shepherd role. Sue had asked, Why not take Cybill Shepherd herself? Her client was cast—at a cut-rate salary of $25,000. Begelman now warned Bogdanovich that if he insisted on using Shepherd in *Nickelodeon*, he wouldn't honor the studio's commitment to put her in *Taxi Driver*. As a favor to Shepherd, Bogdanovich cast her friend Jane Hitchcock instead. "There are certain women who have a threat," said Bogdanovich. "Ava Gardner had it. Cybill had it. But the girl we used didn't. Jane Hitchcock was good—but she was very Lillian Gish, not Theda Bara."

Columbia refused to let Bogdanovich shoot *Nickelodeon* in black and white, despite the fact that he had had two black-and-white hits. At the time, Orson Welles, broke and down on his luck, was staying with Bogdanovich; Richter remembered the director occasionally lumbering through the room, like an ocean liner dressed in a caftan. Bogdanovich also wanted Welles for a key role in *Nickelodeon*, but Begelman refused to pay his salary. Ryan O'Neal and Burt Reynolds both agreed to chip in $25,000 apiece to cover it, but when Welles found out about it, he said he couldn't ask the two actors to give up so much and bowed out of the project, to be replaced by Brian Keith. In November 1975, the trade papers announced that Bogdanovich's differences with Columbia had resulted in the studio's withdrawal from the picture, but eventually Begelman and Bogdanovich ironed out their differences to the point that *Nickelodeon* could proceed.

Nickelodeon had its sneak preview in Tulsa, and the audience response was middling. On the way back to Los Angeles, when Sue started giving Bogdanovich notes on the picture, he exploded. "I lost it," he recalled. "I really yelled at her—the only time I ever did that with her. I felt she had hurt me on the last two pictures. She didn't support me. I felt the Burt

Reynolds thing hurt *At Long Last Love,* and she didn't support me on Cybill
and black and white for *Nickelodeon.* I was looking for people to blame, I
suppose, so I blamed her for some of it. That was it—the end of the relationship." *Nickelodeon* fizzled on release, and Bogdanovich took time off from
filmmaking and did not return until the release of *Saint Jack* in 1979—by
which time his A-list status was a thing of the past.

The parties in Bel Air were usually bigger than the ones on Dawnridge
Drive, but otherwise they remained essentially the same: carefully chosen
collections of directors looking to cast, actors looking for a part, now and
then a political leader like Henry Kissinger or Jerry Brown, a best-selling,
critically acclaimed author, and visiting figures from the publishing or television journalism worlds of New York. Sue told *Vanity Fair*'s Peter Biskind,
"If my mother had been outside in the rain, she wouldn't have been able to
get in." The fare was the same: simple, satisfying food like brisket, lasagna,
meatloaf, goulash. The smaller affairs were sit-down dinners at a beautifully appointed table, but the larger ones were buffets.
     When it came to entertaining, Sue might as well have taken her cue
from Phyllis McGinley's poem "A Word to Hostesses":

> Hostesses, then, when you are able
> To lure Celebrity to table,
> It is discreet to bear in mind
> He needs the comfort of his kind.
> Fetch other Names. Fetch three or four.
> A dozen's better, or a score.
> And half a hundred might be fitter.
> But even one will make him glitter.

     Jean-Claude was always the model host, keeping the conversation mov-
ing and the atmosphere bubbling, while Sue bore down on business matters. One person who was not often invited to the parties—usually because
he was throwing grand-scale, rival soirees of his own—was the legendary
agent Irving "Swifty" Lazar. "Sue was ballsy and smart, but it was my feeling that she had a mask," observed Barbara Howar, the Washington, D.C.,
columnist, author, and, later, reporter on television's *Entertainment*

Tonight. "I was a good friend of Swifty Lazar, and he was so jealous of her. She had all these big names around her, and that was in the up-the-nose era, with everyone snorting this and that. And Swifty would ask me, 'How much was snorted there?' I would say, 'Not as much as at your Oscar party.'" Still, Sue enjoyed Lazar's company and always bore in mind that he might be useful in getting many of her star clients signed up for lucrative book deals with the major publishing companies in New York.

In 1977, Sue invited Michael Black, who was now representing actors the caliber of Cliff Robertson and Fred Astaire, to one of her parties for the first time. Black wanted to make a good impression and asked her what he should wear. Sue replied, "Honeeey . . . stars can come in pajamas or a robe or a pillowcase. You'll come in a suit." He drove up in his rented Volkswagen, and when he entered the house, Sue, deep in conversation with Columbia's executive vice president of worldwide production, Stanley Jaffe, excused herself and told Black that he wasn't there to eat, he was there to work. Few people had yet arrived, but Black spotted a well-dressed man in the living room and went over to him, as instructed, and introduced himself. Suddenly the doorbell rang and the man politely excused himself to answer the door. Sue, who had witnessed the whole encounter, floated over to Black.

"*Good, honeeey, good.* You almost signed my *butler.* Honeeey, don't sign the help, okay? He's already paid. Stars are coming now—you can introduce yourself to *them.*"

Sue continued to have a warm mentoring relationship with Black—he remained one of the people at ICM with whom she had the greatest rapport. One night, while Jean-Claude was away in France, she called Black and told him, "Honeeey, pick me up tonight. We're going to a party at Jack Nicholson's."

Black arrived at the appointed time in his Volkswagen. When Sue came out to the driveway and spotted the car, she said, "Honeeey, let me give you a tip. If you were a multimillionaire or really powerful, and you drove up in a Volkswagen, people would say you were eccentric. When you're *you,* and you drive up in a Volkswagen, people will say you're lower rung. Not even B-list. And anyway, I can't even fit into that fuckin' car."

In the years to come, Sue remained fond of Black and eventually handed him both Anthony Perkins and Tuesday Weld from her own list. She

launched both of these transfers over dinners at her house, and Black was
given a coveted seat at the table, so that the actors would not feel that they
were being pawned off on a junior agent. "How smart of Sue," said Black,
"instead of having me call Tony Perkins and say, 'Hi, I'm Michael Black,
and I'm your new agent, day to day.'"

Tuesday Weld had not been in evidence on the Hollywood scene for
some time. In 1974, she had turned down the leading part in *The Stepford
Wives* and gone to England with her new husband, comedian and musician
Dudley Moore. The couple had a young son, and Weld had been leading a
very quiet life, but after several years she began to feel cut adrift. "Suddenly," she remembered, "I received a telegram from Sue saying, 'YOU
HAVE NOT BEEN FORGOTTEN.' It was not something she would do. If
you were gone, and not making a picture, you were gone, you know? The
telegram was very touching because she seemed to know the lonely heart of
an actress—because I feel that she had a lonely heart, also."

In 1977, Weld let Sue know that she was eager to work. Sue helped land
her a good role as Diane Keaton's troubled sister in *Looking for Mr. Good-
bar*, a hit about the promiscuous nightlife of a New York City teacher. (The
tag line was "When you can't find love, you take something else.") Weld's
performance earned her an Academy Award nomination for Best Supporting Actress, and she was soon at work in Karel Reisz's *Who'll Stop the
Rain*, opposite Sue's new client Nick Nolte.

Weld was a frequent party guest at Bel Air Road. "Sue mixed people
fantastically, and loved doing it," said the actress. "Once, she said, 'Woody
is going to pick you up.' I had never met Woody Allen. I was on one of my
exercise sprees, and he came in his limo to pick me up and I said, 'Let's
walk up there to Bel Air.' He said, 'Walk? Are you kidding?' He had the
chauffeur follow us for forty-five minutes. You don't walk in Bel Air."

Upon her return from England, Weld was reasonably sure that Sue would
want to represent Dudley Moore as well. But Sue turned him down, telling
Weld, "Honeeey, he's too short, and he's big in England, but nobody knows
him here, and I don't think it's going to work out." Sue turned Moore over to
Lou Pitt. "If it didn't present itself as a big, beautiful bouquet," observed
Weld, "she didn't work on it, let's say." Lou Pitt did very well with Moore,
who had an attention-getting supporting part in the 1978 comedy *Foul Play*
and the following year became a star in Blake Edwards's *10*. "When Sue

would miss an opportunity like that, she had the disappointment and rage
of an actress missing a part," observed Weld. "It was even worse. When she
didn't get the client after the client was handed to her, she could have a fit."

She missed another chance at an important client when she refused to
sign Burt Reynolds's girlfriend Sally Field. A 1960s TV sitcom star in
lightweight fare like *Gidget* and *The Flying Nun*, Field was a back number
by the mid-1970s. Her last attempt at a TV series, *The Girl with Something Extra*, had flopped, but in 1976 she suddenly emerged as a strong
dramatic talent, first in the feature film *Stay Hungry*, and crucially in the
role of a hideously abused girl with multiple personalities in the made-for-
television drama *Sybil*, which earned her a Best Actress Emmy. When Field
began making a move toward big-screen stardom, Sue remained unim-
pressed. Reynolds urged her to sign Field as a client, and Sue bluntly declined. "She said, 'Burt—are you out of your mind?'" recalled Rona
Barrett. "'You're crazy. No—I'm not handling her.'" Soon Reynolds left Sue
for another agent.

Around this time, Tuesday Weld was offered a promising script about a
young North Carolina woman who works in a textile factory and finds herself an unlikely labor union organizer. "I turned down *Norma Rae* because
I thought it was depressing and I didn't want to do it," said Weld. Sue felt
her client had made the right decision: she saw nothing at all in Harriet
Frank, Jr., and Irving Ravetch's script and found the subject matter grimy
and completely without interest. *Norma Rae* was a big hit when it was released in 1979, and earned Sally Field much acclaim and the Best Actress
Academy Award. Weld didn't care, certain that she would not have won the
Oscar had she played Norma Rae. But Sue told Rona Barrett, "You know
what kind of a schmuck ass I was? I didn't take that little five-feet-one Sally
Field and I lost Burt." To others she assumed her default position of having
a tantrum, telling them that she hoped Burt Reynolds—famous for wearing
hairpieces—would die of cancer of the scalp.

Jean-Claude, meanwhile, was making progress of his own professionally.
He had adapted the script for and directed his first movie, a French espionage thriller based on a novel by Pierre Boulle. *Le Point de Mire* was released in the fall of 1977, and with a cast headed by Annie Girardot and
Jacques Dutronc, it received some positive reviews but didn't make much of

an impression on the public. Jean-Claude hoped more than anything that he could start directing American films, and although Sue frequently spoke to studio executives and stars about him, she never represented him, for fear that it might appear nepotistic. Neither she nor Jean-Claude wanted him to be known in Hollywood solely as the husband of Sue Mengers, but finding work for him turned out to be a major challenge when he had no impressive credits on his resume. Everyone found him a charming and engaging host and a witty raconteur, but no one was willing to give him a directing job.

Sue always credited Jean-Claude with being a big part of her success. Always, she said, if it came down to a choice between her husband or show business, Jean-Claude would win easily. "How effective would Gerry Stutz and Helen Gurley Brown be without their Davids?" she asked *Women's Wear Daily*. "When I have a meeting, my head doesn't have to wander . . . 'Who, dammit, am I going to have dinner with?'"

"I often had the feeling that Jean-Claude was sitting back and watching the world cavorting around," said Jacqueline Bisset. "He was there, and part of it, but there was a degree of him sitting back. I rarely saw him sit forward in his seat. He sat with his back against the cushion, and he always seemed to be finding his way around Sue. And Sue was a very big personality. You did not want to go up against her." Frequently, however, Jean-Claude did engage Sue in fiery arguments across the dinner table. Many of Sue's friends and clients who liked Jean-Claude also felt that he maintained a rather condescending attitude toward his wife. He loved to discuss international politics—he leaned strongly to the right—and literature, while Sue, who was all but apolitical, wanted to share the latest piece of Hollywood casting and who was sleeping with whom. Jean-Claude often ridiculed her narrow interests in front of others. "I was not a great fan of Jean-Claude's," said Barry Diller. "I think he treated Sue poorly. He belittled her in public, or he took humorous advantage negatively of Sue, much, much more than she did of him."

With Sue devoting so many hours of the day to her job at ICM, Jean-Claude was inevitably left to play the role of the Hollywood husband with too much time on his hands. He often corresponded with authors whose books he admired, and occasionally, an epistolary friendship developed. One such relationship was born when Jean-Claude read Max Apple's collection of stories, *The Oranging of America*, which received considerable critical acclaim when it was published in 1976. Apple was teaching English literature at Rice University, and after corresponding with him, Jean-Claude flew to Houston for a visit. "He was a real French intellectual," recalled Apple. "I hate to pigeonhole, because he wasn't a type, but he talked ideas. Later I came to work a little in the movie industry, and it's not about ideas! I felt as comfortable with him as if he were an academic colleague. On the other hand, he was living the high life in a mansion in California, surrounded by glamorous people, and obviously he was drawn to that."

Occasionally Apple would come to stay for a week or so at Bel Air Road, and he was aware of the constant squabbling between Sue and Jean-Claude. When Apple told Jean-Claude that his teaching salary at Rice was only $12,000, Jean-Claude was horrified. "Our cook makes more than that!" he exclaimed, and tried to get Apple to move out to Los Angeles. For a time they worked together on a comedy script about a women's health club; Sue had arranged some start-up money through Columbia Pictures. Occasionally they dined with Barbra Streisand and Jon Peters. Apple observed Jewish dietary rules; one evening they went to a sushi restaurant in Beverly Hills, and before Apple would take a bite, Streisand had to have the chef come to the table to assure them that everything was kosher. Eventually Apple abandoned the script idea because he needed to attend to his wife, who suffered from multiple sclerosis, and his contact with Jean-Claude became less and less frequent.

Michael Caine had remained Sue's client throughout the 1970s, and during one of his trips to California to make a picture, he came to the house and met Jean-Claude. "You know something?" Caine said. "I used to knock around with a guy in Paris, and you remind me of him."

"Michael—it's me," said Jean-Claude.

The two old friends spent the evening getting caught up and reminiscing about the day, years ago, when they had met at a discothèque on Saint-Germain. Jean-Claude discussed his various investments with Caine; he studied the market closely and was already investing in Los Angeles real estate and would go on to do very well with various stock purchases, such as Intel.

Sue's client Herbert Ross was directing a film version of the Neil Simon play *California Suite*, about the problems of various guests at a Los Angeles luxury hotel. There was a key role Ross was having trouble casting, and one night, Sue invited Caine and Ross to dinner and seated them next to each other. Soon enough Ross cast Caine as Sidney Cochran, the gay husband of neurotic, Oscar-nominated actress Diana Barrie (Maggie Smith); the two are flown in from London and, holed up together while waiting to attend the Academy Awards ceremony, they hash out the problems of their marriage. "That was my big break for a big Hollywood movie," said Caine. "I wouldn't have got that without Sue."

Caine received excellent reviews for *California Suite*—both critics and audience members seemed to admire his courage in playing a gay man—and Sue engineered a dramatic increase in his salary. Caine received $1 million for being one of many stars in *The Swarm*, disaster-movie expert Irwin Allen's thriller about an attack by killer bees. "Henry Fonda, Richard Widmark, Olivia de Havilland," Caine recalled. "I thought it was going to be great. But they couldn't make bees interesting. We had loads of illegal immigrants in sheds destinging the bees. Every now and then, someone would yell 'HOT ONE!' and you would get stung." Sue thought these stories were hilarious, but she urged Caine to concentrate on the million-dollar salary and look ahead to the next movie, which would almost have to be better.

At Bel Air Road, the official reason for the parties often masked a web of ulterior motives. In the spring of 1978, Sue and Jean-Claude threw a party for Pauline Kael, the widely read film critic of *The New Yorker*. But it was clear there was a much more colorful drama going on in the second ring, as Sue went from guest to guest railing about Herbert Ross, who had just left her to sign with William Morris.

The real focal point of the evening, however, was John Travolta, whose performance in *Saturday Night Fever* Kael had recently reviewed enthusiastically. To Sue, Travolta was no longer "that fucking sweathog"; he was the hottest thing in pictures (and about to get even hotter, with the June release of his next movie, *Grease*). She spent the entire night pursuing him in a series of conversations that moved from room to room, and Travolta remained polite and charming but stubbornly elusive. As Sue recalled years later, "I was in a group and somebody passed me a joint. At the moment I took it, I saw him across the room looking at me, and I knew right then that I would never represent him."

• • •

It was inconceivable to Sue that some people might not actually care about money. When they told her they didn't, she simply refused to believe them. As if to ward off any possible lingering doubts that she might have taken another path in life, she armed herself with the position that everyone dreamed of fame, glamour, wealth; she often proclaimed that on Oscar night there wasn't a person on earth who didn't fantasize about winning an Academy Award. And occasionally, when she did encounter someone who didn't conform to her ideas, she was baffled.

In March 1978, Fran Lebowitz, the dazzlingly funny essayist for *Mademoiselle* and *Interview*, published her first book, *Metropolitan Life*, which received excellent reviews and quickly landed on the bestseller lists. Lebowitz's grumpy, self-mocking, urban couch potato literary persona matched up beautifully with Sue's. The book became a favorite of Sue's, which was hardly surprising, given that it included such Mengers-like observations as "Even when freshly washed and relieved of all obvious confections, children tend to be sticky. One can only assume that this has something to do with not smoking enough," and "The outdoors is what you must pass through in order to get from your apartment into a taxicab."

After the book's publication, Lebowitz's literary agent at ICM was besieged with requests for interviews. "But," Lebowitz recalled, "I never heard the note of hysteria in my agent's voice as when she called me to say, 'Sue Mengers called.'" Lebowitz was about to leave on a tour to promote the book, and Sue invited her to lunch during the Los Angeles stop. "There were no cell phones and no modern communications system," said Lebowitz, "and there was a constant stream of calls about the meeting with Sue, where I was supposed to be, where I was supposed to be standing. She had two secretaries who kept calling, and I nicknamed them January and February.

"So the day arrived when I was going to have lunch with Sue. And at a quarter to one, I called my agent and said, 'No one, including January and February, after all these phone calls saying to be out front, has asked me where I am!' And my agent said, 'Don't be ridiculous. You're at the Beverly Hills Hotel. Sue just assumed that. There's only one place that she would come to pick someone up from New York. So just be outside.'" Lebowitz did as she was instructed, and at the appointed hour Sue pulled up in front of the hotel in her silver Mercedes. As they drove to Ma Maison for lunch, Sue told Lebowitz that she had received an offer from David Begelman for $250,000 for the film rights to *Metropolitan Life*. "That was a huge sum at the time," said Lebowitz, "but I said, 'Sue, I do not want to sell this book to the movies.'"

Sue was stunned that Lebowitz would decline so large an amount, and protested, "This could be your 'Fuck you' money!"

Lebowitz, who had never heard the term, asked what it meant.

"That's when you have enough money that you can say 'Fuck you' to people," explained Sue, as she pulled up at a traffic light.

"How much money is that?" asked Lebowitz.

Sue looked blankly at her.

"Because I am telling you right now, 'Fuck you. I am not selling that book to the movies.' And she never believed me. She didn't believe me decades later."

They proceeded to Ma Maison, where an endless line of celebrities stopped at Sue's table to pay court. "It was like being in Las Vegas with Frank Sinatra," said Lebowitz. "They would all stand there, and she never asked anyone to sit down. Ursula Andress was in the restaurant, and she was incredibly beautiful, and Sue starts talking about how stupid Ursula Andress is because she has affairs with all these movie stars and she doesn't get any of them to marry her—she doesn't close the deal. She acts like a man. She thinks she can do whatever she wants. She has affairs with men like they have affairs with women. That was a central thing to Sue with women: they had to get married. Sue was extremely conscious of the brief life span of a movie star."

Recently, it had been in the news that Sue had signed a new contract with ICM for $600, 000. At the end of the lunch, Sue and Lebowitz passed a table where several actors' managers were sitting.

"Sue, we just wanted to tell you how fantastic it was, what you did, and how much we respected you for what you did," they told her, and Lebowitz recalled that the men went on talking about respect for several minutes. "I was thinking to myself, 'What did she do? Did she save a child from a burning building?' So I said to Sue afterward, 'What did you do?' And she said, 'I signed my new contract at ICM.' I said, 'That's what they respect you for? You mean, they're afraid of you?' Of course, in Hollywood, that means the same thing. I found that very funny."

In 1978, Sue took the risky step of embroiling herself in the biggest Hollywood scandal in some time. In February 1977, Academy Award–winning actor Cliff Robertson received a 1099 form for unreported 1976 income in the amount of $10,000. Knowing that he had never gotten such a check for that sum, Robertson began digging around. A preliminary investigation revealed that the check had been ordered by David Begelman, still riding high as the head of Columbia Pictures. (That fall, the studio would release Steven Spielberg's *Close Encounters of the Third Kind,* which would become one of the era's great successes.) Begelman initially said he had ordered the check as payment for some work Robertson had done on the promotional tour for Brian De Palma's mystery drama *Obsession,* released by Columbia in 1976. Studio employees suspected that Begelman had forged Robertson's signature on the back of the check, which was soon confirmed by an official from the Wells Fargo Bank in Los Angeles, where the check had been cashed. Columbia dealt leniently with Begelman, initially suspending him with a paid vacation and later reinstating him. Further investigation, however, uncovered the fact that Begelman had misappropriated additional money, totaling $65,000—a bizarrely minuscule amount, but given the money he was ultimately in charge of, enough to ensure his firing from the studio. The affair became known in the press as "Hollywoodgate."

What was baffling to many was why Begelman had stolen the money in such a clumsy manner that was so easily traced. If he had needed funds, he could have gotten them from any of his powerful friends in Hollywood—chief among them Ray Stark, one of many major players in the industry who came immediately to his defense. One day Begelman entered Ma Maison, and everyone gathered in the restaurant rose to give him a standing ovation.

Dissatisfied with the studio's handling of the scandal, Cliff Robertson and his irate wife, Dina Merrill, went public with it in the *Wall Street Journal.* The story continued to snowball: a reporter for *New West* magazine soon unearthed the fact that Begelman's Yale background was an invention. The fact was that Begelman suffered from torturous self-destructive impulses, and the need to lie constantly. Early in his career, he had fabricated a tony Ivy League background for himself, when, in fact, his upbringing was closer to Sue's.

Sue had enormous difficulty in comprehending Begelman's crime, which was so alien to her determined, focused, practical nature. The two had had their differences; Begelman was livid with her for telling Goldie Hawn to distance herself from Julia Phillips, who was planning to produce a screen version of Erica Jong's bestseller *Fear of Flying* as a big release for Columbia in 1978. But her loyalty to her friends was never more apparent than in her response to the Begelman scandal. Although he was no longer a part of her close inner circle, she felt that she owed him an enormous debt, because it was he who had launched her career in the agency major leagues. In addition, she adored Begelman's wife, Gladyce—and Begelman had been instrumental in getting *Point de Mire* set up for Jean-Claude. In collusion with Ray Stark, she began soliciting statements of support for Begelman from many of her powerful clients and friends in the industry, urging them to send them to Herbert Allen of Allen & Co., the New York investment bank that had owned a considerable share in Columbia for years. When Jack Nicholson refused to write such a statement, she wrote it for him and put his name on it—which infuriated the actor when he learned of it.

Sue telephoned Boaty Boatwright, who had recently left her home base in London for a quick trip to New York, asking her to urge her clients to send telegrams of support to Allen as well. Boatwright's client Norman Jewison was in Japan at the time, and Boatwright did as Sue asked, writing a statement and putting Jewison's name on it. "I figured, What's he going to do—never speak to me again?" recalled Boatwright. "But he did say, 'Boaty, you should have asked me.'" All in all, Sue was remarkably successful in getting stars to rally to Begelman's cause. Begelman was well liked in Hollywood, and Sue got a certain leverage out of the threat that many stars might not be willing to work at Columbia if Begelman was no longer a presence there.

Sue and Ray Stark also put pressure on Liz Smith not to report on the Begelman matter in her widely read column in the *New York Daily News*. Stark flew to New York for the express purpose of dissuading Smith from printing the story. Unlike Joyce Haber, Smith was a responsible, careful reporter who was interested primarily in objective journalism. "Ray Stark thought he owned me because he had met me through press agents, and would invite me to his house," said Smith. "He ordered me not to write the

Begelman story. I said, 'Ray, it's not me writing it! It's Cliff Robertson telling me to my face the truth. He's not a liar, and I've known him since he was an unknown, so he trusts me.'" Smith assured Stark that a few evenings as a guest in his private screening room did not mean she owed him a thing. The *Washington Post* analyzed the Begelman scandal in an article that ran on Christmas Day 1977, but it received little attention. Smith took the story, reworked it while giving the *Post* credit, freshened it with some comments that Robertson gave her, and got credit for bringing the story to a new level of public consciousness. Sue ultimately forgave Smith for running the story because it was politically expedient to do so.

Cliff Robertson found the 1980s a difficult time professionally and became certain that he was being denied work because he had spoken out against a beloved figure in the industry—though Sue always denied that she had ever in any way participated in his alleged blackballing. To her, Robertson's time as a star was long past, and he would have found film roles hard to come by even without his involvement in Hollywoodgate.

After leaving Columbia, David Begelman would become CEO and president of MGM in 1980. Soon it was reported in the trade papers that Begelman was on the verge of appointing Sue as the studio's executive vice president. Sue, however, denied the rumors, claiming that she had every intention of honoring her lucrative ICM contract.

Having pulled off the spectacular maneuver of getting Gene Hackman $1 million for the abysmal *Lucky Lady*, Sue now felt free to take the million-dollar fee and parlay it whenever she felt it appropriate. At times she could be downright capricious. George Segal remembered that Sue represented him for a single film, Universal's *Rollercoaster*, in 1977. The character Segal was playing was supposed to be carrying $1 million in extortion money in a briefcase, and Sue told Universal that she felt it was only fair that the actor got $1 million in salary. Ultimately, Segal received $750,000, then his going rate. "These were crazy numbers at the time," the actor remembered. "The salaries were going up—but that's what they were good at, at an agency like ICM."

At other times, Sue was simply aware that the studio wanted a particular star so desperately that it was willing to pay the price. For United Artists' *A Bridge Too Far* in 1977, she got Ryan O'Neal $1 million for five days' work.

The schedule stretched to seven, so the producer took an expensive watch off his wrist and handed it to O'Neal as payment for the extra two days. "I didn't tell Sue," said O'Neal. "She would have wanted part of the watch." *A Bridge Too Far*, top-heavy with million-dollar star salaries, seemed not to have a chance of recouping its $25 million cost, especially when greeted with weak reviews; fortunately, the box-office response in Europe was far healthier than in the United States, and the film eventually grossed in the neighborhood of $50 million.

O'Neal did not want to reprise his role as Oliver Barrett IV in *Oliver's Story*, Paramount's sequel to *Love Story*, and repeatedly turned down the script—until roughly a week before filming was set to begin in Boston and New York. The real inducement was the reported $3 million, plus a percentage of profits, that Sue negotiated for him. This time it turned out to be Paramount's folly: when *Oliver's Story* was released in December 1978, it was greeted with poor reviews and disappointing attendance. O'Neal was the subject of widespread criticism for the size of his salary, and it was felt that he hadn't been worth it—but Sue, ever loyal, disagreed, always falling back on the question, Why should the producers make all the money?

The prominent Los Angeles attorney Kenneth Ziffren, who was representing O'Neal at the time, received a fond keepsake from the negotiations for *Oliver's Story* that underlined Sue's basic attitude toward her job. It was a booking report that stated that O'Neal would be the first-position star in the film for a salary of $3 million. There was only one other notation: "Remainder of terms, call Ken Ziffren."

When Stanley Jaffe was casting his comedy about a kids' baseball team, *The Bad News Bears*, he phoned O'Neal to say he wanted to cast Tatum in the starring role, even though she had never played baseball. Several years earlier, O'Neal had gotten in a scuffle with Jaffe at a Hollywood party, and Tatum had kicked the producer in the knee. Jaffe was willing to let bygones be bygones, but O'Neal decided to have a little fun with him, and when Sue got an offer to engage Tatum for $150,000, O'Neal turned it down. Sue went back repeatedly to Jaffe, who agreed to raise Tatum's salary, but O'Neal kept refusing until the amount was $450,000 plus ten points of the gross after breakeven. O'Neal then remarked to his daughter, "Now I think I have to buy you a glove."

Sue delighted in driving such hard bargains, especially as she observed the strange phenomenon of films like *Star Wars* and *Close Encounters of the Third Kind* setting records at the box office. These were not Sue's kind of pictures; she had no interest in sci-fi and special effects, or in anything that might be spinning around in space. She regarded such films as part of a new attempt to infantilize the audience—the movies as one big boy's adventure story—and could not have been more dismissive of the huge merchandising component attached to them. In 1976, she guessed wrongly when she told a reporter, "Actually, I think it's a good time for new people, because if anything I think the trend is going to be back to low budget. . . . I think the studios are too nervous to keep on rolling the dice on two or three pictures. God forbid if they don't have a *Jaws* or whatever; then they're in a lot of trouble." Hollywood was in the midst of another immense change, one as sweeping as the one that had rocked it in the late 1960s. But this time, Sue was not able to fully embrace it.

CHAPTER FOURTEEN

1979-1980

On January 27, 1979, Sue was taking a Sunday night flight from Los Angeles to New York when a passenger on the plane attempted a hijacking. The hijacker's demands were unusual: to have Charlton Heston read a message on television. The 131 other passengers included Sue's friend philanthropist Max Palevsky, Dean Paul Martin, veteran actor Sam Jaffe, and Theodore Bikel. After several hours the plane was stormed and the hijacker subdued, with no fatalities among the passengers or crew. Sue told her seatmates, "If anything happens to me, take care of my coat."

When the news broke, Ed Limato, who had left New York to join the ICM team in Los Angeles, telephoned Joan Harris at home and told her to take the company car and meet Sue's plane at John F. Kennedy Airport. When Sue saw Harris, she asked, "What the fuck are you doing here?"

"Great greeting, Sue," Harris responded. "Your good friend Ed was afraid you were going to have the vapors from the attempted hijacking." Sue dismissed the company car and ushered Harris into her waiting limousine and on to Elaine's restaurant on Second Avenue, where the two had a midnight drink. There she told Harris what she also told several other friends: the worst part of the hijacking attempt had not been the panic that ensued, the feeling that she was about to die. The worst part had been Theodore Bikel, who insisted on trying to calm everyone by playing his guitar and singing "Hava Nagila." Sue told *Vanity Fair*'s Peter Biskind, "There is nothing worse than Theodore Bikel. Nothing. And so I was thinking, I'm gonna die listening to Theodore Bikel, and he wouldn't fuckin' sit down and shut up." But she seemed most incensed by the demand to have Charlton Heston deliver a message. She told everyone that she could have gotten the hijacker Barbra Streisand.

Boaty Boatwright met Sue at her suite at the St. Regis hotel, and remembered that after all the trauma of the hijacking, Sue had no difficulty calling the front desk to tell them she hated the suite and would need to be moved to a different one.

The following day, Sue had one of her carefully orchestrated face-to-face encounters with her mother when the Tramonts threw a seventieth-birthday party for Ruth. Her friends from her Rego Park neighborhood were in attendance, as well as many of the Sender relatives. Jean-Claude continued to get along with Ruth far better than Sue did, and he was a model host at the party, making certain that his mother-in-law remained the center of attention and effortlessly charming all her friends. Ruth, who had gotten even stockier with the years, wore an orchid corsage, while Sue, dressed in a sand-colored caftan, did her best to behave during the party, smiling indulgently when an enormous cake with strawberries was wheeled out with "HAPPY BIRTHDAY, MOTHER" written across the top.

Around Hollywood there was still much speculation that Sue might move into a top executive post at one of the studios, but the talk faded after Sherry Lansing became senior vice president of production at Columbia Pictures, while the studio was being run by David Begelman. Lansing was not the first female studio executive; in the mid-1970s, after a distinguished career at Bantam Books in New York, Marcia Nasatir had become a vice president at United Artists. But Lansing was still in her early thirties when her career took off, and unlike Sue, she had a personal style that her male colleagues did not find threatening. While Sue would derisively dismiss the ideas and concerns of studio heads and fellow agents if she found no merit in them, Lansing had developed great skill at taking the emotional temperature in a boardroom.

Lansing had begun her career as an actress, discovered by Howard Hawks, who cast her as a Native American girl in his 1970 John Wayne Western, *Rio Lobo*. But Lansing's beauty, charm, and intelligence, so immediately apparent in life, were less evident on-screen. She quickly found that she hated acting in movies and moved to the other side of the camera, becoming a five-dollar-an-hour script reader. In 1975, Daniel Melnick, who was heading up production at MGM, hired her to be the studio's executive story editor. Lansing quickly impressed her bosses with the acuity of her editorial insights. While still a junior player, she had inadvertently crossed swords with Sue: studio executives David Goodman and Frank Rosenfelt were throwing a surprise birthday party for Daniel Melnick, and had accidentally left Sue off their guest list. Lansing, in charge of invitations, hadn't noticed the oversight, and over the years Sue would remind her, jokingly and occasionally not so jokingly, of the slight. For some time the two women kept a respectful distance from each other. When Lansing rose to fame, Sue simply said that she had always assumed that if a top studio job would be offered to a woman, it would be offered to her first. And she didn't hesitate to say the same thing to Lansing's face. "People who are very caustic I am usually not that friendly with because they frighten me," observed Lansing. "I think—When is this going to turn on me?"

When Melnick left MGM for Columbia in 1977, he took Lansing with him, and in 1980 she was named president of Twentieth Century Fox, becoming the first female studio head in history. Always, Lansing showed a remarkable prescience for developing a story that would connect with what was happening or was about to happen in the world. In 1979, *The China Syndrome*, a drama about the attempts to cover up a near-meltdown at a nuclear power plant, was released by Columbia just two weeks before the Three Mile Island disaster. *Kramer vs. Kramer*, a marital drama that Lansing sponsored at Columbia the same year, appeared at a time when divorce in America was reaching record-high levels.

Despite the difference in their ages, Sue and Lansing shared much common ground. Lansing's mother had also escaped from Nazi Germany and was an intensely scrutinizing, endlessly critical parent. "I was a reflection of my mother," said Lansing. "If I went out the door not looking the way she thought I should look, she felt that was a bad reflection on her." Sue and Lansing both had a relentless work ethic that drove them to put in long hours. "I would look at other people running studios who didn't work so hard," Lansing recalled, "who didn't read every draft of the scripts, didn't go to sneak previews, didn't go to the test screenings, and I would say, 'I wish I could do that, but I can't.'" Sue admitted to Lansing that she was also driven to the arduous work of reading scripts, chasing down studio executives, listening to her clients' concerns and anxieties over the phone. To her clients, Sue often downplayed this aspect of her job. Ryan O'Neal remembered her saying to him, "Honeeey, I don't read 'em. I just book 'em." But it wasn't true, O'Neal believed, because he saw her go home with a stack of scripts every weekend.

Many people felt that Sue and Lansing shared another quality: a belief that theirs was essentially a man's world, and that certain things were, and perhaps even should be, beyond the grasp of women. But the differences between Sue and Lansing were equally striking. Lansing remembered the first time an executive hugged her in a meeting, and how accepted it made her feel. She practiced a positive, supportive attitude when dealing with people, and hugging became something of an overall metaphor in her career. Toni Howard recalled that if someone presented Lansing with a bad idea, the harshest thing she could usually bring herself to say was "Honey, I just can't put my arms around that."

"I never got hugs from my mother," Lansing recalled. "Sue never got hugs from her mother." The difference between the two women was that Sue responded by shutting down, using sarcasm and wit to keep people at an emotional distance, while Lansing expressed a genuine warmth and kindness that proved an enormous asset in the business.

Given how brusque and dismissive Sue could be, it surprised many that she was interested in psychiatry; in fact, she had seen an analyst regularly for many years. "She had so many wounds from childhood," said Carole Bayer Sager. "When one engages in therapy, it's not usually out of curiosity, but because you feel some pain or discomfort or inability to live in a certain way. Sue hated her mother."

Many who worked in and around the entertainment industry would later observe that they could feel an almost palpable turning of the earth as the 1970s gave way to the 1980s. There was a general feeling that the great cultural and social explosion of the 1970s had contracted, that the experimentation and expansion that had marked so much of the previous decade was tapering off into something much safer and more conservative. In his 2011 memoir *Lucking Out*, writer James Wolcott recalled his segue moment incisively: In December 1980, after he and his friend Pauline Kael attended a screening of a mediocre romantic drama, *The Competition*, their cab driver told them that John Lennon had been shot outside the Dakota apartment building on West Seventy-second Street. It was the moment, Wolcott wrote, "when the doorknob turned and the seventies were truly over."

Historians and biographers often categorize the passing of decades quite rigidly; in truth, eras often come to an end more subtly and imperceptibly. Throughout the 1970s, a great film—like *The Last Picture Show*; *The Godfather* and *The Godfather: Part II*; *Cabaret*; *The Conversation*; *The Long Goodbye*; *Harry and Tonto*; *Next Stop, Greenwich Village*; and *Nashville*—was not the rare, isolated occurrence it had been previously. Directors and writers were responding to the altered landscape of American life in that period with a new depth and edge—not in the synthetic way they had mostly responded to World War II, but in a bracing, unsentimental, highly personal way seldom experienced on the American screen.

But by the end of the decade, studios were rapidly losing the spirit of risk taking that had yielded such remarkable results. With production costs skyrocketing, everyone became focused on maximum box-office return, and not merely a respectable profit on a worthwhile picture. Pauline Kael, who took a leave of absence from her critic's post for an abortive fling at film producing in 1979 to 1980, later wrote in *The New Yorker* that studios didn't "want to make any movies that they can't protect themselves on. Production and advertising costs have gone so high that there is genuine nervous panic about risky projects." For Kael, this had a dreadful effect on moviemakers' creative spirit, since executives "postpone decisions because they're fearful, and also because they don't mind keeping someone dangling while his creative excitement dries up and all the motor drive goes out of his proposal."

Some bizarre distribution trends were starting to indicate the way things were going in Hollywood. *The Rose*, a drama starring Bette Midler as a Janis Joplin–like rock singer, was produced on a budget of $9.25 million, but its distribution budget (including prints and advertising costs) ballooned to $7.2 million. *Alien*, the biggest box-office hit of the summer of 1979, had a distribution budget of $9.2 million, surpassing its production cost of $8.9 million. According to the trade papers, even a "small" film like Peter Yates's *Breaking Away*, a sleeper hit for Twentieth Century Fox in the summer of 1979, had a production cost of $2.9 million and a marketing budget of $3.65 million.

In a way, what was happening in Hollywood in the late 1970s heralded the great social change that was about to transform the rest of the country. The November 1980 election of Ronald Reagan as president launched a profound split in the national consciousness. When Reagan asked in his campaign against President Jimmy Carter, "Ask yourself, are you better off than you were four years ago?" many people answered with a loud and resonant no. The economy became more of a central issue than ever: the increasing influence of the multinational corporate mentality was being felt in daily American life as it had never been felt before, and a large chunk of the population wasn't resisting it at all. The spirit of revolt of ten years earlier seemed all but dead; rising public apathy, and the overall turn inward, were reflected by the pitifully small voter turnout for the election of 1980.

What this all ultimately meant for Hollywood wasn't yet fully apparent to Sue, whose focus in reading a script remained on finding a good, compelling story with strong roles for her stars and making sure that it landed them fat salaries. She did not have the gift of being several jumps ahead of movie trends, predicting what was about to happen in the industry at large.

Although 1979 was not a good year for American films, it did not distress Sue unduly. As always, her paramount concern was to find the right vehicle for Streisand. It was a tough task: the star had not been happy with either *Funny Lady* or *A Star Is Born* and remained highly selective about material. Sue had turned down a number of scripts for her out of hand because she thought them inappropriate, including *Julia*, which became a big hit for Twentieth Century Fox, with Jane Fonda and Vanessa Redgrave. And Sue was dead set against Streisand's dream project, an original screen musical based on Isaac Bashevis Singer's story "Yentl the Yeshiva Boy," which the star envisioned as her move into writing and directing. The project had first come up when Streisand's friend Valentine Sherry mailed her a copy of the Singer story. She soon learned that David Begelman had already vetoed the idea, the first in a long line of resounding nos that Streisand heard whenever she mentioned her interest in the project. And few nos were more insistent than Sue's; she could not conceive that there would be an audience for Streisand playing a twenty-eight-year-old woman, a spinster starving for knowledge and education, who disguises herself as a boy and winds up falling in love with a fellow student of Talmudic law. And she would be *singing* the whole time.

Probably no one else in Streisand's circle thought that the "Yentl" project was a good idea, either; it was virtually the only thing in Streisand's career that Sue and Jon Peters agreed on. "Sue was always against *Yentl*," remembered Streisand. "She would say, 'How can you play this? . . . You're going to play a *boy*?'" Sometimes Sue was downright derisive about the idea in front of other people—not noticing that she was hurting her friend's feelings.

Sue's producer friend John Heyman remembered how disdainful Sue was of the entire project, but stopped short of interpreting her attitude as some sort of internalized anti-Semitism or veiled discomfort with her own Jewish identity. "Her Jewishness was a Jewishness of convenience," said Heyman. "She was Jewish when she was with Jews and she wasn't when she was with anti-Semites. The persona was crystal clear: It doesn't matter how things are. They have to look right. That is the key to Sue."

In the meantime, Michael Black read a script by Gail Parent and Andrew Smith called *The Main Event*, about a woman who loses her personal fortune and tries to put her life back together by promoting a broken-down prizefighter. Sue knew the script was second-rate, but she thought it might turn out to be a commercial hit for Streisand and Ryan O'Neal. Sue had failed to get anywhere with *The Bodyguard*, and O'Neal had suffered three box-office disappointments in a row with *Barry Lyndon*, *A Bridge Too Far*, and *Oliver's Story*. The part of the prizefighter appealed to O'Neal, who was a boxing aficionado with a twice-broken nose to prove it, and when Streisand said she wouldn't do the film unless he did, O'Neal came around.

The Main Event had originally been developed by producers Howard Rosenman and Renee Missel as a vehicle for Nick Nolte and Susan Blakely, fresh from their success on television's *Rich Man, Poor Man*. Michael Black was representing Rosenman, and when he read the script, he formulated what Rosenman later called "the most brilliant idea." Black told Rosenman and Missel that he was going to give the script of *The Main Event* to Sue to read. For some time she had been looking for a vehicle for Diana Ross and Ryan O'Neal, who were having a romance. Ross had been represented by Sue for a few years, but her film career had not fulfilled the promise of *Lady Sings the Blues*. Ross had most recently starred in the disappointing film version of *The Wiz*, directed by Sidney Lumet—a project that Sue had never been terribly excited about—and needed a hit. Universal had trouble booking *The Wiz* into a number of theaters in the American South, and although many of the studio heads loved the idea of an interracial love story, they were reluctant to go near it.

Barbra Streisand, Black informed Rosenman, had to be in principal photography on a picture by September 1, 1979, as per her long-standing deal with First Artists—and if she didn't choose something soon, Warner Bros. had the contractual right to insist she do any third-rate script it had lying around. Black pressed the script on Sue, telling her it was "like Tracy and Hepburn," and when Sue read it, she perceived its potential. The problem was that the script was at MGM and needed to be moved to Warner Bros. as a proposed project for First Artists.

The day after Sue read the script, she phoned Rosenman. "Honeeey . . . how do you like this? 'HOWARD ROSENMAN PRESENTS BARBRA STREISAND AND RYAN O'NEAL IN *THE MAIN EVENT!*' You'd be the first producer ever to work with her, other than Ray Stark and Jon Peters, that piece of shit."

She went on to ask if Rosenman had a tuxedo. When he replied that he did, she told him to take it to Holloway Cleaners and have it cleaned and pressed. "Then," Sue said, "when the movie opens, go to Holloway Cleaners, get your suit, bring it home and take off the plastic, go to the opening, and kiss Barbra Streisand." In other words, she was telling Rosenman that he was going to have nothing to do with the movie.

And he didn't—not much. Sue threw a big party on Bel Air Road to introduce Rosenman to Streisand and orchestrated the entire evening, down to telling him how to dress. "Wear those white painter's pants and your cowboy boots and your Ralph Lauren tweed jacket and a beautiful plaid shirt and that gorgeous belt that you have from Lalaounis," she instructed Rosenman. "Barbra is very swayed by young, chic men." Rosenman did as he was told, but when he showed up at Sue's, he felt like the least important person in a roomful of stars. At one point in the evening, Sue manipulated the crowd so that she created a private space in the living room for just Streisand, Jon Peters, and Rosenman, who went to work charming the actress to the point of introducing a conversational gambit Sue had suggested. Rosenman's parents were both Israeli. "Speak Hebrew to her," Sue advised. "Barbra will really be swayed by all that Jew talk."

Once Rosenman and Streisand had met, the next step for Sue was to get the material away from MGM, who had an option on it, and into production at Warner Bros. "This is what you're going to do," Sue told Rosenman. "Dick Shepherd, who runs MGM, is married to Louis B. Mayer's granddaughter. They are now separated and sleep in separate beds. He is very pretentious. He changed his name from Silberman to Shepherd. Go into that office and tell him you are fed up with his nonsense, and that his real name was Dick Silberman and that he and his wife sleep in separate beds. Get him riled up. He's such an amateur, this one."

Rosenman did as he was told. In a production meeting at MGM also attended by Renee Missel, Sherry Lansing, and several others, Richard Shepherd began his vision for *The Main Event*: he was going to hire Neil Simon to rewrite the script. Rosenman spoke up and protested that he was too young to make a Neil Simon movie. Everyone in the room stared at him, and he went on as Sue had instructed, railing at Shepherd that he was a pretentious piece of shit, and saying that everyone knew that he and his wife slept in separate beds and that he had changed his name from Silberman. Leaving the entire room dumbstruck, Rosenman stormed out. Shepherd dumped *The Main Event*, and Warner Bros. picked it up with Streisand and O'Neal.

During the film's preproduction phase, however, O'Neal began to get nervous. During the shooting of *What's Up, Doc?*, Peter Bogdanovich had been in complete command, down to acting out scenes for the two stars. On *The Main Event*, Streisand seemed to have total control over director Howard Zieff, taking over the wardrobe tests and many other facets of preproduction.

"It's all corny and silly," remembered O'Neal, "and I'm watching it, and I don't like it. So one night on the phone, I said to Sue, 'Have you seen the wardrobe she wants to wear? You've got to talk to her, but don't tell her I told you.'"

The Main Event was released in the summer of 1979 with the biggest opening-weekend gross of any film that year. It was a flimsy and mechanical comedy with a cheesy title song, yet it grossed over $40 million on an $8 million budget. Streisand didn't care for the end result, but Jon Peters, who was heavily involved in its production, loved it. Streisand resumed work on her screenplay for *Yentl* and continued the search for backers, while Sue continued to heap scorn on the project.

Several of Sue's other longtime clients were busy working in 1979. In November, Anthony Perkins opened on Broadway in Bernard Slade's new play, *Romantic Comedy*, which would run for 396 performances. Michael

Black accompanied Sue to the opening and remembered how the paparazzi mobbed her the moment she stepped out of her car.

After years of inactivity during her marriage to Steve McQueen, Ali MacGraw resumed filming in 1978, appearing in Sam Peckinpah's *Convoy*, a deal Sue had set up. By now she was separated from McQueen and needed to work. *Convoy* was followed by Paramount's *Players*, a romantic drama set in the world of professional tennis and produced by Robert Evans. Sue negotiated the leading female part for MacGraw, so the picture would serve as a temporary (platonic) reunion of her favorite golden couple. When it was released in November 1979, the picture received snide reviews and did disappointing business.

Neither *Convoy* nor *Players* accomplished anything other than to remind producers that Ali MacGraw was once again available for work. But in late 1979, Sue had strong-armed Sidney Lumet, who was still her client, into casting MacGraw in the leading female role in Lumet's new project, *Just Tell Me What You Want*. Written by Jay Presson Allen (based on her novel), it was a sophisticated comedy about a New York magnate and his mistress, who disagree on which direction their relationship will take. Lumet demanded that MacGraw read for the part but he was impressed by what she was able to do with it and agreed to cast her. It provided MacGraw with her happiest filmmaking experience.

"This was the best thing that she ever did for me as an agent," said MacGraw. "She fought for it, and it was a real piece of high-end agenting, with a big salary attached, and some work to be proud of. Sidney did two weeks of book-memorized rehearsal—unheard-of. If he saw something in an actor, he knew how to get it out, as much as it was ever going to come. That's not true of many directors. You'd better come to work prepared to blow their minds, because they are not going to be watching you." MacGraw drew positive reviews for her performance, and although *Just Tell Me What You Want* was not a hit, it received much attention for its climactic fight scene, in which MacGraw bashes Alan King with her purse in the middle of Bergdorf Goodman.

The year brought much better luck to Sue's other golden girl, Candice Bergen. Alan J. Pakula, by now a client of Sue's old friend Boaty Boatwright, had turned out some of the decade's most stimulating and sophisticated movies, including *Klute* and *All the President's Men*. Pakula was now casting his newest film, a low-key adult comedy called *Starting Over*, starring Sue's former client Burt Reynolds as Phil Potter, a divorced man fumbling his way through single life.

One night at Bel Air Road, Sue seated Candice Bergen next to Pakula at dinner. Conversation naturally turned to his new film. A few days later when she read the script, Bergen was immediately drawn to the starring part of Marilyn Holmberg, the plucky spinster schoolteacher looking for a man who will respect her. Sue lost no time knocking down this idea, assuring Bergen that the choice role in the script was Jessica, Reynolds's no-talent wife, who ends her marriage in search of success as a songwriter, which she miraculously achieves. Initially Bergen was offended by the idea; the part of the wife was definitely a secondary one. "But Sue was absolutely right," the actress commented years later. "What was I thinking? The fact that I was thinking of doing the lead in that movie was *nuts*. I was not equipped to do it—and naïve enough not to know."

In 1971, in a rather harsh review of Bergen's performance in *Carnal Knowledge*, *The New Yorker*'s Pauline Kael wrote that she had always felt that the actress "suggested some bright possibilities as a comedienne." Sue agreed, hoping for some of the actress's wit and charm to register on-screen in a splashy way that they had so far failed to do. Her instincts paid off, and Bergen gave a deft comic performance as the hopelessly narcissistic wife. She hilariously executed her off-key screeching of Marvin Hamlisch and Carole Bayer Sager's pitch-perfect parodies of late 1970s pop ballads, and she was rewarded with her best reviews to date; Kael acknowledged that Bergen gave "the film its only surprises." The following February, Bergen received her first Academy Award nomination, for Best Supporting Actress. Her father, Edgar Bergen, had died recently. "My father would have been so proud, I thought," the actress wrote in her memoir, "but more important, so was I."

Starting Over would sharply redirect Bergen's career path. Soon she was cast in another attention-getting comic role, as a self-dramatizing novelist in George Cukor's final picture, *Rich and Famous*. But by that time, Bergen had been receiving pressure from other trusted associates to leave Sue, with the assurance that she could get better parts. Sue's sharp, personal criticisms only exacerbated the situation, and soon Bergen left her for agent

Joan Hyler at William Morris, regarded by some as a Sue Mengers wannabe. The actress recalled that Sue's reaction was one of betrayal and shock; Bergen's departure also seemed to vindicate Sue's feelings about how weak and untrustworthy actors were, and how foolish she herself was to invest anything of herself in her friendships with her clients. The morning Bergen's name was included among the Academy Award nominees for *Starting Over*, Sue sent her a curt telegram that read, "CONGRATULATIONS. LOVE, SUE." Bergen interpreted it as a gesture of barely concealed contempt, but the two of them would manage to remain relatively friendly for many years.

Sue's obstinacy would often vex those sitting on the other side of the negotiating table. In the late 1970s, Frank Price, chairman and CEO of Columbia, had developed a comedy called *Used Cars*, and felt Ryan O'Neal would be perfect for the lead. But Sue rejected the idea. Price felt that her prejudice against the project stemmed from the fact that director Robert Zemeckis and producer Bob Gale, who also collaborated on the script, were relatively new filmmakers. "I think Sue could only be persuaded by accepted industry opinion and a 'name' director. I think it would have worked had Ryan done the movie, and that would have given his career a needed boost. Had it missed, Sue could have explained that Ryan did it to encourage talented young filmmakers and never expected a big hit. But I think the kind of judgment required—judging the material and the potential of a no-name director, was foreign to her." *Used Cars* was eventually made with Kurt Russell in the lead, and had a middling reception in 1980.

Not long after, producer Brian Grazer approached Sue about the possibility of Barbra Streisand's appearing in a comedy-fantasy he was developing called *Splash*. Sue looked over the script and handed it back to Grazer, snapping, "Not enough lines." The picture was a huge hit when it was released in 1984 with Daryl Hannah and Tom Hanks, and made stars out of both.

By 1980, Michael Caine's career was badly in need of rejuvenating. He had appeared in two consecutive failures, Irwin Allen's *Beyond the Poseidon Adventure* and Michael Ritchie's abominable *The Island*. He was becoming one of those odd phenomena in Hollywood: actors who retain their major stature even after appearing in a long string of flops. Sue felt that Caine badly needed a wild card, a complete change of pace, to shake up audiences' complacent attitude toward his screen persona. In late 1979, she received the script for Brian De Palma's thriller *Dressed to Kill*. De Palma was exceedingly hot at the time, yet an oddly underemployed director. Despite excellent press for his 1976 hit *Carrie*, it had been a year before he was able to line up another project, *The Fury*, for which Sue got him $300,000 and turned the rest of the negotiations over to Bob Bookman. When Sue read the script of *Dressed to Kill*, a kind of erotic fantasia on Hitchcockian themes, she thought Caine should play the transvestite psychiatrist. "I didn't think there was a problem with doing this," said Caine. "I do think American actors were sometimes wary of doing that sort of part. They thought they would lose their female audience. But I wasn't a movie star like that, so I could do anything like that and get away with it. Also, I was married with two kids, so nobody thought I was gay in the first place."

Dressed to Kill was another Sue Mengers package: cast in the leading female role of the prostitute was a new client, De Palma's talented young wife, Nancy Allen, who had appeared in *Carrie*, *I Wanna Hold Your Hand*, and Steven Spielberg's soon-to-be-released *1941*, which had excellent word of mouth. Allen met Sue at a Hollywood dinner party also attended by Martin Scorsese, George Lucas, and Steven Spielberg. At the time, the actress was represented by Allan Badiner, but Sue sidled up to her at the dinner and said, "Fuck Allan Badiner. *I* want you!"

Dressed to Kill was initially developed as a Ray Stark production, but trouble started between producer and director when Stark insisted on Suzanne Somers for the part of the hooker, and De Palma rejected the idea, insisting that he had written the part for Allen. At this point, George Litto, a talented producer who had been De Palma's agent years earlier, swept in and told De Palma that he could secure him a $1 million salary on *Dressed to Kill* if the production was moved to American International Pictures (later Filmways). "AIP was a little different from Ray Stark," Nancy Allen said with a laugh. "But Brian wanted to go for the bigger deal and he probably figured he would have more control at AIP." It was a potentially explosive situation, given Sue's close friendship with Stark, but Allen felt that "Sue was okay with it as long as Brian was happy. This was not the biggest fish she had to fry at the time."

Allen's professional connection with Sue was short-lived. The actress, confident that the forthcoming *1941* would be a big hit, was disappointed in the featured billing that George Litto offered her on *Dressed to Kill*. When she complained about it to Sue, her hurt feelings were swiftly dismissed. "She said, 'At this rate of dealing, it's not even worth it.' It was a big deal for me to ask, but I felt strongly about it. After the movie was over, George said, 'You were really good in it. You deserve to have your billing moved up,' and he went to Michael Caine, who said yes. But Sue was kind of funny that way. She told me, 'You don't tell them you're a star. They tell *you* you're a star.' In other words—be quiet." Soon after *Dressed to Kill* was released in the summer of 1980, to strong reviews and big box office, Allen returned to Badiner.

In the midst of all these successes, Sue became more Sue-like than ever before. The persona was well established; now it was being refined and perfected. Every day, she would barrel into the offices of ICM, to be met by one of her secretaries at the elevator. "Get me Ray Stark!" Sue would bark. "Get me Bob Evans! Send this script back to Sid Sheinberg!" Her colleague Arnold Stiefel remembered, "You knew she was in the business. And you weren't."

By now agent Ed Limato was clearly bent on entering the ICM Personality Sweepstakes, and would parade around the offices in his bright red and bright yellow jackets, carrying a red-rimmed or gold-rimmed coffee cup to match. Limato had an office a few doors down from Sue and had a young gay secretary who was both devoted to him and wanted to send the message to everyone that his boss was just as important as Sue. One day, when Sue began hollering to her assistants, "Get me Barbra! Then get me Ryan!," Limato's secretary called out, "Ed! Ed! Exciting news! Patrice Munsel on line three! She's calling from that dinner theater in Maine. *Call Me Madam* has been extended!" Sue thought this was hilarious. As she passed by Limato, she purred, "Don't keep Patrice waiting, Ed."

After the confusion over Barbra Streisand's appearance at the Royal Film Performance of *Funny Girl*, Sue was determined never again to commit another such faux pas. For years she studied the lives of the British royal family, mastering all the finer points of protocol and memorizing the distinctions

among recipients of the OBE, CBE, and DBE on the Queen's annual honors
list. By the time she had completed her education, she could practically di-
agram complete family trees dating back generations, including the most
obscure members of the nobility.

In London in the fall of 1978, at a party at the home of drama critic
Kenneth Tynan and his wife, Kathleen, Sue had once again met Princess
Margaret, whose rebellious nature and sophisticated, party-girl persona
were bound to appeal to her. Sue told the princess that if she happened to
be in Los Angeles, she would love to throw a party for her. In March 1979,
she received a call from the princess's social secretary informing her that
the princess would be in California that fall and would love to take Sue up
on her offer. "It seemed like we did nothing from March to October but plan
this party," recalled Sue's former assistant, Cindy Pearson. The reception
was held only weeks after the Irish Republican Army murder of Lord Mount-
batten, so security was at a maximum. "The party was on a Saturday night,"
said Pearson, "and several days before, Scotland Yard people were sent
with bomb dogs to smell the house." A third-floor bathroom was locked
after the dogs had cleared it, and no one could use it until the princess's
arrival.

It was Sue's most elaborate and exclusive gathering yet, and had she
never thrown another party, it would have cemented her reputation as Hollywood's most imaginative hostess. The evening validated the old cliché: if a
bomb had gone off at Bel Air Road, half of Hollywood really would have
been obliterated. Sue was furious with Steve McQueen for having poisoned
himself with cocaine and not shown up, but his presence was scarcely
missed, given that the guest list included Barbra Streisand, Jack Nicholson,
Candice Bergen, Michael Caine, Robin Williams, Neil Diamond, Ryan
O'Neal, John Travolta, and Gregory Peck. Helicopters hovered outside the
windows of the house: Sue sat with Princess Margaret for most of the evening, and Michael Caine remembered, "They got on like a house on fire."
On this particular night, there was no cocaine set out in sugar bowls, although Jack Nicholson recalled that "Sue accused me of ruining her connection to the royal family. At the party Gore Vidal kind of nudged me into
offering Princess Margaret a sample of illegal substance. She declined. But
Sue forever said that I had destroyed her chance to be invited into the

queen's boudoir, where she hoped to go." There was a formal sit-down dinner for which Sue produced all her best china and silver. (In the days leading up to the event, many of Sue's friends and clients thought she was going to have a nervous breakdown; late in the game, she frantically telephoned Marcia Diamond to bring over her buffet plates, because they matched Sue's set, and she feared she didn't have enough.) In the end, all her efforts paid off beautifully, as everyone judged the event a complete success. Sue always denigrated the evening, claiming that she had failed to charm Princess Margaret. The guest of honor lived up to her reputation by having a healthy amount to drink as the evening went on; Michael Black recalled that "Princess Margaret got a little sauced and was definitely coming on to John Travolta."

Sue and Jean-Claude had always shared a caustic wit; their ability to top each other's remarks had enlivened the dinner parties at both Dawnridge Road and Bel Air Road. Sometimes, however, their epigrammatic jousting curdled into something much more unsettling—less a John Van Druten comedy and more of an August Strindberg drama. There were evenings when Jean-Claude's resentment at being an underemployed Hollywood husband would boil over. Sue would goad and bait him, then playfully retreat into her Baby Doll routine—"Jean-Claude, honeeey, come light Susi's cigarette"—which would make him even angrier.

Rona Barrett and her husband, Bill Trowbridge, often socialized with Sue and Jean-Claude. "When we were out together," Barrett remembered, "my husband and I thought we were seeing the Wars of the Roses. They could be so angry and nasty and mean to each other. I think there had been a moment when Sue thought she was never going to get married. I couldn't always get into Jean-Claude's brain, but I would say that he saw something in her that really interested him, and I think he had a great fascination with heavier-set women. There was something about Sue: when she was all dressed up, she was so attractive—and so unusual. But underneath it all, Jean-Claude was never her type. Never."

Sue wanted Jean-Claude to work more than he did, certain that it would take only one financially successful film to push his career down the road. She felt that Jean-Claude should definitely pursue directing, since most screenwriters were treated so abominably in Hollywood. She frequently complained that writers not only were underpaid but were subject to directors' mercurial egos; a script might be accepted by an actor, only to be rewritten by the director prior to the first day's shooting. (She also believed that directors were underpaid, most of them getting somewhere in the neighborhood of $250,000 to $500,000, with very few making as much as $750,000.)

Jean-Claude's taste in movies was excellent—he was particularly drawn to Louis Malle's work—and he favored complex, slightly off-center ideas for pictures. But he never had sufficient clout or enough of a track record to land a good Hollywood film. Then, in 1980, he came up with an idea that seemed as if it might land him the Hollywood success he had been chasing for so long. The concept was unusual—a comedy with semiserious overtones about people in Los Angeles who work at night. David Susskind had agreed to produce at first, but then suddenly reneged.

At the time, Sue knew about a special arrangement that Jerry Weintraub and Leonard Goldberg had to produce a string of films for Universal, anything they wanted, as long as the budget didn't exceed $4 million. The hugely expensive *1941* had opened at Christmas 1979 and turned out to be far from the hoped-for blockbuster, and the studio was opting for more low-budget films in the near future. Since the idea for *Night People*, as it was originally called, had started with Jean-Claude, Sue managed to sell him as director, and with the film being such a low-stakes project, Universal approved him. W. D. Richter, who had recently had a winning streak with his scripts for Philip Kaufman's remake of *Invasion of the Body Snatchers* and Stuart Rosenberg's *Brubaker*, was hired to write the screenplay. When Jean-Claude read it, he was delighted: it was just the kind of offbeat movie he longed to make, a comedy that didn't target its laughs with direct hits, but one in which the humor emerged through the characters and atmosphere. He was thrilled when Universal green-lighted the script.

The story dealt with George Dupler, who has served for twenty years as an executive of a Los Angeles drugstore chain. In the opening scenes he loses his temper, punches his boss, and throws a chair through the office window. Because he's a senior staff member, he's dealt with leniently: he is demoted to become manager of one of the company's all-night drugstores in a nondescript part of town. While his professional life is falling apart, George learns that his son, Freddie, is having an affair with an older married woman, a blond, suburban housewife named Cheryl Gibbons. George meets with Cheryl to talk her out of seeing his son; it turns out she is a daffy and completely untalented aspiring songwriter, whom George falls in love with himself.

Sue set to work getting her clients into *All Night Long*, as the film was eventually titled. Gene Hackman, with his Everyman persona, was ideal for the part of George. Sue and Jean-Claude both felt that the role of Cheryl would make an excellent change of pace for Barbra Streisand—but Streisand, deeply occupied with *Yentl*, passed on it. W. D. Richter recalled that when Hackman heard Streisand had been approached about playing Cheryl, he had been thrilled by the prospect. "It was a way for Hackman to realign himself in the Hollywood superstar structure by being in a romantic comedy opposite Barbra Streisand. When Barbra passed, I think for honest reasons, Gene was crestfallen." Tuesday Weld also declined the role, which inflamed Sue. Loni Anderson, then very hot because of her hit TV series, *WKRP in Cincinnati*, was pursued for a time, but the part finally went to Lisa Eichhorn.

Along with Meryl Streep, Eichhorn was considered the fastest-rising young actress in films. She had scored an immense critical success in John Schlesinger's 1979 World War II drama *Yanks*, earning two Golden Globe nominations for her performance. "The real discovery of *Yanks* is Lisa Eichhorn," wrote Kathleen Carroll in the *New York Daily News*. "She is absolutely enchanting." Eichhorn's work in James Ivory's *The Europeans* and Larry Peerce's *Why Would I Lie?* had also been well received, and now there was talk of a possible Academy Award nomination for her superb portrayal of an alcoholic in the critically acclaimed independent movie *Cutter and Bone* (later retitled *Cutter's Way*).

The cast rehearsed for two weeks. In the evenings, Eichhorn would go to Gene Hackman's house for a swim and further discussions about their roles in the film. She was in awe of Hackman and remembered later that their time alone was "getting perilously dangerous, because I knew he was a married man. I was intrigued by him, so it was, 'Okay—I think I'd better go home now.'"

A little over three weeks into shooting, Jean-Claude had finished only a few of Eichhorn's scenes. She remained thrilled to be working with Hackman. "I remember we shot this scene where we were sitting opposite each other in a coffee shop," Eichhorn recalled. "And Gene looks at me and says, 'You are so beautiful.' I didn't grow up with anyone telling me I was beautiful. He said, 'You are luminescent on-screen.' I remember the word. 'Luminescent.'"

W. D. Richter was on the set at the time and recalled that Hackman seemed to be withholding something vital from Eichhorn in their scenes together. "Jean-Claude was a nice man," said Richter, "but he was confronted with this horrible realization that Hackman was going to subvert the process because he so resented being opposite Lisa Eichhorn. He would be a pain in the ass to her, do weird little actorish things to her in her close-ups, making it hard for her to be at her best. We could tell from the dailies it was not working. He was being cold to her in a weird, subtle way, and none of the Hackman charm was coming through."

Eichhorn does not remember having the impression that Jean-Claude was upset with her performance. He would occasionally ask her for another take, to try doing something a little differently. Just business as usual.

At the time, it was widely reported that Sue worked for months beating Barbra Streisand into submission to accept the part of Cheryl and "save" *All Night Long*. What really happened was that Sue was determined to have a big star play the part of Cheryl to help drive her husband's movie to box-office victory. When she saw the rushes, she complained to Jean-Claude that the chemistry between Hackman and Lisa Eichhorn was all wrong. "Honeeey, the rushes on Lisa Eichhorn are a *horror*," Sue told Michael Black at the ICM offices. The question of Barbra Streisand's taking the leading role arose once more.

Streisand was still holed up at her house on Carolwood Drive with the script of *Yentl* and was getting an acute case of cabin fever. She had poured an enormous amount of time and energy into work on the project, and she wanted something that would take her out of herself for a while so she could return to *Yentl* refreshed.

One night, when Streisand was a guest at Bel Air Road, Sue asked if she would reconsider playing Cheryl, telling her that she was sure she could get her a $4 million salary.

"I felt very alone, tired and frustrated," Streisand remembered. "She offered me her husband's movie that was only six weeks' work, which would have been a nice respite from my writing. And it was playing a ditzy, untalented housewife. Martin Scorsese had offered me *Alice Doesn't Live Here Anymore*, and it was the part of an untalented singer, and I remember at the time I thought, 'How the hell do I do that?' Then she told me she would get me more salary for *All Night Long* than any man or woman had made, so that intrigued me, too." Streisand, after looking at the script again, agreed, provided the financial deal was approved by Universal.

Sue called Leonard Goldberg at home on a Saturday and blurted out, "Barbra wants to do the movie." At first Goldberg didn't know what she was talking about, and when she explained her plans for *All Night Long*, he replied, "Sue, this doesn't make sense."

"What doesn't make sense?" asked Sue. "I'm telling you that you can have Barbra Streisand."

Goldberg held firm. "Is this a new pattern?" he asked. "We're going to shoot a movie with unknown people and then show it to stars to see if they want to do it?"

"I'm doing you the courtesy of calling you as producer," said Sue. "I could call Sid Sheinberg at Universal, and if you don't wish to discuss it with me, I *will* call Sid Sheinberg."

Goldberg immediately phoned Ned Tanen, Universal's president of production, who jubilantly said, "Great! We'll shut down and then we'll start up again!" Goldberg emphasized how costly Streisand's casting would be, and Tanen responded, "It's Barbra Streisand! We'll do it."

Jerry Weintraub recalled that he was as appalled by the entire deal as Goldberg was. "I said to Sid Sheinberg, 'How can you do that? It makes no sense.' I thought it was wrong. The whole picture wasn't as much money as Barbra's salary. I said, 'If you're going to do that, I'm not going to stay involved.' But that's what Universal and Sheinberg wanted, so as long as they paid me, I was fine."

What is astonishing is that Sue, with all her professional savvy, did not grasp that she was tossing her husband into a potentially explosive situation. Not one person in her professional circle believed that putting Streisand in Jean-Claude's film was a good idea. "I begged her not to do it," said

David Geffen. *"Begged* her." So did Robert Evans. So did many others. But Sue would not be dissuaded. With Streisand above the title, *All Night Long* was sure to be a big hit, and after a career of waiting for the phone to ring, Jean-Claude would finally enter the golden circle of Hollywood's bankable directors.

CHAPTER FIFTEEN

1981-1982

For everyone concerned, *All Night Long* looked like a project to inspire envy—the Hope Diamond of Hollywood, 1980. It was supposed to give Barbra Streisand a much-desired change of pace as an actress. It was supposed to provide Gene Hackman with an A-list romantic leading-man luster that had eluded him, especially in recent years, when he had been appearing mostly in middling action movies. It was supposed to catapult Jean-Claude into the top ranks of directors. It was supposed to cement Sue's reputation as the most powerful woman in Hollywood—someone who had gambled by pairing her most potent star client with her unknown husband, and won. But *All Night Long* turned out to be the Hope Diamond only in terms of the attendant curse it transmitted to almost everyone involved.

On Mother's Day weekend 1980, Lisa Eichhorn was visiting her parents in Connecticut when the phone rang at one in the morning. It was Jean-Claude, who said simply, "It's not working."

Eichhorn didn't quite catch his meaning. When, after a stiff silence, he repeated, "It's not working," she replied, "What can I do? What can we do to fix it?"

"You don't understand," said Jean-Claude. A heavy silence followed, and Eichhorn thought, I'm going to make him tell me. And then he did.

"We're replacing you."

"Oh," said Eichhorn, trying hard to recover from how stunned she was. "Who is replacing me?"

"This should make you feel better," said Jean-Claude. "Barbra Streisand."

"I later read, subsequent to that, that they fired me and then Barbra Streisand stepped in," Eichhorn said. "But on that night, Jean-Claude told me that she was taking my place. If I had been replaced by Sissy Spacek or Amy Irving, I would have understood it. It would have been devastating to be replaced by a peer, but it was more devastating to be replaced by someone who wasn't a peer. I couldn't get my head around it."

Eichhorn kept hold of her emotions until Jean-Claude hung up, but then collapsed, sobbing. When she had regained some degree of composure, she telephoned her business manager, Jay Julien, to tell him what had happened. Julian responded, "The motherfuckers have to pay you." And they did—Eichhorn received her full salary of $250,000.

The next day, she got on a plane to Los Angeles, and as soon as she arrived at her rented house in Benedict Canyon, the phone began ringing incessantly. Among the calls she received was one from Sue's good friend Warren Beatty. "I had an unlisted number," Eichhorn said, "and I don't know where Warren Beatty got it. But he said, 'Hi, Lisa. It's Warren Beatty. So sorry. Is there anything I can do?'"

According to *All Night Long*'s lead editor, Marion Rothman, Jean-Claude strongly resisted replacing Eichhorn. "He was so opposed to it," said Rothman. "He really did think she was a lovely actress. I don't know what sort of arm-twisting went on, how they convinced him of it. But he was desperate to have Lisa in the film."

The press jumped on the story gleefully, some reporters taking pains to portray the situation as a turf war between ICM and William Morris, since Eichhorn was a WMA client. Eichhorn's agent, Ed Bondy, turned out to be no help at all in dealing with the fallout. Bondy had a long history of making abusive comments to the actress, calling her a "stupid cunt," and saying, "I want to suck your boyfriend's dick." Years later Eichhorn stated, "There's a part of me that feels he had some of the best actresses in Hollywood so he could destroy them."

Somehow, the decision was made to portray the incident as Eichhorn's failure to deliver. Jean-Claude complied, assuring the press that she had been miscast, but Leonard Goldberg disagreed with Richter's assessment of Eichhorn. Decades later Goldberg recalled that there was nothing wrong with the rushes of Hackman and Eichhorn. "You didn't walk out thinking, 'Wow, what's going on between them is explosive,'" said Goldberg. "But they were fine. They worked well together, and I didn't see any trouble between them." Once Jean-Claude began to speak to the press, Jay Julien vowed to Eichhorn that he would "make sure the motherfucker never makes another movie."

The press played along with the campaign against Eichhorn; it was widely reported that her interpretation of Cheryl Gibbons had been too ethereal and not earthy enough. Ed Bondy tried to make light of it in the press, implying that any actress had to be philosophical when she found herself replaced by Barbra Streisand.

Being fired from *All Night Long* changed the entire trajectory of Eichhorn's fast-rising career. Suddenly the phone stopped ringing. Bondy, perhaps fearing Sue's enormous influence around town, remained neutral in the matter. Eventually Eichhorn would leave William Morris for Creative Artists Agency, which was fast emerging as the hot new agency in town. But her career would never recover the momentum it had in the late 1970s and early 1980s.

Production on *All Night Long* was suspended for several weeks. The original cinematographer, Tak Fujimoto, was fired and replaced with Philip H. Lathrop, and Adam Baldwin, in the role of Freddie Dupler, was replaced by Dennis Quaid, fresh from his success in 1979's *Breaking Away*. W. D. Richter remembered that when he heard of Streisand's casting, he girded himself for substantial rewrites, but neither Jean-Claude nor the producers asked him for any. Streisand's recollection is that she was dissatisfied with the second half of the script and felt it needed considerable work, which Sue, Jean-Claude, and the producers promised her would be done. As filming went on, no changes were forthcoming.

Streisand behaved with consummate professionalism, and Hackman was thrilled to be working with her. "I love Gene Hackman," said Streisand. "That's one of the reasons I said yes. But Gene was very hard on Jean-Claude. And I was trying to protect Jean-Claude, in a way, because I felt so bad for him." Apart from that, filming went smoothly, and generally everyone seemed pleased—except the studio executives, who seem never to have grasped the film at all. Jean-Claude was thrilled that the great composer Georges Delerue had agreed to score the film; Jean-Claude loved the music Delerue had written for many of François Truffaut's pictures, including *Jules and Jim* and *Shoot the Piano Player*.

Marion Rothman recalled the trip to Paris to arrange for the score. The weather in France was cold, and on the way to LAX, Sue insisted on stopping off at a Beverly Hills furrier to pick up a new sable coat she had ordered. Once they landed in Paris, Sue and Jean-Claude checked in at the Bristol and arranged to meet the others for dinner at a favorite neighborhood bistro of Jean-Claude's. After dinner, Jean-Claude insisted that they take the Metro back to the hotel. Sue began screaming, "I don't take subways! I'm not in New York anymore! I'm not a secretary anymore!" But they all got on the Metro anyway. "It was at the height of the time in France when they were having a big campaign against using furs," said Rothman. "Sue was clutching her sable, terrified, refusing to sit down."

Once the score was recorded, though, the studio refused to use it. "The music was rather whimsical," said Rothman. "It gave the film a certain light feeling, in the spirit of artistic rebellion." Jean-Claude was heartbroken when Delerue's music was rejected, and felt once more as if he had only minimal control over the project.

In the end, *All Night Long* was something genuinely unusual: a gentle, subtle comedy that couldn't easily be placed in any kind of formulaic, descriptive box. Thanks to Jean-Claude's touch, it had an almost French feel to it; the comic and dramatic points were dealt with almost allusively. There was just a shade of Robert Altman's affect in Jean-Claude's dealing with the ordinary yet crippling problems of this group of yearning, unfulfilled Los Angeles suburbanites with their cookie-cutter ranch houses, their dead-end jobs, their unmemorable dinners at crummy restaurants. Hackman's performance was his finest in years, and the supporting cast was admirably filled out by Quaid, Diane Ladd, Kevin Dobson, Jean-Claude's great friend from Paris Annie Girardot, and seasoned Hollywood character actors such as Ann Doran and Irene Tedrow. As the dazed Cheryl, Streisand gave a thoughtful performance in a kind of role new to her, registering nicely on-screen in her scenes with Hackman. The movie was edited and prepared for a March 1981 release.

When Streisand, who had insisted that Gene Hackman receive top billing, saw advance copies of the movie's print ads, she was appalled. "It was a dark comedy, strange—not ha-ha," she recalled. "It was badly sold, like *Up the Sandbox*, which showed a cartoon of me being strapped to a baby bottle. And in *All Night Long*, it was me with my skirts hiked up going down a fire pole, which sold the movie completely wrong. It was really a little European kind of film. So I just felt totally betrayed.

"I had no control. They were paying me a lot of money. People always talk about, 'Oh, she wants control.' Yeah—you're damned right I want control. I had no control over that film."

A major studio preview was held in Houston. Leonard Goldberg remembered seeing a long line around the block, and overhearing ticket holders standing in line saying, "I hear Barbra is even better than she was in *What's Up, Doc?*" and "I heard Barry Gibb is in it"—because Streisand had just recorded a hit record, "Guilty," with Gibb. Goldberg turned to Jean-Claude and said, "I'd like to go across the street to a bar and start drinking."

After the preview ended, Goldberg and Jean-Claude began looking for someone who responded enthusiastically. Jean-Claude spotted a group of five young boys and girls laughing and seemingly enjoying themselves. When they approached the group, they realized they were completely stoned. "We loved it," one of them said. "The color purple is in it!" Goldberg remembered that Jean-Claude looked stricken—more so when he saw the comments on the preview cards, which were not particularly positive. The audience had believed it was seeing a quintessential Barbra Streisand picture, one in which she would play the assertive, wisecracking sort of part she had made famous in so many of her earlier films. Her laid-back appearance and style in *All Night Long* threw them completely. Perhaps if the picture had featured a leading lady known for eccentric character roles— someone like Veronica Cartwright or Diana Scarwid—it might have fared better. But too many people were unable to judge the film's merits fairly.

Many of the reviewers were, too. In *Time*, Richard Corliss condemned the film for the "worst miscasting of Streisand, in a role vacated by Lisa Eichhorn and suitable only for the young Minnie Pearl." In the *New York Daily News*, Kathleen Carroll found the picture "in total disarray." But not all the notices were unfavorable. Pauline Kael wrote an extremely positive review of the film in *The New Yorker*, drawing comparisons between Jean-Claude's sensibility and that of Ernst Lubitsch or Jacques Tati. In *Newsweek*, David Ansen found that the film "displays surprising moments of reflection and feeling," and *New York Magazine*'s David Denby considered it "a benign, even-tempered piece of work" in which the sterile nature of American life wasn't "emphasized or caricatured; it's just there, waiting to be noticed." "When the substitution of Streisand for Eichhorn was made," recalled Jean-Claude's friend film critic Michael Sragow, "I think there was a lot of bad feeling directed toward the movie. I'm still not sure at what point it became clear that was going to be reflected in the reviews." Sragow himself gave the picture a very strong early review in *Rolling Stone*, but it got lost in the avalanche of negative notices. Audiences couldn't reconcile the cheesy ad campaign with what they saw on the screen, and, not knowing what to make of it, urged friends to stay away. In major cities everywhere, an anticipated long run was cut short to a few weeks. The picture didn't come close to making back its cost, which had of course mushroomed with the addition of Streisand's superstar salary.

From the time the film opened, critics dredged up the Lisa Eichhorn story and accused Sue of double-dealing in order to advance her husband's career. In his *New York Times* review, Vincent Canby thoroughly savaged the picture. "Mr. Tramont, from the hints available in *All Night Long*," he wrote, "has no discernable style or point of view about comedy." Canby also delved into the politics behind the Streisand substitution, naming Sue as the responsible party. "Ordinarily, this sort of information has no place in a review," Canby admitted, "but *All Night Long* is such an oddity that it invites fantasies about how it ever came to be in the form we can see on the screen today."

In a *Times* interview shortly after the picture opened, Jean-Claude made a wan attempt at damage control. "My wife and I have been together eleven years," he said. "If she had the ability to force Barbra to do a picture with me, I wish she had used it sooner." He added that he did not consider the movie a failure, because "failure is to be doing things that you don't want to do. I think there are very successful failures in the world."

Streisand was still smarting over the fact that her request for rewrites had been ignored and that the print ads had misrepresented the tone of the film. Sue, she felt, had not gone to bat for her, and she felt as betrayed as Peter Bogdanovich had over the black-and-white photography and casting of Cybill Shepherd in *Nickelodeon*. Then there was the matter of Sue's antagonistic attitude toward *Yentl*.

She invited Sue to her home on Carolwood Drive and told her, "We just don't have the same taste in material, and I think that I should have a different agent. We'll still be close friends."

After a stunned silence, Sue responded, "I won't be your friend if I'm not your agent."

Streisand was shocked by Sue's reaction. "It was like, 'what?'"

Streisand, who often acknowledged her own capacity for cutting off people who had deeply hurt her, decided on the spot to drop Sue from her life. "My career was the only thing that mattered to her," she said, "so I shut her off from that, too."

For years Sue had warned her friends in the agency business that it was a mistake to think of clients as friends, while she herself had broken that rule constantly. Ali MacGraw was a friend, as was Candice Bergen and, to a lesser degree, Tuesday Weld. But no client had occupied a more important place in her life than Barbra Streisand had. They will all leave me, Sue said over and over. All except Barbra. Because Barbra and I are like sisters.

"Sue didn't think it was that hard to be an agent until late in her career at ICM, when they started to leave her," said David Geffen. "And she was very bitter about it. Barbra's leaving her was painful because she thought that she and Barbra were soul mates. It never occurred to Sue that there would come a time when Barbra would leave her. And after that, she would always say, 'They all leave.'"

Sue railed to her closest friends that Jon Peters had been behind Streisand's decision to stop working with her. She denounced him as an idiot who was so uneducated that he had to have the development girls read scripts aloud to him. Sue knew that part of Streisand's perfectionism was her habit of perpetually second-guessing herself. She was certain that Peters had spoken against both *The Main Event* and *All Night Long*, and that was why she was now out in the cold.

Many producers and agents in Hollywood believed that an actress was past her prime by the age of thirty. In the case of many of the biggest names of the 1970s, their talent and versatility could extend the Hollywood age cutoff to around forty. By the spring of 1981, Streisand was thirty-nine years old. Goldie Hawn was thirty-six, Jill Clayburgh thirty-five, Candice Bergen thirty-five, Faye Dunaway forty, Ali MacGraw forty-two, Jane Fonda forty-three, Dyan Cannon forty-four. In a short time, their peak years as movie actresses would be behind them, and an entire era that Sue had played a crucial role in orchestrating would be over.

Sue had relished having so many of the top stars of a defining epoch in American movie history: the sheer quantity, as well as the quality, of her clients had given her a greater sense of personal and professional security.

But Barbra Streisand had always been the linchpin of her client list, the biggest star in the entertainment world and the closest and most powerful reminder to Sue of her own exalted stature in Hollywood. Through no fault of Streisand's, her departure was more than a little death for Sue, who chose to interpret it as a mammoth and devastating failure. For the moment, she did her best to carry on as if nothing had changed.

CHAPTER SIXTEEN

1981–1986

When Sue felt defeated, there was no reaching her. Just as she loved to luxuriate in the successes of her friends and clients, she seemed determined to wallow in her own failures. Marlo Thomas remembered that Sue always telephoned her and offered encouragement when something had gone well in her career. When *All Night Long* opened to bad reviews, Thomas telephoned Sue to commiserate, sharing her feeling that it was easy to be congratulatory but often difficult to express oneself to friends when they had experienced a flop. "I called her and said, 'I'm so sorry about this,'" recalled Thomas. "'That's so unfair. Jean-Claude did a fine job on that picture.' And Sue said, 'I don't appreciate this at all. I would rather not talk about it, and I don't think you should have called me about it.' I realized that for her, hiding from it was better. There was something in her that couldn't take what she felt was an impression of negativity or maybe feeling sorry for her, even though I was doing it out of the kindness of my heart. But I felt an iciness on the other end of the phone that I had not felt before and didn't feel after."

With the departure of Streisand, there was nothing for Sue to do but continue trying to secure the best for her other clients and hope that she could attract new stars as the 1980s rolled onward. But given her intense connection to Streisand, it was probably impossible to avoid a trickle-down effect when dealing with the remainder of her client list. So many of her brightest gems were now fading. With the record-breaking successes of *Raiders of the Lost Ark* and *E.T.*, Steven Spielberg would become the most powerful player in Hollywood, and his elated kid's spirit had infected ticket buyers. The movie audience that had seemed so willing to embrace unusual, gripping, adult material in the 1970s seemed quietly to be withdrawing; moviemakers were chasing an audience that was looking for ways to rejoice in a second childhood. The more remote that remarkable decade of moviemaking became, the less happy and fulfilled Sue seemed.

For one thing, it wasn't nearly as much fun scrambling to keep her roster of stars' careers afloat as it had been making deals for them when they were at their peak. Among her new director clients was Michael Cimino, who had earned the 1978 Academy Award for Best Director for his brilliant work on *The Deer Hunter*. In November 1980, Cimino's second effort, *Heaven's Gate*, was released. An epic story set against the Johnson County War in 1890s Wyoming, *Heaven's Gate* had a huge cast headed by Kris Kristofferson. But Cimino's directorial excesses—he reportedly demanded as many as fifty takes on many of the scenes—led to immense cost overruns, and the picture became the greatest disaster of the era, returning a little over $3 million on a final production budget of $44 million. Instead of being treated by the industry as an anomaly, *Heaven's Gate* was viewed as an object lesson in the foolishness of allowing star directors to proceed without strict oversight, and it was used by many commentators and studio executives as a warning to many of the finest artists of the 1970s.

The Main Event had restored Ryan O'Neal to box-office favor, but that proved to be only temporary. Jeffrey Lane remembered attending a party at Alana Stewart's house around this time; O'Neal was in another room, and Sue said to those in her immediate group, "Ryan's as cold as ice." She had been having trouble finding a quality script for him, and in 1981 O'Neal had starred in a weak comedy, *So Fine*, for Warner Bros. When the film was being readied for autumn release, the studio's chairman of the board and co-chief executive officer, Robert Daly, received an urgent call from someone in the Warner Bros. publicity department saying that O'Neal's agent had refused to allow his appearance on *The Tonight Show* to promote the movie. Daly called Sue, who reiterated that O'Neal would not take part in the program. When Daly asked why not, Sue said, contemptuously, "Would Cary Grant go on *The Tonight Show*?" Daly assured her that if he had Cary Grant, he wouldn't be calling her, and that Warner Bros. hoped to make many pictures with O'Neal and that she was making a tactical error by being so obstinate. But Sue held firm: no *Tonight Show* for O'Neal.

O'Neal still commanded a good salary and above-the-title billing, but *So Fine* went nowhere, and O'Neal clashed with Sue over his next project, *Partners*, a comedy in which he played a cop who goes undercover to solve a series of murders of gay men in Los Angeles. The movie featured a forced, abrasive script by Francis Veber. The picture was originally set to star James Caan, but when Paramount rejected his brother as coproducer, Caan walked out, and Sue pressed O'Neal to replace him. "It never felt good, that picture," said O'Neal. "But she told me to do it. She lived a high life, and she's got to bring commissions into the agency."

Sue faced a tough, complicated agent-client situation with *Prince of the City*, released by Warner Bros. in the late summer of 1981. She was representing Brian De Palma, who was developing a screenplay with the acclaimed Broadway playwright David Rabe; Robert De Niro was in line to star. It took De Palma some time to get a workable script and a commitment from De Niro, and many at ICM doubted that the director would ever deliver. The deal hadn't yet been closed, and Sue suddenly discovered that her colleague Mike Medavoy was negotiating the same property as a De Niro project with Sidney Lumet. "I shouldn't be telling you this," Sue told De Palma, because Lumet was also a client of the agency. Medavoy and Lumet had assumed that they could keep De Niro on the project while going behind De Palma's back and pushing him out, but De Niro's Italian loyalty carried the day, and he said that he had agreed to make the picture with De Palma and no one else.

"If Sue hadn't said anything," observed De Palma's then-wife, Nancy Allen, "he could have had more people involved and had David Rabe working longer. It could have been a debacle. Sue also put together a dinner with Jon Voight, trying to persuade him that he could play an Italian—but Jon Voight didn't think so." Eventually, Lumet made the picture with Treat Williams—a future client of Sue's—in the lead; it was a critical success but a box-office disappointment when it was released in 1981.

Another rising actor Sue snapped up around this time was Christopher Walken, who, after a fine track record on the New York stage, had made a stunning impression in Michael Cimino's *The Deer Hunter* and won the 1978 Academy Award for Best Supporting Actor. She became Walken's agent around the time he filmed Steve Martin's critically acclaimed but unpopular *Pennies from Heaven*, released by MGM at Christmastime 1981. (*Pennies from Heaven* was one of the commercial failures that cut short David Begelman's tenure at MGM.) Walken recalled her saying to him, "Chris, when you come to Los Angeles, people will invite you to parties and you will socialize, and go out and meet people. Stay in the hotel. Learn your lines and go to work. And keep to yourself.' She thought it was better for me to keep myself spare. Very good advice for an actor." Walken echoed the recollections of other clients that Sue urged him just to keep

going—-sometimes the picture would work out well and sometimes it
wouldn't. But he was thrilled with the way that she consistently increased
his movie salary, and he was dazzled by being invited to parties at Bel Air
Road, where he could mingle with the likes of Jack Nicholson and legends
like Billy Wilder.

Wilder and his wife, Audrey, were frequent guests of the Tramonts; the
cynical edge of Wilder films such as *The Lost Weekend, Sunset Boulevard,*
and *Ace in the Hole* was a good match for Sue's own sensibility, and Jean-
Claude was plainly in awe of the veteran director. But after a time in the
mid-1980s, Wilder stopped going, telling his close friend Robin Hurlstone,
"There's nothing worse, *Schätze,* than a self-hating Jew."

The Wilders were present at one memorable dinner party in July 1982,
attended by Joan Collins, Michael Cimino, Anjelica Huston, and the guest
of honor, Joan Juliet Buck, whose first novel, *The Only Place to Be,* had just
been published. Later in the evening, Jerry Brown, still governor of California, appeared. "Why am I wasting my time talking to you?" Buck joked to
Joan Collins as Brown came over to speak to her. The two of them fell into
an intense conversation, and soon enough, Buck recalled, "the room was
spinning."

Two days later, Buck raced out of a movie to call Sue to thank her for the
party. "MRS. BROWN?" said Sue excitedly. "HONEEEY, YOU'RE MRS.
BROWN. HE CALLED ME FOR YOUR NUMBER." At the time, Buck
was married to journalist and author John Heilpern, but Sue encouraged
her to pursue an affair with Brown. "I remember at one point writing in my
diary, 'Am I doing this for me or for Sue?'" recalled Buck. "It was one of the
headiest things that ever happened to me in my life. Years earlier, in Paris,
Sue had been adamant about the Rothschilds, which was strange, because I
was single when I was with Eric. But it was about power—who had the
power. It was what you do."

Sue's dinners were most enjoyable to those stars who were riding high. For
anyone who happened to be experiencing a career lull, they could be excruci-
ating, as Cher discovered in the late 1970s, when the only work she could
find was modeling assignments for *Vogue.* "I remember one night when
Barbra and Warren and Ryan and Ali were all there," said Cher. "I thought,
'I have to get the fuck out of here.' Sue was always very funny and nice to
me, but I didn't add to the dinner. I was friends with all of those people—I

had known Warren since I was sixteen—but not in the way they were friends with each other." Cher never became a client, but as she emerged as a top film star and respected actress in the 1980s, with successes such as *Silkwood* and *Moonstruck*, Sue's admiration for her only increased.

One disarming quality that Sue continued to reveal at her parties was her ability to laugh harder at her own professional missteps than she did at anyone else's. Early in 1982, she was briefly handed Lucie Arnaz as a client. Despite an unimpressive start in the business playing second fiddle to her famous mother on *Here's Lucy*, Arnaz had enjoyed some solid successes in the theater, notably in the national company of *Seesaw* and in Broadway's *They're Playing Our Song*. In 1980, she had costarred with Neil Diamond and Laurence Olivier in the disappointing remake of *The Jazz Singer*, and she was eager for a film that would raise her profile.

Sue came up with two offers: Lawrence Turman's comedy-drama *Second Thoughts*, and another script, for a supernatural thriller. Arnaz read both and felt that *Second Thoughts* definitely offered the better acting opportunity; in the thriller, she would yield the foreground to a lot of special effects, and she feared she would be lost. Sue agreed with her. "In the thriller, you're going to have mud all over your face and you're not really acting, and what are you going to get out of that? *Second Thoughts* is being made by these great people at EMI." *Second Thoughts* turned out badly and almost went straight to video. The movie Sue encouraged Arnaz to turn down was *Poltergeist*—and Sue loved dining out on the story.

Around this time, Sue briefly represented rising actress Beverly D'Angelo, who had earned terrific reviews for her acting and singing as Patsy Cline in 1980's biopic of Loretta Lynn, *Coal Miner's Daughter*. "The film had been edited," D'Angelo recalled, "and what was remaining was not fully the blood I had on the tracks. It had been explained to me that *Coal Miner's Daughter* was not *The Patsy Cline Story*. So I was vulnerable to being poached." D'Angelo left her agent, Rick Nicita, and signed with Sue, who told the actress she had "cachet." When D'Angelo pressed her on the matter, Sue replied, "Did you read that review in the *New York Times*? He mentioned your overbite. That's money in the bank!" Their association lasted about eight months, during which time Sue failed to land the actress a job. When D'Angelo telephoned Sue to tell her it wasn't working out, Sue replied, "I didn't much like you anyway."

The most attractive and glamorous women in Hollywood and New York continued to pass through Sue's living room. In the early 1980s, one of the era's most notable pop icons became a client of Sue's. Farrah Fawcett, the new woman in Ryan O'Neal's life, was eager to parlay her television stardom into movie success. Until now, her big-screen films had failed, but in 1981 she drew strong reviews for her performance in a high-quality made-for-television movie, *Murder in Texas*, based on the best-selling Thomas Thompson book *Blood and Money*. Sue advised her in this transition to better material: in 1983, Fawcett took over the demanding leading role in the hit off-Broadway play *Extremities*. Praise for her performance as a would-be rape victim who turns the tables on her attacker made it far easier for her to be taken seriously as an actress. By 1984, Fawcett had received an Emmy nomination for her performance as an abused wife in the TV-movie *The Burning Bed*. It was a transition not unlike the one Sue had helped Ann-Margret pull off in *Carnal Knowledge*—which she continued to point to as one of her proudest achievements as an agent.

Sue also took an abiding interest in the career of Tina Sinatra, who had segued from being an actress to becoming an agent. Sinatra began this new phase of her life by working with Arnold Stiefel, who had opened his own management firm in the 1970s. When Sue read about Sinatra's job in the Hollywood trade papers, she gave her an encouraging telephone call. "Just remember, baby," she said, "you have to get the clients. You're pretty. Let somebody else close the deal. You don't worry about that." Sue was fond of Tina's mother, known as "Big" Nancy, who lived next door in Bel Air. Around Tina's famous father, Sue was endearingly coquettish and tongue-tied, and used to tease Tina about her stepmother, Barbara Marx, by saying, "One date. Give me one date with your father, and Barbara will be history. Nobody else will matter." In the mid-1980s, Tina persuaded Sue, as well as Stan Kamen at William Morris, to read scripts with an eye toward finding a possible vehicle for her father. Sue came across several that were being developed for the likes of Clint Eastwood or Gene Hackman and brought them to Frank Sinatra's attention—but in the end he wasn't interested enough in taking on a full-scale movie role.

Sue also passed useful information on to Tina from time to time. Tina became romantically involved with Columbia president Daniel Melnick, who had a script in development that he hoped would be a vehicle for Mick

Jagger. Sue, who had briefly worked with Jagger in the mid-1970s without coming up with any firm movie offers, called Tina and told her she should get herself to New York immediately and meet with Jagger to see if the Stiefel Office could sign him. "I got on a plane, got in at midnight, went to bed, went to the meeting, got on a plane at four, and came back," Tina remembered. "We didn't get him, but we got in the running because of her. It wasn't the only time she did that." Later, when the Stiefel Office lost Robert Wagner and Natalie Wood as clients, Sue, who knew that Tina had once dated Wagner for nearly a year, was the first person to call both Stiefel and Tina. "She said, 'This is a low blow. Don't let it get you down,'" recalled Tina. "She wasn't losing people yet, but she knew it was shitty and hurtful, and she was sensitive to it. That's the kind of person she was."

Around the office, Sue continued to be both strict and supportive with those she deemed worth her time. Hildy Gottlieb, who became a servicing agent at ICM after working at a smaller agency, J. Michael Bloom & Associates, remembered the challenge of dealing with Sue in the early 1980s. Gottlieb had no clients of her own; she was essentially a covering agent, assigned to find out what projects were in development at certain studios and then report back to the top agents, who would place calls to the studio heads. Sue would barge into Gottlieb's office with a list of her top clients, tape it to Gottlieb's telephone, and forbid her to speak to the studio vice presidents about any ICM clients but hers.

Gottlieb's breakthrough came when she discovered comedian Eddie Murphy, flying to New York City every month to catch him in his regular gig on NBC's *Saturday Night Live*, and set about trying to get him work in the movies. At the time, Gottlieb was dating the popular director Walter Hill, whom she later married. When Gregory Hines dropped out of a film Hill was developing, *48 Hrs.*, Gottlieb went to work getting Murphy the part. Sue would make withering comments about how Gottlieb was wasting her time on a lowbrow client, but once Paramount released *48 Hrs.* at Christmas 1982 and it became a huge hit, Sue suddenly became her champion.

She subjected Gottlieb to her style of sisterly tough love. "ICM gave me a big raise and a bigger office, and Sue said to me one day, 'You're not dressed right.'" There was a store on Rodeo Drive, Lina Lee, and Sue called the manager and asked him to keep the store open late while her colleague came in to shop. She also sent Gottlieb to a top L.A. hair stylist.

"It was a nice way of reaching out and supporting me—in her own way," said Gottlieb.

Sue was also quite helpful to junior agent John Burnham, who got his start in ICM's television department. She was impressed that, at a big industry party, Burnham had the confidence to engage the somewhat unapproachable Barry Diller in conversation. "We're going to get you out of that fucking TV department," she said, "and into the movie department." Within months she had proven true to her word. Burnham was stunned by the daily image of Sue on the phone, with her legs propped up on her desk, while one assistant rolled pot into the tobacco end of a cigarette, and another would hand her the joint. "She would inhale and say 'Uh-*huhhhhh*,'" recalled Burnham, "which was an indication that she was holding in the hit of pot. And then she would say '*Yeeeeees*,' and she would exhale. Once, in a staff meeting, she left a vial of coke on top of the table, and Jeff Berg, right in her face, got very angry."

Sue came to Burnham's aid when he was trying to get James Mason a promising villain role in Sidney Lumet's forthcoming courtroom drama *The Verdict*. She called Lumet and urged him to cast Mason, but the director declined on the grounds that Mason was British and he wanted a genuine New Englander. (Elsewhere at ICM, Lou Pitt was desperately trying to wangle the role for his client, Christopher Plummer.) After haranguing Lumet repeatedly, Sue told Burnham she was giving up and that Mason should call the director himself. Mason did—and got the part and an Academy Award nomination for Best Supporting Actor of 1982.

Martha Luttrell had been a partner in a small but successful agency, Robinson/Luttrell & Associates, representing a handful of clients such as Carol Burnett, James Garner, and Alan Arkin. In 1983, ICM bought the agency, and Luttrell learned that her time at ICM was going to be dramatically different from the professional existence she had known previously. "In meetings we would laugh at Sue and Michael Black until we cried," said Luttrell. "Michael would come to meetings and he would give his report as Bette Davis or Carol Channing. We had so much fun in those days."

Sue made for good entertainment value out of the office, too. Hair stylist Alex Roldan remembered the first time he was hired to dress Sue's hair. Roldan was working at Elle, a salon on Beverly Boulevard near ICM's offices, and had several prominent clients, including actresses Susan

Sullivan and Linda Gray. One day he was called to go to Sue's office to braid her hair. She was pleasant enough, but as Roldan had his hands in her hair, she took a call.

"Hi, honeeey," said Sue. "How are you? How's the family? Uh-huh. Yeah. Oh, great. What? You WHAT? YOU JUST TRY AND DO THAT, YOU MOTHERFUCKER!"

Roldan was shaken, but he returned to style her hair many times after, and she was always cordial. "It was clear that this was a woman who didn't bullshit," he said. "And she never dished it with me about the industry. No gossiping about her clients."

Sue continued to pull off relatively spectacular agenting coups during the early to mid-1980s. But increasingly her old enthusiasm seemed to be wanting. It seemed to many of her friends that in losing Streisand, she felt that she had lost the best part of herself. The game was simply not nearly as much fun as it had been when she knew that Streisand was her trump card in Hollywood. Try as she might to muster her old excitement in working out deals for Michael Caine and Christopher Walken, it wasn't the same. She had spent so much time telling what she believed to be the naked truth to her clients and friends—always, she felt, for their own good—that it was impossible for her now to be lulled into lying to herself. A kind of low-grade depression slowly overcame her as she realized that the glory years she had enjoyed in the 1970s were coming to an end.

For that reason she found it difficult to see as much of Robert Evans as she had in the past. Evans had represented for Sue the epitome of Hollywood's creative spirit: the gambling instinct, the confidence in material that might seem questionable to the moneymen, the delight in playing close to the line that had all been such an integral part of moviemaking in the 1970s. But Evans had recently entered a period of sharp professional decline. In 1980, he had been convicted of cocaine trafficking. He then became immersed in the production of Francis Ford Coppola's *The Cotton Club* and appeared as optimistic that the film would equal his past successes with Coppola as David O. Selznick had been hopeful that the execrable *Duel in the Sun* would somehow match *Gone with the Wind*. But *The Cotton Club*, despite its many virtues, received mostly poor reviews and failed at the box office, posting enormous losses. For Evans, a shadow was cast over the entire project because of the 1983 contract killing of one of the film's major financial backers, promoter Roy Radin—a crime in which Evans soon found himself implicated. When he took the stand at a preliminary hearing in the case in 1989, he pleaded the fifth and was eventually absolved of any guilt—although rumors continued to circle around Hollywood that he had had a hand in Radin's death. It made Sue inexpressibly sad to see someone she had believed in so strongly and worked with so joyously fall on hard times. She told close friends that it was probably best that they now socialized less—that neither she nor Evans could stand to watch the other one grow old.

Very occasionally Sue made contact with friends from the old days in Utica. Adele Rosen had been living in Montecito with her husband for decades when she and Sue were reunited in the mid-1980s. Rosen invited Sue and Jean-Claude to lunch. "Oh, God, your hair is too short!" Sue exclaimed when she entered the house. She spent the afternoon pumping Rosen for information about their old sorority gang from Utica and dropped endless stories about Barbra Streisand. "She took out her weed and smoked the whole time," said Rosen. "And she did not ask permission. It was a great afternoon."

With many of her celebrated friends, she continued to paint her life as being inferior to theirs; over time, it was a topic she raised habitually, without expecting any kind of solution or definitive answer. Marlo Thomas had remained a close friend after the demise of *That Girl* in 1971, and Sue was perpetually telling her that Thomas had a perfect life, and that in the next life, Sue wanted to be her. She envied Thomas's warm and supportive relationship with her father, Danny, and repeatedly told the actress that it had contributed mightily to her professional success, just as her own father's weakness continued to make Sue doubt herself. Fathers were an incessant topic of conversation. "It was like a quilt of things she wanted," observed Thomas. "She thought that her fearlessness came from fighting, clawing her way up, and my fearlessness came from a more confident place."

Sue kept adding to her client list, but with little of the passion or prolificacy she'd had in the 1970s. In the wake of Cathy Moriarty's Academy Award–nominated performance in Martin Scorsese's *Raging Bull*, Sue began representing her. Their working relationship didn't last long, but Sue loved the fact that Moriarty was part owner of Mulberry Street Pizzeria in Beverly

Hills. "She was sweet and tough and endearing," recalled Moriarty. "I would get a call, and she would say, 'I need a white spinach pizza *now*. Can you do that?' She was outside of delivery range, but we always did it." Soon Moriarty was being represented by Sue's good friend Toni Howard, who later landed her a choice role in *Soapdish*.

Sue also began working with Eric Roberts, who was already impressing Hollywood with his dramatic range and versatility. He had played a tough street kid in *King of the Gypsies*, a literate, buttoned-up young man in *Paul's Case*, and a World War II sailor in *Raggedy Man*. He survived both a brutal car accident and being fired by director Geraldine Fitzgerald from the Broadway production of Bill C. Davis's *Mass Appeal*, and then was cast by Bob Fosse as Paul Snider, the obsessive loser husband of Dorothy Stratten in the controversial *Star 80*, released in the autumn of 1983. It was a tricky role, in which the entire drama hinged on the embarrassment that the audience felt for him, and Roberts recalled that he began living and breathing the part. The film was too downbeat and disturbing to catch on with audiences, but Roberts went on to give impressive performances in a number of major Hollywood films, including Andrey Konchalovskiy's *Runaway Train* and Dušan Makavejev's *The Coca-Cola Kid*, both released in 1985. Roberts's salary for *Star 80* had been $60,000, but Sue succeeded in jumping it to $500,000, and it escalated from that point.

Like Moriarty, Roberts wasn't with Sue for long, but he remembered that she never pressed him to do anything he disliked. This may well have been a sign of her increasing boredom with her job. Roberts recalled, "She would say, 'The studio wants you to do this. It's my mission to hand you the script. I don't like it. You may like it. I hope not.' That's how she would make it clear. She was a cool chick, and she let me know, as a young actor, how to be cool."

In 1983, Sue negotiated a strong deal for Ali MacGraw to appear in several episodes of the immensely popular nighttime television soap opera *Dynasty*. MacGraw would portray Lady Ashley Mitchell, a love interest for Blake Carrington (played by John Forsythe), and Sue arranged for her to be paid $350,000 for thirteen episodes—a remarkable salary for the time. "I was terrible in it." MacGraw laughed. "I have a tremendous respect for the people who can do it—the energy you need to come up with for spouting off that kind of rubbish is a real skill. Joan Collins did it wonderfully. But it was the most amazing amount of money I ever saw in my life. I came from a very real background, so it was a lot. Also, I had misspent a lot, and if I don't have that kind of money, I'm okay." But Sue didn't think MacGraw would be okay without that degree of income, and constantly fretted that her friend had not adequately prepared herself for the future.

After *Dynasty*, MacGraw was cast in the coveted leading role of Natalie Jastrow in *The Winds of War*, the big-budget miniseries based on Herman Wouk's best-selling novel. That deal was mostly negotiated by ICM agent Andrea Eastman, and Sue was not intensely involved. "Sue's personality was so enormous that the agent expertise part was the least interesting thing about her," observed MacGraw. "She had power and everybody wanted to be in touch with her, but that's different from saying, 'This is an amazing, visionary person who I know is going to hand-hold me through this minefield so that I am protected.'" After *The Winds of War*, MacGraw's career slipped into lower gear, and she also left Sue's roster, but they remained close for the rest of Sue's life. It was around this time that Ruth Sender enraged her daughter by asking her if she had any clients of importance left.

In the fall of 1983, Barbra Streisand's once-in-a-lifetime movie, *Yentl*, was released. It generally received very good reviews and did tremendous business, eventually earning over $40 million. Streisand and Sue had not communicated since the break over *All Night Long*, but after seeing *Yentl* in a public screening on opening day at the Village Theatre in Westwood and being overwhelmingly moved and impressed by it, Sue sent Streisand a telegram that read, simply, "BRILLIANT." It was the beginning of a reconciliation of sorts—but their friendship never regained the buoyant momentum it had had in the 1960s and '70s. Many people continued to believe that Sue's connection to Barbra had been unhealthy, like that of an obsessive fan who works her way into a position of prominence in a star's life. "I always thought," said Jerry Weintraub, "that Sue believed she *was* Barbra."

By now Sue and Jean-Claude had purchased an apartment in Paris. It wasn't large, but it was beautifully situated at 3 place André Malraux, a short walk from the Louvre, where Jean-Claude loved to go day after day to gaze at his favorite paintings. Friends remember having the impression that this second home represented Sue's agreeing to live in Jean-Claude's world part of the time after he had spent so much of their marriage living in hers.

But she characteristically did so in a grudging way, protesting to her friends that she loathed spending time in Paris. After a brief and rather disastrous fling at private French lessons, she gave up any serious attempt to speak the language, sometimes falling back on her German if the situation called for it. Jean-Claude frequently went to Paris alone for one- and two-month stretches.

Intimate friends believed there were other reasons for Jean-Claude's liking to go off to Paris by himself. Sue told many of her close friends, often in an almost boastful way, that Jean-Claude's sexual tastes leaned to the kinky. Several in her inner circle were made aware that when Jean-Claude did spend time on his own in Paris, he liked to frequent after-hours clubs that specialized in seeing women put in submissive positions. A certain amount of this leaked out into Hollywood gossip circles, and Sue's detractors were eager to connect the dots psychologically: a man who had spent nearly fifteen years in Hollywood flailing professionally, married to one of the most powerful women in town, harbored a quietly perverse streak about seeing women dominated.

The couple's own sexual dynamic seemed a complete mystery. Sue's general attitude toward what was sexually viable vexed many of her close friends. She told many in her intimate circle that she had not told Jean-Claude she loved him until they had been together for ten years. And even in her basest recounting of men and women together, she gave the advantage to men. She often said that she didn't understand the point of foreplay. "Just get hard and get in," recalled Lili Zanuck, wife of Twentieth Century Fox chief Richard Zanuck. "Which is bizarre, because most of us are not like that. Sue used to say to me, 'I didn't know if I was attractive to a man unless I saw a hard dick. It if was stiff, I knew I was attractive.'"

Even now that Barbra Streisand was no longer on the roster, Jean-Claude complained incessantly about how much time Sue's work consumed, and their fights became regular occurrences. As the job paled for her, Sue began to lash out indiscriminately, telling her clients that they hadn't gotten a certain job because they were getting old, or because they were overweight, or because they had behaved badly at a party. Most stars are not inclined to accept such criticism, no matter what the motivation may be. And many of them sensed that Sue's honesty was at least partly motivated by her growing sense of frustration with the business. She continued to complain that Gene Hackman was a typically thoughtless, ungrateful client because he hadn't thanked her in his Oscar speech of 1972. In 1983, Hackman left her for another agent.

The world that she had so desperately longed to be part of, she now believed was responsible for everything that was going wrong in her life. Ever since she had entered show business, her driving obsession had been to become as relevant as she could possibly be. Now, she told friends, she could feel herself becoming irrelevant. Many people later posited that Sue's decline came about because she grew more famous than many of her clients, but in retrospect, that seems beside the point. "Her decline," said David Geffen, "came from the fact that she started to hate her clients. After Barbra left, she started to hate them, and when the others left, she *really* hated them." Sue's contempt was fearless, epic, freely vented and unleashed, and indiscriminate. It was one thing to be angry that a client had left; it was another to wish that he would get cancer and die. She frequently told friends that she would rather be a whore in a Turkish prison than work with actors any longer.

"Managing people was difficult for Sue," said her longtime ICM colleague Lou Pitt. "And I'm convinced that if you don't know how to manage people—your colleagues, your assistant, the head of an agency, the head of a studio—then you won't succeed." Sue had passed on the likes of Arnold Schwarzenegger, Jessica Lange, and Dudley Moore when they were young and had yet to break through, always saying, "I need a star."

As an agent, her one-trick-pony nature was finally catching up with her. She was not strong at helping her fading clients rethink themselves in other media. Cher once commented that she couldn't get arrested in Hollywood before she gave a critically acclaimed performance in a 1982 Broadway flop, *Come Back to the 5 and Dime, Jimmy Dean, Jimmy Dean*; suddenly, the movie business took notice of her. But even though Broadway had revived the careers of many a fading star, Sue seldom encouraged her clients to go to New York to do a play, and television she saw as worthwhile only for the money it offered.

Once, in the 1980s, she was desperately looking for a project for Ryan O'Neal, and she was forced to appeal to ICM's television department for help. A junior television agent had a script that seemed exactly what she was looking for. Lou Pitt asked if he might help the young agent with the pitch, because he knew how Sue could be if she was in one of her moods. The young agent wanted to do it himself, and when he transmitted the offer, Sue snapped, "I wouldn't have my client do that!"—making her young colleague feel insignificant. "It was hurtful, and it was wrong, and I told her that," said Pitt.

During the Christmas holidays of 1984, Sue and Jean-Claude went to Venice, where they stayed at the Gritti Palace. Christopher Walken was shooting the James Bond film *A View to a Kill* in England, and he and his wife, Georgianne, joined the Tramonts in Venice over New Year's. Gore Vidal met them there and took them on a sightseeing trip that included the San Michele Cemetery, the burial place of Sergei Diaghilev and Igor Stravinsky. Jack Lemmon and Felicia Farr were also staying at the hotel and became part of the group. The Tramonts' enthusiasms were typically divided: Jean-Claude reveled in the art and history of the place, Sue in the food and the glittering company. For several years, Walken had enjoyed a strong friendship with Jean-Claude independent of his business relationship with Sue; Walken regarded him as "such a wholesome, healthy man, and such good company."

Walken remained a busy star character actor throughout the 1980s, and he always expressed his gratitude to Sue for negotiating excellent deals for him. He never moved into the position of being able to carry films as a leading man, unlike Michael Caine, who continued to combine the aura of a character actor and leading man to impressive effect. Caine felt that much of his success was owed to Sue's excellent judgment of the scripts submitted and her freedom to encourage him to take risks, as she had with *Dressed to Kill*. Another big leap for Caine came in 1981, when she negotiated a deal for him to star in the film version of Ira Levin's long-running Broadway hit *Deathtrap*. Sidney Lumet was set to direct, and Sue urged him to cast Caine as the gay playwright Sidney Bruhl. *Deathtrap*'s big shocker scene came when Caine had to kiss Christopher Reeve, playing his lover Clifford Anderson. "Neither of us had mouth-kissed a man before," Caine said. "We drank a bottle of brandy between the two of us, and then we forgot the lines! Afterward, I was in Miami in a bookstore for a pee, and I went to the Gents, and it was locked. Next door was the Ladies, and I thought, 'I'll go in.' The door handle goes down, and there's a sixty-year-old woman inside. I said, 'It's all right, love—I'm a lesbian.' Without a pause, she said, 'No, you're not. I saw you kiss Superman!'"

Sue was later instrumental in Caine's being cast in Woody Allen's *Hannah and Her Sisters*, about the roundelay of romantic and professional frustrations of a New York theater family. Sue read the script and told Caine she thought he should play the part of Elliot, a successful but perennially dissatisfied Manhattan investment whiz who is married to one sister (Mia Farrow) while lusting after another (Barbara Hershey). She got in touch with Allen, who told her up front that this picture, like all of his pictures, was being filmed on a tight budget and he could not promise anything close to Caine's going salary level. Allen had never done any business with Sue in the past. "She would not hesitate to pitch an actor or actress to me who was wrong for my project," he said. "She epitomized the kind of Hollywood agent's mentality and ethics and scruples, and I had no interest in dealing with her on business. Everything she ever said to me about my films was always that I was a genius. She only said, 'Oh, this film is so great, you're so brilliant, and so-and-so would love to meet you.' I never believed a word she said; it reeked of standard agent sincerity. I will say that over the years, she was always very nice to me and never seemed to want anything in return."

If Allen thought that his long-standing friendship with Sue would have generated some negotiating leniency on Sue's part, he was wrong. "I needed Michael Caine for the film," said Allen, "and appropriately—because her ethical commitment was to Michael—she drove a hard bargain. I couldn't afford much, and she would not sell us Michael for lower than a certain fee. Eventually we paid it. We loved Michael, and he was great. But I know it was more than we could afford." In the end, Sue's efforts paid off: when it was released early in 1986, *Hannah and Her Sisters* was both a critical and a box-office success, and earned Michael Caine the Academy Award for Best Supporting Actor, leading to yet another upswing in his career.

On May 24, 1985, Eugene Sender died at the age of eighty-one. Ruth's marriage to him had provided her with security and companionship, helping her to overcome the memories of George's suicide. It might have been expected that Sue would now spend more time with her mother, but that did not happen. More often than not, on the couple's visits to New York,

Jean-Claude was dispatched to visit Ruth, while Sue remained at a safe distance, as always.

Sue had difficulty keeping a steady line of help at home. At Bel Air Road, she barely if ever opened a refrigerator door; everything was brought to her, and she would have been hard pressed to do as much as boil an egg in the expansive kitchen. Several servants came and went, but the mainstay, who arrived in the mid-1980s, was Virginia Portillo, a lovely, elegant, even-tempered woman from Honduras. Virginia made much of Sue's lifestyle possible, and Sue, no matter what derisive comments she might make behind Virginia's back, came to depend on her completely.

Portillo kept the household running smoothly. "Virginia was elegant and charming and kind," said Ali MacGraw. Portillo would remain with Sue for twenty-five years—which were to include many of the most difficult years of Sue's life.

In the summer of 1985, Sue was delighted when Jean-Claude received an unexpected job offer. For years Michael Black had been attempting to land him a directing job, but after the debacle of *All Night Long*, interest was minimal. Black was particularly focused on pursuing projects that were being filmed in Europe, given Jean-Claude's sensibilities and facility with languages, but Black recalled that the standard response from producers and studio executives toward employing him was "Interesting, interesting. . . ." Sue frequently spoke with Black about her desire for Jean-Claude to work more, about her enduring belief in his abilities. For his part, Black felt that Jean-Claude was so erudite and well read that he would have made a first-class movie critic.

The offer was to direct a made-for-cable movie called *As Summers Die*. Jerry Schatzberg was originally assigned to the project, partly because he wanted to work with James Caan, who was set to star. Schatzberg's disenchantment with the project began when the producers fired Caan prior to the start of shooting; he was also opposed to the casting of Jamie Lee Curtis as a Southern belle. But after one day's shooting, he was suddenly out—with the entire company stuck in Waycross, Georgia. An emergency replacement was needed, and Jean-Claude was available.

As Summers Die was a familiar story of Southern greed and bigotry, concerning members of a wealthy family who scheme to get the farm of an elderly black woman (Beah Richards), who had been left the property years earlier by the family's unorthodox and now failing matriarch (Bette Davis). The stars were Scott Glenn and Jamie Lee Curtis, both extremely popular at the time. The cinematographer was Ernest Day, who had been Freddie Young's camera operator for many of the big David Lean epics, and who knew how to create a marvelous visual scope and light the Southern settings so they showed up wonderfully on film.

Alan Caso, camera operator on *As Summers Die*, remembered that Jean-Claude was relaxed and respectful and eager to seek out advice from others on the crew. "Some people want your help but don't want you to know," said Caso. "He would say to me, 'What do you think about this? How do you want to block this?' He trusted me very early."

Jean-Claude treated Bette Davis very deferentially, and although she was still recovering from the debilitating stroke she had suffered two years earlier, Caso remembered that she was "a very stoic woman. She never wore her ills on her sleeve, and arrived every day ready to work." Throughout, Davis had some difficulty retaining her lines, and on the final day of filming, she was scheduled to shoot her big climactic scene in the courtroom—nearly six pages of dialogue. Davis was supposed to wrap by three in the afternoon, as she had to board a plane later that evening, but in take after take, she couldn't remember the script. Jean-Claude was patient. "We went through magazine after magazine of film," Caso recalled, "and finally she makes it all the way through. I had been partying with the crew the night before, and I fell asleep on the camera. Jean-Claude woke me up by saying, 'How was it, was it good?' I said, 'Yeah, it was great.' The film was shipped off to L.A., and it's literally a week later before we saw the dailies. The longest week of my life. I was sweating it, but it was all fine."

Jean-Claude's behavior during the final stages of *As Summers Die* was puzzling. Wende Phifer Mate, who was one of the editors, recalled that he largely absented himself from the process. "Usually, you can't keep the director out of the editing room," said Mate. "But he just wasn't around much." When *As Summers Die* aired in May 1986, it received respectful but not outstanding reviews—not surprisingly, since the film is marred by a curious lack of momentum. It was the last film project Jean-Claude would undertake.

There were other reasons Sue was beginning to feel like a stranger in a strange land. After its modest beginnings, CAA was by now flourishing, a fierce competitor that was fast burying ICM in its ability to sign stars and get them topflight deals. In February 1986, Stan Kamen of William Morris died, and many of his powerhouse clients were cut adrift. Kamen had been a brilliant agent but had erred in not establishing a succession plan at William Morris, and CAA swooped down on the unanchored clients, signing them up one after the other. "Sue and Stan Kamen and Sam Cohn were all very boutique oriented," observed Ron Meyer, then part of the voracious CAA team. "No one else was allowed to touch their clients. And I think that hurt their agencies."

Sue's on-the-town personality was growing increasingly irrelevant in a Hollywood that was becoming dominated by an infusion of MBA candidates with no particular passion for the movies but simply an interest in making money. The social aspect of doing business, which had been one of her major assets for years, was beginning to seem quaint in the numbers-driven world of Ronald Reagan's 1980s. Over at CAA, it was an endless parade of Armani suits and a tightly controlled, highly corporate attitude, with very little flamboyance or room for outsized, colorful personalities. One-on-one dinners in restaurants with clients were the norm; there were no big parties. Two of the only big holdovers were Swifty Lazar and Ed Limato, with their Academy Award extravaganzas.

Ovitz and Meyer and the other CAA agents had a firm grasp on how the business was changing. "Sometimes the agent has the power, sometimes the studio executive has all the power," explained Sherry Lansing. "It all depends. During the packaging heyday, if you got two top stars, studios would do the phone book with them. Then, when enough of those movies flop, it's all about the script. Then there's a long period when movie stars are dead. Or they want special effects. But Sue's style of agenting changed." Studio executives were no longer willing to tolerate her calling them up and screaming at them or making them feel stupid; the movie business was now about the nice, soft, seductive sell—the CAA way.

"Sue used to call me three times a week and ask me, 'What are you doing?' 'What's going on?'" remembered Jerry Weintraub. "And I would say, 'I don't have time to talk about nothing. I'm so busy.' A lot of this place lives on that information gathering. But it doesn't go anywhere at the end of the day. It doesn't get you anywhere."

Guy McElwaine had returned to ICM, and time had done nothing to warm his relationship with Sue. He remained very cuffs-and-collars, California polished—and Sue remained the aggressive street fighter. Sue's office was on the seventh floor, McElwaine's on the eighth, and they spent as little time together as possible. Jim Wiatt, who became an agent at ICM in the late 1970s, recalled going into Sue's office for a meeting to have her say, "What—Guy's not available?" Occasionally, she would egg McElwaine on to talk about some of his notable conquests in both business and romance, only to deflate him immediately. One day she asked him, "Guy, who are your greatest *schtupps*?" McElwaine thought for a moment and said, "Juliet Prowse. And then probably Martha Hyer."

"Oh, Martha-for-Hyer." Sue sighed. "Oh, well, Guy. Bobby Evans fucked *Ginger Rogers*."

By the mid-1980s she was even more lax about details than she had been early on. "She would rely on others," said Wiatt. "She would tell me to finish up work on a deal, or she would tell Michael Black or Jeff Berg to do it. She didn't need to be great on details. She was spending her time being larger than life and getting people on the phone and doing things most people couldn't do." She also made brutal fun of Berg behind his back for his tendency to explain everything to everyone, as if they were his intellectual inferiors.

Sue became increasingly frustrated when she couldn't pull off a deal. She pressed Sid Sheinberg at Universal on a daily basis to cast Ryan O'Neal as Bugsy Siegel in the movie about the gangster that the studio was preparing. (It was a picture that had been in development for years; Peter Bogdanovich had been set to direct it in 1976.) "It was absurd," recalled Sheinberg. "Bugsy was dark haired, very 'Jewish' looking, and Ryan O'Neal oozes Irishness." The film was eventually made with Warren Beatty, much to Sue's everlasting regret.

She constantly reminisced about the exciting days of the late 1960s and early '70s. To her old friend Boaty Boatwright, Sue had often seemed a little like Barbara Stanwyck's Stella Dallas—the woman standing outside, watching through the window as the glamorous wedding takes place. At one point in the late 1970s, Sue's ICM colleague Sybil Christopher had attended a party in New York that Diane von Furstenberg had thrown for Sue. The cream of New York society was in attendance, and Christopher asked the guest of honor, "Sue, who are all these people?"

"I don't know," said Sue. "But I can't believe they're all here just because they want to meet me."

As Boatwright had observed, even most of the people who became justi-
fiably angry with her needed to seek her favor. But Sue no longer cared—or
at least pretended she didn't.

At work, as she pursued star clients and failed to land them, she more
and more often directed her poison darts at herself. She would stroll down
the hall to fellow agent Martha Luttrell's office and, after asking her if she
had any chocolate, would inquire, "What little cunt are you signing? My
day? Honeeey, I'm so cold I couldn't sign Totie Fields's legs." She was also
deeply wounded by several more losses on her roster around this time—
particularly Sidney Lumet, who had long been one of her most prominent
director clients.

"She was bored," said John Heyman. "She was a tap dancer—a genuine performer. The lights would go on, and she would be ready to do her act.
I think she was fed up with it."

Sue had no tolerance for being bored. And with Jean-Claude's directing
career still a disappointment, and the affront to her self-esteem that *All
Night Long* had wrought, she saw no point in staying in the game.

In early March 1986, Michael Caine received a call from Sue.

"Michael, it's not fun anymore. I'm going." She made exit calls to all of
her other clients as well, cleaned out her desk, and withdrew to Bel Air
Road, with no idea of what lay ahead.

"We regret Sue's decision, but we also respect it," announced ICM
chairman Jeff Berg. "She is a great agent and a wonderful colleague, and
all of us at ICM wish her nothing but the best."

CHAPTER SEVENTEEN

1986–1991

More often than not, major public figures who make the decision to retire—
or have the decision made for them—are unable to keep themselves from
indulging in a bit of self-justifying spin. They tell the press that they have
had all the fun and excitement of being at the top; that they want to devote
themselves to other projects while they are still young enough to do so; that
they want to spend more time with their family.

Sue, to her credit, said very little publicly about her decision to leave
ICM when she was only fifty-four. There was, in fact, little she *could* say.
The last few years at the agency had not been particularly fun or exciting,
and she had no interest in any other projects. She did tell some of her close
friends that perhaps she and Jean-Claude could really get to know each
other now that she didn't have a band of unruly movie-star children to look
after. But she did not approach retirement with great joy or anticipation.

She had no immediate financial worries—Jean-Claude knew a great
deal about the stock market and he had invested her ICM salary quite
adeptly in a keenly diversified portfolio—and passed most of her days
lounging around the house, smoking pot heavily, puffing on Gauloises,
splashing in the pool. She and Jean-Claude spent considerable time in
Paris, though Jean-Claude continued to go there for months on end by himself, at which point Sue complained loud and long that he had abandoned
her once again. When Marlo Thomas would telephone her from New York,
telling Sue that her husband, Phil Donahue, was spending a few days by
himself at their house in Connecticut, Sue would routinely chastise her,
telling her what a wonderful husband she had and how foolish it was for her
to let him out of her sight for any length of time.

Her attitude toward men remained as old school as ever. "Her bottom
line was always about men," observed Toni Howard—and although she
considered that there wasn't one capable of fidelity, the idea of a straying

husband seemed not to bother her much. She loved to counsel her women friends on how to keep their husbands happy—and how to keep their mouths shut when the men were talking, an instruction she would frequently issue at the dinner table. She often claimed that Jean-Claude kept mistresses stashed away—there were also rumors that he was an occasional client of Madam Alex, the noted A-list Hollywood hooker—and that she was well aware of what kind of kinky things he was up to in Paris.

Her own attitude toward Paris remained strangely ambivalent; she was happy enough to spend a short time there but was always eager to get home to Los Angeles, to find out what her friends were up to and to keep her ear to the ground about what was happening in the movie business.

In 1986, Sue and Jean-Claude attended the wedding of Douglas Wick and Lucy Fisher. She had met Fisher several years earlier and was not pleased when, in the summer of 1981, Fisher and Sue's former ICM colleague Paula Weinstein spent the summer in Ravello, where they became quite friendly with Gore Vidal and Howard Austen and wound up having dinner with them nearly every evening. Sue had always been particularly possessive about her friendship with Vidal, even though she criticized him frequently. "There was a picture of me sitting in Gore's lap," said Lucy Fisher-Wick, "and he wasn't that kind of guy, usually. That really got Sue's goat, and she decided to get to know me better, because if I could be sitting in Gore's lap, well . . ."

Fisher followed the correct Sue Mengers-approved path for women: she married a smart, successful man. Wick's parents were close friends of Ronald and Nancy Reagan. At Douglas and Lucy's wedding, Sue told screenwriter Patricia Resnick that she would give her five hundred dollars if she cut in on Nancy Reagan on the dance floor. Resnick did it and danced with the First Lady, much to Sue's delight.

She made several lengthy stays at Vidal's house in Ravello, with Jean-Claude, or with Boaty Boatwright, Alana Stewart, or other friends. She still loved the water, loved walking nude on the beach and splashing in the ocean. She and Jean-Claude also made frequent trips to New York, eventually subletting producer David Chasman's apartment in the Museum Tower at Fifteen West Fifty-third Street. Sue liked seeing her New York friends on a more regular basis, but the Tramonts didn't keep the apartment for long since they found New York too expensive, and she wasn't keen on being around so many career-driven people when she herself wasn't working.

When the Tramonts were in New York, Sue often spent time on Fire Island, which she had come to love as a young woman. On one occasion, she and Jean-Claude spent several rainy days in a beach house with David Geffen and Fran Lebowitz, who later recalled it as one of the funniest times of her life. When they were on Fire Island, Jean-Claude did a series of beautiful charcoal drawings of Sue lying on the beach, taking the sun and reading a book. She later had them framed and displayed in their home.

Occasionally, during these years, Sue would wonder aloud if she should have had a child, but she usually dismissed the subject almost as soon as she had brought it up. She continued to show little interest in the children of her close friends. Some people felt that she made an exception for Anthony Perkins and Berry Berenson's two young sons, Osgood and Elvis, but Osgood Perkins remembered it differently. "She was friendly and funny and available," he said, "but it was clear that she had no business with children and children had no business with her. I never thought it was anything exclusive or nasty. It was kind of like a 'that doesn't interest me' stance. I got it as a child. It was honest, in a world where all adults pretend they want to know what the kid is talking about, or want to hold something dirty the kid has brought them. They put on their best game face. But I could count on Sue not to pretend, not to bullshit me."

She spent the occasional weekend at Max Palevsky's house in Palm Springs. At the time, the town was not frequented by Hollywood elite to the degree that it would be later, but Palevsky's wealth and social standing made it acceptable for Sue to go there. Palevsky and his wife, Jodie Evans, also treated a group of friends, among them Sue and Fran Lebowitz, to a trip to Israel in the summer of 1986. Palevsky's connections with the Israeli government got several members of the group to the top of Masada in a helicopter (which turned out to be illegal, since the gusts from helicopter blades had been causing erosion of the land). Sue, who had never been entirely comfortable flying, developed a certain phobia about it after surviving the hijacking incident in 1979, and refused to board the vehicle, even when assured that it was being manned by a top Israeli fighter pilot.

Fran Lebowitz, a nonobservant Jew, gratefully accepted the invitation to fly onto the top of Masada, and laughed at the others in the group who chose to walk up. "Only Jews would think it was a mountain," said Lebowitz. "It's a big hill! You're supposed to walk to the top and get some sort of blessing. If you don't want to walk, or don't need a blessing, they have a kind of monorail. And that's how Sue went. She arrived before we did, and as we were landing, everyone was looking to see who this was. It was a military helicopter, and there was a certain amount of nervousness as to why it was landing there. And then these Americans jumped out."

Sue, no doubt with a trace of envy, said to Lebowitz, "You really know how to make an entrance."

But the real high point of the trip was a private audience with Prime Minister Shimon Peres. Everyone in the group of Americans was quite respectful, asking him questions about Israel. "But Sue sat there with him, gossiping about movie stars!" remembered Lebowitz. "He wasn't interested in anyone else's earnest little questions. Sue was saying, 'Did you know that so-and-so is fucking so-and so?' He was riveted. He was completely charmed and completely fascinated by her."

As the months passed, it became clear that Sue was not inclined to reinvent herself. Perhaps the first invention of her persona had proven more strenuous than anyone realized. Though she showed no interest in a second act, either within the movie industry or outside it, she continued to ferret out information on all the latest studio deals, which pictures were doing business and which weren't, who was sleeping with whom—and she began to follow the new young actors closely. Glenn Caron, producer of the hit television series *Moonlighting*, recalled a night in 1988 when he and Sue were among the dinner guests at Ray Stark's house. The rocky years with Streisand had not affected Sue's relationship with the star's one-time producer; she continued to quote him to anyone who would listen. "Ray never said anything wrong, according to Sue," recalled Fran Lebowitz. "Every single thing he told her, she believed."

Stark enjoyed screening yet-to-be-released films in his art-filled living room; if his guests didn't seem interested in one movie, he would start up another. On this particular evening, Gore Vidal and Shirley MacLaine gave thumbs down to the first picture Stark screened, so he switched to Donald Petrie's low-budget *Mystic Pizza*. The lights went down, and the second an unknown Julia Roberts appeared on the screen, Sue stood up and pointed at her image and declared, "Oh, my God! This girl is a star!" Caron said, "I remember thinking how prescient and how brave, to make such a public declaration in front of so many accomplished and opinionated people."

By 1988, Sue confessed to feeling restless. Unlike Jean-Claude, she was not a born traveler. She did not possess his deep interest in European history and architecture and culture, and still spoke only the most rudimentary French and practically no Italian. She enjoyed living her own version of *la dolce vita*, but she could not remotely be said to be a genuine member of the international set. In the end, her heart was only in Hollywood. By now, they had sold the house on Bel Air Road for well over $2 million, and she and Jean-Claude had found a new house that they liked. It was a lovely "downsizing" alternative: a 4,400-square-foot salmon-colored house at 1207 Lexington Road in Beverly Hills, designed by John Elgin Woolf, who had created homes for such golden-age stars as Cary Grant, Loretta Young, and Barbara Stanwyck. The house was built on a curve around an egg-shaped swimming pool surrounded by Greek columns. It had a large living room and a formal dining room, a library, and three bedrooms. It was run-down and in need of a new roof and upgraded plumbing, but Sue and Jean-Claude fell in love with it. Jean-Claude went to work overseeing the repairs and furnishing it, which he did on a tight budget, picking up things almost entirely from auctions. He had an expert eye for interior design, and had the place redone in earth tones, largely terra-cotta and celadon green, with blue-and-green Belgian tapestries on the walls and Aubusson pillows scattered around. "It had an old-world, faded-aristocracy look," remembered Joanna Poitier, "like you had inherited these pieces from your great aunt." In the new house, Sue continued to surround herself with her favorite symbols of gracious, high-end living—excellent china and silver for the dinner parties they still gave, Pratesi sheets, vases of orchids—all of it sheer perfection, as if she were creating the ultimate movie set.

It was then that she began to receive a long series of phone calls from her friends who worked at the William Morris Agency. The once-potent talent firm was in a state of chaos. Since the death of Stan Kamen, none of the other established William Morris agents in top positions—among them, Walt Zifkin, Roger Davis, and president Norman Brokaw—was thought to possess the right combination of traits to take over and lead the company. Leonard Hirshan, the veteran agent who had guided the careers of Clint Eastwood, Sophia Loren, and many others, was head of Morris's motion picture group, but it was generally conceded that he, too, was no Stan Kamen. Hirshan was best at working with individual talent, but he was not a born administrator, nor someone with the vision to pull together a company that was rapidly falling into disarray.

By now the coolly calculating Mike Ovitz, the outwardly soft-spoken and relaxed Ron Meyer, and the rest of the "CAA boys," as they were commonly known around Hollywood, had risen to a position of enormous power. While Sue admitted that she never gave much thought to an actor's career more than one to two years in the future, CAA specialized in long-term strategy. Ovitz believed that team management, not individual agent power, was the key to success, and his client list included Barbra Streisand, Steven Spielberg, Sydney Pollack, Tom Cruise, Dustin Hoffman, Michael Douglas, Sylvester Stallone, Barry Levinson, and Bill Murray. Mike Ovitz was a corporate player on a level unimaginable to most of the employees of the William Morris Agency; in 1988 he was a key figure in the negotiations that would result in the $3.4 billion sale of Columbia Pictures to the electronics conglomerate Sony, after the studio's previous multinational owner, Coca-Cola, had proven too gun-shy about the volatile nature of the movie business. Morris's board felt that perhaps it needed an established talent wrangler to sign new stars and rejuvenate a client roster that was now topheavy with over-the-hill actors. And as 1988 went on, those conversations began to center more and more on Sue.

At first she claimed not to be interested. But several of her close friends and allies at the firm were deeply committed to the cause and launched a campaign to persuade her to come back to work. Ed Limato, who had left ICM for William Morris some years earlier, was particularly eager to have her come aboard and had done a great deal to sell the board of directors on the idea. So had John Burnham, the young agent she had befriended at ICM, who had also decamped to William Morris; Toni Howard, now a Morris agent as well; and Boaty Boatwright, by now settled in the company's New York office. (Unlike Sue, Boatwright disliked Los Angeles and preferred to base herself in either London or New York.)

Sue's employment by William Morris became an incredibly protracted process; the older men on the board were divided about whether or not they wanted her, and they went back and forth over the terms of the deal. One temporary obstacle was the question of autonomy. Although Limato had urged her hiring, he had assumed he would be running the motion picture division along with Sue, who thought otherwise and said simply, "There is no co-running. I run it."

Eventually the board offered her a three-year contract as senior vice president with an annual salary of $1 million, plus stock in the company. But they stopped short of giving her a position on the board, and Sue, strangely, did not insist on it. Privately she made jokes to her friends about the doddering old men running the company and seemed not to doubt for a moment that she would ultimately maneuver her way around them with no difficulty. The board members, for their part, were openly contemptuous of her for being an older woman. "Even though they were all a decade older than Sue," remembered Elaine Goldsmith-Thomas, at the time a Morris agent, "they felt they were impervious to criticism and to ageism."

Of all the agents at William Morris, few loved his star clients quite as much as Ed Limato. While he had a reputation for being vindictive—in his office hung a double-decker row of photos of his top stars, and when any of them left him, his or her picture was moved to the bottom row—but he had not made a habit of indulging in the "I hate actors" invective that Sue had during her waning days at ICM. On April 6, 1988, the day Sue was to begin at William Morris, Ed Limato, who had been mysteriously missing in action for several days, announced he was leaving the company. Sue's decision that he would not be running the movie department with her had upset Limato. He had telephoned Toni Howard the day before to inform her he was departing, and when Howard asked if it was all right for her to tell Sue, Limato agreed.

"Sue," Howard said, "you may not want to come to William Morris, because Ed is leaving." But Sue, while startled by Limato's decision, underestimated his power and cunning, as she had often done in the past. On the day that Limato left, so did Richard Gere, Michelle Pfeiffer, Mel Gibson, and Denzel Washington.

This exodus of top talent immediately cast a shadow over Sue's arrival. Her return also inspired a flood of articles in the press, many of them breathless, but a few poisonous. "Who with a little HEAT still exists whom Mengers might lure back?" wondered *Los Angeles Business Journal*. "Peter Bogdanovich? Michael Cimino? Paula Prentiss? . . . Gabby Hayes?"

The country was then about to emerge from eight years of Ronald Reagan's revolutionary reimagining of the U.S. economic structure. The accepted ethic was that it was all about coining money, in a way that it had not been, at least not as exclusively, during Sue's years at ICM. Sue had always aggressively pursued the top dollar, but the corporate machinations perfected by CAA bored her. She thought that doing business should be fun as well. But agents weren't giving parties much anymore. She wasn't going to sign top clients because they enjoyed hearing her funny stories, smoking her quality pot, and dining on her chicken potpie; she was going to sign them only because she could outmaneuver the competition in the increasingly complex numbers game, and that had never been her strength.

From the beginning, Sue's return to the agency business was a halting, stumbling affair. Many of the clients she pursued were happy at CAA or one of the other agencies in Hollywood and saw no point in making a switch now that they were comfortably settled and prosperous. Her most painful realization concerned her roster from her glory days at ICM, whom she assumed she would have little difficulty in re-signing. When she let them know she was back, all of them said that that was very nice, but they would stay where they were.

Now there was plenty of opportunity to curse her ex-clients into the depths of hell, to wish cancer or AIDS on them, when they declined to come back to her. Ryan O'Neal declined, as did Michael Caine, Gene Hackman, Sidney Lumet, and Cybill Shepherd, now riding high on TV's *Moonlighting*, and perhaps still smarting from the time, a few years earlier, when she had gone to Sue for career advice and Sue had told her to forget it, that she was permanently washed up in the business. The one yes came from the everloyal Christopher Walken.

But it was going to take much more than Walken's presence on her roster to win back some of her lost stature. Many people in Hollywood relished the fact that her position in the industry had slipped. One story that got around quickly was that Jean-Claude had observed that he used to be married to Barbra Streisand's agent; now he was married to Treat Williams's.

This turned out to be just a story, as Williams claims he was never represented by Sue. Many of Sue's friends feared that Toni Howard was right: you couldn't say "I hate actors" as often as Sue had done and expect that people wouldn't remember it. Cher disagreed with this observation. "Sue adored her clients," she said. "I mean, she didn't love them all the time. We're just obnoxious, self-centered children. How can you love us all the time?"

It didn't take Sue long to realize the mess that William Morris was in— and in her new position, she had only limited power to fix some of it. Unlike ICM, Morris leaned toward penny-wise and pound-foolish, paying some of their best agents in the $60,000 range and denying them company cars. There was also a profound sense of entitlement: the executives insisted that the assistants dress expensively, even if their salaries couldn't support anything more than a basic wardrobe. Sue herself could be crudely dismissive of Morris's younger staff members. Jeff Field, who had worked as John Burnham's assistant and was burning to be promoted to an agent, initially did not receive much support from her. She regarded him as a greedy upstart, and it was only after he demonstrated a talent for bringing in new clients that she began to take him seriously. He was involved in signing Kelly Lynch, and later intently pursued Emily Lloyd, who was extremely hot at the time. "She finally realized I was an aggressive young agent with no fear," said Field. "The only way I was going to get in her good graces was to do something that would put me on the map in a positive way."

She could still give excellent advice to her colleagues. Johnnie Planco, an agent at William Morris at the time, remembered what a tough taskmaster she could be. Scott Glenn was preparing to succeed John Malkovich in Lanford Wilson's long-running Broadway hit *Burn This*, and Sue told Planco to go to New York to see the play and sign Glenn on pain of death. Planco thought it seemed like a fool's errand, but did as he was told. When he met Glenn backstage, the two of them hit it off, and he succeeded in signing him. Planco immediately called Sue, who said, "Listen to Mama and see what happens?"

Sue detested the condescending old-boys'-club attitude of the older men on the staff but took great pleasure in her relationships with new female colleagues, among them Elaine Goldsmith, and she was happy to be working with her old friends Toni Howard and Boaty Boatwright. But she was quite brutal about the quality of the talent they were representing. After reviewing each of the individual agents' client lists, Sue pronounced, "You all have crap!" She was determined to bring star power into the agency but repeated her earlier mistake of not putting enough focus into developing young actors into major stars. Among Elaine Goldsmith's clients who had yet to break through were Tim Robbins and Julia Roberts. "Without stars, honeeey, *you'll* never be one," she told Goldsmith. She spoke dismissively of Roberts, apparently having forgotten the night when she saw her in *Mystic Pizza* at Ray Stark's house. Goldsmith rather defensively pointed out that Roberts was about to star in the film version of Robert Harling's stage hit *Steel Magnolias*, directed by Sue's old client Herbert Ross.

"SALLY FIELD is starring in *Steel Magnolias*, honeeey," snapped Sue. "OLYMPIA DUKAKIS is starring in *Steel Magnolias*. DARRYL HANNAH! SHIRLEY MACLAINE! JULIA ROBERTS NOBODY KNOWS!" In the fall of 1989, when *Steel Magnolias* was released, Julia Roberts got serious attention from the press and was the only cast member to be nominated for an Academy Award. Sue lost no time in telling Goldsmith, "I *told* you she was a movie star."

But the stars continued to be elusive, no matter how many tricks Sue pulled out of her hat. She arranged a signing meeting with Geena Davis shortly after the actress's Academy Award–winning success in 1988's *The Accidental Tourist*. Toni Howard, J. J. Harris, and Elaine Goldsmith were all present, and they gave Davis the hard sell, talking about current hot projects and about female executive power.

"Geena, let's be honest," said Sue. "If you don't sign, I'm going to blame Elaine. And then Elaine is going to blame J. J. And J. J. is going to blame Toni, and we're all going to point the finger at each other."

Geena Davis laughed but shortly afterward signed with CAA.

At the regular Wednesday staff meetings, there was a lot of grandstanding on the part of many of the agents. Someone would begin to brag about a deal for a star client that was nowhere close to set, and Sue would start to make masturbatory gestures. At other times, when someone else was speaking, she would mutter under her breath, "These people are such *schtumies*." Sitting across the table, Toni Howard, worried that the others would think Sue was losing her grip, would make discreet hand signals to attempt to get her to stop.

One of William Morris's few top female stars at the time was Anjelica

Huston, who was being pursued by director Stephen Frears to play hard-bitten con artist Lilly Dillon in his upcoming film *The Grifters*. Huston, however, was hedging. "I was worried," recalled Huston, "because there was a scene where Lilly gets slammed in the stomach with a bag of oranges and her insides are so messed up from it, she shits in the corner. I said to Toni Howard, 'I don't know if I can do this. It's graphic.' Howard suggested that she speak with Sue, who several years earlier had turned Huston down as a client because, bizarrely, she felt that Huston was too much like Ali MacGraw.

Huston showed up for a meeting with Sue at William Morris. The first words out of Sue's mouth were "If Stephen Frears wants you to take a shit in the corner, that's exactly what you should do." Years later, Huston remembered it as the kind of advice she always responded to, and gave kudos to Sue, whom the actress felt was "unparalleled in her honesty."

Whatever the obstacles she was facing at Morris, work didn't occupy every second of Sue's life; she retained her curiosity about other people and was constantly seeking to expand her social circle. When Robin Hurlstone, a tall, handsome, British art dealer, became Joan Collins's new lover in the late 1980s, Collins lost little time in bringing him to Sue's for an unveiling. Hurlstone recalled that he was so intimidated by Sue that he wasn't able to speak.

"Honeeey," Sue finally said, "you haven't had a line in twelve pages."

Hurlstone was deeply touched by the notice she took of him and came to love both her and Jean-Claude deeply. "I think the fact that Jean-Claude and I adored each other made my relationship with Sue even stronger," said Hurlstone. "He was kind of a touchstone in a way. He was terribly funny, terribly observant, and well read. Extremely adept on many subjects that I love—art, travel, France." Hurlstone introduced Sue to many people, such as the celebrated art historian John Richardson.

Sue introduced Hurlstone to many of her "twinklies." One day during lunch, she confessed to him that she was bored with Los Angeles and wanted to meet someone interesting. Hurlstone promptly telephoned Elton John and invited him to lunch at Sue's house. John was apprehensive, since he had met her a few years earlier and found her terrifying, but he agreed to show up. When Hurlstone called Sue to tell her he was bringing John and his partner, David Furnish, for lunch, Sue was impressed. "Tell me," she asked, "is there anything they can't eat, apart from pussy?"

In his ongoing friendship with the Tramonts, individually and as a couple,

Hurlstone was often brought up short by how unguarded they were. Jean-Claude confessed to Hurlstone his decades-old affair with Jean-Pierre Aumont. Sue appeared to be completely aware of it and not the least bit concerned; one evening, when Collins and Hurlstone were entertaining the Tramonts at their home in Saint-Tropez, the conversation turned to married men who were secretly sleeping with other men. "Oh, my honey had a few experiences like that when he was a baby," Sue said dismissively. Jean-Claude pointed out to her that at the time of his affair with Aumont, he had been twenty-eight.

A few minutes later the group got onto the subject of circumcision.

"My honey is circumcised," said Sue.

"No, I'm not," said Jean-Claude.

"Yes, you are."

Jean-Claude was incredulous: "For God's sake, we have been married for all these years, and you don't know?"

"Baby Sue" purred, "I thought it was rude to look."

In mid-1989, the *Los Angeles Times* ran an article titled "William Morris: Is the Movie Luster Slowly Fading?" that placed much of the blame for the company's lethargic performance on Sue.

As she repeatedly failed to work the magic that had been expected of her at the company, Sue's way of expressing herself became even sharper and more brutal. "Everyone was a *schwarze*, a kike, a cunt, or a cooz," Marcia Diamond said with a laugh. Often the objects of her conversational wrath were the men on the board of directors at William Morris. When dealing with them face to face, Sue might exercise diplomacy, but behind their backs she would often lay them out flat. "I'm working for these fucking old Jews," she would say to John Burnham. "They're so fucking stupid." One of the board members for whom she had the least degree of respect was Lee Stevens, William Morris's president and chief executive officer. Stevens was a rather starstruck man who had been at Morris since he started working in the mailroom in 1953. In 1988, after Stevens had just returned to the office after brain surgery, John Burnham mentioned to Sue, "I just ran into Lee Stevens."

"No difference, right?" she replied.

In February of the following year, Stevens died of lymphoma at Cedars-Sinai Medical Center.

As always, when she expressed affection for someone with whom she worked, it could come in the sharpest, most unexpected way. In early 1989, Elaine Goldsmith needed help with a promising script by J. F. Lawton called *Three Thousand*. A dark story about a prostitute and her john, *Three Thousand* found its way from fledgling-independent to mainstream-studio picture when it landed with Jeffrey Katzenberg at Disney. There it sat for months until Katzenberg made the decision to assign it to director Garry Marshall and try to build it into a mainstream romantic comedy, which would soon be retitled *Pretty Woman*. "It was Jeffrey Katzenberg who transformed *Three Thousand* into *Pretty Woman*," recalled Goldsmith. "Julia had been loosely attached to the darker, smaller version of this film, but all bets were off once it went to Disney. We had to campaign hard to get it for her." Goldsmith had lobbied the company's head of production, David Hoberman, and producers Laura Ziskin and Steve Reuther, but the final call was Katzenberg's. And by all accounts, it wasn't happening very quickly. "The process took months," recalled Goldsmith. In the interim, Roberts had committed to a small independent film for a different company. Ten days later, Disney put *Three Thousand* on the fast track and officially offered Roberts the movie. "The question wasn't 'Should we do *Three Thousand*?'" said Goldsmith. "The question was 'How can we do it?' We needed help. We needed guidance. We needed Sue. And she delivered. It was like watching a master chess player negotiating the moves, massaging the egos, flirting, cajoling, threatening, pushing her way through, until ultimately we had a victory. I sat at her feet and watched in absolute awe and admiration. Without Sue Mengers, I'm not sure Julia would have been able to do *Pretty Woman*. That's the truth."

It was a complicated effort to move the independent picture aside, but once that was accomplished, Goldsmith informed Sue of one other issue: Julia Roberts wouldn't do nudity.

"SHE'S PLAYING A HOOKER?" screamed Sue. "WHAT THE FUCK DID SHE EXPECT?" Then she picked up the phone and called Roberts, saying sweetly, "Honeeey, if I had your body, I would be shopping naked down the aisles at Gelson's." Roberts laughed but was resolute. "It was a lot of dancing, and a lot of conferences," Elaine Goldsmith recalled, "and it was a lot of pressure—I was twenty-nine years old. How lucky were we to have Sue?"

When Risa Shapiro moved from William Morris's New York office to Los Angeles at the end of 1989, Sue made sure she got situated in the proper place. She asked Shapiro where she was shopping around for a home, and when Shapiro told her, she said curtly, "Too far east." Sue immediately telephoned the owner of a nice building that was two blocks from the William Morris offices; when Shapiro got an apartment there, Sue sent the owner a magnum of champagne. "She had a tendency to fight with those she really loved," said Shapiro. "I don't like to fight, so she didn't fight with me. But she was like a parent. She had no children, but she was the mother to everyone."

By now Sue's prospects at Morris had become so discouraging that she had begun opening staff meetings with "Well, guess who turned me down today?" She was smoking more and more pot during the day, and when she did, her manner often became increasingly fuzzy and eccentric.

One day, after failing to land Richard Pryor and Mickey Rourke, Sue returned to the office in a state of utter defeat and said, "I couldn't get Mickey *Rooney* if he came back now." It was pure Sue: another executive might easily have deflected the blame, but she assumed the responsibility for her own poor performance.

Toward the end of 1989, John Burnham and Mike Simpson were abruptly named codirectors of William Morris's West Coast motion picture division. Initially, it appeared that Sue was still in charge. She thought that Burnham and Simpson were going to supplement her, that her status as a show-business legend made it impossible for her to be supplanted. Gradually, though, it became clear to her that she was being marginalized, and it stunned her to think she could have been maneuvered out of the way by the men on the board. The idea that she would have to share her clients with the men on the staff was appalling to her. "It wasn't based on a new sense of teamwork," said Goldsmith. "It was based on fear—the fear that the people running the agency didn't have enough heavyweights."

"Mike Simpson and I got her job, not nefariously, but just openly," said John Burnham years later. "She felt I was a little bit of a quisling. But she both didn't want to do the job anymore and undid herself. I didn't chase down her job and nip at her heels. But it was awkward. She was a good coach, sort of—but she was arbitrary. She thought some people were morons, and she would piss all over them, and you have to be more democratic as a coach. Sue had the likes and the not-likes."

Sue's contract with Morris was set to run until April 1991. For most of

1990, she kept up appearances, coming in to the office, collecting her salary, making attempts to sign clients—but she knew that the game was all but over for her. When *Pretty Woman* was released in March of that year, she had the great satisfaction of watching Julia Roberts become an enormous box-office star, the biggest in years—and she was happy to tell Elaine Goldsmith how proud she was of her, personally. But Roberts was not a client Sue had brought to the agency.

By the fall of 1990, it was made clear to her that William Morris would not renew her contract. In December, she announced that she would not be staying until the end of her term; her contract was being bought out.

She left quietly. In the wake of Sue's departure, Toni Howard, Elaine Goldsmith, Risa Shapiro, and Boaty Boatwright all turned in their resignations and moved on to other posts.

Sue's brief time at William Morris marked the first genuine failure of her life. Putting Barbra Streisand and Jean-Claude together for *All Night Long* and ultimately losing Streisand had been a severe misstep—but she had built up enough success at that point to absorb it, had she really cared to. The William Morris episode was another matter entirely. Had she been brought into the job with less fanfare, she might have had an easier time of it. But it had been announced to the world that she was going to revive a sleeping giant—and she had proven unable to do so.

Why, exactly, did Sue have so much trouble reactivating her career at the Morris office? Certainly Toni Howard's theory about her increasing bitterness toward actors carries some weight. And her prime motivation for accepting the job had been the money; her heart was never fully in it. "She was ambivalent," said Paula Weinstein, "and there's no greater impediment to being successful."

But there was another factor that was far more significant: in 1988, when she began the job, she was well into her fifties and had been away from the business for two full years—a decade, at least, in Hollywood time. She was unquestionably perceived as something of a dinosaur by the rest of the industry—and a female dinosaur at that, which is particularly unforgivable in Hollywood.

"The clients didn't stay away because she wasn't good," said Elaine Goldsmith. "They stayed away because the word around town was that she was old. The truth was that Mike Ovitz was fifteen years younger than she was, from a different generation, and it was easy to see that he was a younger, more viable choice—a better, newer version.

"That's what happened to Sue. And it was heartbreaking to see her vulnerable. Hard to see it, and hard for her to show it."

CHAPTER EIGHTEEN

1992–1997

Now that Sue was out of the business for good, she might have written a best-selling memoir or made a small fortune on the lecture circuit, regaling her audience with anecdotes from her prime years as a Hollywood power broker. But she was not comfortable with the role of the salty showbiz veteran, retailing her autobiography for profit. With a few exceptions, she seemed to have a distaste for coming out to take one more bow, like Sophie Tucker, waving a ragged copy of the sheet music for "Some of These Days" over her head.

Instead, she shifted into a different role. Rather than being the brilliant, fast-talking guest on a top-rated talk show, she was to be its hostess, drawing out the best from the people around her table, yet somehow always managing to remain the center of attention. In the future, she would complain loud and long about having to go to anyone else's house, anyone else's yacht, anyone else's villa, to do "a morning, afternoon, and evening show." For the most part, the Sue Mengers Show would now be staged exclusively at home; the legend would continue but mostly within the walls of 1207 Lexington Road.

Although she occasionally fretted about money, Jean-Claude had continued to invest her earnings well, and during the economic boom of the 1990s, she got richer and richer without taking on a paying job, apart from a very occasional appearance speaking at a university. But she was anything but isolated. She began spending more and more time with her close circle of women friends, who retained her comic label "the Dyke-ettes"— the regular members of the club being Boaty Boatwright, Toni Howard, Ali MacGraw, Joanna Poitier, Marcia Diamond, Alana Stewart, Sherry Lansing, and Lili Zanuck. From time to time others joined the group, including Angie Dickinson and Anjelica Huston. Over long lunches of tuna fish sandwiches and soup, plus generous hits of pot, the women would gossip about the business, but most often about the men they had slept with—often in precise, even clinical, detail. Sue would goad them, allegedly in the interest of naked honesty, and while some would occasionally bristle and keep a temporary distance, there was seldom a lasting breach of friendship. The tougher Sue was on them, the more the Dyke-ettes seemed to interpret her behavior as a gesture of affection from the den mother of an exclusive club. And there was no camouflaging the fact that she deeply loved her closest friends, no matter how cruel her wit could be at times. "Those of us who felt that affection believed it," said Ali MacGraw, "in spite of the barrage of negativity and criticism."

Sue's women's club meetings were like something out of a Jackie Collins novel, or Truman Capote's story "La Côte Basque, 1965"—gatherings of Hollywood's elite, talking about their husbands, their lovers, their career triumphs and mistakes. The conversation tended to be hilariously funny, with lots of tart-tongued advice thrown in. To her older women friends who were desperately looking for new romances, Sue would often intone, "RE-TIRE THE PUSSY." But there was plenty of room for serious matters as well. "People would talk openly about anything," said Alana Stewart. "She brought that out in you. She didn't like it if little groups of people talked amongst themselves. She liked to be at the center of things. She would say, 'HELLO? I'M HERE?' She was a narcissist, but not at the exclusion of everyone else."

Lili Zanuck was a late initiate into the Dyke-ettes, but had the pedigree and record of achievement to belong: Lili had made a considerable name for herself in films, especially after winning the 1989 Best Picture Academy Award for producing the unexpected box-office hit *Driving Miss Daisy*. "Sue once accused me of having an intimacy problem," said Zanuck. "And I said, '*You're* the one who went ten years without telling Jean-Claude that you loved him.' She never wanted you to kiss her goodbye or hug her. As time went on she got a little better about it, but she didn't really like it. She would say, 'Okay, okay—I got it.' I would say, 'Sue, I am so happy to see you,' and she would say, 'As you should be.' I would tell her that I was never going to meet anyone with a mind like hers and she would say, 'No, honeeey, you're not.'"

Perhaps because she envied Zanuck for being married to such a major player in Hollywood, Sue often tried to provoke her friend about her marriage. "Dick and I would talk a lot on the phone," Zanuck recalled. "And Sue would say, 'You know why he's calling you: he doesn't trust you.' I would say, 'No, Sue—he misses me.' I had a marriage where if we saw the other one's car in the driveway, we'd get excited, because that meant one of us was home. Sue never really had that."

Several of the Dyke-ettes found themselves in a state of perpetual ambivalence about how to take her criticism. She might claim to detest Ruth, but it certainly appeared to the others that she was channeling her mother in her endless scrutiny of her friends' private and professional lives. Many of them struggled not to take a defensive position in the face of her searing evaluations of their weak points—and Lili Zanuck called her on it more than most did.

But even when Sue talked the toughest, she inspired a deep loyalty among her friends. Boaty Boatwright remained very much in Sue's camp, although the two women could be honest with each other and frequently had disagreements. Sue would tease Boaty about her incessant optimism, but again, she was happy for her friend's success. The two women continued to see a great deal of Gore Vidal, even though they both found him to be increasingly high maintenance as the years went by. "Whenever Gore was around, it was like 'Gore doesn't want to go out tonight' or 'Gore isn't doing this,'" observed Boaty's son, Patrick Baker. "Boaty and Sue loved Howard Austen, but they always seemed a little bit disappointed in Gore. They were the two mother hens, trying to keep him in line."

In 1991, one of the Dyke-ettes struck marital gold, as defined by Sue. Although she had never represented him, one of her favorite people in the business was William Friedkin, whose industry peak had coincided with her own, with *The French Connection* and *The Exorcist*. Friedkin loved talking to Jean-Claude and Sue about the many things that interested him on an intellectual level, particularly politics, art, and literature. Friedkin and Sherry Lansing's whirlwind romance and marriage surprised many in Hollywood, since they seemed in some ways an odd pairing: Friedkin had long since developed a reputation for being brilliant but headstrong and sharp-tongued, while Lansing was known as a good girl who wanted everyone to be happy. The couple eloped, and when they came back to Los Angeles, Lansing returned a call from Sue, who told her, "You will never be bored a day in your life." Sue and Lansing had known each other only casually for years, but now, because Lansing had fallen in love with Friedkin, she was somebody Sue became curious about.

The Sue that Lansing befriended was someone who worried incessantly over her girlfriends—worried that their husbands weren't treating them properly, worried that they hadn't put enough money away for the future. She loved to try to camouflage her concern behind her brilliant wit, but it was obvious to Lansing just how much she cared. "She was a moosh-face. I used to tell her that," said Lansing. Sue routinely called Lansing "Rosemary," after the Kennedy sister who had been lobotomized, simply because Lansing was so positive and seemed to like everyone with whom she came in contact. Often, if someone in the lunch group said something mean or negative about someone else, Sue would chime in with "Be careful—Rosemary is upset that you said that."

Sue and Lansing often discussed their tough, scrutinizing mothers. They would tell each other stories, and Sue would conclude, "It's a tie." "I think that most women who are successful had mothers who criticized them every day of their lives and never gave them the love they wanted," said Lansing. "That's why we kept striving. I would tell her about the horrible things my mother did and we would laugh. It was a bond. She always said she hated her mother. But I don't think she *really* did. If we hadn't had the mothers we did, would we have stayed in our hometowns and married the gas station attendant? I don't know."

Sue's friendship with Lansing was distinct from the ones she enjoyed with the other Dyke-ettes in one important respect: Lansing made it clear early on that she had no interest in talking about business in social situations. "I never said to Sue in my life, 'Do you think I should make this movie?'" Lansing recalled. "My friends had nothing to do with work, and if they wanted to talk about work, they weren't friends—it was a business meeting. Sue and I talked about our friends. Our marriages. Getting older. She would say to me, 'You can't possibly like everybody.' If she thought you were being disingenuous, she would call you on it." As much as Sue admired Lansing and was delighted by her success, she held fast to her belief that no one in the industry could read a script and predict automatically whether or not it would turn into a hit movie. She simply believed that some people were luckier than others.

Given her enormous intelligence and drive and original point of view on so many subjects, it was surprising that Sue seemed so uninterested in channeling herself into a new phase of her professional life. There were offers to teach, to consult, to write a book—all of which she spurned like unworthy lovers. After leaving William Morris, she did agree to be represented by her old ICM colleague Sam Cohn, who pitched a proposal for a memoir to several major publishing houses, including Doubleday and Random House. Ultimately she claimed that none of the offers was lucrative enough—she considered a mere $1 million advance insulting, given what others had received—and as time went on, she became increasingly dismissive of the very idea of writing a book, claiming, "I'm not going to talk about the size of somebody's dick." She was to a certain extent imprisoned by her past: having moved among the Hollywood elite for so many years, she had made up her mind that nothing else could possibly pass as a substitute. She was no longer in the film business, and would not be again. Yet the business remained her touchstone.

The movie industry in Los Angeles is filled with people who are never entirely sure what anyone else in the profession thinks of them. As time went on, Sue's unapologetic take on the politics of the movie business became her calling card. People who had never met her sought out her company because they knew she would give them a dose of straight talk. Ironically, what she had failed to do when she returned to William Morris, she succeeded in brilliantly as a hostess, dispensing advice to anyone who cared to come to Lexington Road to hear it. "She talked to me like I was her," said Joan Juliet Buck. "Which, I suppose we all do. Anyone we like, we think is us—that's why we like them. So it was wonderful to be brought into her life and be treated as part of her life, and hear all her secrets."

To a degree, she still operated in agent mode when she handed out advice to her actor friends. Liam Neeson was a frequent guest at Sue's, following his enormous success in Steven Spielberg's *Schindler's List* in 1993. Sue was also enormously fond of his wife, actress Natasha Richardson, always telling Neeson, "She's a classy broad. DON'T fuck this up." She was deeply concerned about where the actor's career might head after the peak of *Schindler's List*. "I was a jobbing actor," recalled Neeson. "If the script seemed okay and the money was good and the project had a good director, I would go for it. There wasn't any rhyme or reason. But she would try and corral me and say, 'You're hot. Do some action movies. The art stuff you can do when you're sixty.' I would laugh, but I sort of took it on board, you know?"

Frequently Sue would shock her guests by the seeming toughness of her views on social trends and current events. When Los Angeles erupted in riots after the 1992 acquittal of police officers that participated in a video-taped beating of suspect Rodney King, she was downright scathing about the public sympathy directed at the rioters. She often ridiculed people who were on welfare, brusquely saying that their real problem was that they were lazy. In Hollywood, where liberalism is mostly worn as a badge of honor, her views were not always received well, and friends frequently objected to her offhand racist comments, which sometimes seemed to indicate a certain internalized anti-Semitism. She believed in the Second Amendment, but she wasn't hawkish; she saw no sane reason for anyone to have an AK-47 stashed in his closet. On the topic of gun control, she could tweak the liberal stance of Hollywoodites who employed heavily armed security teams to patrol their property. "The nicest way you can say it is that she wasn't politically correct." Fran Lebowitz laughed. "But it went, in my opinion, beyond that. I think she thought that when people she knew expressed opposite opinions, that they were hypocrites. She thought it was a kind of pretension."

When her friends called her, she could be astonishingly blunt. "What do you want?" was often her response on picking up the phone. Then she would usually stay on the line for nearly an hour. Almost always it was she who chose the moment to terminate the conversation. Ali MacGraw or Sherry Lansing or Boaty Boatwright would wind up a lengthy story, and Sue would sigh and say, "Can I go now?" She remained, as Lillian Hellman once wrote of Dorothy Parker, a tangled fishnet of contradictions. She loved to gather people around her table, loved hearing their secrets and stories, even the ones she already knew, since some new wrinkle or nuance might be revealed in the retelling. But after all these years, it was still difficult for her to receive affection. She was, in fact, a person of tremendous needs, but Jean-Claude fulfilled many of them. Sometimes she would get upset if someone brought her flowers or a present. When Ali MacGraw was invited to dinner and brought her a hostess gift, Sue chided her, telling her that she couldn't afford these little extravagances. Yet she made exceptions for her wealthy friends, whom she expected to offer palpable evidence of their affection for her. When Marlo Thomas admired a spectacular sapphire-and-diamond ring that David Geffen had bought her, Sue shrugged and said, "Oh, he could have afforded more than this."

Can I Go Now?

Robin Hurlstone recalled that by now Jean-Claude was "sick to the back teeth of Beverly Hills and everything that lay within it." Whenever he saw the possibility of spending several weeks in Paris, he seized it. Sue complained if she had to accompany him, and she complained if he left her behind. Once, when she was protesting having to make another trip to France, she mentioned that she could have considered it a permanent residence if she had been guaranteed she would be in the constant company of Marie-Hélène de Rothschild and Jacqueline de Ribes. "I thought, 'Jesus Christ— you just retired,'" said Lili Zanuck. "'Can't you go hang out with your husband in Paris?' I had enough early success that if I never saw another 'twinklie' again, it would be fine. And the idea that at her age, it was still about 'twinklies'—I thought, how sad, how insecure."

Sue's definition of acceptable "twinklies" could be amazingly indiscriminate, and her pursuit of one major artist shocked and incensed Fran Lebowitz. During a trip to Germany, Sue sought out Third Reich filmmaker Leni Riefenstahl, a close personal friend of Adolf Hitler's and director of the Nazi propaganda film *Triumph of the Will*. Sue and Jean-Claude met Riefenstahl for tea, and when they returned to Los Angeles, Sue told Lebowitz how fascinating they had found the director.

Sue was hardly the first person to make allowances for Riefenstahl based on the director's reputation as an artist; she was generally heralded, despite the content of *Triumph of the Will*, as the preeminent female filmmaker of the twentieth century. Perhaps had Riefenstahl been officially convicted of a war crime, Sue might have felt differently. That a Jewish refugee would take tea with a celebrated Nazi was inexplicable to Lebowitz— yet Sue was suspicious of her outraged reaction.

"Do you mean to tell me that you wouldn't have gone to tea with Leni Riefenstahl?" Sue asked, incredulous.

Lebowitz said that unequivocally she would not, and told Sue about her student days at New York University, when Riefenstahl's book of photographs, *The Last of the Nuba*, had been published and the artist found herself the toast of the NYU faculty—"which was in itself," observed Lebowitz, "a kind of Third Reich enclave." But Sue would not back down from her position. Riefenstahl was a star—and that alone was justification for spending time in her presence.

When Sue did join Jean-Claude in Paris, their arguments often rivaled the ones they had in Los Angeles. Sue claimed to friends that the best part of retirement was the chance to spend more time with her husband, though he didn't always seem as keen on the prospect. "When it was bad," remembered Robin Hurlstone, "they were like two acids bubbling away in the same bottle." One evening in Paris, Hurlstone was planning to meet the Tramonts at the Ritz for dinner. The Ritz was only about a seven- or eight-minute walk from their apartment. He was waiting in the bar when Jean-Claude, decked out in an immaculate gray flannel suit, came storming in, irate. They had gotten halfway to the Ritz when Sue refused to walk another step because her heels were too high. Jean-Claude had no luck hailing a taxi, and Sue said, "Don't worry. My Robin will come and rescue me." Hurlstone took one of the Ritz cars and went to look for her; she was sitting at a café on the rue Saint-Honoré, smoking a cigarette. When he returned with her to the Ritz, Jean-Claude was nursing a cocktail and fuming. "He was very grumpy, and I tried to jolly them along, but then he had had enough and stormed out," said Hurlstone. "But I never saw her get angry with him about anything. She was just Baby Sue."

She still delighted in the occasional opportunity that gave Jean-Claude a chance to shine professionally. A memorable one took place in the late fall of 1990, at San Francisco's famous revival theater, the Castro. Weeks earlier, Jean-Claude's film critic friend Michael Sragow had published *Produced and Abandoned: The Best Films You've Never Seen*, a collection of essays about films that failed undeservedly. The Castro programmed a concurrent series of movies discussed in the book, one of which was *All Night Long*. Sue and Jean-Claude flew up for the event, which drew a sizable crowd. Director Philip Kaufman, whose movies *Invasion of the Body Snatchers* and *The Right Stuff* Jean-Claude deeply admired, was in the audience and came up to tell him how much he loved the film. "Jean-Claude was just sort of beaming," recalled Sragow, "and Sue sat down on the couch in the mezzanine and watched and was delighted that he was having this experience. I sat down with her for a minute or two, and she clutched my hand and pressed my knee and smiled. She wanted to drink in her husband getting his due in this setting."

While abroad, she continued to play matchmaker whenever she had the chance. Matt Pincus, the son of Sue and Boaty's close friend, former actress Suzanne Storrs, was someone she took an interest in when he was a

teenager, a self-confessed anarchist and a punk with a Mohawk. She kept
tabs on him over the years, and in 1994, when Matt was spending his junior
year of college in Paris, they saw a fair amount of each other. She helped
him handle some of the details of renting his apartment, and once, when he
was ill, took him to a Parisian doctor she knew. Matt's girlfriend for most of
his college years was black, and Sue called him in Paris to ask, "You like
black girls, don't you? I've got a good one for you." She proceeded to set him
up with Sidney and Joanna Poitier's eldest daughter, Anika. "There was
nothing happening," recalled Pincus, "but Sue was really interested in the
whole thing."

Even though Sue was out of the business, she was still the subject of
occasional magazine and newspaper articles. In 1994, Susan Orlean wrote
a profile of her for *The New Yorker* called "After the Party." The Sue that
Orlean encountered was a rather sad woman cut adrift without any meaningful professional purpose in life. "I feel just like the Queen Mother, because I have this association with Hollywood but no function there anymore.
I'm just like her," Sue told Orlean. "Only not as rich." Orlean was left with
the erroneous impression that Sue was struggling financially, but she correctly assessed Sue's feeling that she had never quite belonged to the golden
circle of Hollywood—that she had merely been useful, and now she no longer
was. "I found it so interesting," said Orlean. "Who doesn't want to be part of
the in crowd? Isn't that everybody's story in a way? It was one of the few times
I interviewed someone when I felt like I could see through her skin." The encounter threw Orlean slightly; she was affected by it for days after.

Now that Sue was no longer the queen bee of Hollywood, she admitted
to Orlean, and to many of her friends as well, she felt she had wasted her
time there. But this was probably mostly misplaced frustration. Her attraction to the world of glamour and money and power that Hollywood represented was so overwhelming that she was unable to rid herself of it. In a
way, she was like someone who gives up drinking but still longs to associate
with people who drink.

In the summer of 1994, Sue and Jean-Claude traveled frequently with Sidney and Joanna Poitier—to Europe, the Bahamas, and even to Deer Valley,
Utah, where the others skied and Sue enjoyed the après-ski time. Anika

Poitier remembered that once, while seated in the first-class section of a nonsmoking flight, she smelled cigarette smoke. She looked around and saw Sue discreetly blowing smoke into her pocketbook. Johnnie Planco also recalled seeing her on a flight in the mid-1990s. Sue asked the attendant if it was a smoking flight and was told that it was not. Two hours later, when the plane was at cruising altitude, she grabbed the attendant by the sleeve and demanded to see the pilot. "If I don't have a cigarette, I'm going to die," she pleaded. "We're going to have to land."

That summer Paramount released *Forrest Gump*, which pulled in enormous grosses and would go on to win the Best Picture Academy Award and Tom Hanks's second consecutive Best Actor Oscar. It was hardly Sue's kind of picture; she had no interest in Hanks's characterization of the slow-witted, openhearted Forrest. But she was thrilled for the film's success because Sherry Lansing, chairman of Paramount since 1992, was in the midst of an enviable string of successes, and *Forrest Gump* was one of her biggest. Sue delivered one of her classic backhanded compliments to Lansing: "I hated that movie more than life itself. How could you have known to make that movie? Now I know that you're a genius."

Full-on retirement meant that Sue was less physically active than she had ever been. Since leaving William Morris, she had put on a great deal of weight. She spent more and more time lounging in her bedroom, watching television and munching on chocolate chip cookies. Jean-Claude, who remained as trim and fit as ever, harangued her perpetually about her eating and her chain-smoking of both joints and Gauloises, but she brushed aside his concerns. She made the occasional trip to Canyon Ranch, the famous health spa in Tucson, Arizona, where she would (usually halfheartedly) attempt to get herself in some kind of reasonable shape. She was curiously touchy about visiting doctors too often—as if she was afraid of what they might tell her, or afraid that she might get sick simply for having consulted one.

In May 1995, while making a visit to New York without Jean-Claude, Sue unexpectedly decided to take a sentimental journey back to some of her old haunts in the Bronx and Queens. She wondered aloud to Elaine Goldsmith and her husband-to-be, Dan Thomas, what the old neighborhood looked like, which prompted Goldsmith to sweep into action. The three of them drove to the Bronx, Sue in a hooded pullover that Thomas thought

made her look like Obi-Wan Kenobi, and past the candy store that she used
to frequent. Sue's memories tended to be on the negative side, of being bul-
lied for her German accent—which is a surprising recollection, if one believes Arthur Segaul's claim that she lost her accent at an early age. But she
seemed to harbor a certain affection for the Bronx, telling Goldsmith and
Thomas that it had helped instill true grit in her. "Sue would go out of her
way not to give the group the sense that she had a loss of control of her emotions," said Dan Thomas. "I did notice, though, that her way of getting misty
was not telling me to move on. The pattern that sort of developed was 'I
don't care about that, let's keep going,' and the moments when she wouldn't
kick the horse with the spurs were when I got the sense that she wanted to
enjoy whatever jumped out at her."

Eventually they made their way to Queens, where Sue enjoyed herself
enormously over lunch at the Pastrami King on Queens Boulevard. They
also telephoned Ruth to tell her that they would be stopping by for a visit
after lunch. They drove up and down Austin Street and Yellowstone Boulevard and 108th Street, and when they finally pulled up in front of Ruth's
apartment building, Thomas got out to open Sue's door.

"No," she said. "I can't do it," and asked him to get back in the car.

"Are you sure?" Thomas replied. "You're right here."

"Don't force me to do this," Sue said. "I'll explain it to my mother later."
With that, the three of them drove back to Manhattan.

That summer another reminder of her earlier days surfaced. David Begelman had fallen on even harder times since the Columbia Pictures scandal of the 1970s, in which Sue had defended him so vigorously. His tenure
as CEO and president of MGM had not been a success, except for a few
isolated hits such as *Poltergeist*. When MGM absorbed United Artists, Begelman attempted a lateral move but was soon out of the company altogether. He then partnered with sports mogul Bruce McNall in the Gladden
Entertainment Corporation (named for Begelman's then-wife, Gladyce, a
great friend of Sue's, who died of leukemia in 1986), but later declared
bankruptcy, reportedly because the company was unable to make payments
in excess of $4 million to actors, directors, and writers.

On August 7, 1995, Begelman checked into the Los Angeles Century
Plaza Hotel under the name of Bruce Vann and shot himself. The details of
George Mengers's suicide—his checking into the Times Square Hotel

under the name of Oscar Dale—must surely have resonated deeply with
Sue. But, to the surprise of Begelman's widow, Annabelle, Sue did not attend the funeral.

In the summer of 1996, the Tramonts traveled together to France. They
made their way through the south, winding up in Saint-Tropez at the home
of Joan Collins and Robin Hurlstone. While there, Jean-Claude complained
that one of his nipples was itching constantly. Hurlstone suggested that perhaps he was allergic to whatever laundry detergent was being used to wash
his clothes.

But the persistent itch turned out to be a symptom of something far more
serious: tests at the American Hospital of Paris revealed prostate cancer
that had metastasized to his spinal cord. Sue and Jean-Claude came home
to Los Angeles, where he underwent hormone treatment and radiation. But
it was a fast-moving cancer that soon had spread to other organs in his body.

Sue saw to it that Jean-Claude got the best possible nursing care at
home, and she was aided immeasurably by Virginia Portillo, Ana Maria
Calito, and the rest of the household staff. It was a terrible time: Jean-
Claude was filled with rage and frequently lashed out at her. He railed that
she was the one who had abused herself with pot and food and cigarettes
and no exercise for so many years. He had always assumed that he would
outlive her, as had Sue, and this reversal of their expectations seemed brutally unfair. Although they had always argued, these outbursts were almost
more than Sue could bear.

On December 27, 1996, Marcia Diamond received a frantic call from
Sue telling her that Jean-Claude's condition had abruptly worsened. Diamond immediately arrived at the house. Having weathered the terminal illness of a loved one a year earlier, she instantly recognized that Jean-Claude
probably had only a few hours left. Sue was going to phone for an ambulance, but Diamond discouraged her, telling her she was in no shape to deal
with an ambulance. Virginia and another housekeeper, Ori Miranda, honored Mexican tradition by tying a scarf around Jean-Claude's head. He was
clutching one of the throw pillows that Marlo Thomas had given them several Christmases earlier. Virginia and Ori knelt down before the window in
prayer. Jean-Claude died shortly afterward.

Sue called Leo and Barbara Sender in New Jersey and explained to

them that she had not been able to call Ruth to tell her the news. She asked
if the Senders would mind going out to Queens to tell Ruth in person. They
later remembered that the moment they walked in, Ruth instantly knew
why they had come.

A full Roman Catholic Mass was held for Jean-Claude at Saint Victor
Church on Holloway Drive in West Hollywood, which Marlo Thomas arranged. A handful of mourners attended, including Virginia and Ori, Sidney and Joanna Poitier, and Candice Bergen. When Sue, unfamiliar with
the customs of the Catholic Church, walked in and saw the altar spilling
over with beautiful red and white flowers, she said to Bergen, "Candy, look
what Marlo's done!"

"It's Christmas," explained Bergen. "Marlo didn't do this."

Over the years, Sue had repeatedly told both friends and interviewers
that if it ever came down to a choice between Jean-Claude or her career, it
would be the easiest choice in the world. Whatever the frequency and depth
of their disagreements, Jean-Claude had represented to her a life that stood
apart from Hollywood and her professional achievements, one that had sus-
tained her in the years after she lost her career. Now, it seemed to many of
her friends, she had lost just about everything she had ever cared about.

CHAPTER NINETEEN

1998–2001

The biggest blow Sue faced after the death of Jean-Claude was the discovery in the first half of 1998 that she had developed throat cancer, which seemed even crueler than losing her husband. At first, she was terrified that, even if she recovered, she would have to undergo a laryngectomy, and she could not imagine a life in which she would be unable to speak freely. Joanna Poitier drove her to her chemotherapy treatments, which were followed by a round of radiation. In July 1997, she had written to Gore Vidal and Howard Austen that she was still in the middle of radiation treatment and having difficulty talking. "However," she assured them, "don't prepare for my dirt nap yet." Sue did recover, but no matter how strongly her friends urged her to give up her pot and cigarettes, she refused to even consider it.

On Christmas Day 1998, Ruth died at her home in Rego Park. Leo Sender made all the arrangements with a funeral parlor on Queens Boulevard. Sue flew to New York, and when the undertaker asked her if there was a special outfit Ruth should be buried in, she responded, "My mother was never a fashion plate, and I don't think she's going to start now."

Ruth's death triggered an enormous emotional collapse. For two weeks, Sue holed up at the Sherry-Netherland, seeing no one. Many of her friends felt that since Jean-Claude's death, she'd sought to portray her marriage as far more idyllic than it really had been for either of them. But in the case of her mother, she did the opposite, painting Ruth in ever darker hues whenever she spoke of her.

In Jean-Claude's absence, David Geffen stepped in and demonstrated his devotion as a friend. Sue, in turn, expected to be treated as if she were his consort, no matter who the man in his life happened to be at any given moment. She still insisted on being called "Mrs. Geffen" and she frequently demanded that he fly her in his private plane, even when the destination was his private yacht. Geffen seemed happy to oblige his old friend, and when others would express astonishment that she couldn't simply fly first-class on a commercial flight, she would tell them not to give it another thought—it was the least that Geffen could do for her. Geffen showed his loyalty in other ways, too, such as buying her the only high-quality pieces of jewelry she had ever owned. But for Sue, it never seemed to be quite enough. "The entitlement," said Elaine Goldsmith-Thomas, "was a little crazy."

Periods of great camaraderie between Geffen and Sue were often followed by months of frozen silence between them. "She would be very rude," recalled Geffen. "She would get to a point where I would say, 'That's it— I'm out of here.' I wasn't going to stand for too much abuse. She abused everyone. If she did something that was so beyond the pale, I wouldn't speak to her for a while, and she would call me up and say, as Baby Sue, 'I did bad. I'm a bad girl.' I would forgive her. And that would be the end of it." But other friends felt that Geffen was deeply hurt by her frequent attacks, especially whenever she summoned the word "faggot."

She continued to show a maternal side to several of her friends, but it had traces of the kind of mothering she had received from Ruth. Both before and after Elaine Goldsmith married Dan Thomas in 1995, Sue would harangue her to lose weight, telling Elaine it could only help her marriage. "DON'T FUCK THIS UP!" she would remonstrate.

Late in 1998 Sue flew by private jet to New York—the last time she would make the trip. She was staying at the Pierre when she received a call from Elaine asking if she could come to see her. Sue brusquely informed her that she didn't have time, but when Elaine explained that she and her husband had recently separated, Sue told her to come over immediately. Sue held Elaine while she cried and poured out her problems. Instead of berating her for not hanging on to her husband, Sue told her how accomplished and successful she was and assured her that she could achieve anything. "Honeeey," she said, "nothing will make you feel better than a new signing." Shortly thereafter, Elaine signed Jennifer Lopez. "There you go!" crowed Sue. "Now you can forget him!" But she was delighted when Elaine and Dan were reunited a short time later.

She also cautioned Elaine not to make the same mistakes she had made. "Learn from me," she would say. "Your clients are *not* your friends." And yet, Elaine observed, she seemed terribly stung if Barbra Streisand didn't call her.

In 1999, Marcia Diamond was diagnosed with cancer, and during the course of Marcia's treatments, which lasted over nine months, Sue sent Virginia over every two weeks with an enormous pot of homemade chicken soup. That same year, Sue suffered another major health setback. One day Virginia telephoned Sue's assistant, Sandra Leoncavallo, at home to tell her Sue was having trouble breathing but didn't want a doctor. Later she was rushed to Cedars-Sinai Medical Center, where she was diagnosed as having suffered a heart attack. She underwent a successful quadruple bypass, but once she recovered, there was no discernible change in her habits: she still ate poorly and chain-smoked, though she did acknowledge that she had narrowly escaped dying.

Friends urged her to consider a more healthful lifestyle, but she couldn't be less interested. When she went out to lunch, she usually favored chain restaurants that served rich, fatty food, like Hamburger Hamlet and the Cheesecake Factory. Joanna Poitier was the most consistently present member of her close circle, seeing her often and telephoning every day. If something happened to delay her call, Sue would snarl a message on Poitier's answering machine: "THE WIDOW TRAMONT COULD BE DEAD. WHAT THE FUCK DO YOU CARE?" Sue would frequently tell her friend how lucky she was to be married to as fine a man as Sidney Poitier. "Sidney could do no wrong," recalled Joanna. "If anything was wrong, it was my fault. She was all about the man."

As always, Sue absorbed information obsessively, reading nonstop and delving into areas that occasionally surprised some of her friends. She questioned the distinguished art historian and author John Richardson about art dealer Larry Gagosian. "I had done a series of exhibitions for Gagosian," said Richardson, "and you couldn't tell her anything, because she knew it already. So I helped her fill in parts of the map she wasn't quite clear about, and she liked her map to be very, very clear."

One of Sue's favorite pastimes was reading each month's issue of *Vanity Fair*, which over the years had maintained an enviable track record of publishing smart, incisive pieces on celebrities from the arts, business, society, and politics, both present and past. Graydon Carter, the magazine's well-connected editor in chief, was a frequent guest at her house whenever he found himself in Los Angeles, which was often. When Sue praised a recent issue of *Vanity Fair*, she would tell him, "It's like Proust."

Carter had come into her life when Jean-Claude was still alive, and he could easily see that part of Sue left with him. It was clear to Carter and many of her other friends that she was becoming more withdrawn. "I think an underlying reason for her depression is that she wanted to have a man all the time in her life," said Carter. "When you called there, they still said, 'Tramont residence.'"

The idea of Sue's writing a memoir was revived briefly, and John Burnham arranged a meeting with his friend Daphne Merkin, a superb essayist and fiction writer who was then working as a film critic for *The New Yorker*. Merkin was in Los Angeles writing a piece on Diane Keaton, and Burnham put together a lunch for the three women. "Diane, as I recall, was slightly horrified by her," said Merkin. "That abrasive quality is not so much her type. I found Sue unexpectedly more interesting than I thought I would. She was shrewd—but not *only* shrewd. She was far more interesting than that." There was considerable discussion afterward about the book, which the two women wanted to call *When I Was Alive*, which was how Sue often referred to her heyday. But once again, Sue ultimately shied away from the idea, as it would involve a level of work to which she did not care to commit herself. But as Graydon Carter observed, her reluctance may have partly been her recognition that "unavailability is your greatest asset."

She was no longer highly visible around Los Angeles at screenings or premieres, and one reason her dinner invitations became so coveted was because they were handed out to such a select few. "Her friendship was an endorsement that went further in Southern California than winning an Academy Award," said Carter. Writing a book would mean that much of her personal mystique would be dissipated, and she wanted to preserve that for as long as she could.

Sue still remained very much involved in her former profession, as a kind of unofficial observer and consultant. The phone rang constantly with queries and invitations from producers, actors, studio heads. She enjoyed performing the Sue Mengers Show around a dinner table for a small group of the Hollywood elite; at the same time, she was beginning to resent it. Daphne Merkin recalled, "I sort of felt the air go out of her at the end of the lunch or at the end of the evening." At that point, Sue would retreat to her bedroom and television, puffing on a few more joints and eating sweets in bed. Virginia Portillo and the rest of the staff continued to look after her affectionately, which Sue clearly appreciated, though she was guarded about how she expressed her gratitude. Jean-Claude had made arrangements to provide for Virginia generously, asking her to promise to look after Sue, who he knew would be lost without her. "When Jackie Onassis died, she left her housekeeper fifty thousand dollars," she told Boaty Boatwright. "My Jean-Claude left Virginia enough to *buy* Honduras."

In the spring of 2000, Sue got her strongest blast of media attention in some time when Peter Biskind's lengthy feature article, "When Sue Was Queen," appeared in the April issue of *Vanity Fair*. Biskind was a contributing editor at the magazine and the author of the critically acclaimed study of 1970s moviemaking, *Easy Riders, Raging Bulls: How the Sex-Drugs-and-Rock 'n' Roll Generation Saved Hollywood*, published in 1998, a book for which he had interviewed Sue. He made two separate trips to Los Angeles to interview her for the *Vanity Fair* piece, and also spoke with many of her former clients and colleagues. The result was a memorable profile that captured a woman who was crankily fading into old age but still vitally proud of what she had accomplished during her peak years. Biskind's profile was so vivid that it seemed as if the movie version of her life was probably in the works before the magazine even went to press, and Sue was pleased with it. She sent Biskind a large gift basket from Zabar's, which he later recalled was "something that never happened before or since" with any of his profile subjects.

Of course, she was compelled to undercut her own enthusiasm. When Graydon Carter visited her in Beverly Hills shortly after the article appeared, he bent down to give her a kiss, and Sue said, "Modest?"

"What do you mean?" Carter asked.

"You call this place 'modest'?"

"I realized that Peter had written that she lived in a modest John Woolf house," Carter recalled. "One word out of that whole story, and that's what she hung on to."

Sue would also grant the occasional interview to writers who were under contract to do histories of the movie business. Rachel Abramowitz interviewed her roughly a half dozen times for her history of women executives in Hollywood, *Is That a Gun in Your Pocket?*, published by Random House in 2000. Abramowitz recalled Sue as seeming sad and depressed during many of their sessions together. "She wasn't easy," said Abramowitz. "I had to pull a little to get the stories out of her. And then she would have these little flashes into who she had been and she would get happy in those moments."

Sue spent much of her time with friends discussing the overwhelming changes in the movie business, which was now entirely in the hands of the multinationals. The Harvard MBA mentality, on the rise for years, had completely overtaken the major studios. The love of movies that Sue had felt, both in herself and in many of the people she had once worked with, had been replaced with a desire to get the fattest and fastest payout possible. Sue was stunned by the fate of executives like Mike Ovitz, who had left CAA in 1995 to become president of the Walt Disney Company. By January 1997, he no longer had the job, having been let go by Disney chairman Michael Eisner, and walked away with a reported $38 million in cash and around $100 million in company stock—which many in Hollywood considered a staggering severance package. As comedy writer Bruce Vilanch observed, "What else is a kid at Harvard Law supposed to think except, 'Holy shit—I want some of that!'"

Star salaries had escalated to something beyond anything Sue had dreamed of during her salad days. In 1995, Universal had signed Sylvester Stallone to a nonexclusive three-picture agreement worth $60 million, which included plenty of perks and back-end guarantees. In the same year, Universal and Casey Silver had worked out a deal for Jim Carrey to receive $20 million for a single film, *Liar Liar*, which was anticipated to be the big Christmas movie of 1996. As Peter Bart wrote in *Variety* in 1998, "The movie business isn't a business anymore except for the stars and their agents. None of the corporate owners want to make movies. They just want to find a sucker who'll put up the money."

Sue found most of this hard to fathom. One day while Mike Ovitz was still at CAA, Bob Bookman was visiting her, and she asked, "Bobbeee . . . what is Mike Ovitz's secret?" Bookman replied that it was simple: Ovitz believed that clients should be shared, and that an agent gained the bulk of his compensation through salary and not what was booked. Sue replied, "That's such bullshit." She couldn't understand how the agency business could be structured differently from the way it had been during her heyday.

By 2001, even Sue's old friend Sherry Lansing, who had enjoyed a remarkably successful run as the chairman of Paramount's Motion Picture Group, could see the end of her own road in the film industry. Paramount had recently completed *Lara Croft: Tomb Raider*, starring Angelina Jolie. When Lansing saw the final cut, she was horrified by how bad it was and told her vice chairman and chief operating officer, Rob Friedman, that she would have to meet with the director and producer to figure out how to fix it. Lansing recalled Friedman saying, "It will be fine. We're going to open 28.6 and then we're going to do 2.5 rather than 3 multiple, and we'll make 'x' amount of dollars, and I've cut 3 spots and they've already tested 60, which is a high number." Lansing recalled thinking, "*Whaaaat?*" From that point on, she knew that word of mouth on a film no longer mattered: marketing was now more important than the movie itself.

Sue's dinner parties continued to be a prime gathering place for people in show business. At one memorable evening in mid-2000, the guests included Candice Bergen and her new husband, Manhattan real estate tycoon and philanthropist Marshall Rose, Jack Nicholson and his then-girlfriend Lara Flynn Boyle, Joan Collins, and Robert Downey, Jr., who had recently been released from the California Substance Abuse Treatment Facility and State Prison, where he had been serving a term on drug-related charges. Bergen's first husband, Louis Malle, had died of cancer in 1995, and this was the first time that many people in the room had met Rose, whom Bergen described as "very much a straight arrow." At the table, the evening's high point came when Joan Collins turned to Downey and inquired, wide-eyed, "Ooooh! What do you do for sex in prison? Don't you get *horny?*" Rose dealt with it all quite gracefully, but he looked as if he had been dropped down the rabbit hole.

One evening in the fall of 2000, the guests included Anjelica Huston, Graydon Carter, Sue's former client Anne Bancroft, and her husband, Mel Brooks, who was holding forth at dinner about a new Broadway musical he was planning based on his famous film *The Producers*. He was acting out the part of Max Bialystock, the shyster producer whose plot to profit from a flop show backfires when it turns out to be a hit. After dinner, Huston and Carter were driving home and Carter said, "That is the worst idea I ever heard." Huston agreed. Four months later the musical version of *The Producers* was a record-breaking Broadway smash, with premium seats selling at five hundred dollars a ticket.

For years, Sue had admired the writing of Frank Rich, former theater critic of the *New York Times*, who was now an incisive, brilliantly informed, and immensely readable op-ed columnist for the newspaper. She had also followed closely the work of Rich's wife, Alex Witchel, and her lively coverage of the New York theater beat in the *Times*. She met Rich and Witchel one evening in 2000 at David Geffen's home, the old Jack Warner mansion in Beverly Hills that Geffen had purchased for $47 million and spent more than that refurbishing and landscaping. Sue made Rich and Witchel double over with her entrance line: "I just spent a hundred dollars getting my hair blown out. You'd better be worth it."

That night, Geffen was about to give the Riches a tour of his famous art collection, but Sue said to Witchel, "No, you won't take a tour of the art. You will talk to me." She grilled Witchel about her life and work and finally blurted out, "I want to tell you something. You're not blond enough. This is my business. I tell people what they should do in their lives. I'm always right. You would look much better blonder." Witchel went straight home and got blonder immediately.

Throughout the dinner, also attended by Warren Beatty, Sue smoked incessantly. David Geffen's chef had prepared a low-fat meal of fish and vegetables. Sue had ordered a steak in advance but she scarcely touched her plate. Finally Geffen pointed out that he had provided the steak because she had requested it—wasn't she going to eat it? Sue asked Geffen and Beatty if they wanted to try it, and they both tasted it. Witchel remembered thinking, "These men can afford a million steaks, but here they are, eating off Sue's plate in Jack Warner's mansion." When dessert was served, Geffen asked a servant to bring out some expensive artisanal chocolates that he loved. "I don't eat that shit," said Sue. "I eat See's." Rich and Witchel would be frequent guests at Sue's in the years to come, and she always insisted on putting together a dinner party for them that comprised above-the-line Hollywood names. She couldn't imagine that they might want to come just to see her; she still felt it her duty to provide a generous sampling of twinklies.

She had become increasingly dependent on the presence of twinklies. Having stars around her table had once been a way of doing business; now it seemed to be her way of reminding herself that she had once mattered— as was her custom of turning on the *60 Minutes* interview so any newcomers could see it on arriving. If there were shades of Norma Desmond in such behavior, she leavened it with her fascination with everything and everyone on the current Hollywood scene.

Despite being enormously judgmental, Sue could be oddly forgiving—but if one of her twinklies failed to show up at a party, she kept score assiduously. In early 2000, Mitch Glazer and Kelly Lynch were invited to dinner with Graydon and Anna Carter and Mel Brooks and Anne Bancroft. Glazer had worked on the screenplay for the first *Charlie's Angels* movie, and received a call from Bill Murray, who was doing one of Glazer's scenes on a night shoot and needed his presence on the set. Glazer called Sue to apologize, saying he would have to back out of dinner. "FUCK THAT GUY! GET OVER HERE!" she shouted into the phone. It turned out to be an indelible evening, with Brooks holding forth brilliantly, and Sue made sure Glazer heard about it for years afterward.

In 2000 Elaine Goldsmith-Thomas, frustrated by the limitations of being an agent, began to explore other career possibilities. At first, Sue discouraged her, trying to convince her that being an agent was the only thing she knew how to do. In a classic case of projection, she told Elaine, "You want to leave because they're going to leave you." But Elaine longed to write and produce, and when she did leave to join Revolution Studios in New York, Sue was supportive. She did the opposite of what most people do: while she frequently underestimated her friends' talents, she inevitably boasted about them behind their backs.

In December 2002, Goldsmith-Thomas's first film as producer, *Maid in Manhattan*, starring Jennifer Lopez, enjoyed a huge first weekend. When Elaine called Sue to tell her that the movie had opened in the number-one box-office spot, Sue corrected her by crediting the head of Revolution Studios: "JOE ROTH's movie opened at number one!" Elaine replied that she had produced it and her name was on the screen. "*Best boys* have their names on the screen. *Gaffers* have their names on the screen," answered Sue. Toni Howard later telephoned Elaine to tell her that Sue had called to say, "Elaine's movie is number one. And it says, 'Produced by Elaine Goldsmith-Thomas' on the screen.'"

It became increasingly apparent, though, that Sue was unable to camouflage her resentment of some of her close friends who were continuing to work. Boaty Boatwright, who had reinvented herself repeatedly and kept herself vital in the business, was occasionally a target. Boaty's daughter, Kara Baker, recalled, "Sue could say some mean things to my mother. Boaty would make a deal, and Sue would pooh-pooh it. And yet Sue loved hearing Boaty talk about whom she was out with every night, which parties she was going to. Sue lived vicariously through Boaty."

Just as she considered herself the only one who could criticize her close friends, Sue was by far the only one who could take potshots at Barbra Streisand. She delighted in Elaine's success in guiding the career of Julia Roberts, but she frequently reminded Elaine that Roberts couldn't touch Streisand.

Ali MacGraw remembered a night when she, Candice Bergen, and Streisand were gathered at Sue's house. Streisand launched into a lengthy discussion of *The Way We Were* and began to describe in detail all the scenes that had been cut, which in her opinion (one she shared with screen-writer Arthur Laurents) had undermined the story. She then began to talk—again, in great detail—about a sequel that had been discussed in the 1990s. It felt as if no one else had spoken for around twenty minutes. Finally, Sue said, "Can we skip to *Yentl*?"

For several years, Carrie Fisher had been a fairly regular guest at Sue's house. Sue had known her during her early years of acting success in *Star Wars*, *The Blues Brothers*, and *Hannah and Her Sisters*, but she didn't quite treat her as a real grown-up talent until Fisher had a big success as an author with her 1987 best-selling novel, *Postcards from the Edge*. "Once I started writing," said Fisher, "I think she was able to accept me without feeling she was compromising something in herself. If you got invited to Sue's house, it was *you*. You couldn't assume someone else was welcome. I was usually brought by David Geffen."

In February 2001, Fisher's latest project, *These Old Broads*, aired on ABC. An inside-showbiz comedy about the fraught television reunion of three former movie costars (played by Shirley MacLaine, Joan Collins, and Fisher's mother, Debbie Reynolds), the film was loaded with in-jokes—one of which was that the character of Beryl Mason, the agent who brokers the TV comeback, was played by Elizabeth Taylor, who had famously broken up Reynolds's fan-magazine-approved marriage to Eddie Fisher back in the 1950s. Another in-joke was that the character of Beryl—and Taylor's performance—was clearly inspired by Sue. Taylor wasn't very good in the part—her attempt at a Bronx accent kept sliding into something that sounded vaguely Cockney—and there was some difficulty prior to the shooting, when Taylor made fun of Reynolds behind her back for being a Goody Two-shoes. "Sue probably didn't think *These Old Broads* was all that great," said Carrie Fisher. "But I think she liked that I was in the middle of a fight there, that I got along with Elizabeth and could broker a sort of peace between Elizabeth and my mother. I remember I went to Sue for advice on who should broker it, and how."

When two of Sue's old friends, Barry Diller and fashion queen Diane von Furstenberg, decided to get married in 2001, Sue was fascinated, and continually attempted to pry information about the couple out of mutual friends. "My house in the country is on the same road as Diane von Furstenberg and Barry's," said John Richardson. "So she was always trying to squeeze information, rumors, stories out of one about the 'Vondillahs,' as she called them. There was a lot of 'Vondillah' talk. I was a bit wary, because I'm extremely fond of them and wanted to stay on good terms with them."

On September 11, 2001, word quickly spread in Hollywood circles that Anthony Perkins's widow, Berry Berenson, had been on board American Airlines Flight 11 out of Boston's Logan Airport when it had been hijacked by terrorists and crashed into the North Tower of New York's World Trade Center. Boaty Boatwright was at home in a panic, like everyone else trying to make sense of the ordeal. The phone lines had been down all day, but the first call Boaty got was from Sue, who was in tears, telling her friend, "Berry Berenson was on that plane that crashed." Sue had spent considerable time with Berenson after Perkins's death in 1992, and had been a good friend to their children, Osgood and Elvis. In the context of Sue's own life, Berenson's death felt like the closing of some kind of final door.

CHAPTER TWENTY

2002–2011

As Sue reached her seventies, an invitation to her home increasingly provided visitors a glimpse into a glorious era in Hollywood's past. She continued to insist that all newcomers be ushered in to see the *60 Minutes*
interview—"proof of when I was alive," as she still loved to say. She took
pleasure in reminiscing about her glory days, and was invariably honest
about the sting that accompanied those memories, since they became more
and more distant. She still spent much of each day in bed, making her way
through piles of trashy entertainment magazines, watching television, and
eating all the things that were only going to make her gain more weight. She
often seemed at risk of becoming a self-parody or a figure of pity. But just
when she might appear to be irretrievably wrapped up in her own past, she
could stagger her new, younger friends with her insights into their careers
in the movie industry.

Despite her abhorrence of exercise and love of rich, fatty foods, she
didn't entirely convey the image of an unhealthy person. She was heavy, but
still remarkably pretty, with thick, lustrous hair that she had expensively
maintained. Her skin was also remarkable: it had naturally the "mystic
glow" that women's fashion magazines were always advocating. Perhaps the
best thing she did for herself in terms of health was to get plenty of sleep,
sometimes as much as eighteen hours a day. As much as she resented critical suggestions being passed her way, she still relentlessly scrutinized her
good friends, always pointing out that their hair looked awful or that they
had gained weight, or that they were wearing unflattering colors.

In December 2003, Kelly Lynch and Mitch Glazer invited Sue to a party
at their house to celebrate Glazer's fiftieth birthday. She had been friends
with the couple for years and had often given them career advice, becoming
quite piqued with Lynch when she turned down the part eventually played
by Sharon Stone in *Basic Instinct*—especially when the salary offer escalated to $1 million. On this particular occasion, the other guests at the

Glazers' party included Robert Evans, Graydon and Anna Carter, Owen Wilson, and Lisa Eisner.

As usual, Sue smoked pot throughout the evening and at one point disappeared for a long time. When the other guests went to investigate, they discovered she had locked herself in one of the Glazers' bathrooms and was too stoned to figure out how to get out. Lisa Eisner was yelling at her to hang on, and Sue kept screaming, "LISA EISNER, SHUT THE FUCK UP!" She was now beginning to panic over being trapped in an enclosed space, and Glazer had to go outside, remove the bathroom window screen, and climb in to rescue her. When he strolled over to the door and easily turned the doorknob, Sue sat down on the toilet, laughing uncontrollably at her inability to figure out how to undo the lock.

She was becoming more selective about going out in the evening, but she continued to have enough energy for ladies' lunches at home. Sue Naegle, at the time entertainment president of HBO, remembered the affectionate atmosphere that prevailed at the lunches—as well as the feeling that she had better sit down at the table with something to say if she was going to be in the company of Anjelica Huston, Ali MacGraw, Joanna Poitier, and Lili Zanuck. Sue's taste in food remained as unpretentious as ever. At lunch one day, Ali MacGraw took a bite of her cheesecake and remarked how delicious it was.

Without looking up from her plate, Sue replied, "Costco."

She continued to be helpful in terms of offering career advice. In early 2004, Universal was casting the part of the free-spirited mother of bride-groom-to-be Greg Focker (Ben Stiller) in Jay Roach's comedy *Meet the Fockers*, and Sue pushed for Barbra Streisand to play it. Streisand did do the film, which became a big box-office success when it opened in December 2004. Jack Nicholson, among others, urged her to press Streisand to pay her a commission, since the film was something Sue had brought to her attention. Sue never said anything to Streisand about it, but privately groused that her old friend should have paid her something.

Her attitude toward Streisand remained very push and pull. Jack Nicholson remembered, "I didn't see Sue and Barbra in one another's company that much. Barbra is a private kind of person in her way, and mostly, she would probably have seen Sue by herself." By now Streisand was happily married to actor James Brolin, whom Sue approved of and referred to as "a

saint" to her friends as well as to Streisand herself. The two women still saw
each other socially, but Sue had not come close to putting aside her bitterness over their earlier break. John Burnham remembered telling Sue
about a party he had attended at which he had a long and pleasant conversation with Streisand. Sue responded with a nasty and dismissive crack
about her old friend.

Dinners at Lexington Road continued to reflect their hostess's hard-and-
fast rules. Sue could not tolerate lateness or inappropriate attire—which
sometimes meant that she didn't like it if her guests had dressed too for-
mally when she had stipulated that the evening was to be casual. She insisted on approval of any guests that they might be bringing. "If you wanted
to bring someone, she would say, 'Who is that?'" Fran Lebowitz remembered. "And unless you could say, 'He won the Pulitzer Prize last year,' she
might not say yes. And even then that would sometimes not be good
enough."

Her literary taste, which had mostly leaned toward biography and the occasional social or cultural history, began to expand a bit. For several years,
Gore Vidal had urged her to read important fiction, and she suddenly became
willing to immerse herself in titles that turned up on the syllabuses of English
literature courses. She still held very few strong political convictions, and
many of those seemed designed purposely to rankle her liberal friends in
Hollywood; she remained up on current events, but the world of politics itself
generally bored her. She was less interested in candidates' political platforms
than in how good they were in bed. A bit later on, William Friedkin, who had
by now branched out from films to become a highly successful director of
staged opera in both the United States and Europe, induced her to accompany him to concerts of the Los Angeles Philharmonic at the spectacular new
Walt Disney Concert Hall. "She loved that," recalled Friedkin. "At the inter-
missions, I would have to take her outside so she could smoke grass."

As time went on, particularly if she wasn't feeling well and was in a
prickly mood, she could occasionally misstep socially. One person she was
clearly ambivalent about was Nora Ephron. Sue was impressed by Ephron's
accomplishments, which also served to remind her of her own inactivity.
She would make sarcastic comments to friends about Ephron's expertise not
only as a writer and director, but as a cook and hostess. One night in 2003,
Frank Rich and Alex Witchel attended a dinner at Ephron's house that

included Sue and a number of notable comedy talents, including Steve Martin, Will Ferrell, and Ferrell's writing partner, Adam McKay. Ephron had prepared the pork roast from the popular *Mustards Grill Napa Valley Cookbook*, and Sue began to cruise down the memory lane of old Hollywood. The longer she talked, the more the other guests began to struggle visibly to sustain their concentration. Witchel recalled, "I could tell that Adam McKay and Will Ferrell were thinking, 'Is class over yet?' It was unlike Sue, because she usually read a room very well."

Every year, as movie awards season approached, Sue would drive herself into a state of mild frenzy. She wanted to entertain on a grand scale, giving a series of lunches and dinners for nominees who happened to be in town, assembling the best tables of twinklies possible. It wasn't an easy task, because social demands were great during awards season, and she would become highly stressed as she juggled menus and invitations, making sure that all the china and silver were in order. In 2005, she threw a luncheon for her former client Sidney Lumet, who, despite five nominations, had never won a competitive Oscar; now the Academy had voted him an Honorary Award for his body of work. Quentin Tarantino was among the guests. Sue, who had never forgiven Lumet for not joining her roster when she was flailing at William Morris, made a toast: "I want to thank Sidney Lumet for letting me have this lunch because the only way I could get Quentin Tarantino to come was to meet Sidney."

She combed the newspapers and magazines, searching for new talents she might consider worthy of a dinner invitation. Alessandra Stanley and Maureen Dowd, whose work she had been reading carefully in the *New York Times* for years, were both summoned to Lexington Road and became regular lunch and dinner guests. For several years, Sue had followed the work of the young writer Claire Hoffman in the *Los Angeles Times*. Hoffman was a friend of John Burnham's, and Sue asked him to make introductions. In the summer of 2006, she invited Hoffman to a dinner party, at which the other guests were Gore Vidal, Oliver Stone, Frank Rich and Alex Witchel, and Jack Nicholson. When Nicholson let it be known that he would like to date Hoffman, Sue called her and warned her against it. "It will mean you're a slut," she cautioned.

A few months later, one of Hoffman's editors at the *Los Angeles Times* asked her to work up a few advance obituaries that would be ready to go

when the subjects passed away. The editor told her she should telephone
Sue to get information beyond what the newspaper already had on file and
assured Hoffman that Sue would find it all very funny.

Sue did not find it amusing at all.

"WHAT THE FUCK?" she screamed into the phone. "You think I'm
about to die? This is so insulting!" and hung up. As a way of apologizing,
Hoffman sent her champagne and chocolates, and Sue did call her back
and forgave her. But Hoffman remembered, "There was an emotional intensity that I couldn't quite plug into. I felt like I insulted her well-being."

In September 2007, Sue, who still complained that she had never been
thanked in an Oscar acceptance speech, was delighted when Tina Fey accepted her Emmy for Outstanding Comedy Series for *30 Rock*, and thanked
her daughter, her parents, the show's viewers, and Sue Mengers. Sue was
also watching when the category of Outstanding Reality Program came up.
Sue was dismissive of the other nominees, including Cesar Millan for *The
Dog Whisperer*, hoping that her favorite, Kathy Griffin, would win for *My
Life on the D-List*. When Griffin's name was announced, Sue was thrilled—
and a few seconds later, convulsed with laughter when Griffin delivered her
acceptance speech:

"A lot of people get up here and thank Jesus for this award. I want you to
know that no one had less to do with this award than Jesus. He didn't help
me a bit. If it was up to him, Cesar Millan would be up here with that
damned dog. So all I can say is, Suck it, Jesus! This award is my God now."

As Christian groups denounced Griffin, the Academy of Television Arts
& Sciences nervously shuffled its feet, trying to come up with a position on
the controversy, and CNN put together a panel of experts to gauge the ap-
propriateness of the comedienne's remarks. Griffin loved being at the center
of the storm, and in the midst of it, her stand-up agent at ICM called to say
she had received a fax from Sue Mengers, inviting her to dinner.

Griffin accepted immediately and researched Sue's life by reading Peter
Biskind's *Vanity Fair* profile. "I paid for professional hair and makeup like
I was a princess from Dubai," she said, "and I put on a Chanel dress and
Chanel shoes and did all the things I thought you were supposed to do when
you are wealthy and in show business." She drove up in her Maserati with a
gift of expensive sweets from a top Beverly Hills chocolatier. When she entered the house, she thought her head would explode: lining the living room

were Natasha Richardson, Angie Dickinson, Tina Fey, David Geffen and his boyfriend, Jeremy Lingvall, Lorne Michaels, and Neil Diamond.

As a joke, Griffin had decided to walk in holding her Emmy, which made Sue collapse in laughter. "This Kathy Griffin won an Emmy," Sue announced, "and she said something so shocking and appalling that I decided she deserved a seat at my table." Later in the evening, Jack Nicholson strolled in and Sue proclaimed, "The king is here!" When Nicholson spotted Griffin's Emmy, he looked at her as if she had escaped from an institution, but Griffin broke the tension by saying, "Jack, I'm going to put this in the bathroom, so when you go in there and do your blow or whatever people do at these parties, you can look at a real award."

Griffin came to Sue's several times. There were moments she waited for at each party, such as the one in which Sue would yell, "GRAAAAAASSS!" and Ori would come running in to light the joints. Frequently Sue would quote a line or two from the previous week's episode of *My Life on the D-List* and crow, "That this fearless cunt would *say* this!" She also was fascinated by Griffin's tough-talking, sagacious, drinking-wine-out-of-the-box mother, who popped up frequently on *D-List*. Griffin told Sue that her mother was a natural, a star in her own right, who knew exactly how to flip the switch once the camera began to roll. Sue seemed delighted, and perhaps, thinking of Ruth, more than a little envious.

Frequently Sue would talk to Griffin about Jean-Claude. She always spoke of him with great love and affection, and Griffin, who had heard some of the stories about their differences and cataclysmic arguments, found herself thinking, "No harm, no foul. If she wants to revise history this way—do it. If Liza Minnelli wants to act like Judy Garland was the greatest mom in the world, it's fine with me. So have another joint, Sue, and enjoy it."

One night, the guests included Brad Grey, who had succeeded Sherry Lansing as chairman and CEO of Paramount, Broadway producer Michael Butler, actress Megan Mullally, comedian Garry Shandling, and Griffin. In the days leading up to the party, Griffin had had to get special permission to bring Mullally by citing her friend's multiple Emmy Awards for playing Karen on *Will and Grace* and her appearance in the Broadway show *Young Frankenstein*, but Sue finally deemed her worthy of a place at the table. During dinner, Brad Grey was looking at his phone incessantly, because his wife, Cassandra, was madly texting photos from the prêt-à-porter runway shows in Paris. "Jesus Christ, Brad, put your phone down." Griffin laughed. "This is Sue Mengers! She's probably got stories about the times she saved your sorry career. What do you do now? Do you still manage Andy Dick? Is it true you were sleeping with Sandy Gallin at those seventies parties—is that how you got this job? Now do something useful and go get someone some coffee."

Sue was doubled over, but she wasn't laughing at all when Garry Shandling strolled in quite late. She had planned the evening as a sort of blind date between Shandling and Griffin, because she didn't approve of Griffin dating a "civilian"—someone not in show business. "Honeeey, you'll need a wealthy older man," she advised. "Stop with these younger men: go with an older man who will take care of you." Griffin thought the whole thing was a long shot, and as the guests walked to their cars afterward, she pulled Shandling aside and asked him how he had enjoyed their date. He was dumbfounded when she told him what Sue had planned. "Kathy," he said, "I was shaking in my boots. I was in the most vicious lawsuit with Brad Grey and I haven't seen him in years. It was bitter and contentious. You will never know how you got me through the night with the stuff you were saying to him. No one talks to Brad that way!" As she drove home, Griffin realized that the whole evening had been carefully "cast" by Sue, who not only wanted to play matchmaker, but had decided that the tension between Shandling and Grey had lasted long enough.

After one memorable evening at Sue's, Griffin made a serious tactical error: the following night she went on *Piers Morgan Tonight* and talked in some detail about the dinner party. Sue was incensed: there were certain rules at her gatherings that she assumed were clear, such as not asking to have your photo taken with the other guests, and never talking publicly about what had been discussed. She told Griffin that she felt she should telephone all the other guests from that evening and apologize personally, but she forgave her to the extent of inviting her to another party some time later.

Friends continued to nag Sue to stop smoking and try to pull herself into some sort of reasonable physical shape, but she brushed aside their concerns. In the past she had made semiregular trips to spas in Hampshire, England, and Quiberon, France, as well as to Canyon Ranch, but it was harder now to get her even to consider the idea of any kind of exercise. Years earlier, Carole Bayer Sager had introduced Sue to her close friend Bette Midler. Over time, Midler and Sager both became deeply concerned about the state of Sue's health and pushed her to do something other than take up a sedentary position on the couch. The two women decided to try to take her to Canyon Ranch to lose weight and get some exercise. As always, Sue was concerned about the mode of travel, and once Sager's husband, Robert Daly, arranged for a limousine to take her to a private plane, she agreed to make the trip to Tucson.

At the ranch, Sager and Midler got settled in and then went to fetch Sue at her bungalow and take her to lunch. It was difficult for Sue to walk, and the two women held her up on either side as they went into the main dining room. Sue got an appointment with a ranch therapist, who told her that the reason she was in such bad shape was that she had never properly mourned the death of Jean-Claude—that she had responded to it by simply refusing to live. Midler and Sager thought that perhaps here was progress at last. But Sue could not summon the strength or courage to delve into the suggestion.

Every morning, Sager and Midler would knock on her door, decked out in their Canyon Ranch gear, ready to take her for a walk. "GO AWAY!" Sue would shout through the door. For the rest of their stay at the ranch, she didn't leave her room.

For some time, Sue had been pondering how her money might best be distributed after her death. Apart from remembering a few close friends, she was beginning to give thought to some sort of major charitable contributions. In 2008, she was approached by William Friedkin, who had become friendly with Sabine de La Rochefoucauld, the public relations director (and later curator of ancient works) of the Louvre. Because Jean-Claude had loved the Louvre so deeply, Friedkin thought that it might be an excellent place for Sue to remember in her will. Sabine de La Rochefoucauld traveled to Los Angeles that year, and Friedkin arranged a meeting with Sue. De La Rochefoucauld found her abrupt and gruff yet in some respects surprisingly warm. Sue asked questions about Sabine's four children and spoke lovingly of Jean-Claude, and of the possibility of scattering his ashes from the roof of the Louvre. She smoked hashish throughout the meeting, which she ended abruptly after it was verbally agreed that Sue's donation would be

directed to the museum's capital endowment fund, with the money generated from that going to restoration of works of arts in all departments.

In mid-2008, HBO approached Sue about doing a documentary on her
life. Frank Rich had begun working at HBO as a consultant, and Sue was
intrigued by the idea, provided that Rich would interview her on camera as
well as produce the film. Sue developed a nice telephone friendship with
Sheila Nevins, president of HBO Documentary Films. At some point, however, they hit a sticking point about exactly what Sue would talk about on
camera. Rich pointed out that she would have to discuss the people she
worked with in some detail, and Sue, worried as always about discretion, vacillated. Eventually she asked for an exorbitant amount of money, although she
surely knew that subjects of documentaries are seldom paid anything. It was
undoubtedly her way of making the project, like the memoir, fade away—
which it soon did. Later, HBO's Sue Naegle pitched the idea of a series in
which Sue would interview all of each year's Academy Award nominees, but
the response Naegle got was, "Who in the hell would want to see that?"

It might have sounded as if she was mocking her own status, but Sue was
still quite aware of her power to command the best of Hollywood's younger
talents: Eva Mendes, Jennifer Lopez, Ryan Phillippe, Matt Dillon, Tina Fey,
Jennifer Aniston, Jon Hamm, and Sean Penn all were guests at her table.
(Once, Sue became irritated with Lili Zanuck because Lili had been out of
town for an extended time and hadn't called every day to check on Sue. When
Lili returned, Sue deadpanned, "I've replaced you with Jennifer Aniston.")
And the old group of friends remained deeply loyal. Jack Nicholson was always on hand to drive her anywhere she wanted to go, and Joanna Poitier
spent day after day chauffeuring her from one doctor to the other.

She could be sharper than ever with her oldest friends. Several well-
intentioned people attacked her for spending so much of her time watching
television. Sue told Jack Nicholson, "They say that watching television is so
boring. But really, Jack, it's not as boring as most of your friends."

Some of the old guard drifted away. After the Canyon Ranch incident, Carole Bayer Sager did not come around as often. Candice Bergen also withdrew.
For some time, Bergen and a number of other friends had been put off by Sue's
attitude toward them; they felt they were boring her, that when they spent time
around her, she would rather be smoking pot or watching *Access Hollywood*.
One night at a dinner party, Sue betrayed a confidence, something that Bergen

had told her under duress. "It was a group of ten people," Bergen remembered, "and it stopped things cold. And that was after a lot of 'I hate this, I hate that.' And I just thought . . . I can't. I rarely spoke with her after that."

Sue also saw less and less of Gore Vidal. Howard Austen had died of brain cancer in the fall of 2003, and Sue had deeply grieved the loss of her old friend. She had often told Boaty Boatwright over the years that the only reason Vidal cared about either of them was because of their closeness to Howard. "Gore would be going on about something, bloviating," said Jack Nicholson, "and Sue would lean over and pantomime a masturbatory gesture."

For years, she had been troubled by Vidal's lack of manners, such as never sending thank-you notes or flowers when she had invited him to one of her dinners at Lexington Road. She denounced him for being cheap and mean-spirited—especially when he was drinking. And as Vidal's drinking intensified after Howard's death, Sue lost patience, just as Vidal found her increasing dependence on pot difficult to take. She was also annoyed when, in the fall of 2006, he published a memoir, *Point to Point Navigation*, and failed to mention her name once.

But the deepest rifts came with Lili Zanuck and David Geffen. In the peculiarly Mengersesque ambivalence where her female friends' professional accomplishments were concerned, Sue alternately praised Zanuck and put her down, telling her that she was nothing more than her husband's shadow. After being on the receiving end of too much of Sue's ugly behavior, Zanuck withdrew for a year, returning to a degree at the very end of Sue's life, mostly because she found her mind so endlessly fascinating.

But Sue's greatest degree of cruelty was reserved for her most powerful ally, her professional "husband," David Geffen. She angered him on occasion by failing to show up when he had gone to great expense to transport her to a special vacation. Once, he arranged for a private plane to fly her to his private yacht, and she decided at the last minute not to go, leaving him with a bill for the plane in the amount of $120,000; when friends chided her for her thoughtlessness, she laughed the matter away, claiming that Geffen could well afford it. She could also be unaccountably vicious to him, telling him that the only reason people were nice to him was because of his money. Geffen, who had forgiven her so many times, was continually angered and wounded by these outbursts.

As always, her vindictiveness retained its comic dimension. Although they had seen each other occasionally over the years and things had been

friendly enough on the surface, she had never really forgiven Dominick
Dunne for the rumors he had spread about Jean-Claude. In 2007, it came to
her attention that *After the Party*, a documentary about Dunne, was making
the rounds of L.A. screening rooms, in search of a distributor. She had
heard that Dunne had recently been diagnosed with cancer, which would
claim him two years hence. Sue got hold of a copy of the DVD. Midway
through, Dunne, interviewed on camera, told the story about losing his
movie-producing career because he told people that Jean-Claude Tramont
was really Jack Schwartz.

Dominick's son, Griffin, was in Los Angeles at the time, shooting a film
and staying at a rented house. One afternoon, the telephone rang and the
voice on the other end said, "Sue Mengers for Griffin Dunne." Griffin happily accepted the call.

"Griffin, honey, it's Sue. How are you? Listen—is your father dead yet?"

Assuming that she was joking around, Griffin laughed and told her no,
but she would be at the top of his call list when it happened.

"Goddammit. I wish he was dead. I hate that fucking asshole. I want
him dead. That story about Jean-Claude's name being Jack Schwartz is
bullshit. How dare he say that? I've never been so insulted."

Griffin pointed out that his father was really telling the story on himself,
and that he didn't think she should take offense.

"Fuck him," said Sue. "I'm going to sue those filmmakers and sue him."

Griffin, uncertain why she was telling him all this, responded that of
course she could do that if she wanted. And then the entire mood of the
conversation changed.

"Anyway—enough of that. Griffin, I'm serving chili at the house tonight. Warren Beatty's going to be here, and Lauren Hutton's in town. Why
don't you come on over?"

After many years of devoted support, Sandra Leoncavallo stopped working as
Sue's assistant. She was replaced by April Schulte. Sue conducted the interview in bed, complimenting Schulte on what nice hair she had, but telling her
she didn't care for the color. Schulte's duties included financial management,
and in time she was increasingly occupied with Sue's battery of doctors.
Schulte recalled her relationship with Sue as warm but occasionally contentious. There were certain rules that Schulte was happy to observe, namely

that Sue slept a great deal of the time and did not care to be disturbed unless she received a telephone call from someone she absolutely was keen to speak with. She read the *Hollywood Reporter*, *Variety*, and the *Washington Post* every day, but was spending more and more time in bed.

Still, she roused herself to give frequent dinners. By this point, her dining room was scarcely ever used; the meals were served in the living room around the long, rectangular coffee table. There were two long sofas facing each other, and she could usually manage to seat four on each. She still favored a starter course of a cup of homemade soup and a heavy entrée, followed by a chocolate dessert or a fruit tart from Bailey's Bakery in Beverly Hills. She had never drunk more than a bit of wine or champagne, but now she didn't even do that. Her joints still rested in the little filigreed silver-plate Art Nouveau box on the table, and she still chain-smoked cigarettes.

Her connection with celebrities was now essentially all she had. It saddened some of her old friends to see her interests and outlets become ever more limited, to have to confront more and more, each time they were around her, the core of depression and sadness. "It was unhealed," said Ali MacGraw. "Hollywood provides people with the illusion that the 'stuff' is going to make it okay—the dress, the car, the Beverly Hills Hotel, the 'A' table in the hot restaurant. And it doesn't. You still have to do the work on the inside. And my own feeling is that although she was very bright, she never got close to the scary stuff, because for the longest time, she had the wherewithal to do anything she wanted. She worked very, very hard. Her clients were her life." Beverly D'Angelo remembered attending a gathering with Sue and Robert Evans around this time and thinking that the two friends resembled two old lions.

Sue refused to believe that not everyone was as celebrity obsessed as she was; she continued to think it was the universal common denominator, whether or not people chose to admit it. She would ask April Schulte if she was excited about Woody Allen coming to the house for dinner; when April registered indifference, Sue would respond, "Everybody is a starfucker. You are, too!"

But her concern for those who made her daily life possible would come out in glancing ways. She might rail to her friends about the housekeeping staff being Third World people, but her gratitude to Virginia and Ori often seeped through. She detested pets—she often said the only animal she liked was the one on her plate—but when Schulte's dog died, Sue offered to buy her another one that she could bring with her to Lexington Road. "I know you're here late a lot of the time," she told Schulte. "So if you want the company, I'll buy you one. Just keep the little bastard on the other side of the house. And tell that little fucker if I hear it bark, I'm going to cut its goddamned tongue out!" April chose not to take her up on her offer.

In early 2011, during Oscar season, Sue had a party for Tom Hooper, whose acclaimed film *The King's Speech* had been nominated for multiple awards. The guests included Boaty Boatwright (who represented Hooper), Anjelica Huston, and Tim Robbins. Early in the evening, Sue had a sort of seizure. Huston, expert in an emergency, took immediate command of the situation, instructing everyone on how to move the table and give Sue enough air. When Sue began to revive a bit, she looked at Boaty and Huston and said, "Don't worry—you're both in the will."

In April 2011, Sue made one of her rare forays away from home, attending the wedding of Brad Grey and Cassandra Huysentruyt at Grey's Bel Air mansion. The couple had wanted Sue to feel chic, so they had bought her a special caftan to wear for the occasion. She arrived in a wheelchair, escorted by Jack Nicholson, and she was delighted to be part of the starry gathering, which included Tom Cruise and Katie Holmes, Jennifer Lopez, and Brad Pitt. "Jack was holding his arm out," recalled Barbara Davis, wife of Marvin Davis, the former owner of Twentieth Century Fox Studios, "and she was holding on to his arm and they came in as the most elegant couple. It made her feel so good." It was Sue's final public outing.

In June, while spending a few days in Palm Springs, Sue sprained her ankle badly. "She was on a rampage," April Schulte remembered. "She was furious that this would happen to her. In the hospital, she was yelling and screaming at the staff—the worst patient imaginable." At home, she had a very difficult recovery, and her muscles were so flaccid that it took several people to lift her off the bed.

Now she became more reluctant than ever to leave the house. She was so distraught that it was difficult even to get her to the doctor. Her housekeepers hated the idea of her smoking marijuana in the car, but April finally told them it was all right for her to have two puffs because it helped take the edge off.

By now she was taking a plethora of medications. She had developed a mild form of diabetes, for which she took Lantus. She took Lipitor to control her high cholesterol, since modifying her diet seemed out of the question, and she loved to eat in bed, which brought on acid reflux. She took Zofran to control her bouts of nausea, and after a series of mild strokes, she was also placed on a low dose of an antiseizure medication. In 2009, she had had a bout with hydrocephalus—water on the brain—that involved the complicated procedure of implanting a shunt in her brain. While she was at UCLA Medical Center having the surgery, Joanna Poitier and Sherry Lansing went to visit her. When they entered her room, Sue gasped; then a small tear escaped. Sue told them she couldn't believe they had shown up. Sherry leaned over her bed to kiss her and said, "There's one condition, Sue: you can't say one mean word to us for one full year." She later recalled that Sue kept her promise.

Sue was fearful and mistrustful of doctors—except for one, a handsome Beverly Hills internist, Dr. Joshua Trabulus, whom she had a crush on and always referred to as "Fabulous Trabulus." Mostly she hated talking to doctors directly and often insisted that Joanna Poitier or April Schulte act as intermediary. She stopped dyeing her hair. On most days, she seemed to find it difficult to reach for a positive thought about any aspect of her life.

Sue became as dependent on April as she had been on Sandra Leoncavallo. Although she still refused to discuss her mother except in the most oblique way, she would occasionally impart a stunning revelation to April. In mid-2011, Sue told her that years earlier she felt an abortionist had taken away her life on an operating table. "I think at that point, even though she had not wanted children, she regretted that she had not had them," said April.

Holiday time was particularly poignant. Her friends would be occupied with their families, and Sue would sneer, "They're with those horrible children, horrible grandchildren." Then she would tell April, "I'm glad you don't have family, because then you can stay here with me." April had a son in college, but she didn't mind spending holidays at Lexington Road; she knew that Sue needed her more than her son did.

Even in her final year, Sue was occasionally involved in Hollywood deal making. When Anjelica Huston wasn't sure she should take the role of Eileen Rand in *Smash*, NBC's forthcoming series about the world of Broadway musicals, Sue told her she would be crazy not to do it. Around the same time, Sue's old friend Lorne Michaels, along with John Goldwyn and Evan

Goldberg, was producing a comedy in development at Paramount called *The Guilt Trip*, about the uneasy relationship between a middle-aged Jewish inventor and the loving mother who has always vexed him with her irritating personality quirks. The part of the mother was exceptionally well written, and all concerned were certain it could provide Barbra Streisand with a wonderful acting opportunity. "There was a long courtship for it," said Lorne Michaels. "We did readings."

Eventually John Goldwyn called Sue to ask if she might try to persuade Streisand to take the role. Sue told him to wait by the phone. Fifteen minutes later she called Goldwyn, saying, "I just got off the phone with Barbra. She's not sure about the script, and I said, 'Barbra, you're never sure about the script. But it's not 1975 anymore. Things don't wait. If you commit to the movie, I assure you they will work on the script.'" About three months later, Streisand committed to do the film. "I've always believed," said Goldwyn, "that Sue making that call to Barbra might have been the thing that closed it. If she was on your team, there was no more loyal adviser, no better friend, no one smarter about what you should or shouldn't do."

When *The Guilt Trip* was released at Christmas 2012, it didn't fare well at the box office, but Streisand gave one of the most convincing and beautifully modulated performances of her career. "I think," said Michaels, "that Sue never wavered in her regard for Barbra's talent."

Sue constantly expressed her terror of her life coming to an end. Throughout much of 2011, she would tell April, "I'm dying." She made April promise that when she eventually passed, she would be wearing her wedding dress—and to make sure she died at home, not in a hospital. She also extracted a promise from April that no one would be around. "She didn't want anyone to see her in some inglorious state," explained Schulte. Despite her extreme neediness, she retained her deep-seated discomfort with overt displays of affection. When her closest friends attempted to hug her as they were leaving the house, or tell her they loved her, she would stiff-arm them, saying, "Yeah, yeah—I get it." How fitting, then, that she would want to die alone—or at least say that she did.

That fall, Sue had a mild transient ischemic attack, but refused to go to the hospital, despite her doctors' warnings that she might suffer a major, debilitating stroke. She chose to have her meals in bed. Eventually, she aspirated food particles and developed pneumonia. Her breathing became wet and labored, and doctors were fairly certain that she was suffering from blood clots in her pulmonary system. On Wednesday, October 12, she passed into a state of semiconsciousness, and Skirball Hospice was called in to supervise her passing away. Joanna Poitier was on hand every day, and April was in constant touch with Ali MacGraw and Boaty Boatwright, who were determining whether they should come immediately or wait a few days. April called them both and told them that if they were planning to come, they should do so immediately. They were both at the house on Saturday, October 15.

Boaty, in a highly pensive state, had telephoned her son, Patrick Baker, married and still living in Los Angeles, and asked him to drive her to Sue's house, telling him that she would need him to be with her all day long. Baker later remembered that the look he saw on his mother's face when she walked over to Sue's bed was unlike anything he had ever witnessed: she was staring into the eyes of her oldest friend, who was going to die in a matter of hours.

Later that day, Alana Stewart stopped by, as did Cassandra Grey and Sue's good friend Jane Semel. Word had gotten out that Sue was near the end, and the telephone began to ring incessantly. April asked Patrick to help field calls. Michael Caine phoned, not realizing how sick Sue was, and asked to drop by later in the day, but Patrick discouraged him from doing so. Caine was stunned, thanked him, and hung up the phone. Joanna Poitier showed up, and she and Boaty made sure Sue was comfortably propped up with pillows and looked her best. A bottle of champagne was opened, and the women began lightening the mood in the way Sue would have approved of most—by telling stories about all the women who had slept with Jack Nicholson, Ryan O'Neal, and Warren Beatty. They talked about their own lives and how Sue had helped shape them. Julia Roberts called to say goodbye, as did a tearful Barbra Streisand.

The doorbell rang, and Barbara Davis showed up for a brief, unannounced visit, initially mistaking Patrick for a member of the household staff. When she asked him what he did, he said, "I'm a film producer."

"Oh," said Barbara Davis. "My husband and I used to own Fox." She was polite and charming, but when she realized what was really happening, she bowed out and let the closest friends continue their process of saying goodbye.

Around five in the afternoon, as the others were gently rubbing Sue's feet and reminiscing, Joanna said, "Patrick, you have to take one for the team. You have to smoke Sue's joint and get her high."

Virginia walked in holding the silver box stacked with joints. Even though Patrick, fit and athletic, had not smoked in years, he lit up a joint, sat very close to Sue, and began blowing deep hits of smoke into her face.

"Every time I did it," said Patrick, "I almost saw this . . . happiness. After twenty minutes, I said I had to stop. I was baked."

Cassandra Grey returned with her husband, Brad, just as Boaty emerged from the bedroom in tears. Sue had died a few moments earlier. No one wanted gossip columnist Nikki Finke to get hold of the news first, so Boaty asked the Greys to keep the matter quiet until she had telephoned Graydon Carter and Frank Rich in New York. Soon the telephone began to ring, but Patrick Baker made no comment and referred all the callers to ICM's publicity department. The rabbi and the medical examiner arrived, and eventually Joanna went home to her husband and Ali went to Robert Evans's house, where she was staying, leaving Boaty and Patrick alone. In a departure from Jewish law, Sue had left instructions that her body was to be cremated. There was to be no funeral or memorial service.

The following morning every major newspaper in the country ran an obituary for Sue. Michael Cieply's in the *New York Times* was headlined "SUE MENGERS, HOLLYWOOD AGENT, DIES AT 79," and featured a large photo of her with Farrah Fawcett and Ryan O'Neal at Studio 54 in 1981. "Brilliant, schmoozy and often devastatingly funny," wrote Cieply, "Ms. Mengers broke through a glass ceiling to become one of the first women to wield true power in the agency business. She captured the spirit of an era in which agents could be as colorful as their clients."

Epilogue

Given Sue's emotional state in the final years of her life—the sedentary existence, the increasingly bitter mind-set about so many things—it is not surprising that there was some general confusion about her estate. Over the years, she had asked a few of her friends about serving as her executor; at one point she raised the matter with Lili Zanuck, because she felt that Zanuck was highly organized and efficient. Eventually, as far as everyone close to her was concerned, she had settled on Sherry Lansing for the same reasons.

It was surprising, therefore, when it was discovered that she had not made the necessary emendations to the will to have Lansing in place as executor. That duty fell to her original choice, David Geffen—much to Lansing's relief.

The amount of money Sue had left behind surprised even some of her closest friends. The total value of the estate was $13 million—the final tribute to Jean-Claude's savvy as an investor. The bulk of the estate was to be divided between two beneficiaries, which Sue identified only in the most general terms: half was to go to support the restoration of art in either Paris or Venice; the other half was to aid old people. Since she had already been in conversations with the Louvre for some time, Geffen made the decision that it would receive one half of the largest share. The other half Geffen earmarked to establish the Sue Mengers Outpost at the Motion Picture & Television Country House and Hospital, the famed residence for retired and ailing film industry professionals.

For years Sue's will had been in a state of perpetual revision; if she got angry at someone, out they went. In her later years, she talked endlessly to friends about making a new will, but she never got around to contacting a lawyer about it. This was somewhat in keeping with the way she had functioned as an agent—making sure the big picture was set, and then losing interest in the finer points. In the final version, there were a few bequests to friends and employees: significant ones to Boaty and Ali and smaller but still ample ones to Fran Lebowitz, April Schulte, and Virginia Portillo. A set of silver candlesticks was left to Candice Bergen.

In the middle of sorting out the details of the estate, Geffen discovered something that shocked him, and he immediately placed a call to Lansing, who had frequently defended Sue or made excuses for her behavior over the years. Geffen pointed out that he had been right in his assessment of his old friend: she had been just as duplicitous and mean-spirited as he'd thought. Lansing asked what he meant, and Geffen responded that Sue had always promised to leave Tom Korman a sizable amount of money as a thank-you for giving her her real start in the agency business. As the years went by, Korman had fallen on hard times financially, and surely the bequest from Sue would be most welcome.

Now, Geffen told Lansing, Sue had proven once and for all what a bitch she really was: she had crossed Korman's name out of the will. Lansing was shocked and for several weeks began to question her own judgment of Sue. "I'm thinking, did I really love this woman? Was she really this mean underneath it all?" Lansing remembered. She telephoned Toni Howard to vent. "Maybe I really had a naïve, stupid view of her," said Lansing. "I mean, she didn't leave any money to Tommy Korman."

"That's because he died seven years ago," Howard replied.

The house at Lexington Road was listed just a few weeks after Sue's death. It moved quickly, selling in mid-December to entertainment lawyer Allen Grubman and his real estate agent wife, Deborah, for $6.2 million.

In the spring of 2012, arrangements were made to distribute Sue's ashes, as well as Jean-Claude's. Sue's will stipulated that her ashes were to be scattered in France by a circle of her closest women friends; their trip was to be paid for by the estate. The decision was made to scatter the ashes in Paris. Candice Bergen felt the idea was wrongheaded, because Sue had never been enthusiastic about spending time there. Still, it was the place Jean-Claude had loved most, and she had loved being with him—so Paris was chosen as their final resting place. At the last minute, Joanna Poitier, Marcia Diamond, and Toni Howard were unable to make the trip, so the responsibility fell to Ali MacGraw, Sherry Lansing, and Boaty Boatwright.

Brad and Cassandra Grey arranged for the ashes to be delivered to Boaty in New York via Paramount's private plane. There was engine trouble in the Midwest, and the plane had to land in Appleton, Wisconsin. When Cassandra Grey telephoned Boaty to tell her where they were, Boaty laughed. "Miss Sue is *not* happy." Appleton turned out to be only a brief detour, and the plane went on to New York. Boaty and Ali then traveled together from New York to Paris with the ashes, and checked into the suites at the Plaza Athénée that Sue's estate had provided for them. There they were joined by Sherry Lansing, who was staying at the Hotel Meurice, and the three of them laughed and reminisced about their friend.

The three women, not realizing that the ashes had already been mixed in California by Joanna Poitier, mixed them again. They then took the bags to the Louvre and began scattering the contents around the trees and the sculpture garden. When someone looked at them quizzically, Sherry said brightly, "Fertilizer!" Because Sue had loved the water so much, they decided to scatter the rest in the Seine. At a magazine stand, Boaty pointed out to Ali a black-and-white photo of Steve McQueen, naked from the waist up, on his motorcycle. A group of Japanese tourists spotted them as they were tossing the ashes into the water, but made no attempt to interfere or call a policeman. The final stop was Sue and Jean-Claude's old home at 3 place André Malraux, where they scattered the last of the ashes at the fountain in front of the apartment building. Then they retired to a favorite restaurant that Boaty knew about, had lunch and champagne, and continued telling stories about Sue.

One quality that unites so many people of exceptional accomplishment is the desire to be remembered. Politicians, most of them, want to ensure that they leave some sort of legacy; so do business executives, authors, actors, and musicians. Foundations arise all over the world bearing the names of the famous, guaranteeing that they will not be forgotten after they are gone, by the work that continues to be attached to their names. The need to "give back" has proven to be one of the hardiest clichés of modern life.

Sue had, as many of her obituaries pointed out, done a great deal to break the glass ceiling for women in the agency business. But it had never been her driving ambition, never her conscious intention, to be any kind of feminist trailblazer. As fond as she was of many of her female colleagues, she had very little interest in being a mentor to other women. If they failed to conquer the man's world of business as she had—well, then, that was their problem. And in the end, it isn't just the bare facts of her accomplishments in the business world that matters most. Her genuine legacy is the *way* in which she did it all—the style, the cunning, the wit, the incomparable panache that she brought to her work and her life. That was the source of so much of her originality, and the source of so many people's endless fascination with her.

These qualities were captured by John Logan in his one-character play *I'll Eat You Last*, which opened on Broadway in the spring of 2013, with Bette Midler playing Sue. The play was produced by Graydon Carter, and the opening was attended by many of her close friends and clients, including Boaty Boatwright, Ali MacGraw, and Ryan O'Neal. The curtain rose to reveal Midler as Sue, dressed in a turquoise caftan, reclining on a sofa. At every performance the applause greeting Midler was electrifying and long lasting. When it finally died down, she delivered Logan's opening line: "I'm not getting up," which led to another rolling burst of applause and laughter. All her close friends were certain that Sue would have reveled in the play's success.

Late in her life, Sue was talking to Fran Lebowitz and David Geffen about her miserable early working experiences.

"I can't believe it," Geffen blurted out. "Didn't anyone see your talent?"

Lebowitz glared at him and said, "You have zero idea of what it's like to be a girl. *Zero.*"

But Sue left sentiments like that for others to express. She did not feel that the women's movement owed her anything, and she had no need whatsoever to "give back"—the very idea would surely have both appalled her and made her laugh derisively.

Yet it is hard to believe that she did not want to be remembered. Why else had she always worked so hard, always kept herself in sight as a woman of glamour and power, someone who knew the best, moved with the best, commanded the best, and ultimately deserved the best? In her early years, achieving those things must have seemed at times almost ridiculously remote and unattainable, even to her—her own version of the green light that Gatsby gazed at across the water from Daisy Buchanan's dock.

It would be a mistake to gauge Sue's life as the tale of the triumph of some sort of (figuratively) ugly duckling. Such a view is reductive, despite the rags-to-riches trappings of her story, which seem almost to be lifted from the pages of a Fannie Hurst novel. Her life is perhaps more of a cautionary tale about a woman of astonishing intellect and wit and drive who never developed the command of her inner demons, and as a result never quite relished her success as much as she might have. As brilliant as she was, her gnawing hunger to become a star in her own right trumped everything else—and that ultimately led to a kind of slow, painful unraveling. And at the core, there was the ambivalence that Paula Weinstein spoke of, always rattling away within her. "Sue should have taken a lesson from Sam Cohn," observed Frank Price. "Sam always supported the client. When I was trying to control the budget on *All That Jazz*, there was nothing Sam wouldn't do to defend Bob Fosse. What a client wants is that kind of loyalty." As hard as Sue worked for her clients, her sense of herself was ultimately too strong for her to become subsumed entirely into their lives. She didn't simply want to serve them; she craved their love and respect, too. And during the intoxicating era of the 1970s, she must have believed, most of the time, that she really had them.

In her later years, she cleverly maintained a key position in the grand scheme of Hollywood. As Daphne Merkin observed, the last years of Sue's life at times resembled a sort of trompe l'oeil: in a town that routinely discards yesterday's celebrities and chases after the newest, biggest, and brightest, Sue maintained an enviable niche, drawing new people to her as the years went by. She might like to play the charming misanthrope, yet there was something about her, even at her meanest, that was not exactly misanthropic. She cared deeply about many of the brilliant people who passed through her life, some of whom stayed permanently. If it was all but impossible for her to show that her loved ones meant anything to her—if it was easier for her to berate and ridicule them—there was an enormously childlike part of her that simply expected them all to understand.

In the end, she really did become the Queen Mother she had described herself to Susan Orlean as being. If she limited herself by being viewed as a symbol of the daring and originality and fun and excess of Hollywood's glorious 1970s, at least she was as vivid a symbol as anyone could have asked for.

On June 11 and 12, 2012, a sale of items from Sue's estate was held at Bonhams, the Los Angeles auction house. Among the choice lots were a pair of

David Arquette's portraits of her, with her trademark tinted glasses, as well as her neoclassical walnut writing desk and various other pieces of furniture and artwork.

Several friends attended the auction, buying up little mementos here and there. Toni Howard bid on a few of Sue's purses, thinking a couple of them might make nice gifts.

When she got home, she opened one of them. There, resting at the bottom, was one of Sue's neatly rolled joints.

Toni did make a present of the purse—with the joint still in it.

ACKNOWLEDGMENTS

When I was growing up in the 1970s, Sue Mengers was quite visible—more visible than any agent had ever been, more even than Swifty Lazar with his big black glasses designed to command attention. Sue Mengers wore glasses, too—hexagonal and tinted pink, which became a kind of trademark, like Rose Marie's bow. I can remember seeing Mengers interviewed on CBS's *60 Minutes* and reading a few of the many profiles of her that appeared in print around this time; she seemed to be right in the vortex of the exciting work that was going on in 1970s Hollywood. As the seventies faded into the distance, I began to see her as a symbol of that era, as I saw the Eagles, Steely Dan, Robert Altman, Robert Evans, Mary Tyler Moore, Carol Burnett, Chick Corea, Martin Scorsese, and Claude Bolling. To that list I would add Barbra Streisand. Obviously, Streisand transcended the era, as all classic performers do— yet there is something about the searching, politically aware, artistically inquisitive Streisand that for me will always be inextricably linked to the 1970s. It was a glorious moment in pop culture, and it makes me smile, as I write this, just to think about it.

Still, when my brilliant and imaginative agent, Edward Hibbert of Donadio & Olson, suggested Sue Mengers as the subject for my next biography, I wasn't sure it was right for me. That was before my research led me into the most fascinating odyssey I have undertaken as a biographer. I am glad that Edward persisted in steering me toward this book, tartly brushing aside my doubts and reservations. Any writer is lucky to have one person in his life whose opinion he can always trust. For me, that person is Edward, and I am thrilled to have him as my friend and representative.

Once I began the research, I realized immediately that I was going to discover this book largely through interviews. Sue's assistant, April Schulte, gave me the hard news that, at Sue's instructions, her entire business archive had been destroyed. So much for any hope of recovering interoffice correspondence, letters, and the like.

Fortunately, in Los Angeles doors began to open. William Friedkin, whose work as a director I have admired for years, was instrumental in getting this process started—as was his wife, Sherry Lansing. I won't forget their support of this project when I needed it most.

Polly Bergen, the former wife of Sue's mentor Freddie Fields, provided welcome encouragement and fascinating memories when I spent a day with her at her home in

Connecticut. I know how keenly the New York show business community feels her absence.

In Los Angeles, I embarked on a series of eye-opening interviews. One of the first was with Lili Zanuck. We met at the Beverly Hills Polo Lounge, and I can still remember the rush of feeling the book start to take shape in my head as Lili and I spoke.

Sue's longtime colleague Toni Howard of ICM also proved unfailingly generous. We met for lunch at Craft in Century City, and after some initial nervousness about my taping our interview, Toni put her trust in me. She gave this project her blessing and encouraged many hard-to-reach people to speak with me.

Another member of Sue's close circle, Joanna Poitier, was always willing to answer any stray questions I might have and to share with me the photo albums of Sue's mother, Ruth Sender, which Sue entrusted to Joanna.

Sue's colleague Michael Black offered invaluable help and friendship from the day we met, as well as the best vocal impersonation of Sue I have yet to hear. Michael helped me secure interviews with a number of people, including his gifted client Tuesday Weld. I once flew to Los Angeles for a weekend mostly so I could have dinner with Michael and a mutual friend, Barbara Howar, at Craig's in West Hollywood. The evening was more than worth it.

After a few months' work, I had the good fortune to meet Sue's client and good friend Ali MacGraw. Ali is a biographer's dream source. I turned to her many times for guidance throughout my work on this book, and she never failed me.

The true godmother of this book is Sue's oldest friend, Boaty Boatwright. Sue and Boaty met in the 1950s and were friends for six decades. Boaty called or e-mailed me weekly to suggest possible interview subjects, and when I was having trouble getting through to someone, she always intervened on my behalf. Previously, I had known Boaty only as a legendary figure in the agency business; now I know her as a loyal and delightful friend and unwavering ally. Without her this book would never have pulled itself together, and she has my everlasting thanks.

Thanks also to the many other friends, clients, and colleagues of Sue's who spoke with me: Rachel Abramowitz, Nancy Allen, Woody Allen, Diana Anderson, Max Apple, Lucie Arnaz, Jonathan Axelrod, Kara Baker, Patrick Baker, Judy Balaban, Rona Barrett, Barbara Barrie, Peter Bart, Keith Baxter-Wright, Annabelle Begelman, Richard Benjamin, Candice Bergen, Peter Biskind, Jacqueline Bisset, Peter Bogdanovich, Bob Bookman, Joan Juliet Buck, Gail Lumet Buckley, John Burnham, Kate Burton, Michael Caine, Dyan Cannon, Glenn Caron, Graydon Carter, Alan Caso, Marge Champion, Cher, Sandra Church, Marya Cohn, Joan Collins, Douglas Cramer, Mart Crowley, Robert Daly, Beverly D'Angelo, Constance Danielson, Kim Darby, Barbara Davis, Joel Dean, Sabine de la Rochefoucauld, Marcia Diamond, Angie Dickinson, Barry Diller, Griffin Dunne, Lisa Eichhorn, Dr. Mark Elias, Harvey Evans, Robert Evans, Jeff

Field, Bertram Fields, Carrie Fisher, Joan Fisher, Roz Slakter Fisher, Stephen Fry, Penny Fuller, Elizabeth Gabler, Art Garfunkel, David Geffen, Robert Getchell, Jack Gilardi, Mitch Glazer, Leonard Goldberg, Elaine Goldsmith-Thomas, John Goldwyn, Dorothy Goodale, Hildy Gottlieb, Elliott Gould, Joel Grey, Kathy Griffin, Stephanie Wanger Guest, Barbara Hale, Wynn Handman, Joan Harris, Joyce Harris, Nick Haslam, Brooke Hayward, Buck Henry, Jerry Herman, John Heyman, Claire Hoffman, Barbara Howar, Esme Howard, Robin Hurlstone, Anjelica Huston, Rachel Igel, Stanley Jaffe, Anne Jeffreys, Jay Julien, Lucille Kall, Jay Kanter, Marthe Keller, Michael Korie, Seymour Kover, Ellen Kramer, Alan Ladd, Jr., Jeffrey Lane, Robert Todd Lang, Lionel Larner, Fran Lebowitz, Sandy Lieberson, George Litto, Trini Lopez, Donald Loze, Martha Luttrell, Kelly Lynch, David Mamet, Edward Markley, Wende Phifer Mate, Mike Medavoy, Daphne Merkin, Ron Meyer, Lorne Michaels, Bette Midler, Sylvia Miles, Liza Minnelli, Cathy Moriarty, Wendy Stark Morrissey, Sue Naegle, Liam Neeson, Phyllis Newman, Jack Nicholson, Lynda Obst, Ryan O'Neal, Susan Orlean, Suzanne Palmiero, Cindy Pearson, Larry Peerce, Osgood Perkins, Matt Pincus, Lou Pitt, Johnnie Planco, Anika Poitier, Virginia Portillo, Jane Powell, Paula Prentiss, Frank Price, Harold Prince, Carole Radziwill, Tamara Rawitt, Rex Reed, Frank Rich, John Richardson, W. D. "Rick" Richter, Joan Rivers, Eric Roberts, Alex Roldan, Frank Rose, Adele Rosen, Karen Rosenfelt, Howard Rosenman, David Rothenberg, Marion Rothman, Harvey Sabinson, Carole Bayer Sager, Beverly Sanders, Alvin Sargent, Hannalore Schatz, Jerry Schatzberg, Robert Schear, Paul Schrader, April Schulte, Joel Schumacher, George Segal, Arthur Segaul, Barbara Sender, Leo Sender, Stuart Sender, Risa Shapiro, Sid Sheinberg, Richard Shepherd, Tina Sinatra, Liz Smith, Michael Sragow, Alessandra Stanley, Alana Stewart, Arnold Stiefel, Barbra Streisand, Dan Thomas, Marlo Thomas, Jane Trichter, Larry Turman, Harry Ufland, Bruce Vilanch, Christopher Walken, Lesley Anne Warren, Paula Weinstein, Jerry Weintraub, Eric Weissman, Tuesday Weld, Jim Wiatt, Lucy Wick, Alex Witchel, David Yarnell, Jerry Zeitman, and Kenneth Ziffren.

For help in uncovering facts about Sue's early life in Utica, New York, I owe a great debt to the Oneida County Historical Society, and in particular to ace researcher Mary Anne Buteux. Thanks also to James Kelly and Emily Ostertag, who helped track down details about Sue's beginnings.

I am also grateful to the staffs of the Margaret Herrick Library of the Academy of Motion Picture Arts and Sciences in Los Angeles; the UCLA Film & Television Archive; the New York Public Library for the Performing Arts at Lincoln Center; the Houghton Library at Harvard University (special thanks to Peter Accardo); the Howard Gotlieb Archival Research Center at Boston University; the Paley Center for Media; the Wisconsin Historical Society (special thanks to Lee Grady); the Lilly Library at Indiana University; the NBC Universal Archives (special thanks to William Bartlett), and the Harry Ransom Center at the University of Texas, Austin.

My thanks to Graydon Carter and his wonderful staff at *Vanity Fair*—especially to deputy editor Mark Rozzo.

Thanks also to Boaty Boatwright's assistants, Kevin McEleney and Meredith Duff, who made my life much easier by chasing people down for me. I also received valuable help in a variety of areas from Molly Barnett, Brenda Berrisford, Sandy Bresler, Peter Carzasty, Melanie Chapman, Jeremy Conrady, Marty Erlichman, Alexandra Ferick, Ray Freer, Percy Gibson, Priscila Giraldo, Dick Guttman, Jill Hattersley, Byron Lane, John Manis, Michele Schweitzer, Shelby Shaw, David Zippel. And Alexandra Krug, Eric Price, Eliza Roberts, and especially Kathryn Leigh Scott, who repeatedly opened her Beverly Hills home to me during my research trips to California.

Special thanks to Jim Di Giovanni for his enthusiastic support of this project from the very outset.

As always, my gratitude to the staff of *Opera News*, my employer of many years: editor in chief F. Paul Driscoll, who has always been supportive of my work as a biographer; publisher Diane Silberstein; editorial production coordinator Elizabeth Diggans; plus Gregory Downer, Louise T. Guinther, Tristan Kraft, Maria Mazzarro, Henry Stewart, Mariah Wakefield, and Adam Wasserman.

A big hand to a fine group of friends in New York who supported this book in a variety of ways: Patricia Bosworth, Ronald Bowers, Erik Dahl, Polly Frost, Craig Haladay, Jessica Hirshbein, Jill Krementz, Arlo McKinnon, Francesca Mercurio, Steven and Lisa Mercurio, Eric Myers, David Niedenthal, Patricia O'Connell, Rebecca Paller, Judy Rice, Ray Sawhill, Michael Slade, and Tracy Turner.

I must express my ongoing gratitude to my editor at Viking, Rick Kot. This is our third book together, and once again I have benefited from his sure guidance. Thanks also to Rick's assistants Nick Bromley and Diego Núñez, and to Jane Cavolina, as fine a copy editor as I've come across.

Finally, there are three important anchors in my life: my partner Scott Barnes, to whom the book is dedicated; my remarkable father, Jack Kellow; and my brother, Barry Kellow, who is never too busy to talk to me about anything and everything.

Brian Kellow
New York City
April 2015

NOTES

INTRODUCTION

2 "I was a little pisher": "Mengers' the Name—Hollywood's the Game," *60 Minutes*, CBS, January 26, 1975.

2 "Sue had a tough weekend": Author interview with Lionel Larner, January 29, 2012.

2 "I remember coming into the offices": Author interview with Phyllis Newman, September 20, 2013.

3 "I never invited anyone": Susan Orleans, "When Sue Was Queen," *New Yorker*, March 21, 1994.

CHAPTER ONE: 1901–1946

5 "My mother, the Gorgon": Author interview with Ali MacGraw, April 23, 2013.

5 "I should have been *you*": Author interview with Marlo Thomas, August 28, 2013.

6 "was wrong, as the pitch of a note": Eudora Welty, "June Recital," *The Collected Stories of Eudora Welty* (New York: Harcourt Brace Jovanovich, 1980), 305.

6 "The war came": Ibid.

7 "I'll call you in the morning": Author interview with Patrick Baker, June 12, 2013.

7 "*Aaach!* If I have to see any more Jews": Ibid.

7 "I'm an outdoor educator": Ibid.

7 "I'm an Alpinist": Ibid.

7 "You know what? Jews own banks": Ibid.

8 "Sue's father was not well enough off": Author interview with Dr. Mark Elias, September 22, 2013.

8 thirty-one-year-old "merchant": Log of the SS *Koenigstein*, August 15, 1938.

8 "What I remember about her": Author interview with Dr. Mark Elias, September 22, 2013.

9 "A bar on practically every corner": Author interview with Dorothy Goodale, September 8, 2012.

10 "You rounded the corner": Ibid.

10 "Because her mother was working": Author interview with Arthur Segaul, February 24, 2014.

10 "When she started speaking": Ibid.

10 "She had a flair for the dramatic": Author interview with Dr. Mark Elias, September 22, 2013.

12 "I couldn't speak": Author interview with Lucille Kall, September 21, 2013.

12 "At camp, I had a sister": Ibid.

12 "She was chutzpah personified": Author interview with Rosalind Slakter Fisher, September 21, 2013.

13 "My dad had a dry goods": Author interview with Adele Rosen, September 29, 2013.

CHAPTER TWO: **1946-1950**

15 "**To Rozy—the girl with the big heart**": Inscription on back of photograph of Sue Mengers, sent to Rosalind Slakter Fisher, 1947.

16 "**It was almost if there was a force field**": Author interview with Seymour Kover, December 29, 2012.

17 "**not Rita Hayworth attractive**": Ibid.

17 "**Betty taught us to have a certain accent**": Ibid.

17 "**We were challenged to be creative**": Ibid.

18 "**What happens to someone who is a happy-go-lucky person**": Author interview with Sherry Lansing, January 11, 2013.

19 "**German Jews think**": Ibid.

19 "**Dear Roz, Don't you dare**": Inscription on the back of a photo sent from Sue Mengers to Rosalind Slakter Fisher, ca. 1950.

CHAPTER THREE: **1950-1957**

20 "**I always thought that Ruth and Sue**": Author interview with Barbara Sender, June 6, 2014.

21 "**was welcomed like a promise**": Jan Morris, *Manhattan '45* (New York: Oxford University Press, 1987), 4.

22 "**I was Patsy Reuben's best friend**": Author interview with Judy Balaban, August 22, 2013.

25 "**Who ever heard of an entertainer**": Author interview with Jerry Zeitman, January 12, 2013.

26 "**Most of the pictures Grace did**": Author interview with Jay Kanter, November 20, 2013.

26 "**She sang a few lines**": Ibid.

26 "**Jay, you're going to ruin this business**": Ibid.

27 "**a deal at Fox for two or three pictures**": Ibid.

27 "**Dress British, think Yiddish**": Author interview with Jerry Zeitman, November 30, 2014.

27 "**I always turned down being interviewed**": Author interview with Jerry Zeitman, January 12, 2013.

28 "**They did insist on one thing**": Author interview with Jay Kanter, November 20, 2013.

28 "**She had somehow negotiated**": Author interview with Judy Balaban, August 22, 2013.

29 "**We became friends on the phone**": Author interview with Joan Fisher, June 21, 2013.

CHAPTER FOUR: **1957-1959**

30 "**Mr. Power, I will get him on the phone**": Author interview with Boaty Boatwright, March 6, 2013.

31 "**If I said, 'Red, this is junk'**": Author interview with Wynn Handman, March 12, 2014.

31 "**small potatoes. Not classy**": Author interview with Sylvia Miles, December 28, 2013.

31 "**Oh, honey, *you're* never going to make it**": Author interview with Lionel Larner, March 21, 2012.

32 "**She went down to the mailbox**": Ibid.

32 "**Baby Sue's smart**": Ibid.

32 "Once I had to go out to Fire Island": Ibid.
33 "Mother? *Mother?*": Ibid.
33 "Are you kidding?": Ibid.
33 "You know, when Lionel came here": Author interview with Lionel Larner, January 29, 2013.
33 "Well, some girls go on dates": Ibid.
34 "This is Billy Rose": Author interview with Lionel Larner, March 21, 2012.
35 "took our breath away": Author interview with Jerry Herman, March 19, 2013.
36 "Hi, I'm Flora Roberts": Ibid.
36 "Melina Mercouri and Jules Dassin": Ibid.
36 "Joe Sweeney doesn't read": Author interview with Lionel Larner, March 21, 2012.
36 "I don't think you understand me": Ibid.
36 "And I told you, Joe Sweeney doesn't read": Ibid.
36 "Joe Sweeney doesn't *work*": Ibid.
36 "Jolson had the dough": Michael Braun, undated interview with journalist Audrey Wood.
37 "The theater today is wide open": *Newark News*, July 8, 1958.
38 "They used to call her": Author interview with Joan Fisher, June 21, 2013.

39 "*What does an agent do?*": Arthur Kopit, *End of the World* (New York: Hill and Wang, 1984), 17.
39 "In *theory*, an agent": Ibid.
40 "I got my first Broadway job": Author interview with Barbara Barrie, February 2, 2013.
41 "banked on the general uncertainty": Tom Kemper, *Hidden Talent: The Emergence of Hollywood Agents* (Berkeley: University of California Press, 2010), 92.
41 "The studio handled everything": Author interview with Jane Powell, October 23, 2012.
42 "I was heartbroken": Author interview with Anne Jeffreys, November 21, 2013.
42 "I figured I might as well": Author interview with Barbara Hale, March 7, 2013.
43 "I used to sharpen": Author interview with Robert Schear, February 6, 2013.
44 "It had to be Nathan's": Ibid.
44 "Oh, darling, they just *hated* you": Author interview with Barbara Barrie, February 2, 2013.
44 "Sorry, he's not going to": Author interview with Robert Schear, February 6, 2013.
44 "Phyllis was a powerhouse": Author interview with Barbara Barrie, February 2, 2013.
45 "Didja call for a table?": Author interview with Robert Schear, February 6, 2013.
45 "And then it was Jule Styne!": Author interview with Lionel Larner, March 21, 2012.
45 "All the big guys had a secretary": Author interview with David Rothenberg, April 12, 2013.
46 "She thought I was nothing": Author interview with Barbra Streisand, January 19, 2014.
46 "Oh, I know who *you* are!": Author interview with Boaty Boatwright, March 6, 2013.
46 "We are?": Ibid.
46 "Marty Balsam!": Ibid.
46 "No, he hasn't slept with me yet": Ibid.
46 "Well, he has with *me*!": Ibid.
47 "Sue Sondheim . . . Sue Sondheim": Ibid.

47 "nearly putting her eye out": Peter Biskind, "When Sue Was Queen," *Vanity Fair*, April 2000.
48 "I knew Gore": Author interview with Judy Balaban, August 22, 2013.

CHAPTER SIX: 1963–1966
50 "Sue went over to work for Tom": Author interview with Lionel Larner, January 29, 2013.
50 "I don't think he did very well": Author interview with Stephanie Wanger Guest, February 8, 2013.
51 "I came up zero": Author interview with Elliott Gould, August 13, 2012.
53 "Kay? Kay *who*?": Author interview with Lionel Larner, January 29, 2013.
54 "I think Sue and Gore": Author interview with Nicky Haslam, May 14, 2013.
55 "I think that Howard was able": Author interview with Boaty Boatwright, March 6, 2013.
55 "Gore wants to fuck you": Author interview with Lionel Larner, March 21, 2012.
55 "swinging all through Greece": Letter from Sue Mengers to Gore Vidal, November 11, 1965.
56 "Fuck David Merrick!" Peter Biskind, "When Sue Was Queen," *Vanity Fair*, April 2000.
57 "I thought I would faint": Ibid.
57 "I guess Constance finally got her box": Author interview with Lionel Larner, March 21, 2012.
58 "Gore, dear: I find myself": Letter from Sue Mengers to Gore Vidal, November 11, 1965.

CHAPTER SEVEN: 1966–1968
60 Fields's then-wife, Polly Bergen, claimed: Author interview with Polly Bergen, June 29, 2012.
61 "People said he was sleazy": Author interview with Polly Bergen, June 29, 2012.
61 "Sue was going into a world": Author interview with Peter Bart, July 21, 2014.
62 "I thought David Begelman": Author interview with Elliott Gould, August 13, 2012.
63 "I remember walking into Sue's office": Author interview with Polly Bergen, June 29, 2012.
63 "Tell him Baby Sue is calling": Ibid.
63 "Dear Mr. Hitchcock": Letter from Sue Mengers to Alfred Hitchcock, August 18, 1967.
65 "Oh, Otto": Author interview with Lionel Larner, March 21, 2012.
65 "After all, who knew?": Author interview with Jerry Schatzberg, February 3, 2015.
66 "small, deft, beautifully performed thriller": *New York Magazine*, October 28, 1968.
66 "She was there all the time": Author interview with Osgood Perkins, July 15, 2013.
68 "You're going to love Elliott Gould": Author interview with William Friedkin, January 30, 2012.
68 "I was sort of new": Ibid.

CHAPTER EIGHT: 1968–1969
70 "She was still in New York": Author interview with David Yarnell, September 17, 2013.
71 "an irritating little faggot": Author interview with Ali MacGraw, May 31, 2014.
71 YOU SWORE TO ME: Author interview with Boaty Boatwright, March 6, 2013.
72 "I hope you don't mind": Author interview with Marcia Diamond, April 17, 2013.
72 "It turned out that he was her date": Author interview with Joanna Poitier, January 12, 2013.
73 "She would say, 'Oh, your hair'": Ibid.

73 "Even the people who got angry": Author interview with Boaty Boatwright, March 6, 2013.

73 Sue called Evans "Prick": Author interview with Robert Evans, January 15, 2014.

73 Evans called her "Mengela": Ibid.

74 "Sue was a master": Author interview with Douglas Cramer, November 23, 2013.

74 "Sue liked me": Author interview with Trini Lopez, January 10, 2014.

74 "Who told you?": Author interview with Lili Zanuck, February 3, 2014.

74 "Trini Lopez": Ibid.

74 "I don't want reviews": Ibid.

75 "How do I sign Oskar?": Author interview with Diana Anderson, May 17, 2014.

75 "I didn't see any character": Jack Hirschberg interview with Barbra Streisand, 1969, Jack Hirschberg collection, Margaret Herrick Library.

75 "In fact, I'm too easy": Ibid.

75 "A song, you know": Isobel Lennart, screenplay of *Funny Girl*, Columbia Pictures, 1968.

76 "Sue was perfect": Author interview with Jeffrey Lane, March 6, 2013.

76 "But Barbra's the star": Ibid.

76 "Princess Margaret wasn't that crazy about ladies": Ibid.

77 Excuse me, Mrs. Onassis—I just wanted to say": Author interview with Boaty Boatwright, February 10, 2015.

77 "David had a keen mind": Author interview with Constance Danielson, April 10, 2014.

78 "She didn't care who she stepped on": Author interview with Rona Barrett, July 23, 2012.

79 "like that song in *A Chorus Line*": "The *Playboy* Interview: David Geffen," *Playboy*, September 1994, 56.

79 "I'd rather die than fail": "Inventing David Geffen," *American Masters*, PBS documentary, 2012.

80 "William Morris had a strict policy": Author interview with Harry Ufland, January 24, 2013.

80 "Why do you spend all this time": Ibid.

81 "Sam didn't care about money": Author interview with Toni Howard, January 11, 2013.

81 "I thought we were doing": Author interview with Harold Prince, October 8, 2013.

81 "I went back to New York": Ibid.

82 "He was a real showbiz kid": Ibid.

82 "What do you want to cast": Author interview with Toni Howard, January 11, 2013.

82 "Oh, Susie's *scared*": Author interview with Joan Collins, November 16, 2013.

82 "She was quite fearful": Ibid.

82 "Don't worry, honey": Peter Biskind, "When Sue Was Queen," *Vanity Fair*, April 2000.

CHAPTER NINE: 1970

85 "I had one line": Author interview with Ali MacGraw, April 23, 2013.

85 "exactly the right mixture": *New York Times*, April 4, 1969.

85 "makes up for all the fashion models": *Village Voice*, April 3, 1969.

85 "I fell in love with Sue": Author interview with Ali MacGraw, April 23, 2013.

86 "I do love my clients": Author interview with Risa Shapiro, March 27, 2013.

87 "Battle of the Network Caftans": Author interview with Bruce Vilanch, January 10, 2013.

87 "Look, Mike Nichols isn't exactly": Ann-Margret, *My Story* (New York: G. P. Putnam's Sons, 1994), 203.

87 "I'm not a technical actress": Ibid., 204.

88 "quiet, soft, moving performance": *Newsweek*, July 5, 1971.
88 calling it "simp pathos": Pauline Kael, *Deeper into Movies* (New York: Atlantic Monthly Press, 1973), 284.
88 "I was good in *Carnal Knowledge*": Candice Bergen, *Knock Wood* (New York: Simon & Schuster, 1984), 222.
89 "the Doris Day of the Counter-Culture": Digby Diehl, "Kim Darby Has Rich Girl's Shoulders," *Show*, February 1970.
89 "The first thing she said to me": Author interview with Kim Darby, August 23, 2013.
89 "In those days": Ibid.
89 "Scripts were piled up": Ibid.
89 "She was always on the phone": Ibid.
90 "Otto was famous": Author interview with Dyan Cannon, April 3, 2013.
91 "It was an emotional scene": Ibid.
91 "You could not reason with him": "Dyan Cannon Explodes in Preminger's New Film 'Such Good Friends,'" *Show*, February 1972.
91 "Sue took me on": Author interview with Michael Caine, February 28, 2013.
92 "She would call me and say": Ibid.
92 "I was putting sugar in my coffee": Ibid.
92 "No disagreements": Ibid.
92 "Through Bob Evans": Author interview with Joan Collins, November 16, 2013.
93 "starts with the inestimable": *Focus on Film*, No. 1, 1970.
93 "I don't care if the critics": *New York Daily News*, October 31, 1971.
93 "It reeked of success": *New York Times*, November 7, 1971.
93 "She wanted me to work": Author interview with Tuesday Weld, March 11, 2013.
94 "I think one reason everybody": Ibid.
94 "doubtful there will be the kind": *Variety*, February 16, 1970.
95 "Sue Mengers, a big agent": Diary of Peter Bogdanovich, September 24, 1970.
95 "We think an excellent film": Letter from Sue Mengers to Peter Bogdanovich, October 26, 1970.
95 "Sue was sort of outrageous": Author interview with Peter Bogdanovich, December 13, 2013.
96 "Instantly, Dick Zanuck said": Author interview with William Friedkin, July 28, 2013.
96 "On the first day he was great": Ibid., January 30, 2012.
96 "You can't do this movie!": Ibid.
96 "I almost fell asleep": Ibid., July 28, 2013.
97 "I went upstairs alone": Author interview with Elizabeth Wilson, May 3, 2007.
98 "It was the scene where Hackman": Author interview with William Friedkin, July 28, 2013.
98 "He delivered a great performance": Ibid.
99 "If the formula of *Love Story*": *Chicago Sun-Times*, January 10, 1971.
99 "they are crying for themselves": *New York Times*, January 10, 1971.
99 "Howard Rubin *sucks*": Author interview with Ryan O'Neal, May 27, 2013.
99 "Sue didn't find people off the street": Ibid.

CHAPTER TEN: 1971–1972
101 "The wonderful thing about Sue": Author interview with Kenneth Ziffren, October 8, 2012.

101 "She said, 'I don't get why'": Author interview with Mike Medavoy, July 19, 2013.

101 "We set up this important meeting": Author interview with Richard Shepherd, November 13, 2013.

102 "Sue was the greatest negative seller": Author interview with Barry Diller, July 15, 2013.

102 "I've just talked to my wife": Author interview with Kim Darby, August 23, 2013.

103 "He never laid hands on me": Ibid.

103 "It was more than terrible": Author interview with Elliott Gould, August 13, 2012.

104 "They both had a kind of irreverent": Author interview with Jack Nicholson, October 27, 2014.

104 "a film festival": Robert Evans, *The Kid Stays in the Picture* (New York: Hyperion, 1994), 273.

104 "There was so much about the fairy-tale piece": Author interview with Ali MacGraw, April 23, 2013.

105 "She said, 'Oh, God'": Ibid.

106 "I'm trying to convince Ali": Robert Evans, *The Kid Stays in the Picture* (New York: Hyperion, 1994), 247.

106 "I think Sue was so angry": Author interview with Ali MacGraw, April 23, 2013.

107 "The only thing I liked": Author interview with Peter Bogdanovich, December 13, 2013.

107 "I left the office producing": Ibid.

107 "Just go see *Love Story*": Ibid.

107 "Have lunch with him": Ibid.

108 "Barbra was having a thing": Ibid.

108 "You're going to hate me": Ibid.

108 "I'm having a difficult time": Ibid.

108 "*What's Up, Doc?*, you're calling it?": Ibid.

108 "Barbra was funny": Author interview with Ryan O'Neal, May 27, 2013.

108 "Have a good tan": Ibid.

109 "Barbra is great": Ibid.

109 "Listen—we're too close": Ibid.

109 "She knew I was always on the prowl": Author interview with Buck Henry, December 4, 2012.

109 "*The Last Picture Show* is a masterpiece": *Newsweek*, October 11, 1971.

110 "Before that, we were just good friends": Author interview with Barbra Streisand, January 19, 2014.

111 "fear of total public acceptance": *Village Voice*, November 9, 1972.

111 "It was great networking": Author interview with Joel Schumacher, January 23, 2014.

112 "a major above-the-title sex life": Author interview with Ali MacGraw, April 23, 2013.

112 "Jean-Claude was one of the most": Author interview with Candice Bergen, November 11, 2013.

112 "She thought, what—Velveeta?": Ibid.

113 "I think Sue couldn't believe it": Author interview with Ali MacGraw, June15, 2014.

CHAPTER ELEVEN: 1973–1974

114 "If I ask Joan Harris": Author interview with Joan Harris, May 10, 2013.

115 "I think she had the impression": Ibid.

115 "We were the kind of girls": Author interview with Ali MacGraw, April 23, 2013.

115 "tiny and tough": Author interview with Candice Bergen, November 11, 2013.

116 "He just was not the kind of guy": Author interview with Ali MacGraw, June 15, 2014.

116 "Oh, all right": Author interview with Tuesday Weld, March 11, 2013.

116 "She gave my daughter": Ibid.

116 "When you were there": Author interview with Jacqueline Bisset, December 17, 2012.

116 "I think it's difficult": Ibid.

117 "a metaphysical mystery": Author interview with Larry Turman, July 26, 2014.

118 "I know no actor cooler": Letter from Stephanie Phillips to Fred Zinnemann, July 27, 1971.

118 "I have a conviction": Letter from Stephanie Phillips to Fred Zinnemann, August 10, 1971.

118 "She said, 'You've got to do this film'": Author interview with Jacqueline Bisset, December 17, 2012.

118 "You're not going to do it": Ibid.

118 "See, I know what heat is": Paul Rosenfield, *The Club Rules: Power, Money, Sex, and Fear—How It Works in Hollywood* (New York: Warner Books, 1992), 142.

119 "If I had closed that day": Ibid., 138.

119 "They figure, 'If she's got Barbra'": "Dialogue on Film: Sue Mengers," *American Film*, November 1976.

119 "Honey, shoot me down a Tab!": Stephen Sondheim and Anthony Perkins, screenplay of *The Last of Sheila*, Warner Bros., 1973.

120 "Take the character Dyan plays": Cynthia Grenier, "The Munificent Seven," *Village Voice*, June 28, 1973.

120 "open-faced, typical hero": Letter from Stephen Sondheim to Author, January 30, 2013.

120 "You've got to help me": Author interview with Howard Rosenman, October 3, 2013.

120 "And Dyan Cannon *was*": Ibid.

121 "a curious woman": Author interview with Dyan Cannon, April 3, 2013.

121 "I just had a call": Ibid.

121 "a director between jobs": *New York Daily News*, October 29, 1973.

122 "The parties were totally constructed": Author interview with Richard Benjamin, January 10, 2013.

122 "I was always interested!": Author interview with Paula Prentiss, January 10, 2013.

122 "'Sew your blue jeans'": Ibid.

123 "Did she really read": Author interview with Richard Benjamin, January 10, 2013.

123 "Ryan's *out*": Ibid.

123 "She kept right on going": Ibid.

123 "There aren't too many people": Ibid.

124 "It's kind of an end-of-the-West Western": Author interview with Peter Bogdanovich, December 13, 2013.

125 "Ryan has to be directed": Ibid.

125 "peppy, coarse, funny": *Time*, May 28, 1973.

125 "to Bogdanovich's extraordinary flair": *Village Voice*, June 21, 1973.

125 "She didn't deal with the back end": Author interview with Peter Bogdanovich, December 13, 2013.

125 "What eighty thousand dollars?": Author interview with Ryan O'Neal, May 27, 2013.

125 "But I won the Academy Award": Ibid.

125 "Let me explain something": Ibid.

125 "Maybe I'd better do another picture": Ibid.

125 "She never treated me as a child": Tatum O'Neal, "My Starry Nights with Sue," *Daily Beast*, October 23, 2011.

126 "Any agent who thinks that way": "Super Agent for Super Talent," *Hollywood Reporter*, 1975, forty-fifth anniversary issue.

126 "She was totally obsessed": Author interview with Barbra Streisand, January 19, 2014.

126 "Sue knew how to push your buttons": Ibid.

127 "Yes, darling": Ibid.

127 "'Great. We would agree": "Super Agent, for Super Talent," *Hollywood Reporter*, 1975, forty-fifth anniversary issue.

129 "directed by Larry Peerce": *New York Times*, November 22, 1973.

129 "Instead of telling the actors": Author interview with Griffin Dunne, May 25, 2013.

129 "I liked him": Author interview with Keith Baxter-Wright, May 10, 2014.

130 "This picture should be subtitled": *Dominick Dunne: After the Party*, documentary film, 2008.

130 "In drinking and talking out of school": Author interview with Griffin Dunne, May 25, 2013.

130 "Congratulations on those wonderful numbers": Author interview with Joan Rivers, July 19, 2013.

131 "You cannot divorce Freddie": Author interview with Polly Bergen, June 29, 2012.

131 "What are you talking about?": Ibid.

132 "Each side was as dazzled": Author interview with Joan Juliet Buck, August 2, 2013.

132 "Now listen, Joanie": Ibid.

132 "She always teased me": Author interview with Jack Nicholson, October 27, 2014.

133 "colder than Baskin-Robbins": Robert Evans, *The Kid Stays in the Picture* (New York: Hyperion, 1994), 263.

133 "Bobbeee . . . I fibbed": Ibid.

133 "If I thought the pussy looked good": Author interview with Lynda Obst, April 3, 2013.

134 "Jon is a formidable figure": Author interview with Lesley Ann Warren, July 23, 2013.

134 "Jon urged me to explore": Ibid.

135 "She hated Jon Peters": Author interview with Barbra Streisand, January 19, 2014.

136 "What do these five famous names": "Mengers' the Name . . . Hollywood's the Game," *60 Minutes*, January 26, 1975.

136 "I thought you'd never ask": Ibid.

136 "Of course, I don't know": Ibid.

137 "It's gonna pay off": Ibid.

137 "Golda Meir had power": Ibid.

137 "Do you ever pinch yourself": Ibid.

137 "Oh, yeah": Ibid.

137 "It was cool and white": Author interview with Ali MacGraw, June 15, 2014.

138 "she told the *New York Times*": Elaine Louie, "Inside Five Famous Women's Closets," *New York Times*, August 28, 1977.

140 "We trusted Phil Weltman": Author interview with Ronald Meyer, June 23, 2014.

140 "Stanley Kubrick said": Author interview with Ryan O'Neal, May 27, 2013.

140 "You're going to represent": Author interview with Paula Weinstein, January 22, 2014.

140 "It was one of my first moments": Ibid.

141 "Do you have anything for my Ali?": Author interview with Michael Black, January 9, 2013.

141 "But I'm hungry!": Author interview with Ali MacGraw, April 23, 2013.

141 "She looks at me": Ibid.

142 "I don't think Sue": Author interview with Boaty Boatwright, October 3, 2013.

142 "Sue called me one day": Author interview with Peter Bogdanovich, December 13, 2013.

143 "By the time the picture was over": Ibid.

143 "a stillborn picture": Pauline Kael, "The Rear Guard," *New Yorker*, March 24, 1975.

143 "Will you for Chrissake stop": Author interview with Peter Bogdanovich, December 13, 2013.

144 "a production of *The Three Musketeers*": Author interview with Michael Black, January 9, 2013.

144 "for the film *The Three Musketeers*": Ibid.

144 "Coming soon . . . *The Further Adventures*": Ibid.

144 "I never paid anybody": Author interview with Alan Ladd, Jr., March 11, 2013.

145 "If a couple of these studios": James Powers, "Dialogue on Film," *American Film*, November 1976, 36.

145 "Aaach," she muttered: Author interview with Michael Black, January 9, 2013.

145 "I was like a kid": Ibid.

146 "You would say, 'I tried'": Author interview with Jack Gilardi, November 19, 2013.

146 "I never felt she was condescending": Author interview with Elizabeth Gabler, April 26, 2013.

147 "Get me Barbra": Author interview with Michael Black, August 21, 2013.

147 "What is this 'rolling breakeven?'": Ibid.

147 "the pictures being done": "Super Agent for Super Talent," *Hollywood Reporter*, forty-fifth anniversary issue, 1975, 62.

148 "This fuckin' cunt": Author interview with Michael Black, August 21, 2013.

148 "Oh, dear. Baby Sue was wrong": Ibid.

149 "Now, listen, Pussy": Author interview with Rex Reed, October 18, 2014.

149 "What *is* it, Barbra?": Ibid.

149 "This is a snap": Ibid.

149 "Honeeey, keep that to yourself": Author interview with Jonathan Axelrod, March 9, 2015.

149 "I decided not to sue": Ibid.

149 "Are you kidding?": Ibid.

151 "that fucking sweathog": Author interview with Michael Black, January 9, 2013.

151 "Rules are made to be broken": Anthony Shaffer, screenplay of *Death on the Nile*, Paramount Pictures, 1978.

151 "Bobbee." Sue sighed: Author interview with Bob Bookman, October 1, 2014.

151 "Bobbee . . . are you still": Ibid.

152 "It's not about reality": "The *Playboy* Interview: David Geffen," *Playboy*, September 1994, 57.

152 "Am I in the will?": Author interview with David Geffen, February 4, 2013.

153 "What he had us do": Author interview with Nancy Allen, May 30, 2010.

153 "Put it on Mr. Melnick's account": Author interview with Bob Bookman, October 1, 2014.

153 "This was all for her mother": Author interview with David Geffen, February 4, 2013.

154 "Mike did not feel L.A.": Author interview with Candice Bergen, November 11, 2013.

154 "Honeeey," Sue said once: Author interview with Lou Pitt, April 16, 2013.

CHAPTER THIRTEEN: 1977–1978

155 "I would be digging out": Author interview with Joan Harris, May 10, 2013.

155 "Every chance she would get": Author interview with Joel Dean, July 11, 2012.

156 "I always kind of regretted": Author interview with Peter Bogdanovich, December 13, 2013.

157 "I was sitting in Peter's Bel Air office": Author interview with W. D. Richter, April 26, 2013.

157 "There are certain women": Author interview with Peter Bogdanovich, December 13, 2013.

157 "I lost it": Ibid.

158 "If my mother had been": Peter Biskind, "When Sue Was Queen," *Vanity Fair*, April 2000.

158 "Hostesses, then, when you are able": Phyllis McGinley, "A Word to Hostesses," *The Love Letters of Phyllis McGinley* (New York: Viking, 1954), 85.

158 "Sue was ballsy and smart": Author interview with Barbara Howar, August 21, 2013.

159 "Honeeey . . . stars can come": Author interview with Michael Black, January 9, 2013.

159 *"Good, honeeey, good"*: Ibid.

159 "Honeeey, pick me up tonight": Ibid.

159 "Honeeey, let me give you a tip": Ibid.

160 "How smart of Sue": Ibid.

160 "Suddenly, I received a telegram": Author interview with Tuesday Weld, March 11, 2013.

160 "Sue mixed people fantastically": Ibid.

160 "Honeeey, he's too short": Ibid.

160 "If it didn't present itself": Ibid.

160 "When Sue would miss an opportunity": Ibid.

161 "She said, 'Burt'": Author interview with Rona Barrett, July 23, 2012.

161 "I turned down *Norma Rae*": Author interview with Tuesday Weld, March 11, 2013.

161 "You know what kind of a schmuck": Author interview with Rona Barrett, July 23, 2012.

162 "How effective would Gerry Stutz": Karen Winner, "Eye View," *Women's Wear Daily*, September 16, 1974.

162 "I often had the feeling": Author interview with Jacqueline Bisset, December 17, 2012.

162 "I was not a great fan": Author interview with Barry Diller, July 15, 2013.

163 "He was a real French intellectual": Author interview with Max Apple, October 3, 2013.

163 "Our cook makes more than that!": Ibid.

163 "You know something?": Author interview with Michael Caine, February 28, 2013.

163 "Michael—it's me": Ibid.

164 "That was my big break": Ibid.

164 "Henry Fonda, Richard Widmark": Ibid.

164 "I was in a group": Quoted in James Reginato, "Sue Mengers: What Makes an Agent Run," *W*, February 2006.

165 "Even when freshly washed": Fran Lebowitz, *The Fran Lebowitz Reader* (New York: Vintage, 1994), 40.

165 "the outdoors is what you must pass through": Ibid., 22.

165 "I never heard the note": Author interview with Fran Lebowitz, February 6, 2013.

165 "There were no cell phones": Ibid.

166 "That was a huge sum at the time": Ibid.

166 "This could be your": Ibid.

166 "That's when you have enough": Ibid.

166 "How much money is that?": Ibid.

166 "Because I am telling you": Ibid.
166 "It was like being in Las Vegas": Ibid.
166 "Sue, we just wanted to tell you": Ibid.
166 "I was thinking to myself": Ibid.
168 "I figured, What's he going to do": Author interview with Boaty Boatwright, September 24, 2013.
168 "Ray Stark thought he owned me": Author interview with Liz Smith, January 13, 2014.
169 "These were crazy numbers": Author interview with George Segal, July 17, 2013.
170 "I didn't tell Sue": Author interview with Ryan O'Neal, May 27, 2013.
170 "Remainder of terms": Author interview with Kenneth Ziffren, October 8, 2012.
170 "Now I think I have to buy": Author interview with Ryan O'Neal, May 27, 2013.
171 "Actually, I think it's a good time": James Powers, "Dialogue on Film," *American Film*, November 1976.

CHAPTER FOURTEEN: 1979-1980
172 "If anything happens to me": Author interview with Boaty Boatwright, September 24, 2013.
172 "What the fuck are you doing here?": Author interview with Joan Harris, May 10, 2013.
172 "Great greeting, Sue": Ibid.
172 "There is nothing worse": Peter Biskind, "When Sue Was Queen," *Vanity Fair*, April 2000.
174 "People who are very caustic": Author interview with Sherry Lansing, January 11, 2013.
174 "I was a reflection": Ibid.
174 "I would look at other people": Ibid.
174 "Honeeey, I don't read 'em": Author interview with Ryan O'Neal, May 27, 2013.
175 "Honey, I just can't put my arms": Author interview with Toni Howard, August 23, 2013.
175 "I never got hugs": Author interview with Sherry Lansing, January 11, 2013.
175 "She had so many wounds": Author interview with Carole Bayer Sager, September 30, 2013.
175 "when the doorknob turned": James Wolcott, *Lucking Out: My Life Getting Down and Semi-Dirty in Seventies New York* (New York: Doubleday, 2011), 253.
176 "want to make any movies": Pauline Kael, "Why Are Movies So Bad? or, The Numbers," *The New Yorker*, June 23, 1980.
176 "postpone decisions because they're fearful: Ibid.
177 "Sue was always against *Yentl*": Author interview with Barbra Streisand, January 19, 2014.
178 "Her Jewishness was a Jewishness": Author interview with John Heyman, October 2, 2013.
179 "like Tracy and Hepburn": Author interview with Michael Black, March 30, 2015.
179 "Honeeey . . . how do you like this?": Author interview with Howard Rosenman, October 3, 2013.
179 "Then when the movie": Ibid.
179 "Wear those white painter's pants": Ibid.
179 "Speak Hebrew to her": Ibid.
179 "This is what you're going to do": Ibid.
180 "It's all corny and silly": Author interview with Ryan O'Neal, May 27, 2013.
181 "This was the best thing": Author interview with Ali MacGraw, April 23, 2013.

182 "But Sue was absolutely right": Author interview with Candice Bergen, November 11, 2013.

182 "suggested some bright possibilities": Pauline Kael, "Pipe Dream," *The New Yorker*, July 3, 1971.

182 "the film its only surprises": Pauline Kael, "Three Pairs," *The New Yorker*, October 26, 1981.

182 "My father would have been so proud": Candice Bergen, *Knock Wood* (New York: Simon & Schuster, 1984), 327.

183 "CONGRATULATIONS. LOVE, SUE": Author interview with Barbra Streisand, January 19, 2014.

183 "I think Sue could only be persuaded": Author interview with Frank Price, June 17, 2014.

183 "Not enough lines": Author interview with Barbra Streisand, January 19, 2014.

184 "I didn't think there was a problem": Author interview with Michael Caine, February 28, 2013.

184 "Fuck Allan Badiner": Author interview with Nancy Allen, January 14, 2013.

184 "AIP was a little different": Ibid.

185 "She said, 'At this rate of dealing'": Ibid.

185 "Get me Ray Stark!": Author interview with Arnold Stiefel, December 10, 2013.

185 "You knew she was in the business": Ibid.

185 "Get me Barbra!": Ibid.

185 "Ed! Ed! Exciting news!": Ibid.

185 "Don't keep Patrice waiting": Author interview with Michael Black, March 30, 2015.

186 "It seemed like we did nothing": Author interview with Cindy Pearson, April 14, 2014.

186 "The party was on a Saturday night": Ibid.

186 "They got on like a house on fire": Author interview with Michael Caine, February 28, 2013.

186 "Sue accused me of ruining": Author interview with Jack Nicholson, October 27, 2014.

187 "Princess Margaret got a little sauced": Author interview with Michael Black, August 21, 2013.

187 "Jean-Claude, honeeey": Ibid.

187 "When we were out together": Author interview with Rona Barrett, July 23, 2012.

189 "It was a way for Hackman": Author interview with W. D. Richter, April 26, 2013.

189 "The real discovery of *Yanks*": Kathleen Carroll, *New York Daily News*, September 19, 1979.

189 "getting perilously dangerous": Author interview with Lisa Eichhorn, April 23, 2015.

190 "I remember we shot this scene": Author interview with Lisa Eichhorn, April 23, 2014.

190 "Jean-Claude was a nice man": Author interview with W. D. Richter, April 26, 2013.

190 "Honeeey, the rushes on Lisa Eichhorn": Author interview with Michael Black, August 21, 2013.

191 "I felt very alone": Author interview with Barbra Streisand, January 19, 2014.

191 "Barbra wants to do the movie": Author interview with Leonard Goldberg, February 20, 2013.

191 "Sue, this doesn't make sense": Ibid.

191 "What doesn't make sense?": Ibid.

191 "Is this a new pattern?": Ibid.

191 "I'm doing you the courtesy": Ibid.

191 "Great! We'll shut down": Ibid.

191 "It's Barbra Streisand!": Ibid.
191 "I said to Sid Sheinberg": Author interview with Jerry Weintraub, August 21, 2013.
191 "I begged her not to do it": Author interview with David Geffen, February 4, 2013.

CHAPTER FIFTEEN: 1981–1982

193 "It's not working": Author interview with Lisa Eichhorn, April 23, 2014.
193 "What can I do? What can we do to fix it?": Ibid.
193 "You don't understand": Ibid.
193 "We're replacing you": Ibid.
193 "Oh": Ibid.
193 "This should make you feel better": Ibid.
193 "I later read, subsequent to that": Ibid.
194 "The motherfuckers have to pay you": Ibid.
194 "I had an unlisted number": Ibid.
194 "He was so opposed to it": Author interview with Marion Rothman, August 21, 2014.
194 "stupid cunt": Ibid.
194 "I want to suck": Ibid.
194 "There's a part of me": Ibid.
194 "You didn't walk out thinking": Author interview with Leonard Goldberg, February 20, 2013.
194 "make sure the motherfucker": Author interview with Lisa Eichhorn, April 23, 2014.
195 "I love Gene Hackman": Author interview with Barbra Streisand, January 19, 2014.
196 "I don't take subways!": Author interview with Marion Rothman, August 21, 2014.
196 "It was at the height of the time": Ibid.
196 "The music was rather whimsical": Ibid.
196 "It was a dark comedy": Author interview with Barbra Streisand, January 19, 2014.
197 "I hear Barbra is even better": Author interview with Leonard Goldberg, February 20, 2013.
197 "I heard Barry Gibb is in it": Ibid.
197 "I'd like to go across the street": Ibid.
197 "We loved it": Ibid.
197 "worst miscasting of Streisand": *Time*, March 9, 1981.
197 "in total disarray": *New York Daily News*, March 6, 1981.
197 "displays surprising moments": *Newsweek*, March 16, 1981.
197 "a benign, even-tempered piece of work": *New York Magazine*, March 23, 1981.
197 "emphasized or caricatured": Ibid.
197 "When the substitution of Streisand": Author interview with Michael Sragow, August 2, 2013.
198 "Mr. Tramont, from the hints": *New York Times*, March 6, 1981.
198 "Ordinarily, this sort of information": Ibid.
198 "My wife and I have been together": *New York Times*, March 13, 1981.
198 "failure is to be doing things": Ibid.
198 "We just don't have the same taste": Author interview with Barbra Streisand, January 19, 2014.
198 "I won't be your friend": Ibid.
198 "It was like, 'what?'": Ibid.
199 "Sue didn't think it was that hard": Author interview with David Geffen, February 4, 2013.

CHAPTER SIXTEEN: 1981–1986

201 "I called her and said": Author interview with Marlo Thomas, August 28, 2013.

202 "Ryan's as cold as ice": Author interview with Jeffrey Lane, March 6, 2013.

202 "Would Cary Grant": Author interview with Robert Daly, January 17, 2014.

203 "It never felt good, that picture": Author interview with Ryan O'Neal, May 27, 2013.

203 "I shouldn't be telling you this": Author interview with Nancy Allen, January 14, 2013.

203 "If Sue hadn't said anything": Ibid.

203 "Chris, when you come to Los Angeles": Author interview with Christopher Walken, February 15, 2013.

204 "There's nothing worse, *Schätze*": Author interview with Robin Hurlstone, January 20, 2013.

204 "Why am I wasting my time": Author interview with Joan Juliet Buck, August 2, 2013.

204 "the room was spinning": Ibid.

204 "MRS. BROWN?": Ibid.

204 "I remember at one point": Ibid.

204 "I remember one night": Author interview with Cher, December 16, 2014.

205 "In the thriller": Author interview with Lucie Arnaz, January 10, 2014.

205 "The film had been edited": Author interview with Beverly D'Angelo, February 2, 2015.

205 "Did you read that review": Ibid.

205 "I didn't much like you": Ibid.

206 "Just remember, baby": Author interview with Tina Sinatra, August 22, 2014.

206 "One date. Give me one date with your father": Ibid.

207 "I got on a plane": Ibid.

207 "She said, 'This is a low blow'": Ibid.

207 "ICM gave me a big raise": Author interview with Hildy Gottlieb, February 16, 2014.

208 "We're going to get you out": Author interview with John Burnham, March 20, 2013.

208 "She would inhale": Ibid.

208 "In meetings we would laugh at Sue": Author interview with Martha Luttrell, February 11, 2014.

209 "Hi, honeeey," said Sue: Author interview with Alex Roldan, January 16, 2014.

209 "It was clear that this was a woman who didn't bullshit": Ibid.

210 "Oh, God, your hair is too short!": Author interview with Adele Rosen, September 24, 2013.

210 "She took out her weed": Ibid.

210 "It was like a quilt": Author interview with Marlo Thomas, August 28, 2013.

211 "She was sweet and tough": Author interview with Cathy Moriarty, July 2, 2014.

211 "She would say, 'The studio wants'": Author interview with Eric Roberts, August 20, 2013.

211 "I was terrible in it": Author interview with Ali MacGraw, April 23, 2013.

212 "Sue's personality was so enormous": Ibid.

212 a telegram that read, simply, "BRILLIANT": Author interview with Barbra Streisand, January 19, 2014.

212 "I always thought": Author interview with Jerry Weintraub, August 21, 2013.

213 "Just get hard and get in": Author interview with Lili Zanuck, February 3, 2014.

214 "Her decline": Author interview with David Geffen, February 4, 2013.

214 "Managing people was difficult for Sue": Author interview with Lou Pitt, April 16, 2013.

214 "I need a star": Ibid.

215 "I wouldn't have my client do that!": Ibid.

215 "It was hurtful, and it was wrong": Ibid.
215 "such a wholesome, healthy man": Author interview with Christopher Walken, February 15, 2013.
215 "Neither of us had mouth-kissed": Author interview with Michael Caine, February 28, 2013.
216 "She would not hesitate to pitch": Author interview with Woody Allen, May 21, 2013.
216 "I needed Michael Caine for the film": Ibid.
217 "Virginia was elegant": Author interview with Ali MacGraw, April 23, 2013.
217 "Interesting, interesting. . . . ": Author interview with Michael Black, September 26, 2013.
218 "Some people want your help": Author interview with Alan Caso, May 11, 2013.
218 "We went through magazine": Ibid.
218 "Usually, you can't keep the director": Author interview with Wende Phifer Mate, May 10, 2013.
219 "Sue and Stan Kamen": Author interview with Ron Meyer, May 8, 2013.
219 "Sometimes the agent has the power": Author interview with Sherry Lansing, January 11, 2013.
219 "Sue used to call me three times a week": Author interview with Jerry Weintraub, August 21, 2013.
220 "What—Guy's not available?": Author interview with Jim Wiatt, February 11, 2014.
220 "Guy, who are your greatest *schtupps*?": Author interview with Bob Bookman, October 1, 2014.
220 "Juliet Prowse. And then probably Martha Hyer": Ibid.
220 "Oh, Martha-for-Hyer": Ibid.
220 "She would rely on others": Author interview with Jim Wiatt, February 11, 2014.
220 "It was absurd": Author interview with Sid Sheinberg, January 8, 2014.
220 "Sue, who are all these people?": Author interview with Boaty Boatwright, March 6, 2013.
220 "I don't know": Ibid.
221 "What little cunt are you signing?": Author interview with Martha Luttrell, February 11, 2014.
221 "She was bored": Author interview with John Heyman, October 2, 2013.
221 "We regret Sue's decision": *Los Angeles Times*, March 4, 1986.

CHAPTER SEVENTEEN: 1986–1991
222 "Her bottom line was always about men": Author interview with Toni Howard, January 11, 2013.
223 "There was a picture of me": Author interview with Lucy Fisher-Wick, July 8, 2014.
224 "She was friendly and funny and available": Author interview with Osgood Perkins, July 15, 2013.
225 "Only Jews would think it was a mountain": Author interview with Fran Lebowitz, February 2013.
225 "You really know how to make an entrance": Ibid.
225 "But Sue sat there with him": Ibid.
225 "Ray never said anything wrong": Ibid.
226 "Oh, my God!": Author interview with Glenn Caron, June 20, 2014.
226 "I remember thinking how prescient": Ibid.
226 "It had an old-world, faded-aristocracy look": Author interview with Joanna Poitier, January 12, 2013.
228 "There is no co-running": Author interview with John Burnham, March 20, 2013.

228 "Even though they were all a decade older": Author interview with Elaine Goldsmith-Thomas, August 27, 2014.
228 "I hate actors" invective: Author interview with Toni Howard, January 11, 2013.
228 "Sue, you may not want to come to William Morris": Ibid.
229 "Who with a little HEAT": *Los Angeles Business Journal*, April 1988.
229 "I hate actors": Author interview with Toni Howard, August 16, 2013.
230 "Sue adored her clients": Author interview with Cher, December 16, 2014.
230 "She finally realized I was an aggressive young agent": Author interview with Jeff Field, April 11, 2013.
230 "Listen to Mama": Author interview with Johnnie Planco, September 9, 2014.
231 "You all have crap!": Author interview with Elaine Goldsmith-Thomas, December 19, 2013.
231 "Without stars, honeeey": Ibid.
231 "SALLY FIELD is starring": Ibid.
231 "I *told* you she was a movie star": Ibid.
231 "Geena, let's be honest": Ibid.
232 "I was worried": Author interview with Anjelica Huston, December 16, 2013.
232 "If Stephen Frears wants you": Ibid.
232 "unparalleled in her honesty": Ibid.
232 "Honeeey, you haven't had a line": Author interview with Robin Hurlstone, January 20, 2013.
232 "I think the fact that Jean-Claude": Ibid.
232 "Tell me": Ibid.
233 "Oh, my honey had a few experiences": Ibid.
233 "My honey is circumcised": Ibid.
233 "No, I'm not": Ibid.
233 "Yes, you are": Ibid.
233 "For God's sake, we have been married": Ibid.
233 "I thought it was rude to look": Ibid.
233 "Everyone was a *schwarze*": Author interview with Marcia Diamond, April 17, 2013.
233 "I'm working for these fucking old Jews": Author interview with John Burnham, March 20, 2013.
233 "I just ran into Lee Stevens": Ibid.
233 "No difference, right?": Ibid.
234 "It was Jeffrey Katzenberg": Author interview with Elaine Goldsmith-Thomas, December 19, 2013.
234 "The process took months": Ibid.
234 "The question wasn't 'Should we do *Three Thousand?*'": Ibid.
234 "SHE'S PLAYING A HOOKER?": Ibid.
234 "Honeeey, if I had your body": Ibid.
234 "It was a lot of dancing": Ibid.
235 "Too far east": Author interview with Risa Shapiro, March 27, 2013.
235 "She had a tendency to fight": Ibid.
235 "I couldn't get Mickey *Rooney*": Author interview with John Burnham, March 20, 2013.
235 "It wasn't based on a new sense of teamwork": Author interview with Elaine Goldsmith-Thomas, December 19, 2013.
235 "Mike Simpson and I got her job": Author interview with John Burnham, March 20, 2013.
236 "She was ambivalent": Author interview with Paula Weinstein, January 22, 2014.
236 "The clients didn't stay away": Author interview with Elaine Goldsmith-Thomas, December 19, 2013.

CHAPTER EIGHTEEN: 1992–1997

238 "a morning, afternoon, and evening show": Author interview with Elaine Goldsmith-Thomas, December 19, 2013.

239 "Those of us who felt": Author interview with Ali MacGraw, March 18, 2015.

239 "RETIRE THE PUSSY": Ibid.

239 "People would talk openly about anything": Author interview with Alana Stewart, August 19, 2013.

239 "Sue once accused me of having an intimacy problem": Author interview with Lili Zanuck, February 3, 2014.

239 "Dick and I would talk a lot on the phone": Ibid.

240 "Whenever Gore was around": Author interview with Patrick Baker, June 12, 2013.

240 "You will never be bored": Author interview with Sherry Lansing, September 10, 2012.

241 "She was a moosh-face": Ibid.

241 "Be careful—Rosemary is upset": Ibid.

241 "It's a tie": Ibid.

241 "I think that most women who are successful": Ibid.

241 "I never said to Sue in my life": Ibid.

242 "I'm not going to talk about the size": Author interview with Joan Juliet Buck, August 2, 2013.

242 "She talked to me like I was her": Ibid.

242 "She's a classy broad": Author interview with Liam Neeson, April 30, 2013.

242 "I was a jobbing actor": Ibid.

243 "The nicest way you can say it": Author interview with Fran Lebowitz, February 16, 2013.

243 "What do you want?": Author interview with Ali MacGraw, April 23, 2013.

243 "Can I go now?": Author interview with Sherry Lansing, January 11, 2013.

243 "Oh, he could have afforded more": Author interview with Marlo Thomas, August 28, 2013.

244 "sick to the back teeth of Beverly Hills": Author interview with Robin Hurlstone, January 20, 2013.

244 "I thought, 'Jesus Christ, you just retired'": Author interview with Lili Zanuck, February 3, 2014.

244 "Do you mean to tell me": Author interview with Fran Lebowitz, February 16, 2013.

244 "which was in itself": Ibid.

245 "When it was bad": Author interview with Robin Hurlstone, January 20, 2013.

245 "Don't worry. My Robin": Ibid.

245 "He was very grumpy": Ibid.

245 "Jean-Claude was just sort of beaming": Author interview with Michael Sragow, August 2, 2013.

246 "You like black girls": Author interview with Matt Pincus, November 15, 2013.

246 "There was nothing happening": Ibid.

246 "I feel just like the Queen Mother": Susan Orlean, "After the Party," *The New Yorker*, March 21, 1994.

246 "I found it so interesting": Author interview with Susan Orlean, August 19, 2014.

247 "If I don't have a cigarette": Author interview with Johnnie Planco, September 8, 2014.

247 "I hated that movie more than life itself": Author interview with Sherry Lansing, January 11, 2013.

248 "Sue would go out of her way": Author interview with Dan Thomas, January 6, 2014.

248 "I can't do it": Ibid.
248 "Are you sure?": Ibid.
248 "Don't force me to do this": Ibid.
250 "Candy, look what Marlo's done!": Author interview with Candice Bergen, November 11, 2013.
250 "It's Christmas": Ibid.

CHAPTER NINETEEN: 1998–2001
251 "However," she assured them: Letter from Sue Mengers to Gore Vidal and Howard Austen, July 10, 1997.
251 "My mother was never a fashion plate": Author interview with Barbara Sender, June 6, 2014.
252 "The entitlement": Author interview with Elaine Goldsmith-Thomas, December 19, 2014.
252 "She would be very rude": Author interview with David Geffen, February 4, 2013.
252 "DON'T FUCK THIS UP!": Author interview with Elaine Goldsmith-Thomas, December 19, 2014.
252 "Honeeey," she said, "nothing will make you feel better": Ibid.
252 "There you go!": Ibid.
252 "Learn from me": Ibid.
253 "THE WIDOW TRAMONT COULD BE DEAD": Author interview with Joanna Poitier, January 12, 2013.
253 "Sidney could do no wrong": Ibid.
253 "I had done a series of exhibitions": Author interview with John Richardson, February 12, 2013.
253 "It's like Proust": Author interview with Graydon Carter, November 7, 2013.
254 "I think an underlying reason": Ibid.
254 "Diane, as I recall": Author interview with Daphne Merkin, June 19, 2013.
254 "unavailability is your greatest asset": Author interview with Graydon Carter, November 7, 2013.
254 "Her friendship was an endorsement": Ibid.
254 "I sort of felt the air go out of her": Author interview with Daphne Merkin, June 19, 2013.
255 "When Jackie Onassis died": Author interview with Boaty Boatwright, March 6, 2013.
255 "something that never happened before or since": Author interview with Peter Biskind, September 13, 2013.
255 Sue said, "Modest?": Author interview with Graydon Carter, November 7, 2013.
255 "What do you mean?": Ibid.
255 "You call this place 'modest'?": Ibid.
255 "I realized that Peter had written": Ibid.
256 "She wasn't easy": Author interview with Rachel Abramowitz, June 18, 2014.
256 "What else is a kid at Harvard Law": Author interview with Bruce Vilanch, January 10, 2013.
256 "The movie business isn't a business anymore": Peter Bart, "No More Mr. Nice Guy," *Variety*, December 14, 1998.
256 "Bobbeee . . . what is Mike Ovitz's secret?": Author interview with Bob Bookman, October 1, 2014.
256 "That's such bullshit": Ibid.
257 "It will be fine": Author interview with Sherry Lansing, January 9, 2013.
257 "*Whaaaat?*": Ibid.

257 "very much a straight arrow": Author interview with Candice Bergen, November 11, 2013.
257 "Ooooh! What do you do for sex in prison?": Ibid.
257 "That is the worst idea I ever heard": Author interview with Graydon Carter, November 6, 2013.
258 "I just spent a hundred dollars": Author interview with Alex Witchel, May 9, 2013.
258 "No, you won't take a tour": Ibid.
258 "I want to tell you something": Ibid.
258 "I don't eat that shit": Ibid.
259 "FUCK THAT GUY!": Author interview with Mitch Glazer, October 2, 2013.
259 "You want to leave": Author interview with Elaine Goldsmith-Thomas, December 19, 2014.
259 "JOE ROTH's movie": Ibid.
259 "*Best boys* have their names": Ibid.
259 "Elaine's movie is number one": Ibid.
260 "Sue could say some mean things to my mother": Author interview with Kara Baker, July 17, 2013.
260 "Can we skip to *Yentl?*": Author interview with Ali MacGraw, June 15, 2014.
260 "Once I started writing": Author interview with Carrie Fisher, April 2, 2013.
261 "Sue probably didn't think": Ibid.
261 "My house in the country": Author interview with John Richardson, February 12, 2013.
261 "Berry Berenson was on that plane": Author interview with Boaty Boatwright, March 6, 2013.

CHAPTER TWENTY: 2002-2011
263 "LISA EISNER, SHUT THE FUCK UP!": Author interview with Mitch Glazer, October 2, 2013.
263 Sue replied, "Costco": Author interview with Sue Naegle, August 1, 2013.
263 "I didn't see Sue and Barbra": Author interview with Jack Nicholson, October 27, 2014.
263 referred to as "a saint": Author interview with Barbra Streisand, January 19, 2014.
264 crack about her old friend: Author interview with John Burnham, March 20, 2013.
264 "If you wanted to bring someone": Author interview with Fran Lebowitz, February 6, 2013.
264 "She loved that": Author interview with William Friedkin, January 30, 2012.
265 "I could tell that Adam McKay": Author interview with Alex Witchel, May 9, 2013.
265 "I want to thank Sidney Lumet": Author interview with Boaty Boatwright, November 20, 2013.
265 "It will mean you're a slut": Author interview with Claire Hoffman, August 21, 2014.
266 "WHAT THE FUCK?": Ibid.
266 "There was an emotional intensity": Ibid.
266 "A lot of people get up here": Kathy Griffin, Emmy Award acceptance speech, September 8, 2007.
266 "I paid for professional hair": Author interview with Kathy Griffin, January 10, 2014.
267 "This Kathy Griffin won an Emmy": Ibid.
267 "Jack, I'm going to put this in the bathroom": Ibid.
267 "GRAAAAAASSS!": Ibid.
267 "That this fearless cunt would *say* this!": Ibid.

267 "No harm, no foul": Ibid.
268 "Jesus Christ, Brad, put your phone down": Ibid.
268 Griffin dating a "civilian": Ibid.
268 "Honeeey, you'll need a wealthy older man": Ibid.
268 "Kathy," he said: Ibid.
269 "GO AWAY!": Author interview with Carole Bayer Sager, September 30, 2013.
270 "I've replaced you with Jennifer Aniston": Author interview with Lili Zanuck, May 16, 2015.
270 "Who in the hell": Author interview with Sue Naegle, August 1, 2013.
270 "They say that watching television": Author interview with Jack Nicholson, October 27, 2014.
271 "It was a group of ten people": Author interview with Candice Bergen, November 11, 2013.
271 "Gore would be going on": Author interview with Jack Nicholson, October 27, 2014.
272 "Sue Mengers for Griffin Dunne": Author interview with Griffin Dunne, May 25, 2013.
272 "Griffin, honey, it's Sue": Ibid.
272 "Goddammit. . . . I've never been so insulted": Ibid.
272 "Fuck him," said Sue: Ibid.
272 "Anyway—enough of that": Ibid.
273 "It was unhealed": Author interview with Ali MacGraw, April 23, 2013.
273 "Everybody is a starfucker": Author interview with April Schulte, December 7, 2012.
274 "I know you're here late": Ibid.
274 "Don't worry—you're both in the will": Author interview with Boaty Boatwright, September 20, 2013.
274 "Jack was holding his arm out": Author interview with Barbara Davis, November 22, 2013.
274 "She was on a rampage": Author interview with April Schulte, December 7, 2012.
275 "There's one condition, Sue": Author interview with Sherry Lansing, March 4, 2015.
275 "Fabulous Trabulus": Author interview with Joanna Poitier, January 12, 2013.
275 "I think at that point": Author interview with April Schulte, December 7, 2012.
275 "They're with those horrible children": Ibid.
275 "I'm glad you don't have family": Ibid.
276 "There was a long courtship for it": Author interview with Lorne Michaels, December 12, 2013.
276 "I just got off the phone with Barbra.": Author interview with John Goldwyn, May 5, 2013.
276 "I've always believed": Ibid.
276 "I think," said Michaels: Author interview with Lorne Michaels, December 12, 2013.
276 "I'm dying": Author interview with April Schulte, December 7, 2012.
276 "She didn't want anyone to see her": Ibid.
276 "Yeah, yeah—I get it": Author interview with Lili Zanuck, February 3, 2014.
277 "I'm a film producer": Author interview with Patrick Baker, June 12, 2013.
278 "Patrick, you have to take one": Ibid.
278 "Every time I did it": Ibid.
278 "SUE MENGERS, HOLLYWOOD AGENT, DIES AT 79": *New York Times*, October 16, 2011.
278 "Brilliant, schmoozy and often devastatingly funny": Ibid.

EPILOGUE

280 "I'm thinking, did I really love this woman?": Author interview with Sherry Lansing, January 11, 2013.

280 "Maybe I really had a naïve, stupid view of her": Ibid.

280 "That's because he died seven years ago": Ibid.

281 "Miss Sue is *not* happy": Ibid.

281 "Fertilizer!": Ibid.

282 "I can't believe it": Author interview with Fran Lebowitz, February 13, 2013.

282 "You have zero idea": Ibid.

283 "Sue should have taken a lesson": Author interview with Frank Price, June 17, 2014.

BIBLIOGRAPHY

Abramowitz, Rachel. *Is That a Gun in Your Pocket?: Women's Experience of Power in Hollywood*. New York: Random House, 2000.

Ann-Margret. *My Story*. With Todd Gold. New York: G. P. Putnam's Sons, 1994.

Bergen, Candice. *Knock Wood*. New York: Simon & Schuster, 1984.

Biskind, Peter. *Easy Riders, Raging Bulls: How the Sex-Drugs-and-Rock 'n' Roll Generation Saved Hollywood*. New York: Simon & Schuster, 1998.

Bogdanovich, Peter. *Who the Hell's in It: Conversations with Hollywood's Legendary Actors*. New York: Ballantine, 2005.

Brown, Helen Gurley. *Sex and the Single Girl*. New York: Bernard Geis, 1962.

Bruck, Connie. *When Hollywood Had a King: The Reign of Lew Wasserman, Who Leveraged Talent into Power and Influence*. New York: Random House, 2003.

Carroll, Peter N. *It Seemed Like Nothing Happened: The Tragedy and Promise of America in the 1970s*. New York: Holt, Rinehart and Winston, 1982.

Dunne, Dominick. *The Way We Lived Then: Recollections of a Well-Known Name Dropper*. New York: Crown, 1999.

Dunne, John Gregory. *The Studio*. New York: Farrar, Straus & Giroux, 1969.

Edwards, Anne. *Streisand: A Biography*. New York: Little, Brown, 1997.

Eliot, Marc. *Steve McQueen: A Biography*. New York: Random House, 2011.

Evans, Robert. *The Kid Stays in the Picture*. New York: Hyperion, 1994.

Friedkin, William. *The Friedkin Connection: A Memoir*. New York: HarperCollins, 2013.

Gould, Lois. *Such Good Friends*. New York: Farrar, Straus & Giroux, 1970.

Haber, Joyce. *The Users*. New York: Delacorte Press, 1976.

Hackett, Pat, ed. *The Andy Warhol Diaries*. New York: Grand Central, 1989.

Hofler, Robert. *Party Animals: A Hollywood Tale of Sex, Drugs, and Rock 'n' Roll Starring the Fabulous Allan Carr*. New York: Da Capo, 2010.

Jaffe, Rona. *The Best of Everything*. New York: Simon & Schuster, 1958.

Kemper, Tom. *Hidden Talent: The Emergence of Hollywood Agents*. Berkeley: University of California Press, 2010.

Kohn, S. Joshua. *The Jewish Community of Utica, New York, 1847–1948*. New York: American Jewish Historical Society, 1959.

Lebowitz, Fran. *The Fran Lebowitz Reader*. New York: Vintage, 1994.

McClintick, David. *Indecent Exposure: A True Story of Hollywood and Wall Street*. New York: Morrow, 1982.

McGilligan, Patrick. *Jack's Life: A Biography of Jack Nicholson*. New York: W. W. Norton, 1994.

MacGraw, Ali. *Moving Pictures*. New York: Bantam, 1991.

Mair, George. *The Barry Diller Story: An Inside Look at Hollywood's Power Player*. New York: John Wiley & Sons, 1997.

Mann, William J. *Hello, Gorgeous: Becoming Barbra Streisand*. New York: Houghton Mifflin, 2012.

Nelson, Nancy. *Evenings with Cary Grant: Recollections in His Own Words and by Those Who Knew Him Best*. New York: William Morrow, 1991.

Obst, Lynda. *Hello, He Lied: And Other Truths from the Hollywood Trenches.* Boston: Little, Brown, 1996.

O'Neal, Tatum. *A Paper Life.* New York: HarperCollins, 2004.

Phillips, Julia. *You'll Never Eat Lunch in This Town Again.* New York: Random House, 1992.

Prince, Stephen. *A New Pot of Gold: Hollywood Under the Electronic Rainbow, 1980–1989.* New York: Charles Scribner's Sons, 2000.

Rapf, Joanna E., ed. *Sidney Lumet Interviews.* Jackson: University Press of Mississippi, 2006.

Reed, Rex. *People Are Crazy Here.* New York: Delacorte, 1974.

Rose, Frank. *The Agency: William Morris and the Hidden History of Show Business.* New York: HarperCollins, 1995.

Rosenfield, Paul. *The Club Rules: Power, Money, Sex, and Fear—How It Works in Hollywood.* New York: Warner Books, 1992.

Seaman, Barbara. *Lovely Me: The Life of Jacqueline Susann.* New York: William Morrow, 1987.

Sharp, Kathleen. *Mr. & Mrs. Hollywood: Edie and Lew Wasserman and Their Entertainment Empire.* New York: Carroll & Graf, 2003.

Susann, Jacqueline. *The Love Machine.* New York: Simon & Schuster, 1969.

Vidal, Gore. *The Essential Gore Vidal.* New York: Random House, 1999.

Wasson, Sam. *Fosse.* New York: Houghton Mifflin, 2013.

Winecoff, Charles. *Split Image: The Life of Anthony Perkins.* New York: Dutton, 1996.

Wood, Audrey. *Represented by Audrey Wood.* With Max Wilk. Garden City, NY: Doubleday, 1981.

INDEX